SECOND EDITION

ENCOUNTERS WITH CHILDREN:
Pediatric Behavior and Development

SECOND EDITION

ENCOUNTERS WITH CHILDREN:
Pediatric Behavior and Development

SUZANNE D. DIXON, M.D.

Professor of Pediatrics
Department of Pediatrics
University of California, San Diego
La Jolla, California

MARTIN T. STEIN, M.D.

Professor of Pediatrics
Department of Pediatrics
University of California, San Diego
La Jolla, California

 **Mosby**
Year Book

St. Louis   Baltimore   Boston   Chicago   London   Philadelphia   Sydney   Toronto

Sponsoring Editor: Stephanie Manning
Assistant Editor: Jane Petrash
Assistant Director, Manuscript Services: Frances M. Perveiler
Senior Production Assistant: Maria Nevinger
Proofroom Manager: Barbara Kelly

1 2 3 4 5 6 7 8 9 0 UG MA 96 95 94 93 92

Library of Congress Cataloging-in-Publication Data
Dixon, Suzanne, D.
Encounters with children: pediatric behavior and
   development/Suzanne Dixon, Martin Stein. — 2nd ed.
       p. cm.
     Includes bibliographical references and index.
     ISBN 0-8016-1432-5
     1. Child development. 2. Child development—
   Testing. 3. Behavioral assessment of children. I. Stein,
   Martin T. II. Title.
     [DNLM: 1. Child Behavior. 2. Child Development.
   WS 105 D621e] RJ131.D59 1991
   305.23'1—dc20   91-27366
   DNLM/DLC   CIP
   for Library of Congress

CONTRIBUTOR LIST

ELIZABETH BATES, Ph.D.

Professor of Psychology
Department of Psychology and Linguistics
University of California, San Diego
La Jolla, California

HEDI J. BREHM

Specialist, Video Review for Children
La Jolla, California

MARY CAFFERY, R.N., M.S.N.

Department of Pediatrics–Infectious Disease
University of California, San Diego
La Jolla, California

SUZANNE D. DIXON, M.D.

Professor of Pediatrics
Department of Pediatrics
University of California, San Diego
Director of Newborn Services, Family Maternity Care Center and Special Babies Program
University of California, San Diego Medical Center
La Jolla, California

HEIDI FELDMAN, M.D., Ph.D.

Associate Professor of Pediatrics
Director, Child Development Unit
Children's Hospital of Pittsburgh
Pittsburgh, Pennsylvania

MARIANNE E. FELICE, M.D.

Professor of Pediatrics and Psychiatry
Vice-Chair, Department of Pediatrics
Director, Division of Adolescent Medicine
University of Maryland
Baltimore, Maryland

PETER GORSKI, M.D.

Assistant Professor of Pediatrics and Psychiatry
Divison Head, Behavioral and Developmental Pediatrics
Department of Pediatrics and Psychiatry
Northwestern University Medical School
Evanston Hospital
Chicago, Illinois

MICHAEL J. HENNESSY, M.D.

Assistant Clinical Professor of Surgery
Division of Orthopedic Surgery
Department of Surgery
University of California, San Diego
La Jolla, California

PAMELA KAISER, M.N., C.P.N.P.

Assistant Clinical Professor of Pediatrics
Division of Behavioral and Developmental Pediatrics
Department of Pediatrics
University of California, San Francisco
San Francisco, California

PHILIP R. NADER, M.D.

Professor of Pediatrics
Department of Pediatrics
University of California, San Diego
La Jolla, California

NICHOLAS PUTNAM, M.D.

Associate Clinical Professor of Psychiatry
University of California, San Diego
La Jolla, California

LYNN I. RICE, R.N., C.P.N.P.

Clinical Instructor of Pediatrics
Division of Adolescent Medicine
Department of Pediatrics
University of California, San Diego Medical Center
San Diego, California

JOHN E. SCHANBERGER, M.D.

Emeritus Clinical Professor of Pediatrics
Department of Pediatrics
University of California, San Diego
La Jolla, California

MARTIN T. STEIN, M.D.

*Professor of Pediatrics
Department of Pediatrics
University of California, San Diego
La Jolla, California*

ROBERT D. WELLS, PH.D.

*Director of Behavioral Science Training
Assistant Clinical Professor
Departments of Pediatrics and Psychiatry
University of California, San Francisco
San Francisco, California*

JOHN B. WELSH, M.D. *

*Clinical Professor of Pediatrics
University of California, San Diego
La Jolla, California
Deceased

FOREWORD TO FIRST EDITION

This is a wonderful, timely book. Written for primary care practitioners who care for children and their families, it will meet an increasing need in pediatric care. At a time when the Task Force of the American Academy of Pediatrics has recommended a knowledge of child development for all pediatricians, when the American Nursing Association has developed a career for graduate nurses in primary care (the Pediatric Nurse Practitioner), and at a time when the public is for more support and guidance in parenting roles, the Committee on Psychosocial Development of Children and Families of the Academy of Pediatrics has published a series of guidelines for primary care physicians to enhance their attention to child and family development on routine visits to their caregiver. These guidelines are a help, but they need just such a volume as this to enhance their meaning and their value. The "lists" of items to be identified at these routine visits will be of no value to either pediatrician or targeted family unless they form a bridge for communication between the physician and parents and child. If the questions are asked simply as questions, the parents will feel bombarded by a new set of demands to answer in a relatively meaningless fashion. The already-too-pathological model of looking for and identifying failures in the patient will be made into a longer list by developmental questions aimed at looking for failures in the child and in the parent. If, on the other hand, with this textbook as a backdrop, the primary caregiver can participate in the enormous richness of the child's and parent's development as his or her area to share with families, he or she will feel the excitement of the developing child and family. If he or she can understand and participate in the emotional and cognitive development of the child, as well as in his* physical development, the caregiver will feel the rewards of a deepening relationship with the parents in his or her care, for the child's development is the language of the parent. If the caregiver demonstrates a real understanding and gives a sense of caring for these aspects of the child's development, every parent will feel supported and cared for. In these days, new parents are no longer backed up by extended families, by strong cultural belief systems, or by support systems which are meaningful in the area about which they care the most—becoming a successful parent. As women must go to work (and over half of mothers of young children are in the work force now), their need for backup, for information and for guidance in their precious job of childrearing is even greater. It is a time when we, as caring physicians and PNPs, can play a vital role in advocacy for the child and in enhancing the joy and assurance of the parenting role. Our opportunity to play a vital role in the family with attention to anticipatory guidance is out of proportion to the time and effort it will take from us. Each routine visit will become valued and valuable to us as well as to parents. If we

---

*For simplicity's sake, I shall use the masculine pronoun for the child, the feminine for the parent.

indeed transmit a sense of caring, of joining in each parent's job of parenting, we can establish rewarding roles for ourselves.

Having been in pediatric practice for 35 years now, I know that I personally would have "burned out" 25 years ago if I had not shared the child's development as a mutual goal with parents in my care. The quest for physical disease and for physical milestones is too sparse and unrewarding for most active physician minds at routine visits. They all too quickly become "routine." But the kind of shared knowledge and the kind of relationships with each family which this book will enhance at each visit can make the practice of primary care an act and a pleasure.

In Stein's chapter on interviewing, he displays the respect for children which underlies each subsequent chapter. He and Dixon give one a real sense of "how" to make and keep a working relationship with each set of parents at each visit. For it is within the context of relationships that a caregiver can be of any meaningful help to parents. Also, as the relationship deepens over time, the shared values deepen. I find that I no longer need to search for meaningful questions with the patients with whom I have developed a relationship. They bring me the important questions all too readily. Hence, each visit should be seen as an opportunity to strengthen and deepen the relationship between you and the parents. This is the reason why the child's development is such a critical ground for shared understanding.

Enhancing your relationship is also a reason for being sure that you hit "paydirt" in at least one area at each visit. You can recognize "paydirt," for the parent will lean forward, her face will become intense as her involvement with what you are saying becomes more and more obvious. I always try to be sure that I touch on one meaningful area for each parent and that I provide an opportunity for her (and him) to share the intensity of her own feelings as we approach such an area. With this concept of paydirt in mind, the concept of anticipatory guidance is a powerful one, because every parent will recognize her need for information and support you are offering as she approaches a new developmental phase in the child. If she can share her own feelings and anxiety with you as you share your developmental knowledge with her, you will be of real value to her.

Coincident with our capacity for conquering and preventing physical disease, we are becoming more sensitized to our capacity for the prevention of psychological disorders and for improving the quality of life for the children in our care. Prevention, intervention, and quality of life are becoming catchwords in pediatrics. Plasticity, the capacity of a developing organism to find pathways around a deficit or to recover from an insult, is a concept we can all utilize in pediatrics if we are aware of its forces and have a deeper understanding of its mechanisms in development. This book can provide such an understanding for pediatricians and for nurse practitioners.

The format of each chapter is economical and helpful. The theoretical base for the developmental processes which can be profitably addressed at each stage of development is excellent. The attention to deepening the relationship with parents and child is accompanied by specific questions which will help the practitioner. The section on what to observe, how to observe is followed by specific suggestions of how to share this with parents at each visit in infancy and toddlerhood. Sharing the developmental exam with parents is the most powerful way of achieving an effective working relationship to improve the child's outcome that I have found. I can then couch advice and anticipatory guidance without threat to our relationship or to the parent's feeling of competence because we have shared this mutually satisfying observation. I need this kind of communication at each visit. These chapters by Dixon, Stein, and Kaiser are rich in these values for all those involved in primary care.

Stein prepares us in the perinatal period for preventing the "vulnerable child syndrome." Dixon says "parents of premature infants are premature, too." Kaiser addresses the important issue of mothers dealing with sibling rivalry in the post partum period. Each chapter addresses the cognitive and social progress of the child and the appropriate parental responses which one can elicit at each well baby visit. The meaning and use of stranger anxiety at 8 months, of magic and fantasies in the third and fourth years are beautiful essays and should be read by all who are interested in small children.

Putnam and Nader address the issues of the preschool and school-aged child in the same valuable format. Pediatric practitioners will not only better understand the developmental issues, but the practical questions and observations of each area which should be addressed are clear and helpful.

Marianne Felice outlines the issues of preadolescence and adolescence for practitioners in a sympathetic way which will allow us to respect the adolescent's turmoil and need for privacy, but which will also help us to enhance our relationship with him and to address his issues in a straightforward, helpful manner. I find that adolescents with whom I've grown up are extremely grateful for my continued deep involvement with them. Although they may guard themselves with me from time to time, they use me in crises—drugs, sex, and other acting out periods—and remember my caring relationship later by bringing their own children to me. I now have more grandchildren than children in my practice. A real reward for all these years!

The last two chapters are as helpful as any in the book. The chapter on which books to have available by Felice, Caffery and Kaiser is very good. The marvelous chapter on children's drawings—their meaning and their use in enhancing a pediatrician's relationship with his parents—is by John Welsh, a pediatrician practicing for 35 years. It is not only delightful but insightful and wonderful in presenting a whole new system for communication and for diagnostic work with children.

I wish I'd written this book, for it is sure to be a classic for pediatric practitioners. In their famous longitudinal study of the development of temperament, Thomas and colleagues found that the relationships of families with the observer pediatricians proved to be amazingly effective in alleviating potential psychological problems: 68% of the patients with mild or moderate symptoms improved markedly and 50% with real psychopathology improved with their team's preventive approach. I believe that pediatricians and pediatric nurse practitioners are in a unique position to provide the kind of relationship, insight, and therapeutic support which most parents will utilize to prevent disorders in their children. But pediatricians will need an understanding of normal development and of establishing supportive relationships in working with families to do that. This volume will go a long way toward providing that for primary caregivers.

T. Berry Brazelton, M.D.
Professor of Pediatrics
Harvard School of Medicine
Chief, Child Developmental Unit
Children's Hospital Medical Center
Boston, Massachusetts

BIBLIOGRAPHY

Brazelton TB: Anticipatory guidance. *Pediatr Clin North Am* 1975; 22:553.

Brazelton TB: Developmental framework of infants and children: A future for pediatric responsibility. *J Pediatr* 1985; 27:14.

Brazelton TB: Developmental framework of infants as an opportunity for early intervention for pediatricians, in Green M (ed): *The Psychosocial Aspects of the Family.* Skillman, NJ, Johnson and Johnson Publishers, Lexington Books, pp 53–65.

Committee on Psychosocial Development of Children and Families. *Guidelines for Health Supervision.* Evanston, Ill, American Academy of Pediatrics, 1985.

Thomas A, Chess S, Brick HG: *Temperament and Behavior Disorders in Children.* New York, University Press, 1968.

PREFACE TO THE SECOND EDITION

Several forces continue to provide the imperative to infuse a developmental perspective on health supervision visits for children and make the issues presented here more timely. Research in child development continues to provide new insights into developmental processes and the social and cultural forces that shape them. This demands that the clinician continue to upgrade knowledge and skills in this area. Parents continue to ask for help in interpreting new information and making sensible application of it. This book proposes to help in that process.

Economic forces continue to squeeze the health care of children, demanding more than ever that we focus our assessments and interventions and provide sophisticated developmental surveillance rather than widespread screening or other costly measures. This volume supports this kind of clinical role, breaking the check list model and generic screening of all. Enhanced physical and mental health, decreased inappropriate use of emergency visits, and increasing parental competency will, in the end, prove this to be a more efficient approach as well as one more satisfying to clinicians and families.

Health and social issues have had their impact on this edition. We now discuss working mothers' concerns at an earlier age. AIDS, homosexuality, and the impact of poverty, domestic violence, and very low birthweight on children receive new and expanded coverage. In order to respond to requests for more information on the school-aged child, we have added a new chapter with a new focus. The judicious use of videos with this age group gives us new opportunities to explore developmental, social, cultural, and economic issues *with* our kids. A list of resources is provided with this volume.

The identification of developmental delay has always been part of the pediatric mandate. Research has shown that while major difficulties, particularly in the motor domain, are unlikely to be missed by the pediatric provider, subtler forms of dysfunction, particularly in cognition, language, and interpersonal skills, are often missed in pediatric encounters. While formalized testing of all children is not warranted, a broad mandate for "developmental surveillance" within the context of primary health care is now emerging. The clinician orchestrates a series of activities that include parent questionnaires, selected assessments, judicious referral, and, importantly, astute clinical observation and interview based on in-depth knowledge of child development, family, and cultural issues, and the continuities of issues over time. It is in this activity that this book will be useful. Developmental surveillance requires knowledge, skills, and the ability to guide, anticipate, and focus on basic processes of developmental change. This concept raises the cognitive demands on the clinician and relegates the use of questionnaires and screening assessments to a subsidiary position.

Special families have become the majority of families, forcing us to address generically the functions of the family rather than specific role expectations. The impact of divorce, adoption, and foster care now appear to stay with children even beyond the period of immediate stress. Parental drug and alcohol abuse are now identified as more prevalent than ever. Maternal depression has been shown to have a profound effect on children. Overall, poverty continues to be the biggest pathogen for over 50 million children, influencing physical and psychological well-being.

Pediatric advocacy has never been more important from the office to society. Clear perspectives on the developmental tasks and needs of children is even more important. We are indebted to our colleagues in behavioral and developmental pediatrics, psychology, psychiatry, sociology, and education for the new insights and perspectives in this edition. We are also grateful for the increasing integration of these disciplines in education, prevention, intervention, and advocacy for children and families. A difference will be made for them one office visit at a time.

SUZANNE D. DIXON, M.D.
MARTIN T. STEIN, MD

PREFACE TO THE FIRST EDITION

The purpose of this volume is to suggest one explicit approach to the integration of child behavior evaluation and developmental assessment into the practice of pediatric primary care. With increasing frequency, pediatric caregivers seek out this integration as they attempt to meet the psychosocial as well as the physical needs of their patients (Reisinger and Bires, 1980). As much as 40% of a primary care practitioner's time may be spent in assessment and counseling in matters that pertain more to psychological growth than physical growth (Chamberlain, 1974). Parents' concerns, laid out in questions to their pediatric caregivers, are largely in psychosocial areas (McCune et al., 1984; Hickson et al., 1983). Indeed there is evidence that psychosocial factors may go unrecognized as a basis for many encounters or illnesses and may be the source of poor compliance and complicating factors in the most ordinary of pediatric encounters (Starfield et al., 1980). Many factors may be contributing to this recent and growing emphasis in pediatrics, i.e., a decrease in morbidity from infectious disease, improved perinatal conditions with resultant decrease in mortality, smaller families, a decrease in the extended family support structure, and a growing consciousness of the impact of psychological factors on the future of children (Yancy, 1975; Hickson et al., 1983). In addition, there has been an increase in pediatric care providers, so that now there are more pediatricians, pediatric nurse practitioners and physician's assistants who are involved in the direct care of children. Family medicine residencies now offer a greater exposure to the care of pediatric patients in the context of their families. Particular needs of children find more focus in these specialized settings and with practitioners specially trained in the care of children.

The specialty of pediatric medicine, in itself a young discipline, grew out of both a sociological and medical awareness of childhood as a distinct period of life. Prior to this century, children were viewed as miniature adults and adolescence was not recognized as a special period of life at all. An awareness of the extent and complexity of the differences in physiology of both sick and well children has emerged in the 20th century. The technology of medicine has been applied to the study of organ ontogeny, embryology, cell physiology, and the basis for physiologic growth regulation. Children form marvelous models for study of physiologic maturation. The study of psychological growth of children and its impact on their overall well-being has increased in the second half of this century and is beginning to show a significant effect on pediatric medicine.

In light of these changes, the significant gap in the attention to and remediation of behavioral problems in comparison with the attention received by somatic dysfunction is striking (Starfield and Borkowf, 1960). The disciplines of psychology, sociology, education, psycholinguistics, neuropsychology, anthropology, and child psychiatry are all adding new information to the data bank on normal and abnormal development. We know more today than ever about the development of the child (Elkind, 1981). In spite of the increasing degree of sophistication and specificity, this data base is not often seen as readily applicable to clinical settings. Scholarly journals from these social science disciplines are usually not read by clinicians, or if they are, the studies seem unintelligible, complex in design and analysis, and are written in seemingly foreign tongues. Practical answers to the issues presented every day in clinical practice seem elusive. The clinician may feel himself like a rat in a maze looking for a way out when he attempts to enter the world of social sciences. This volume was developed in response to the need to infuse child development into pediatrics with a scholarly approach that is still practical and focused.

TRAINING IN BEHAVIOR AND DEVELOPMENT

There are many good reasons why the social and behavioral sciences may seem an alien territory for the clinician. Traditional training programs have offered little in formal education in the behavioral sciences (Dworkin et al., 1979). Newer programs, in line with recommendations of the Task Force for Pediatric Training (American Academy of Pediatrics, 1978) are beginning to have this input (Richmond, 1975). Most programs, however, still rely upon casual integration of behavior and development into training. Many institutions report that they lack trained personnel and a curriculum to do this in a more formal way. When this kind of integration is attempted in many pediatric training programs, it is presented as "soft" (i.e., intuitive versus scientific) and as such is given little time or credibility. This may be a reaction to limitations in available professional expertise and to information found in the medical literature on psychosocial issues. This body of information is largely ignored in traditional training programs and the new material that is constantly under development in the professional social science world is not readily integrated into medical curricula.

The level of scholarly input in behavioral medical science has not kept up with that of the physical sciences. Written material that is presented for the clinician in a readable form is often from "a pathological model"—an emphasis on delays in development or behaviors that indicate pathology (Brazelton, 1975). It is assumed that the disease model of physical illness can be utilized in a similar fashion when assessing child development and behavioral issues. Although surveillance for developmental disability remains an important part of pediatric practice, it is not what clinicians find most often among their daily concerns. In general, they must deal with a normal child growing up in her own style, at her own rate in a family interested in optimizing its children's lives, and not just avoiding psychoses or other major handicaps.

In the conceptualization and organization of this book, we have sought to remediate some of these gaps in professional child health training. We have developed an approach that is different than a disease surveillance model. This volume is designed to be used as part of formal child health training programs as well as a guide to "mid-career" clinicians who want to upgrade their knowledge and expertise in this area. Indeed, some of our most gratifying responses to this work have been from the well-established physicians who are delighted with the new dimensions this material adds to their practices.

A SYNTHESIS

From the literature of pediatrics, psychiatry, anthropology, and psychology, salient and clinically relevant points in child development have been refocused in a form that we hope the clinician will find readable, digestible and easily integrated into clinical pediatric practice. It serves as an outline of child development for the clinician.

This work presents a model for considering one or more aspects of development at each health supervision encounter. We have attempted to integrate issues of both parent and family development into this model.

This is a how-to-do-it book—how to integrate the monitoring, supporting, and assessing of developmental processes into the usual course of pediatric care. It is the transposition of behavioral science into primary care settings. This transposition allows the clinician to vary his approach to well child care with each encounter. The child and the family have different agendas at different ages; so should the clinician. This changing agenda instills a freshness into the practice of pediatrics that in our experience adds to professionalism and enjoyment in primary care. Casey and Whitt (1980) and Hoekelman (1975) have shown this reordering of well child care to include changing developmental concerns does not result in a decline in the quality of surveillance of medical care. In addition, this approach may even be cost-effective in the delivery of comprehensive preventive medicine, the foundation of pediatrics. This clinical model of practice does not represent a deviation from the basic philosophy of pediatric care. Rather, it allows for the integration of behavioral issues and traditional pediatric care in a way that is practical, intellectually secure, and palatable to pediatric clinicians.

THE DEVELOPMENT OF THIS BOOK

We, the authors and contributors, are active pediatric caregivers, working in an urban primary care center of a university hospital and/or in private practice. We all participate in medical student, nurse practitioner, housestaff, and fellowship training in addition to maintaining our own practices. Clinical and basic research supplement our primary focus as clinicians. We have all struggled with the process and content of teaching behavioral pediatrics within primary care. We have participated in curriculum development and have experimented with many formats for presenting behavioral and developmental concepts and skills. Some of the material fits into lecture form; most is best presented in seminars through assigned readings and discussion of topics presented in an abbreviated form here. Some of the most effective but costly teaching occurs individually with students and residents as we discuss or examine a specific patient; we use the model presented in this book in that setting.

As teacher-clinicians in general pediatrics, the need for this book was identified by the pediatric housestaff. As clinicians we stretched our imaginations in order to discover ways to teach normative development at each well child encounter, identifying basic issues and moving away from the pathologic model. To spark enthusiasm for primary care issues in residents, whose minds were preoccupied with intravenous orders and respirator settings, we soon realized that the *dynamic* changes in children from visit to visit had to be identified and placed in precise focus. Residents could not be allowed to slip into monotonous listing of developmental milestones, or they lost interest and enthusiasm. Each visit was seen as a unique challenge, and the residents requested that we write down the principles and focus of our teaching methods. They did not want another textbook, but a practical how-to-do-it manual. With this handbook, we have attempted to meet that need.

The volume then is a practice manual, a curriculum component for clinicians at several stages in their own professional development, an outline of child development presented in a novel and clinically relevant way. This work grew out of pediatric primary care and we hope it adds excitement and vitality to that setting.

SUZANNE D. DIXON, M.D.
MARTIN T. STEIN, M.D.

REFERENCES

American Academy of Pediatrics: *The Future of Pediatric Education: The Task Force Report.* Evanston, Ill, American Academy of Pediatrics, 1978.

Brazelton TB: Anticipatory guidance. *Pediatr Clin North Am* 1975; 22:533–544.

Casey PH, Whitt JK: Effect of the pediatrician on the mother-infant relationship. *Pediatrics* 1980; 65:815–820.

Chamberlain RW: Management of preschool behavior problems. *Pediatr Clin North Am* 1974; 21:33–47.

Dworkin RH, Shonkoff JP, Leviton A, et al: Training in developmental pediatrics: How practitioners perceive the gap. *Am J Dis Child* 1979; 133:709–712.

Elkind D: *The Hurried Child: Growing Up Too Fast, Too Soon.* Redding, Mass, Addison Wesley, 1981.

Hickson GB, Altemeier WA, O'Connor S: Concerns of mothers seeking care in private offices: Opportunities for expanding services. *Pediatrics* 1983; 72:619–624.

Hoekelman RA: What constitutes adequate well baby care? *Pediatrics* 1975; 55:313.

McCune Y, Richardson M, Powell J: Psychosocial health issues in pediatric practice: Parents' knowledge and concerns. *Pediatrics* 1980; 74:183–190.

Reisinger KS, Bires JA: Anticipatory guidance in pediatric practice. *Pediatrics* 1980; 66:889–899.

Richmond JB: An idea whose time has arrived. *Pediatr Clin North Am* 1975; 22:517–523.

Starfield B, Borkowf S: Physician's recognition of complaints made by parents about their children's health. *Pediatrics* 1960; 43:168.

Starfield B, Gross E, Wood M, et al: Psychosocial and psychosomatic diagnosis in primary care of children. *Pediatrics* 1980; 66:159–167.

Yancy WS: Behavioral pediatrics and the practicing pediatrician. *Pediatr Clin North Am* 1975; 22:685–694.

ACKNOWLEDGMENTS

The ideas presented here have their origins in the work of several major contributors to pediatrics and child development. To these mentors and models we would like to present our thanks and respect. We hope that the condensation and translation of their work has not been too devitalizing.

T. Berry Brazelton, M.D., has been a leader and a role model in this area for many years. Never wavering from his firm identity as a pediatrician, he has with a positive approach infused broad understanding of child development into clinical medicine.

Dr. Benjamin Spock believed in developmental pediatrics before it was born, and served as the midwife at its birth. His practical advice and definition of what is proper pediatric territory still guides and inspires us all.

Drs. Morris Green, John Kennell, Sally Province, Marshall Klaus, Albert Solnit, Milton Senn, Leon Yarrow, Barbara Korsch, Julius Richmond, Stanley Freedman, and many others have all made important contributions to the pediatric literature, solidifying our data base and directing its integration into clinical practice. Dr. Lewis Fraad provided direction and insight into the developing child for hundreds of pediatric residents and medical students; we are dedicated to his influence in our clinical practice. Dr. William Nyhan served as a model of the wise clinician and supportive chairman.

We would like to especially acknowledge the contributions of Dr. John Welsh for his long-standing application of developmental insights into practice, which served as a model for all of us. He operationalized much theoretical material, making it always seem new, exciting, and important. His 38 years of pediatric practice testified to the economy, usefulness, and the enjoyment of this model. His death in 1989 left a large legacy for us all.

An extra thanks to Michael and Mary, Ryan, Colin, and Neil, and Joshua and Ben for their giving us the time, the encouragement, and active participation that it takes to get it all done.

A special thanks to Harriette Iddings and Andrea Cody without whose clerical support this work could never have been accomplished. Thank you also to Michelle E. Lambert from the University of California for her fine illustrations. The young artists who shared themselves through their drawings are acknowledged with much appreciation.

SUZANNE D. DIXON, M.D.
MARTIN T. STEIN, M.D.

CONTENTS

"My family on a hike." By girl, age 11½.

CHAPTER **1**

Basic Perspectives: Biases and Format

SUZANNE D. DIXON, M.D.
MARTIN T. STEIN, M.D.

KEY WORDS

DEVELOPMENTAL MONITORING: SCREENING VERSUS SURVEILLANCE
DEVELOPMENTAL MODEL
INDIVIDUAL DIFFERENCES IN DEVELOPMENT
ANTICIPATORY GUIDANCE
CHILD DEVELOPMENT AS PEDIATRIC SCIENCE

The contents and form of this work present an eclectic approach to child development and a model to apply these principles in a particular clinical setting—pediatric primary care. It would seem appropriate to lay out some general and pervasive concepts that are part of this work.

THE DEVELOPMENTAL MODEL

Our model is one familiar to pediatricians—a developmental one. That is, our expectations of children change qualitatively with age. Developmental work appropriate at one age is inappropriate at an earlier age or at a later one. This model encompasses several tenets. First, developmental work is a self-fueling, ongoing process that requires energy, physical and psychological. It occurs in distinct stages, with later stages building on the achievements of a prior stage. For the child, each stage is characterized by a new understanding and feeling about himself and his place in the world. To understand the child's development at any one point in time, one must assess what has gone before. This developmental history cannot be captured by a checklist of developmental milestones; it is much more complex than that. This model implies an ongoing active interaction between the child and his world over time. "Developmental surveillance" (Dworkin, 1989) within the context of a primary care relationship rather than widespread screening implies the use of a focused developmental history and clinical observations through time. A child's development cannot be explained exclusively by his own neurodevelopment or by what the environment pours into him. Both the child himself and his environment synergistically determine his own path, his own personal history. It is futile and foolish to doggedly attempt to dissect "nature and nurture," the child from his experience. This newer dynamic and interactional understanding of child develop-

3

ment makes the care of children both exciting and demanding. Development cannot be seen merely as moving along a predetermined path, passing sign posts on schedule or not.

The second tenet behind this work is that development in any one child is not a smooth continuum but a series of spurts and lulls. Periods that precede a developmental advance are, in general, times of disorganization, not only in the particular area (e.g., motor or language) but in other areas of functioning as well. The clinician can share that anticipation of growth and change with families as they attempt to cope with that seemingly unexplained turbulence. "Lull periods" are busy too but are characterized by the polishing of new skills and by the elaboration of related skills, insights, and relationships. These "stagnant" periods should be viewed in balance and their richness highlighted rather than as times of anxiety for the family or of lassitude in the child.

Third, all areas of development—physical, social, motor, and so forth—are interrelated. Accomplishments, compromises, strengths, and weaknesses in one area mutually affect events in all other areas. Sometimes, but not always, these overlap in predictable ways, particularly when one area of functioning is compromised. One may anticipate difficulties in the development of some competencies if there are disabilities, deficits, or unusual strengths in another area. For example, a premature infant with a preponderance of extension posturing may have secondary compromises in the cognitive sphere; the child cannot bring her hands to midline to see what interesting things those hands can do, which then limits active exploration of the environment. This results in delayed cognitive development by that fact alone. Other factors may, of course, independently impact on the development of this child.

In another example, an infant with nonorganic failure to thrive secondary to psychosocial deprivation may be visually hypervigilant with "radar eyes" as if increasing visual experiences will compensate for a deficit in responsive auditory and emotional inputs. In a hospital setting, it is not unusual to observe young children who are immobilized for a prolonged period develop an expressive language delay that may last beyond the period of immobilization. They pull back to allow for the exercise of coping skills in handling that stressful situation. Regressions in language functioning should not only be expected but be seen as healthy adaptive response to an extraordinary stress.

These interrelations require us to see that children do not exist only at one point in time, nor can one aspect of the child be considered in isolation, or without an understanding of the child's circumstances. Deviations in development or unusual behaviors may testify to an intact adaptive child in an unusual or unhealthy situation. The whole child and his environment must be considered as one with an interrelated history that is the foundation for understanding the present.

BASIC APPROACHES

Some biases or at least some points of view pervade this work. Most important is the idea that *children are normal until proven otherwise*. Although we seek to impart expertise and a recognition of deviations in behavior and development, we hope to avoid fostering yet another disease-oriented generation of pediatric clinicians, marauding for neurological or psychological disease, fueled by pathological findings only. Most unusual behaviors are both explainable and adaptive if seen within the broader context of an individual child and family strengths, weaknesses, and life stresses. We hope to excite the clinician by the complexity of *normal* development, coping strategies and the vagaries of human variation. Cross-cultural, socioeconomic, geographical, and even political forces are active in shaping the boundaries of normal versus abnormal.

Second, our initial approach in forming an intervention or a plan of guidance for a family is to *define and play into the strengths, in the child, in the family, and in the environment.* This in no way implies a denial of deficits or difficulties in any of these areas; it merely means putting efforts where they are likely to pay off, where there are capacities and energies (Brazelton, 1975). Many things cannot be completely remediated or fixed. We must teach children to build detours if they reach roadblocks in development rather than hammer against fixed barriers. This implies an understanding of *fundamental and dynamic* bases of behavior and development, not just the expected behaviors themselves. This approach is analogous to the formulation of a therapy based on an understanding of pathophysiology versus developing a symptomatic cure. The therapy approach implies an indepth understanding of the basic process; a symptomatic cure is inherently limited. At times both comprehensive therapy and symptomatic cures for behavioral difficulties may be appropriate. For example, an encopretic child's symptoms often respond to simple behavior modification techniques augmented by dietary fiber and a cathartic; when accompanied by significant delays in social development and family dysharmony, a more comprehensive developmental model must be utilized, but the cathartics may still be necessary. A wheezing child needs bronchodilators as well as removal of the allergen from the environment; the clinician uses both approaches. In behavioral medicine, a complete black bag of therapies includes some quick cures to be used wisely within a comprehensive understanding of the issues and the long-term goals.

Third, we recognize, respect, and enjoy the *variations in development* that arise from individual differences in children, families, cultures, and social circumstances. These differences do not undermine our understanding of normative development; they, in fact, define these basic processes more clearly and add richness to our clinical experience. We hope to make clinicians comfortable with these variations but with firm boundaries of knowledge of the true universals of development. In fact, developmental variations are not unlike normal variations pediatricians recognize and interpret in the physical growth or disease processes of children. The science of developmental medicine provides a structure, and within that context there is nothing "soft" in this tolerance for individual variation. Developmental assessments themselves may have their best justification in keeping that framework in front of the clinician who is schooled well in child development (Meisels, 1989).

Fourth, we extend the pediatric mandate to provide preventive care to include mental health. We see *anticipatory guidance* (Brazelton, 1975; Reisinger and Bires, 1980; Telzrow, 1978) as the expected model for health supervision care. Physicians can have an impact insofar as they guide and support parents *in their own* problem-solving in the daily care of their children (Casey and Whitt, 1980; Chamberlain et al., 1979; Gutelius et al., 1977). Within this approach, parents are guided in seeing in advance the changes the child is likely to exhibit. Parents work out their own approach using expert advice as needed. Pat answers to issues usually do not further this process of growth except on the rare occasion when immediate and dramatic success in child management is needed to restore energy to the family system. The immediate stress relief solidifies the relationship between clinician and family so that other work can proceed. Each intervention should have spillover to other times and other areas.

Our perspective is that the child develops within the context of a family, and some of our best predictors of developmental outcome are familial factors. We also believe that the family is the medium for change in children (Chamberlain et al., 1979). If the clinician is to support optimal development for children, it can only be through an understanding of the family as a unit. Support for families has been shown to be effective in improving the outcome of health supervision visits (Wasserman et al., 1984). This approach implies a *growing sense of confidence in the competence of parents* that is mutually built by the clinician and family over time. It is an approach that also assumes that the "guide," the clinician, has a solid understanding of normative development, as well as an ongoing relationship with an individual family over time. This relationship is the most effective tool the clinician has, particularly in the areas of preventive mental health and education (Senn, 1948). It is built over time as clinician and family unit share in the resolution of the many minor and few major crises in the care of the child. This relationship is a powerful tool; it is the essential difference between primary care and subspecialty medicine. Even the pattern of use of health care can give us clues to measures of family interaction that may have profound influence on the child. Conversely, interactional factors may in turn determine appropriate or inappropriate use of health care (Harris et al., 1989).

In this volume we hope to outline how that tool might be developed consciously and utilized to its most effective advantage. We believe that this approach not only provides for the most optimal care of families but also is efficient in that the clinician can effect change in the daily environment of the child, not just around a particular problem or issue. The clinician can influence how a family or a school perceives and handles a youngster, how new issues and problems are managed or highlighted for intervention. Our sense of effectiveness in primary care is dramatically enhanced through a rethinking of our daily work in this context. Feeding problems, sleeping problems, and frequent visits for minor illnesses are the matrix on which this relationship is built in early childhood. The wise clinician will make use of these daily and seemingly trivial concerns. The relationship that develops through longitudinal primary care is our most powerful clinical intervention and our greatest personal reward.

THE ORGANIZATION OF THIS BOOK

The principles of development in this book follow an anticipatory guidance model. Each section is determined by the timing of the pediatrician's usual health supervision encounters with a child and a family as outlined by the American Academy of Pediatrics (1985). These frequent visits in the early years of a child's life for well-child care have been criticized as ineffective and costly (Hoekelman, 1975) when outcome measures are limited to evaluation of physical growth, recognition of physical disease, and immunization levels. This guide follows the recommended schedule of visits and allows for a varied and expanded agenda for these encounters to include specific behavioral and developmental assessment. Outcome measures then are broadened to include preventive mental health, enhanced parental competence (including an acceptance of normal developmental variations), and early identification and remediation of behavioral problems.

One or more aspects of development have been selected for discussion and assessment for each well-child office visit. In this way the clinician can review this developmental process, focus the visit, and offer some anticipatory guidance in this area. Clearly, additional or alternate areas of development in a particular child or family may emerge as important at any given encounter; cross-referencing the chapters will be helpful in addressing these. We use the "Well Child Check Sheet" (Jones and Johnson, 1980; see Appendix) and *Guidelines for Health Supervision* (AAP, 1985) to provide a listing of many brief points to be covered at each assessment. However, this volume suggests an alternate format, particularly useful for a family one sees over time. Questionnaires and developmental checklists may be used in addition by office personnel, with concerns addressed by the clinician. However, we believe that the clinician should be able to set these in a broader context and participate in a dialogue with the family. This means a controlled, carefully orchestrated encounter that varies widely from age to age and family to family. This book presents a higher level of professional expectation than a checklist format. This is in line with the newer concept of *developmental surveillance* as described by Dworkin (1989a). This approach appears to be a more efficient use of the clinical encounter time.

All aspects of development at any given age are not presented at each interval in this work. Through cross-reference of chapters and review of tables in the Appendix, the scope of child development will become available to the reader. We have proposed to do something different from the checklist format that has been available to pediatric caregivers for some time. We are suggesting that each visit address one or more areas in depth. This allows for an extension of understanding of that area, both back to its foundations at an earlier time and forward in anticipation of future developments. This approach has been more satisfying to clinicians and parents than a mere tabulation of new skills, yes-no answers or pass/fail on any given scheme. The opportunity to look beyond the immediate behavior to see its origins, its foundations, and its adaptive significance is rewarding. This is our goal for the clinician and the family.

The issues chosen for each encounter are those that appear most dominant and salient for most families at a particular time. Maturation of skills or areas of concern can be seen as subtopics of a major theme. A more comprehensive understanding can be gleaned by examining these broad fundamental concepts at any one point in time and seeing behaviors as the outward evidence of developmental work in progress or as an outcome of task completion. This transcends individual, familial, and cultural differences that tend to be distracting and deceiving. The *basic* developmental tasks are there to be negotiated.

This approach does not add additional time to health supervision visits. It is designed to sensitize the clinician's eyes and ears to phenomena that testify to normal or deviant developmental work. If one keeps developmental concepts appropriate to a given age in one's mind, one's observation of the child, the family, the responses to a stethoscope or reaching for a tongue blade become development assessments in themselves. One gets more mileage out of every clinical encounter. For busy clinicians in practice, wary of even greater demands on their time, this approach should have an appeal. IT MEANS WORKING SMARTER, NOT MORE.

Overall, the book provides a minicourse in child development for all child health care providers and for practitioners of pediatrics in particular. Each chapter can be used as a seminar topic for more extensive review of the issue by both trainees and those in practice. This is a core curriculum in child development for the clinician dealing with children.

There are many things that this book is not. It makes no pretense to be a complete textbook on child development; many good volumes are available (e.g., Clarke-Stewart et al.,

1985; Gardner, 1978; Hetherington and Ross, 1981; Kopp and Krakow, 1982; Mussen et al., 1980; Rutter, 1981). These offer expansions on the ideas presented here, as well as on topics that we had to leave behind. We hope that the reader will be enticed to look at one or more of these for more scholarly input into this aspect of pediatric practice. This book is not a handbook of primary care pediatrics or one of general pediatrics. These broad subjects have been presented by others (Barnett, 1972; Behrman and Vaughn, 1983; Chow et al., 1979; Fernholt, 1980; Hoekelman, 1978; Oski et al., 1990; Rudolph, 1977). We assume that the readers are (or are becoming) astute clinicians with a broad knowledge of pediatric illness, prevention, and treatment. This manual builds on that base to allow for the regular integration of behavioral issues into clinical medicine. This volume includes discussions of behavioral problems but is not organized around a problem approach as are other texts (Block and Rash, 1981; Gabel, 1981; Gelfand et al., 1982; Hoekelman and Friedman, 1980; Jellinek and Herzog, 1990; Lavigne and Burns, 1981). A more expanded discussion of these behavioral problems may also be needed by the modern pediatric clinician.

In summary, this book presents a model for the integration of behavioral and developmental issues into primary care pediatrics with application for training and practice. A clinican builds on a solid base of knowledge in the behavioral and biologic sciences. Child development constitutes a real science; it may be the "basic science" of pediatrics and must be assimilated before it can be applied to clinical practice.

We have laid out one model—a way to begin to build a matrix of knowledge and experience in behavioral pediatrics. Our hope is that this approach will make primary care pediatrics a continuing challenge and point to a way to discover the joy and excitement in following up children over a period of time.

DEVELOPMENTAL MONITORING: SCREENING OR SURVEILLANCE?

Clinicians who care for children traditionally have relied on various forms of screening tests developed to detect developmental delays. Screening tests seek to identify those children at high risk for significant, unsuspected deviations from normal development. The most widely accepted test in pediatric practice is the Denver Developmental Screening Test (DDST), a test designed for office and community settings to screen whole populations for delays in motor, language, and social skills up to 6 years of age (Frankenburg, 1973). Some clinicians use the DDST for each patient; the majority have modified it in the form of checklists for each health supervision visit or questionnaires given to parents (Lim and Stein, unpublished manuscript, 1990).

Although the DDST was designed to be an acceptable test, simple to perform, economical, and reproducible, carefully constructed evaluation studies challenge its validity (Meisels, 1989a). In fact, the low test sensitivity of the DDST (i.e., high false negative rate) may be a generic problem with developmental screening tests rather than specific to the DDST (Dworkin, 1989). Furthermore, some clinicians have inappropriate expectations for the DDST, using it for purposes not originally intended, such as identifying developmental delay in biologically vulnerable infants (Sciarillo et al., 1986), screening specifically for speech and language problems (Borowitz and Glascoe, 1986), and identifying moderately to severely developmentally delayed children (Meisels and Margolis, 1988).

The assessment of a child's developmental growth in the context of pediatric practice can be more efficiently monitored when development coexists with other aspects of child health.

A child's development is ongoing and dynamic, so much of the subtlety, individuality, and variability of development is missed or blurred when limited to developmental checklists. Parental concerns, clinical observations of a child during an office interview, physical examination at the time of an illness, and assessment of the family history for genetic diseases yield significant data about child development in the context of a general pediatric practice.

As mentioned earlier, this process of monitoring has been conceptualized as developmental surveillance. Paul Dworkin (1989b) has summarized its components:

> Developmental surveillance is a flexible continuous process that is broader in scope than screening, whereby knowledgeable professionals perform skilled observations of children throughout all encounters during child health care. Surveillance encompasses all primary care activities related to the monitoring of the development of children. It includes obtaining a relevant developmental history, making accurate and informative observations of children, and eliciting and attending to parental concerns. Emphasis is placed on monitoring development within the context of the child's overall well being, rather than viewing development in isolation during a testing session.

REFERENCES

American Academy of Pediatrics: *Guidelines for Health Supervision.* Evanston, Ill, American Academy of Pediatrics, 1985.

Barnett HL (ed): *Pediatrics,* ed 15. New York, Appleton-Century-Crofts, 1972.

Behrman RE, Vaughan VC: *Nelson Textbook of Pediatrics.* Philadelphia, WB Saunders Co, 1983.

Block RW, Rash FC: *Handbook of Behavioral Pediatrics.* Chicago, Year Book Medical Publishers, 1981.

Borowitz KC, Glascoe JP: Sensitivity of the Denver Developmental Screening Test in speech and language screening. *Pediatrics* 1986; 78:1075–1078.

Brazelton TB: Anticipatory guidance. *Pediatr Clin North Am* 1975; 22:533–544.

Casey PH, Whitt JK: Effect of the pediatrician on the mother-infant relationship. *Pediatrics* 1980; 65:815–820.

Chamberlain RW, Szumowski EK, Zastowny TR: An evaluation of efforts to educate mothers about child development in pediatric office practice. *Am J Public Health* 1979; 69:875–885.

Chow MP, Durand BA, Feldman MA, et al: *Handbook of Pediatric Primary Care.* New York, John Wiley & Sons, 1979.

Clarke-Stewart A, Friedman S, Koch J: *Child Development: A Topical Approach.* New York, John Wiley & Sons, 1985.

Dworkin PH: British and American recommendations for developmental monitoring: The role of surveillance. *Pediatrics* 1989a; 84:1000–1010.

Dworkin PH: Developmental screening—expecting the impossible? *Pediatrics* 1989b; 83:619–622.

Fernholt JDL: *Clinical Assessment of Children: A Comprehensive Approach to Primary Pediatric Care.* Philadelphia, JB Lippincott Co, 1980.

Frankenburg, WK: Pediatric screening: *Adv Pediatr* 1973; 20:145–175.

Gabel S: *Behavioral Problems in Childhood: A Primary Care Approach.* New York, Grune & Stratton, 1981.

Gardner H: *Developmental Psychology.* Boston, Little, Brown & Co, 1978.

Gelfand D, Jenson W, Drew C: *Understanding Child Behavior Disorders.* New York, Holt, Rinehart & Winston, 1982.

Gutelius MF, Kirsch AD, MacDonald S, et al: Controlled study of child health supervision: Behavioral results. *Pediatrics* 1977; 60:294–304.

Harris ES, Weston, DR, Leiberman, AF: Quality of mother-infant attachment and pediatric health care use. *Pediatrics* 1989; 84:248–254.

Heatherington EM, Ross H: *Child Psychology.* New York, McGraw-Hill Book Co, 1981.

Hoekelman RA: What constitutes adequate well baby care? *Pediatrics* 1975; 55:313.

Hoekelman RA, Friedman S: *Behavioral Pediatrics.* New York, McGraw-Hill Book Co, 1980.

Hoekelman RA (ed): *Principles of Pediatrics: Health Care of the Young.* New York, McGraw-Hill Book Co, 1978.

Jellinek MS, Herzog DB: *Massachusetts General Hospital Psychiatric Aspects of General Hospital Pediatrics.* Chicago, Year Book Medical Publishers, 1990.

Jones B, Johnson DD: Well child check sheet. *Clin Pediatr* 1980; 19:290–292.

Kopp CB, Krakow JB (eds): *The Child.* Reading, Mass, Addison-Wesley Publishing Co, 1982.

Lavigne JV, Burns WJ: *Pediatric Psychology.* New York, Grune & Stratton, 1981.

Lim R, Stein MT: A survey of developmental screening practices among pediatricians. (Unpublished manuscript, 1990.)

Meisels S: Can developmental screening tests identify children who are developmentally at risk? *Pediatrics* 1989; 83:578–585.

Meisels SJ, Margolis LH: Is the early and periodic screening, diagnosis and treatment program effective with developmentally disabled children? *Pediatrics* 1988; 81:262–271.

Mussen PH, Conger JJ, Kagan J: *Essentials of Child Development and Personality.* New York, Harper & Row Publishers, 1980.

Oski F, DeAngelis C: *Principles and Practices of Pediatrics.* Philadelphia, JB Lippincott Co, 1990.

Reisinger KS, Bires JA: Anticipatory guidance in pediatric practice. *Pediatrics* 1980; 66:889–899.

Rudolph AM (ed): *Pediatrics.* New York, Appleton-Century-Crofts, 1977.

Rutter M (ed): *Scientific Foundations of Developmental Psychiatry.* Baltimore, University Park Press, 1981.

Sciarillo WG, Brown MM, Robinson NM, et al: Effectiveness of the Denver Developmental Screening Test with biologically vulnerable infants. *J Dev Behav Pediatr* 1986; 7:77–83.

Senn M: The psychotherapeutic role of the pediatrician. *Pediatrics* 1948; 2:147.

Shelov SP, Mezey AP, Edelman CM, et al: *Primary Care Pediatrics.* New York, Appleton-Century-Crofts, 1984.

Telzrow RS: Anticipatory guidance in pediatric practice. *J Cont Educ Pediatr* July 1978, pp 14–27.

Wasserman RC, Inui TS, Barriatua BS, et al: Pediatric clinicians' support for parents makes a difference: An outcome-based analysis of clinician-parent interaction. *Pediatrics* 1984; 74:1047–1052.

ADDITIONAL READINGS

Alrich R, Robertson W, Smith D: *Trends in Pediatric Education and Practice, 1959–1982.* Seattle, University of Washington, 1983.

American Academy of Pediatrics: *The Future of Pediatric Education: The Task Force Report.* Evanston, Ill, American Academy of Pediatrics, 1978.

Chamberlain RW: Management of preschool behavior problems. *Pediatr Clin North Am* 1974; 21:33–47.

Dworkin RH, Shonkoff JP, Leviton A, et al: Training in developmental pediatrics: How practitioners perceive the gap. *Am J Dis Child* 1979; 133:709–712.

Elkind D: *The Hurried Child: Growing Up Too Fast, Too Soon.* Reading, Mass, Addison Wesley Publishing Co, 1981.

Gordis L, Markowitz M: Evaluation of the effectiveness of comprehensive and continuous pediatric care. *Pediatrics* 1971; 48:755.

Green M: Training the pediatrician in the psychosocial aspects of school health. *Zero to Three.* Washington, DC, National Institute of Clinical Infant Studies, June 1982.

McCune Y, Richardson M, Powell J: Psychosocial health issues in pediatric practice: Parents' knowledge and concerns. *Pediatrics* 1980; 74:183–190.

Richmond JB: An idea whose time has arrived. *Pediatr Clin North Am* 1975; 22:517–523.

Starfield B, Borkowf S: Physician's recognition of complaints made by parents about their children's health. *Pediatrics* 1960; 43:168.

Starfield B, Gross E, Wood M, et al: Psychosocial and psychosomatic diagnosis in primary care of children. *Pediatrics* 1980; 66:159–167.

Yancy WS: Behavioral pediatrics and the practicing pediatrician. *Pediatr Clin North Am* 1975; 22:685–694.

"My own self." By Colin Hennessy,
age 4½.

CHAPTER **2**

Setting the Stage: Theories and Concepts of Child Development

SUZANNE D. DIXON, M.D.

The child has been seen from many perspectives. Theoretical models of child development have both derived from and determined these perspectives. The study of the child has flourished in the 20th century; we know more now than ever before about this phase of human development (Elkind, 1981). This gradient in knowledge is likely to continue into the 21st century and perhaps even find some convergence of views (Kagan, 1984). The pediatric clinician cannot be expected to be the developmental psychologist, psycholinguist, child psychiatrist, or behavior therapist. However, a basic knowledge of some major theories of development help in the understanding and evaluation of children in clinical settings. In addition, new sources of information or old sources with newer input (e.g., *Journal of Behavioral and Developmental Pediatrics, Journal of Pediatric Psychology, Developmental Medicine and Child Neurology,* and *Pediatrics*) provide an integration of behavioral science and medical conditions that address many issues of clinical interest. The clinician will do well to understand the theoretical bases on which these research efforts are based. My own experience with adding the study of the theories of child development to residency and fellowship training is that it enhances the expertise of trainees in clinical dealings with children. Older staff physicians have requested many of these materials as well, sensing that some new understandings of these theoretical perspectives will provide an enrichment for their considerable personal experience.

In this volume we have taken an eclectic approach to child development, pulling some concepts and applications from several different schools that seem to make sense in specific clinical settings. Insights from several perspectives enable a clinician to see a child and the family in many lights. As clinicians we may highlight one or more of these based on our own perspective, the needs of a child, and the therapeutic modalities available to us. Different periods of development themselves seem to fit one perspective better than other periods. The clinician may choose from these theoretical spotlights to direct one or more on a particular child with a particular concern. This approach, however, must be based on firm knowledge of these perspectives.

In this chapter I have cited some primary references as well as more general overviews. The books by Crain (1980) and Salkind (1981) will be useful to the clinician with limited time to devote to this area. I have drawn heavily from these synthetic works.

MATURATIONAL THEORY

One model of maturational theory presents the child as a developing neurophysiologic organism. This is the perspective most familiar to pediatricians deriving from the study of embryology and developmental physiology and from the study of physical growth. In this model, behavior depends entirely on neurologic maturation, built on a base of reflexes that emerge and disappear at specific ages. This maturational theory is built on the observations of Rousseau (1762) of the sequential unfolding of the capacities of the immature organism. The child is seen as an immature or incomplete organism, moving in predictable patterns of behavior during the course of continuous maturation. Gesell (1945, 1946) and other proponents (Illingsworth, 1960; Knobloch, et al., 1980) of this model provided us with extensive information on the course of normal and delayed development. The earliest systematic observation of development came out of this approach (Gesell, 1946; McGraw, 1943). Much of the prevalent emphasis in medicine and psychometrics on milestones in early development comes from this perspective and remains an important part of our evaluation of children. In particular, motor development, which is striking in infancy, follows this prototype most closely. In traditional medical education the maturational model predominates, possibly because it most closely approximates other medical modes of maturation over time. It does so by allowing for easy clinical assessment and for the systematic classification of children as delayed, deviant, or normal based on the timing of emergence of specific skills (Illingsworth, 1960). Development is seen as a continuum, and the child's place in the continuum compared with that of his age-mates is the basis for a diagnostic formulation. Although Gesell (1946) recognized the importance of temperament and individual differences, his overall emphasis was on the unfolding of behavioral sequences regulated by genes (Gesell, 1945). The child's environment may have been an impact in a subordinate way; it may have detrimental impact impeding developmental sequence; it may fail to provide for the necessary conditions of maturation (Gesell, 1943). The environment itself did not determine behavior.

I accept part of this model as it emphasizes the processes of maturation over time: the predictable emergence of the patterns of (particularly) motor behaviors and neurological maturity as a foundation for behavior. Many basic developmental assessments used early in life (Bayley, 1969; Frankenberg and Dodds, 1975; Knobloch et al., 1980) are clinically useful in identifying children with delayed development (Gesell and Amatruda, 1965) and assessing the impact of intervention programming for very young children. I believe, however, that this model alone does not allow for the role of the child's environment, particularly for the role of the interpersonal milieu, in his development. Nor does it allow for the individual variations. The lulls and spurts of maturation in many areas are not explained adequately through this model. The neurophysiologic set is dry and perhaps extreme; it does not explain enough and leaves little room for flexibilities in the developmental processes of the growing child. Some of the poor predictors in early assessment based on this scheme may be explained by these gaps in this theoretical model. Affective and cognitive development are not adequately explained by this model and are only tightly squeezed into its framework. The major contribution of maturational theory stems from the valuable norms it has provided for the beginning of the systematic observation of development in children.

PSYCHOANALYTIC THEORY

Freud made a significant contribution to our understanding of the child's affective and emotional development through his retrospective observations and thoughtful theoretical formulations (Brenner, 1974; Crain, 1980; Freud, 1905, 1959; Hall, 1954). He drew our attention to the consequences of childhood experience on later life. His model now has been expanded and modified by the neo-Freudians: Anna Freud (1965), Mahler et al. (1975), and Erikson (1950), among others. This model emphasizes the importance of the unconscious and conscious mental processes that allow children to develop the concept of themselves as individuals and their place in society. This process results from the interface of the child's inner needs or drives with the demands of the external world around him, which, by necessity, are viewed as conflicting. Psychoanalytic theory provides a guide to understanding these processes and results of those conflicts.

The main stages of these theories are outlined in Table 2-1 (Freud, 1905; Hall, 1954). The act of feeding is central to the earliest (oral phase or infancy); the pleasures and demands of elimination (the anal phase), in the second stage toddler years; and the identification of self as a sexual person during the phallic stage (ages three to seven). The latency (school-age) period is characterized by an increase in control of sexual drives (i.e., bodily pleasures and aggressive tendencies). Adolescence encompasses the genital stage in which relationships with other individuals grow and mature while the child separates from his parents. The

TABLE 2-1.
Psychoanalytic Theory

Stage	Age	Erogenous Zone	Central Activities	Interpersonal Focus
Oral	Birth–1½ yr	Mouth	Feeding; sucking; biting	Self (primary narcissism); separation from mother
Anal	1½–3 yr	Anal area	Elimination	Rebellion vs. compliance with parental demands; fear of loss of parental love
Phallic (Øedipal)	3–6 yr	Genitals	Genital exploration; imitating adult roles	Sexual attraction to opposite-sex parent; identification with like-sex parent after a period of rivalry
Latency	6–11 yr	None (?)	Increased control of sexual and aggressive drives; socially accepted activities	Self among like-sex peers; identification with powerful or effective heroes
Genital	Puberty– adulthood	Genitals	Taking "flight" from the family; denial of pleasures; intellectualization	Separation from parents; successful extrafamilial relationships

nature of the child's experience with his parents in these stages is central to the child's emotional maturation. Successful resolution of the specific inner conflicts and intrapersonal contacts that each stage brings leaves the child ready for a new level of emotional and social maturity. Disruptions or abnormalities at a specific stage (e.g., anal) result in psychic difficulty (e.g., obsessive behavior) that continues into adult life, resulting in conflicting difficulties (neuroses) or major psychological disturbances (psychoses).

Orthodox freudian theory has not been submitted to rigorous scientific scrutiny and has been built on retrospective analyses of childhood memories as they survive in the adult mind. These observations have an inherent cultural, historical, and perhaps a male bias (Erikson, 1959; LeVine, 1973; Malinowski, 1927; Thompson, 1950). Although the semantics of this theory are now a part of everyday life (e.g., ego, libido, freudian slip, repression), full acceptance of every aspect of this theory may be difficult in many clinical settings. It is not a comprehensive developmental theory but deals primarily with affective growth in a stage sequence manner. However, some concepts from these works add substantially to our understanding of the child. First, children do have an active mental life even before the emergence of speech, and this life contributes to the child's adjustment both then and later. Freud made us aware of the power of the unconscious wishes and thoughts to influence both present and future behavior. Much of the child's behavior cannot be understood without an understanding of this stage-locked process of active assimilation of a child's life experiences in forming a concept of self. Second, the place of the child's interpersonal experience with those whom he loves, most often his parents, is central to his overall adjustment and later functioning as an individual. Later relationships with others are determined in part by these primary interactions and the gradual process of separation and individuation. Freud taught us that people, even little people, have an unconscious life and that any new life experiences are met by forces from that life, both past and present. Or, as stated by Hall and Lindzey (1975), freudian theory "tries to envision a full bodied individual living partly in the world of reality and partly in the world of make believe. . . . "

NEO-FREUDIANS

Margaret Mahler et al. (1975) taught us that a child's mental and physical relationship with his mother gradually moves from one of total symbiosis to independence through a series of stages in the first 3 years of life. These predictable landmarks of emotional development allow for the child's increasingly solid sense of himself as an individual, unique, and competent person.

Erik Erikson (1959, 1963), advancing and broadening psychoanalytic theory, formulated a very useful structure in which to understand the stages of emotional development throughout the life cycle, as shown in Table 2–2. Each stage is characterized by negotiation of one central issue. Without successful resolution of this issue, the individual is left developmentally arrested or handicapped for further development. The earlier stages are the foundation for later development, which is fueled by biological maturation and social expectations. Erikson's schema is attractive because it subsumes developmental tasks that seem otherwise unrelated. In addition, the broadness of the stages leaves plenty of room for healthy physical and cognitive development, as well as emotional change, because these are organized under the cen-

TABLE 2-2.
Erikson's Stages of Development

Stage	Age	Issue
1	Birth–1½ yr	Trust vs. mistrust
2	1½–3 yr	Autonomy vs. shame and doubt
3	3–6 yr	Initiative vs. guilt
4	6–11 yr	Industry vs. inferiority
5	Adolescence	Identity vs. role confusion
6	Young adulthood	Intimacy vs. isolation
7	Adulthood	Generativity vs. stagnation
8	Old age	Ego integrity vs. despair

tral developmental theme. Erikson's stage theory is not time locked and allows for individual variation in the rate and acquisition of various developmental processes. That variation is based on forces of culture, family, and the changing demands of society. The broadness of Eriksonian theory is also one of its weaknesses in that it leaves the clinician a bit "at sea" in terms of evaluating specific behavior. Primary research based on Erikson's theory is just beginning. Erikson (1963) moved freudian theory from the dark shadows of Victorian neuroses to include a vision of healthy normal development that spans the life cycle. In addition, similar to most pediatric clinicians, he believed that "the child can be trusted to obey the inner laws of development." Under this umbrella, child rearing becomes a child-response event rather than a prescriptive or adult-directed process; the child can influence rather than being completely determined by environmental forces.

BEHAVIORALISTS: LEARNING THEORY

Most students of even the most basic psychology course are familiar with environmental learning theory (Pavlov, 1927; Skinner, 1927; Watson, 1924). The proponents of this theory postulate that only behavior is worth studying and that the environment is a source of behavioral change. The environment supplies patterns of reinforcement or reward that shape and determine the child's response. The child learns through a series of responses to his behavior and an association between his behavior and the actions of the environment. Behaviors that are rewarded stay; those ignored or punished disappear or are "extinguished" with predictable regularity. Watson (1924) believed that development of the infant could be entirely determined by these responses. Development is seen as a continuum of increasing elaborate chains of behaviors and associations. Internal mental processes and innate maturation are minimally influential on this course.

Behavioral theory is very attractive because it is easily understood and has clinical usefulness in modifying patterns in behavior that are disturbing or maladaptive. Also, this theory can be easily demonstrated in laboratory settings or in clinical settings where behavior can be counted, timed, rewarded, or punished. Its usefulness in real life clinical situations is less clear. Much literature has been made available to parents on behavior modification techniques (Azrin and Fox, 1981; Patterson, 1976) for altering disturbing behavior in their children. Many programs for mentally retarded or autistic children (Lovas, 1973) depend heavily on these techniques to manage disruptive behaviors and to teach simple skills. Programmed learning in many educational programs is based on the premise of immediate response to a behavior (i.e., an answer) and then adding in small increments association to the original response for sequential learning. There is no doubt that in many situations programmed learning provides a useful teaching tool. In some situations behavioralist techniques have been found beneficial when one is interested in *changing the behavior alone.* Other situations may arise in which behavior modification may be used to demonstrate to a child the possible favorable consequence of a new response on his part. A frequently used clinical example is the use of rewards to help asthmatic children learn to understand and manage their symptoms more effectively.

However, the ready application of this theory in practice takes no account of the person's inner life—motivation, emotions, or internal mechanisms of behavior. The mental life of the child, the innate forces of maturation, and the complexity of self-identity are not taken into account by rigid adherence to this theory. I believe that all behavior means something, no matter how maladaptive or obtuse. Children especially tell us things by their actions, their behavior, things that we should not ignore or minimize or try to alter by surface change alone. We should look for the cause rather than providing the symptomatic cure through behavior modification techniques as a uniform prescriptive medication. In addition, behavioralists cannot account for the powerful driving force in any one child that propels him forward to try out new skills, ideas, and experiences, all without any apparent reinforcement to achieve. It is as if the child has a drive for inner competence (White, 1959). Clinicians who subscribe exclusively to behavioralists' theory will find much they cannot explain in children; clinicians who know nothing about behavior modification will be without resources in situations in which behavior itself must be changed for the good of the child or family. The learning theorists taught us the use of the constant learning children do and how the environment influences them. However, they have underestimated the inner competencies of the child and his changing developmental perspective.

SOCIAL LEARNING THEORY

Cognitive social learning theorists, led by Bandura and his followers (1963, 1971), postulate a more elaborate learning milieu to explain both social and object-related development. A child learns so as to fit into a social organization in which he finds himself (the family, the school, the soccer team, etc.). Children learn through the observation of behavior and its consequences on those around them in these settings. Imitation of models is the predominant mode of learning under this theory, so that the models and the environment have central importance in determining what, when, and how a child learns. Through the processes of attention, retention, motor reproduction, and reinforcement, the child learns new skills, attitudes, and strategies in an ongoing continuing way (Bandura, 1965). Again, the contribution of the child's own internal resources and initiative is viewed as less important, and the child's readiness for learning is minimized. Social learning theorists have emphasized the importance of social structures to a child's growth. Socialization is the process by which a child acquires sex-appropriate behaviors and develops culturally defined mores for aggression, moral judgments, prosocial behaviors, and appropriate daily living activities. Although a child's development is initially fueled by reinforcement from without, maturation under this model involves the internalization of an ongoing reward structure.

Through many well-designed laboratory experiments, primarily with older preschoolers and school-aged children, Bandura (1965) has demonstrated the importance of models, both real-life and those inanimate models presented in the mass media. The influence of a society as a whole on the child is seen through these experiments. When a child's behavior is deviant or maladaptive, Bandura would have us look back on the models the child has available and change those if change is desired in the child. Social learning theorists have demonstrated clearly that punishment and commands do not change behavior (Crain, 1980). Preaching must be exceedingly forceful and prolonged to effect any change. For pediatric clinicians this perspective may offer clear insights into some behavioral problems, particularly in the older child, and lead to some therapeutic change in the environment. The forces, messages, and rewards operative in the child's milieu must be taken into account when formulating an intervention. However, the clinician may wish to retain a developmental perspective on the child and consider the child's own contribution to the issues laid out in a clinical setting.

SOCIOBIOLOGY

A new theoretical school based on the direct observation of both animal and human behavior is that of sociobiology. Wilson (1975), Freedman (1979), and others have postulated that all of behavior is predetermined to maximize the chances for self-reproduction within the cultural context of the individual. Behavior is built on the evolutionary adaptation toward this end, based on genetic makeup and innate response patterns. This theory presupposes that social behavior is determined just as biology is. Although research is meager, this perspective may be helpful in the linkage of physical and psychological processes of development, a combination that the clinician sees all the time. The clinician will find that the behavior of the child is somewhat inexplicable indeed, if it is seen only as part patterns leading to an optimum growth of the species as a whole. However, the power and the force of the attachment between the parent and the child may be explained through this model. Cross-cultural similarities in the generic components of child rearing (Werner, 1979) and their adaptive diversity (Whiting and Whiting, 1975) are also explained by this model.

PIAGETIAN THEORY

Piaget, a Swiss philosopher, made an enormous contribution to our understanding of cognitive development, the capacity to understand and use phenomena in the world around us (Ginsburg and Opper, 1969; Piaget, 1951, 1952; Piaget and Inhelder, 1969). Piaget saw children as active participants in their experiences of life, constantly incorporating experiences (i.e., assimilation) into their own mental and physical structures of action (schema), which change over time. These structures or patterns of behavior and understanding are built and elaborated by the child himself, starting with innate reflexes. When confronted with a new event, the child modifies his behavior and mental structures to handle this (i.e., accommodation). This modification is dependent on a stage-related level of competencies. The quality, not the quantity, of the child's mental structures changes with time in an invariant sequence of stages that are only roughly time locked. The environmental experience fuels the child's

TABLE 2–3.
Piagetian Stages of Development

Stages	Approximate Age	Ways of Understanding	Basic Concepts to Be Mastered
1. Sensorimotor	Birth–2 yr	Through direct sensations and motor actions	Concepts of object permanence, causality, spatial relationships, use of instruments, etc.
2. Preoperational	2–6 yr	Mental processes that are governed by the child's own perceptions and linkage of events; no separation of internal and external reality	Sense of animism; egocentrism; transductive reasoning; idiosyncratic associations
3. Concrete operational	6–11 yr	Child can reason through real and mental actions on real objects; can reverse changes to the world mentally to gain understanding; can reason using a stable rule system	Concepts of mass, number, volume, time
4. Formal operations	12 yr	Abstract thought; can reason about ideas, impossibilities, probabilities, broad abstract concepts	Mastery of ideas and concepts

drive but does not determine it under this model. The child's thinking is qualitatively different from the adult's. These stages are laid out in Table 2–3.

SENSORIMOTOR STAGE

During the sensorimotor period the child knows the world and acts on it only through his sensation and motor acts. Six substages, starting with reflex behavior, exist, as laid out in Table 2–4. For example, in stage one all of the baby's responses are built on reflexes, and he learns with each repetition by assimilating information and making accommodations to the influence of these reflexes on the environment around him. Throughout the sensorimotor period the child develops an increasingly solid concept of the world. He learns that objects exist even when he does not see them (object permanence), that objects exist independent of their place in space or placement relevant to other objects (spatial relationships), that events have causes even when the cause cannot be seen (causality), and that characteristics of objects have implications for functioning (use of instruments, combinations of objects). The child learns things first in relationship to himself (e.g., the spatial relationship of objects around his own body) and within a positive emotional climate. For example, a child develops object permanence for his mother before that of other people or objects if his relationship with her is a good one (Goin-Dé Carie, 1965).

PREOPERATIONAL STAGE

In the period of preoperational thought, 2 to 6 years of age, the child can do mental operations if these are linked to concrete objects. But his thinking is flawed because he can understand reality only from his own viewpoint; he cannot imagine another's perspective literally (i.e., he is egocentric). In addition, he uses his own system for organizing objects and

TABLE 2-4.
Sensorimotor Intelligence

Overall Concept (Approximate Ages)	Stage	Object Permanence	Causality	Spatial Relationships	Use of Intermediaries	Use of Instrument
Reflexes 0–1 mo	1	No response to disappearance	No differentiation of self and external events	Space defined by self		No instrument outside self
I° circular 1–4 mo	2	Follows trajectory but stops with loss; no search	Own actions are cause of all events	Space defined by perception; has depth		Hand is an extension of vision
II° circular 4–10 mo	3	Follows trajectory and waits; reconstructs whole from parts	No separation of cause and effect	Has sense of space around self		Hand and other body parts act on objects
Coordination of schemes 10–12 mo	4	Searches for hidden object, single displacement	Tries for a cause, old schema	Has 3-dimensional space for distal objects	Can use extension of object alone	Objects are extensions of body movements
III° circular 12–18 mo	5	Can follow *visible* displacements	Visible cause	Follows course of objects through space	Makes choices about intermediaries; trial and error	Use of instruments by imitation or trial and error
Early thought >18 mo	6	Can follow *invisible* displacements	Hidden cause	Can move in novel ways through space	Able to assess appropriate intermediary *before* activity	Spontaneous use of *particular* aspect of instrument

TABLE 2–5.
Preoperational Thinking

Question or Statement	Answer or Conclusion
Egocentrism	
Why do flowers grow?	To be smelly for me
Why does the moon shine?	To see me at night
Why do cars go?	To take me to the store
Why did you get a shot at the doctor's?	I hit my brother
Animism	
Why is the sun bright?	Because it's happy
How did you get hurt on your bike?	It threw me off
Do you like to flush the toilet?	No, it wants to suck me in
Why did you spank the table?	It hit me in the head
Idiosyncratic Reasoning	
It must be dinnertime	Daddy's home
That lady wears white	She will poke at me

events in his mind (i.e., idiosyncratic), and he reasons from one particular to another (transductive) when these particulars are linked by perhaps an unrelated event (e.g., it must be night because daddy came home; my earache came because the doctor put that thing [i.e., an otoscope] in my ear). Examples of a child's thinking are presented in Table 2–5.

CONCRETE OPERATIONAL STAGE

In the concrete operational period, the school-aged period, the child can do mental operations in his head if these relate to real objects. He develops rules to organize his experience, and he develops the ability to classify with increasing complexity. He develops stable concepts of mass and number. Piaget defined these stages through experimental operations. The child can imagine a reversal or changes in objects in his head so that he can "conserve" one property of objects (e.g., their number) even when another property (e.g., arrangement in space) is changed. Most schoolwork involves concrete operational activities.

FORMAL OPERATIONS

The adolescent is capable of abstract thought. He can do mental operations on objects that are not real, on concepts, on ideas, on large systems of events. Some people may not reach this level of functioning at all, or in every area, and this kind of mental activity may be particular to Western, rational thought (Dasan, 1977).

Piaget tells us that children are self-propelled; they practice the physical and mental schema they possess, almost to exhaustion and without the necessity of reinforcement from the external environment, although children "assimilate" environmental input in an ongoing way and alter their behavior because of it (accommodation). They are active experimenters with whatever capacities they have and, in that sense, have their own environment. Parents help them by providing a supportive emotional climate and allowing that experimentation. Piagetian approaches in assessment (Casati and Lezine, 1968; Uzgirhis and McVicker-Hunt, 1975) allow us to tap this area of competency when other handicaps are present. Piaget does not allow for any individual or group difference in this invariant sequence of cognitive development, although these variations have been reported by others (e.g., Dasan, 1977).

TABLE 2–6.
Kohlberg's Stages of Moral Development

Level	Concept	Examples
Level I: Preconventional Morality		
Stage 1	Obedience and punishment; fixed rules from above; focus on punishment consequences	It's bad; you'll be punished
Stage 2	Instrumental orientation; relativistic hedonism; there are several sides to an issue; decide by pleasure; bartering	It depends on how you see it; do what you want because either would be OK
Level II: Conventional Morality		
Stage 3	Maintain approval of others; motivation is taken into account; good person orientation; judgments by intentions; well-meaning behavior	It's OK because he meant to . . .
Stage 4	Maintenance of the social order; concept of the *function*, not just the presence of laws	What would happen if we all did . . . ?
Level III: Postconventional Morality		
Stage 5	People make the laws and can change them; personal values lead one to try to change the laws; morality of contract, individual rights	This rule is unjust and should be changed
Stage 6	Universal principles, justice; everyone sees everything from another's perspective; based on conscience-internalized ideals	If it applies to one, it applies to all; justice would be best served by . . .

Kohlberg (1974) has followed Piaget in the application of stage theory to moral development, as well as cognitive development. He has made specific observations on *the way* (i.e., not the content) of children's ethical decisions. These stages follow a sequence that is coordinated with cognitive development (Table 2–6).

Both Piaget and Kohlberg (Crain, 1980) have been criticized for their lack of extensive experimental support of their work, especially in varying cross-cultural and socioeconomic settings, although some research in these areas appears to support the theories, particularly in young children (Dasan, 1977; Werner, 1979). Adolescent and adult mental processes appear to show greater variation dependent on the environment. Large-scale normative data (Parmelee et al., 1968) and standardized tests based on Piaget's model (Uzgirhis and McVicker-Hunt, 1975) are recent developments. These may be particularly important in settings in which areas of development are known to be compromised (e.g., motor, visual handicaps) and in which one would like to know *how* a child is learning in order to design an intervention.

SUMMARY

As clinicians, we do not have to commit to one theoretical perspective or another. No one school has all of the answers; nor can any theory explain the richness of even one child's behavior to its completeness. Table 2–7 lays out some of the crossovers in the comparison of many of these perspectives. One can see similarities in observation and hope that the future

TABLE 2-7.
Perspectives of Human Behavior

Age	Theories of Development				Skill Areas		Psychopathology
	Freud	Erikson	Piaget	Kohlberg	Language	Motor	
Birth–18 mo	Oral	Basic trust vs. mistrust	Sensorimotor	"Amoral"	Body actions; crying; naming; pointing	Reflex sitting, reaching, grasping, walking	Autism; anaclitic depression; colic; disorders of attachment; feeding, sleeping problems
18 mo–3 yr	Anal	Autonomy vs. shame, doubt	Symbolic (preoperational)	Stages 1–2	Sentences; telegraph jargon	Climbing, running	Separation issues; negativism; fearfulness; constipation; shyness, withdrawal
3–6 yr	Oedipal	Initiative vs. guilt	Intuition (preoperational)	Stages 1–3	Connective words; can be readily understood	Increased coordination; tricycle; jumping	Enuresis; encopresis; anxiety; aggressive acting out; phobias; nightmares
6–11 yr	Latency	Industry vs. inferiority	Concrete operational	Stages 2–5	Subordinate sentences; reading and writing; language reasoning	Increased skills; sports, recreational cooperative games	School phobias; obsessive reactions; conversion reactions; depressive equivalents
12–17 yr	Adolescence (genital)	Identity vs. role confusion	Formal operational	? stages 4–6; variable	Reason abstract; using language; abstract manipulation	Refinement of skills	Delinquency; promiscuity; schizophrenia; anorexia nervosa; suicide
17–30 yr	Young adulthood	Intimacy vs. isolation	Formal operational	Stages 4–6	Reason abstract; using language; abstract manipulation	Refinement of skills	Schizophrenia; borderline personality; adjustment disorders; development of intimate relationship and difficulties with relationships
30–60 yr	Adulthood	Generativity vs. stagnation	Formal operational	Stages 4–6	Reason abstract; using language; abstract manipulation	Refinement of skills	Depression; self-doubts; career development issues; family, social network; neuroses
≥60 yr	Old age	Ego integration vs. despair	Formal operational	Stages 4–6		Loss of functions (?)	Involutional depression; anxiety; anger; increased dependency

24

brings some convergence of these many perspectives. Included are the major language and motor milestones for each age, although these are more fully developed in later chapters. The developmental difficulties and frank psychopathology appear at various ages. Although the severe forms of most of these difficulties are rare, they represent to some degree a failure or a delay in coping with various developmental issues.

At this point in history, there is an abundance of knowledge on a child's development. The pediatric clinician will do well to pack some of these supplies into his "mental black bag" every day as he goes "into the field" that is his office so he can use this knowledge in his close interactions with children and their families.

REFERENCES

Azrin N, Fox R: *Toilet Training in Less Than a Day.* New York, Simon & Schuster, 1981.

Bandura A: Influence of model's reinforcement contingencies on the acquisition of imitative responses. *J Pers Soc Psychol* 1965; 1:589–595.

Bandura A (ed): *Psychological Modeling.* Chicago, Atherton, Aldine, 1971.

Bandura A, Walters R: *Social Learning and Personality Development.* New York, Holt, Rinehart & Winston, 1963.

Bayley N: *Bayley Scales of Infant Development.* New York, Psychological Corp, 1969.

Brenner C: *An Elementary Textbook of Psychoanalysis.* New York, Anchor Books, 1974.

Casati I, Lezine I: *Les etapes de l'intelligence sensori-mortrice.* Parmelee AH, Kopp C, Sigman M (trans-eds), UCLA revision and translation, 1968.

Crain WC: *Theories of Development: Concepts and Applications.* Englewood Cliffs, NJ, Prentice Hall, 1980.

Dasan PR (ed): *Piagetian Psychology: Cross-Cultural Contributions.* New York, Gardner Press, 1977.

Elkind D: *The Hurried Child: Growing Up Too Fast, Too Soon.* Reading, Mass, Addison-Wesley, 1981.

Erikson EH: Identity and the life cycle, in Klein GS (ed): *Psychological Issues.* New York, International Universities Press, 1959, vol 1.

Erikson EH: *Childhood and Society,* ed 2. New York, WW Norton & Co, 1963.

Frankenburg WK, Dodds JB: *Denver Developmental Screening Test.* Denver, LADOCA, 1975.

Freedman D: *Human Sociobiology: A Holistic Approach.* New York, Free Press, 1979.

Freud A: *Normality and Pathology in Childhood: Assessments of Development.* New York, International Universities Press, 1965.

Freud S: Three contributions to the theory of sex, in *The Basic Writings of Sigmund Freud.* Brill AA (trans), New York, Modern Library, 1905.

Freud S: *Collected Papers.* New York, Basic Books, 1959, vol 2–5.

Gesell A: *The Embryology of Behavior.* New York, Harper & Row Publishers, 1945.

Gesell A: The ontogenesis of infant behavior, in Carmichael L (ed): *Manual of Child Psychology.* New York, John Wiley & Sons, 1946.

Gesell A, Amatruda C: *Developmental Diagnosis,* ed 2. New York, Harper & Row Publishers, 1965.

Gesell A, Illg F: Infant and child in the culture of today (1943), in Gesell A, Illg F (eds): *Child Development.* New York, Harper & Row, 1949.

Ginsburg H, Opper S: *Piaget's Theory of Intellectual Development.* Englewood Cliffs, NJ, Prentice-Hall, 1969.

Goin-Dé Carie T: *Intelligence and Affectivity in Early Childhood.* New York, International University Press, 1965.

Hall C: *A Primer of Freudian Psychology.* New York, Mentor Books, 1954.

Hall C, Lindzey G: *Theories of Personality,* ed 2. New York, John Wiley & Sons, 1975.

Illingsworth RS: *The Development of the Infant and Young Child: Normal and Abnormal,* ed 1. London, Livingstone, 1960.

Kagan J: *The Nature of the Child.* New York, McGraw-Hill Book Co, 1984.

Knobloch H, Stevens F, Malone A: *A Manual of Developmental Diagnosis: The Administration and Interpretation of the Revised Gesell and Amatruda Developmental and Neurologic Examination.* Hagerstown, Md, Harper & Row Publishers, 1980.

Kohlberg L: Development of moral character and moral ideology, in Hoffman ML, Hoffman LW (eds): *Review of Child Development Research.* New York, Russell Sage Foundation, 1974, vol 1.

LeVine R: *Culture, Behavior and Personality.* Chicago, Aldine Publishing Co, 1973.

Lovas OI: *Behavioral Treatment of Autistic Children.* Morristown, NJ, General Learning Press, 1973.

Mahler MS, Pine F, Bergman A: *The Psychological Birth of the Human Infant: Symbiosis and Individuation.* New York, Basic Books, 1975.

Malinowski B: *Sex and Repression in Savage Society.* New York, Harcourt Brace Jovanovich, 1927.

McGraw M: *The Neuromuscular Maturation of the Human Infant.* New York, Columbia University Press, 1943.

Patterson GR: *Living With Children: New Methods for Parents and Teachers.* Champaign, Ill, Research Press, 1976.

Pavlov IP: *Conditioned Reflexes.* Anrep GV (trans), London, Oxford University Press, 1927.

Piaget J: *Play, Dreams and Imitation in Childhood.* New York, WW Norton & Co, 1951.

Piaget J: *The Origins of Intelligence in Children.* Cook M (trans), New York, WW Norton & Co, 1952.

Piaget J, Inhelder B: *The Psychology of the Child.* Weaver H (trans), New York, Basic Books, 1969.

Rousseau JJ: *Emile, or Education* (1762). Foxley B (trans), London, JM Dent & Sons, 1948.

Salkind NJ: *Theories of Human Development,* ed 2. New York, John Wiley & Sons, 1981.

Skinner BF: *About Behaviorism* (1927). New York, Alfred A Knopf, 1974.

Thompson C: Cultural pressures in the psychology of women, in Mullahy P (ed): *A Study of Interpersonal Relations.* New York, Hermitage Press, 1950.

Uzgirhis IC, McVicker-Hunt J: *Assessment in Infancy: Ordinal Scales of Psychological Development.* Chicago, University of Illinois Press, 1975.

Watson JB: *Behaviorism* (1924). New York, WW Norton & Co, 1970.

Werner EE: *Cross-Cultural Child Development: A View From the Planet Earth.* Monterey, Calif, Brooks-Cole Publishing Co, 1979.

White R: Motivation reconsidered: The concept of competence. *Psychol Rev* 1959; 66:297–333.

Whiting B, Whiting JWM: *Children of Six Cultures: A Psychocultural Analysis.* Cambridge, Mass, Harvard University Press, 1975.

Wilson EO: *Sociobiology: The New Synthesis.* Cambridge, Mass, Harvard University Press, 1975.

"Talking to my doctor." By Ryan Hennessy, age 7.

CHAPTER **3**

Interviewing in a Pediatric Setting

MARTIN T. STEIN, M.D.

KEY WORDS

EDUCATIONAL MODEL
DUAL PATIENT
NONVERBAL COMMUNICATION
PROCESS AND CONTENT
EXPLANATORY MODEL
ACTIVE LISTENING
TRANSFERENCE

"Families are the focal element of life's circumstances, and the primary context within which life is experienced, especially for children" (Schor, 1988). By temperament and through training experiences, pediatricians tend to focus on the child's symptoms, developmental skills, and behaviors and spend less time assessing areas of family strengths, stresses, and life-event changes. By incorporating both the parent (or parents) and the child as equal players during the clinical interview, the clinician will find that important information about family function, including marital discord, depression, economic and social uncertainties, along with specific data about the child, will surface. This model supports the notion, confirmed by research and clinical experience, that the developmental potential for most children is affected by the environment in which they live (Cohen and Parmelee, 1983; Werner et al., 1968). Family-directed interviewing also encourages data generation about the child's home environment, which has been shown to have an important impact on a child's development (Casey and Bradley, 1982).

The clinical practice of preventive pediatric care is built on an educational model. When the clinical interview is directed in a manner that provides an educational experience for the parents, child, and clinician, expanded possibilities emerge from the encounter. By orchestration of the style and content of the interview, an educational perspective augments the practice of pediatrics. The manner in which questions are asked, the types of questions asked, the direction of the questioning (to the parent and the child), and the actual interaction with the child herself are the critical components of the interview that control not only the informational data base but also what the parent and child become mindful of in the broader context of growth and health.

This educational model for the clinical pediatric interview should follow a pattern in which information exchange is dynamic for the three participants:

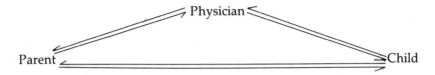

The clinician acquires information from the parent and child that generates a broad, socio-medical data base. The parent and older child receive information from the clinician that should be diagnostic, prescriptive, and educational. During the interview, parent-child inter-actions provide the clinician an opportunity to assess developmental skills of the child, as well as parenting skills and the dynamics of family interaction. When clinicians encourage the kind of interchange that allows for this educational dynamic to occur, the rewards of the clinical interview can be a shared learning experience. Careful engineering of this process can provide for long-term gains in an understanding of the family.

THE DUAL PATIENT

The pediatric interview encompasses the notion of the dual patient. The parent and the child are the patient, both as individuals and as a family unit.

Although most of the historical facts during an interview will originate from the parent, the child often provides important clues through verbal and nonverbal interactions. In addition, the interview should provide information and supportive care of the "third patient," the interaction between the child and his family unit, through direct questioning of the participants and observation of their interaction. A frequent shortcoming of the pediatric interview is seen when the physician, rather than actively involving the child, communicates exclusively with the parent. In the 3-year-old, expressive and receptive language skills provide the child with the ability to communicate symptoms and concerns to the clinician. Questions should be directed to children with age-appropriate words and eye contact that will encourage the child's participation. A direct interaction with a child of any age acknowledges the important contribution any individual child has on his own child rearing, health, and development. An appreciation for the "dual patient" directs the clinician's attention to concerns of both the parent and the child. This approach enhances traditional pediatric advocacy for the needs of the child.

NONVERBAL COMMUNICATION

Information from the clinical interview is derived from two major sources: verbal and nonverbal communication. Verbal information refers to the data that patients tell us about themselves, the core of the traditional medical history. Nonverbal information refers to those observations we make about the style, timing, emotive ambience, and flow of the interview. Facial expressions, posture, movements of the extremities, and the quality and tone of speech are examples of important observations that frequently provide clues to critical aspects of a child's life and family environment. Interactional behaviors are also part of the nonverbal data base—how the baby is held, fed, stroked, spoken to, looked at, and so on. Similarly, the relationship between an older child and parent should be observed and assessed during the interview. Observations about communication style and content regarding discipline and self-help skills (e.g., undressing and getting onto the examination table) can provide important clues about parent-child relationships, as well as developmental capacities. In fact, motor, social, adaptive, and individual temperament skills can be assessed in the young child by observing the child's activity while one is obtaining the medical history from the parent.

Nonverbal information should be treated with the same respect as verbal information. In this manner, clinicians should learn to make these observations and to trust what is observed. Nonverbal data are as real as verbal statements and, therefore, should be incorporated into the medical evaluation. Often it gives clearer and more important information. These observations should be written in the medical record and given diagnostic status when appropriate (e.g., the sad child, rule out depression; the parent with multiple tics and a halting voice, parental anxiety; the active, difficult to cuddle infant, an active infant temperament). They should be incorporated into the problem list to assure appropriate attention during follow-up care.

Nonverbal cues given by parents and children are a component of the "process" portion of the interview compared with the "content" portion. Although the process of an interview is interwoven with the content at all times, it is helpful for the clinician to be aware of the two components as separate (Rosenthal et al., 1979). In that way, verbal data can be understood within the context of nonverbal statements that were generated simultaneously by the parent or the child and monitored by the sensitive clinician. For example, the mother of a normal 2-month-old infant who demonstrates her anxiety as she states her concern about multiple minor somatic symptoms is understood with more clarity when nonverbal observation suggests maternal sleep deprivation since the birth of the child.

POSITIONING THE PARTICIPANTS

There are aspects of the interview environment, controlled by the clinician, that determine the quality and quantity of data that will be obtained. The clinician and parent should be physically positioned at the same level to ensure eye contact and to prevent a subservient positioning effect. The decision to conduct the interview in a sitting or standing position will change with the type of visit. For a new patient or a new problem that requires an extensive history, sitting down with the parent and child may encourage greater information exchange, as well as allowing the clinician to provide more attention to nonverbal cues. For an established patient with an acute illness, the history may be taken while the parent and clinician are both standing. A young child who is ill may remain in the arms of the parent. The placement of chairs in an examination room and the proximity between clinician and patient influence the style and content of the interview. A desk between a practitioner and the parent and child can act as a barrier to optimal communication. Picking up a chair and moving it closer to a parent may facilitate the exchange of information.

Some clinicians prefer to examine the child while taking the history. Although this may be a necessity on occasion when time is very limited, simultaneous interviewing and physical examination runs the risk of shortchanging both aspects of data collection. The clinician is not free to establish eye contact with the parent or to communicate effectively with the child. Critical nonverbal data will be missed.

TABLE 3–1.
Pediatric Examination: A Developmental Approach

Age (Approximate)	Developmental Stage	Approach to Physical Examination
0–6 mo	Symbiotic (not fearful of strangers)	Usually easy to examine infant on table; start with least invasive parts of examination (abdomen, cardiac, pulmonary, nodes, etc.)
6 mo–3 yr	Separation-individuation (fear of strangers initially followed by the toddler clinging to parent)	Examine while standing parent holds the child or while infant is in parent's lap; approach the child gently; use of toys, peekaboo games, keys, flashing otoscope may be helpful
3–6 yr	Preschool age: age of initiative (a period of fantasy play and increasing verbal ability)	Communicate with child in simple language; explain procedures and ask child to participate in examination; make use of child's interest in fantasy
6–12 yr	School age: age of industry (a period of cognitive growth; growing interest in and ability to understand cause and effect)	Recognition of child's ability to understand procedures leads to cooperation; an explanation of bodily functions and results of assessment are helpful
12 yr	Adolescence: age of identity (heightened awareness of body and its perceived effect on others)	Respect privacy during examination; careful explanations help

The placement of the child also determines the quality and tone of the interview (Table 3–1). Infants less than 6 months of age can be placed either in the parent's lap or on the examining table. However, some infants less than 6 months of age will not settle down when placed on the table. With children between 6 months and 2 or 3 years, because of the emergence of stranger awareness and the accompanying need to be close to the parent, interviews are conducted most efficiently while the child is sitting on the parent's lap. This position is reassuring to the child. The physical examination can be performed in the same position with a cooperative child of this age. A child less than 2 years of age should not have to cope with direct eye contact from the clinician while being examined. This distancing will reassure the child. When the clinician is interviewing parents of the older child, the child may be occupied with a request to draw a picture of his or her family. Not only a distracting maneuver, the family picture may provide helpful insights into the child's visual-motor skills and psychological development. It directs the child's expected anxiety into an activity in which he is in charge and can regain control of the circumstances to some degree (see Chapter 31). The adolescent patient should be interviewed separately from the parent as a way to show an appreciation for the teenager's separate identity and to encourage the development of a trusting relationship between patient and clinician. Parents of an adolescent may also need help in realizing their child's maturation and increasing independence. The clinician's behavior models that acknowledgment. To maximize the quality of the interview of a child at any age, the clinician should position himself at the level of the child. For the clinician of tall stature, the importance of positioning is especially important when interviewing young children and parents. Allow the younger child to scan you at a distance first and become familiar with you. Eye-to-eye contact is an intense, invasive interpersonal maneuver and may be very threatening to the child less than age 2 years or to a child at any age if it is presented very early in an interview.

VERBAL AND EMOTIONAL COMMUNICATION WITH CHILDREN

When interviewing a child who has achieved true language skills, the clinician can speak directly to the child to ask the child questions and to listen carefully to responses. It is helpful to remember that receptive language development is often ahead of expressive language. A 2-year-old toddler may understand as many as 300 words, but expression may be limited to 50 words. Children may reveal information that the parent is either unaware of or has suppressed. In addition, allowing the child to participate in the interview provides an opportunity to assess language development and auditory functioning. Furthermore, it provides the child with an experience to participate actively in the visit to the physician, which may encourage a sense of responsibility and participation in one's personal health and medical care. It may also provide a model for parents in listening to and respecting the opinions of the child.

The clinician's interactions with the child during the interview and physical examination provide an opportunity for modeling certain behaviors for the parent. Holding, rocking, and stroking the infant while talking to the parent can give the young, uncertain mother a chance to observe effective soothing techniques. Providing firm discipline to the uncontrolled toddler with a concise and authoritative statement can help the parent experience the effect of appropriate limit setting and control. Giving a 5-year-old the choice of carrying out a venipuncture or tuberculin skin test in either the right or left arm may illustrate to the parent the value of providing options for the child when options exist without presenting options that are really nonnegotiable. In addition, the clinician may demonstrate to the parent the powerful effect of reflecting on a child's feelings when an emotional response is intense. For example, to the tearful youngster about to undergo a painful procedure, the physician might say, "You're worried that the stick is going to hurt, aren't you?" The altered emotional response to these "feedback" statements is often dramatic and encourages further communication about the child's feelings (Gordon, 1975). In general, clinicians should be sensitive to the effect their behaviors vis-à-vis the child have on the parent's behavior and style of child rearing. These models are more effective than any amount of formal instruction or critiques of the parents' own behavior.

STRUCTURING THE INTERVIEW

Structuring the well-child medical interview is helpful in assuring complete data collection, as well as providing a framework for controlled digressions. An *opening statement* should include an introduction by name if this is the first visit. A concerned, friendly, and empathetic atmosphere can be established by a warm introduction associated with immediate eye contact with the parent. Some clinicians find that an extended hand assists in the development of a new medical relationship. For well-child visits, a brief statement about the goals for the visit may be helpful at the beginning of the interview. This can be followed by asking, "What areas of your child's health would you like to discuss during this visit?" A similar question might be directed to the older child.

The *content* of the well-child interview is dependent on the child's age and the significant developmental themes at that period of age. Specific chapters in this book will provide guide-lines for each age. *To encourage a developmental perspective for the well-child visit, one should organize questions and educational information around the major developmental issues at a particular age. In this manner, specific goals can be established for each visit.* For example, the visit when the infant is 6 months of age highlights the emerging motor skills of grasping and reaching out. Advice about solids (especially finger foods), toys, and poison prevention should be provided to parents in the context of specific current and anticipated developmental skills. The chapters on each health supervision visit in this book prepare clinicians for this task. The content of the clinical interview, both data gathering and instruction, for each age will be outlined in subsequent chapters.

Parents appreciate a *summary statement* after the history and physical examination. When the child's health and development is satisfactory, it should be expressed positively, emphatically, and with enthusiasm. The parent should be congratulated on the care and health of the child. These supportive statements encourage a high level of self-esteem with regard to parenting skills and strengthening of the relationship between parent and clinician. When a problem has been uncovered and discussed during the content portion of the visit, it may be helpful to review the problem briefly during the summary statement. This should include an assessment of how serious the clinician judges the problem to be and the plan he advises. The parents' and child's options should be clearly stated. The parents may raise an important question or concern at this time as their options are reflected back to them.

Each well-child visit should terminate with a *closing statement* that allows the parent and older child to express an uncovered problem or concern. "Was there anything else you wanted to bring up?" may encourage the surfacing of an emotional-laden problem that the parent or older child is able to express only after a feeling of trust has been established at the end of a visit. These out-the-door (OTD) questions may be frustrating in a busy clinical setting as the visit is about to end. However, they frequently reflect significant parental concerns. If time for an adequate response is not available, a statement such as "It sounds like something we should talk about when we both have more time together" may be followed by arranging for the next available appointment if the area is of a nonemergent nature. Although the clinician should not feel obligated and time pressed to answer all OTD questions, interest and concern can be expressed with an immediate appropriate follow-up arrangement as part of a new contractual agreement.

Each clinician develops a personal style for interviewing that optimally encourages the establishment of a helpful and healthy therapeutic relationship with children and parents. If education, guidance, and developmental monitoring are the objectives of well-child visits, a flexible, empathetic, and compassionate approach is helpful to assure optimal communication between the clinician and the family. Awareness of tools available to the clinician in constructing the interview will create a form and foundation for the art of medicine.

OPEN AND CLOSED QUESTIONS—Open-ended questions (e.g., "How is your baby doing?" "What's new with the baby's development?" "What do you like about your baby?") generate more spontaneous, less structured responses. They allow the parents to bring up problems of greatest concern to them. They acknowledge the parents' responsibility in establishing priorities in the interview. The interview should start with these. Open-ended questions allow the child or the parents' "explanatory model" (Klineman et al., 1978) of the illness or problem to come out. This is the first step in meeting the family's needs for understanding an issue.

Open-ended questions can be followed by closed-ended questions that are focused, specific, and more concrete (e.g., "Is the baby sitting up without support?" "How is breast-feeding going?" "Are you getting any help with child care?"). These provide important concrete data and shift the control of the interview to the interviewer. The clinician's explanatory model and agenda for the interview can be brought out by the careful use of these questions.

PAUSES AND SILENT PERIODS—When emotionally difficult issues are discussed, the use of silent periods is extremely beneficial. It allows the patient time to collect thoughts and to express feelings. It carries with it the message that you care enough about the patient to take the time to listen to his deepest concerns about the child and family. This is not wasted time.

REPETITION OF IMPORTANT PHRASES—When a patient makes a statement that appears significant from either verbal or nonverbal cues but stops the communication abruptly, the clinician may choose to repeat or interpret an important phrase that was mentioned. This encourages further exploration, clarification, or modification by the patient. For example, a mother of a 6-month-old infant was told that her child, who had previously exhibited normal development, demonstrated signs of spasticity. When the meaning of this finding was discussed with her, she said that she had worried about her son's breathing problems at birth (respiratory distress syndrome). There was a period of silence followed by a statement from the clinician: "You worried about the baby's breathing at birth?" The mother was then able to express her concern about the need for ventilation and oxygen supplementation during the perinatal period and her ongoing fear that it would affect her child's brain development.

ACTIVE LISTENING—Active listening refers to the process of giving undivided attention to what a person is saying through words and body language. It requires, above all, the ability to concentrate. The assumption underlying active listening is that the patient will provide most of the important information spontaneously if given an opportunity. The clinician who listens actively utilizes open-ended questions, pauses and silences, and repetition of important phrases. She also reads facial and body movements that express important emotions. It is a skill that can be learned and is one of the most effective and efficient ways to build a complete data base.

TRANSFERENCE—Well-child pediatric care is based on the development of a long-term relationship with families. When continuity of health care is provided in this framework, a special relationship develops between the caregiver and the patient. In pediatric practice, parents usually have significant respect and admiration for their child's physician; it is the foundation for a trusting, long-term relationship. This relationship is the single most powerful tool in effecting change for the child. It is also one of the rewards of primary care. At the same time, and to various degrees, as a result of this close and special relationship, a parent may respond to the pediatrician as someone who is symbolically and psychologically identified with another important person in his or her own life, past or present. For some mothers, the symbolic attachment may be a father or a mother, for others, an uncle or other important person in their lives. This "transference" phenomenon may surface only at times of deep emotional expression such as overwhelming joy, relief, and admiration for the clinician after a successful therapeutic intervention. It may also be the unconscious source of hostility directed toward the clinician by the parent of a child with a chronic, functionally disabling illness. An appreciation of parental reactions mediated by transference may assist the clinician in providing more appropriate and helpful responses during medical interviews and in understanding some aspects of the interaction. In addition, at other times it will allow for an understanding of strong personal feelings experienced by the clinician. With this insight, one does not get rid of transference in an interaction but acknowledges it, uses it for the healthy energy it provides, and keeps in check the less helpful aspects of its presence.

Recent studies of the pediatric interview through videotape records have documented those clinical skills to which parents are most responsive. Process and outcome measures such as parental understanding of a diagnostic label and compliance with a medical regimen have been measured and correlated with specific traits of clinicians that yield optimal results. Effective interviewing skills go a long way toward optimal results. Dr. Barbara Korsch (1971), a pioneer in pediatric interview research, suggests that the following traits produce the most effective medical encounters:

1. Pay attention to the *concerns of patients.* Three open-ended questions will elicit most parental concerns for the child with a problem: "Why did you bring Johnny to the clinic today? What worried you most about him? Why did that worry you?"

2. Acknowledge the parent's expectation for the medical visits and the parent's explanation of the child's problem. Parents may bring to the visit their own *explanatory model* of illness and health. It is important to bring that model to the surface and show the parents that you understand their perception—whether it is similar or different from your own.

3. Parents need an *explanation of the diagnosis and cause.* If the medical explanation is inconsistent with the parents' own understanding, the clinician should try to reconcile the difference. For example, the parent who believes that the child acquired a cold from rain exposure may be assisted by the statement, "The cold was caused by a virus he acquired, rather than by your taking him out into the rain."

4. Nurture the *doctor-patient relationship.*

5. *Limit medical jargon.* This is often a protective barrier for yourself. One uses jargon to establish power over another, to hide ignorance when one feels threatened. Rather than hide behind words, try to deal with the situation directly.

6. Most parents prefer a *friendly, professional attitude* rather than an authoritative, business-like stature or an overly casual manner.

7. *Attend to parental anxieties* as manifested by nervousness and tension during the interview. Examples of this include "You look nervous to me today . . . is there something you want to bring up?" "You don't seem to accept my explanation of his sore throat."

These skills can be acquired during medical training or in pediatric practice. As with most aspects of learning, supervision is extremely helpful in gaining insights into interviewing techniques. A one-way mirror provides an opportunity for observing interviews. A videotape of a patient encounter can be played back in front of the student and teacher. Videotaping has the advantage of allowing comments periodically as the tape is stopped and replayed. Medical centers with teaching programs usually have video facilities that can be utilized by pediatricians in practice as a form of continuing education.

Communication is the high technology of the twenty-first century. But without computers, satellites, or forms of artificial intelligence, the primitive art of communication during the medical interview remains a powerful and effective way to gather data, teach, and develop the specifically human way of connecting with another human being empathetically and therapeutically. We owe it to ourselves and our patients to develop these skills optimally.

RECOGNIZING HIDDEN AGENDAS

At its best, the clinical interview yields information that will elaborate upon a particular diagnosis or parental concern. The priorities set by the clinician, nurse, or telephone receptionist can enhance or suppress important information. Two studies suggest strategies for more effective acquisition of data while strengthening the relationship between the child's clinician and parent by inquiring about specific behavioral concerns.

The Pediatric Symptom Checklist (PSC) (see Appendix) was developed as a screening test for psychosocial dysfunction among school-age children seen in general pediatric practices (Jellinek and Murphy, 1988). While in the waiting room, the parent is asked to complete a 35-item list of symptoms by approximating their occurrence—never, sometimes, or often; scored 0, 1, and 2 respectively. (See appendix for PSC behaviors.) Twenty-eight points or above constitutes a positive screen. Comparison studies with the established Children's Global Assessment Scale given blindly to the same sample of children revealed that about 15% of middle class school age children would screen positive compared to 24% of economically disadvantaged children. Using 28 points as a positive screen, the sensitivity of test is 95% (5% false negatives) and the specificity is 68% (32% false positives).

Commentary—While screening checklists in clinical practice are limited by their tendency to oversimplify complex developmental issues, they have the advantage of bringing clues to the child's behavior into the pediatric encounter that can then be elaborated on. In addition to the PSC, other investigators have developed parent-generated checklists for preschool behavior problems (Willoughby and Haggerty, 1964) and school age behaviors (Rutter, 1970; Connors, 1970; and Goyette, 1978). Epidemiological studies indicate that up to 15% of school-age children have a disorder of psychosocial dysfunction and that pediatricians identify only a small percentage of these disorders during most office visits (Costello, 1986). Some clinicians may find the PSC helpful in setting the agenda for health supervision by giving the parent (and child) the message that behavioral concerns are appropriate and discussion is encouraged during the visit.

Parents who bring children to a physician for an illness visit not infrequently are motivated to come to the office because of a concern that is not immediately apparent. The "secondary diagnosis" often originates from a behavioral, psychosocial, or developmental uncertainty that the parent may be unaware of at the time of the visit or one that seems inappropriate to bring to the attention of the child's clinician.

Bass and Cohen (1982) investigated ostensible and actual reasons for seeking care in a pediatric office practice. Over a 3-month period, they asked each parent of 370 children who came for a sick visit, "What are you concerned about?" When the parent responded with a physical symptom, she was asked "Is there anything special about the (fever, cold, or infection) that causes your concern?" Among the 370 office visits, 34% of the parents expressed a fear not verbalized initially that appeared to worry them about a more serious condition than could be anticipated from the ostensible reason for the visit.

	Patients
Vulnerable child syndrome	39
Parent thought the worst	30
Parents' fear of cancer or leukemia	10

	Patients
Authority figures raised concerns	10
Illness lasted "too long"	9
Death of relative or friend	8
Travel or moving	7
Symptoms of "vital organs"	7
Absent parent	5
	125 (34%)

These parental concerns reflect fears and anxieties about their child's health that provide insight into family functioning and parental perceptions that are critical to the growth and development of their child. Ten percent of the children were seen as "vulnerable" to their parents as a result of a previous illness or event in either the life of the child, a family member, or a close friend (Green, 1964). Providing the parent with a brief opportunity to express their hidden agenda may be therapeutic in itself. The clinician then has a window of opportunity to place the symptom in perspective and, when appropriate, reassure the parent about the health of her child and the limited duration of the current illness. When these fears create significant or chronic parental anxiety, a future visit is necessary.

These explorations in causality are the rewards of sensitive interviewing. For the child and family, the therapeutic value is as important as unraveling the pathophysiology of a cardiac murmur. The long-term benefit comes from the relationship that begins to be built when clinicians give parents the message that their concerns are important and worthy of their time.

REFERENCES

Bass LW, Cohen RL: Ostensible versus actual reasons for seeking pediatric attention: Another look at the parental ticket of admission. *Pediatrics* 1982; 70:870–874.

Casey PH, Bradley RH: The impact of home environment on children's development: Clinical relevance for the pediatrician. *J Dev Behav Pediatr* 1982; 3:146–152.

Cohen SE, Parmelee AH: Prediction of five-year Stanford Binet scores in preterm infants. *Child Dev* 1983; 54:1242–1253.

Conners CK: Symptom patterns in hyperactive, neurotic and normal children. *Child Dev* 1970; 41:667–682.

Costello EJ: Primary care pediatrics and child psychopathology: A review of diagnostic treatment and referral practice. *Pediatrics* 1986; 78:1044–1051.

Enelow AJ, Swisher SN: *Interviewing and Patient Care*, ed 2. New York, Oxford University Press, 1979.

Gordon T: *P.E.T.: Parent Effectiveness Training*. New York, Plume Books, 1975.

Goyette CH, Connors CK, Ulrich RF: Normative data on revised *Connors* Parent and Teacher Rating Scales. *J Abnorm Child Psychol* 1978; 6:221–226.

Green M: The pediatric interview, in Green M, Haggerty RJ (eds): *Ambulatory Pediatrics IV*. Philadelphia, WB Saunders Co, 1990.

Green M, Solnit AJ: Reaction to the threatened loss of a child: A vulnerable child syndrome. *Pediatrics* 1964; 34:58.

Jellinek MS, Murphy JM: Screening for psychosocial disorders in pediatric practice. *Am J Dis Child* 1988; 142:1153–1157.

Klineman A, Eisenberg L, Good B: Culture, illness and care. *Ann Intern Med* 1978; 88:251–258.

Korsch BM, Freemon B, Negrete VF: Practical implications of doctor-patient interactions and analysis for pediatric practice. *Am J Dis Child* 1971; 12:110.

Korsch BM, Gozzi EK, Vida F: Gaps in doctor-patient communication: Doctor-patient interaction and patient satisfaction. *Pediatrics* 1968; 45:855–871.

Liptak GS, Hulka BS, Cassel JC: Effectiveness of physician-mother interactions during infancy. *Pediatrics* 1977; 60:186–192.

Pantell RH, Lewis CC: Communicating with children in the hospital, in Thornton SM, Frankenburg WK (eds): *Child Health Care Communications: Enhancing Interactions Among Professionals, Parents and Children.* Skillman, NJ, Johnson & Johnson, 1983.

Reiser DE, Rosen DH: *Medicine as a Human Experience.* Baltimore: University Park Press, 1984.

Rosenthal R, Hall JA, DiMatteo MR, et al: *Sensitivity to Nonverbal Communication: The PONS Test.* Baltimore, Johns Hopkins University Press, 1979.

Rutter M, Tizard J, Whitmore K: *Education, Health and Behaviour.* London, Longmans, 1970.

Trad PV: *Psychosocial Scenarios for Pediatrics.* New York: Springer-Verlag, 1988.

Werner E, Honzik MP, Smith RS: Prediction of intelligence and achievement at ten years from twenty month pediatric and psychologic examinations. *Child Dev* 1968; 39:1063–1075.

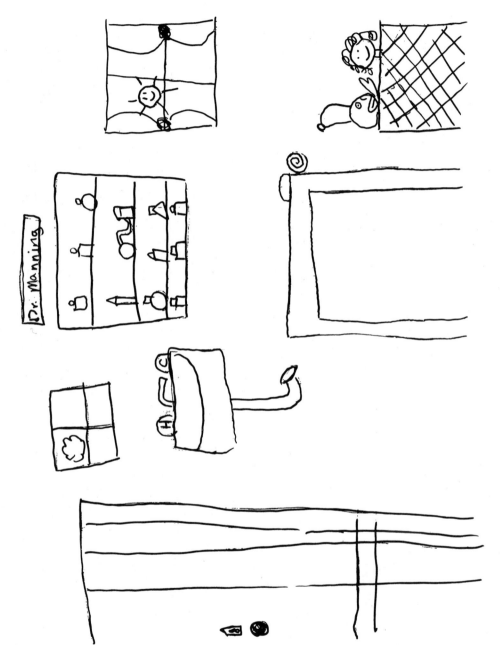

"My doctor's office." By Heather Robinson, age 9½.

CHAPTER **4**

Designing an Office With a Developmental Perspective

MARTIN T. STEIN, M.D.

The physical and social ecology of a medical office that serves the needs of children requires forethought in planning and continuous modification. An appreciation that personnel, space, color, and design can interact to create a positive, health-promoting atmosphere may generate interesting ideas that allow the office environment to enhance child development, parent-child-clinician interactions and assessment of health and development (Weinstein and David, 1987). The pictures or children's drawings selected for the walls, the availability of crawl and walk space and toys in the reception area, and the educational material made available to parents and children are at first seemingly unrelated decisions that create a unique theme in each office.

Whether a new office or clinic facility is planned or modification to an established office seems possible, two useful questions to ask are, "How can we plan to use the available space in a manner that is consistent with the developmental needs of the children and parents who will come to the facility? Can the design promote comfort, relieve anxiety, nurture the parent-child relationship, and maintain a learning and educational milieux simultaneously?" Priorities, budgets, and available space will vary among settings, but some developmental principles are applicable to most pediatric offices:

1. The waiting area should allow for movement and play of children. Flooring, walls, and furniture should consider *the developmental requirements of children* at various age groups.

2. Furniture and play objects can be safe while *engaging and instructive.* A concern for a safe environment should not create a sterile office.

3. *Pictures of children* and their families or *drawings* created by children in the practice invite children to feel comfortable in the office while encouraging conversations about their content with parents and other children.

4. A *tropical fish tank* in the waiting room may help alleviate anxiety and fears that many children experience when visiting a physician's office.

5. *Table and chairs* designed for toddlers and young children and placed in the reception area may encourage a child to separate from her parent, independently open a book, or play with a puzzle. Anxiety may be momentarily decreased as the child learns to manage a fear independent of her parent.

6. *A busy waiting room is like a neighborhood park.* Parents can observe their children learning to play and interact with other children. Toys, books, or a wall board equipped for drawing will make these interactions more interesting for parents and children (Table 4–1).

7. Available paper and marking pens or a chalkboard will *encourage children to draw pictures* that may help them to redirect fears about their symptoms, an infection, or the unrecognizable concern they have experienced in their parent. These drawings can be shown later to the clinician; they may provide valuable insight into the child, family, or illness (see Chapter 31).

8. The observation of children and parents together by the office personnel allows for the collection of data about developmental and interactional issues.

The prevention and health promotion goals that form the foundation for primary care pediatrics can be communicated to patients within the office or clinic setting by means of posters, pamphlets, books (for children and parents), and even instructional questionnaires and videos in the waiting area. Care must be taken not to overwhelm parents with too much information at one time. Bulletin boards and posters directed at a single message and changed frequently (e.g., breast-feeding, car safety, or toddler nutritional requirements) will capture the available interest of a parent. Child-oriented educational displays may promote a useful dialogue between child and parent about a topic of importance. Examples would be a bulletin board devoted to bicycle safety and the use of bicycle helmets, the importance of sunscreen protection, or the health benefits of exercise. Recently, instructional videotapes and patient-generated computer health printouts have utilized newer technologies to engage sustained interest in health promotion materials. One caveat—the literature in primary prevention reminds us that acquired new knowledge does not necessarily bring about change in health behaviors. The design of the waiting area and the attractiveness of the educational materials encourage the acquisition of knowledge. This new information must then be reinforced and elaborated on when one interacts with the child and parent during the office visit. These materials are not a substitute for direct interaction with the clinician.

Some clinicians have been encouraged by the value of parent questionnaires to assess concerns about a child's behavior, school achievement, social interactions, and family functioning that may not surface during a traditional office visit. Standardized questionnaires are available to monitor early child development (Frankenburg, 1987; Humphreys, 1979), psychosocial behavior problems in school-aged children (Jellinek, 1986), school underachievement (Levine, 1980), and adolescent developmental progress (Felice, 1983). Green (1986) has proposed that a "continuity questionnaire" asking open-ended questions be sent to the family before the health supervision visit. We would like to know:

1. Have there been any unexpected or unusual family stresses or illnesses since your last visit?
2. What are some of the things that you are enjoying most about your child?
3. What are your questions or concerns about your child?

The clinical value of any questionnaire is related to how the information is used by the child's clinician. Parent responses provide a beginning to allow further exploration into the child's behavior or family functioning. Parent questionnaires are reliable in detecting devel-

TABLE 4-1.
Suggested Play Materials in an Office Setting and Their Potential Value in Assessing Development and Behavior*

Play Material	Potential Assessment Value	Appropriate Age Level		
		Infant	Toddler	Preschooler
Human figures Miniature doll and family house; hand puppets; doll with clothing and blankets	Functional and symbolic play; child's understanding of family dynamics and peer interactions; role identity; facilitate communication and expression	−	+	+
Miniature cooking utensils and tea set	Sensorimotor, functional and symbolic play; fine motor skills; eye-hand coordination	+	+	+
Car/truck	Functional and symbolic play; realistic play	−	+	+
1-in. colored blocks	Sensorimotor, functional, and symbolic play; fine-motor skills and coordination, i.e., reach and grasp, stacking; spatial orientation; organizational skills; object permanence; attention span and persistence	+	+	+
Toy telephone	Functional and symbolic play; fine-motor skills; speech and language skills; facilitate communication and expression; glean child's insight into his experience	−	+	+
Crayons and paper	Functional and symbolic play; fine-motor skills; sensorimotor integration and perception; allow nonverbal child to express feelings; body image; family dynamics; intellectual functioning; cognitive milestones	−	+	+
Soft foam ball	Gross motor skills; object permanence; vehicle for give and take with clinician	+	+	+
Cardboard books	Fine motor skills; coordination; speech and language; cognitive abilities	+	+	+
Mobile Unbreakable, out of reach	Ability to attend, tune in; visual capacity; distraction during physical examination	+	+	+
Mirror Unbreakable, next to examining table, on wall	Visual capacity; mirror play (5–6 mo); distraction during physical examination	+	+	−
Chalkboard Attached to wall, low enough for toddlers	Fine-motor skills; cognitive skills	−	+	+
Posters Cheerful, related to the child's world, e.g., Sesame Street, encased in plastic frame and cover, on walls and ceiling	Cognitive skills; speech and language; facilitate communication with provider; distraction during physical examination	−	+	+

*Data derived from the following references: Garvey, 1977; Gesell, 1954; Gesell and Amatruda, 1969; Gramza, 1976; Illingworth, 1982.

opmental concerns provided there are no parental barriers to identifying these issues. These also serve to identify the concern for developmental issues that the clinician has in health supervision visits. Finally, a questionnaire allows for the speedy collection of data, freeing up the interview time for more in-depth discussion of topical issues.

Planning and caring for a newborn are pivotal moments in the life of a family. Pediatric practice procedures designed to inform and support the new parent or parents are a good investment insofar as they promote the quality of the relationship between the new mother, father, and clinician. A prenatal visit is an invitation to parents to meet the clinician and review the prenatal course, family history, and expectations for parenting and to share views on child care and the role of a child's clinician (see Chapter 5). Recent use of group prenatal visits, where from three to five couples meet with a pediatrician, have highlighted the value of a group process when parents are experiencing a shared stage in their development. The clinician's time for prenatal education is shortened by the use of this method. An office should be able to accommodate these groups with comfortable adult chairs.

Public health nurses and "older, wiser" pediatricians have reminded us about the value of a home visit when insight into family function and style of child care are available to the child's clinician. Recently, pediatricians who recognize the importance of the neonatal period in setting the stage for healthy development have made a home visit standard practice when the infant is 1 week of age. Other pediatricians have reported that group well-child visits promote parent discussion, support new parents in their concerns about physical and behavioral aspects of infancy, and allow more time for exploration of behavioral issues that may not be explored during traditional visits (Stein, 1977). Parent-infant groups of about five families meet at times of standard health supervision visits during the first 2 years of life. Parental acceptance, physician enthusiasm, and cost effectiveness support the group well-child care model (Osborn, 1985; Osborn and Wooley, 1981).

For the new family with older children, the *initial family interview* is a way to learn about new patients in the context of other family members. All available family members—children, parents, stepparents, half-siblings—are actively encouraged to attend this 30-minute office visit where the family's method of discipline, attitude toward education, reasons for seeking a new physician, and nature of recent family change (divorce, illness, job change), if applicable, are discussed. When the initial family interview was compared with a noninterviewed group of families randomly assigned and followed for 2 years, those interviewed were less likely to have problem visits to the office and twice as likely to have health supervision visits (Karofsky, 1989).

The pediatric and family nurse practitioner can participate in many of these new models of office practice. Group well-child visits, the home neonatal visit, and the initial family interview are some examples. In private practices, community clinics, and managed health care systems, nurse practitioners not only are acceptable but also are seen as valuable to participating parents.

The intelligent use of the telephone in office practice can promote the quality of practice and parent satisfaction while attending to the concerns of the office staff (Schmitt, 1980). A specific time set aside for telephone calls to the office and a system in place for office personnel to triage and manage selected calls has been shown to be associated with enhanced satisfaction about office telephone calls among pediatricians (Fosarelli and Schmitt, 1987). Telephone queries about a developmental concern or a behavior problem often require more time than a call about a sore throat or cough.

Pediatricians and other child care primary clinicians are paid for or salaried as "cognitive" providers of care. Time is limited; behavioral problems in an office practice are between a clinical rock and a hard place; they take time to explore properly and reimbursement schedules limit the financial return. Although the recently proposed reimbursement scheme may change reimbursement patterns in a manner that will support behavioral evaluations and counseling among primary care physicians, at the present time there are some imaginative strategies available to motivated clinicians. One-half day may be scheduled weekly for behavioral problems, school underachievement, dysfunctions in parenting, and problems of adolescence. Some pediatricians who have a special interest in one of these areas have sought additional part-time training. Patients with similar psychosocial disorders are scheduled during a half day when appropriate time is allotted for each evaluation. This system has the advantage of the clinician knowing each week that the pace will slow down to allow a visit of 30 minutes or more, as well as the intellectual stimulation inherent in focusing on behavioral pediatrics without other distractions. This system works best in a group practice where each partner maintains a special interest appointment period.

Other clinicians may find that periodic lectures or discussion with groups of parents that focus on a particular behavioral or developmental topic may be applicable to their practice style. Planned in the early evening, parent groups may be scheduled throughout the year on a regular basis (e.g., a series of discussions about parenting and child development during infancy; another for the toddler stage, preschool, school-age, and adolescent periods). Alternatively, they can be organized around specific common behaviors that most parents are concerned about (e.g., night time awakenings, discipline, sexual curiosity, sibling relationships, divorce). Pediatricians who have planned and participated in group parent discussions have found the experience rewarding, stimulating, and an effective method to explore many common behavioral issues of concern to parents. This approach places the pediatric office as a community resource for primary prevention and advocacy.

REFERENCES

Fosarelli P, Schmitt B: Telephone dissatisfaction in pediatric practice: Denver and Baltimore. *Pediatrics* 1987; 80:28–31.

Karofsky P: Initial family interview. *Pediatr News* 1989; 23:6.

Osborn LM, Wooley FR: The use of groups in well-child care. *Pediatrics* 1981; 67:701–706.

Osborn LM: Group well child care. *Clin Perinatol* 1985; 12:355–365.

Schmitt B: *Pediatric Telephone Advice*. Boston, Little, Brown & Co, 1980.

Stein MT: The providing of well-baby care within parent-infant groups. *Clin Pediatr* 1977; 16:825–828.

Weinstein CM, David TG: *Spaces for Children: The Built Environment and Child Development*. New York, Plenum Press, 1987.

ADDITIONAL READINGS

Felice ME: Adolescence, in Levine MD, Carey WB, Crocker AC, et al (eds): *Developmental-Behavioral Pediatrics*. Philadelphia, WB Saunders Co, 1983.

Frankenburg WK, Fandal AW, Thornton SM: Revision of the Denver prescreening developmental questionnaire. *J Pediatr* 1987; 110:653–657.

Green M: Behavioral and developmental components of child health promotion: How can they be accomplished? *Pediatr Rev* 1986; 109:371–378.

Humphreys LE, Ciminero AR: Parent report measures of child behavior: A review. *J Clin Child Psychol* 1979; 8:56–63.

Jellinek MD, Murphy JM, Burns BJ: Brief psychosocial screening in outpatient pediatric practice. *J Pediatr* 1986; 109:371–378.

Levine MD, Brooks R, Schonkoff J: *A Pediatric Approach to Learning Disorders.* New York, John Wiley & Sons, 1980.

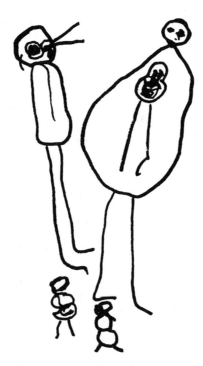

"Father shoots kisses at the (pregnant) mother. Two other kids are there (underneath)." By Colin Hennessy, age 4.

CHAPTER 5

The Prenatal Visit: Making an Alliance With a Family

SUZANNE D. DIXON, M.D.

KEY WORDS

PSYCHOLOGICAL ASPECTS OF PREGNANCY
SIBLING RIVALRY
ROLE OF FATHERS
SLEEP-WAKE CYCLE
RECIPROCAL INTERACTIONS
INFANT TEMPERAMENT
VULNERABLE CHILD SYNDROME

Debbie and Mark Hanson, a soon new family, come in at the end of a busy day, having requested an interview to see if they would like you to take care of their baby, who is expected in 6 weeks. On the telephone, Debbie wants to know if you support breast-feeding and have evening hours for working mothers. She says here she has a list of questions and wants to know if you have any books or pamphlets. Mark expresses no immediate concerns and appears uncomfortable in the office. He says he is worried about being late for his second job helping his dad.

The period of time before an infant's birth is a time of readjustment, concern, anxiety, and some adaptive stress in a family's development. This time, and indeed the time that has gone before it, is the true start of the unborn child's physical and psychosocial development. It is, therefore, the time for the pediatric clinician to begin his or her work. The majority of pediatricians are now inviting prenatal interviews for at least some of their families (Sprunger and Preece, 1982). The American Academy of Pediatrics endorses this practice and encourages pediatricians to become more involved with prenatal anticipatory guidance (Committee of Psychosocial Aspects of Child and Family Health, 1982, 1984). This type of prenatal encounter offers the unique opportunity to begin to build a strong working relationship with a family as the child's advocate. It offers the opportunity to support the necessary psychological development that is demanded by the birth of the child and to gather a unique body of information. Physicians find that this data base gathered in the prenatal period leads to greater efficiency in the later care of the child. Anticipatory guidance begins here in the prenatal period as a prototype for other such encounters of guidance throughout the child's life. It offers the unique opportunity to make an impact on the child's family, even before the infant's birth

49

(Brazelton, 1975; Telzrow, 1978). The prenatal interview, although relatively new to pediatrics, represents the best of care, as well as good business. It allows the physician to establish a strong alliance with a family.

PERINATAL RISK: THE CLASSIC APPROACH, PEDIATRIC STYLE

The data base established here in the prenatal period should include an assessment of physiologic perinatal risk to the unborn child, as well as familial occurrence of inherited disease, history of prior reproductive casualty or success, exposure to toxins, pregnancy events, and the medical history of the parents. These factors are shown in Table 5–1. Pediatric concern for these issues emphasizes to the family the continuities in prenatal and postnatal life. It is the gathering of factual information that is needed for a focused medical assessment of the child. All expectant parents will have concerns about the physical well-being of their child; your questioning is far more likely to be an assurance of your concern rather than a source of *new* worries to a family. These data allow you to provide an accurate assessment of

TABLE 5–1.
Perinatal Risk Factors

Nutritional
  Low weight gain >20 lb
  Excessive weight gain >45 lb
  Unbalanced diet
  Vitaminosis
Infectious
  Viral
    Rubella (check immune status); cytomegalic inclusion; herpes; hepatitis (active disease HsBAg
      carrier); nonspecific vaginitis (rule out *Chlamydia*); syphilis; urinary tract infections
  Bacterial
    Gonorrhea; vaginal discharge; chronic skin infection
  Parasitic
Chemical teratogens
  Alcohol use
  Prescribed medicine
  Street drug use
  Smoking history
  Use of over-the-counter drugs
  Topical drug use (e.g., acne medication—retinoic acid)
Reproductive
  History of this pregnancy
  History of past pregnancy(ies)
  Fetal growth estimates and measurements
  Lactation history
Maternal health conditions
  Endocrine
    Diabetes: prepregnancy, gestational
    Thyroid disease, with or without medication
    Breast abnormalities or difficulties
  Cardiovascular
  Renal
  Neurologic
  Gastrointestinal
  Hematologic
Environmental teratogens
  Occupational exposures
  Exposures related to place of residence

prenatal factors that may influence the development of the child and provide some preventive intervention. The pediatric perspective on these issues may vary somewhat from the obstetric position and call for renewed emphasis on issues that have impact on the infant. So, for instance, the tuberculosis screening test may be seen by the obstetrician as not having the great priority that it does for the pediatric clinician, with whom the specter of neonatal tuberculosis exposure looms very great. Hepatitis B carrier status in a mother means immediate action by the child's clinician after birth and in the months following. The pediatric clinician will offer emphasis to dietary counseling by highlighting the importance of good nutrition for the success of lactation and the intrauterine development of the infant. The public is aware of the danger of drug exposure to the pregnant woman, but the pediatrician's specific concern may be the catalyst for maternal treatment or change. An increased emphasis in the days ahead on environmental toxins is expected to add to a list of concerns. As more women are involved in occupations outside the home, the factors associated with occupational risks need to be addressed. This ascertainment of physical risk and the preventive potential here is certainly a part of the important work to be done in the prenatal interview. Much of this can be gathered on a written form, either before or following the interview (Fig 5–1).

EXPANDING THE HORIZON: PSYCHOLOGICAL ADAPTATION

However, this encounter is too limited if it stops merely with this data base. Parents are particularly open to the establishment of a new relationship with a clinician as they reorder their views of themselves and their relationships with others, a major task of pregnancy (Brazelton, 1981). Parents can rely on your professional support as they try out the new role of a parent of a pediatric patient. Data are gathered with incredible efficiency at this time because of the energy a family brings to the situation and how close the adult needs and feelings are to the surface at this time. In addition, the infant's delightful presence does not distract from the focus on the parents' own developmental progression, an important adaptive process of pregnancy. The dialogue between clinician and the parents becomes a therapeutic alliance around which health and optimal development of the child may be built (Parker et al., 1978). It is this alliance that will allow for the pediatric clinician's effective care of the child in the days after birth.

The prenatal interview gives you the opportunity to clearly indicate your approval and areas of concern, which include the health of the unborn child in the broadest and preventive sense. An anticipatory or preventive model is clearly presented in this setting (Telzrow, 1978), offering a format for future encounters as you establish your territory of concern—psychosocial aspects of development, as well as the physical concerns in the care of the child. Parents can look you over to see if your approaches are in line with their expectations; "misfit" between clinician and parents can thus be avoided.

PSYCHOLOGICAL ADJUSTMENT TO PREGNANCY

These adaptive changes have important implications for the unborn patient. The mental turbulence of this time is both normal and adaptive in mobilizing the family in meeting the needs of the unborn child (Liebenberg, 1973). Excessive stress may alter the family's ability to make these important developmental changes. Severe psychological stress may directly affect fetal growth and perhaps psychological structures of the child as well (Yamamoto and

Prenatal Interview

Date _____

Place _____

Referral Source _____

Mother's name _____ Phone: Home _____
Address _____ Business _____

Father's name _____ Phone: Home _____
Address _____ Business _____

Expected date of confinement _____ Language(s) spoken
Anticipated method of delivery _____ at home _____
Gestational age at interview _____
Obstetrician _____ Hospital _____

G _____ P _____ Ab$_s$ _____ AB$_t$ _____ Maternal Age _____

Previous pregnancy complications _____
Number, sex, and ages of mother's living children _____
_____
Number, sex, and ages of father's living children _____
_____
Household members _____
This pregnancy:
a. month of first prenatal visit _____
b. medications: Vitamins _____ Iron _____ Other _____
c. Presence of: anemia _____ explain _____
   proteinuria _____ explain _____
   glycosuria _____ explain _____
   hypertension _____ explain _____
   spotting _____ explain _____
d. other complications _____
e. ultrasound(s) date(s) _____
   result(s) _____
f. screening tests positive: VDRL _____ Rubella _____ PPD _____ HsBAg _____

Mother's health: _____
   Review of systems: _____
   Alcohol _____ Tobacco _____ Drug use _____
   Occupation _____
   Family history of illness _____
Father:
   Review of systems: _____
   Age _____ Family health history _____
   Occupation _____ Married to mother: Yes _____ No _____
   Living together: Yes _____ No _____

   Health insurance _____
   Special concerns _____

FIG 5-1.
Questionnaire for prenatal interview.

Kinsey, 1976). The loss of a close loved one during pregnancy is a particularly high-risk situation as the energy for attachment to the unborn is drawn off into this other "disattachment" process. Stress between spouses or between expectant parents and grandparents may be seen to some degree in every pregnant family as individuals reorder relationships (Griffith, 1976; Tolor and Digrazia, 1976). Extremes in conflicts may draw energy away from the adaptive changes that are a necessary part of every pregnancy. Indeed, the lack of a female support system may be one of the most significant risk factors for any mother undergoing pregnancy (Kennell, 1982; Rubin, 1976). The isolated, unsupported family represents a very high risk for both psychosocial and physiological adjustments during gestation and beyond (Egeland and Sroufe, 1981). The whole family and the pregnancy context must be taken into account if one is attempting to assess a child's full well-being.

Pregnancy is the time of psychological turmoil for every family and has been described as "a developmental crisis" (Bibring and Valenstein, 1976; Deutsch, 1944). Although the concept of a "crisis" is controversial, pregnancy is a major time of psychological adjustment. Energy is mobilized, reordered, and directed around the unborn child in a process of attachment (Bibring and Valenstein, 1976; Leifer, 1977; Rubin, 1976). Anxiety, conflict, tension, and fears all are normal and necessary emotional components of even the most uncomplicated gestations for both mothers and fathers and for other family members (Bittman and Zalk, 1978; Heymans and Winter, 1975; Hott, 1976; Legg et al., 1974). It is a time for both parents to take on new roles and identities that are consistent with their expectations and responsibilities (Caplan, 1976). Shifts in attention, time allocation, and monetary resources follow from the process of changing priorities within the whole family unit. This process begins by a turning inward (Deutsch, 1944) and a reassessment of old relationships, particularly those between the expectant parents and their own parents. The search for a role model, either conscious or unconscious, and a need to be dependent again are all the bases for this renewed focus on one's own parental relationships. Whether the grandparents of the unborn child are perceived as positive or negative, whether they are present or not, does not diminish their central *psychological* place in this adjustment process. Parents must work through this relationship with their own parents with each new pregnancy (Bibring and Valenstein, 1976; Brazelton, 1981).

THE DEVELOPMENTAL COURSE OF PREGNANCY

A predictable developmental course of adjustment has been described through interviews with pregnant women (Bibring and Valenstein, 1976; Rubin, 1976) as they deal with the four major developmental tasks outlined in Table 5–2. These tasks are (1) seeking a safe passage; (2) finding an assurance of acceptance of the child by significant others; (3) binding in (i.e., bonding) to the unborn child; and (4) learning to give of oneself.

FIRST TRIMESTER

In the first trimester, the inward preoccupation of the mother is largely focused on her changing body. The bodily sensations, most of them unpleasant, serve to repeatedly verify the presence of pregnancy. These conflicting sensations press to resolve any old feelings of anger, guilt, remorse, and disbelief that may linger around the pregnancy (Uddenberg et al., 1976). The baby is not yet a real person to the family, although the mother may become

TABLE 5-2.
Developmental Course of Pregnancy*

Task	First Trimester	Second Trimester	Third Trimester
Seeking safe passage	Focus on maternal health	Avoidance of perceived dangers to the child	Increased feelings of vulnerability; seeking solutions to imagined problems; increased fears and anxieties; increased dreams and tension
Acceptance of the child	Loosening of old relationships; acceptance of pregnancy by significant others	Fantasies of the unborn child in relationship to others	Increased anxieties about the child not meeting expectations
Bonding	Attachment to the idea of pregnancy; ambivalence	Attachment to the child growing at a rapid rate; private sense of shared experience	Disattached to the pregnancy; ready to see the real child; increased fear of losing the child
Giving of oneself	Assessment of cost/ benefit to self in having a child	Decrease in ambivalence; more concrete in planning for the infant	Seeks gifts for self and infant; increased worries about competencies

Adapted from Rubin R: *J Adv Nurs* 1976; 1:367–376.

attached to the *idea* of being pregnant. The fetus is viewed as a change in the mother rather than as a separate individual. Most mothers report feeling tense, edgy, nervous, irritable, and occasionally depressed (Caplan, 1976). For mothers with a history of spontaneous abortions, these feelings are enhanced.

SECOND TRIMESTER

With the onset of fetal movement in the second trimester, there is a marked shift in psychological processes. The mother has an increase in her sense of well-being. She begins to see the developing fetus as a separate individual who is bound to her by a process of individual attachment rather than by general feelings of attachment to the pregnancy as a whole. The mother may have various fantasies about what the child will be like, whom the child will resemble, and how he or she will fit into the family unit. Dreams and imaginings about the unborn child begin at this time, and the mother may actively seek out female support systems and develop and show protective feelings toward the child. Some investigators have suggested that lack of a female support system may be the greatest psychological risk factor (Kennell, 1982). In general, parents increase their efforts to solidify ties with friends, community, and extended family at this time. Early preparation for the baby is a good sign that this second psychological stage has been met. "Nest building" (i.e., the thinking about and preparing a place for the baby) is a positive sign. However, even in the absence of real concrete preparations for the infant, parents may be involved in important internal preparations for the infant's arrival. Indeed, for some families and cultures, physical preparations may be prohibited or viewed as dangerous. However, even in these cases, mothers will be preoccupied with making plans for the infants and themselves (LeVine, 1981). Most older children, even toddlers, now begin to show behavioral change that indicates their awareness that their relationship with mother is changing. These processes are usually adaptive and resolve with time and highlighting to parents the need to "baby" the older child.

THIRD TRIMESTER

The work of the third trimester is that of seeking a safe passage through the turmoil of labor and delivery. The mother becomes disattached to the pregnancy itself but not to the concept of the child, who now becomes a companion for a dangerous adventure ahead. With increasing physical limitations, the mother's feelings of vulnerability and entrapment by her increasing bulk become more real. An increase in passivity and introversion peak at 7 to 8 months in the pregnancy. Troublesome symptoms such as shortness of breath, gastritis, and swollen feet and ankles now appear. Feelings of fear and almost paranoia dominate the mother's thought processes. Parents who have a pattern of coping with stress by drugs or alcohol may be vulnerable to use during this time. Sleep may be erratic, may be lighter, and may change electrophysiologically as well as behaviorally (Petre-Quadens et al., 1967) to be in line with the needs of the infant (Sanders et al., 1975). Sleep is dominated by fears, fantasies, and dreams of the unborn infant (Heymans and Winter, 1975). The mother worries about the delivery and fears damage to the child. At this time, the baby and the mother are perceived as separate individuals but facing a common peril—the safe passage through delivery. Psychological nest building continues through a process of inward direction of thoughts and ideations. Mothers become disinterested in external events and the concerns of others around them as they become more introspective and more preoccupied with their own issues. Mothers in the third trimester often appear irritable and overinterpretive of others' actions through this kind of sensitivity to the interactional variables around them (Rubin, 1976). They focus on microscopic details, appear somewhat disorganized, and are very preoccupied. Late in the third trimester, prenatal interviews are not as successful as those held earlier, because mothers and fathers are focused only on the delivery, on survival of the upcoming events.

Early third trimester offers a unique opportunity for education, counseling, and anticipatory guidance, including the prenatal interview. Mothers are eager to assure a safe delivery and are anxious to make a relationship with a professional who will be in charge of the health of their infant. Fantasies about deformity and calamities and dreams that have imagery of damaged infants are very common. Mothers will seek out professional consultation to ward off these possible impending difficulties through reassurance and the promise of help. A mother might also experience difficulty focusing on external affairs and the activities of others. She may have a growing doubt about her own competence. She may seek out professional help to confirm her own competencies in a role about to be undertaken—that of motherhood (Seiden, 1976).

FATHERS

Although research in this area is sparse, the adjustment process for fathers in pregnancy is very real (Bittman and Zalk, 1978; Hott, 1976; Parke, 1981). Fathers' reactions often may be delayed and less intense but appear to be similar to those of mothers-to-be. They do not experience the compelling internal physical presence of the child or regular physical symptoms to drive the adjustment. In addition, a father must work through his sense of loss of the relationship he once had with his wife without the gain of the child's presence. Sexual experiences often change dramatically during pregnancy (Holtzman, 1976). Out of inappropriate fears for the fetus, frequency and variety of sexual experiences may be diminished. Other couples report more frequent enjoyable sexual activities at various times during the pregnancy. In either event, the relationship has changed, and the father's psychological view about the pregnancy may be guided by the way he experiences his new relationship with his wife and, in turn, parallels her experience with the pregnancy, labor, and delivery.

The third trimester may bring anxieties about the child and the delivery. In addition, the actual cost of caring for a child may push some fathers to seek extra work and to develop new strategies for financial future planning. Some fathers will seek out work to balance the anxiety that the impending delivery brings (Obrzut, 1976). Mothers may misinterpret this as "fleeing."

Do fathers make any difference to the delivery and well-being of the infant? Unequivocally yes! Research has shown that in families in which the father is involved and present for labor and delivery, everything goes better (Pederson et al., 1980). Mothers go through labor more easily, and deliveries are smoother. Indeed, the actual effectiveness of child-birth preparation classes may be through the medium of father participation (Parke et al., 1979). Ninety-five percent of fathers in the Park et al. (1979) study reported the delivery as a positive experience. The father's presence at a cesarean section prompts greater involvement with the infant in the neonatal period (DeChateau and Wiberg, 1977) and even into the first months of life (Pederson et al., 1980). Fathers also have a role in aiding older children in their adjustment to pregnancy (Earls, 1976). In one study, fathers increased the time spent with the older child on the average by 34%, and the time allocation was positively related to the ease of the older child's adjustment (Parke et al., 1979). The best predictor of breast-feeding success is the support of the spouse.

In summary, a father's involvement with the pregnancy and delivery bodes well for the family's adjustment. It also makes the pediatric clinician's work easier in supporting the health and well-being of the family. It is well worth the effort to actively encourage and support the involvement of fathers in the child's life before birth. Direct positive support for this involvement should come from the pediatric clinician.

Pregnancy demands an important transition in adult development for both mothers and fathers, a process that is not complete at the time of the infant's birth or beyond. The parents who come in for the prenatal interview will not be the same as those the clinician will meet after the delivery. The pediatric clinician can anticipate the strength of the infant to mold some of the uncertainties, anxieties, and the mild, often adaptive, disorganization seen in most families at this time.

OTHER CHILDREN

The adaptation to the impending arrival of a competitor is a hurdle for any young child (Legg et al., 1974). The birth of a sibling requires readjustment of the child's views of himself and of his place in the family. The parents' own adjustment processes make a child aware of a change in a family long before he is aware of the source of the change. In fact, concealment of the pregnancy not only is impossible but leads to an increase in the anxiety the child may be experiencing because of all of the changes that are occurring. The young child needs to be reassured often of his parents' unwavering love and the security of his life around him. For a child less than 3 years of age whose capacity to understand future events and whose world is largely confined to his family and home, the birth of a sibling may be difficult. This assurance of continuity is particularly important. If changes are needed (e.g., change in beds), they should be done early to allow for accommodation. Young children may enjoy feeling the baby move in utero or accompanying mother for checkups; there are no data to suggest that these activities ease the adjustment. The rehearsal of the specific plans for a child at the time of the delivery is helpful to a young child so that he can anticipate what will happen to him. Mild regressions and an increase in demands by the child are positive signs of a child's sensitivity to an adjustment to the pregnancy and offer testimony to the child's attachment to his parents. There is no reason to expect that having to share one's parents with another child will be greeted with enthusiasm, at least for some period of adjustment. This is true no matter what the spacing interval is between children. The central issue in the adjustment is the parents' continuing psychological availability for the older child.

A parent may have significant feelings of loss in the relationship to the older child with the anticipated arrival of another and wonder if she or he has enough time, energy, and love to share with another child. A sense of urgency about that relationship with the older child, a feeling of pressure to do all that the parent can before the birth of the next child, may be a source of additional tension in a family. These issues run counter to the pulling away, inward turning of mothers at this time. An expectant mother is a new and changeable person with whom the older child must adjust.

Parents can introduce books that deal with the birth of a sibling (see Chapter 32) in the third trimester. Children's questions about the event should be answered clearly and honestly, bearing in mind what might be the *basis* for the specific question (e.g., separation, loss of possessions, special shared activities), as well as the child's developmental level. Medical details are of less interest.

Some families will ask about a sibling's presence at the birth. Research on the effects of this experience is sparse. The clinician may ask the parents to consider this from their older child's perspective: Will the intensity of the emotion be overwhelming or frightening? How will the child respond to an unexpected event as well as the expected events? Who will be present with the *exclusive* job of support for the older child, to monitor this child's responses, answer questions, and give permission to leave? Are the parents willing and able to prepare the older child insofar as they can? Does the child wish to attend the birth and will there be a chance for him to change his mind? A consideration of the child's capacity to deal with fears and fantasy must be brought forward.

Hospital visitation after the infant's birth may ameliorate some of the child's worries about separation. Acceptance of the new baby should not be the goal of this visit; the reassurance of maternal availability and intactness should be. There is no evidence that a hospital visit decreases any of the expected negative behaviors at home. That rivalry appears to need to run its course.

FEARS AND EXPECTATIONS

Fears for self and the unborn child throughout the pregnancy are normal and adaptive (Brazelton, 1981). In one study, 81% of women admitted to fears regarding their unborn infants; 52% imagined them as malformed; 29%, as mentally defective; and 28% regularly feared that their infants would die (Heymans and Winter, 1975). The more highly educated the women, the greater the number of fears they experienced. These worries are healthy in that they prepare parents psychologically for the birth of an imperfect child. This "rehearsal" makes the approaching crisis seem more manageable. Fantasies about a damaged child, worries of destruction of self, or even paranoid thoughts about loved ones are evidence of real psychic work and are, in general, resistant to simple reassurances by the professional or even the forces of logic and statistics. The clinician should attend more to the affect than the factual base. The emotional responses are testimony to the level of caring and the assumption of responsibility that the parent is assuming. They are a measure of the attachment process following its own expected developmental course. Explicit reflections during the prenatal interview on the adaptive significance of this turmoil will help parents see these new experiences as part of a normative process. This may not dissolve their persistent fears and anxieties, but it may allow them to see them in a different light—one that yields acceptance and personal growth. Even some of the expectable changes in behavior come from displaced fears for the infant and for the self as a parent: an increased anxiety level, increased self-preoccupation and need for care, decreased ability to cope with stress, and increase in "maternal" behaviors toward the husband. Parents may also benefit from a reflection of these behaviors and feelings as adaptive.

PARENTAL EXPECTATIONS

Parental expectations for the child that are expressed before birth are highly predictive of the postnatal adjustment process (Paschall and Newton, 1976). These expectations for the child, realistic or not, will become a part of the relationship between infant and parents after the birth. These may be expressed openly at this time; later they may be unconsciously or consciously suppressed. These expectations may be for a certain gender, for a specific physical appearance, or that the child will serve as a substitute for a lost loved one or make up for deficiencies in self. These expectations are to some degree part of every parent's dreams and hopes. However, in extreme or rigid form, set expectations for the unborn child constitute a high risk for poor bonding and integration of the particular child into the family unit. The clinician will find these very near the surface in the prenatal period in contrast to their elusiveness after the real infant arrives on the scene. These unfulfilled expectations may, in turn, be impediments to effective caretaking and attachment. Clinicians may find these issues disguised as sleeping, feeding, and discipline problems later on. Without these early data, the resolution of these problems will be difficult because their bases will be very deeply concealed, usually unconsciously.

All of the turbulent psychological factors that are a part of every parent's journey through pregnancy testify to the inevitable ambivalence that each parent experiences with each new baby. The infant will require time, money, attention, emotional energy, and thought that must be taken from other relationships. The infant's demands are continual, unknown, and unpredictable. It is to be expected that parents approach this new relationship with conflicted feelings (Bibring and Valenstein, 1976). The infant commands such formidable commitment that other realignments and readjustments will inevitably have to be made. The role of the clinician is not to dictate these realignments but to monitor and support a family as they work through these in their own style and in their own way. The clinician is an advocate for the child and may highlight the generic needs of that child if these are not clear to the family.

The prenatal interview allows the clinician to tap the expectations for the child and the parental turbulence in the adjustment process. The physician may also offer some reality test-ing and reassurance for some of the parents' fears. Parents will appreciate being told that most expectant couples have these same concerns and that these fears are part of the adjust-ment process and a measure of the parents' care and beginning attachment to the infant. Normal fears and fantasies do not in and of themselves damage the infant or in any way cause or predict poor parenting.

SINGLE PARENTS

Single mothers present some special concerns for the clinician; the nature of the contract between the clinician and the parent may be slightly altered (Brazelton, 1981). As an increas-ing proportion of any pediatric practice, the single parent's issues warrant some additional consideration and a modified approach that begins in the prenatal period. It is hard to be a parent; it is harder to be a single parent. Isolation from immediate support systems is a regular stress in many cases. Economic, social, and practical management problems are increased dramatically in this group. More important, the decision-making process within that family and the relationships between members are expectedly different than in two-parent families. The clinician's role should also be different if she is an advocate for the child's mental health and optimal development. To act in that capacity, the clinician must examine her own feelings regarding the single parent. The clinician who brings only minimal support, a punitive atti-tude, or mixed feelings of commitment to such a family will not be effective in the role of child advocate.

Several special roles will be expected of the primary caregiver in this situation. The cli-nician may be a sounding board for child management issues for the parent who has no other close support and who is trusted as the pediatric caregiver. These encounters around small matters should be seen as building confidence in the parent without a partner. Confirmation of good ideas and management plans is an important part of that. The clinician should iden-tify this issue in the prenatal period so that the parent uses her services appropriately *early* in the child's life. Within the context of a trusting relationship, this help should not be accu-satory, berating, or dismissed as trivial.

All children need a supportive network of care. The clinician should identify who will be available during labor and after the baby is born as a means to address these issues. Isolation, alienation, and poor self-esteem place the infant at high risk. A "doula," or support person, during the labor will make the delivery go better.

The child of a single parent may be called on to play a more intense and complex role in the family. A closeness develops that sustains the relentless demands of unshared responsi-bility. However, the closeness may make it difficult for the child and parent to separate when it is developmentally appropriate to do so. The clinician's responsibility is to anticipate these times and to support the child's needs for greater autonomy. The demands of other family members force this separation in most two-parent families. These separation difficulties may present in mundane disguise: sleeping, eating, discipline problems (Zuckerman and Blitzer, 1981). The prenatal interview provides the opportunity to lay out that expectation as an offer for particular support. The clinician may anticipate being a bit more direct and directive in the anticipatory guidance of single parents, particularly early in the infant's life—a balancing force, a trail guide for a difficult path.

WORKING MOTHERS

With the majority of women returning to work during their child's infancy, new dimensions loom over a pregnancy. Mothers may unconsciously limit their own attachment to the unborn, knowing they must turn over care to another, as has been shown by Keefer (study in progress, 1990) and Brazelton (1985). This is a dangerous process and should be identified early and prevented if possible. The value of early, supported mothering, the importance and possibility of breast-feeding, and ways to establish and maintain that special relationship with the infant must be discussed, even if the parents do not bring up these issues. Facilitation of contacts with other working mothers, child care resources, and office practices that support working parents all aid this adjustment. Support for parental leave in individual cases and broadly is a proper pediatric role. Child care with a relative, in the child's home, or with small family day-care providers appear to be the best options for care of the infant if available (National Center, 1987), although centers with low provider/child ratios do give good care (Clarke-Stewart, 1989). Most important, the pediatrician must explore his own attitudes and biases about working mothers. Although younger and more clinicians show a trend for more supportive care, negative attitudes prevail in spite of the changed demographics of the American family (AAP and Rubenstein, 1990).

SUMMARY

The developmental work for parents through the prenatal period involves the readjustment of old roles and relationships so that they are prepared to mobilize energies to meet the needs of their individual child. The mental processes during the prenatal period should indicate that the expectant family is attending to the needs of the unborn child and that its members are accepting the new roles and actively working through this adjustment. Certainly the best predictor of the child's outcome is how much the parents care. Turmoil and anxiety are normal, are adaptive, and allow the clinician to monitor, guide, and support the family. Most important, the prenatal interview allows for the development of the beginning of the relationship of a family-caregiver unit (Wolfson and Bass, 1979).

DATA GATHERING

SETTING THE STAGE

Allow about 30 minutes for the interview if possible; invite both parents to participate at a time that is convenient for both of them and for you. Four to eight weeks before birth appears to be the ideal time. The end of the morning or afternoon office hours may provide the necessary quiet time in a pediatric practice. Provide at least two comfortable adult chairs in the office setting and provide these in a position where eye-to-eye contact is possible. Ask the parents to fill out a medical history before the interview and review it before your interaction with them.

Each clinician will have her own style in doing prenatal interviews, and this will vary on parental factors as well. However, this encounter can be maximized by having a format set at least to begin. Many pediatric clinicians may be slightly uncomfortable at first without the presence of a child; a set agenda will help to ameliorate this discomfort.

Group pediatric prenatal visits are a new option for some practices, often attached to childbirth, breast-feeding, or sibling preparation classes. These sessions offer the opportunity to efficiently review your own philosophy and practice plan and to answer questions. Information can be given to the group and productive discussion. Many families respond to the group support, and this may lay the foundation for group health supervision visits. All such group formats should include some private time with each couple to address their particular concerns and begin to establish an individual relationship.

OBSERVATIONAL DATA

Note who comes and why. Assess the interaction between the parents as they enter the room for the interview process. Be aware of the general affect; some degree of anxiety and apprehension would be expected. Determine the degree of comfort with the pregnancy: behavioral and verbal, both mother and father. Note the patting of the abdomen by the pregnant woman as an indicator of a positive attitude. Note the use of pronouns or names for the unborn child and the type and quantity of questions asked.

WHAT TO ASK

The format of questions outlined in Table 5–3 provides for the control of the interaction to flow from the clinician to the parents.

A discussion of the specifics of your contract with the family should include the following: your availability and backup plans, the schedule for seeing the infant in the neonatal period and beyond, some general statements about your own philosophy of pediatric care, and your fee schedule and payment options.

A summary statement about your understanding of the interview's content and process will allow for a resolution of differences or highlight areas of omission.

SPECIAL REFERRALS

Call or make a note of the obstetrician regarding special concerns from a pediatric perspective.

State terms of your own availability at the time of the birth (e.g., another clinician may provide care for the baby in the hospital in some circumstances).

Recommend prepared childbirth, breast-feeding, or other parenting classes if these have not already been attended.

Refer to social service agency or public health nurse for diagnostic aid and support system, if indicated.

Nutrition referral should be made if indicated by nutritional history or economic needs.

Suggest appropriate readings (see Appendix).

ANTICIPATORY GUIDANCE

Encourage open discussion between parents of the subjects addressed in the interview.

Advise the parents that it may be wise to plan to get help (e.g., a relative, friend, or employee) in the immediate postnatal period but to limit (most) visitors for about 2 weeks.

Encourage class attendance or reading as a supplement but not as a substitute for your own care.

Reassure that fears, fantasies, and feelings of loss of control are normal, adaptive, and a good indicator of care.

TABLE 5–3.
Questions to Be Asked in Prenatal Visit

Question	Objective
How are you feeling?	Lay the territory to include parents' well-being; assess response to the situation overall.
Ask how the pregnancy has gone (expand to cover medical events, life stresses, etc., as noted on the medical history form and your own individual outline, i.e., a pregnancy history from a pediatric standpoint).	Gather data for objective risk factors and the parents' perception of them as well; assess general response to the pregnancy and the perception of the pregnancy as high risk (whether it is by medical criteria or not).
Turn to the father and ask how the pregnancy has gone for him.	Assess the father's perceptions and concerns about his wife and baby and his own adjustment to the pregnancy.
Was this a planned pregnancy?	Assess the place of the child in the relationship, parents' adjustment to pregnancy, and degree and nature of adjustment for child's health.
Do you have other children at home? What are their ages and sexes? Have you cared for an infant before? What was that experience like?	Assess the family structure; note the child's place in it; assess experience and expectations for infant care; locus of control, i.e., do parents see themselves in control of this event?; preparedness, general information on the subject; open opportunity to give information or your own preferences about the delivery event; may tap in on particular anxieties or fears in the third trimester; assess unrealistic or rigid expectations; when appropriate, assert that you think that the parents are in charge.
Ask how do you plan to feed the baby? (expand to include a diet history during pregnancy, preparation for nursing).	Assess realistic planning for the baby and advise; reaffirm parents' control of this option, emphasize the importance of nurturance in general; offer the opportunity to say how you feel about the situation; assess maternal nutrition vis-à-vis the infant; assess specific breast-feeding preparations; do not push a decision if the family is not ready.
If the infant is a boy, will you have him circumcised? (Address question to the father.)	Assess individuation of the baby; bring the father into the decision-making process; open this topic for a two-way discussion, providing objective information on circumcision (i.e., the lack of clear medical indications) and the procedure itself (Wallerstein, 1980).
Have you purchased a carseat?	Show interest in safety and caretaking; assess the parents' anticipation of the needs of the infant.
How long have you lived in this area? Where do most of your family live?	Assess family support systems; assess the realignment of old relationships.
Who will be available to help you after the baby comes?	Assess support systems; assess the realignment of old relationships; tap in on parents' relationship to their own feelings.
Do you have other responsibilities outside the family?	Assess the mother's other areas of responsibility and stress; assess what realignment of these is anticipated; some areas of ambivalence and concern may be discussed.

Continued.

TABLE 5–3 (Continued).
Questions to Be Asked in Prenatal Visit

Question	Objective
Are you working outside your home? What are your job plans? Do you have any ideas about the time you will return to work? Are you attending school? Have you made plans for the infant's care?	Assess the psychosocial situation of the family; assess the mother's perception of her role in her career or education and as a mother; assess realistic planning for infant care.
Do you have any worries about your infant? Most parents do have some concerns about the child. Would you like to share any of those with me? Is there anything in your past history that makes you think you have some special worries about your child?	Open discussion of concerns directly, but also use this setting to respond to affect and perhaps deeper concerns; provide information about common fears, fantasies, and dreams during a normal pregnancy.
For families with other children: How are your other children reacting to your pregnancy? What things have you done to prepare them for the birth? Most parents have some worries about how they'll manage to have enough time and love for more than one child. Do you share any of these concerns? What are the specific arrangements you've made for that child at the time of the baby's birth?	Assess the realignment of family relationships; assess the plans for readjustment around the care of the infant; assess the maternal and paternal feelings toward the attachment to their children who have already been born.
Do you have any questions?	Set a model for pediatric visits, i.e., you are open to questions and waiting for the parents to take the lead.

Emphasize good nutrition and safety planning for the infant and congratulate the parents on advance planning and responsibility in initiating the interview process.

Emphasize that it is important to approach the birth with some flexibility so that unforeseen events (e.g., anesthesia or a cesarean section) can be weathered with adaptation and grace.

Emphasize planning for sibling response.

REFERENCES

American Academy of Pediatrics, Rubenstein, C: What pediatricians really think about working mothers. *Working Mothers* April 1990 (Reprinted in *AAP News* May 1990.)

Bibring GL, Valenstein AF: Psychological aspects of pregnancy. *Clin Obstet Gynecol* 1976; 19:357–371.

Bittman SJ, Zalk SR: *Expectant Fathers.* New York, Hawthorn Books, 1978.

Brazelton TB: *On Becoming a Family: The Growth of Attachment.* New York, Delacorte Press/ Seymour Lawrence, 1981.

Brazelton TB: *Working and Caring.* Reading, Mass, Addison-Wesley Publishing Co, 1985.

Brazelton TB: Anticipatory guidance. *Pediatr Clin North Am* 1975; 22:533–543.

Caplan G: *Emotional Implications of Pregnancy and Influences on Family Relationships in the Healthy Child.* Cambridge, Mass, Harvard University Press, 1976.

Clarke-Stewart KA: Infant day care: Maligned or malignant? *Am Psychol* 1989; 44:266–273.

Committee on Psychosocial Aspects of Child and Family Health: The prenatal visit. *Pediatrics* 1984; 73:561–562.

Committee on Psychosocial Aspects of Child and Family Health: Pediatrics and the psychosocial aspects of child and family health. *Pediatrics* 1982; 79:126–127.

DeChateau P, Wiberg B: Long-term effect on mother-infant behavior of extra contact during the first hour post partum: II. A follow up at three months. *Acta Paediatr Scand* 1977; 66:145–151.

Deutsch H: *Psychology of Women.* New York, Grune & Stratton, 1944.

Earls F: The fathers (not the mothers): Their importance and influence with infants and young children. *Psychiatry* 1976; 39:209–226.

Egeland B, Sroufe LA: Attachment and early maltreatment. *Child Dev* 1981; 52:44–52.

Griffith S: Pregnancy as an event with crisis potential for marital partners: A study of interpersonal needs. *JOGN Nurs* 1976; 5:35–38.

Heymans H, Winter ST: Fears during pregnancy. *Isr J Med Sci* 1975; 11:1102–1105.

Holtzman LC: Sexual practices during pregnancy. *J Nurs Midwife* 1976; 21:29–38.

Hott JR: The crisis of expectant fatherhood. *Am J Nurs* 1976; 76:1436–1440.

Kennell JH: The physiologic effects of a supportive companion (doula) during labor, in Klaus MH, Robertson MO (eds): *Birth, Interaction and Attachment.* Pediatric Round Table Series, New York, Johnson and Johnson Baby Products Co, 1982.

Legg C, Sherick I, Wadland W: Reaction of preschool children to the birth of a sibling. *Child Psychiatry Hum Dev* 1974; 5:3–39.

Leifer M: Psychological changes accompanying pregnancy and motherhood. *Genet Psychol Monogr* 1977; 95:55–96.

LeVine S: *Wives and Mothers: Gusii Mothers of East Africa.* Chicago, University of Chicago Press, 1981.

Liebenberg B: Prenatal counseling, in Shereshefsky PM, Yarrow LJ (eds): *Psychological Aspects of a First Pregnancy and Early Postnatal Adaptation.* New York, Raven Press, 1973.

National Center for Clinical Infant Programs: Infant day care: A continuing dialogue, in *Zero to Three.* Special Reprint, Washington, DC, NCCIF, September 1987.

Obrzut LE: Expectant fathers' perception of fathering. *Am J Nurs* 1976; 76:1440–1442.

Parke RD: Fathers, in Bruner J, Cole M, Lloyd B (eds): *The Developing Child Series.* Cambridge, Mass, Harvard University Press, 1981.

Parke RD, Power TG, Tensley BR, et al: The father's role in the family system. *Semin Perinatol* 1979; 3:25–34.

Parker WB, Keefer C, Brazelton TB: *The Prenatal Period: An Opportunity for Pediatricians.* Cambridge, Mass, Harvard Medical School, 1978.

Paschall N, Newton N: Personality factors and postpartum adjustment. *Primary Care* 1976; 3:741–750.

Pederson FA, Naslow MT, Cain RL, et al: Caesarean birth: The importance of a family perspective. Paper presented to the International Congress on Infant Studies, New Haven, Conn, 1980.

Petre-Quadens O, DeBarsy AM, Devos J, et al: Sleep in pregnancy: Evidence of foetal sleep characteristics. *J Neurol Sci* 1967; 4:600–605.

Rubin R: Maternal tasks in pregnancy. *J Adv Nurs* 1976; 1:367–376.

Sanders L, Stechler G, Julra H, et al: Primary prevention and some aspects of temporal organization in early infant-caretaker interactions, in Rexford EN, Sanders LW, Shapiro T (eds): *Infant Psychiatry.* New Haven, Conn: Yale University Press, 1975, pp 187–204.

Seiden AM: The maternal sense of mastery in primary care obstetrics. *Primary Care* 1976; 3:717–726.

Sprunger L, Preece EW: Characteristics of prenatal interviews provided by pediatricians. *Clin Pediatr* 1982; 20:778–782.

Telzrow R: Anticipatory guidance in pediatric practice. *J Cont Educ Pediatr* 1978; 20.

Tolor A, Digrazia PV: Sexual attitudes and behavior patterns during and following pregnancy. *Arch Sex Behav* 1976; 5:539–551.

Uddenberg N, Fagerstroom CF, Hakanson-Zaunders M: Reproductive conflicts: Mental symptoms during pregnancy and time in labor. *J Psychosom Res* 1976; 20:575–581.

Wallerstein E: *Circumcision: An American Health Fallacy.* New York, Springer Publishing Co, 1980.

Wolfson J, Bass L: How the pediatrician can foster optimal parent-infant relationships. *Semin Perinatol* 1979; 3:101–105.

Yamamoto KJ, Kinsey DK: Pregnant women's ratings of different factors influencing psychological stress during pregnancy. *Psychol Rep* 1976; 39:203–214.

Zuckerman B, Blitzer EC: Sleep disorders, in Gabel S (ed): *Behavioral Problems in Pediatrics.* New York, Grune & Stratton, 1981, pp 257–272.

ADDITIONAL READINGS

American Academy of Pediatrics, Committee on Standards of Child Health Care: *Standards of Health Care.* Evanston, Ill, American Academy of Pediatrics, 1972.

Doering SG, Entwisle DR: Coping mechanisms during childbirth and postpartum sequelae. *Primary Care* 1976; 3:727–739.

Entwisle DR, Doering SG: *The First Birth.* Baltimore, Johns Hopkins University Press, 1981.

Klaus M, Kennell JH: *N Engl J Med* 1980; 303:597–600.

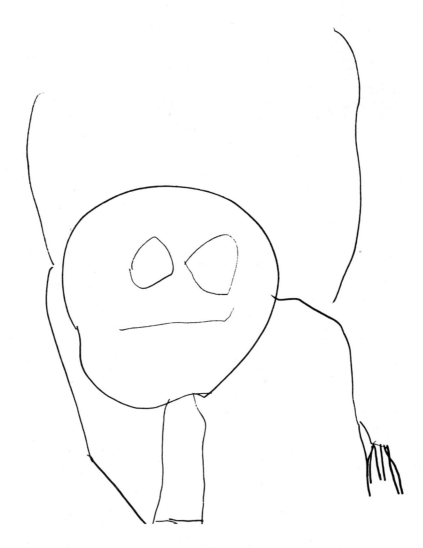

"A baby." By Heather R., age 3½.

CHAPTER 6

The Newborn Examination: Innate Readiness for Interaction With the Environment

SUZANNE D. DIXON, M.D.

KEY WORDS

PERCEPTUAL DEVELOPMENT
NEONATAL VISION AND HEARING
NEONATAL MOTOR BEHAVIOR
PRIMITIVE REFLEXES
INTERSENSORY COORDINATION
POSTPARTUM ADJUSTMENT

Jessica, born without complications, was to be examined at 1 hour of life. Her body was relaxed under the warmer, her hands and feet bluish. Her respirations were even. She scanned the environment with head to one side, fingers in her mouth. When her father spoke, she startled, and her eyes shifted toward him. Gradually she turned to find his face and then stared intensely at him, until her eyes crossed. She closed her lids briefly and then found his face again. Her father said he was in love already. Then she turned pale, moved restlessly, and spit up mucus. Jessica's father jumped back and called for the nurse.

The full-term human infant enters the world fully equipped to negotiate the dramatic physiologic changes and behavioral adjustments required for postnatal life. These capacities enable him to begin the job of learning about his world and participating in his central interactive setting, his family (Brazelton, 1969). The newborn does not just function on a reflex level; primitive reflexes only attest to neurologic adequacy and provide a behavioral base on which he builds social and cognitive structures (Brazelton, 1977). These structures emerge through direct interaction with the environment. The neonate is fully capable of participation in the social world with abilities to discriminate and direct selective attention.

The goal of the newborn examination is to assess the full range of infant competencies and to monitor the process of postpartum adjustment. In addition, the initial visit with the newborn and his family offers the opportunity to participate in and perhaps facilitate the initial getting acquainted period for baby and his family. The first step toward attachment and parenting requires assurance that the infant is intact and is successfully negotiating the postpartum adjustment. The newborn examination offers the opportunity to assure the family of the infant's physiologic and behavioral integrity (Tronick and Brazelton, 1975).

SENSORY CAPACITIES

The remarkable sensory capacities of the newborn infant are receiving increasing emphasis and research in clinical settings with each passing year (Lewin, 1977; Tronick et al., 1979). Clearly, the newborn's sensory capacities are far greater than was previously believed. Not only are the infant's capacities well developed in each sphere of perception, but a substantial degree of coordination between senses is evident, even in the neonatal period. Or, as stated by Bower (1977), "The newborn lives in a unified perceptual world with some degree of intersensory coordination."

VISION

The neonate's visual system is intact at all levels (Bronson, 1984). The human infant can see faces and objects when they are presented in a range of his best focal distance, 8 to 12 in., although his depth of focus may actually cover a wider range. Retinal structures, especially rods, are well developed at birth, but lens mobility is limited, preventing clear focus through a wider range of distances. Foveal structures are less well developed, and central focus is less than in older infants and adults. Acuity is limited primarily by retinal immaturity. Acuity and improved accomodation proceed rapidly in the first 4 months. Extraocular movements allow for slow tracking of objects up to 180 degrees horizontally, perhaps briefly vertically, but not diagonally in the newborn period. Infants are very sensitive to light, perhaps more so than adults, and will open their eyes in light that is considered dim by adult standards. The infant in utero will slowly turn to a light source placed on the mother's abdomen. The infant clearly has the capacity to see a three-dimensional image as evidenced by a primitive reaching and the ability to blink as an object approaches (Bower, 1977). This capacity has been demonstrated, even controlling for air movement and sound cues that may warn the infant of the approaching object. This defensive response is more elaborate and less automatic than a reflex behavior and attests to the complex integration of visual and motor action, even in the newborn period. Blind infants do not demonstrate this blink response in the defensive situation. Additional laboratory studies have shown that infants demonstrate differential attention to visual displays that have high contrast, curved lines over straight, bright colors rather than dull colors, and many elements as opposed to few (Miranda, 1970). Infants are sensitive to symmetry. Visual fixation time on one of paired stimuli that differed along these dimensions has been used as an index of "preference" (Fanz, 1963).

"Color preference" has been studied in the same way, but the results are equivocal, because color is inevitably confounded by brightness, and infants do prefer moderately bright objects. Infants probably can discriminate red, green, and yellow but not blue when intensity is controlled (Adams et al., 1986).

The human face draws much attention from the human newborn; even scrambled schematic faces draw more attention than random field designs. Facial presentations that more closely resemble real human faces, particularly the upper part of the face and the eyes, draw increasingly more scanning and fixed attention from the infant as he matures. Infants are programmed from the start to seek out and visually explore stimulating visual displays. This is particularly true of the human face. Infants will preferentially look at their mothers' faces even without sound or smile (Field et al., 1984) even as neonates.

The human newborn can successfully imitate an interesting visual display, such as the mother sticking her tongue out (Melzoff and Moore, 1977). This capacity implies marvelous intersensory and motor coordination. The infant must be in a quiet, alert state and allowed enough time to process that interesting display held out for imitation. This can be demonstrated even in a 1-day-old infant.

The importance of visual input for the infant is illustrated through derangements in the visual system. An impairment of vision such as that present with cataracts may prevent the development of *functional* pattern vision if it is not corrected during the first 6 months of life; subtle residua of newborn visual compromise have been noted in children who have this condition, even for 1 week. Without binocular input, for even short periods of time, there may be impairments that are long-lasting. Frank cortical blindness in the case of severe esotropia is the extreme of a continuum of behavioral and perceptual compromise. The infant is vulnerable to alterations in vision, even up to the third year of life. Early visual compromise of any duration is to be avoided at all cost.

A newborn's visual capacities can be demonstrated at their fullest only when the infant is in a quiet, alert state and all distracting stimuli, even his own motor movements, are minimized. Visual performance may be limited to brief periods and may be overridden, especially early on, by physiologic events (e.g., bowel movements, hiccups).

The newborn's higher visual processing can be seen by observing the whole face and body when visual stimuli are presented. When attentive, the infant may initially startle slightly and then shut down bodily movements as he focuses on the visual display. His facial muscles will lift, and his palpebral fissures will widen, giving him a bright, softened look. Brief periods of attention will cycle with periods of inattention, gaze aversion, and possibly even asleep times (Brazelton, 1977). The infant, thereby, will limit the duration and the complexity of the visual events he must handle at any one point in time. Gaze is the capacity under the infant's control from early on and he can modulate his experience by exercising that control. Maturation and recovery from birth or illness are characterized by increasing duration of these alert periods and the ability to respond to increasing complexity of stimuli. Infants who readily habituate to visual stimuli and show a strong preference for novelty are more likely to show more advanced development (Borenstein and Sigman, 1986). The ability to attend to salient features is supported by mothers who draw selective attention to objects in the environment for visual scanning.

AUDITION

The infant can hear and is responsive to sounds even in the uterus. The cochlea is operative beginning 4 months before term. Neurologic structures enable the infant to discriminate between different tones and intensities at 32 weeks' gestation. The ability to clearly direct attention to auditory input may even be seen in 28-week-old premature infants (Volpe, 1971). The fetus will turn to familiar sounds and show habituation to repeated, familiar sounds.

Although fluid is present in the middle ear for several days after birth, the newborn is attentive and responsive to his sound environment, especially the sound of the human voice, particularly that of his parents. His threshold may be 10 to 20 dB higher than adult thresholds.

The infant will respond to a pleasant auditory signal, such as a voice or soft rattle, in ways similar to his response to visual stimuli: an initial alerting startle, a brightening of expression, and a diminishing of body activity. The infant may then turn toward the sound after a short delay and search for it. The infant's eyes will move toward the sound even before he moves his head or body. This testifies to the coordination of the auditory and visual systems (Kearsley, 1973). Female voices in highly modulated tones (i.e., "baby talk") produce the most consistent orientation response. Lower tones such as those produced by male speakers produce a quieting response in the newborn when he is upset. Perhaps the father's role in quieting the upset infant is mediated through this capacity. Short bursts of modulated human speech produce a greater behavioral response than unpatterned speech or speech of a greater or lesser duration. Adults in general speak to infants in short bursts of 5 to 15 seconds, the same time unit that produces this differential auditory attention. Soft, low-pitched lullabies and particularly the human heart tones produce decreased activity and decreased crying in the newborn. Even while continuing to cry, the infant coordinates his cry with the lullaby within seconds, eventually quieting. Lullabies around the world have the same rhythms that appear soothing to the infant. In contrast, "game songs" produce either alerting or behavioral disorganization (Lopez, 1991). The sound of his own cry or other newborns' cries produce dramatic increase in distress and crying. Clearly, by 1 month of age, and often in the immediate newborn period, an infant can distinguish between his own mother's voice and another's. This has been demonstrated through differential quieting and through a differential sucking response (McCall, 1979). The infant will work harder sucking to receive the reward of a taped recording of his mother's voice as opposed to that of another person. He will often quiet immediately on hearing his mother in the room.

Work with high-speed film (Condon and Sander, 1974) has shown that newborns readjust their ongoing body movements to the voice patterns of those speaking around them and will do so more consistently if the speaker is their mother or at least someone speaking in their family's native language. Pure tones, runs of babble, and other nonspeech tones do not produce this differential response. Early interactional synchrony attests to complex integration of the newborn's behavior, auditory and motor.

Infants fail to respond to auditory stimuli if it is loud (e.g., hand clap), or aversive (e.g., "white noise" in a nursery) or if confounded with other stimuli (e.g., loud voice with an overly animated close face). The infant shuts out these adversive auditory events very successfully and may even appear to have impaired audition under these conditions. One must provide a pleasant auditory event without distraction to demonstrate an appropriate response.

Some infants will be more responsive to sound than others; visual displays will produce a greater behavioral attention with other infants. These individual differences may be noted even in the newborn period and will highlight the special behavioral profile of an individual child. Both avenues of perception, vision and audition, can be used successfully by the infant to gather experience, to calm himself, and to change state (i.e., fall asleep or maintain alertness).

TASTE AND SMELL

Studies have demonstrated that infants have an acute and sensitive sense of taste. The infant's taste buds are of greater number and are more widely distributed than those of an adult. Even while in utero, infants can demonstrate an alteration in sucking frequency when sugar is introduced into the amniotic fluid. This differential response to varying sugars and to sucrose at varying concentrations is consistently demonstrated in full-term infants. This seeming preference for sweet taste and discrimination is demonstrated through the infant's ability to habituate to a single taste, with an increasing response to a new taste added. Complex patterns of taste preference are shaped by experience during the first year of life; however, the infant is already directed to avoid aversive tastes that in nature are largely poisonous and to seek out those that are sweet and differentially nourishing (Crooks and Lipsitt, 1976). Breast milk is sweeter than formula and may be preferred on this basis.

Smell is well developed in newborns and has been shown with increasing documentation to be of major importance as the infant orients to his environment (Self et al., 1972). The infant can successfully localize odors and may demonstrate preference through differential turning away and orienting toward unpleasant and pleasant odors, respectively. Infants as young as 5 days of age can differentiate by smell alone the breast pad of their own mother from that of other mothers' pads. The mother's smell rather than that of breast milk seems to be the determining factor (MacFarlane, 1975). Smell is thought to play an important role in familiarization with parents in the first week of life, giving us another reason to hold the infant close.

PHYSIOLOGICAL FACTORS

The first days of life are characterized by dramatic physiologic shifts. The smoothness of these shifts and the infant's ability to weather this turbulence attest to maturity and competency. Steady improvement in stability is to be expected, although each infant will vary in his or her degree of physiologic regularity based on maturity and the turbulence of labor, delivery, and the postpartum period. Skin color, skin perfusion, the degree of acrocyanosis and its increases with stress are important to characterize. The response to and recovery from undressing, handling, reflex assessment, and even social interaction give us an indication of the infant's vulnerability, margin of tolerated stress, and maturity. Observations of the lability of these physiologic factors, done in a consistent way during the course of the newborn examination, allow us to make an assessment of individual differences, the processes of maturation, and the immediate perinatal recovery process.

STATE BEHAVIOR

Infants exist in at least six states of consciousness (Prechtl and Beentema, 1975): quiet sleep, active sleep, drowsiness, quiet alert state, active alert-fussy, and crying. They move through these states in cycles with some regularity. Responsivity to some outside stimuli, physiologic processes (e.g., heart rate, breathing) and even reflex behaviors based on motor tone vary with these cycles.

The clear characterization of each state and the regular movement from one state to another testifies to a neurologic competency and maturity. The intact newborn can resist outside disturbances during sleep and even awake states by shutting out these intrusive events. Noises, lights, and even painful stimuli will be behaviorally and electrophysiologically ignored with successive presentation (Brazelton, 1977). This process is called *habituation*. The adaptive, protective nature of this capacity is obvious. The infant protects his own vulnerability to noise and light stimuli through a process of selective inattention. In the active state, repeated stimuli that are exactly the same are successively ignored (Hutt et al., 1968). When a new stimulus of even a slight variation is presented, the infant will again redirect attention toward the altered, now moderately novel, stimuli (Kagan, 1970). Habituation, then, can be an outcome measure by which we assess the infant's sensitivity to minor changes in his environment. These may include changes in visual acuity, auditory perception, smell, taste, and position sense. Renewed attention, often associated with heart rate changes, testifies to the infant's ability to detect change in his environment and direct his attention to this "new" information.

The first hours and days of life are characterized by irregularities in the wake-sleep cycle, prolonged periods of drowsiness, and often short periods of alertness. Neurologically intact infants under the care of one caretaker will show progressive gains in state cycle stabilization (Sander et al., 1970). However, many infants will remain somewhat irregular and unpredictable as part of their individual temperament profile and the slope of their recovery after birth (Brazelton, 1969). Most infants in the first days of their life will benefit from a little help in establishing a regular wake-sleep cycle. Although the cycle is innately determined and is present in utero to some degree before the disturbance of birth, this stabilization is facilitated through the care of a regular caregiver. Regular feedings, variations in illumination and sound, and close bodily contact with another human being all work toward a stabilization of this state. Consistent illumination, continuous noise, many caregivers, and an irregular response to crying and distress (all characteristic of a hospital nursery) will make it more difficult for the infant to have periods of sound sleep and periods of bright alert attentiveness. We do neither mothers nor healthy infants any favors by bringing the babies to the nursery "so mother can sleep." This just confounds the postpartum adjustment for both and makes sleep an area of delayed adjustment when they go home.

MOTOR BEHAVIORS

Motor behaviors are built on a set of primitive reflexes originating in the brainstem (Table 6–1). These reflexes are indicators of general neurologic integrity, and each has its own developmental course (Table 6–2). These reflexes are based on muscle tone, which, in turn, in the normal infant, varies with the state of consciousness. Therefore, in addition to noting the presence, absence, or asymmetry of these reflexes, the clinician should also assess active and passive tone within the context of several states, with the infant asleep and awake. Hypotonia and hypertonia are each appropriate in different states of consciousness, but the persistence of these through several states is worrisome. For example, plantar and palmar grasp may be sluggish in active sleep, when tone is diminished, but brisk in a cry state when tone is increased.

Learned volitional behaviors are built on reflexes. For example, the reflexive suck becomes

TABLE 6–1.
Reflexes of the Normal Full-Term Infant

Reflex	Normal Response*
Deep tendon reflexes	
Biceps	Brisk response without spread
Knee	Crossed adductor response with knee jerk
Ankle	Ankle clonus up to 10 beats
Palmar hand grasp	Closure over finger
Plantar grasp	Flexion of toe and forefoot
Babinski	Toe extension, with or without initial flexion
Moro	Extension and abduction of the arms followed by flexion and adduction; cry may or may not be present
Tonic neck reflex	Long latency; not fully developed; increased tone, leg extension on side of head direction, flexion in contralateral arm and leg; this response is the basis for asymmetries in tone and reflexes when the head is not in midline
Placing	Extension of leg with dorsal stimulation
Stepping and walking	Range from minimal weight-bearing to several brisk steps

*Asymmetries that are consistent and demonstrated when the head is in the midline are always abnormal.

specific for the breast or the bottle early in the first days of life. It becomes coordinated to milk flow characteristics of each and becomes part of a complex pattern of behavior between a mother and infant. The tonic neck reflex enables the infant to watch his hand movements so that gaze and reach become linked—the first step toward volitional reach. Reflexes provide an opportunity for the infant to interact with the environment so that experiences can begin immediately and are the beginning of both cognitive and affective growth (Piaget and Inhelder, 1969).

The manner of execution of "random" movements gives clues to neurologic competency, inborn patterns of coordination, and even individual style. Persistent jitteriness and tremulousness, especially in both asleep and alert states, attest to a neurologic immaturity, perinatal stress, or metabolic abnormalities. Jerky movements in arcs of 45 degrees or less are worri-

TABLE 6–2.
Ontogeny of Neonatal Reflexes and Tone*

Reflex and Muscle Tone	Age of Emergence	Age of Disappearance
Tonic neck reflex	35 wk, peak at 44 wk	7–8 mo
Moro	28 wk incomplete, 37 wk complete	3–6 mo
Head turn in prone	37 wk	Variable
Palmar grasp	28 wk	2 mo
Trunk incurvation	28 wk	4–5 mo
Placing, stepping	37 wk	2–4 mo
Ankle clonus, up to 5–10 beats	33–35 wk (?)	1 mo
Pupillar response	32 wk	Never
Flexor tone, lower extremity	32 wk	> 1 yr
Flexor tone, upper extremity	36 wk	? > 1 yr

*Adapted from Volpe JJ: *Neurology of the Newborn.* Philadelphia, WB Saunders Co, 1971.

TABLE 6–3.
Clinical Assessment of Capacities of Newborns: Trends in the First Days of Life

Vision	Follows face without voice in arc of 30 to 180 degrees horizontally when quiet and alert; face "softens"; shuts down motor activity when attention is directed at a visual display (e.g., face of examiner); hand and mouth activation with pleasant visual display; blinks at looming object (e.g., stethoscope)
Audition	Eyes shift to positive sound source; turns to soft sounds (e.g., soft rattle, voice); shuts down motor activity to listen to pleasant sound; ignores, startles, or cries in response to loud sounds (e.g., clap)
Smell	Aversive response to strong smell (e.g., alcohol wipe near nose)
Taste	Increase of sucking to sucrose solution vs. water
State regulation	Has increasingly regular wake/sleep patterns (nurses' notes regarding newborn); goes to sleep with aversive maneuvers on general examination (e.g., circumcision, PKU* stick); has clear, although brief, quiet-alert times; progressively easier to waken for feedings or wake periods
Physiological stability	Gradual moderate skin color changes during the course of the examination; increasingly less mottling, acrocyanosis; heart and respiratory rate vary with state changes (note during examination and in medical record); increasing tolerance for a pediatric examination without showing signs of stress (e.g., color changes, gaze aversion, abrupt state change to cry or sleep)
Vestibular	Responds to rocking with quieting; opens eyes when held upright in a dim room; turns head to direction of an upright spin
Motor	Observe posture and active tone within context of state (e.g., hypertonia to some degree expected while crying, hypotonia is normal in sleep); observe tremulousness (mild to moderate appropriate in cry states) and jerky movements; the greater the arc of movement of the arms, the greater the maturity of the child; assess primitive reflexes; asymmetries and marked extremes need repeat assessment and, perhaps, further evaluation

*PKU = phenylketonuria.

some in the full-term infant. Ankle clonus, greater than two beats, and many startles throughout the regular pediatric examination or with minimal handling are of similar concern in the term infant. However, these motor abnormalities do not carry predictive significance beyond the newborn period. These should be monitored over a period of time and should be taken as clues indicating the possibility of other adjustment difficulties rather than as being diagnostic or prognostic in themselves.

All in all, the infant's perceptual and behavioral repertoire is geared toward initiating and maintaining positive social interactions between infant and parents. It is through this interaction that the infant's physical and psychological nurturance is sustained. Cognitive and effective growth is dependent on this process. The infant comes fully equipped for this vital work. These capacities are shown in Table 6–3.

THE BIRTH EXPERIENCE

The impact of perinatal events on the development of the family unit is profound. Labors that are attended by supportive people, particularly the father, tend to be shorter and less fraught with complications (Parke, 1981). The mother's experience of labor and delivery are much more positive in these circumstances. Clear knowledge of the expectancies of the events of labor and delivery allow the family to feel that they are in control of this natural process and to move through it with an enhanced feeling of competency and fulfillment. Prepared childbirth training offers help on several levels: educating, laying out expectations, calming fears, and offering the support of the whole group of parents. Certainly, labors are shorter and medication is needed less often after these preparations.

A delivery that is surrounded by a continuation of that controlled, orderly, peaceful experience would seem to smooth the infant's transition to extrauterine life. Although it has not yet been shown statistically to alter infant behavior, the delivery techniques that allow for this gradual transition may appear to be advantageous, at least to some observers (Leboyer, 1975). These techniques utilize softened lights, quiet, and the placement of the newborn into a water bath at 98°F. Gentle massaging, soft talking, and rocking are said to mollify the abrupt transition in the usual hospital delivery in the United States. Caution must be given, however, that the parents and the infant, not the obstetrician, orchestrate this event and that good medical care can be in no way compromised in the rigid adherence to this or any other delivery practice. The pediatrician can serve as the child advocate, being sure that the infant's needs come first—medical, social, and psychological.

Many workers have described the behaviors and importance of the first minutes and hours of life toward ultimate attachment between infant and parents (Klaus and Kennell, 1976). Immediately following the birth, the heightened feelings of near ecstasy (and relief!) on the parents' part and the prolonged sense of alertness on the infant's part prepare both partners for the initial meeting. This experience may have long-term positive effects on the child's subsequent development, especially in circumstances of high risk for attachment. A quiet time together immediately after birth, before any medical procedures, is certainly optimal. However, this is not always possible, and some parents have no positive feelings toward the infant at this time of "bonding." Feelings of failure can ensue if expectations for this peak experience are not met. Birth is the beginning of a relationship and, as in any human relationship, it is as variable as the people involved. Sensitivity to the feelings of parents, both positive and negative, will allow the infant's physician to support this process as it proceeds in its own individual way.

Cesarean section, especially if it is unanticipated, may result in feelings of failure and unmet expectations on the part of parents. In addition, children delivered by cesarean section may tend to be drowsy, slow feeders and often poorly responsive to their parents' attempts at early social interaction. Mothers indeed may feel more pain from the incision and have a more prolonged recovery course than mothers of infants born by vaginal delivery. *No* long-term developmental consequences have been demonstrated for those children when confounding variables are controlled. Infants delivered by cesarean section may require more time and patience getting themselves behaviorally organized in the immediate newborn period, but long-term detrimental effects are *not* apparent in populations of infants who have not experienced perinatal distress. Particular patience and support of the family unit is necessary after the cesarean delivery. However, fathers may be even more involved with infant care after a cesarean section birth (Parke, 1981), and this has long-term positive consequences.

Medication given to the mother during labor and delivery affect the infant's behavior, ranging from hypotonia after epidural and spinal anesthesia and magnesium administration, to frank depression of respirations if inappropriate medication is given immediately before delivery (Brackbill, 1967; Brazelton and Robey, 1965). Even a small amount of drugs may make a mother less alert for her early interactions with her infant, and the infant may be poorly responsive to her.

Infants of diabetic mothers have behavioral abnormalities, as well as metabolic problems. They tend to be drowsy, hypotonic, have long latency for response, and have only brief periods of alertness. Some of these behavioral abnormalities are shared with hyperbilirubinemic infants, particularly those undergoing phototherapy. No systematic studies of polycythemic infant behavior have been done, but many clinicians have observed that these infants tend to be lethargic, even without demonstration of frank hyperviscosity or correction of their hematocrit levels. The combination of polycythemia and hypoglycemia may have profound behavioral effects. Infants born of mothers with pregnancy induced hypertension (PIH) may be behaviorally disorganized, even if not undergrown. They need more patience in the first days of life, allowing for more behavioral recovery. Breast-feeding initiation is often slower in these pairs, usually because of both maternal and infant factors.

Circumcision is a stressful event that predictably alters the infant's behavior, both during and after the procedure (Dixon et al., 1984). This is especially true if the circumcision is done without anesthesia. Parents should anticipate that their son will have a prolonged period of sleep and may then be unavailable for social interaction for the next 12 to 24 hours. These behavioral alterations appear to be self-limited. The dorsal penile nerve block provides a safe and effective local anesthesia during a circumcision (Kirya and Werthmann, 1978).

Minor or major physical deformities may strongly influence a parent's response to the infant. Every effort should be made to correct these early, if possible, to both ensure a good result and to decrease any barriers to attachment for the parents.

Behavioral abnormalities may impact on development for a long time after the perinatal period (Korner, 1974). Researchers have shown that parents' first perceptions of their infants are lasting, and these, in turn, affect their behavior toward the child (Broussard et al., 1971). The biologically programmed system designed to commit parents to their infants may be hampered by these seemingly benign events. Parents may harbor feelings of the infant's vulnerability long after seemingly benign difficulties have resolved (e.g., neonatal jaundice). This may be particularly true in situations in which resources for parenting are few and pressures on individual families are great. Anticipation of these behavioral differences in an open discussion with the parents may facilitate the family's adaptation to their particular infant. They should be helped to see these difficulties as transient and should be given ways and a broad timetable to mark recovery. They will become partners with the physician in marking the stabilization, maturation, and growth in organization of their infant in the first hours and days of life. The early period of getting acquainted is facilitated for all parents by rooming in. An infant's proper place is with his mother and father. The infant's wake and sleep cycles stabilize early in rhythm with those of the mother. Breast-feeding goes more smoothly, and parents are allowed to practice their new roles in a supportive environment. The infants have prolonged periods of alertness when protected from the disorganizing effect of the nursery. Clinicians should do all that they can to influence hospital policies to allow for this immediate and continuous contact within safe limits of care.

WHAT TO OBSERVE

In examining the infant, you should observe the following:

1. The infant's response to all the examiner's maneuvers (see the following section). The examination itself is a social interaction and presents a gradient of stress from very positive to moderately adversive.

2. The nurses' and parents' handling of the infant. This handling is determined by *both* the caretaker and the infant.

3. Your own responses to the infant.

4. Nursing record for regularity of state, response to procedures (e.g., bath, phenylketonuria [PKU] stick), and difficulties with caretaking.

5. Parents' impression and handling of the infant.

6. Maternal (and paternal) fatigue, stress, and ill health.

WHAT TO ASK

Questions to be asked and the objectives of each question are presented in Table 6–4.

WHAT TO ASSESS

Begin assessment in a quiet, dimly lit room. Observe the infant's response to your own maneuvers. Order the examination with the least noxious and intrusive items first. Watch the infant move from sleep to awake states; observe these transitions themselves and as a base for other observations.

Bring the infant to an alert state by uncovering and undressing him. When the infant is alert, present a bright object of moderately small size (e.g., red ball of 3-in. diameter) at his focal distance. Move object slowly, horizontally and vertically, to assess infant's tracking and whole performance in visual processing.

Repeat the visual assessment using your face and then using face and voice together. (The combined stimulus is more compelling than the single one for term infants; stressed and immature infants may find the combined stimulus too complex and, therefore, aversive.) He

TABLE 6–4.
Questions to Be Asked During Newborn Examination

Questions	Objective
How are you? How did the delivery go? Did things go as you had planned?	You care about parents as people; assess whether expectations were fulfilled.
How is he/she the same/different than you expected?	Assess perceptions of the child; note any discrepancies with your own.
Do you have any special worries or concerns about him/her?	Answer concerns.
Ask about any maternal medical concerns (e.g., maternal fever, ABO or Rh incompatibility)	Assert the locus of control with them.

will show you that you have exceeded your limit by turning away, looking away, or with gagging or color change.

With the infant held securely above eye level, often wrapped to avoid interference of motor activity, talk softly to him. Wait for his response. Having an alert look, turning his eyes toward you, and then turning his head toward you is the expected response, if given time and a positive auditory cue.

During this time, note the infant's irritability, changes of motor tone with state of consciousness, and the amount of tremulousness and startles. This assessment gives you an idea of the infant's maturity, neurologic integrity, and physiologic stability. This first assessment provides a basis of comparison for subsequent assessment, allowing you to monitor the infant's recovery. In addition, these are the infant behaviors with which his caretakers build their impressions, expectancies, and patterns of early interaction.

Complete the usual pediatric examination from the least disturbing and intrusive assessment to those portions of the examination expected to cause more disturbance.

A full neurologic examination, with careful assessment of active and passive tone, and the presence, character, and vigor of the reflexes should be done.

During periods of crying (e.g., after the test of the Moro reflex), the infant should be carefully observed to assess the maneuvers he has used to quiet himself and the amount of effort needed by the examiner to quiet the infant.

Clinicians should see themselves as a barometer of the infant's behavior. If one feels that this infant is behaviorally vulnerable, he probably is, and the parents will feel that too. If the child is particularly attractive, it may be because the infant is exceptionally well organized.

SPECIAL REFERRALS AND TREATMENTS

Good medical management is, of course, the first necessity.

Children born of diabetic mothers or mothers who received medication during labor and delivery, those born after long labors or labors complicated by PIH, or those born by cesarean section are expected to have a more prolonged recovery, with mild hypotonia, lethargy, and drowsy states. These behaviors should be anticipated but not ignored by the primary care physician. These behaviors may herald or mask significant metabolic problems (e.g., hypoglycemia) or the presence of sepsis. These infants require increased vigilance for these medical problems. Secondary difficulties such as poor feeding, jaundice, and mild dehydration may ensue from the behavioral abnormalities. The parents' initial perceptions of their child are shaped by these early difficulties. The clinician can place these transient behaviors in perspective, as part of the recovery process. Extra efforts to alert the infant, especially around feeding, will require extra nursing help.

Swaddling, quiet rooms, and dim lights are helpful to all infants, but especially to those experiencing drug withdrawal or drug effect, prenatal alcohol exposure, and any other events that result in a hyperirritable, hyperresponsive state.

Even mild hyperbilirubinemia and phototherapy lead to significant alterations in infant behavior. These drowsy, floppy, or jittery infants appear to be poorly responsive to caretaking maneuvers, even into the second week of life, after discontinuance of the phototherapy. The behavioral changes in the child should be explained to the parents and assurance of its transiency made.

Wake-sleep cycle regulation for the infant is facilitated by close interaction with a single caretaker. Rooming in is beneficial for babies and parents, almost without exception. There is a differential response to the infant, day and night, that facilitates the infant's organization.

The initial newborn examination is an opportunity to assure parents that the infant is physically and behaviorally intact. Congratulations are in order for producing a lovely baby. This reassurance and an added sense of competency as being reproductively sound are necessary to begin the work of caring for and caring about the infant. Unmet expectations for the delivery, or the infant, or any intercurrent concerns are to be laid in clear perspective. The clinician should specify as exactly as possible the degree of appropriate concern for a given problem or process of adjustment. Parents should not be expected to weigh these, both major and minor, without the clear input of the clinician. Both parents' choices in care options should be presented clearly, and the clinician should join in an alliance to support the infant's postnatal adjustment and reorganization.

REFERENCES

Adams RJ, Maurer D, Davis M: Newborn discrimination of chromatic from achromatic stimuli. *J Exp Child Psychol* 1986; 41:267–281.

Borenstein MH, Sigman MD: Continuity in mental development in infancy. *Child Dev* 1986; 57:251–274.

Bower TGR: *The Perceptual World of the Child.* Cambridge, Mass, Harvard University Press, 1977.

Brackbill Y: *Infancy and Early Childhood.* New York, Free Press, 1967.

Brazelton TB: *Infants and Mothers: Individual Differences in Development.* New York, Delacorte, 1969.

Brazelton TB: Neonatal behavioral assessment scale. *Clinics Dev Med* No. 50. Philadelphia, JB Lippincott Co, 1977.

Brazelton TB, Robey J: Observations of neonatal behavior: The effect of perinatal variables, in particular that of maternal medication. *J Child Psychiatry* 1965; 14:613.

Bremner JG: *Infancy.* New York, Basil Blackwell, 1988.

Bronson G: The postnatal growth in visual capacity. *Child Dev* 1974; 45:887–890.

Broussard E, Sergay M, Hartner S: Further considerations regarding maternal perception of the firstborn, in Hellmuth J (ed): *Exceptional Infant.* New York, Brunner-Mazel, 1971.

Condon WS, Sander LW: Synchrony demonstrated between movements of the neonate and adult speech. *Child Dev* 1974; 45:456–462.

Crooks CK, Lipsitt L: Neonatal nutritive sucking: Effects of taste stimulation upon sucking rhythm and heart rate. *Child Dev* 1976; 47:518–522.

Dixon S, Snyder J, Holve R, et al: Behavioral effects of circumcision with and without anesthesia. *Dev Behav Pediatrics* 1984; 5:246.

Fanz RL: Pattern vision in the newborn infant. *Science* 1963; 140:296–297.

Field T, Cohen D, Garcia R, et al: Mother-stranger discrimination by the newborn. *Infant Behav Dev* 1984; 7:19–26.

Hutt C, Von Bernuth H, Lenard HG, et al: Habituation in relation to state in the human neonate. *Nature* 1968; 220:618.

Kagan J: The determinants of attention in the infant. *Am Scientist* 1970; 58:298–306.

Kearsley RB: The newborn's response to auditory stimulation: A demonstration of orienting and defensive behavior. *Child Dev* 1973; 44:582.

Kirya C, Werthmann MW: Neonatal circumcision and penile dorsal nerve block: A painless procedure. *J Pediatr* 1978; 96:998–1000.

Klaus M, Kennell J: *Maternal-Infant Bonding.* St Louis, CV Mosby Co, 1976.

Korner A: The effect of the infant's state, level of arousal, sex and ontogenic stage on the caregiver, in Lewis M, Rosenblum L (eds): *The Effect of the Infant on the Caregiver.* New York, John Wiley & Sons, 1974.

Leboyer F: *Birth Without Violence.* New York, Alfred Knopf, 1975.

Lewin R (ed): *Child Alive.* Garden City, NY, Anchor Press, 1977.

Lopez S: The effect of the lullaby and game song on the behavior of the newborn, doctoral dissertation. LaJolla, California, University of California, San Diego, Department of Music, 1991.

MacFarlane A: Olfaction, in *The Development of Social Preference in the Human Neonate.* Ciba Foundation Symposium No. 33, 1975.

McCall RB: *Infants.* Cambridge, Mass, Harvard University Press, 1979.

Melzoff AN, Moore MK: Imitation of facial and manual gestures by the human neonate. *Science* 1977; 198:75–78.

Miranda SB: Visual abilities and pattern preferences of premature and full term infants. *J Exp Child Psychol* 1970; 10:139–205.

Parke R: *Fathers.* Cambridge, Mass, Harvard University Press, 1981.

Piaget J, Inhelder B: *The Psychology of the Child.* New York, Basic Books, 1969.

Prechtl H, Beentema D: *The Neurological Examination of the Full Term Newborn Infant.* Philadelphia, JB Lippincott Co, 1975.

Sander LW, Stechler G, Burns P, et al: Early mother-infant interaction and twenty-four hour patterns of activity and sleep. *J Am Acad Child Psychiatry* 1970; 9:103.

Self PA, Horowitz FD, Paden LY: Olfaction in newborn infants. *Dev Psychol* 1972; 7:349–363.

Tronick E, Als H, Brazelton TB: Early development of neonatal and infant behavior, in Falkner F, Tanner JM (eds): *Human Growth.* New York, Plenum Publishing Corp, 1979, vol 3.

Tronick E, Brazelton TB: Clinical uses of the Brazelton Neonatal Behavioral Assessment, in Friedlander BZ, Sturitt GM, Kirk GE (eds) *Exceptional Infant.* New York, Bruner-Mazel, 1975, vol 3.

Volpe JJ: *Neurology of the Newborn.* Philadelphia, WB Saunders Co, 1971.

"Mom changing baby's diaper." By
Eric Ries, age 6½.

CHAPTER 7

The Hospital Discharge Examination: Getting to Know the Individual Child

MARTIN T. STEIN, M.D.

KEY WORDS

NEWBORN DEVELOPMENTAL CAPACITIES
QUIET-ALERT STATE
NEONATAL "PERSONALITY"
HABITUATION
ANTICIPATORY GUIDANCE
VULNERABLE CHILD SYNDROME

A 35-year-old mother gave birth to her first child—a healthy, full-term boy. Respiratory distress developed shortly after birth. A chest radiograph was consistent with congenital pneumonia, and the baby was treated intravenously with antibiotics for 10 days without complications.

The mother was a successful manager in a retail business before her marriage 1 year before the birth of the baby; she worked throughout the pregnancy. On the third postpartum day, she appeared anxious, at times withdrawn, and distant. Prompted by a concerned nursing staff, the baby's pediatrician reviewed the course of the pneumonia with the mother and emphasized the infant's excellent progress and prognosis.

At the same time, she explored the mother's feelings about the baby and about herself. By means of open-ended questions and active listening (Chapter 3), the pediatrician allowed the mother the opportunity to tell her own story. She had been sexually abused repeatedly as a school-aged child and during early adolescence. Abuse by her father had resulted in strained and limited relationships with men in her past. She felt conflicted and ambivalent about her infant son; the pneumonia at times seemed a punishment for these ambivalent feelings. She was uncertain about her ability to nurse and care for the baby.

Listening to her "ghosts-in-the-nursery" story (Freiberg, 1959), the pediatrician pointed out that all parents—mothers and fathers—experience feelings at the time of a child's birth that recall past childhood experiences. Events, people, and emotions from the parental past often surface in the neonatal period. Unknowingly, they bring about moods, perceptions, and physical symptoms that appear to have no clear origin. Recognizing the normalcy of these "ghosts," the clinician is in a position to help the parent recognize and cope with ambivalence and vulnerability.

At the baby's 9-month health supervision visit, this mother reminded the pediatrician of the time they spent together during the baby's first week of life. She commented that the insight she gained into her conflicting feelings was as important to her as the expertise in management of the baby's pneumonia.

With shorter newborn hospital periods in recent years, the time between delivery of the baby and discharge may be as brief as 6 hours, rarely longer than 2 days in the uncomplicated delivery. Nevertheless, in most cases, by the time of the discharge examination, several important developmental tasks are under way for the main cast of characters.

FOR THE MOTHER

The ecstasy of the birth process came and quickly went. She is usually preoccupied with feeding the newborn and thinking about care at home. Although the mother is reassured that results of the initial physical assessment were normal, lingering thoughts about birth defects are not uncommon. The mechanics of child care are important at this time. The special physical and behavioral characteristics of her own child now impact on the daily care of the child. She may be just beginning to deal with these in the development of effective caregiving. If nursing, many new mothers are unsure of their ability to nurse at this early stage: Will I have enough milk? How will I know I have enough milk? Will the milk be of high quality? What if the baby does not learn to nurse well? Having said this, most mothers are educationally available and show a readiness to acquire new information about their baby at the discharge examination (Brazelton, 1963). The early experiences of feeding and care have brought forth concerns, observations, and an energized attention toward the care of the infant (Klaus et al., 1972). A minicrisis looms as the discharge approaches and the support of the hospital team is withdrawn. The chance of possessing the infant without interference or observation is the positive side to the impending separation.

FOR THE FATHER

When involved with the birth process and as a frequent visitor at the hospital, the father is often elated; the ecstasy following birth is somewhat more subdued but, at the same time, more prolonged than his wife has experienced. A period of "engrossment" has been described among fathers who experience a profound attachment to the newborn beginning at the time of delivery (Greenberg and Morris, 1974). Not overwhelmed with concern about breast-feeding, some fathers are more available than mothers to information about various aspects of the child's development at this time. Even for the father who has not been significantly involved before the infant's birth, this time is critical. The real presence of his own unique infant captures fathers in ways that might not have been anticipated. The child is real now, and a hesitant father may be looking for ways to be part of the child's care (Yogman, 1980).

FOR THE NEONATE

After the first 24 to 48 hours of extrauterine life, the baby has completed many profound physiologic adjustments (cardiovascular, neurologic, pulmonary, and gastrointestinal) to prepare her for a placenta-free environment. The rate at which neonates make these adjustments varies tremendously. Persistent acrocyanosis, gagging on secretions, delayed micturition or defecation, and feeding irregularities are not uncommon. They represent normal developmental tasks for the neonate. Parental responses to these variables set the stage for future interactions.

From this brief description of the developmental dynamics taking place, it can be seen that the time of the hospital discharge examination offers the clinician a remarkable opportunity to assist the parents in responding to the needs of their own baby, as well as to respond to parental needs directly.

From nursing notes, parental reporting, and clinical observations, the baby's style of regulating sleep-wake cycles may be known (see Chapter 6). Providing parents with an appreciation for and understanding of their baby's remarkable capacities to regulate states of alertness and sleep will help the parents adapt to their baby at home.

A neonate spends about three fourths of a 24-hour period in either quiet or active sleep (Parmelee et al., 1974). These cycles are disrupted at birth but become reestablished when under the care of one individual over time. When she arouses for about 6 to 8 hours each day, only about 10% of the time is spent in a quiet-alert state. The importance of this brief period is that it is during these moments that the new baby is responsive to social, interaction and active mental processing of environmental events (Wolff, 1959). Visual, auditory, tactile, and olfactory capacities are most available during the quiet-alert state. As parents become more knowledgeable about state changes, they become better prepared to interact with their new baby at these available times. They will begin to see their infant as a social, interactive real person. Through these encounters the baby's own patterns of sleep and wakefulness are perceived as a predictable foundation on which to build a relationship.

The newborn's innate capacities for state regulation and alternating between sleep-wake cycles are influenced by her environment and caretaking (Brazelton, 1973). Bright nursery lights, excessive noise (machines or conversation), and frequent random handling all serve to stimulate the neonate and disrupt her own efforts at organization. Swaddled in a receiving blanket and left to rest on her side in a bassinet, the neonate will move from quiet to active sleep and from a quiet-alert state to active crying by herself. Timely lifting and gentle soothing will settle most babies. Depending on her innate temperament, a baby will respond to nursing routines and to soothing techniques in a variety of ways. Some hyperresponsive babies require less handling and tighter swaddling. Other hypoactive babies may, at times, require more tactile, verbal, or visual stimulation. The infant's responses to the nursery routines and caretaking reflect the child's own temperamental makeup. The behavior of neonates varies between cultural groups because they are both the recipients and shapers of these group differences. Perinatal and genetic factors contribute to this delightful variation. How the infant is handled is, in turn, influenced by her own behavior. Motorically strong infants elicit vigorous handling by their caretakers. Poorly responsive infants tend to be left alone. Visually alert infants are looked at and talked to frequently. Mothers who are encouraged to hold their normal newborns an extra few hours each day report less crying during the first 3 months of life (Hunziker and Barr, 1986).

The notion that babies are affectively different the moment they are born is helpful for the new parent to understand and observe in their infant (Thomas and Chess, 1977). Teaching parents to respect those differences while helping them to define their newborn's own personality can be a rewarding clinical experience. It will also help in making management plans with the family. Equally important is the notion that, although the newborn enters the world with personality and perceptual capacities to notice caregivers, she is also capable of interacting reciprocally (Lozoff et al., 1977). The baby is capable of some mutuality in interactions from the start. The baby is learning about the world through interactions with her own parents as individuals. Many parents will know this intuitively; others require information and demonstration for verification. The discharge examination is an ideal time to teach these developmental capacities to parents—to show them how their behaviors and responses can positively influence the new baby. A demonstration of the behavioral capacities of the infant has been shown to dramatically improve the parents' interaction with the child (Olson et al., 1981). The discharge examination is an intervention, as well as a strategy of assessment. In addition, the mother's perception of her infant is a powerful predictor of her interaction with the child. The discharge examination provides the opportunity to observe and influence this process.

Whenever possible, examine the infant at the mother's bedside. This will provide a broader data base with regard to mother-infant interactions. Let the mother know when you plan to perform the discharge examination to encourage the father's presence. That you are interested in both parents is an important message for the father and mother to hear at this early moment in family development.

Insofar as the parents' earliest impression of the newborn infant may be lasting, what you say about the baby may have a lasting influence on the way they perceive her now and in the future.

WHAT TO OBSERVE

The following should be observed at the time of examination:

1. How is the baby held—by the mother, by the father?
2. Do they seem comfortable with the baby?
3. Is there an eagerness to take the baby home or, through questions the parents ask or the tone of their voice, can you detect concern or anxiety in anticipation of the trip home?
4. What is the initial psychological state of the baby? Can you observe and define state changes during the examination? What is the parents' response to these changes? Have they learned any soothing techniques?
5. If the baby is being fed when you enter the room, observe the mother's comfort during feeding. If nursing, does she appear at ease with the baby and herself?

WHAT TO ASK

Questions to be asked during the discharge examination are presented in Table 7–1.

ASSESSMENT DURING PHYSICAL EXAMINATION

PHYSICAL FINDINGS

Because this will typically be the second examination of the baby, it is usually only necessary to perform a screening examination to detect abnormalities that may have gone undetected at the time of the initial assessment. Physical findings with a higher yield of abnormalities at this point in time are summarized in Table 7–2. Abnormalities or minor variations noted on the initial examination should be reviewed again.

TABLE 7–1.
Questions to Be Asked During Discharge Examination

Question	Objective
How is nursing (feeding) going? Do you have any questions about feeding the baby?	Assess comfort with feeding, especially if breast-feeding; are there expressed ambiguities or unreal concerns?
Let's review nursing procedures—frequency, night feedings, hydration, maternal rest, and diet.	Clarify any misconception and provide a solid early foundation for successful nursing.
Babies usually have from ten bowel movements each day to one every third day; does that surprise you?	Assess knowledge of gastrointestinal tract function, while giving information that may be helpful at home.
There are "entitlements" of birth—sneezing, hiccuping, spitting up milk! You needn't bother yourself about these normal events.	Anticipatory guidance.
You seem very comfortable holding your baby	Positive reinforcement of intuitive parental behavior.
Do you have a carseat to secure the baby in on the way home?	Anticipatory guidance; assess commitment to use the carseat and emphasize the high value you place on its use.
Will someone be helping you with the baby?	Anticipatory guidance; assess support system.

DEVELOPMENTAL ASSESSMENT

Many aspects of the initial neurobehavioral examination might be repeated at this time for two reasons: (1) to assess maturation of the infant while he is recovering from the birth experience and (2) to demonstrate to the parents some of the remarkable visual, tactile, and auditory capacities their young neonate is capable of performing. Specific responses that are easy to elicit and instructive for parents include visual alertness to a parent or the examiner; response to a soft bell or rattle; ability to settle self (or be settled) after a test of Moro reflex;

TABLE 7–2.
Screening Examination to Detect Abnormalities

Sign	Disorder
Cardiac murmur; abnormal second heart sound; absent femoral pulses	Congenital heart disease
Hip click	Congenital dislocation of hip
Cyanosis	Pulmonary, cardiac, metabolic, or infectious disorder
Jaundice	Hyperbilirubinemia
Parietal swelling	Cephalohematoma
Excessive increase in head circumference (often difficult to assess due to resolution of molding or caput succenadeum)	Hydrocephalus
Forceps marks	Facial trauma
Adequacy of early feeding	Level of hydration;
Infection; cardiac, pulmonary, central nervous system, and metabolic pathology	Tachypnea; tachycardia; hypothermia or hyperthermia

neonatal grasp, stepping, and rooting reflexes; and truncal tone when held in a prone position.

This assessment may be an ideal time to comment on the baby's "personality"—her unique way of responding to various sensory stimuli, both noxious (e.g., Moro reflex or foot stimulation) and pleasant (e.g., human voice and face). Helping the parents to perceive their infant as a person with a personality at this early stage encourages more complex and developmentally appropriate interactions at home. The clinician's goal should be to demonstrate that the baby's responses are far more than primitive reflexes and that the parents can interact with and modulate the infant's behavioral responses. Parents who are shown these capacities from the start will demonstrate more responsive caretaking as the child grows.

Some parents are impressed by the demonstration that the baby can be shown to habituate to a repetitive noxious stimulus, such as scratching the bottom of a foot or presenting the baby with a bright light. The shutting down of the response (leg withdrawal or eyes blinking in these examples) demonstrates to the parents that the infant's brain is organized to the degree that it can "interpret" and shut out unwanted environmental inputs. This kind of demonstration raises the parents' appreciation of the competencies of the infant for managing environmental stresses and demands.

During the neurobehavioral examination, the baby will have moments of neuromuscular and vocal release; for example, she will cry vigorously while the examiner is initiating a Moro reflex. This is an important fleeting moment of which to take advantage. The baby who settles down by herself with minimal or no outside input demonstrates a mature form of state regulation—from active crying to quiet alertness. Congratulate the infant! Let the parents know how impressed you were by this behavior. Most babies will not settle down left to their own accord; they require a soothing hand on the abdomen, a reassuring, rhythmic voice, or, more likely, they need to be lifted and gently swung against a warm chest of a loving caregiver. Let the parents know that this is normal behavior as the baby moves from one psychological state to the next. They will discover the most effective pathway toward calming behaviors for their own baby. Emphasize that each baby has her own way of regulating these states and of responding to parents.

ANTICIPATORY GUIDANCE

NUTRITION

NURSING BABIES

Allow the mother to express her concerns about her milk—its quality and quantity. Remind her that weight loss is common (and expected) in all babies. Neonates lose between 5% and 10% of birth weight in the initial week of life, and it will not harm the infant. Breast milk appears thin and bluish but is high in protein and fat in spite of this appearance. Review feeding frequency (approximately every $2\frac{1}{2}$ to 3 hours in the initial few weeks) and duration (10 to 15 minutes on each breast at each feeding). Let her know that often a baby who nurses well on one side is content and will fall asleep before completing the opposite breast; point out that this is common, and awaken the infant to feed on the other side. She should begin the next feeding on the unfinished side. Review the mother's diet; in general, a healthy prenatal diet, supplemented with a multivitamin and including consumption of a minimum of 2 qt of fluid each day is sufficient for adequate milk production. The key words are a *high-protein* diet with adequate *fluids* and a *vitamin* supplementation for the mother. Full-term nursing newborns probably do not require vitamin supplementation, although some clinicians prefer to supplement the baby's feeding with vitamin D. If the infant will not receive sufficient sunlight exposure (Hayward and Stein, 1987) or if the maternal diet will be low in vitamin D, breast-fed babies should receive a vitamin D supplement of 400 IU (AAP, 1979). Reviewing these facts at the time of discharge goes a long way in reassuring the mother about the adequacy of her milk and in assuring optimal infant growth. Leave this topic by congratulating the mother on her decision to nurse her baby.

Teach mothers, and fathers, that nursing is a *learned experience* for both mother and baby. The woman who deftly nursed her infant probably started out unsure of her nursing ability; with 1 week or so of practice, the nursing synchrony between the new mother and baby is usually established. Patience, information, and reassurance are required to ensure the initiation and continuation of nursing.

At the time of the discharge examination, nursing can be enhanced by emphasizing the following:

1. Feed the baby on demand. Most babies awaken to feed at 2- to 3-hour intervals.
2. To establish your milk supply, do not allow the baby to go more than 4 hours between feedings during the first week of life; this includes evenings. After the first week, when nursing is established, the duration between feedings may be longer.
3. Do not supplement with a bottle in the first month. Encountering an artificial nipple early may discourage your baby from learning and enjoying the more complex sucking mechanism required when nursing.
4. Do not use a pacifier during the first few weeks. Some babies, those who are more fussy, seem to settle when a pacifier is given judiciously after a week or two. Do not overuse it!
5. Talk to your physician, other mothers, nurses, friends, and relatives who have direct experience or knowledge about nursing. Although nursing is a personal experience between you and your baby, the wisdom of the ages has passed down a shared foundation to ensure the longevity of nursing. Make use of others! Consult a local lactation specialist if difficulties persist.
6. Find a relaxing, comfortable, and quiet place in your home to nurse your newborn. Your milk production and the availability of the milk ("let-down reflex") are inhibited by tension. Call your physician or physician's nurse if you think you need assistance with stress reduction.
7. At the first office visit (within 1 week after discharge from the hospital), your physician will review nursing, check the baby's weight, and be available to assist you. These early visits ensure success.

Breast-feeding represents both a nourishing and nurturing experience for the baby but also has some psychosocial effects on other family members. Some fathers are prepared to enjoy observing the love and comfort created by breast-feeding; their participation should be encouraged. Other fathers may experience a feeling of abandonment or loss as the nursing mother develops an extraordinarily close relationship with the baby that is not available to the father. These paternal feelings are not uncommon, and they can be anticipated. Fathers may need to be supported through this period by pointing out to them that there are other ways they can express their love for the baby, such as changing and dressing, singing, rocking, and carrying. Once the unbilical cord has fallen off, bathing the infant, followed by a soft massage with a small amount of baby oil, provides the father with an especially valuable and sensual moment with his son or daughter.

Siblings may also be affected by the time and attention the nursing mother directs toward the baby. Jealousy and rivalry are expected; it should not be seen as problematic but as a reflection of the parents' strong bond to the older child who now seems threatened by the intrusion of this time-consuming infant. Anticipating sibling reactions as the expanded family leaves the hospital to go home may help dampen the reaction, but the goal should not be complete alleviation. Recruiting grandparents, aunts, uncles, and neighbors, in addition to dad, to spend extra time with the older child will assist in the adjustment and enhance further developmental growth.

FORMULA-FED BABIES

Support the mother in her decision to feed the baby formula. Whatever the reason, it is hers, and she needs the full support of her baby's clinician. Point out that commercial formulas are made to ensure complete nutrition for babies, including adequate amounts of vitamins. Let her know that her baby will grow well on formula and that she will satisfy not only nutritional but also emotional needs of the baby. Review the formula preparation with the parents. In households supplied with chlorinated water, sterilization is not necessary. Wash bottles and nipples with hot, soapy water, rinsing well. Review the form of formula the family will purchase—powder, concentrate, or ready-to-feed—and explain the importance of proper dilutions; instructions are available on the formula can. Because formula from a bottle is simpler to suck compared with nursing at the breast, and gastric emptying is slower with formula, feeding at intervals of 3 to 4 hours is usually satisfactory for the neonate.

SOOTHING PATTERNS

A parent can be taught specific maneuvers that will settle a crying baby while showing that she has the ability to help her baby at a time of distress. Enhanced parent-child interactions result. During the discharge examination (or at the time of a postpartum newborn class taught by a staff nurse), a fussy newborn can be soothed with a hand rubbing the back, a finger stroking the cheek, or a soft voice. A more irritable infant can be held by the clinician with an open palm supporting the chest and the opposite hand around the buttocks; as the baby is held horizontally in this position, she is moved gently to the right and left of the examiner, always visible to the parents. This simple repositioning maneuver frequently settles the infant, the crying diminishes, and the parents are amazed! At that moment, move the baby into a vertical position facing the parents. Her eyes will open, and the parents invariably will smile. You have given them a powerful experience as the baby's innate propriosensory response capacities are utilized to demonstrate how parents can modulate their own infant's behavior. Most parents find it useful to have the baby's clinician state emphatically that responding to an infant's cry will not "spoil" the child. The classic study by Bell and Ainsworth (1972) showed that consistency and promptness of the maternal response was associated with a decline in frequency and duration of infant crying. More recently, when mothers of normal newborns were encouraged to carry their babies for a minimal prescribed time each day, both the daily crying duration and evening crying time diminished compared with that of control infants (Hunziker and Barr, 1986).

PHYSICAL NEEDS

CAR RESTRAINT

The evidence is now overwhelming that proper car restraints significantly reduce morbidity and mortality in the event of an automobile accident. Informing the new parents about your concern for the newborn's safety at this time expresses your interest not only with the baby's physical and emotional well-being but also with the safety of the environment (Berger et al., 1984). Some hospitals have "first-ride" programs that provide literature and rent-a-carseat availability. The child's clinician should be the child's advocate at this point and ensure that all babies go home in a proper car restraint. Parents should be helped to separate their own proper desire to cuddle the infant with the child's undisputed need for safety.

SLEEPING ARRANGEMENTS

Have the parents anticipated the infant's arrival by preparing a place for the infant to sleep? An infant crib or cradle is the choice of most American families. In some cultures, it is customary for the newborn to sleep with her parents. Anticipatory guidance should ensure that the sleeping place is safe and within reasonable proximity to the caretaker. Babies may be placed down on their side (right side down encourages gastric emptying) or, after the umbilical cord has dislodged, on the abdomen, a position that may prevent regurgitation of gastric contents.

CLOTHING

Garments should be loose fitting, lightweight, and fire retardant. The decision to use either cloth or paper diapers rests with the parents' esthetic, economic, or ecological interests.

Whatever the infant wears, she should be able to move all extremities freely and rotate her neck to maximize interaction with the environment. Her hands should be free to explore the tactile aspects of the environment and to use hand-to-mouth activities to soothe herself.

BATHING

Once the umbilical cord stump has dislodged and the umbilicus is dry (usually 1 to 2 weeks after birth), the baby may be bathed. A bathroom sink or a shallow, plastic, oval-shaped tub is a suitable place for the bath. The water temperature should be monitored carefully to simulate skin temperature; it should be neither chilled nor too hot. The baby's head should be controlled with the parent's one hand while the other hand is free to wash. A mild soap or simple baby soap may be used.

Bathing can be a wonderful experience for the parents of a neonate. The warm water and gentle soaping is soothing to most babies. At the same time, it provides the parents with an ideal moment to interact in a reciprocal fashion with an infant who seems to be totally enjoying the experience. Visual, auditory, and tactile skills are available to make this an exciting moment in the coming together of the new family.

Fathers, in particular, may find bathing the baby an especially rewarding experience. It offers a sensual interactive moment between the baby and the father. Some fathers have commented that bathing their young infant was a time of ummatched closeness. It provides an opportunity of paternal-infant attachment. After the bath a gentle, light massage with light baby lotion enhances this experience.

PREVENTING THE "VULNERABLE CHILD SYNDROME"

Some parents attach lasting significance to either a minor medical illness or a significant medical or surgical crisis that is transient. In either case, the child survives in relative good health without major physical sequelae. The parents' concern for the child's health continues at an inappropriate level even though the child has recovered fully. These "vulnerable children" later demonstrate difficulty with separation, infantilization, bodily overconcerns, and poor school performance (Green and Solnit, 1964).

The vulnerable child syndrome may be an outgrowth of the early neonatal period, even with apparently healthy newborns. Transient events from the time of labor and delivery to the discharge examination might be viewed as potentially catastrophic by parents, such as brief abnormalities during fetal monitoring, a cesarean section, a nuchal cord, and mild and transient respiratory distress.

Contemporary nursery practices have carried with them numerous interventions to monitor the baby's transition (radiant warmers and heat probes), prevent disease through screening (phenylketonuria/thyroxine skin punctures), and either monitor or treat common neonatal problems (e.g., jaundice). For some mothers, the cumulative effect of these hospital routines is to internalize a feeling that "something may be wrong with my baby." Standard well-child care for hospital staff may be interpreted as sick care by a mother, especially in the sensitive postpartum period. Even mild to moderate jaundice in the first week can be associated with early termination of breast-feeding when assessed 1 month after birth; this association was found even when mothers were given written and verbal materials about the benign nature of jaundice (Kemper et al., 1989). To prevent parental overconcern, parents must be given clear and detailed explanations for even minor deviations from the usual perinatal course. Whenever possible, medical interventions should be kept to a minimum. For example, phototherapy and temporary cessation of breast-feeding should be prescribed only when the degree of hyperbilirubinemia may be dangerous to the child (Meisels, 1988). Jaundiced nursing neonates usually require more nursing, not less. When parental anxiety is detected, they should be given the opportunity to express their concerns. A review of the neonate's course at the discharge examination provides an opportunity to detect parental misconceptions and anxieties. Distorted perceptions about the baby can be addressed frankly and promptly. Following up this discussion at the first office visit may go a long way in preventing the vulnerable child syndrome.

REFERENCES

American Academy of Pediatrics: *Pediatric Nutrition Handbook*. Evanston, Ill, 1979, p 130.
Bell SM, Ainsworth DS: Infant crying and maternal responsiveness. *Child Dev* 1972; 43:1171–1190.
Berger LR, Saunders S, Armitage K, et al: Promoting the use of car safety devices for infants: An intensive health education approach. *Pediatrics* 1984; 74:16.
Brazelton TB: The early mother-infant adjustment. *Pediatrics* 1963; 32:931.

Brazelton TB: *Neonatal Behavioral Assessment Scale.* Philadelphia, JB Lippincott Co, 1973.

Fraiberg S: *The Magic Years.* New York, Charles Scribner & Sons, 1959.

Green M, Solnit AJ: Reaction to the threatened loss of a child: A vulnerable child syndrome. *Pediatrics* 1964; 34:58.

Greenberg M, Morris N: Engrossment: The newborn's impact on the father. *Am J Orthopsychiatry* 1974; 44:520–530.

Hayward I, Stein M, Gibson M: Nutritional rickets in San Diego. *J Dis Child* 1987; 141:1060–1062.

Hunziker UA, Barr RG: Increased carrying reduces infant crying: A randomized control trial. *Pediatrics* 1986; 77:641–648.

Kemper K, Forsyth B, McCarthy P: Jaundice, terminating breast feeding, and the vulnerable child. *Pediatrics* 1989; 84:773–778.

Klaus MH, Jerauld R, Kreger NC, et al: Maternal attachment: Importance of the first postpartum days. *N Engl J Med* 1972; 286:460.

Lozoff B, Brittenham GM, Trause MA, et al: The mother-newborn relationship: Limits of adaptability. *J Pediatr* 1977; 91:1–12.

Meisels MJ, Gifford K, Antle CE, et al: Jaundice in the healthy newborn infant: A new approach to an old problem. *Pediatrics* 1988; 81:505–511.

Olson R, Olsen G, Pernia J, et al: Use of the Brazelton neonatal assessment scale as an early intervention with adolescent parents in the newborn period. Paper presented at the Ambulatory Pediatric Association, San Francisco, May 1981.

Parmelee A, Weiner W, Schultz H: Infant sleep patterns: From birth to 16 weeks of age. *J Pediatr* 1974; 65:576.

Thomas A, Chess S: *Temperament and Development.* New York, Brunner-Mazel, 1977.

Wolff PH: Observations on newborn infants. *Psychosom Med* 1959; 21:110.

Yogman MW: Development of the father-infant relationship, in Fitzgerald H, et al (eds): *Theory and Research in Behavioral Pediatrics.* New York, Plenum Press, 1980, vol 1.

"Babies in nursery with machines."
By Ryan Hennessy, age 8.

CHAPTER 8

The Special Care Nursery: Unlocking the Behavior of the Vulnerable Neonate

SUZANNE D. DIXON, M.D.
PETER GORSKI, M.D.

KEY WORDS

PREMIE'S BEHAVIOR
DEVELOPMENTAL COURSE OF PREMIES
GRIEF REACTIONS
PREMIE BODY LANGUAGE
NICU ENVIRONMENT
DEVELOPMENTAL SURVEILLANCE IN PREMIES
VULNERABLE CHILD SYNDROME

Jason Merrill, who has an adjusted age of 36 weeks even though he was born 5 weeks ago, is a patient in the neonatal intensive care unit (NICU). He is now ready for discharge. His parents, Carolyn and Bill, have been very involved with his care since he was born. They seem to be a competent professional couple who have waited a long time for this infant and who have asked a lot of good questions throughout the hospitalization about his condition. Although they did meet the respiratory therapist to learn about the home monitor and to review cardiopulmonary resuscitation (CPR), their visiting has really decreased in the last week. The nurses report they have no more expressed stored breast milk to give Jason. A discharge conference has had to be rescheduled twice. When the parents did come in at night, they became very angry at the dust on the bassinet and the emesis around Jason's mouth. The neonatologist asks you for help handling this "difficult family" and seeing what you can do about the breast milk and the discharge conference.

The birth of an infant prematurely or with perinatal illness presents a developmental crisis for a family and for the infant herself. Neither the child nor the family is optimally prepared for the demands of postnatal life and the adjustment that the premature newborn demands. Neurodevelopmental immaturity, physiological and behavioral vulnerability, and the extraordinary caretaking tasks contribute to this requirement. The birth of an infant with no problems is a challenge at best; a birth under extraordinary circumstances calls for even greater levels of coping and adaptation. The clinician caring for the premature or sick neonate must address his efforts toward developing strategies to optimize the infant's capacities for healing and recovery, along with developmental work based on maturation. The family requires support through both the predictable and the individual aspects of this crisis. The primary care clinician has dual therapeutic opportunities in his interactions with a child and family under these circumstances. The primary care professional is in the best position to monitor the infant's emerging capacities as she recovers and grows. As important, he has recurrent chances to observe and support the parents' emotional challenges created by their special circumstances.

The parent must be helped to see the infant as she really exists, with both strengths and weaknesses. This implies a clear delineation of the child's physiological and behavioral capacities at that point in time and clear counsel around effective caretaking activities for the future. The clinician must then renegotiate a contract for the care of the special baby. This contract must spell out the role of the primary care clinician, the specialists needed by the child, other community services, and the family. The role of the family will be the most important in the long range. Attachment to the child as a person may take a long time; the primary care clinician must, with special knowledge and patience, follow this through, marking progress and facilitating it through observation and support. This approach implies the clinician's responsibility for restoring a sense of competency and confidence in parenting in a family in which these factors have been assaulted by the less-than-expected circumstances of the child's birth. The child's own fragility may be the most important limiting factor in these circumstances.

The clinician cannot meet all of the physical and psychological needs of the child directly but must support the development of the family into an effective, appropriate, adaptive caregiving unit, no matter what a particular child might require. The family is both the object of stress and the agent for recovery on behalf of a "special needs" child. The clinician must support that process if he is to effect long-lasting adaptation to the special needs child. This role definition is substantially different from that of the neonatal staff who often have the main professional role during a child's acute illness. Their focus is on the distinct period of time when the child requires their care, whereas the primary care clinician will always see the hospital discharge as not the end but a beginning. Neonatal medicine acknowledges the key role of the family in their patient's long-term outcome (Beckwith and Cohen, 1978; Beckwith et al., 1976; Sameroff, 1981), and most neonatal units make active efforts to include families in care. However, in infant special care nurseries, the survival of a child through rapid advances in technology will always be the main focus (Gottfried et al., 1981). Depending on geography and training, the primary care physician may be more or less involved in the management of the acute neonatal illness but will always be involved in the important work of helping a family rebuild around a particular child.

The family's perception of the child and their own feelings of competence are not always directly related to the severity of the perinatal illness. Even conditions that the clinician may regard as relatively minor, insignificant, or transient may set the groundwork for a permanently altered perception of the child by the family. Green and Solnit (1964) have highlighted the important dimensions of the "vulnerable child syndrome." In this syndrome, a child with an imagined or real illness in early life experiences an altered attachment to her parents. There is a long-term perception of the child as being vulnerable to illness, and the child is also viewed as both fragile and incapable of acceptance of age-appropriate limit setting and clear guidance. This perception of vulnerability leads to intrafamilial stress and an alteration of expected attachment behaviors between the child and the parents. In our own work in the rural region in Sub-Saharan Africa, the residual effects of this early impediment to attachment had long-term nutritional consequences; our observations are in parallel to those in this country (Dixon et al., 1982). It appears that there are universal consequences of perceiving one's offspring as vulnerable in early life. The clinician must be sensitive to this as a basis of many later problems (e.g., problems with sleep, eating, discipline, and school phobias) as related to this *altered perception* in the newborn period. The severity of the vulnerable child syndrome is not correlated with the severity of perinatal illness but with the parents' perceptions of the child's initial and ongoing fragility. The clinician can ask questions and make observations that provide a clue to unrealistic parental perceptions. The observations of nurses in the special care nursery are often critical in assessing the parents' perception of the child. Of course, the perceptions may change as the baby's condition improves or worsens. Maintaining a vulnerable outlook in the face of improvement or normalization defines this syndrome. We must work toward the prevention of the premature establishment of this perspective. Because the child may be physically and behaviorally more fragile, it is expected that all parents feel anxious and insecure when taking over care of the infant. Through frequent visits (especially in the first month) and clear plans and directions, the primary care physician can instill in parents both a sense of resilience in the child and competence in themselves. This process, as well as the growth chart, should be monitored frequently.

Recent research indicates that children who experience relatively minor complications of the perinatal period, such as minor intrauterine growth retardation (Als et al., 1976), hyperbilirubinemia (Telzrow et al., 1982) or maternal diabetes (Yogman et al., 1982), sustain alterations of behavior that affect their ability to interact with their families. The child then perpetuates the parents' perception that things are not quite right with her and that she requires extraordinary care that may be beyond their limits of providing (Newman, 1982) or that she is unrewarding or unresponsive to their caregiving (Brazelton, 1981a). Even in these minor circumstances, the clinician should anticipate that there may be some extra hurdles to overcome in spite of his own perception that things are just fine. When a child is born prematurely or with major perinatal illness, the child's ability to meet any of the behavioral demands of postnatal life are substantially compromised. Initially these infants are physiologically unstable, require extraordinary surveillance and monitoring, and are very poor participants in social interactions (Osofsky and Danzer, 1974). The infants' limitations predominate in these situations. Thus, one must think of the premature infant as sick, stressed from illness, and undergoing recovery rather than as just immature.

IMPACT OF THE ENVIRONMENT

The long-standing effects of bombarding the immature infant with input from extrauterine environment even when illness is not a factor is still under investigation (Duffy, 1985). The data suggest that there are associations between acute fluctuations of systemic hemodynamics and concurrent environmental events and caregiver interventions (Gorski and Huntington, 1988; Linn et al., 1985; Long et al., 1980a, 1980b). These, in turn, appear to alter important central nervous system parameters, including intracranial pressure changes and brain oxygenation. There is a direct relationship between these factors and hypoxemia, apnea, bradycardia, and cerebral circulation and autoregulation (Brazy, 1988; Perlman and Volpe,

1985). Investigators have examined the sensory characteristics of NICUs, along with infant behavioral and physiological responses to the caretaking activities in this environment (Gaiter, 1985; Gorski et al., 1983; Gottfried et al., 1981; High and Gorski, 1985; Linn et al., 1985). Results have shown the NICU environment to be one that provides both sensory overload and deprivation (Gottfried, 1985; High and Gorski, 1985). These studies found that infants experience a bombardment of stimuli from sheer numbers of different caregivers and procedures each day. At the same time, however, very little social contact and long intervals of social isolation are also present. High and Gorski (1985) also discovered an absence of temporal contingency between the sleep or awake state of infants in an NICU and the onset of either medical or custodial care. Less than 10% of cries are heeded. From the infant's view, this is a chaotic, nonresponsive, and, in many ways, aversive environment.

The impact of prematurity itself may be long standing (e.g., Vohr and Garcia-Coll, 1985). Whether the clinician is faced with a "well" premature infant or one recovering from serious illness, this child requires altered care based on individual needs and competencies. In these cases, he needs extraordinary measures of protection (Brazelton, 1981b) and measured intervention to bring out the best in his behavioral capacities to overcome physiological instability (Als et al., 1979). This requires new skills on the part of parents and other caretakers, because the infant's needs and response are subtly expressed and not intuitively obvious.

The behavior of the premature infant can be confusing to even an experienced caregiver. His facial expressions have a limited range (Frodi et al., 1978), his body movements may be few and his cries nonexistent or irritating (Lester, 1987). The latency of his responses may be so long that it is difficult to connect one activity with the response. Social interactions that are so exciting with a full-term infant may cause him to turn away, become mottled, or even stop breathing (Goldberg, 1979; Gorski, 1983; Gorski et al., 1983). He may actively avoid eye contact, a very negative message to those who would like to interact with him. At other times his unremitting irritability seems to resist all of the usual consoling and comforting measures. All of these behaviors run counter to what is usually expected of infants. Without some special knowledge and some techniques to make sense of the premature infant's behavior, caregivers will feel ineffective, frustrated, angry, and perplexed. Conversely, if the clinician can interpret some of the confusing messages and help a family to develop effective caregiving patterns, there will be an enhancement of competency and confidence. The child's energy can be directed toward recovery and developmental work rather than toward defending herself against an insensitive, overwhelming environment. The attachment of parent to infant is enhanced by this mutually satisfying relationship (Brazelton, 1981a; Ounsted et al., 1974).

The infant uses body language to signal both positive and negative responses to the various life experiences. Even a short period of observation during the nursery rounds, treatment sessions, and examinations will demonstrate many of these. Some of these behaviors are listed in Tables 8–1 and 8–2. Adverse stimuli will vary from infant to infant and will change as the infant matures. Aversive stimuli for the premature infant tend to be overwhelming or high levels of input: bright lights, noise, rapid movements, two or more simultaneous inputs (e.g., movement of the infant and speech to her). In addition, aversive behaviors emerge when there are rapid changes in input, even if the level of input is low. Transitions between one activity (e.g., feeding) and another (e.g., vital sign checks) may produce considerable disruptions. Even the transitions to sleep or to wakefulness may be prolonged and accompanied by much physiological instability (Als et al., 1985).

TABLE 8–1.
Body Language of the Premature Infant*

Approach Behaviors

Sounds
Hand clasp
Foot clasp
Finger folding (moving fingers in flexion pattern)
Tucking body inward
"Soft" body movements
Mouthing
Suck-search
Sucking
Hand holding
Locking visually or auditorially and thus cutting down on motor movement
"Ooh" expression on face
Cooing

*Adapted from Als H, Lester B, Brazelton TB, et al: Dynamics of the behavioral organization of the premature infant: A theoretical perspective, in Field TM, et al (eds): *Infants Born at Risk: Behavior and Development.* Jamaica, NY, Spectrum Publications, 1979.

PREMATURE PARENTS

The parents too are "premature" and have special processes of recovery that have impact on the child, and these must be acknowledged by the clinician. They have not completed the developmental work of pregnancy, and, in addition, they must put energy into the resolution of the complex feelings that emerge as a consequence of their infant's birth. The predictable course of response to the loss of a loved one has been described in many settings (Bowlby, 1980; Lindemann, 1944). The initial response of denial and anger give way to depression and

TABLE 8–2.
Body Language of the Premature Infant*

Avoidance Behaviors

Spitting up
Gagging
Hiccuping
Bowel movement: grunting and straining
Grimaces, lip retraction
Trunk arching
Finger splaying
Airplane posture: all four extremities going backward
Sitting in air (flexing forward)
Coughing
Averting gaze

*Adapted from Als H, Lester B, Brazelton TB, et al: Dynamics of the behavioral organization of the premature infant: A theoretical perspective, in Field TM, et al (eds): *Infants Born at Risk: Behavior and Development.* Jamaica, NY, Spectrum Publications, 1979.

guilt and, finally, resolution. These same stages of grief reaction are apparent in the parental response to an infant born prematurely or with neonatal illness. Parents truly have lost a valued person in the form of the hoped-for or imagined child, and their grief comes from that separation. They must resolve that grief to attach themselves to the *real* child that is now before them, to see that child as separate from their image. The grief reaction must run its course through the various stages of denial, anger, depression, and resolution. Clinicians must monitor this process and not be surprised at the turbulence and seemingly inappropriate responses or anger that may be leveled at them or others as a result of this process. These are healthy reactions and over the long run will produce emotional energy that will enable the family to reorganize around the real child. Short-term counseling may be necessary in achiev- ing resolution of this process in some cases. Many anxious calls, trivial questions, requests for laboratory values, and reluctance to be discharged from the hospital or leave the office are manifestations of this anxiety. One must not be distracted into answering these demands at a superficial level only; they must be seen as opportunities to support a parent's recovery of competence and self-esteem. The positive side of the family dynamic is that fathers are more often active in the care of their premature infants than are fathers of full-term infants (Haw- thorne et al., 1978). Pressed into extraordinary service early and frequently in the hospital, they remain more involved with care later on (Parke, 1981). In addition, in families in which the father is supportive and involved, the mothers visit more often and participate more reg- ularly in their infant's care (Minde et al., 1978). The smart primary care clinician will cultivate a real involvement of fathers of high-risk infants as an effective way to infuse energy into the whole family system.

PARENTS AND THE SPECIAL CARE NURSERY

The experience of the special care nursery adds to a parent's feelings of incompetence, poor self-esteem, and guilt that are born with the child with special problems. These feelings originate in the birth of an infant who is not quite the baby they expected, who has problems, and who is not perfect. Parents harbor guilt and anger at their own threatened reproductive competence and their inability to care for the infant (Brazelton, 1981a). The special care nurs- ery adds to these feelings by overtly or covertly giving the message to parents that they cannot take care of the baby or that something they did caused the baby's difficulties. Expert nurses, therapists, and physicians must take over, because the family has failed. Parents are left with little confidence and little energy to assert themselves, to learn new skills, make decisions, or to get to know their infant. Even in the best of circumstances, the special care nursery envi- ronment itself leads to these feelings. This does not imply that nurses or physicians are insen- sitive to parents' needs; rather, it speaks for the fact that the high technology and overwhelm- ing care requirements for sick and premature infants give these unspoken messages to families. In addition, nurses must attach to their infant charges if they are to give the best of care. Both technology and the necessary substitute caretakers compete with and undermine the parents' abilities to become part of their infant's life. The lack of ability to experience any sort of intimacy with their own child, any sort of privacy, or any sort of caretaking regime without the surveillance of the nursing staff adds stress in the special care nursery environ- ment for parents. Only 2% of human contact experienced by the infant is from the parents, according to one careful study (Gottfried et al., 1981). Most families will, in addition, experience extreme financial pressures around the care of their infants. Spending days, to weeks, to perhaps months in the special care nursery requires extraordinary adaptive skills at a time when parents are least able to muster these resources. Sparse visiting, lack of telephone calls, lack of initiative, or angry accusations are more often adaptive responses to overwhelming stress rather than a measure of disattachment to the child or lack of appreciation of the expert care. The clinician may have to interpret these behaviors to the staff on the NICU and display considerable patience with families. He must grant them a "grace period" in which to recover.

As discharge approaches, parental anxiety increases (Brazelton, 1981a). The demands of unrelenting care, the lingering sense of inadequacy, and the fear of further damaging the infant all contribute to this. This may be manifested as decreased visiting, anger, accusations, or the proposal of impediments. The clinician should recognize the need to withdraw before this new step (Klaus and Kennell, 1976), to support it while still holding firm on the discharge plan with as specific a course as can be anticipated. The development of a notebook for all instructions, appointments, important telephone numbers, and critical observations helps to channel this energy into a useful mode. The reflection on these feelings as normal and as a testimony of caring will help parents put the feelings into perspective. The *explicit* agreement of *frequent, scheduled* calls and visits appears to generate earlier independence in a family rather than relying on an ad hoc arrangement. A more expanded "debriefing" should be set up 6 weeks to 3 months after discharge. A conference at discharge should be very concrete, focused on short-term goals and expectations and plans.

Social service evaluation for significantly sick neonates' families should be routine and should be also offered to other families who may perceive their infant as vulnerable or damaged. Parental support groups and parent programs have been shown to be remarkably successful and are gaining political strength as well. Parents themselves may be the best support for other parents in this difficult adjustment crisis. The parent-to-parent movement, particularly for families of premature infants, has the potential of becoming a powerful force to help families through this significant adjustment period. The clinician should arrange such encounters and such support systems, because families are usually unable at this time to do a lot of this resource acquisition themselves. Parenting groups, particularly for children with specific problems of known outcome (e.g., Down syndrome), and with other professionals may be significantly more helpful to families than the clinician himself during this adjustment phase. It must be appreciated that the clinician, no matter how caring or responsive, may be perceived as part of the problem by the family, as one who perpetuates the high-technology interventions and prevents the seemingly free experience between the child and family. The clinician must weather this assignment of guilt and see it as part of the adaptive resolution. Other resources must be mobilized for a family because the physician often maintains this somewhat scapegoat role.

GETTING TO KNOW EACH OTHER

To learn the infant's signal system, parents must spend time in the nursery. The clinician can add structure to these sessions after the child is medically stable. The parents can be asked to monitor their own infant's response to caregiving. Effective soothing, especially through transitions and modulated use of the infant's alert times, are new skills to be learned. Nurses should share their own observations and techniques, but they must be given a new agenda.

The family is ready for discharge when the parents can tell the nurses what is most helpful for their own infant. Nurses must welcome these remarks as measures of success rather than assaults. Parents are ready when they see their infant as an individual with communicative intent—a person who can be known and understood. Parents can reach this level only after they are sure that the infant will survive and are confident that they can cope with the child's needs. Skills in CPR, monitor use, medication administration, and so forth should be seen as building tools for parental coping, as well as necessities for infant survival. These skills free parents to see their infant as manageable, understandable, and lovable.

FOLLOW-UP OF PREMATURE INFANTS

The early developmental course of the premature infant is rarely "normal" (Davis and Thoman, 1987; Telzrow et al., 1982); it will usually show some deviation from our expectations of that for the full-term child. Motor tone will be altered, with some increase in extensor tone, especially prominent during the first year (Fitzhardinge and Ramsay, 1973; Prechtl, 1968). The tone of the extremities will be unbalanced in most infants, with the lower extremities showing greater tone than the upper extremities. Transient dystonia may occur periodically throughout the first year (Drillien, 1961). The long-term consequence of these alterations is confusing at best. Although the incidence of cerebral palsy increases with decreasing birth weight and more severe cerebrovascular complications (Weisglas-Kuperus et al., 1987), the alteration of tone noted early in development is not reliably predictive as it occurs during the first year. Asymmetries of tone and persistent tone abnormalities are more worrisome than fluctuations and early hypertonicity. *Distinctly asymmetric* neurological examinations at 1 year of age are likely to remain abnormal and require special interventions (Vohr and Garcia-Coll, 1985). The premature infant appears to smile and show some increases in social competency before his adjusted-age expectations; however, other evidences of behavioral accelerations are based on postconceptual age.

It is clear that we should make adjustments in our expectations commensurate with a child's postconceptual age rather than his chronological age, beginning with a correction in the growth chart and how we label an office visit. Even within this framework, there are alterations to normal developmental course, and these detours are likely to be more clearly defined in the future. Long-term follow-up studies (Siegal, 1985; Fitzhardinge and Ramsay, 1973) lag behind technological advance, so that the clinician should be cautious of statistics based on the care of populations that have now changed. For the clinician without all the normative data, a few expectations guide our surveillance of the premature infant. Behaviors that require lower extremity extension may be accelerated—the ability to bear weight on the lower extremities, to walk in an infant walker, or even to sit in an infant seat. These are not true accelerations in motor development but only manifestations of increased muscle tone. Devices such as the walkers should be avoided in these cases.

The best assessment of motor competencies is an observation of free play. If one can do only one such assessment, the highest yield is at 8 months of corrected age. The pincer grasp should be developing and used in play. The hips should have good mobility, and the child should have a reasonably stable sit position. The child should have an active curiosity about the environment. He should turn to the parent for support and show the beginnings of wariness; pouting and other gesture language should be emerging. The clinician should systematically assess each of these areas and be familiar with appropriate screening instruments (e.g., Gesell and Knobloch). Major delays should elicit referrals before 1 year. Fixed positions or postures may also need therapy. Language delays may need a repeat hearing assessment.

Visual and auditory alerting and language skills appear to follow the adjusted-age expectations (Sigman and Parmelee, 1974). However, visual-motor tasks (e.g., finding a hidden object) may be delayed during the first year even among premature infants who have had benign perinatal courses (Janowsky, 1985). Indeed, well past infancy, sensory integrative challenges may contribute to problems of attention and processing. Consequently, school performance, learning, and social behavior may suffer. Premature infants do not cry as vigorously or as loudly as infants born at term. Even at 40 weeks' postconceptual age, oral structures may be somewhat altered because of the premature birth, with lack of tongue molding, complicated by nasogastric tubes and delayed feedings. Alterations in oral structure may mean alterations in feeding patterns and later in speech.

Children cared for in the bright light and continuous sound environment of the special care nursery will maintain immature state alterations for the first several months after discharge. It will be more difficult for these infants to settle down for sleeping, they may have long periods of irritability when waking and falling asleep, and they may find it difficult to come to a quiet-alert state for sustained periods (Sigman and Parmelee, 1979). One should expect, however, that once removed from the stressful environment of the NICU, the baby will demonstrate increasing competency at state regulation in a quieter, more predictable environment, although normalization of this sleep pattern is rarely achieved. After 1 year, sleep disorders are more common in children who had perinatal difficulties (Bernal, 1973), and these may persist. Difficulty with making transitions from one activity to another may also be impaired well beyond discharge from the nursery. These are predictable, should be so identified to parents, and are not diagnostic of either poor parenting or neurological damage in themselves. Irritability and sleep difficulties should decrease at 4 to 5 months of postconceptual age in most children.

There is a high incidence of hearing disorders among premature infants. These difficulties cannot be detected in office settings and require formal assessments. A brainstem auditory evoked response (BAER) should be done near discharge, followed by visual reinforced audiometry or other behavioral audiometry when the child is sitting stably and again at age 12 to 15 months. Even normal results of these tests do not rule out a subtle high-frequency loss that will impact on school learning. Another preschool test is advised if any speech or language difficulties persist.

The clinician's time is well spent in supporting these behaviorally fragile neonates and their premature families during this developmental crisis. Although the range of disability in any one family may go from mild to very severe, it is still worth supporting all members of that unit toward creating a mutually responsive and caring environment. Studies of the outcome of sick and premature infants are coming together in one direction: they support the fact that the single most important variable in long-term developmental outcome for these vulnerable children is the responsiveness of the child's caretaker to the child during the first year of life (Beckwith and Parmelee, 1987; Beckwith et al., 1976). With the exception of severe insult directly to the central nervous system (e.g., severe intracranial hemorrhage or meningitis) and a chronic hypoxic state (severe bronchopulmonary dysplasia), the developmental outcome depends less on medical events and perinatal circumstances than it does on the family's ability to meet the needs of an individual child, as summarized by Sameroff (1981).

This is not surprising, given what we know overall about children. If a parent can learn to provide contingent and consistent interactions and appropriate responsiveness for a high-risk infant, the infant's chances for learning and long-term developmental adjustment are augmented. If a parent continues to be unable to read the child's signals and fails to meet the child's needs on both a physical and behavioral level, the child experiences the world as noncontingent and chaotic (Watson, 1981). The basic prerequisites for emotional and cognitive growth are undermined. If he has basic perceptual and cognitive disabilities to start out with, these added insults make his developmental work all the more difficult. Each child's optimal developmental outcome depends on the parents' ability to become effective in dealing with their own individual child (Lozoff et al., 1977). This effectiveness, in turn, leads to stronger attachment and bonding, with the parents' self-esteem and confidence restored, and provides for the care of even the most challenging child.

In most circumstances, the primary care clinician can do little about the particular perinatal insults that the child sustains except provide optimal perinatal medical care and referral as needed. The primary care clinician's work begins while planning the hospital discharge from the special care nursery. At this time, the clinician must accurately characterize the needs, strengths, and weaknesses of an individual child and family. He must come together with other professionals to provide a cohesive plan for care that meets and optimizes development. This optimization must occur through the medium of the family, and, therefore, the family must be seen as the medium for change for an individual child. This does not imply an impotency on the part of the health care professional to provide care with any meaning over the long run for the child; rather, it means that the clinician's approach toward meeting the child's developmental needs must be directed through the family. A sense of professional accomplishment is enhanced when the clinician sees his own role as one of supporting the family unit through this developmental crisis. The primary care physician may be in a better position than a neonatologist or other medical specialist to view the broad picture of this infant and family. Often less involved with the technology of neonatal care, the primary care clinician can offer the broad perspective and see beyond the walls of the special care nursery, beyond all the machines, technology, and bright lights to the child and the family. He can offer perspective and common sense in discharge planning, as well as hospital care of the vulnerable neonate. The clinician's role is to identify strengths and to build on them in each family unit. This does not imply ignoring the difficulties, the vulnerabilities, or the incapacities of the high-risk infant; rather, it implies looking for those avenues in which effective change can be made with both the infant and the family.

DATA GATHERING AT DISCHARGE

It is assumed that the primary care clinician has been observing or has reviewed the course of the infant and is aware of the resolved or lingering medical concerns. Specific plans for these need to be laid out in very concrete, short-term schedules.

WHAT TO OBSERVE

1. The clinician will ask the NICU nurses to begin to keep records of the infant's awake and sleep times for at least 1 week before discharge. The regularity of these state changes are an indicator of neurobehavioral integrity and maturation. It also gives a base on which to evaluate at home change.

2. The clinician should observe the parents while they are feeding and handling their infant. Competence and confidence should be evaluated. Supportive comments and suggestions should be offered. The clinician should work with the NICU staff to identify specific training needs.

3. The infant record should indicate increasing regularity of vital signs, weight gain, alertness, and activity. The parents should be able to describe these processes and identify the infant's individual characteristics.

WHAT TO ASK

Questions to be asked when the infant is to be discharged from the special care nursery are presented in Table 8–3.

EXAMINATION

It is essential that the primary care clinician and the family examine the baby *together* before discharge. As the clinician observes the baby first in sleep, through gentle talking, moving, undressing, and examining, he should narrate his reading of the infant's behavior, both positive and negative. Parents should be asked to comment as well, so that everyone is seeing the *same* infant. The level of stimulation that the infant tolerates should be noted. Signals of overstimulation, physiological instability, and fatigue should be met with a rest period, a pulling back of stimulation, and a period for recovery.

If the infant becomes alert, the clinician should demonstrate alerting and orienting to voice, then a face, and then both together. If overload occurs, this should be pointed out to the parents as evidence of the child's limits. Considerable support for extremities, head, trunk,

TABLE 8–3.
Questions to Be Asked at Discharge From the Special Care Nursery

Questions	Observation
How is the baby doing?	Level of attachment—are the parents answering with a shrug of bewilderment, with a list of laboratory values, or with personalized, accurate observations of their infant's response to them?
Is the baby ready for discharge:	Assess the parents' understanding of readiness issues; gather data from their perspective about the infant.
Are *you* ready to take (name) home?	Assess readiness and response—expand to include specifics of readiness, special needs; assess parental adjustment.
Who will be at home to help?	Assess support systems, intrafamilial concerns, level of father's involvement; assess sibling and family needs.
Do you feel comfortable with (name)?	Evaluate feelings of inadequacy; reassure parents of normality of anxiety; evaluate specific areas in which parents' skills are inadequate.
Do you have any questions about the infant's hospital course?	Open the discussion for any questions about the perinatal events; be honest about your level of concern vis-à-vis these events.
What things would you like to see happen before you take (name) home?	Establish locus of control with parents; develop a plan to meet these wishes if possible; explain if not.

and temperature control may be needed to demonstrate the brief periods of alertness. The *cost* to the infant or difficulty the infant experiences for these periods should be noted so that this may be observed at home, hopefully tracking an improving course.

The general pediatric examination, including a detailed neurological evaluation, should proceed. Any areas of abnormality, as well as encouraging signs, should be clearly stated. The clinician should carefully describe the behaviors that represent the next step in improvement.

A summary statement by the clinician should open a discussion with parents about the evaluation. An unrushed pause and encouragement may be needed. It is not to be expected that all issues or concerns will be laid out and discussed at this time; rather, this discussion sets a pattern for ongoing developmental surveillance.

ANTICIPATORY GUIDANCE

The planning for discharge begins on admission as the clinician interprets the issues, weighs them for families, and lays out a strategy for treatment and follow-up. This plan is expanded, revised, and updated through the child's course. The clinician should attend or chair a multidisciplinary team conference with the family before the infant's discharge from the hospital. This should be planned well in advance and have good preparation. The goal of this conference is to review the hospital course, to make plans for follow-up, and to review any treatment plans. A readiness assessment should include input from all disciplines and should include an assessment of behavioral maturity, as well as physiological stability.

A notebook with all of the infant's needs, resources to meet those needs, warning signals, appointments, medications, and telephone numbers of specialists and staff can be most helpful. Most parents remember very few specifics without such an aid. Highlight one or two resources, including the primary care pediatrician, to work with the parents in coordinating the multiple services.

Appropriate community agency referrals should be initiated even if services may not be needed immediately. Few parents are able to do this on their own. Parent support groups have been shown to be very helpful and effective. The physician should help support the development of these groups.

The follow-up plans should be explicit, frequent, and scheduled before the infant's discharge from the hospital. The NICU staff may designate one nurse to follow-up with a call in 1 or 2 days to ease the transition. Explicit permission "to visit" after discharge is also helpful as parents attempt to separate from the nursery.

The parents should have demonstrated competency in every aspect of their infant's care. They should have rehearsed what will be needed in emergencies.

Instruction in infant CPR and appropriate emergency action will relieve fears rather than generate them. A telephone should be in the house and transportation plans made. Videos, dolls, and pamphlets should supplement *direct* teaching in this and other areas.

An iron-deficient infant is an irritable infant. Appropriate vitamin and iron supplementation should be initiated even in the absence of frank anemia. Check the hematocrit value at discharge.

The clinician should describe the infant by his *postconceptual age* so that expectations are more nearly realistic. Always do this correction at the beginning of each encounter.

Be sure an accurate head circumference is done at the time of discharge.

Parents should be encouraged to stay overnight, if possible, before discharge.

MINIPROGRAMS

The development of a behavioral intervention plan should be initiated either before or in lieu of a formal intervention program for selected infants. The clinician will pick one or two areas of concern and set very small goals. For example, if the infant sleeps erratically, the parents might be asked to keep a sleep record to see if this improves over a period of 2 weeks. If the infant has difficulty tolerating a bath, the parent and the clinician can devise supports (e.g., swaddling half the body) so that the child can begin to at least tolerate, if not enjoy, that experience. By setting short-term goals, both the parents and the clinician can gain a sense of progress and recovery.

DIFFICULTIES AND PLANS

The irritability of many high-risk infants is a major hurdle that often emerges some weeks after discharge. The development of effective soothing and the avoidance of overloading situations will ameliorate but not obliterate this process. Swings, swaddling, waterbeds, and pacifiers all may help. This problem is more baby determined than parent determined. Parents can take hope from knowing that premature infants, like all full-term infants, increase the amount and intensity of crying for the first 6 to 8 weeks after term.

The transition to full breast-feeding is a process that takes weeks to months. A gradual course of decreasing supplements and use of a lactation device (Lactaid) will be helpful. The mother should increase pumping to eight times daily for a period of 7 to 10 days before discharge. The preterm infant should be able to nurse at breast before discharge for part of a feeding or for all of some feedings.

Periodic visual and hearing assessments should be planned at 6-month intervals, more frequently if abnormalities are noted at discharge. Special psychological assessments will be required into school age. Parents should be told that this is routine and does not imply concern for their child. Specialized follow-up services are needed beyond what the primary care clinician can do.

It should be explicitly stated that even though he is ready to go home, the premature or high-risk infant still requires a period of recovery and will take at least some small developmental detours. A comparison with a full-term infant is to be avoided. Stress for the family and infant should be minimized during this adjustment and recovery time.

Home visiting, sometimes including a predischarge or postdischarge visit, is very helpful if done by the NICU staff or others who knew the infant in the hospital. Discharge plans become realistic, and teaching can be focused. Follow-up and compliance are increased at least threefold when a visit is made.

A review of the perinatal course should be added to the 6-week to 3-month visit if a discussion has not been opened by the parents before that time. The 8- to 9-month visit should be expanded to allow for a play observation and a structured developmental assessment. A formal neurological examination should be done at 1 year at minimum. For high-risk children, special attention should be paid to a language assessment at 2 to $2\frac{1}{2}$ years of postconceptual age. A preschool examination should place added emphasis on visual-motor integration tasks (e.g., figure copying). Disabilities in this area should trigger *immediate specific* testing, not just a standard intelligence test.

Every visit should end with a delineation of the infant's and parents' strengths and gains over time, however small. A pregnancy following the birth of a premature or ill infant may be a time of particular anxiety and stress for a family. The clinician should be alert to this possibility when seeing his former premature infant as a toddler or preschooler. Lingering anxiety may be the source of problems in the child and family. The clinician should be alert to the possible vulnerable child basis for sleep, feeding, separation, and play problems. Going back to the perinatal period may be both the most efficient and efficacious way to deal with that.

REFERENCES

Als H, Lawhon G, Gibes R, et al: Individualized behavioral and environmental care for the VLBW preterm at high risk for chronic lung disease. Paper presented at the Society for Research in Child Development, Toronto, April 1985.

Als H, Lester B, Brazelton TB: Dynamics of the behavioral organization of the premature infant: A theoretical perspective, in Field TM, et al (eds): *Infants Born at Risk: Behavior and Development.* Jamaica, NY, Spectrum Publications, 1979.

Als H, Tronick E, Adamson L, et al: The behavior of the full term yet underweight newborn infant. *Dev Med Child Neurol* 1976; 18:590–602.

Beckwith L, Cohen S: Preterm birth: Hazardous obstetrical and postnatal events as related to caregiver-infant behavior. *Infant Behav Dev* 1978; 1:403–411.

Beckwith L, Cohen S, Kopp C, et al: Caregiver-infant interaction and early cognitive development in preterm infants. *Child Dev* 1976; 47:579–587.

Beckwith L, Parmelee AH: EEG patterns of preterm infants: Home environment and later IQ. *Child Dev* 1986; 57:777–789.

Bernal JF: Night waking in infants during the first fourteen months. *Dev Med Child Neurol* 1973; 15:760–769.

Bowlby J: *Attachment and Loss. Loss: Sadness and Depression.* New York, Basic Books, 1980, vol 3.

Brazelton TB: *On Becoming a Family: The Growth of Attachment.* New York, Delacorte, 1981a.

Brazelton TB: Early intervention: What does it mean? in Fitzgerald HE, Lester BM, Yogman MW (eds): *Theory and Research in Behavioral Pediatrics.* New York, Plenum Press, 1981b.

Brazy JE: Effects of crying on cerebral blood volume and cytochrome aa^3. *J Pediatr* 1988; 112:457–461.

Davis DH, Thoman EB: Behavioral states of premature infants. Implications for neural and behavioral development. *Dev Psychobiol* 1987; 20:25–38.

Dixon S, Keefer C, Tronick E, et al: Perinatal circumstances and newborn outcome among the Gusii of Kenya: Assessment of risk. *Infant Behav Devel* 1982; 5:11–21.

Drillien CM: The incidence of mental and physical handicaps in school age children of very low birth weight. *Pediatrics* 1961; 27:452–464.

Duffy FH: Evidence for hemisphere differences between full terms and preterms by electrophysiologic measures. Paper presented at the Society for Research in Child Development, Toronto, April 1985.

Fitzhardinge PM, Ramsay M: The improving outlook for the small, prematurely born infant. *Dev Med Child Neurol* 1973; 15:447–459.

Frodi AM, Lamb ME, Leavitt LA, et al: Fathers' and mothers' responses to the faces and cries of normal and premature infants. *Dev Psychol* 1978; 14:490–498.

Gaiter JL: Nursery environments: The behavior and caregiving experiences of full-term and preterm newborns, in Gottfried AW, Gaiter JL (eds): *Infant Stress Under Intensive Care.* Baltimore, University Park Press, 1985, pp 55–81.

Goldberg S: Premature birth: Consequences for the parent-infant relationship. *Am Sci* 1979; 67:214–220.

Gorski PA: Fostering family development following preterm hospitalization. In Ballard, RA (Ed.): *Pediatric Care of the ICN Graduate.* Philadelphia, WB Saunders Co, 1988, pp 27–32.

Gorski PA, Huntington L: Physiological measures relative to tactile stimulation in hospitalized preterm infants. *Ped Res* 1988; 23:210A.

Gorski PA: Premature infant behavioral and physiological responses to caregiving interventions in the intensive care nursery, in Call JD, Galenson E, Tyson R (eds): *Frontiers of Infant Psychiatry.* New York, Basic Books, 1983, pp 256–263.

Gorski PA: Hole WT, Leonard CH, et al: Direct computer recording of premature infants and nursery care. *Pediatrics* 1983; 72:198–202.

Gottfried AW: Environment of newborn infants in special care units, in Gottfried AW, Gaiter JL (eds): *Infant Stress Under Intensive Care.* Baltimore, University Park Press, 1985, pp 23–54.

Gottfried AW, Wallace-Land P, Sherman-Brown S, et al: Physical and social environment of newborn infants in special care units. *Science* 1981; 214:673–675.

Green M, Solnit AJ: Reactions to the threatened loss of a child: A vulnerable child syndrome. *Pediatrics* 1964; 34:58–66.

Hawthorne JT, Richards MPM, Callon M: A study of parental visiting of babies in a special care unit, in Brimble-Combe FSW, Richards MPM, Robertson NRC (eds): *Early Separation and Special Care Nurseries.* London, Simp/Heinemann Medical Books, 1978.

High PC, Gorski PA: Recording environmental influences on infant development in the intensive care nursery, in Gottfried AW, Gaiter JL (eds): *Infant Stress Under Intensive Care.* Baltimore, University Park Press, 1985, pp 131–155.

Janowsky JS: Cognitive development and reorganization after early brain injury. Thesis, Department of Psychology, Cornell University, 1985.

Klaus MH, Kennell JH: *Maternal-Infant Bonding.* St. Louis, CV Mosby Co, 1976.

Lester BM: Developmental outcome prediction from acoustic cry analysis in term and preterm infants. *Pediatrics* 1987; 80:529–534.

Lindemann E: Symptomatology and management of acute grief. *Am J Psychiatry* 1944; 101:141.

Linn PL, Horowitz FD, Fox HA: Stimulation in the NICU: Is more necessarily better? *Clin Perinatol* 1985; 12:407–422.

Long JG, Lucey JF, Philip AGS: Noise and hypoxemia in the intensive care nursery. *Pediatrics* 1980a; 65:143–145.

Long JG, Philip AGS, Lucey JF: Excessive handling as a cause of hypoxemia. *Pediatrics* 1980b; 65:203–207.

Lozoff B, Brittenham GM, Trause MA, et al: The mother-newborn relationship: Limits of adaptability. *J Pediatr* 1977; 91:1.

Minde K, Trehub S, Corter C, et al: Mother-child relationships in the premature nursery: An observational study. *Pediatrics* 1978: 61:373–377.

Newman LF: Parents' perceptions of their low birthweight infants. *Paediatrician* 1982; 9:182–190.

Osofsky JD, Danzer B: Relationships between neonatal characteristics and mother-infant interaction. *Dev Psychol* 1974; 10:124–130.

Ounsted C, Oppenheimer R, Lindsay J: Aspects of bonding failure. *Dev Med Child Neurol* 1974; 16:447–456.

Parke RD: *Fathers.* Cambridge, Mass, Harvard University Press, 1981.

Perlman JM, Volpe JJ: Episodes of apnea and bradycardia in the preterm newborn. Impact on cerebral circulation. *Pediatrics* 1985; 76:333–338.

Prechtl HFR: Neurological findings in newborn infants after pre- and perinatal complications, in Jones JHP, Viesez H, Troelstra JA (eds): *Dysmaturity and Prematurity*. Leiden, Netherlands, Droese, 1968.

Sameroff AJ: Longitudinal studies of preterm infants, in Friedman S, Sigman M (eds): *Preterm Birth and Psychological Development*. New York, Academic Press, 1981.

Sigman M, Parmelee AH: Longitudinal evaluation of the high risk infant, in Field TM, et al (eds): *Infants Born at Risk: Behavior and Development*. Jamaica, NY, Spectrum Publications, 1979.

Sigman M, Parmelee AH: Visual preferences of four month old premature and full term infants. *Child Dev* 1974; 10:687–695.

Telzrow RW, Kang RR, Mitchell SK, et al: An assessment of the behavior of the preterm infant at 40 weeks gestational age, in Lipsitt L, Field TM (eds): *Infant Behavior and Development: Perinatal Risk and Newborn Behavior*. Norwood, NJ, Ablex Publishing Corp, 1982, pp 85–96.

Vohr BR, Garcia-Coll CT: Neurodevelopmental and school performance of very low birth weight infants: A seven-year longitudinal study. *Pediatrics* 76:345–350, 1985.

Watson JS: Perception of contingency as a determinant of social responsiveness, in Thoman EB (ed): *Origins of the Infant's Social Responsiveness*. Hillsdale, NJ, Erlbaum Publishers, 1979.

Weisglas-Kuperus N, Uleman-Vleeschdrager M, Baerts W: Ventricular hemorrhages and hypoxic-ischaemic lesions in preterm infants: Neurodevelopmental outcome at $3\frac{1}{2}$ years. *Dev Med Child Neurol* 1987; 29:623–629.

Yogman MW, Coles P, Als H, et al: The behavior of newborns of diabetic mothers. *Infant Behav Dev* 1982; 5:331–340.

ADDITIONAL READINGS

Ballard RA, *Pediatric Care of the ICN Graduate*, Philadelphia, WB Saunders Co, 1988.

Cohen BD: *Born at Risk*. New York, St Martin's Press, 1981.

Desmond MM, Wilson GS, Alt EF, et al: The very low birth weight infant after discharge from intensive care: Anticipatory health care and developmental course. *Curr Probl Pediatr* 1980; 10:5.

Galinsky E: *Beginnings: A Young Mother's Personal Account of Two Premature Births*. Boston, Houghton-Mifflin, 1976.

Gottfried AW, Gaiter JL (eds): *Infant Stress Under Intensive Care*. Baltimore, University Park Press, 1985.

Hack M, Fanaroff AA, Merkatz IR: The low birth weight infant: Evolution of changing outlook. *N Engl J Med* 1979; 301:1162–1165.

Harrison H: *The Premature Baby Book*. New York, St Martin's Press, 1983.

Knoblock H, Stevens F, Malone AF: *The Revised Developmental Screening Inventory*. Albany, NY, State Office of Mental Retardation and Developmental Disabilities, 1980.

Korones SB: Physical structure and organization of neonatal intensive care units, in Gottfried AW, Gaiter JL (eds): *Infant Stress Under Intensive Care*. Baltimore, University Park Press, 1985.

Lester BM, Zeskind PS: The organization of crying in the infant at risk, in Field TM, et al (eds): *Infants Born at Risk: Behavior and Development*. Jamaica, NY, Spectrum Publications, 1979.

Nance S: *Premature Babies: A Handbook for Parents.* New York, Arbor House, 1982.

Newman LF: Social and sensory environment of low birthweight infants in a special care nursery. *J Nerv Ment Dis* 1981; 169:448–455.

Schulman CA: Alterations of the sleep cycle in heroin addicted and "suspect" newborns. *Neuropediatrics* 1969; 1:89–100.

Schulte FJ: Neurophysiological aspects of brain development. *Mead Johnson Symp Perinat Dev Med* 1975; 6:38–47.

Seligman MR: *Helplessness: On Development, Depression, and Death.* W.H. Freeman, 1975.

Sell EJ (ed): *The Follow-up of the High Risk Newborn—A Practical Approach.* Springfield, Ill, Charles C Thomas, Publisher, 1980.

Shaywitz SE, Capanilo BK, Hodgson ES: Developmental language disability as a consequence of prenatal exposure to ethanol. *Pediatrics* 1981; 68:850–855.

Starr A, Amlie RN, Martin WH, et al: Development of auditory function in newborn infants revealed by auditory brainstem potentials. *Pediatrics* 1977; 60:831–839.

Strauss ME, Lessen-Firestine JK, Starr RH, et al: Behavior of narcotic-addicted newborns. *Child Dev* 1975; 46:887–893.

Swafford LI, Allan D: Pain relief in the pediatric patient. *Med Clin North Am* 1968; 52:131–136.

Tyson J, Schultz K, Sinclair JC, et al: Diurnal variation in the quality and outcome of newborn intensive care. *J Pediatr* 1979; 95:277–280.

Vourenkoski V, Lind J, Partanen T, et al: Spectrographic analysis of cries from children with maladie du cri du chat. *Ann Paediatr (Paris)* 1966; 12:174–180.

Ward SLD, Schuetz S, Krishna V, et al: Abnormal sleeping ventilatory pattern in infants of substance-abusing mothers. *Am J Dis Child* 1986; 140:1915–1920.

Thoman EB: Sleep and waking states of the neonate, rev ed. Unpublished data, 1985. Available from EB Thoman, Box U-154, Department of Psychology/Behavioral Neuroscience, 3107 Horsebarn Hill Rd, University of Connecticut, Storrs, CT 06268.

Thoman EB, Acebo C, Dreyer CA, et al: Individuality in the interactive process, in Thoman EB (ed): *Origins of the Infant's Social Responsiveness.* Hillsdale, NJ, Erlbaum Publishers, 1979, pp 305–338.

Thoman EB, Denenberg VH, Sieval J, et al: State organization in neonates: Developmental inconsistency indicates risk for developmental dysfunction. *Neuropediatrics* 1981; 12:45–54.

Thoman EB, Graham S: Self-regulation of stimulation by premature infants. *Pediatrics* 1986; 78:855–860.

Thomas A, Chess S, Birch HG, et al: *Behavioral Individuality in Early Childhood.* New York, New York University Press, 1963.

Tronick E, Wise S, Als H, et al: Regional obstetric anesthesia and newborn behavior: Effect over the first ten days of life. *Pediatrics* 1976; 58:94–100.

Turkewitz G, Birch HG, Moreau T, et al: Effect of intensity of auditory stimulation on directional eye movements in the human neonate. *Anim Behav* 1966; 14:93–101.

Turkewitz G, Lewkowicz DJ, Gardner JM: Determinants of infant perception, in Rosenblatt J, Beer C, Hinde R, et al (eds): *Advances in the Study of Behavior.* New York, Academic Press, 1983, pp 39–62.

White J, Labarba R: The effects of tactile and kinesthetic stimulation on neonatal development in the premature infant. *Dev Psychobiol* 1976; 9:569–577.

Williamson PS, Williamson ML: Physiologic stress reduction by a local anesthetic during newborn circumcision. *Pediatrics* 1983; 71:36–40.

Wolff PH: Observations on newborn infants. *Psychosom Med* 1959; 221:110–118.

Wolff PH: The causes, controls, and organization of behavior in the neonate. *Psychol Issues* 1966; 5(monogr 17):1–105.

Woodson R, Drinkwin J, Hamilton C: Effects of nonnutritive sucking on state and activity: Term-preterm comparisons. *Infant Behav Dev* 1985; 8:435–441.

Woodson R, Hamilton C: The effect of nonnutritive sucking on heart rate in preterm infants. *Dev Psychobiol* 1988; 21:207–213.

Yakovlev PI, LeCours A: The myelogenetic cycles of regional maturation of the brain, in Minkowski A (ed): *Regional Development of the Brain in Early Life*. Philadelphia, FA Davis, 1967, pp 3–65.

Zeskind PS, Lester BW: Acoustic features and auditory perceptions of the cries of newborns with prenatal and perinatal complications. *Child Dev* 1978; 49:580–589.

Zeskind PS, Lester BM: Cry features of newborns with differential patterns of fetal growth. *Child Dev* 1981; 51:207–212.

"Our family with our baby." By boy, age 4¾.

CHAPTER 9

Five Days to Four Weeks: Making a Place in the Family

PAMELA KAISER, M.N., C.P.N.P.

SUZANNE D. DIXON, M.D.

KEY WORDS

POST PARTUM ADJUSTMENT
BREAST FEEDING
MATERNAL DEPRESSION
SIBLING RIVALRY

Mrs. Ferris brings in her 3-week-old son, Ethan, for a weight check, carrying him in a plastic carrier. This term infant has been gaining slowly with breast feeding. He awakens very quickly when unwrapped on the examining table and immediately starts to cry. Mrs. Ferris sits quietly, mechanically getting out a new diaper for the infant. She appears pale and tired and is less well dressed than usual. Melissa, her 3-year-old, plays with the examining room toys, throwing a small car across the room. Her mother jumps up quickly and scolds her. Melissa dissolves into tears and then sucks her thumb. You notice that Melissa has on diapers. Mrs. Ferris says she's thinking of starting bottle feeding. She looks tearful.

The early neonatal period after hospital discharge is usually filled with turmoil and adjustments for all members of the family. These individuals must struggle to fit themselves and the infant into a family unit that has irrevocably changed. The infant, too, is working, using his capacities for learning and adaptation to fit into his caretaking unit. He must capture those around him, building his own secure web of sensitive caretaking. His physical and psychological needs are met by those members who will learn to understand his signals and generate appropriate responses. Each infant's particular temperament, physiologic stability, stamina, and behavioral characteristics determine how those needs are met. The parents' perception of the child, as it is formed during this time, is a powerful predictor of their own interaction with the child over the long term; this, in turn, has major consequences for the child's development. Parental self-esteem and the sense of competence in the parenting role are influenced dramatically by the events of the first months. Feelings of competency energize the overall work of parenting. This is an important time for the child and all the family members.

The clinician's role during this first month of life is critical to monitor and support the development of synchrony in the family unit while evaluating the infant's growth and physical well being. It is expected that this process of adjustment will not be without turmoil. This turbulence is evidence of healthy developmental work being performed. More serious difficulties occur in families whose members are not free of other concerns in order to invest in making a place for the infant and a new role for themselves. Particularly when there are no extended family members available, the clinician has a special role of support and guidance. The clinician may need to provide extra energy here to help refocus the family on the particular needs of the infant and, indeed, of all the family members.

The family must get on track with the infant. This is done through the generation of successes in each member's experience around the care of the infant through sensitive observations, and through some thoughtful suggestions on seemingly small matters of management, the clinician can ensure that everyone, including the infant, grows during the adjustment process. It is in the course of this daily care that this psychological realignment is accomplished.

INFANT SOCIAL DEVELOPMENT

The infant begins life with a full set of equipment with which to interact with his environment. Evidence of the baby actively participating in the social interactions includes his movement in rhythm to the human voice (Condor and Sander, 1974), selective orientation to her own mother's milk by 6 days of age (McFarlane, 1975), and visual fixation on the human face different from that of any other kind of visual stimuli (Bower, 1966). The infant's early behavioral repertoire includes socially directed behaviors used in ways of eliciting and terminating interactions (Givens, 1978; Stern, 1977). Directed gaze is important to the bonding between infant and his family in this culture.

It is observed that the baby widens and brightens his eyes as he fixates and tracks his parents' movements and scans their faces. This has a powerful, positive effect on the adults, locking them into a relationship with him. Gaze aversion, conversely, is often actively used by the infant to either avoid or take a break from an interaction. In addition to gaze, the infant can demonstrate readiness for interaction with body language, e.g., smooth, cyclic movements of extremities, or slowing down body movements, open hands, and mouthing. Behaviors that signal withdrawal from caregivers, either to modulate the level of input or to avoid insensitive or overwhelming interaction, include back arching, pulling away, hand to head, increased body tension, and diffuse jittery movements of extremities. Parents may need to have these behaviors identified as communication from their infant, particularly if the infant has difficulties locking in with his own parents. Additionally, attentive mothers and spectral analysis can distinguish different types of cries by the time the infant is 2 days of age. These types of cries include those for hunger and pain.

Smiling is a powerful social "tool," progressing from a reflexive activity to a responsive activity elicited by external events such as a human face, gaze, or voice and then to spontaneous behavior produced to elicit response to others at the age of 6 to 8 weeks (Hetherington and Parke, 1979). The laugh appears by 4 months of age as a response to external stimuli and delightfully draws social attention and amazement from caregivers. Baby talk, including feeding sounds, cooing, and then babbling, is another mode of initiating interactions. These soft vocalizations come out of a positive social interaction sometime in the first month. By the second month, most infants will engage in verbal "dialogues" with their mothers using these sounds. This unfolding of patterns and building of a relationship begins in the first days of life (Brazelton and Cramer, 1990).

The infant's interactional pattern emerges with each parent over the first days and weeks of life. During this acquaintance period the family members develop reciprocal relationships, often rhythmic—smooth and modulated with mothers, more evenly intense and positive with fathers (Dixon et al., 1981). This "waltzing" or "turn-taking" (Brazelton et al., 1974) can be observed in periods of engagement that increase in frequency and duration during the first weeks of life (Hill and Eriks, 1980). Balanced harmony is largely dependent upon the parents' contingent responses and their sensitivity to the child's visual, verbal, and motor cues. Individual variation in both infant and parental temperament is a significant factor in the development of the style and form of this interaction, but not in its basic structure. Its appearance attests to the basic foundation of all other aspects of development to follow. The infant participates in these by developing predictable patterns of behavior; the parent participates by being a good observer and reading the infant's cues closely. The caretaking activities are the matrix upon which this synchrony is built. Being successful with the infant's care and being able to see pattern and meaning in the infant's behavior enable the parents to grow in their role and to meet the child's physical and psychological needs. Close physical contact early on enhances the attachment process immediately and down the line (Aisfeld et al., 1990).

The breast-feeding situation in particular emphasizes the basic interactional nature of the infant's behavior within a family. Each partner brings characteristics to this interaction (Table 9–1). The infant is born with reflexes but these must be quickly adapted to the feeding interaction with his own mother. The infant's temperament, state regulation, physiologic variables, and behavioral organization all contribute to that process. Likewise, the mother's nutrition, hydration, psychological state, and rate of recovery enter into the equation as well. There is a variable time of adjustment for both partners, when rhythms and behavioral patterns of individuals are melded into a successful interaction. Through this medium, both partners learn about themselves as well as the other. Personal, cultural, and group differences are evident here as they are in other situations of interaction. The clinician should be *very* familiar with the practical advice and support required for successful breast-feeding. Within that context, the foundation for later interactions is laid down, as well as the nutritional basis for

TABLE 9–1.
Interactional Nature of Breast Feeding

Infant Characteristics	Maternal Characteristics
Reflexes	Nutrition
Temperament	Hydration
State regulation	Psychological state
Physiologic variables	Recovery stage
Behavioral organization	Concepts of parenting
Residual of/recovery from delivery influences	Extent and use of support
Neurologic maturation	Psychosocial history
	Residual of pregnancy and delivery circumstances
	Role models

physical growth. The success that is realized with optimal nursing energizes the whole inter-actional system. Support of nursing, therefore, does not have only nutritional, immunologic, and infectious disease consequences but psychosocial ones as well. The first 2 weeks of life are the toughest as these patterns are set. Mothers may feel that they have been reduced to a milk machine at this point. The clinician can help them see this broader perspective as well as provide practical management advice. The setting of family priorities (feeding for the infant, rest and good nutrition for the mother) may need to be explicitly explored.

For mothers who decide not to nurse their infants, the basic interactional synchrony must be the basis for the feeding situation. The feeding time should provide close physical contact and attention to the infant's behavioral cues and contingent responsiveness. Nurturance in the broadest sense should be the outcome here as in the breast feeding situation. Even greater vigilance is needed if these broader needs will be consistently met as this kind of physical and emotional contact is not automatic with bottle feeding. Obviously, bottle propping is never appropiate.

Observation of the mother feeding the infant in the office offers the best opportunity to assess the synchrony that is developing between mother and infant. In addition, direct obser-vation offers opportunities for support, specific suggestions, and direct reflection on the baby's behavior. This situation provides a very economical way of observing the interaction between mother and infant. This should be a set part of the examination at least once in the first 2 weeks of life and more often if the adjustment process seems to be moving along slowly or with difficulty. An effective way to observe nursing without altering standard office routines is for the office nurse or medical assistant to suggest that the mother nurse the baby after measurements are taken, while waiting for the clinician, as the history is initiated. The clini-cian is able to observe nursing. A planned office visit within the first week enables the clini-cian to intervene if difficulties are identified. A delayed first office visit often means that a preventable problem with feeding or an opportunity for better adjustment has been lost. Optimally, the visit should be planned within 1 week after hospital discharge for new parents and no longer than 2 weeks for those with prior experience.

POSTPARTUM "BLUES" AND DEPRESSION

Adjustments by parents to a new baby do not come automatically, nor do they emerge in a neutral emotional atmosphere. Some turbulence occurs in most families. Postpartum "blues" is a normal, transient phase in the adaptation process. Most women experience some sadness in a mild form during this time that is related to exhaustion, physical depletion, and hormonal changes. Contributing factors are sleep deprivation due to demanding caregiving responsibilities to the newborn as well as changes in role and body image. Household and other child care duties may be overwhelming. While letting go of their former relationship of "two," the married couple begins to incorporate this "third person" who generally upsets the most established home routines and patterns, e.g., mealtimes, "talk" times, social activities, and sexual patterns. Being home all day and delaying career or academic pursuits often adds to the ambivalence and role conflict many women experience. Economic uncertainty also may compound the stress. The single mother's difficulty during this time may be heightened by her sense of aloneness if supporting individuals or groups are absent. Existing family stresses usually get worse, rather than better, at this time.

As a result of these factors, new mothers must cope with many unanticipated feelings (Kane, 1980). They are often overwhelmed by the chaos this new baby seems to have created. During their "baby blues," women may feel unusually dependent on others or even intimidated by would-be supporters (Barber and Skaggs, 1975). The clinician may be caught up in the adjustment process as the new mother turns to him or her as a resource. Many women are confused and embarrassed by their inexplicable crying, indecisiveness, and fatigue during these first few weeks. Clinicians may be frightened by this excessive dependency and emotionality unless they see it as a transient process of normal adult development. Clinical features of severe depression are immobolizing indecision, impaired cognitive functioning, irritability, and changes in sleep and appetite. The usual onset is within the 30-day period after birth (Kane, 1980). Most new mothers resolve these feelings by 6 to 8 weeks postpartum. Ongoing success as a parent with renewed self-esteem will aid in the resolution of the turbulence. Help and frequent acknowledgment of maternal competencies are the tools that are available for the pediatric caregiver to assist this process. Encouragement to reach out to support systems will enable the family to cope.

Persisting and/or severe symptoms of depression require psychiatric referral, clearly beyond what can be provided in a primary care setting. Mothers may experience a prolonged depressive state accompanied by sleep disturbances, anorexia, constipation, agitation, and a sluggish affect. They may develop an altered way of thinking such as talking about past, present, and future events in a negative or unrealistic way that expresses a radical departure from the prenatal personality. There may be a significant impairment in the mother's ability to function. Suicidal ideations, delusions, and hallucinations may be uncovered, both by specific questioning, or following an unusual response to a routine question. These mothers may require significant respite care as well as psychiatric referral. Most studies report high rates of recovery from the acute phase of this illness. Mothers with a history of psychiatric illness, those with a history of drug abuse, those with a recent loss (e.g., death of parent), or isolated mothers with other major life stressors are significantly more vulnerable to severe depression or psychosis in the postpartum period. Parents of preterm, ill, or handicapped children also are more vulnerable during resolution of grief. As the pediatric clinician may be the mother's only source of medical contact in the first month postpartum, these symptoms may only surface during pediatric health supervision visits with specific questioning and with a sensitivity to these issues. It becomes the pediatric clinician's responsibility to identify the need for further evaluation and possible treatment. If the mother requires psychotropic drugs, the pediatrician should evaluate the extent of the drugs' excretion in breast milk and the availability of another provider until the mother is well.

Maternal depression and mental illness are a pediatric issue. Although the mother's well-being is clearly at risk in this circumstance, the baby's is too. New studies suggest that even brief periods of depressive behavior have profound effects on the infant's behavior (Zucherman, 1987). With a prolongation of symptoms, these effects may have long-lasting effects on the child (Weisman et al., 1987; Tronick, 1978). This may be mediated through the lack of reciprocal interaction with the infant (Brazelton and Cramer, 1990). Many adverse child-rearing conditions may affect the infant through the medium of maternal depression

(Beardslee et al., 1988). The pediatric clinician cannot afford to ignore this condition in parents if he or she wants to support optimal development in the child.

REACTIONS OF OLDER SIBLINGS

Sibling rivalry is a predictable, normal, and healthy response to the birth of a new brother or sister. Since it demonstrates that the older child is appropriately attached to her parents and that she is able to respond to a perceived threat to the parent-child relationship, the emergence of behaviors that reflect sibling rivalry should be viewed in a positive way. Ambivalence toward the baby, evidenced by the ongoing shift between positive and negative behaviors, is to be expected. Indeed, its absence may be worrisome. Sibling rivalry is not a disease but a manifestation of psychological health and an impetus for developmental progress.

Behavioral manifestations of sibling rivalry can take several forms. *Aggressive* behavior is directed most commonly toward the mother but also may be directed toward the baby, father, playmates, oneself, or toys. Aggressive behavior more likely occurs when the older sibling is a toddler. Accelerations in this tension are likely to occur when the new baby becomes increasingly socially engaging at 4 to 5 months of age and when he becomes mobile during the last half of the first year. Open hostility may be mollified to more subtle intrusive behaviors directed at the younger child, such as pulling the pacifier out of the baby's mouth. *Naughtiness,* or doing things contrary to family rules, occurs frequently at the times when the mother is busy with the baby. This strategy serves both to increase the tension in the household and to verify the continuing power of the toddler to alter the behavior of those around him. A careful history of when these behaviors occur may highlight to the family for the first time that these are not "random" but dependent on a particular situation. On the other hand, some children are *overly compliant,* or overly solicitous to the infant. Perhaps the child fears being totally replaced if she misbehaves, so the child becomes "extra good" to assure her place in the family, or she is so frightened of her own aggressive/angry feelings that she holds them tightly in check. This is a very costly strategy. *Regressive and dependent behaviors* are usually seen in the form of clinging and demanding behaviors. Other possible regressive behaviors include sleep disturbances, stuttering, thumb sucking, bed wetting, and baby talk. These generally decrease but may not entirely disappear during the year following the sibling's birth. Over this period of time, the child becomes confident of a new place in the family, with its status and privileges. Additionally, she usually develops her own relationship with the younger child.

The arrival of a younger sibling can evoke positive behavioral changes as well as the negative ones, even in the early, get-acquainted period. Dunn and Kendrick (1982) report gains in the older child's independence and mastery, particularly with regard to self-help skills, e.g., dressing and feeding. The child may gain skills and a growing sense of competency through the participation in "her" baby's care. She may be able to reflect on her own growth and development as she sees the baby's emerging capabilities. She may try out new ways of dealing with the little stranger, initiating and maintaining interactions in which she bears the burden of greater understanding. She will learn to laugh at the antics of the baby and grow in confidence as she learns to make the infant laugh, play games, and imitate. This is an opportunity for growth if understood and supported.

Some factors are correlated with a *positive* response to the infant. Enhanced signs of affection and interest in the baby are correlated with same sex pairs in children whose mothers allow the older child to participate in the baby's care and discuss the baby's needs and behavior with them. However, an overemphasis on behaving "like a big girl (boy)," with demands for more grown-up behavior, is very costly for the child. It is a high price to pay for continuing parental love. It does not allow for the working through of the inevitable negative feelings that are there, or the recuperative process of acting like a baby oneself. Breast-feeding the second baby does not compound stress for the first child (Dunn and Kendrick, 1982).

Certain factors have been shown to intensify an older child's *negative* responses at the time of the sibling's birth. An intense, close relationship between the first child and his parents prior to the baby's arrival is correlated with the child's increased hostile and aggressive behaviors. Temperamentally intense children, who are slow to approach new situations in general, have more difficulties. An extremely withdrawn behavior is more likely in children whose mothers experience severe postpartum exhaustion and/or depression. There is conflicting evidence regarding the effects of child spacing on the sibling's response, that is, whether or not a narrow age gap intensifies rivalrous behavior (Dunn and Kendrick, 1982; Schubert et al., 1983). The child's own issues and coping strategies differ at varying ages but an adjustment period appears at all ages.

Severe responses in younger children may be markers of a long-standing family adjustment problem, not just that associated with the infant's birth. The pediatrician or clinician may be the only professional to see the family at this time of crisis when the issues are very close to the surface. He then is able to suggest a more extensive evaluation of the family as a whole.

There are several *parental* factors that affect the parents' own response to the child's behavior. These include the parents' own ambivalence toward the new baby, guilt in feeling less attached to the new baby, and mourning over the loss of the previous family structure. Parents may be surprised, embarrassed, or disappointed to see the older child's rivalry after their concerted prenatal efforts to prevent it. Certainly, the parents' physical exhaustion in the caring for the new baby diminishes their ability to meet the other child's needs physically and psychologically. It is not surprising that the relationship between a mother and her firstborn changes after the arrival of the second baby. Second-time mothers show less affection for, spend less time with, and have more confrontations with their firstborn (Dunn et al., 1981; Weiss, 1981) after the birth of the infant. It is no wonder that birth order has a profound effect on child development (Maccoby, 1976; Najonc and Markus, 1975).

SUPPORT FOR THE NEW FAMILY

Families and cultures show wide variations in the type, extent, and duration of support given to a new family. Support systems may functionally include emotional support, baby care and/or advice, or homemaking tasks. The baby's father, extended family (especially grandparents), friends and neighbors (with or without children of their own), and various members of the health-care team may be part of the support structure. Many studies show that the number of friends a new mother has is correlated with her success in parenting, attesting to the power of this network.

The amount and kind of support may be constructive or undermining. Some new parents may resent the intrusion of "taking over" of their perceived role. Sometimes support systems offer divergent and even contradictory advice, leading to the new parent's sense of confusion and anxiety in feeling caught in between two "authorities." Other new parents feel fearful and overwhelmed when the support systems are withdrawn, e.g., when the grandparents return to their own home. Some visitors may take away more energy than they leave; the clinician would do well to inquire about the cost/benefit ratio of the supports. In general, the availability and use of this social network should be supported.

Subcultural differences in role expectations are evident in the way families work out the patterns of activity when a new infant arrives. In some situations, the grandmother takes over—to do less would make a mother feel abandoned. In others, relatives are expected to supply large amounts of food and clothing. Most cultures have a period of at least 1 to 2 months postpartum of relative seclusion and care of the new mother whose sole roles are to recover and feed the neonate. Every family needs this protected time to gain strength and to do that mental reorganization. Cultural and economic issues may dictate what form this time period takes. Parents asked to return immediately to work, without this protected time, may protect themselves against "too close" an attachment (Brazelton, 1988, personal communication) and may be reluctant to invest in breast feeding. Clinicians should encourage use of some protected time—actively and at the first or second office visit.

DATA GATHERING

HISTORY

Begin with open-ended questions about the infant. (What new things is the baby doing? In what ways can you tell that he knows you?) The physician also should ask more focused questions regarding the infant's hearing (Does he turn to sounds?), seeing (Does he enjoy seeing things?), feeding behavior (How does he act while being fed?), irritability/soothing preference (What seems to work best to settle him down? What upsets him? How can you tell if he doesn't like something or is enjoying something?), activity patterns (How predictable is he? How regular are his sleep patterns? Is he easily awakened? How long are his alert periods? Does he like his bath?).

Open-ended questions regarding the parents' adjustment are important also: (How are *you* feeling? How are *you* dealing with all this? Are *you* eating/sleeping well?). If any concern appears in content or affect, have the mother describe yesterday in detail.

If there is minimal response, explore further by stating possible feelings the mother may be experiencing, e.g., "Many moms describe this time as so exhausting and discouraging they feel overwhelmed, frightened by the responsibility. Some have feelings of regret or even negative feelings about having the baby. Have you experienced any of these feelings?"

Similarly, the clinician needs to pursue the father's reactions and involvement. Does he hold and feed the baby, change diapers, help with housework? What does he think the baby is like? This is best done directly by inviting father's participation in health supervision visits.

The clinician also needs to evaluate the siblings' response. If only positive responses are given, be suspicious—although some sibling adaptive behaviors may not manifest until months after the birth of a baby. Give permission for parent to discuss possibly negative behaviors with you now or in the future, e.g., "Most children show some negative reaction to the new baby at some point. This is a normal response to feeling somewhat replaced." If negative behaviors are described, pursue how these are perceived and handled by the parent.

The availability and use of support systems should be specifically explored, including the affect that surrounds those reports. "How does your family feel about the baby? How is having grandparents around—positive or negative on a scale of 1–10?" "Are there any friends/neighbors with kids you can depend on?" "Who is cooking (cleaning, shopping)?" The alone and isolated mother or couple are at very high risk for difficulties in the adjustment to parenthood.

OBSERVATION

SOCIAL DEVELOPMENT

Be sensitive to the rhythms of interaction between parents and child. Point out to the parents the infant's body language during the history taking and examination. This is a wonderful opportunity to inform parents about their infant's ability to communicate with them. Note the baby's responsiveness to parents. How easily is he consoled? How well does he maintain eye contact? The clarity of the baby's cues are important. Are his needs and moods easy or difficult to "read"? Note the parents' sensitivity to the baby's cues. Do they pick up on the baby's subtle behaviors that require parent readjustment? How do they console the infant? Note comfort in handling the baby. Keep in mind individual and cultural difference in the parents' sensory mode with the baby, e.g., talking, touching, eye contact, and grooming behavior.

The feeding situation offers an *excellent* opportunity to observe social development and interaction between baby and parent. Note maternal affect, latency to respond to questions, the amount of physical and verbal activity on the parents' part. Note any slowing of movement or responsiveness or evidence of fatigue.

If the older child is in the room, observe his interactions with the baby and parents. Note any affect changes in the child and the parents' response to him. If the father or grandparents are present, note their interactions with the baby and the mother and other children. Who holds the baby? How do they respond to the baby's distress, e.g., bowel movement, crying? Is dad helpful and consoling? Does anyone talk for mom, e.g., giving history, asking questions? Provide a positive comment about the value of an extended family's presence during the office visit.

EXAMINATION

Direct the parent to sit with the baby on her lap in order to maximize your opportunity to observe their interactions. The infant should turn to a voice. Interact (play/smile) with baby to evaluate response, as well as to role model. Observe visual and auditory responses in this context. Comment aloud about baby's social behavior and individuality. Encourage parent to hold and talk with baby often at home. Explain that narrating their activities with their baby encourages and promotes language development. Give reassurance that baby cannot be "spoiled" at this age. This holding will, in fact, decrease crying overall (Barr, 1991). Quick responses to cries, effective soothing, and close human contact lead to less crying in the second year and fine developmental progress in general.

Ask mother specifically about her mood, feelings, and behavior. Allow the mother to cry and use touch contact if it seems comfortable. Attempt to restore confidence, e.g., "You're doing a good job; it takes a while to adjust to this baby and to get to know one another." Enhanced self-esteem energizes new parents. Even minor concerns (e.g., diaper rash, mild jaundice) may impinge upon the parents' feeling of competence. Clinicians should be careful to put problems in a clear perspective and to be unequivocal in their praise and support of positive things about the infant, both physical and behavioral. Be explicit about your availability to discuss feelings further. If there is sadness, ask specifically about hallucinations or feelings of doing harm to self or others. If these are present, referral is indicated.

REACTIONS OF OLDER SIBLINGS

If an older sibling is present, acknowledge and focus on him first. Ask specific, separate questions of him rather than only asking: "Do you help with the baby?" Give praise for any recent developmental achievements the parent may have mentioned and/or any helpfulness shown toward parent and baby. Ask about his interpretation of the baby, e.g., "Does he cry a lot? Is he not as much fun as you thought he'd be?"

Explain to the parents the positive aspects of their older child's behavior changes. For example, "Although I'm sure it's frustrating to see your older child behaving this way, it's actually very healthy behavior. He is clearly demonstrating that he is attached to you and highly values his relationship with you." Reassure them that no matter what preparation was made prior to the baby's arrival, children will have hurt and resentful feelings—this is real and natural. The goal here is not to minimize the negative behaviors, but to help the older child get through and gain from this experience.

Acknowledge the adjustment process all second-time parents experience when learning to "juggle" their availability to the needs of two or more children. It takes time for families to settle into new patterns and rhythms. For many selected families, books for parents and/or children regarding these issues can be helpful (see References).

Encourage parents to continue "special time" with the older child alone on a daily basis; a realistic time frame may be 10 to 15 minutes. Emphasize the importance of physical affection or "snuggle time."

Encourage parents to discuss the new baby's needs and behavior with the older child and to allow his participation in the baby's care. Children often benefit from duplicating these activities with their own dolls; these play experiences should be encouraged.

Plan structured activities for the older child during the baby's bath and feedings so there is a distraction that is attractive to the older child.

The child should not be expected to "share" all his toys, even if he has outgrown them. Reserving some items that are his alone and providing his own special place in which to keep them are important. Sharing his parents on a permanent basis is hard enough.

Urge parents to minimize changes in the older child's life for a while. Such changes as moving to a new bed and/or new room or starting nursery school should ideally occur a few months prior to the new baby's arrival or after some weeks of adjustment.

Displaced aggression can be released through play, e.g., Play-Doh, Nerf balls, foam ball and bat. As long as the younger child cannot defend himself, hitting should not be allowed and leaving the two alone should be avoided. The intensity of the parents' message that children must not hurt others is a most powerful factor in helping children learn to appreciate others' feelings.

The need to be tolerant of regressive behavior should be stressed. Most parents will be reassured to learn that most of the lapses in developmental achievements are temporary.

SUPPORT FOR THE NEW FAMILY

If the father is present, be sure to include him rather than directing comments, eye contact, and questions only to the mother. Direct some questions to him specifically, e.g., "What do you think about this baby? How do you handle his fussy periods? How is the baby affecting your sleep, your work?"

If the grandparent holds the baby for the majority of the visit, ask the mother to hold the baby during the examination in order to allow an opportunity to observe interaction and comfort in handling. If the father or grandparent entirely dominates the visit, the clinician will need to more overtly direct some questions to the mother. Solicitous and supportive inquiry should be the goal. Judgmental comments or rigidly preconceived ideas of optimal family interactions should be avoided. Appreciation of the individual path that each family takes to readjust around the new baby enriches the clinician's professional life. Members of each family should be given appropriate support while they mark their own trail.

REFERENCES

Ames LB, Haber CC: *He Hit Me First: When Brothers and Sisters Fight.* New York, Dembner Books, 1981.

Anisfeld E, Casper V, Nozyce, M, et al: Does infant carrying promote attachment? An experimental study of the effects of increased physical contact on the development attachment. *Child Dev* 1990; 61:1617–1627.

Barber V, Skaggs M: *The Mother Person.* New York, Schocken Books, 1975.

Barr R, McMullen SF, Spress, H, et al: Carrying as colic therapy: A randomized controlled trial. *Pediatrics* 1991; 87:623–630.

Barr RG, Elias M: Nursing interval and maternal responsiveness: Effect on early infant crying. *Pediatrics* 1988; 81:529–536.

Beardslee WR, Zuckerman BS, Amaro H, et al: Depression among adolescent mothers: A pilot study. *J Behav Dev Peds* 1988; 9:62–65.

Bell SM, Ainsworth MDS: Infant crying and maternal responsiveness. *Child Development* 1972; 43:1171–1190.

Bower TGR: The visual world of infants. *Sci Am* 1966; 215:80–92.

Brazelton TB, Koslowski B, Main M: The origins of reciprocity: The early mother/infant interaction, in Lewis M, Rosenblum L (eds): *The Effect of the Infant on Its Caregiver.* New York, John Wiley & Sons, 1974, p. 59.

Brazelton TB, Cramer BG: *The Earliest Relationship,* Part III. Reading, Mass, Addison-Wesley, 1990.

Brazelton TB: *Working and Caring.* Reading, Mass, Addison-Wesley, 1985.

Condon WS, Sander LW: Neonate movement is synchronized with adult speech. *Science* 1974; 183:99–101.

Dixon SD, Yogman M, Tronick E, et al: Early infant social interaction with parents and strangers. *J Amer Acad Child Psychiatry* 1981; 20:32–52.

Dunn J, Kendrick C, MacNamee R: The reaction of first-born children to the birth of a sibling: Mothers' reports. *J Child Psychol Psychiatry* 1981; 22:1–18.

Dunn J and Kendrick C: *Siblings.* Cambridge, Mass, Harvard University Press, 1982.

Gates S: Children's literature: It can help children cope with sibling rivalry. *Matern Child Nurs J* 1980; 5:351–352.

Givens D: Social expressivity during the first year of life. *Sign Lang Stud* 1978; 20:251–274.

Hetherington EM, Parke RD: Emotional development, in Hetherington EM, Parke RD (eds): *Child Psychology: A Contemporary Viewpoint.* New York, McGraw-Hill Book Co, 1979, pp 215–218.

Hill V, Eriks J: Turn-taking in the caregiver-infant interactional system, in Barnard K (ed): *Nursing Child Assessment Satellite Training. Learning Resource Manual.* 1980, pp 44–49.

Kane F: Postpartum disorders, in Kaplan HI, Freedman AM (eds): *Comprehensive Textbook of Psychiatry*, ed 3. Baltimore, Williams & Wilkins Co, 1980, vol 2, pp 1343–1347.

Lawrence R: *Breastfeeding.* St Louis, Mosby–Year Book, 1989.

Maccoby E: *Patterns of Child Rearing.* Stanford, Calif, Stanford University Press, 1976.

MacFarlane JA: Olfaction in the development of social preference in human neonates, in *Parent-Infant Interaction.* Ciba Foundation Symposium No. 33, pp 103–133. Amsterdam, Elsevier, 1975.

Najonc RB, Markus GB: Birth order and intellectual development. *Psychological Review* 1975; 82:74–88.

Schubert HJP, Wagner ME, Shubert D: Child spacing effects: A comparison of institutionalized and normal children. *Dev Behav Pediatrics* 1983; 4:262–266.

Stern D: The infant's repertoire, in *The First Relationship: Infant and Mother.* Cambridge, Mass, Harvard University Press, 1977.

Sweet P: Suggestions for siblings and parents: Sibling preparation reading list for parents and children. *Obstetrics Clinic* Minneapolis, University of Minnesota Hospitals, 1980.

Tronick EZ, Als H, Adamson L: The infant's response to entropment between contradictory messages in face-to-face interaction. *J Child Psychiatry* 1978; 7:1–13.

Weiss JS: *Your Second Child.* New York, Summit Books, 1981.

Weisman MM, Davis-Gammon G, John K, et al: Children of depressed parents. *Arch Gen Psychiatry* 1987; 44:847–853.

Zuckerman B, Beardslee WR: Maternal depression: An issue for pediatricians. *Pediatrics* 1987; 79:110–114.

"Dad goes to comfort baby in cradle."
By Colin Hennessy, age 4.

CHAPTER **10**

Five Weeks to Two Months: Getting on Track

MARTIN T. STEIN, M.D.

KEY WORDS

NUTRIENTS AND NURTURANCE
PSYCHOSOCIAL GROWTH FAILURE
CATCH-UP GROWTH
INFANT COLIC
MATERNAL DEPRESSION

An experienced mother (second child; emergency room nurse) brought her 3-month-old breastfed daughter to the office for a health supervision visit. Following a normal pregnancy and delivery, the child had grown appropriately at the 75th percentile at the 6-week examination. At the current visit, careful measurement revealed no weight gain in 2 months with normal linear and head circumference growth rates. In fact, the child looked well; physical features and developmental milestones were normal. Observation of nursing in the office confirmed an adequate and sustained sucking pattern.

Social history revealed that the father, previously very involved with the family, was out of town for 6 weeks on business. An 18-month-old toddler added to the burden of child care and the mother was not sleeping well. With a normal complete blood count, urinalysis, electolytes, urea nitrogen, and serum glutamic pyruvate transaminase, the mother was instructed to supplement her breast milk with formula and ask friends for occasional assistance with child care.

One week later, at a follow up visit, the mother reported that her sister, a second-year medical student, remarked that "your face looks like you have an endocrine problem." Myxedema was noted by her internist and Hashimoto's thyroiditis with hypothyroidism was diagnosed. On thyroid replacement therapy, the mother's milk production apparently increased and the baby thrived.

This is an unusual case of diminished breast milk production associated with gradual onset secondary to a primary maternal endocrine disorder. At first look, maternal sleep deprivation and a situational depression appeared to account for the poor growth. While the initial evaluation and therapy helped to get this baby's weight back on track, careful follow-up and openness to alternative causes led to the correct diagnosis.

FOCUS OF DEVELOPMENTAL WORK

The period of an infant's life bounded at one end by the first month and at the other by the third month represents a transitional time. Having adjusted to the neonatal period (postpartum physiologic changes and the new extrauterine environment of family), the second month of life is often a settling-in time for infant and parents. Physical growth takes on a new proportion. As the face fills out, the chin "doubles up," and the thigh folds multiply, the fact that the baby is growing so rapidly seems to organize the parents' attention on physical growth at this stage. Feeding the baby consumes much of the mother's time, coupled with concerns about the adequacy of the diet. Furthermore, the times just before, during, and after meals provide moments of optimal social and verbal interactions. By the middle of the second month of life, the parents recognize the infant's ability to smile in response to their smiles! Mutual gaze becomes the preferred form of social interaction. This milestone is enhanced by more frequent periods of visual tracking and the onset of reproducible cooing sounds. When feeding is managed in a secure setting and the parent is emotionally available for social interactions, physical and psychological growth is assured.

Meeting the infant's nutritional needs in terms of appropriate growth requirements becomes the work of this period of infancy. Developmental setbacks at this time usually affect either the quality of the feeding experience (e.g., infant colic or family emotional conflict) or outcome (e.g., failure to thrive).

GROWTH ASSESSMENT

From the time of birth until 6 months of life, infants experience the most rapid rate of growth compared with any other time (with the exception of fetal growth). This is true for stature (length), weight, and head circumference (Fig 10–1). Several decades ago, doubling of birth weight occurred by 5 months of life; today it is not uncommon to record a twofold increase in birth weight before the fourth month. Brain and linear growth are also rapid and predictable at this age. Of course, other organ systems are growing and maturing in function simultaneously.

As child health clinicians, we monitor development as a manifestation of the maturity of the central nervous system and the quality of parentally directed infant interaction. In the same way, physical growth can be monitored as a reflection, at one point in time, of the nutritional adequacy provided the infant and the psychological stability of the environment in which the infant grows.

From studies of emotionally neglected infants in foundling homes, the devastating effect on physical growth from less than optimal tactile, auditory, and visual stimulation has been observed. These infants were given formula (by bottle propping) but were rarely held, spoken to, or engaged visually. The effect was growth failure and an affect that appeared depressed. These infants suffer not only from caloric deprivation (Whitten et al., 1969) but also from the necessary complement of psychosocial stimulation apparently required for optimal growth (Altemeier et al., 1985). If this state is diagnosed early and remediated psychosocially, these infants experience catch-up growth and thrive physically and emotionally. Behavioral changes precede by several days the onset of weight gain regardless of the caloric intake (Rosenn et al., 1980).

The dramatic and tragic examples of psychosocial deprivation and growth failure add to the knowledge base of clinicians insofar as they remind us that adequate physical growth both requires and reflects sufficient nutrients and nurturance in the psychological sense. When an infant is growing along her expected curve on a standard growth chart, it provides

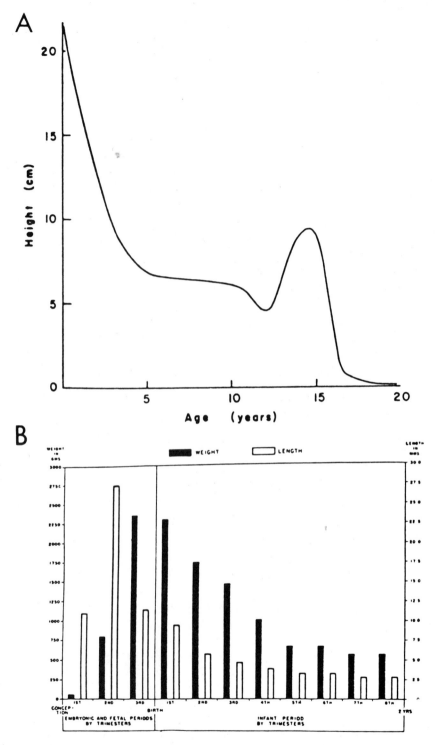

FIG 10–1.
A, an incremental curve showing the rate of height gain. During the first years of life, the growth rate is the most rapid when compared to other periods. **B**, average increment in weight and length by trimesters. (From Valadian I, Porter D: *Physical Growth and Development: From Conception to Maturity.* Boston, Little Brown & Co, 1977. Used by permission.)

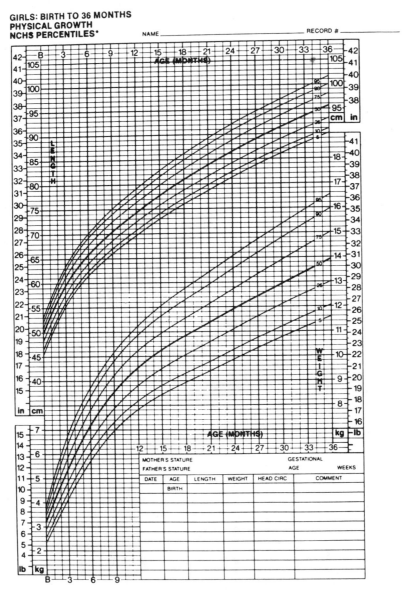

FIG 10–2.
A standard growth curve: birth to 36 months. **A**, length and weight. **B**, head circumference and weight/ length ratio. Both available in separate forms for girls and boys. (From Center for Health Statistics Report, No 3, Supplement NCHS Growth Charts, 1976. Hyattsville, Md, Public Health Administration, 1976. Department of Health, Education and Welfare No [HRA] 76-110.)

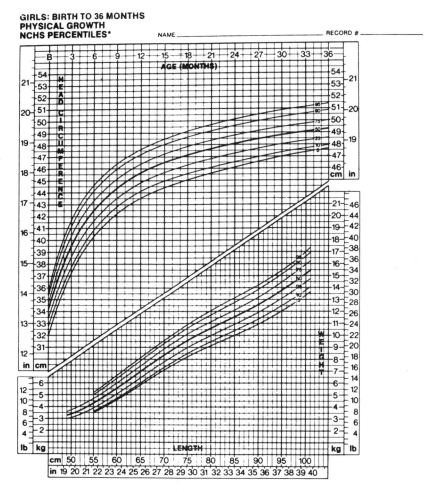

GIRLS: BIRTH TO 36 MONTHS
PHYSICAL GROWTH
NCHS PERCENTILES*

NAME _____   RECORD # _____

FIG 10–2 (cont.).

some degree of objective evidence that both diet and social interaction are adequate. Conversely, early signs of growth failure are clinical signals to assess not only the diet and potential organic illness but also the manner (style) with which the baby is fed, the baby's own temperament, and the psychosocial state of the family. Growth failure in early infancy has devastating effects on parental feelings of competence. Conversely, good growth vitalizes the whole nurturing environment.

The behavior of the small-for-gestational-age infant or that of the infant who postnatally becomes underweight for linear growth is altered. These infants remain hyporesponsive and stay irritable or drowsy for prolonged periods of time. They may show frank gaze aversion, arching, turning away, or marked physiologic instability. These characteristics, in turn, induce feelings of incompetency or disengagement in parents. These infants can be unrewarding for parents, even beyond the neonatal period (Brazelton, 1981).

Standard growth curves should be utilized in clinical practice to assess physical growth. Accurate measurements of weight, length, and head circumference (occipitofrontal measurement) are plotted on these curves at each visit, as shown in Figure 10–2. Growth curves are of tremendous value in clinical practice. They can reassure an anxious parent about the adequacy of growth. In some sense they are like report cards of parenting adequacy. To be helpful to the clinician, however, it must be appreciated that physical growth measurements generate a bell-shaped curve, with 5% of the normal population heavier, longer, lighter, or shorter than the extremes of the charts. Typically, the point at which an infant's measurements are plotted are not as significant as the rate of growth over a period of time. In this way, cumulative measurements over several office visits are usually more revealing than a single measurement. The stature, weight, and head circumference of the parents may also be helpful in interpreting the infant's growth after 6 months of age.

NORMAL VARIATIONS OF GROWTH IN EARLY INFANCY

Postpartum Weight Loss—Extracellular water loss may account for up to 10% of weight loss compared with birth weight. Generally it is greater in breast-fed than formula-fed babies and in infants born of toxemic mothers. Also, breast-fed babies may take longer to regain the weight (usually 1 week for those infants receiving formula, often 2 weeks for breast-fed babies). Premature babies require even longer periods to regain their birth weight; the smaller the birth weight, the longer the period of regaining. Special growth curves for the preterm infant are available.

INTERCURRENT ILLNESS

A brief period of illness in early infancy (e.g., gastroenteritis) is often associated with both anorexia and an increase in metabolic requirements that yield either a plateau in the growth

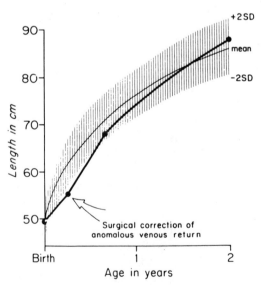

FIG 10–3.
Catch-up growth following corrective surgery in a child with congenital heart lesion associated with growth failure. (From Smith DW: *Growth and Its Disorders.* Philadelphia, WB Saunders Co, 1977. Used by permission.)

curve or weight loss. The illness may, in fact, not be from within the infant, such as maternal breast infection or other maternal illness in a lactating woman or psychosocial deprivation (see the case illustration) or stress.

CATCH-UP GROWTH

After a period of growth failure, a healthy infant has the marvelous capacity to accelerate her growth rate during recovery. This is seen especially in the weight curve, which is most vulnerable to transient caloric depressions and most adaptable by demonstrating dramatic catch-up growth. Depressions in linear growth in infancy testify to the chronicity of the problem, thyroid disease, or long-standing organic illness (Fig 10–3). Premordial (i.e., before birth) growth failure of a severe nature may not catch up; these children will remain small. This is particulary true of those infants with reduction in length for gestational age.

In a healthy premature infant, postpartum catch-up growth is expected to take place (Fig 10–4). Growth parameters in this population should be corrected for the degree of prematurity (i.e., postconceptual age for the first 2 years or up to 3 years in infants born at less than

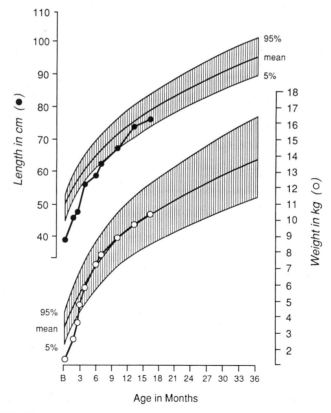

FIG 10–4.
Postnatal growth curve of a 32-week appropriate-for-gestational-age premature infant. The curve demonstrates rapid catch-up growth in a healthy preterm infant.

1,500 g) to better assess growth velocity and relative gains in height, weight, and head circumference.

TOO-RAPID WEIGHT GAIN

Many appropriately nourished infants in the first 6 months of life demonstrate rapid weight gains, often outstripping linear growth. They may appear chubby. Most of these infants, as long as they are not obviously overfed, will decrease their growth rate and "find" their genetic curve between 6 and 12 months of life (Smith et al., 1976). If the infant in this category is breast-fed every 3 to 4 hours, with longer periods at night (or if formula fed, he is consuming no more than 32 oz/day), it is appropriate not to change the diet and to reassess growth after 6 months. Even in many third world populations, these young infants are very "fat" by our expectations but eventually demonstrate a diminished rate of weight gain.

LANDMARKS AND CLINICAL PEARLS OF GROWTH ASSESSMENT IN THE FIRST SIX MONTHS

1. A full-term newborn, determined by gestational age examination, who is less than 2,500 g or less than 45 cm is small and may reflect intrauterine growth retardation. Linear growth depression reflects second trimester growth failure. Absolute or relative underweight babies have usually had late gestation losses.

2. Small-for-gestational-age babies who have the genetic capacity to catch up to the normal range usually show accelerated growth in the first 6 months (Fig 10–5). Failure to show catch-up growth in the first 6 months usually means that growth will continue at a slow rate.

3. A head circumference of less than 32 cm in a full-term newborn represents microcephaly; more than 38 cm represents macrocephaly.

4. Head circumference measurements in the first 6 months of life usually conform to the following schedule: birth to 2 months, 1 cm/2 weeks; 3–6 months, 1 cm/month.

5. Following the reacquisition of birth weight, most babies will grow at approximately 1 oz/day. Weight increases much greater than 1 oz/day often are associated with overweight infants or those undergoing catch-up growth. Premature infants (less than 38 weeks' corrected age) may sustain weight-gain velocities consistent with expected intrauterine growth, higher than those of the infants beyond 40 weeks conceptual age. Weight gain that is less than 0.5 oz/day usually is inadequate.

6. Breast-fed infants who have a decelerated growth rate after 1 month should draw attention to maternal diet and rapid maternal weight loss during this time (i.e., dieting, illness, or strenuous exercise).

7. Occasionally, a baby with a head circumference in the usual or upper range at birth rapidly crosses percentile lines in the first few months and is at or above the 95th percentile. When this curve is maintained in the absence of any evidence for increased intracranial pressure, it usually represents familial macrocephaly, a benign condition. Measurement of parental head circumference will suggest the diagnosis.

SLEEP PATTERNS

Sleep-awake cycles after the first month are highly variable and dependent on the infant's temperament, satisfaction with feedings, and the parents' response to periodic awakenings.

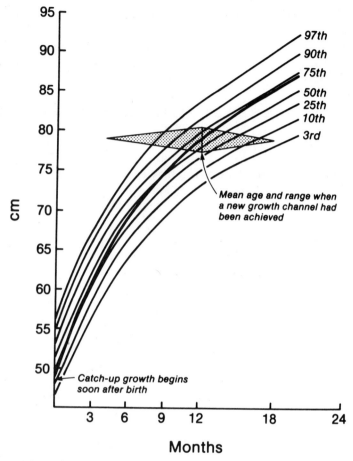

FIG 10–5.
Average linear growth of 18 middle-class normal babies who
had been below the 10th percentile for length at full-term birth
but achieved the 50th percentile or better by the age of 2 years,
by which time their stature correlated well to that of their parents. The catch-up in linear growth began soon after birth, and
a new channel of growth had been achieved by 4 to 18 months.
(From Smith DW, Truog W, Rogers JE, et al: *J Pediatr* 1976;
89:225. Used by permission.)

The early introduction of rice cereal before bedtime does not extend sleeptime (Macknin,
1989). This period represents a transitional time between neonatal sleeping, which is characterized by shorter multiple sleep periods, as well as longer sleep time each day, and the
more organized central nervous system maturation after the third month when each sleep
period is longer (see Figs 11–1 and 11–2). The 2 standard deviation range of maximum longest
sleep time at 6 weeks of age varies from 3 to 11 hours. No wonder that parents of infants

with shorter sleep times seem bewildered when sharing their infants' night time experience with other parents!

Although a child's individual biological determinants dictate most of the variability in sleep patterns at this age, signals from the environment mediate a powerful effect. As early as 10 days of life, infants who roomed in with their mothers slept longer at night than during the day compared with those cared for in the hospital nursery (Sander et al., 1969).

Recent clinical studies suggest that the way a parent responds to an infant at the time of sleep induction and night time awakenings may set long-term patterns. Babies who are settled in a crib while partially awake learn to soothe themselves to sleep compared with those infants who are always nursed or rocked into a deep sleep before being placed into the crib (Ferber, 1985). Associations with falling asleep may be learned at this early time. If an infant has experienced falling asleep alone in her crib, she can reestablish that experience at predictable times of night awakening and soothe herself back to a sleep state.

INFANT COLIC

Parents are confronted with intermittent periods of fussiness in their babies at various times during the initial few months of life. Most parents describe a period of manageable irritability beginning at about 2 weeks of age, peaking between the first and second month, and disappearing by 3 to 4 months. Typically the fussy behavior begins in the late afternoon and resolves in the early part of the evening. Most parents find that by holding, positioning, gently rocking, or feeding the infant, the fussy periods resolve into a comfortable sleep.

The predictability of these events suggests that such diurnal behavior is part of normal development, probably mediated by the central nervous system. The infant wears out (as do parents!) over the course of the day, becoming increasingly unable to modulate her response to environmental stimuli. Colic occurs in babies who are breast-fed and those who are bottle-fed. Boys and girls are affected equally. Premature infants may experience this behavior somewhat later in proportion to their conceptual age and may have this irritability extend to a later age.

When these behavioral outbursts are either more intense or longer in duration (i.e., not limited to the latter part of the day), the term infant colic is used. That it is a more severe form of the diurnal behavior seen in the majority of infants is clear. Why certain infants at this particular age (2 to 3 weeks through 3 to 4 months) express this behavior with more intensity is unclear. Individual temperamental factors seem to be very important. The intensive, hyperresponsive, somewhat hypertonic infant can be spotted in the neonatal period as a likely candidate for colic. Before a diagnosis of infant colic is made, the clinician should have an appreciation for normal crying at this age. In a study of 80 infants from middle class families, crying lasted about 2 hours daily at 2 weeks and progressed to nearly 3 hours daily by 6 weeks in normal infants. It then gradually tapered to about 1 hour daily by 3 months (Fig 10–6). During this interval, most of the crying occurred in the evening (Brazelton, 1962). With this normal pattern in mind, Wessel's definition of infant colic is helpful: Colic occurs when an infant "who, otherwise healthy and well fed, had paroxysms of irritability, fussiness or crying lasting for a total of more than three hours a day and occurring on more than three days in any one week" (Wessel et al., 1954).

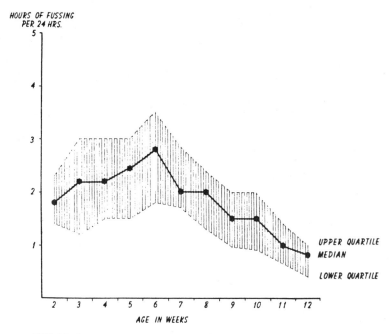

FIG 10–6.
Distribution of total crying time among 80 infants from 2 to 12-weeks old; data derived from daily crying diaries recorded by mothers. (From Brazelton TB: *Pediatrics* 1962; 29:582. Used by permission.)

Many theories have been suggested to explain early infant colic. It was once thought to reflect maternal anxiety, but it is now clear that although severe colic may produce anxiety in parents, most cases are not caused by an overly anxious parent. Humans (especially women) are biologically programmed to respond to infant cries regardless of individual personality differences; lack of success in calming the infant is experienced as failure. However, high-strung parents tend to give birth to high-strung infants. Colicky infants are born, not made.

Because these babies are observed to press their flexed hips against the abdomen during the crying spree and then pass audible flatus at the termination of the episode, it has been suggested that these babies have a form of intestinal dysmotility that produces segmental air-trapping secondary to autonomic dysfunction. Supporting this theory is documentation of lower colonic dysmotility in some infants. Another piece of supportive evidence is that early infant colic resolves in most cases by the end of the third month of life, which correlates chronologically with several behavioral aspects reflecting central nervous system maturation. For example, babies at 4 months of age show more organized sleep-wake cycles, several primitive reflexes disappear, and electroencephalographic (EEG) tracings reveal greater organization. It seems reasonable to assume that higher levels of central organization would be accompanied by maturation of the more primitive autonomic nervous system that, in turn, might modify and regulate gastrointestinal tract motility. Colicky infants tend to have hyperresponsive gastrointestinal tracts that mirror their behavioral response to external stimuli.

Whatever the cause, infant colic (also known as "3-month colic") resolves by the end of the third month in almost every case. When the colic is mild to moderate, simple measures (discussed later on) suffice as the parents learn to modify the behavior through various manipulations. It is the more severe cases of colic that require special attention from the child's clinician. If allowed to continue, these very difficult periods of crying are taxing on parents (as well as siblings and grandparents). The potential for disrupting ongoing attachment behavior between infant and parents exists. In this context, moderate to severe colic represents an interactional problem and requires astute clinical attention.

DATA GATHERING

OBSERVATIONS

As you enter the examining room, observe the interaction between infant and mother (and father, when present). If the infant is being held, observe the comfort of the mother in handling the baby. Does she seem at ease, tense, unsure of herself? At the same time, observe the infant's response. Does she cuddle easily? Is she tense or responsive to her mother? Does the infant's posture and position appear tense with an increase in extension behaviors? Is there evidence of visual engagement between mother and infant? How does the mother talk to the baby—rhythmically and quietly or erratically and with a harsh voice?

If the baby is lying on the examining table, similar observation can be made. Does the mother maintain contact with the baby, with her hand touching the infant or by visual contact? Alternatively, it may be important to be sensitive to the situation in which the infant has been left alone in a corner of the examining table while the mother is seated away from the infant. In this case, the clinician might want to ask herself: Is the mother anxious about the examination, overwhelmed by the office procedures, insecure about her mothering abilities, or depressed? Careful assessment of the initial visual and verbal interactions with the mother may yield clues about how the mother is feeling about herself and about the infant.

The accumulation of these observations will assist the clinician in assessing the individual style, quality, and intensity of the bond between mother and infant; when a father is present, it is remarkable to observe the way in which his presence alters the mother-infant attachment behaviors. In a sense, the family's style of interactional behaviors is available to you for clinical observation at this examination. These observations attain a heightened level of importance when viewed in terms of the requirements for satisfactory growth, particularly in early infancy, in other words, an emotionally nourishing bond between the young infant and its parents.

HISTORY

Questions that should be asked during the history taking and observations during the physical examination are presented in Table 10–1.

TABLE 10–1.
Questions to Be Asked During History Taking and Examination

Question	Objective
History Taking	
How is nursing (or "feeding" when baby is formula fed) going?	Listen carefully to her response to this open-ended question; assess her comfort with nursing; is she self-assured or does she show evidence of insecurity?
Does the baby seem satisfied at the end of a feeding? How do you feel when you are nursing?	Assess *maternal* satisfaction with nursing
How often and for how long do you feed the baby? How do you know when she is hungry?	Assess the mother's settling-in with baby's needs and individual rhythms, as well as an estimation of the amount of milk each day.
Tell me about your own diet (for nursing mothers). How much weight have you lost?	Assess lactating mother's diet; mothers who are back to their prepregnant weight at this time may have difficulty sustaining milk supply through the anticipated increase in caloric requirement at about 2 to 3 mo of life.
How do you manage nighttime feedings? (How often and for how long is the baby fed? . . . In a chair or in bed?) Are you getting enough sleep?	Assess feeding regularity and finding some schedule . . . Is the mother sleep-deprived?
When baby is formula fed, assess amount of milk at each feeding (calculate daily intake). How do you prepare the formula?	Assess quantity of formula and appropriate concentration.
Can you describe your baby's personality? What is she like most of the time?	Assess the infant's temperament and style, and the mother's attentiveness and awareness about these aspects of the baby's development.
Does the baby have a fussy time during most days? Can you describe it to me?	Assess colic-like behavior.
Do you think that your baby cries longer than most infants? What do you do when she cries?	Help parent adapt to periods of difficult infant behavior; explain the expected amount of crying.
In the presence of infant colic, ask: What do you think causes these episodes of crying? When appropriate, what does your husband think?	Assess parent's explanatory model for the behavior; may give clue to most effective therapeutic suggestion for particular family.
Physical Examination	
Obtain accurate measurements of weight, length, and head circumference plotted on standard growth curves.	Assess adequacy of growth (vs. overnourished or undernourished infant); demonstrate rates of growth on chart to parent.
Complete physical examination	Although always important at a health supervision visit, performing a careful physical examination while demonstrating normal findings is particularly important to parents with a colicky baby at this age.
Assess skin texture and turgor, fat folds, and state of hydration.	Evaluate nutrition.
To determine infant temperament, observe the baby at rest on the examining table and during physical examination maneuvers; when weighed and immediately following the DPT* immunization, infant temperament in response to stress can be observed.	Is this an easy baby? An overly active baby? How did the baby respond after the DPT injection? How did the mother or father respond?
If colic appears likely from the mother's history, rule out during routine physical examination: inguinal hernia, corneal abrasion, otitis media, or a thread wrapped tightly around a finger or toe.	Note: These are uncommon causes of paroxysmal crying at this age.

*DPT = diphtheria-pertussis-tetanus.

MANAGEMENT AND GUIDANCE

UNDERNUTRITION

Growth failure at this age usually represents insufficient caloric intake. In breast-fed infants, problems in latching on or continuous ineffective sucking are not uncommon; the correct diagnosis is usually apparent from the history of feeding behavior. Observing the baby feed may be helpful to the mother and to the diagnostician. Improving the mechanics of nursing often resolves the problem, such as pillow support of the baby or mother's arm, helping the mother to encourage the infant to latch on effectively, pointing out that it is normal to suck vigorously, followed by a brief rest period before sucking is resumed.

Insufficient milk may be the problem in some nursing mothers. This may be caused by (1) inadequate amount of fluid in the mother's diet (usually a minimum of 2 qt/day is required), (2) anxiety or depression that may inhibit the let-down reflex as a result of oxytocin suppression or inhibit milk production associated with prolactin secretion, (3) sleep deprivation, or (4) excessive weight loss. Addressing the issue with compassion and knowledge may be sufficient to help the mother reorganize the problem with either her diet or daily schedule. Mild to moderate postpartum depression (see Chapter 9) is usually resolving around this time. Reassurance about the baby's development, coupled with frequent weight checks in the office, may be helpful. For the more severely stressed nursing mother, an appropriate mental health referral, more active involvement of the father (or other member of the extended family), or, *rarely*, formula supplementation may be appropriate.

Formula-fed babies may not be receiving enough milk at each feeding or may be fed too infrequently, or the milk may be inappropriately overdiluted. Corrective measures are simple once the problem is recognized.

With either breast-fed or formula-fed undernourished infants, it may be revealing and often therapeutic to observe the mother feeding the child in the office. Positioning of the baby, maternal-infant eye contact, comfort with feeding, and quality of sucking mechanism—are important characteristics that can be observed. Interactional difficulties can be assessed and corrected.

Less commonly, growth failure at this age is secondary to an organic disorder, either one apparent during the newborn period or one that surfaces during the history or physical examination. Laboratory assessment is seldom indicated at this age until after the interactional, mechanical, and nutritional problems discussed earlier are considered thoroughly.

OVERFEEDING

If the baby's weight curve is greater than 2 SD above the mean, the first step is to repeat the measurements to determine accuracy (especially length). If the data are correct and the baby looks obese, carefully review the feeding pattern over a typical day. Clinical examples:

1. A breast-fed 1-month-old infant is put to the breast every 2 hours (each time she cries) for at least 12 feedings per day, each lasting 10 to 20 minutes.

Diagnosis: Overfeeding.
Therapy: Teach mother other forms of soothing behavior, such as pacifier (after 2 weeks of life), swaddling, rocking, and swinging. Explain the nature and adaptive value of two different sucking behaviors: nutritive and nonnutritive. Some babies seem to want to suck more

frequently; a pacifier is very helpful in these cases. The mother may need to be taught to respond to other needs in her infant (e.g., boredom) with an expanded range of interactions.

2. A breast-fed infant is nursed approximately every 3 to 4 hours for 10 minutes on each side at most feedings.

Diagnosis: This apparently overweight baby is probably not being overfed. Her appetite is vigorous and she looks big. Most of these breast-fed infants will find their genetic growth curve (usually closer to their length curve) after 6 months.
Therapy: Reassure the mother.

3. A formula-fed infant is consuming 40 to 45 oz each day; at 2 months she is given the bottle every 2 to 3 hours.

Diagnosis: Overfeeding.
Therapy: Limit formula to 32 oz/day. Explain baby's nutritional requirements to the mother along with your concerns regarding obesity. Review concept of nutritive and non-nutritive sucking. Suggest pacifier and other tactile soothing techniques. If the baby requires more than 32 oz fluid/day, suggest a water supplement or, alternatively, diluting one bottle each day with water to yield 16 oz from 8 oz of formula.

NIGHT FEEDINGS

If you discover that the baby is awakening every 3 hours through the night, inquire how she is responded to. Parents who pick up the infant at the moment she awakes may be encouraging a long-term pattern of frequent night time awakenings. Point out that even a 2-month-old infant can often settle herself when given an opportunity. A short fussy period will not be harmful. If necessary, a loving pat on the back while the baby remains in the crib may be sufficient to calm the child to sleep. New parents need the reassurance that brief crying periods will be neither emotionally nor physically detrimental to their baby. They will be rewarded by the knowledge that a simple behavioral intervention, initiated and sustained by them, can bring about more restful nights for the baby and parents. Parents can be taught that young babies have a distinguishable cry for hunger compared with pain or the fussy cry characteristic of sleep transitions. As they learn to recognize their own infant's different cries, parents feel more comfortable letting a 2-month-old fuss for a few minutes as she attempts self-soothing behaviors and a return to sleep.

SUPPLEMENTAL BOTTLES

At this stage, many mothers who are nursing successfully choose to continue full-time nursing until after 6 to 12 months when the infant can sit and learn to drink from a cup. For a variety of reasons, other mothers may choose to supplement breast-feeding with either expressed breast milk or a formula. Returning to work or school, plans to wean before the infant's readiness to use a cup, the wish to have an occasional evening or afternoon out without the baby, or a desire to plan for an emergency are the many reasons women may have for supplementation at this time. It may be helpful to ask the nursing mother about her plans as they affect nursing. Helping her to choose between expressed milk and formula, the clinician can play the role of educator rather than decision maker. When bottle supplementation is desired, waiting until after 5 or 6 weeks ensures the establishment of an adequate milk supply and gives the infant and mother enough time to form the psychological attachment and mechanical know-how to safeguard the future of nursing. *What to Expect in the First Year* (Eisenberg et al., 1989) is an outstanding new book for parents on infant care that provides detailed guidelines for supplementation, expression and storage of breast milk.

COLIC ("PAROXYSMAL FUSSING")

In treating the infant with colic, the clinician should follow these steps:

1. Begin with the reassurance, when appropriate, that the findings of the baby's physical examination are normal. Narrating your normal findings for the parents as you examine each body part may be particularly reassuring, such as "the intestinal examination is normal; the bowels feel fine and all the organs in the tummy feel as they should."

2. Discuss "fussiness" and crying at this age in terms of normal patterns (see earlier section). A parent with a colicky baby may find it helpful to see her infant as a variation of what is expected rather than as someone who is abnormal (Taubman, 1984).

3. Assist in the alleviation of parental anxieties that may be exacerbating the paroxysms of crying. Suggesting a time-off afternoon for the mother and brief naps during the day when the baby is sleeping may be helpful.

4. Prevent overstimulation of the baby. Parents of a colicky baby may be doing too much with the baby, such as too frequent feeding or picking her up too often. Teach soothing behavior such as swaddling, gently rocking, or use of a pacifier. Demonstrate to the mother that her fussy infant is soothed by holding the baby vertically away from you and gently and slowly moving him back and forth; this may be enlightening. Some colicky babies respond to a heating pad or warm water bottle against the abdomen. White noise (a hair dryer or vacuum cleaner) placed near the crib is found helpful by some parents (Spencer et al., 1990). A mechanical swing may soothe some of the most fussy infants. Formula change is almost never helpful; these babies are not allergic or intolerant to various formulas for the most part. Even the act of changing a formula may result in the mother seeing her infant as more vulnerable (Forsyth et al., 1985). A double-blind crossover study demonstrated that any initial decrease in colic after elimination of cow's milk diminished rapidly, and only infrequently was the effect reproducible (Forsyth, 1989). Lactose intolerance is rare at this age (Barr et al., 1987). Whether allergic reactions occur to constituents in breast milk is controversial. Some nursing babies seem to improve when cow's milk is removed from the mother's diet (Jakobsson and Lindberg, 1983). Other studies have not supported an association (Evans et al., 1981). Occasionally, elimination of caffeine, chocolate (xanthine), or stimulant medications consumed by the nursing mother will alleviate episodes of colic.

Note that none of these interventions has been studied extensively. They are part of the folklore for colicky babies. They seem to help (parent, baby, or both) in some cases. An intriguing recent study demonstrated that babies whose parents were instructed to hold them for an extra 2 hours each day cried significantly less than a control group of babies (Hunziker and Barr, 1986).

5. Review feeding practices. Encourage quiet feeding times when the mother is comfortable with herself and the baby. This may require a darkened room away from the center of activitiy in a busy house or apartment. Babies who are nursed more frequently overall show significantly less crying and fretting behavior (Barr et al., 1988) of the episodic or colicky type.

6. Medication is generally not advisable except in the most severe cases of infant colic in which the baby's behavior has produced a significant level of parental tension that threatens to obstruct satisfactory interactions between the child and his parents. These situations are often apparent before the office visit as a result of frequent telephone calls about crying and feeding dysfunction. The measures discussed earlier have been tried without benefit.

The use of a mild sedative or antispasmodic preparation for a brief period (a few days to 1 week) in this situation serves to temporarily break the cycle of crying baby leading to tense parents leading to dysfunctional family. It may allow the parents a period of rest and an opportunity to try out other soothing behaviors with a more comfortable infant. A medication that may be used is hysocyamine sulfate (Levsin), 4 to 6 drops three or four times daily.

It should be emphasized that although there are a very few cases suitable for a brief course of medicine, the majority of fussy babies should not receive medication.

7. A positive and optimistic approach is required and beneficial (Carey, 1983). Parents must be told that the baby is normal, there are some measures to be tried, and improvement and resolution will occur. In all but the most severe cases, this conservative approach is rewarded by improvement. It often means that the parents have discovered new ways to relate to and settle their baby. Frequent follow-up telephone calls are usually helpful.

The time invested in the colicky infant and his family is well worth it. The parents will come to understand that this intensity is part of their own infant's style and that this characteristic is one that the child himself must learn to handle. They must be taught to respect and appreciate this infant's vitality, vigor, and excitement. If these broader perspectives are not achieved at this juncture, the colicky infant will come back to haunt the clinician in another guise (sleeping, feeding, or discipline issues).

> But what am I?
> An infant crying in the night:
> An infant crying for the light:
> And with no language but a cry.
>
> Lord Tennyson, "In Memoriam"

REFERENCES

Altemeier WA, O'Connor SM, Sherrod KB, et al: Prospective study of antecedents for non-organic failure to thrive. *J Pediatr* 1985; 106:360–365.

Barr RG, Clogg LJ, Woolridge JA, et al: Carbohydrate change has no effect on infant crying behavior: A randomized controlled trial. *Am J Dis Child* 1987; 141:391.

Brazelton TB: Crying in infancy. *Pediatrics* 1962; 29:579–588.

Brazelton TB: Nutrition during early infancy, in Susking RM (ed): *Textbook of Pediatric Nutrition.* New York, Raven Press, 1981.

Carey WB: "Colic" or excessive crying in young infants, in Levine MD, Carey WB, Crocker AC, et al (eds): *Developmental-Behavioral Pediatrics.* Philadelphia, WB Saunders Co, 1983.

Eisenberg A, Murkoff HE, Hathaway SE: *What to Expect in the First Years.* New York, Workman Publishing, 1989.

Evans RW, Ferguson DM, Allardyce RA, et al: Maternal diet and infantile colic in breast fed infants. *Lancet* 1981; 1:1340–1342.

Ferber R: *Solve Your Child's Sleep Problems.* New York, Simon & Schuster, 1985.

Forsyth BWC: Colic and the effect of changing formulas: A double-blind multiple crossover study. *J Pediatr* 1989; 115:521–526.

Forsyth BWC, McCarthy PL, Leventhal JM: Problems of early infancy, formula changes, and mothers' beliefs about their infants. *J Pediatr* 1985; 106:1012–1017.

Hunziker UA, Barr RG: Increased carrying reduces infant crying: A randomized controlled trial. *Pediatrics* 1986; 77:641.

Jakobsson I, Lindberg T: Cow's milk proteins cause infantile colic in breast fed infants: A double-blind crossover study. *Pediatrics* 1983; 71:268–271.

Macknin ML, Medendorp SV, Maier MC: Infant sleep and bedtime cereal. *Am J Dis Child* 1989; 143:1066–1068.

Rosenn D, Loeb L, Jura M: Differentiation of organic from nonorganic failure to thrive syndrome in infancy. *Pediatrics* 1980; 66:689.

Sander L, Julia H, Stechler G: Regulation and organization in early infant-caretaker interaction, in Robinson RJ (ed): *Brain and Early Behavior*. New York, Academic Press, 1969.

Spencer JAD, Moran DJ, Lee A, et al: White noise and sleep induction. *Arch Dis Child* 1990; 65:135–136.

Taubman B: Clinical trial of the treatment of colic by modification of parent-infant interaction. *Pediatrics* 1984; 74:998.

Wessel MA, Cobb JC, Jackson EB, et al: Paroxysmal fussing in infancy, sometimes called "colic." *Pediatrics* 1954; 14:421.

Whitten CF, Pettit MG, Fischhoff J: Evidence that growth failure from maternal deprivation is secondary to undereating. *JAMA* 1969; 209:1675.

"Smiling kid." By girl, age 5½.

CHAPTER 11

Three to Four Months: Having Fun With the Picture Book Baby

SUZANNE D. DIXON, M.D.

KEY WORDS

INFANT PLAY
SOCIAL INTERACTION
SLEEP ISSUES
TEMPERAMENTAL DIFFERENCES
SLEEP VARIATIONS

   Mrs. Martin brings in her 3-month-old and asks what formula to buy for the infant. She was previously breast-feeding but says the baby does not like to nurse anymore. She is tearful and wonders if it is time she went back to work. She is also concerned because everyone in the supermarket comes up to play with the baby and he will not go to sleep when the two get home; "the whole day gets messed up." She says she has not been sleeping well herself, but the baby "gets along fine without her" all night long.

The child of 3 to 4 months of age is a delightful, cherubic, engaging creature. An increase in alert responsiveness, an expanded behavioral repertoire, and a decrease in reflex-determined behaviors mark a real change in the infant and in the caretaking she both inspires and demands. This new level of organization marks real developmental progress and calls for a shift in emphasis in both the clinician and the family's point of view. The child's newly apparent individuality and increased social needs force this change. Failure to shift parenting gears means parents miss out on the best of infancy.

STATE ORGANIZATION

   By the third or fourth month, the state organization of the child has shown increased stability and reliability. Most infants have shifted their longest sleep time to nighttime hours and have developed reasonably set nap times (Parmelee et al., 1964). Routines for settling to sleep have developed between child and parents (Figs 11–1 and 11–2). The child, if left alone, can usually settle herself back to sleep following the periodic awakenings that occur every 2 to 4 hours during the sleep times. Individual, biologically determined differences are manifest in these abilities as well as in the length of sleep. Some children may be short sleepers and

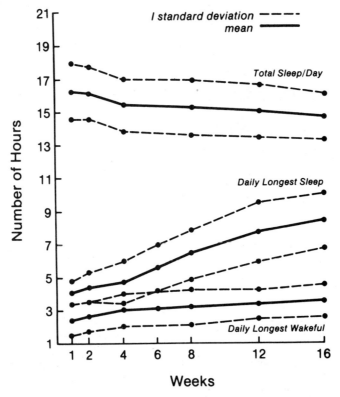

FIG 11-1.
Maturation of sleep patterns; emergence of diurnal pattern over the first weeks of life. (From Parmelee AH, Wenner WH, Schulz HR: *J Pediatr* 1964; 65:576–582. Used by permission.)

some long sleepers; they will have declared themselves by this time and are likely to maintain these characteristics through the life span (Hartman, 1973; Zuckerman and Blitzer, 1981). Preferences for sleep position and the amount of motor activity during sleep also show individual variation.

Sleep shows its own developmental course over time. The cyclic pattern of rapid eye movement sleep (REM) and quiet sleep (NREM) becomes clearer in the first months of life (Fig 11–3); there is a decrease in the relative proportion of REM sleep over the life span and the length of the cyclic pattern (i.e., periodicity) increases from 50 minutes in the newborn to 90 minutes in the average adult. These behavioral and electrophysiologic parameters are markers of neurologic maturation and integrity (Anders et al., 1980). Children with central nervous system, endocrine, or chromosomal disorders, as well as children receiving phenobarbital or other sedatives or even antihistamine therapy, have predictable alterations in the organization and maturation of sleep (Zuckerman and Blitzer, 1981). Premature infants, even those without perinatal complications, will have less regular sleep and will be more difficult to quiet. This will likely continue for the first year but is not predictive of long-term neurological or developmental problems.

Sleep is usually disturbed by periodic awakenings at this age. Some children are able to

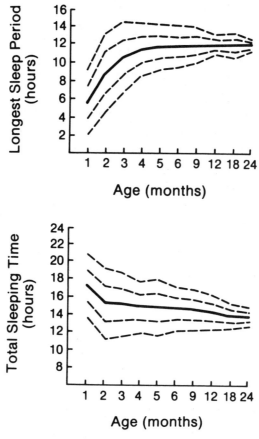

FIG 11–2.
Maturation of sleep patterns in the first months
of life. Mean time of longest sleep time with 2 SD
(*top*) mean and 2 SD of total sleep in 24 hours
(*bottom*). (From Traisman AS, Traisman HS, Getti
RA: *J Pediatr* 1966; 68:608–614. Used by permission.)

quietly settle themselves back to sleep without awakening the parents. These children are
said to sleep through the night. About one third of infants reach a level of arousal that arouses
their parents (Anders, 1979). Some parents are more sensitive and responsive to these noises.
Individual differences exist in children, in parents, in families, in household layouts and
schedules, and even in cultural expectations. In the United States, we expect infants to demonstrate substantial independence in the matter of sleeping. Being awakened by an infant at
night is a violation of expectations, of schedules, and of the time and space allocated for self
and spouse. Therefore, infants who do not "sleep through the night" are viewed as defective
or at least developmentally delayed and certainly as a source of stress. In other cultures,
where schedules are more fluid and independence is not a goal in child rearing, "sleep problems" do not exist (Lozoff et al., 1983; Tronick [written communication, December 1984]);
night wakenings, however, are the usual occurrence in all groups. The introduction of solids

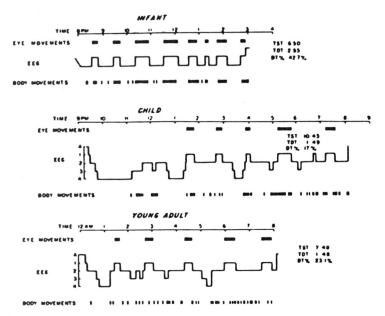

FIG 11–3.
Cyclic pattern of rapid eye movement and quiet sleep. (From Anders TF, Carskadon MA, Dement WC: *Pediatr Clin North Am* 1980; 27:29–43. Used by permission.)

does not effect longer sleep times, although breast-fed infants *may* empty their stomachs sooner than formula-fed infants (Traisman et al., 1966). However, it is the rare infant who awakens because of hunger alone. Maturational factors and environmental issues are the components of this problem. Parents can prolong the awakening through an elaborate inter-action with the infant. Talk, activities, and game playing all will communicate to the infant that this is a time for play, an activity in which he is all too willing to get involved. Quiet comforting, perhaps a quiet feeding, dim lights, and rhythmic soothing (e.g., patting, rocking) will signal the infant that this is the time to sleep (Brazelton, 1975). Breast-feeding mothers may appreciate these quiet, prolonged feedings at night after the distracted, disrupted brief nursings of the infant's busy day. Milk supply will be maintained in spite of the infant's daytime shift in energy investment to the social sphere. With this support and maturation over time, the infant will assume more responsibility for quieting himself. A nightlight will help the infant orient himself and be reassured by the constancy of his room and parents. Some parents who do not get enough time alone with their infants during the day may choose to use the night as a private play time. They must be willing to invest the time to quiet the infant back down, as well as enliven him. The infant may not accept the "quiet time" when the parents attempt this shift. There is no evidence that bringing an infant into the parents' bed is either dangerous, psychologically harmful, or even habit forming at this age (Lozoff et al., 1984). This may be the *least* disruptive pattern for some families to manage sleep and is very common, even into the toddler years (Mandasky and Edelbrock, 1990). On the other hand, the infant's periodic stirrings may not allow his parents any rest, and their interventions to correct that may not allow the infant to quiet himself (Brazelton, 1975), a developmental competency and need. Each family with each child must decide a management plan with the clinician to offer information on sleep pattern and options and to support families in the development of their own solutions.

Sleep at 3 to 4 months of age now becomes more vulnerable to outside disturbances (e.g., the telephone ringing) and to internal turbulence. The excitement of the day's activities may infiltrate the sleep time, so that settling in for the night or staying asleep may be a new problem. These changing developmental processes and issues call for new insights and change in management at this time.

READY FOR PLAY

NEUROLOGICAL MATURATION

The neurological organization of the infant has changed during this interval. The electro-encephalogram tracing shows a dramatic shift toward a more mature pattern, both in electrical wave form and in the cyclic regularities at this time (Parmelee et al., 1964). Most of the primitive reflexes have disappeared. The infant is capable of volitional action on the environment. The tonic neck reflex, reflex hand grasp, and whole body excitation that result from the perception of a positive event have now enabled the child to see his hands and feet. These at first appear separately and then in the midline working together, swiping at objects, and providing interesting tactile and visual input. The activities of the hands come under willed control, although precision in management must wait until later. Muscular control of eye movements has also increased, so the infant can track objects all around the visual field. Eye movements can lead the head and trunk in following. Central nervous system controls and lens mobility have matured so the child can see and follow objects across the room and can maintain fixation on objects for prolonged periods of time. Visual acuity has increased markedly so that small objects with small amounts of contrast (e.g., a button) can be easily seen. The action of the hands in the visual field enables the infant to experiment with depth perception, distance and size relationships, and other perceptual skills that will be at nearly adult levels by 6 months of age. As the psychologist Hans Papousek (1969) has stated, there is "a marked qualitative change in higher nervous function at the third month." This new organizational level enables the child to interact with his family in new and elaborate ways.

COGNITIVE GROWTH

New cognitive skills are evident in the infant's ability to momentarily delay gratification and to link events in his life. The young child of 3 months will stop crying in the nursing position even before the nipple is in his mouth. He may hold back on his vigorous sucking at breast for a few minutes until the milk letdown begins, content in the anticipation of the reward. He may smile as he is eased into a front pack, linking that event to an expected adventure. He may flex his hips readily when placed on the changing table. All of these behaviors indicate that he has been mentally active in assimilating these events that occur consistently around him. He can anticipate and wait (Ginsburg and Opper, 1969).

SOCIAL SKILLS

The human need and drive for social interaction is never more obvious than in the behavior of the 3-month-old infant (Trotter and Thoman, 1978). The child actively seeks out people in the environment for careful scrutiny, attempts at imitation, and delightful elicitations of interactions. The presence of people is more compelling than any other phenomenon (Brazelton, 1975). The 2-month-old infant participates in social exchanges; the 3-month-old can actively initiate the interaction with compelling force. These capacities are vital for development of the many areas of maturation to follow.

Although studies of parent-infant interactions confirm that infants know their specific parents from the earliest weeks of life (Dixon et al., 1981b), the 3-month-old infant offers very dramatic testimony even to the most skeptical parent. At this age, the child will search a room until he finds his parents, will move all extremities in excitement, and arch forward with outstretched arms to urge them to notice, talk, and touch him. Even the temperamentally quiet infant will stop all activity and increase visual regard in parents' presence as if to anticipate the desired interaction. Vocalizing to initiate and sustain an interaction is regular. The 3-month-old has a whole new series of facial expressions to indicate an expanded range of emotional responses: pouting, coyness, disgruntlement, teasing, wariness, insulted, fearful, bored, and so forth. This conveys the image of an interesting and unique personality. The infant can imitate facial expressions and sounds and draws attention with forced coughs, bubble blowing, and "raspberries" (i.e., blowing air through opposed lips). He explores the caregivers' faces through looking at the parts, swiping, poking, and pulling. Parents' clothes and skin offer new safe opportunities to explore the most important part of the environment, his family.

In an interactive setting, the infant has incredible abilities to respond to subtle behaviors (e.g., glances away that are fractions of a second) or underlying emotional tones (e.g., frustration, tension). He is hungry for the social interaction, seeks it out, and learns to play games. The development of "the game" (Stern, 1974) is central to emotional and cognitive growth. The child learns that there is communicative intent in the predictable exchange between caretaker and child. The verbal, tactile, vestibular, and motor games are the elements through which the child learns that he can affect the behavior of others and that his own behavior has meaning (Chance, 1979). It is in the social games of early infancy that the essential elements for cognitive development are initially appreciated by the child: consistency and contingency—the consistency with which he is handled and with which he is answered; the contingency that his own actions produce results, altering the behavior of those around him (Watson, 1978). These social interactions, delivered in the context of caretaking and as individual as the players of the game, are the main event of the infant's day.

The extent of the infant's interest in social interaction is very evident in the feeding behaviors, particularly nursing, at this age. The child simply cannot resist looking around, smiling, cooing, and poking at mom's face during a feeding session. He is now distracted by every sound or sight around him; he may even stop nursing to just look around to be sure he's not missing something. This is very frustrating for most American mothers who are ready for interval feedings rather than continuous feeding and who want to keep up their milk supply through adequate sucking time. There is a danger that nursing will be discontinued at this time because of lack of knowledge and management skills. The mother may interpret the infant's behavior as indicative of *his* desire to wean at this time. The positive force of the child's new social interest should be highlighted, as well as his tendency to overdose on excitement if given the opportunity. At least two feedings per day should be in a quiet, darkened room without distractions. These and other feedings need to be actively choreographed by a mother to allow the infant to concentrate on the task. Other types of vigorous social interactions should be enjoyed at other times. This turbulence does not mean that the infant does not like the breast milk or the mother (in fact, the opposite is true; he loves her even more as a person). He just needs some extra help in maintaining balance in a life that has suddenly gotten more interesting.

Infants work very hard at social play. They are motivated to attend to the social behavior around them and modify their own behavior. Familiar people call forth the most attention; unfamiliar adults elicit wariness, initial unbroken gaze, a tentative bright smile, and then avoidance behaviors, such as gaze aversion and head turning (Dixon et al., 1981b). Rhythms, styles, content of games, and intensity of interactions vary across individuals, socioeconomic groups, and cultures and subcultures (Caudill and Weinstein, 1969; Dixon et al., 1981a), but the basic pattern of game playing with its reciprocal nature, mutually regulated, seems to be a universal pattern of human development (Brazelton, 1975).

For the "game playing" to be successful, mutually enjoyable, and meet the infant's needs for consistency and contingency, some elements are required. The adult must be convinced that these affectionate interchanges are worthwhile. Playing with the infant, holding, massaging, moving, talking to, and nuzzling an infant will not "spoil" the child (i.e., make her more dependent or demanding). In fact, the opposite is true. The more one plays with a baby, the more she will learn ways to amuse herself. Play is a way of learning. Parents who allow themselves to spend this time foster psychological growth. Prompt and appropriate responses build self-sufficiency. The world is experienced as a safe, responsive, predictable, and exciting place to be. Depressed, distracted, or unresponsive parents are a detriment to psychological growth at this time.

OVERDOSING ON FUN

The seductive behavior of the 3-month-old infant is hard to resist. The infant's excitement, interest, charm, and responsiveness draw most caregivers into interactions. The baby's orgasmic smiles, laughs, and total body wiggles are a terrific reward for a few tickles or a play-face expression. Indeed, the investment of effort for the first 3 months is amply paid off in the rewarding baby of 3 to 4 months. Some parents, probably most parents some of the time, will really push the infant beyond the limits of what he can tolerate of this delightful play. Overstimulation is a very real danger if the infant's body language is not heard, particularly for the neurologically, physiologically, or temperamentally fragile child. The parent must be sensitive to the infant's behavioral cues that she is on "overload" and that play must slow down (Lipsitt, 1978). This allows for an organization of the past experiences, a recovery of attentional energy, and some physiological rest. The required pause may be seconds or hours. Some children will be more clear in signaling their overload than others; some children are more sensitive to environmental and interactional stresses than others. Sensitive adults learn this from the individual child and pull back (Stern, 1977). As stated by Catherine Landreth (1967), parents must provide "freedom to do what he [i.e., the child] is capable of and the good sense to stop short of overstimulation." When infants give those cues, parents must not interpret them as personal. The infant is not tired of the parent; he is just tired of playing.

Children who are brought for long periods of time to large gatherings, prolonged trips to large shopping centers, siblings' schools, or long trips may have markedly decreased capacity to handle further stress without overload. Sleep and feeding difficulties are predictable in these contexts. Letting infants at this age "cry it out" may only exaggerate the frenzy at a time when the infant is least able to handle it (Zuckerman and Blitzer, 1981). Quiet containment by a calm adult helps the infant get back under control. This kind of responsiveness restores energy to the child; it does not "spoil" him.

TEMPERAMENTAL DIFFERENCES

Some infants' personalities make their bids for social interaction difficult to interpret, or the style differences between caregiver and parent are very divergent. One infant may signal interactional readiness by serious regard and be overloaded by all but the most gentle play. The child may be perceived as negative, dull, or unappreciative of a parent. The sensitivity and low-key responsiveness may need to be pointed out to a parent worried about the mental capacities of the child or feeling unsuccessful at bids for social interaction. Most caring parents will guard against the feelings of failure by avoiding interaction. Just the opposite is needed here: The parent must gently draw this infant into a mutually regulated, satisfying pattern of interaction. The clinician can foster this new approach through reassurances of the child's integrity and through highlighting these temperamental differences. Modeling this "gentler" approach in the office is effective and rewarding.

At this age alert times are more regular, of longer duration, and can be sustained by interesting events or interactions for all infants. The infant has developed a greater capacity to quiet himself, distract himself, and not wind up to prolonged crying. For most infants, classic "colic" has disappeared by this time, but what may not have disappeared is the highly responsive, intense, and overly reactive infant. This temperamental profile now is seen as the infant who is easily overwhelmed by exciting days, who handles change in scheduling poorly, and who may have sleep difficulties such as falling asleep or restless, disturbed sleep. Vomiting may follow feedings that are frantic and fast, or feedings may be full of wiggles and distractions. For the clinician, the chief complaint, not the basic issue, has changed. The child's own individual makeup must be understood and appreciated for its value.

THE FAMILY AT THREE MONTHS

Parents should be having fun with their infants at this time. Physiological recovery and severe sleep deprivation are usually past, and this enables the mother (and father) to bring new energy to the situation. The infant is usually not seen as physically vulnerable, and the patterns of daily care are stabilized. The parents are very ready to move onto the next level of parenting, that of attention to the individuality of the infant through individual social interaction. Parents should both enjoy and appreciate the infant at this time. However, they will need to broaden their repertoire of responses to the infant's behavior to include play. Feeding in response to every whimper is not enough. Single parents, parents of ill or preterm infants, and overly isolated or stressed parents may hold on the earlier pattern of simply holding and feeding as the only response. Overfeeding may result and may be the clue to this "development arrest" in the family. Maternal depression will now affect the infant's behavior very immediately and profoundly with long-lasting effects (Cohn and Tronick, 1983; Zuckerman and Beardslee, 1987). The baby's behavior and a flattening of responsiveness, the lack of joy in the interaction may be the clue that a mental health referral is needed.

Siblings may reach a new level of organization at this time as well. The baby is able to clearly enjoy the older child's antics and bids for interaction, provided these are not too vigorous or overwhelming. The infant will seem to prefer watching another child if he is not overloaded or stressed. The infant's stability of state and the parents' more rested state allow a little more time for the older child's separate time with his parents. The infant should be adding energy to the unit in the form of love, delight, and active appreciation of the life around him. If not, something is wrong.

DATA GATHERING

WHAT TO OBSERVE

Does the mother enjoy the baby? Is undressing, holding, and waiting sprinkled with game playing, dialogues, and object play? Does the infant visually scan and auditorially monitor the room with a bright, active search? Does the infant monitor your approach, initiate an interaction on a smile cue alone? Are the infant's hands open, active, meeting in the midline? Is the infant beginning to babble in a dialogue fashion with the parent?

WHAT TO ASK

Are you enjoying the baby? What games do you play together? Describe his personality when you play with him. Has his schedule changed? Has *your* schedule changed (e.g., returning to work)? Can you predict his behavior from day to day? What things does he do to settle into sleep? What can you do to settle him? Can he amuse himself for a time? Can he wait for feedings if you come to him? Does he stop crying just with anticipation? How regular is his schedule? Does he awaken during the night or during nap time? What does he do to settle himself back down to sleep? Does he get excited before his bath? Has he discovered his hands, feet? Does he play with both hands together? Does he respond to sound and visual objects easily?

EXAMINATION

During the examination the clinician should ask himself the following questions: is this baby fun to deal with? Does he coo (ahs, ows, i.e., open vowel sounds with the beginning of labial consonants), smile, laugh? How and in response to which stimulus? Are his hands active? When visually regarding things, does he swipe, reach, grasp at these? Does he delight in doing so? Is his reach symmetrical? Have the primitive reflexes disappeared (e.g., tonic neck reflex, grasp reflex, Moro, and walk-in-place reflexes)? Can the child lift head and hands up when prone? Does he repeat a behavior that produced an interesting event (e.g., place a rattle in his hand and see if he understands that his own activity causes the interesting sound)?

Modeling of play interactions during the examination may be particularly important to parents. Point out the baby's smiles as social elicitations. Develop a verbal or motor game with the infant to see his response. Point out the infant's signs of overload or avoidance during the course of the physical examination or even with undressing. Consciously stop, pull back, and point out the infant's behavioral recovery.

Does the parent respond specifically to the infant's style, behavioral cues? Observations during weighing and measuring and after the immunizations may reveal the parent's response to various minor stresses.

ANTICIPATORY GUIDANCE

Some active infants may jettison themselves out of infant seats at this time of increased activity. Therefore, the seats should be retired.

The importance of the child's own active exploration of the world, particularly his own actions, should be emphasized.

Parents should be cautioned about overstimulation in toys and social interactions. Excess fatigue because of the loss of ability to habituate to environmental disturbances is a pitfall to be avoided. Letting the infant "cry it out" will not be helpful.

The surge in activity often produces an increase in appetite and growth at this time.

Emphasize the importance of holding and playing. Infants cannot be spoiled.

Siblings should receive cautious permission to interact with the baby under supervision.

Breast-feeding turbulence is to be expected at this time. Explain its origin and options for management.

Sleep is marked by periodic awakenings. Give the infant the opportunity to develop competency in this area.

REFERENCES

Anders TF: Night waking in infants during the first year of life. *Pediatrics* 1979; 63:860–864.

Anders TF, Carskadon MA, Dement WC: Sleep and sleepiness in children and adolescents. *Pediatr Clin North Am* 1980; 27:29–43.

Brazelton TB: *Infants and Mothers.* New York, Delacorte Press, 1975.

Caudill W, Weinstein H: Maternal care and infant behavior in Japan and America. *Psychiatry* 1969; 32:12–43.

Chance P: *Learning Through Play.* Pediatric Round Table Series no. 3. Skillman, NJ, Johnson & Johnson Baby Products Co, 1979.

Cohn JF, Tronick EZ: Three month old infants' reactions to simulated maternal depression. *Child Dev* 1983; 54:185–193.

Dixon S, Tronick E, Keefer C, et al: Mother-infant interaction among the Gusii of Kenya, in Field T, Sostek A, Vietze P, et al (eds): *Culture and Early Interactions.* Hillsdale, NY, Lawrence Erlbaum, 1981a.

Dixon S, Yogman M, Tronick E, et al: Early infant interaction with parents and strangers. *J Am Acad Child Psychiatry* 1981b; 20:32–52.

Ginsburg H, Opper S: *Piaget's Theory of Intellectual Development.* Englewood Cliffs, NJ, Prentice-Hall, 1969.

Hartman EL: *The Functions of Sleep.* New Haven, Conn, Yale University Press, 1973.

Landreth C: *Early Childhood: Behavior and Learning.* New York, Knopf, 1967.

Lipsitt L: The pleasures and annoyances of infants: Approach and avoidance behavior of babies, in Lipsett L, Reese HW, Bourne LE (eds): *Child Development.* Glenview, Ill, Scott, Foresman, & Co, 1978.

Lozoff B, Wolf A, Davis N: Co-sleeping in urban families with young children in the United States. *Pediatrics* 1984; 74:171–182.

Madansky D, Edelbrock C: Cosleeping in a community sample of 2- and 3-year old children. *Pediatrics* 1990; 86:197–203.

Papousek H: Individual variability in learned response in human infants, in Robinson RJ (ed): *Brain and Early Behavior.* New York, Academic Press, 1969.

Parmelee AH, Wenner WH, Schulz HR: Infant sleep patterns: From birth to 16 weeks of age. *J Pediatr* 1964; 65:576–582.

Stern D: Mother and infant at play, in Lewis M, Rosenblum L (eds): *The Effect of the Infant on Its Caregiver.* New York, John Wiley & Sons, 1974, pp 187–213.

Stern D: *The First Relationship: Infant and Mother.* Cambridge, Mass, Harvard University Press, 1977.

Traisman AS, Traisman HS, Getti RA: The well baby care of 530 infants: A study of immunization, feeding, behavioral and sleep habits. *J Pediatr* 1966; 68:608–614.

Trotter S, Thoman E (eds): *Social Responsiveness of Infants.* Pediatric Round Table Series no 2. Skillman, NJ, Johnson & Johnson Baby Products Co, 1978.

Watson JS: Perception of contingency as a determinant of social responsiveness, in Trotter S, Thoman E (eds): *Social Responsiveness of Infants.* Pediatric Round Table Series no 2. Skillman, NJ, Johnson & Johnson Baby Products Co, 1978.

Willemsen E: *Understanding Infancy.* San Francisco, WH Freeman & Co, 1979.

Zuckerman B, Blitzer EC: Sleep disorders, in Gabel S (ed): *Behavioral Problems in Pediatrics.* New York, Grune & Stratton, 1981, pp 257–272.

Zuckerman B, Beardslee WR: Maternal depression: A concern for pediatricians. *Pediatrics* 1987; 79:110–117.

Zuckerman B, Stevenson J, Bailey V: Sleep problems in early childhood: Continuities, predictive factors and behavioral correlates. *Pediatrics* 1987; 80:664–671.

ADDITIONAL READINGS

Bower TGR: The perceptual world of the child, in Bruner J, Cole M, Lloyd B (eds): *The Developing Child Series.* Cambridge, Mass, Harvard University Press, 1977.

Brazelton TB, Tronick E, Adamson L, et al: Early mother-infant reciprocity, in *Parent-Infant Interaction.* Ciba Foundation Symposium no 33. New York, Elsevier North-Holland, 1975, pp 137–154.

Guilleminault C: *Sleep and Its Disorders in Children.* New York, Raven Press, 1987.

Moore T, Ucko LE: Night waking in infancy. *Arch Dis Child* 1957; 32:333–342.

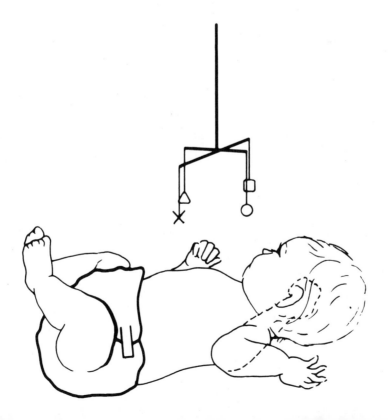

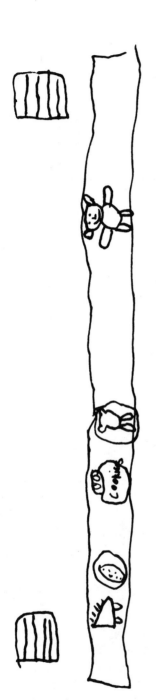
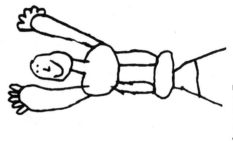

"Reaching Out." By boy, age 7.

CHAPTER **12**

Five to Six Months: Reaching Out to Play

SUZANNE D. DIXON, M.D.

MICHAEL J. HENNESSY, M.D.

PAMELA KAISER, M.N., C.P.N.P.

KEY WORDS

MOTOR DEVELOPMENT
REACH AND GRASP
ONTOGENY OF REACH AND GRASP
HANDEDNESS
OBJECT MANIPULATION IN PLAY
INFANT STIMULATION PROGRAMS

Jason, brought in on time for his third set of immunizations, is a roly-poly passive boy. His mother is concerned because he uses his left hand too much and puts everything in his mouth. She thinks she gives enough formula and cereal but wonders if he is still hungry. She wants to know when she can feed him foods like crackers and breakfast cereal bits. She says her brother is a "lefty" and always had trouble in school. On examination, Jason does reach first for your stethoscope with his left hand but will extend his right hand if the other is restrained. He grabs your pen more accurately with his left hand, shaping his hand before he touches the object. On the right side, his reach is less well directed.

Once he has visually discovered his hands, the child of 5 to 6 months of age now learns what he can do; the sights around him can be explored in an active way. The texture, temperature, shape, and malleability of objects become new dimensions of the world that add interest and excitement to the child's life. The eyes, hands, and mouth work together with an unquench-able appetite to explore everything. The specific way that the skills of reach and grasp are refined during infancy and how these changes make interaction with the external world possible are the focus of this visit.

Monitoring the development of visual-motor skills throughout childhood is part of each pediatric encounter. With the child's new skills, parents have an opportunity to create an environment that provides ample opportunities for the child's exploration. The prototype for this facilitating role is laid down in the middle of the first year with the emergence of reach and grasp.

BASIC PRINCIPLES OF MOTOR DEVELOPMENT

The progress of reach and grasp illustrates some basic principles of motor development. Neurological maturation provides the capacity to use the hands and arms more effectively. Continuities and consistencies are not always seen (Loria, 1980). However, the acquisition of skills in this area (Chandler, 1979) illustrates several general principles about motor development:

1. *Primitive* reflexes must disappear before *voluntary* behavior appears. Thus, the grasp reflexes must be gone before voluntary grasp begins.
2. There is a *proximal to distal* progression of development. This is evident in skill proceeding from the shoulder to the fingers. Thus, *reach precedes grasp.*
3. There is an *ulnar to radial* direction in development. An infant picks up an object on the little finger side and, as maturation occurs, begins to use the thumb side of the hand.
4. *Pronation precedes supination.* Therefore, palm-*down* maneuvers such as picking up objects occur before palm-*up* maneuvers such as putting objects in the mouth.
5. *Grasp precedes release,* in other words, action precedes inhibition.

ONTOGENY OF REACH AND GRASP

The behavior of the newborn and even preterm infant appears to contain precursors of reach and grasp in the form of the coordination of visual processing with hand activity, the presence of grasp reflexes, and some reaching behavior. The newborn in the quiet-alert state and visually fixated on a pleasant sight will begin to have mouthing movements, her hands will open and close, and after considerable latency she will swipe toward the midline with a hand and arm. Her feet and toes may also be activated in this process. Infants as young as 4 weeks respond differently to objects that are in their range of reach than to those that are beyond that range (Bower, 1972); they will swipe at reachable objects but not those that are out of range. The infant may even show the ability to differentiate her approach to two-dimensional versus three-dimensional objects.

In this earliest form of reach, vision initiates these reaches but does not control it accurately. In early infancy, the child cannot make ongoing corrections of his own efforts toward an object (Bower, 1977b). Hand-eye coordination in reach and grasp is evident from the newborn period on (von Hofstein, 1982) and continues throughout childhood (Connolly and Elliot, 1972). However, this lack of fully mature ability, plus the infant's one-handed swipe, makes success very unlikely at this stage. The child swipes with the whole hand and arm as a unit. He will grasp only at those objects he can feel in line with his hand reflexes (Brunner, 1973). This early type of volitional reach disappears at about 4 weeks of age. In a typical clinical setting, we rarely see it because we do not wait out the long latency period, unbind the infant's arms, or provide the truncal support that is needed to observe these skills.

The reflexes of grasp have been described by Twitchell (1955) and are presented in Table 12–1 and Figure 12–1. The timing in the appearance of these reflexes testifies to neurological maturation and integrity. These behaviors are based on motor tone: If tone is increased, these reflexes may be altered in their appearance and the way they are elicited. For example, in the hypertonic infant, every effort must be made to relax the tone through a calm approach and

TABLE 12–1.
Types of Grasp Reflexes

Reflex	Elicitation	Response	Emerges	Disappears
Mental	Touch chin	Hands close	Birth	At 6 wk
Palmar	Touch palm between thumb and index	Hands close	28 wk of gestation	2 mo
Traction	Stretch shoulder adductors and flexors	All joints of the arm flex	2–3 wk, peaks at 6 wk	Up to 5 mo
Instinctive grasp reaction orientation A.	Light touch to radial side of the hand	Open and supinate hand	3–4½ mo	4–5 mo
Instinctive grasp reaction orientation B.	Light touch to ulnar side of the hand	Open and pronate hand	5½–6 mo	6(?) mo
Groping	Light touch to hand on the side	Hand will move toward stimulus	6–7 mo	7 mo (onset reliable volitional grasp)
Grasping	Light touch to the side of the hand	Hand will grasp object	6–7 mo	7 mo (onset reliable volitional grasp)

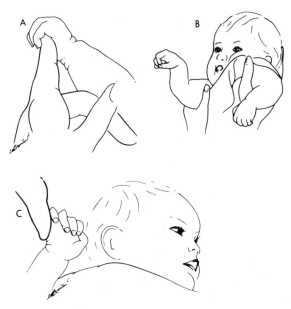

FIG 12–1.
Grasp reflexes. **A,** reflex palmar grasp. **B,** traction orientation grasp, type B, ulnar. **C,** instinctive orientation grasp.

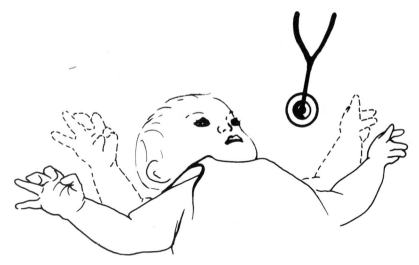

FIG 12–2.
Early infancy contains the earliest elements of reach, hand/arm and foot/leg activation with the presentation of interesting sights.

postural adjustment; these efforts must be done before the observation of reflexes can be made validly. Volitional activation of hands, feet, and mouth may occur even before the reflex grasp disappears (Fig 12–2).

The asymmetrical tonic neck response, peaking at about 6 weeks of age, facilitates the infant's exploration of her own hands. The infant is able to see what interesting things the hands are even before she has the strength and coordination to bring them before her eyes in the midline. Mutual hand grasp comes in at 2 to 3 months after a decrease in the tonic neck response.

By 5 months of age, the automatic grasp responses to objects touching the hand have largely disappeared. Volitional grasp has taken over and now acts independently from reach (Twitchell, 1955). Increasing control of the shoulder musculature, as well as truncal stability (i.e., sitting with slight or no support), enables reach to be more reliable. Fixed-extension postures at the shoulders or weakness may prevent the child from using reach even though she may be able. Applying external support with increase in flexion at the shoulder often allows these reaching abilities to be seen, as in the case of the premature infant. This maneuver is helpful if reach is in question. By 3 to 6 months, the hands should be loosely fisted at rest and both hands activated when the infant attempts to reach. By 6 months, the child should reach across the midline when the contralateral hand is restrained.

White and Held (1966) provide another model to this same progression. They propose that the development of reach and grasp evolves through the following stages: (1) discovery of the hand, (2) visual inspection (regard) of the hand, (3) inspection of objects, (4) swiping at objects, (5) contact of objects, and (6) tactilely inspecting (opening and closing the hand on the object).

Volitional grasp matures with increasing control proceeding downward with decreasing shoulder movement, with more use of the wrist and with increasing use of the fingers as

TABLE 12–2.
Progression of Grasp*

Age (mo)	Term	Pattern Components
1	Nondirected swiping	Arms and legs activated, often beginning with startle; long latency; hands and mouth may open
3–4	Swiping	Moving arm up and down in attempt to contact objects
4	Corralling	Reaching out with entire arm and hand and sweeping arm toward body
4–5	Ulnar-palmar grasp of cube; rotates wrist	Fingers on top surface of object press it into center of palm, thumb adducted, wrist flexed
6–7	Radial-palmar grasp of cube	Fingers of far side of object press against opposed thumb and radial side of palm, wrist straight
6–7	Raking grasp of pellet	Raking object into palm with adducted, totally flexed thumb and fingers
7–8	Radial-digital grasp of cube	Object held with opposed thumb and fingertips; space visible between
7–9	Scissors grasp of pellet	Between ventral surfaces of thumb and index finger
9–10	Pincer grasp of pellet	Between distal pad of thumb and index finger
9–10	Voluntary release	Drops objects when desired

*Modified from Bayley N: *Bayley Scales of Infant Development.* New York, Psychological Corp, 1969; Erhardt RP: *Developmental Hand Dysfunction: Theory, Assessment, Treatment.* Laurel, Md, RAMSCO Publishing Co, 1982; Knobloch H, Stevens F, Malone A: *Manual of Developmental Diagnosis: The Administration and Interpretation of the Revised Gesell and Amatrude Developmental and Neurologic Examination.* New York, Harper & Row Publishers, 1980.

separate units. Also, the child shows increasing ability to anticipate the shape and weight of the object (Table 12–2 and Fig 12–3). That is, as she begins her grasp or reach, near the age of 6 to 8 months, the hand position and the arc of movement reflect the shape and distance away from the object sought, as shown in Figure 12–4. This system coordination, vision and reach, and the higher level of integration that it implies, can be seen even in children who cannot successfully execute a reach or a grasp, such as a child with athetoid movements, hypertonicity, or even an arm in a cast or splint (see Fig 12–4). Again, the clinician should look at the *quality* of the behavior and the basis for it, even when the task accomplishment remains incomplete.

After 4 months of age, reach and grasp are now separate. These can be both visually initiated and visually controlled; the infant can and must make ongoing corrections of her efforts to attain something. Between *4 and 7 months,* visually directed corrective movements can be seen in patterns of grasp. These ongoing corrections are evident throughout, affecting both the direction and velocity of movement. This suggests error correcting movements at this age (Matthew and Cook, 1990). Only when she reaches the desired object in her field of vision will her hand open and a grasp be initiated.

The volitional reach at this time is two handed and symmetrical, at least at its start. The child "misses" and "overshoots," occasionally putting the object in the opposite, available hand. This lucky occurrence and the visual monitoring make success more likely.

Between *7 and 11 months* of age, diminishing dependency on bimanual reach can be demonstrated, and consistent single-hand reach becomes recognizable (Goldfield and Michel, 1986). The transfer of objects is an outgrowth of these midline activities (Fig 12–5). The interest and vigor in the infant's investment in the manipulation of objects at this age make it both easy and exciting for parents and clinicians to begin to be "hand watchers"!

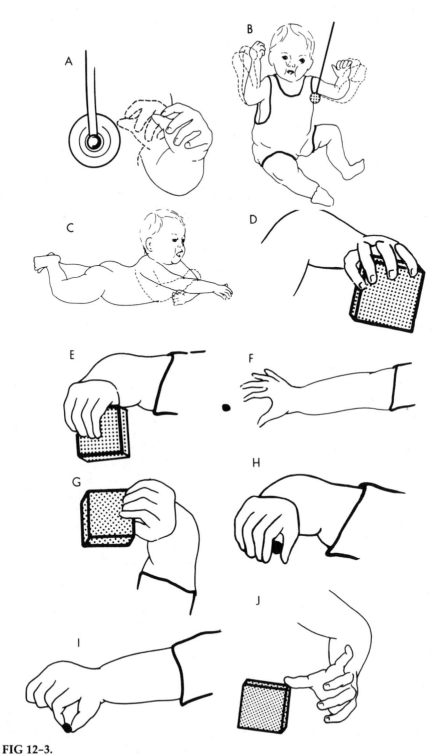

FIG 12–3.
Progression of reach and grasp. **A,** nondirected swiping, 1 month. **B,** swiping, about 4 months. **C,** corraling, about 4 months. **D,** ulnar-palmar grasp of cube, 4 to 5 months. **E,** radial-palmar grasp of cube, 6 to 7 months. **F,** raking of pellet, 6 to 7 months. **G,** radial-digital grasp of the cube, 7 to 8 months. **H,** scissors grasp of pellet, 7 to 9 months. **I,** pincer grasp of pellet, 9 to 10 months. **J,** voluntary release, 9 to 10 months.

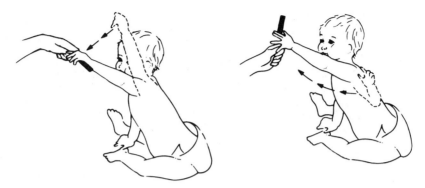

FIG 12–4.
The child anticipates shape of object. Reach is initiated with the hand in position to grasp the object.

INFLUENTIAL FACTORS

Several factors may influence reach-and-grasp behaviors, including distraction, past experience with particular objects, and temperament and general state of the child (e.g., sick, tired, or hungry). Characteristics such as texture, shape, thickness, and density of the object will also play a part. Objects with varying shapes, colors, and characteristics that can be perceived by the child have been shown to provoke the most manipulative behaviors by infants

FIG 12–5.
Transfer of objects from one hand to the other.

FIG 12–6.
Sitting steadily with hips abducted enables child to stretch to limits of play space and use vision effectively in going after objects of varying size and texture.

(Gramza, 1976) (Fig 12–6). As in other areas, moderate novelty elicits more activity on the child's part. Experience with reaching does facilitate more mature forms of reach and grasp in the short term, but there are no data on the long-term implications for this acceleration (Bower, 1977a). Overall, however, an environment filled with a variety of safe reachable objects is fuel for development in this area.

Populations of preterm infants without significant perinatal complications may show specific delays in visual activities even though other areas of development are normal (Vohr and Garcia-Coll, 1985). The lack of hand monitoring in this population due to shoulder girdle weakness and retraction may be at least part of the basis for this. The clinician should pay particular attention to visual motor coordination in this population. Assisting the infant in

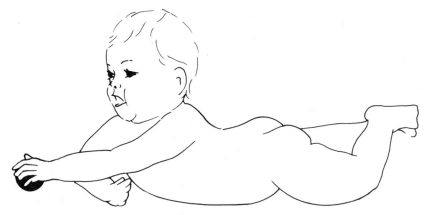

FIG 12–7.
Importance of the truncal stability of the prone posture is seen in situations when child is unwilling or unable to assume this posture. Reach and grasp are facilitated in prone position.

ways that bring the hands into her visual field may preclude these secondary deficits. Prone placement is *essential* to encourage visual-motor manipulations in this population, as well as in children taking a normal pathway. These positions are illustrated in Figure 12–7. Visual exploration with the truncal stability provided while the child is prone makes for a rich learning opportunity.

The preponderance of mouthing behavior in young children of and at objects should be expected as it is an integral part of the infant's exploration and should be seen in the context of reaching. There is no evidence of unsatisfied oral gratification as the basis for the child placing objects in the mouth or even demonstrating mouthing movements when a pleasing object is seen. As reaching and grasping skills mature, children learn to explore their world with increasing hand-to-mouth activity. Within limits of safety, it should be praised and encouraged. Feeding provides the optimal exercise for these emerging skills (Figs 12–8 and 12–9) but lack of food does not usually elicit these behaviors.

Children with asymmetry of reach or grasp in the first 4 months of life are more likely to have a peripheral nerve deficit (e.g., Erb's palsy). Central lesions (e.g., perinatal stroke) will be manifest between 4 and 6 months with increasing asymmetry of spontaneous arm and hand movement, exclusive use of one hand, or asymmetries in movement when the child is upset. This may be observed in free play and exaggerated when the child is crying. Failure to use both hands to pull a cloth off the face also adds to evidence of central dysfunction in this age range. By 6 months both hands should be used in this maneuver, with one predominating or leading as part of the early emergence of handedness.

HANDEDNESS

A child gradually comes to use one hand more frequently than the other; this hand is termed *dominant.* There are many ways to define dominance. A practical definition for the pediatric clinician, though somewhat arbitrary, is that the dominant hand is the hand used

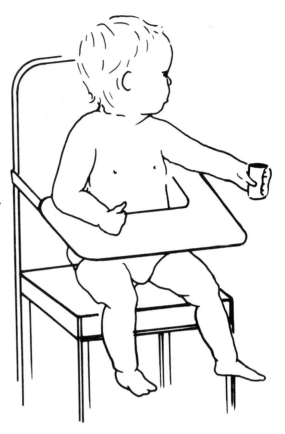

FIG 12–8.
Self-feeding is best initiated when sitting is steady, reach is unilateral, and grasp is at least scissor. The multiple sensory inputs in this situation and opportunities for exploration make it an exciting (although messy!) part of the day.

consistently to hold a spoon, stack blocks, write, and throw a ball. It may *not* be the strongest hand.

However, dominance appears to fluctuate in infancy although there is some suggestion that there may be subtle evidence of laterality even in the first year (Caplan and Kinsborne, 1976). Handedness in newborn infants may even be prefaced by laterality in other reflex patterns (Michel and Hawkins, 1986). Between 1 and $3\frac{1}{2}$ years of age, the dominant hand gradually emerges. Clear persistent dominance appearing in the first 15 months may indicate an impaired peripheral or central control of the other hand (Erhardt, 1982). During this period the other hand proceeds from mirroring the movements of the dominant hand to being passive during the other hand's actions. Normally, clear and consistent handedness is not fully established until 4 to 6 years of age (Mandell et al., 1984), when the majority of children are right-handed. This process is related to differential function maturation of the cerebral hemispheres (Benson and Gerschwind, 1968; Wang, 1980). About 10% to 12% of children will still not have established clear dominance of one hand by school entry.

Left-hand dominance is believed to represent the consequence of less distinct cerebral lateralization, particularly in children and adults who write overhand with the left hand. The

FIG 12–9.
Hands and mouth work together
to explore the world,
independent of hunger and
adequacy of the feeding
situation; this is to be
encouraged.

whole body participates in this laterality of function (e.g., eye, leg, arm, ear), but we focus on hand function because of its central importance in fine-motor functioning (Levy and Levy, 1978). A higher incidence of left-hand preference is seen in young children, with a progressive decrease to an adult rate of 10%. The concept of pathological left-handedness arising from the loss of effective dominant right-hand skill must be distinguished from natural left-hand preference. Early research indicates there is a strong genetic predisposition to dominance (Chamberlain, 1928). Only 2% of children of right-handed parents are left-handed, whereas 42% of children with left-handed parents are left-handed (Erhardt, 1982). To a much lesser degree, handedness is molded by the culture, such as the stigma of being left-handed that may inappropriately persuade parents and teachers to pressure children to use the right hand. There is no specific link between forced use of the nondominant hand and other developmental concerns such as stuttering.

The left-handed child of a right-hand dominant family pedigree warrants careful evaluation. A detailed neurological examination should be performed at school entry or earlier to look for subtle signs of asymmetry of tone and reflexes, the perseverance of mirroring activities, and small amounts of tremulousness and overshooting. Although the majority of these children may demonstrate normal neurodevelopmental skills, in a few, left-hand dominance may be an early clue to a mild central motor disability.

There are innumerable conflicting studies regarding the relationship of dominance to other aspects of development, including speech (especially stuttering), learning disabilities, and mental retardation. The role of hand preference in these conditions has probably been exaggerated in the past (Ayres, 1973; Cratty, 1979; Illingsworth, 1975; Ounsted et al., 1985). Hand preference should be placed in the global assessment of an individual child's health and development, not as a pathological indicator by itself.

PLAY: IMPLICATION FOR DEVELOPMENT

Toys become incorporated into the child's activity with increasing sophistication as reach and grasp mature. The central importance of self-initiated object play should receive emphasis at this time because play is the work of the child!

Play allows for the practice of newly acquired motor skills, used in a variety of circumstances with a range of objects, varying in size, texture, weight, temperature, and so forth. Cognitive functions are established through the *direct* manipulation of objects. An activity is repeated over and over again to experiment with the physical properties of the object. The type of spontaneous activity and the child's choice of toys often give clues to the function that is just at the edge of the child's development. For example, endless fascination with peekaboo tells us that the permanency of objects and people is a current issue. Putting blocks in a cup or pan means that the understanding of space is being discovered (Fig 12–10). This current child-initiated favorite provides valuable clues to cognitive development and is valuable data for current developmental status.

Play serves an *affective* function. Through interactions with toys and people with toys during play, children develop a sense of predictability, mastery, and control. Clinicians frequently observe the good feeling and pride of accomplishment on a toddler's face after successfully stacking several blocks. Play with parents nurtures attachment through shared activities, accomplishment, and shared joy. This is the milieu of language development. Play can also serve the useful function of exploring the child's feelings and experiences. For example, young children experiencing parental separation because of employment or trips may benefit from playing peekaboo or hide-and-seek. Therapeutic play techniques are especially effective for young children with insufficient verbal skills to convey intense feelings of fear, anger, or jealousy. These techniques provide an avenue for preparing even very young children for upsetting experiences such as medical procedures, hospitalization, and surgery. These same

FIG 12–10.
Active experimentation with objects serves the important cognitive work of play. Simple objects allow basic principles to be clear to young child.

situations may bring forth unresolved feelings around stressful events. The pediatric clinician, although not a play therapist, will benefit from a play session with a child, elucidating development and affective themes that may need further evaluation or intervention.

Adult involvement and responsiveness enhance both the quality and duration of a child's play (Chance, 1979). In addition, *mothers and fathers* play differently with their children. Mothers' play styles tend to be more conventional, using toys to stimulate the child's mental capacities and following the child's lead. Fathers, by contrast, engage their children in more physical and novel activities and games (Dixon et al., 1982; Parke, 1981). Some parents feel uncomfortable playing with their children and would benefit from being taught strategies and techniques to facilitate such interaction (Metzl, 1980). For other parents, it should be pointed out that it is not the absolute number or cost of the toys that determines their effectiveness but the way the adult introduces and uses them with the child. Enhancement of developmental potential, coupled with more self-confidence and initiative in the child, are the long-range benefits of parental behaviors such as positive play, nonrestrictiveness, nondirectiveness, descriptive speech, and contingent responses (Clarke-Stewart, 1973; Ramey et al., 1979). On the other hand, *overstimulation* by either intrusive parents or overwhelming and numerous toys can result in the child "tuning out" and disengaging from the activity and the person (Stern, 1977). It may, in fact, be that excessive stimulation by people or toys that becomes overwhelming is more disruptive to development than a sparse environment. Clinicians can practice important preventive mental health by suggesting that the child's needs rather than the parent's wishes determine the play environment, physical and social. Moderate novelty in an unpressured atmosphere to explore freely seems to be the element that most enhances the child's environment. The types of toys and activities are to be determined by the child's developmental level with moderate challenge and some room for innovation on the child's part. An environment that offers a few new experiences, events, people, and objects each day so that a child experiences manageable challenges is the aim. An active and curious response to the environment is testimony to the presence of those qualities. The prototype for this is laid down when the child's hands follow his eye and mind in active exploration beginning in the first year. The pediatric office reinforces the importance of play in a safe environment by having physical space and simple, safe toys available. The use of toys in examination settings further emphasize the developmental dimensions in play.

DEVELOPMENTAL TRENDS

Play should become more complex, more thematic, and have longer segments with time. If not, a problem exists (Garvey, 1977). The play of a developmentally delayed child or a depressed child tends to be slow, sparse, and locked into the particular specific characteristics of the toy or rigidity of use. The handicapped child will have a restricted repertoire of play. This lack of richness in play, what the child does spontaneously with toys, will often provide an additional clinical clue in the evaluation of a child with mental retardation, depression, visual, or language or cognitive handicaps. Clinicians will find that observations of spontaneous play in the office examining room will be an accurate and efficient source of data about a child that often provides more information than a structured neurological examination. Direct inquiries from parents and child care supervisors about a child's play will also add to these observations. Temperamental differences in a child's approach to play can be seen even in the first year—approach to toys, attention span, persistence, and intensity of involvement. To enhance their child's play, parents must recognize and enjoy these early differences and move with their child with increasing complexity of play.

BABY-PLAY ARREST

Some parents have difficulty accepting or responding in a changing way to the child's developmental progress and are reluctant to allow the child to play freely on the floor, in solitary toy play, or in social interactions built on toy play. These families are stuck in more infantilized play patterns. These children are often obese, because feeding is the only response parents offer to fussing behavior, not recognizing the need for novelty and active exploration. During an office visit, the clinician may demonstrate what the child can do with her hands; this experience may begin to effect change in the home interaction, moving the parents to a new level of care. Tolerance for mild levels of frustration in the child will allow the child to perform more elaborate exploration of toys. The basic issue is one of separation from the child to allow for this type of independent, child-initiated play. If this barrier is not breached at this time, the issue may reappear as a sleep problem or difficulty with discipline later. It may also signal a depressed or withdrawn mother who is unable to "let the baby go." Active intervention is needed early to prevent this failing cycle of interaction.

SUMMARY

The emergence of voluntary reach and grasp is the time to look at motor competency, visual-motor coordination, and the appropriateness of the environment in exploring the object world.

DATA GATHERING

WHAT TO ASK

The pediatric clinician should inquire if the infant is achieving developmental milestones for reach and grasp as indicated in Tables 12–1 and 12–2. For example, at 1 to 3 months, does the baby look at his hands a lot? At 4 months, does the baby swipe at objects in his visual space? At 5 months, can the baby reach for and hold onto toys? At 6 months, can the baby transfer an object from one hand to the other? At 7 to 9 months, does the baby feed crackers to himself? At 9 to 11 months, can the baby pick up a pea, raisin, or Cheerio between his thumb and forefinger?

Age-appropriate milestones as delineated in Table 12–3 can provide an assessment scale. The following questions should be asked: At 2 to 3 months, does she increase motor activity (wiggle) when looking at a novel object near her? At 4 months, does she bring her hands to the midline? At 6 months, does she rattle the paper on the examination table or grab her feet? At 7 months, does she explore and manipulate toys, such as hitting them on the table, banging two blocks together? At 10 to 11 months, does she hold a toy out to show you?

Ask if the baby is placed in a variety of positions throughout the day rather than predominantly supine with a monotonous view of the ceiling. Dangling objects in these upright

TABLE 12–3.
Reach Progression

Visual object pursuit	Birth
Arm/body activation (long latency)	2 wk–2 mo
Sustained hand regard	2–4 mo
Arm swipes, bilateral	2–3 mo
Alternating glances	2½–4 mo
Unilateral arm activity	3 mo
Reliable reach to midline	4 mo
Reach for object disappearing beyond visual field	4–5 mo
Unilateral reach	4–7 mo
Hand to hand transfer	5½–6 mo
Finger poke	8–10 mo
Plays midline games	8–12 mo
Visual anticipation of object shape	9–10 mo
Throwing objects	9–18 mo

postures encourage reaching. The child's hands should be free of clothing and restraints. Does the parent play with the infant on the floor?

When asking a parent to describe the child's play, listen for details about the *quality and complexity* of play to determine if it is age appropriate. Inquiry about the child's preferred type of activities and toys may prompt from some parents a vivid and rich description of the child's play. One may need to ask more specific questions with other families. Inquiring what are the child's *three favorite toys* will monitor the child's motor and cognitive skills.

The very inclusion of these questions into the clinical interview dramatizes the important role of play, and the child's exploration of the environment is emphasized. The parent receives the important message that play has significance. The parents' narrative about their child's play behavior helps the clinician screen for such problems as developmental delay, neurological problems, delayed social skills, autism, learning disabilities, and emotional disturbances.

OBSERVATION: WHAT TO OBSERVE

The child's spontaneous play can be observed by setting up the waiting area and the examination room with simple, durable toys, including blocks, cars, dolls, small balls, and books with familiar single pictures. Observe the following:

1. How does the parent play with the infant and facilitate the child's play with the toys?
2. How does the child use the hands and mouth in exploration?
3. What toys does the child choose?
4. Does the child persist with a toy or does the child appear distractible? Has this changed since the last encounter?
5. Does the child use both hands and arms equally? Are the movements smooth?

During the examination from birth through the third year, the examiner should present objects toward which the child can reach. Five objects are suggested: (1) dangling stethoscope; (2) 1-in. cubed blocks with up to six available—begin at 2 months; (3) a raisin or Cheerio— begin at 5 months; (4) a cup and spoon—at 9 months to 1 year; (5) unsharpened pencil or reflex hammer—begin at 4 months.

The raisin offers the child the opportunity to demonstrate fine-motor activity with increasing use of the fingers. The use of both hands equally during the course of this play should be seen. The unsharpened pencil or stick can be presented in the midline horizontally and then vertically to induce reach. The 4-month-old should have a bimanual reach and close the grasp if contact is made. The 6-month-old should anticipate the shape at the beginning of shoulder movement by shaping her hand to an accommodating posture. After 1 year, the child will readily transfer the pencil and will begin to direct it downward to write. By 5 years of age, a mature "writing" grasp of the pencil may be the single best predictor of adequate fine motor skills for school achievement. (The sequence of scribbles and drawings can then be followed to assess visual-motor coordination; sharpen the pencil.) Motor tone, strength and control in the trunk, shoulders, and extremities, and the child's posture should be noted throughout the course of the examination. The disappearance of the reflex grasp should be noted to follow the course outlined in Table 12–1.

The dangling stethoscope should elicit increasingly smooth tracking with activation of mouth, hands, arms, and lower extremities in the newborn period. Swiping should begin at 3 to 4 months of age. The reach should be reliable by 5 to 6 months of age, with both arms participating and the hands opening on contact. With one arm restrained, the child should reach across the midline. By 9 to 10 months of age, the reach should be quite unilateral, although mirroring will be common. Reaching across the midline may not be seen reliably until the second year of life. Movements should be increasingly smooth and there should be increasing use of the elbow and wrist.

A small block should be placed before the child on a surface while the child is sitting on the caretaker's lap. The grasp efforts should proceed as shown in Table 12–2. This activity can be done during the history taking. In the second year and beyond, this activity can move along the continuum of stacking blocks and building imagined structures.

Observe delays or abnormal patterns of the infant's fine-motor behavior. Persistence of primitive reflexes will interfere with the emergence of purposeful fine-motor skills.

In addition to observing laterality, observe what the other hand is doing. For example, at 7 months, is either hand equal in skill? At 10 to 11 months, is the other hand mirroring the active hand? At 12 to 13 months, is the other hand passive but fisted during a manipulation? At 4 to 6 years, is the other hand passive during a manipulation?

ANTICIPATORY GUIDANCE

PLAY ACTIVITIES

The child should be provided with a variety of safe materials to see, touch, and mouth. Parents can facilitate this through positioning the child in a variety of ways in different surroundings with a few simple, safe things to reach for. The office should model this.

When solid foods are introduced after 6 months, the child should be free to explore these herself with her hands. When pincer grasp appears, the child will participate in self-feeding and be effectively reaching for and consuming small soft pieces of cooked vegetables, dry cereal, rice, pasta, and cheese. Every room in the house should have some evidence of the child's work—a play place, her own magazines to tear up, a container of simple objects.

When a clinician has concern about the developmental course or behavioral characteristics about a child's play, referral to a specialist for diagnostic play evaluation or formal developmental testing is appropriate. If the child attends group day care, telephone contact with the teacher often provides a valuable source of information about the child's play behavior. Referral to a public health nurse or clinical nurse specialist may be helpful when there are concerns about the quality of the home environment as it affects development. A complete neurological examination has a higher yield in the child with these historical or observational concerns. Consideration of a primary depression, even in an infant or a young child, should be made when there is a paucity of spontaneous play. Signs of vegetative dysfunction (lethargy, anorexia, or hypersomnolence) are helpful in these circumstances. Children with chaotic, changing, or unresponsive environments are candidates for this kind of depression, presenting as sparse or infantilized play.

Asymmetry of reach or grasp should be taken very seriously because it may signal underlying neurological difficulty. Although subtle differences may be evident, persistent or worsening differences, particularly if they lead to atypical object play, must be investigated. Parents should provide ample opportunities for the child to use the "less mature" hand. However, if these differences persist for 1 to 2 months, further evaluation is indicated.

A former premature infant should be placed with forward shoulder support to allow for good visual monitoring of her hand activity. Prone positioning is particularly important in these groups even though it may take the child awhile to accept this position. Chest support will help this. When the child is seated, a towel under the thighs flexes the hips, thereby relaxing the trunk and facilitating hand movement.

STIMULATION PROGRAMS

Parents should be cautioned about infant stimulation programs that promise gains in development. No program can provide a curriculum that is any better than the baby's own drive to use newly emerging skills in productive ways. These programs perpetuate a feeling prevalent among some parents that they must teach their children developmental skills. This is the wrong perspective. Their role as the primary teachers for their child is one of facilitating the child's own efforts through careful observation and developing a safe environment for the child's exploration. Many "developmentally appropriate" toys are available for purchase, but they do not possess magical qualities in themselves. Good toys are simple, safe, and with bright colors (e.g., blocks and balls). They also leave room for the child's imagination. Excessive concern about stimulation equipment and programs should alert the clinician that these parents may be anxious about their child, feel incompetent as play companions and teachers to their child, cannot appreciate their own child's play needs, or have a distorted view as to what fuels a child's own development. The clinician needs to take these questions seriously, and the underlying parental issues require attention. There is no evidence to date that any of these infant stimulation programs have any long-term effect on development for normal children, provided primary caretakers can respond to their child's needs. Conversely, these programs may put undue pressure on children and families "to succeed." Clinicians can refocus that energy toward a facilitating role for an individual child in a child-directed, home-based program of exploration and discovery.

REFERENCES

Ayres A: Hand dominance and lateralization of cerebral function, in *Sensory Integration and Learning Disorders.* Los Angeles, Western Psychological Services, 1973.

Benson DF, Gerschwind N: Cerebral dominance and its disturbances. *Pediatr Clin North Am* 1968; 15:759–769.

Bower TGR: *The Perceptual World of the Child.* Cambridge, Mass, Harvard University Press, 1977a.

Bower TGR: *A Primer of Infant Development.* San Francisco, WH Freeman Co, 1977b.

Bower TGR: Object perceptions in infants. *Perception* 1972; 1:15–30.

Brunner JS: Organization of early skilled action. *Child Dev* 1973; 44:1–11.

Caplan PJ, Kinsborne M: Baby drops the rattle: Asymmetry of duration of grasp in infants. *Child Dev* 1976; 47:532–534.

Chamberlain HD: The inheritance of left-handedness. *J Hered* 1928; 19:557–559.

Chance P: *Learning Through Play.* Summary of Pediatric Round Table Series no 3. Skillman, NJ, Johnson & Johnson Baby Products Co, 1979, pp 32–33.

Chandler L: Gross and fine motor development, in Cohen M, Gross P (eds): *The Developmental Resource: Behavioral Sequences for Assessment and Program Planning.* New York, Grune & Stratton, 1979, vol 1.

Clarke-Stewart KA: Interactions between mothers and their young children: Characteristics and consequences. *Monogr Soc Res Child Dev* 1973; 38:1–109.

Connolly KJ, Elliott JM: Evolution and ontogeny of hand function, in Blurton-Jonas N (ed): *Ethological Studies of Child Behavior.* New York, Cambridge University Press, 1972, pp 329–383.

Cratty BS: Manipulative behaviors, in Cratty BS (ed): *Perceptual and Motor Development in Infants and Children,* ed 2. Englewood Cliffs, NJ, Prentice-Hall, 1979.

Dixon SD, LeVine RA, Richman A, et al: Mother-child interaction around a teaching task: An African-American comparison. *Child Dev* 1984; 55:1252–1264.

Erhardt RP: *Developmental Hand Dysfunction: Theory, Assessment and Treatment.* Baltimore, RAMSCO Publishing Co, 1982.

Garvey C: *Play.* Cambridge, Mass: Harvard University Press, 1977, p 79.

Goldfield EC, Michel GF: Spaciotemporal linkage in infant interlimb coordination. *Dev Psychobiol* 1986; 19:259–264.

Gramza AE: Response to the manipulability of a play dyad. *Psychol Rep* 1976; 38:1107–1110.

Illingworth RS: *The Development of the Infant and Young Child,* ed 6. New York, Churchill Livingstone, 1975.

Levy J, Levy JM: Human lateralization from head to foot: Sex-related factors. *Science* 1978; 200:1291–1292.

Loria C: Relationship of proximal and distal function in motor development. *Phys Ther* 1980; 2:167–172.

Mandell RJ, Nelson DL, Ceumak SA: Differential laterality of hand function in right-handed and left-handed boys. *Am J Occup Ther* 1984; 38:114–120.

Matthew A, Cook M: The control of reaching movements by young infants. *Child Dev* 1990; 61:1238–1257.

Metzl M: Teaching parents a strategy for enhancing infant development. *Child Dev* 1980; 51:583–586.

Michel GF, Hawkins DA: Postural and lateral asymmetries in the ontogeny of handedness during infancy. *Dev Psychobiol* 1986; 19:247–258.

Ounsted M, Cockburn J, Moar V: Hand preference: Its provenance, development and associations with intellectual ability at the age of 7.5 years. *Dev Behav Pediatr* 1985; 6:76–80.

Parke RD: *Fathers.* Cambridge, Mass, Harvard University Press, 1981, p 37–41.

Ramey C, Farran D, Campbell F: Predicting IQ from mother-infant interaction. *Child Dev* 1979; 50:804–814.

Stern D: *The First Relationship: Infants and Mothers.* Cambridge, Mass, Harvard University Press, 1977.

Twitchell TE: The automatic grasping responses of infants. *Neuropsychologia* 1955; 3:247–259.

von Hofstein C: Eye-hand coordination in the newborn. *Dev Psychol* 1982; 18:450–461.

Wang PL: Interaction between handedness and cerebral functional dominance. *Int J Neurosci* 1980; 11:35–40.

White B, Held R: Plasticity of sensorimotor development in the human infant, in Rosenblath JF, Illingsworth W (eds): *The Causes of Behavior: Readings in Child Development and Educational Psychology.* Boston, Allyn & Bacon, 1966.

ADDITIONAL READINGS

Bayley N: *Bayley Scales of Infant Development.* New York, Psychological Corp, 1969.

Bee H, Barnard K, Eyres S, et al: Prediction of IQ and language skill from perinatal status, child performance, family characteristics, and maternal-infant interaction. *Child Dev* 1982; 53:1134–1156.

Brazelton TB: *Neonatal Behavioral Assessment Scale: Clinics in Developmental Medicine,* no 50. Philadelphia, JB Lippincott Co, 1973.

Collard R: Exploratory and play behaviors of infants reared in an institution and in lower- and middle-class homes. *Child Dev* 1971; 42:1003–1015.

Coons C, Frankenburg W, Garvet P, et al: Home screening questionnaire, in Frankenburg WF (ed): *Developmental Screening.* Denver, University of Colorado Medical Center, 1977.

Cratty BS: Gross motor attributes in early childhood, in Cratty BS (ed): *Perceptual and Motor Development in Infants and Children,* ed 2. Englewood Cliffs, NJ, Prentice-Hall Inc, 1979.

Dixon S, Yogman M, Tronick E, et al: Early infant social interaction with parents and strangers. *J Am Acad Child Psychiatry* 1981; 20:32–52.

Dodwell DC, Muir D, DeFranco D: Responses of infants to visually presented objects. *Science* 1976; 194:209–211.

Dunn J, Wooding C: Play in the home and its implications for learning, in Tizard B, Harvey D (eds): *Biology of Play.* Philadelphia, JB Lippincott, 1977, p 55.

Erhardt RP: Sequential levels in development of prehension. *Am J Occup Ther* 1974; 28:592–596.

Farran D, Ramey C: Social class differences in dyadic involvement during infancy. *Child Dev* 1980; 51:254–257.

Field J: Coordination of vision and prehension in young infants. *Child Dev* 1977; 48:97–103.

Gesell A: The ontogenesis of infant behavior, in Carmichael L (ed): *Manual of Child Psychology.* New York, John Wiley & Sons, 1954.

Gesell A, Amatruda CS: *Developmental Diagnosis.* New York, Harper & Row Publishers, 1969.

Illingworth RS: *Basic Developmental Screening: 0–4 Years,* ed 3. Boston, Blackwell Scientific Publications, 1982.

Knobloch H, Stevens F, Malone A: *Manual of Developmental Diagnosis: The Administration and Interpretation of the Revised Gesell and Amatruda Developmental and Neurologic Examination.* New York, Harper & Row Publishers, 1980.

Piaget J: *The Origins of Intelligence in Children.* New York, International Universities Press, 1952, pp 103–107.

Pollock SL: The grasp response in the neonate. *Arch Neurol* 1960; 5:574–581.

Rubin K, Maiono T, Hornung M: Free play behaviors in middle- and lower-class preschoolers: Parten and Piaget revisited. *Child Dev* 1976; 47:414–419.

Tulkin SR, Kagan J: Mother-child interaction in the first year of life. *Child Dev* 1972; 43:31–42.

Uzgiris IC: Normality in the development of schemas for relating to objects, in Hellmuth J (ed): *Exceptional Infant,* Washington, Special Child Publications, 1967, vol. 1.

Vohr BR, Garcia-Coll CT: Neurodevelopmental and school performance of very low-birth-weight infants: A seven-year longitudinal study. *Pediatrics* 1985; 76:345–350.

Volpe JJ: *Neurology of the Newborn.* Philadelphia, WB Saunders Co, 1981.

White BL, Castle D, Held R: Observations on the development of visually-directed reaching. *Child Dev* 1964; 35:349–364.

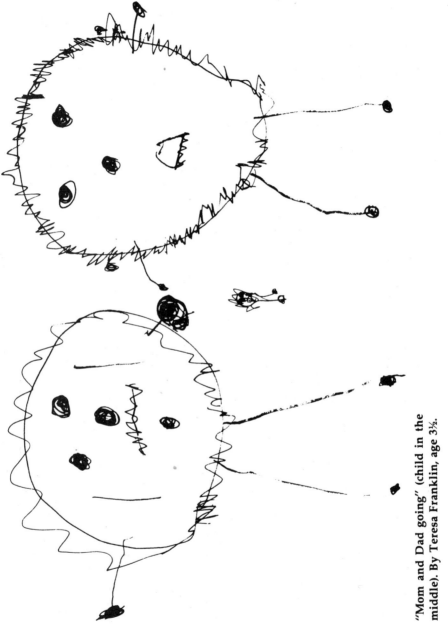

"Mom and Dad going" (child in the middle). By Teresa Franklin, age 3½.

CHAPTER **13**

Seven to Eight Months: Separation and Strangers

PAMELA KAISER, M.N., C.P.N.P.

SUZANNE D. DIXON, M.D.

KEY WORDS

STRANGER ANXIETY
TRANSITIONAL OBJECTS
NIGHT WAKENING
SEPARATION RESPONSE
ATTACHMENT

Katy, an 8-month-old, comes in for suture removal from her forehead. She had fallen out of her highchair during a struggle to get her locked in. She screams and digs into her mother at your approach. Her mother says she just started these "tantrums" and is worried that this injury has made her fearful. She says that even Katy's grandmother cannot take her without protest anymore, and she is waking up crying at night. She believes all of this "bad behavior" was caused by the laceration. Mother says she will just step out quietly while you remove the sutures, because Katy cries even more when she is in the room. Besides, she is really tired, because she has been up three to four times at night with Katy, who has just started awakening again.

The landmark of social development described by Rene Spitz (1946) as "stranger anxiety" is reached after the midpoint of the first year. This event often raises concerns about the infant's relationship with parents and other caregivers. For stranger anxiety to be appreciated in its positive and fullest sense, the infant's response to strangers and parents should be seen in a broader context of social and cognitive maturation. The exclusive bond between parent and child must expand to include others, and yet the stranger now becomes frightening and separations appear stressful. This confusing behavior needs some explanation.

STRANGER RESPONSES

The child has been sensitive to the differences between parents and strangers since his earliest weeks (see Chapter 9) and has shown real preference for the company and games of his parents and other predictable adults (see Chapter 10). This continuum of development makes a quantum change in the second half of the first year. Fear of being touched or picked

183

up when approached by a stranger occurs earlier and elicits more discomfort than fear on sight alone. Fear reactions such as wariness and withdrawal on encounter with a stranger begin to occur between 3 and 9 months of age (Bowlby, 1969b). At this time a more apparent and overtly negative reaction known as *stranger awareness* begins to appear (Tennes and Lampl, 1964). The emergence of stranger anxiety should be viewed as a new stage of both affective and cognitive growth. It reflects the infant's perceptual awareness of unfamiliar persons and novel social interactions (Batter and Davidson, 1979, Bronson, 1972). Familiar care providers are treated as safe sources of comfort in a now clearly unknown land.

The quality of the reaction to strangers is influenced by the infant's developmental age, temperament, presence of illness or fatigue, the stranger's demeanor, and the presence or absence of familiar figures. Conditions that heighten the fear response are unfamiliar surroundings (e.g., an examining room), active approach by the stranger (e.g., moving in quickly to examine the child), close proximity to the stranger, and eye-to-eye contact. In addition, the response to the stranger is more dramatic when the mother is present but not in physical contact with the infant (e.g., mother in chair and child on examining table). Factors that lessen the fearful behavior include a position close to or in contact with the mother or father (Ross and Goldman, 1977), familiarization time in a new setting (Sroufe et al., 1977), and a stranger who approaches with toys and whose behavior is responsive to the infant's cues (Stevenson, 1965). Children who are exposed to many adults during infancy usually have less dramatic response to strangers. Strangers who are similar to the parents in their responses to the child will elicit less anxiety than those who are different, no matter how "good" (i.e., sensitive) they are with children in general. Other children elicit less anxiety than adults in children more than 1 year of age, although the erratic behavior of a toddler may frighten, as well as delight, an infant.

Individual infant temperament modifies the response. Some children sail through this period with a mild behavior change over a short period of time. Other children have predictable and dramatic fear responses that continue full blown until the end of the second year. Dramatic negative responses are not the result of bad experiences in the past or lack of love in the regular environment. These infants are likely to be shy, sensitive, and somewhat slow to warm up. Transitions in people and events may require additional time in these children.

Cross-cultural investigations suggest that infants of all groups studied had the onset and the first peak of stranger anxiety at about 8 months of age. However, in cultures where infants are regularly exposed to many caregivers, the response was less intense, was more easily overcome with a familiarization time, and lasted for a shorter period of time into the second year. In all cultures studied, even those described as "polymatric" (many mothers), the strongest protests came with separation from birth mothers.

THE BASIS FOR STRANGER ANXIETY

The infant can now imagine parents in their absence as a result of the development of the capacity for *object permanence*—the ability to remember an object even when it is not present (Piaget, 1952). A mental image of a parent can at this age be called up even after a separation. The timing of this new development is influenced by the quality of the relationship; an infant with a dysfunctional relationship with her mother develops object permanency for people much later than an infant whose mother has been consistent, contingent, and affectionate (Goin-DeCarie, 1974). The infant's cognitive capacity at this age does not allow her to keep any concept of return in mind (Willemsen, 1979), so every separation is perceived as endless. Over time, with repeated ritualized leave takings and increasing cognitive capacities, she begins to find some relief in her anxious state when a significant person leaves. At 8 months, she has no way to understand that her parent will return; by 18 months, further cognitive capacities allow for additional coping skills.

The signs and rituals of leave taking by a valued adult are linked in the infant's mind so that separation can be anticipated and anxiety builds before the separation (Bowlby, 1969b). The anxiety does not have as its source the anticipation that the child's needs will not be met. Rather, the anxiety is generated at the anticipated or actual separation from a person who has been socially attentive and responsive to the emotional needs of the child. The child is anxious because of separation from a person on whom she has relied to orchestrate her life. This behavior is evidence of an attachment that is held together by needs others than just vegetative ones. Eventually it is the appearance of these same rituals that will help build the skills to anticipate return.

As new motor competencies are discovered and practiced, the child can now move away from a parent by crawling and eventually walking. This can be alarming when previously proximity to the parent was predictable. Mahler et al. (1975) called this new emotion *hatching,* which refers to the realization that the child is separate from her mother, that the mother can leave or the child can leave, and that proximity is not a guarantee during exploratory maneuvers. The drive for mastery and discovery are tempered by the realization that one increases one's distance from the familiar providers.

A child may also become anxious because she is unable to communicate adequately with an unfamiliar adult. She has learned that her needs and desires are conveyed to her familiar caregivers; unfamiliar adults may not recognize the intent of her actions. When separated from their parents, some infants seem to experience themselves in a foreign land where no one speaks their "language."

Another peak of stranger anxiety often occurs at 18 to 20 months of age. This is usually before the development of real language competency. The toddler relies heavily on the nonverbal communication patterns established with her parents. Strangers are not immediately a part of this individualized communication network. The emotional state of this second peak of stranger anxiety has been called *rapprochement* (Mahler et al., 1975). It is observed when the previously secure toddler intermittently checks in with a parent, either running back to a secure base or visually making contact across a room. This resurgence of stranger anxiety at 18 months diminishes gradually as the child's mastery of communication skills reaches a level at which she can communicate with anyone (Bower, 1977).

By $2\frac{1}{2}$ to 3 years of age, the child begins to show decreased distress and increased friendliness with strangers (Maccoby, 1980). This process of socialization and independence is gradual. As the preschool child explores new people and objects, she continues initially to draw closer to her mother and plays less when encountering strangers. Children who are well attached to their primary caregivers use them as bases to venture out in ever-widening circles of exploration; children who are poorly attached to the caregivers do not venture out as readily because they lack that secure attachment (Ainsworth, 1967).

THE WIDENING SOCIAL WORLD: MANAGEMENT OF SEPARATION ISSUES

The opportunity to interact with adults outside the immediate family offers the infant new perspectives. She learns about other people and herself through these social interactions. Her world is richer because of what others can bring to it. Friends, relatives, and other children add vitality to a child's life. The child needs sensitive caregivers, in addition to her parents, to provide that rich experience. The child learns that other adults can be trusted and enjoyed. This is not to replace the parents from their central position but to expand the horizons. The presence of others in the child's life does not dilute the child's bond to her parents.

Alternative caregivers (grandparents, babysitters, etc.) can be introduced in such a way as to support the child's efforts at social expansion without unduly stressing the child. A time of familiarization with the new caretaker, maintaining regular routines and place (if possible), and the initiation of leave-taking routines all make brief separation easier. The most important element, however, is an unambivalent attitude in parents. Parents must be comfortable with the separation before the child can be because she takes her cues from them. Separations that are unplanned, prolonged, or accompanied by exposure to a caregiver who cannot meet the child's needs for consistency and contingency should be avoided at any age, but particularly when these are the dominant developmental issues from about 6 to 18 months. Family vacations, visitation schedules, change of placement, business needs, and career decision must take these needs into account in balancing the priorities in a family.

Bowlby (1969a) has described three phases of response to separations. The first is the familiar *protest*, or screaming, stage evident immediately on separation from the familiar caregiver in the last half of the first year. In the second stage, with prolonged or repeated separations, the child becomes *apathetic*, withdrawn, and sad. Vegetative symptoms of infantile depression, such as increased sleep, poor feeding, weight loss, and developmental regressions, occur. Very prolonged separations produce *detachment*—the indiscriminate social response of the child who is attached to everyone and to no one. Long hospitalizations without the active presence of familiar care providers and situations of neglect may produce this pattern of response to separation.

Long-term studies of poor attachment suggest that there are continuing difficulties with social relationships, personality problems, and delinquency. However, it is difficult to attribute these population findings to lack of "mothering" or the adverse conditions that tend to surround these conditions (Rutter, 1979). Separations, strangers, and mild stresses are part of life; they are opportunities for growth through widening social experience, the development of coping strategies, and the reenergization of parents. The clinician can identify the child's perspective by participating in discussion of family management decisions. The clinician thus serves as the child's advocate by promoting the expansion of the social experiences and lessening any detrimental impact of prolonged separation. This advocacy extends to the cases of foster or adoptive children and those in custody battles and other situations where there are proposed shifts in the primary caregiver or caregivers. This period of life when the establishment of "basic trust" (Erickson, 1977) requires a solid foundation, when stranger anxiety is so prominent, and when attachments are established must be protected from excess and unnecessary separation stress.

Leave takings should be brief, affectionate, and accompanied by a clear statement of return, even for the child who does not understand words or time. These patterns should be clearly established in infancy and maintained over early childhood. Parents should never sneak out, lie about a return time, or promise gifts for each leave taking. Trust is violated, and brief separations are seen as either a punishment or an extraordinary event. Separations that are brief are a regular part of family life and healthy for all concerned. The primary care clinician, who is in a position to observe these behaviors over time, will be concerned if the child's responses are at the far extreme of expected (e.g., no differential response to strangers at any time or severe, sustained anxiety toward strangers that does not change after 18 months). The child's current caretaking environment and medical, developmental, and social history should be explored if such responses are present. Prolonged or traumatic separations fuel excessive anxiety to the appearance of a stranger. Poor attachment to primary caregivers leads to the indiscriminate response. Parental anxiety during separation experiences heighten the child's own response, and this may highlight a "vulnerable child syndrome" (Green and Solnit, 1964) or generalized difficulties with separation.

TRANSITIONAL OBJECTS

Winnecott (1958) and Bowlby (1969a) have pointed out that a young child's attachment to a cuddly object, which they called the transitional object, is consistent with the developmental process of forming relationships. These first treasured possessions are "frequently capable of filling the role of an important, though subsidiary, attachment 'figure'" when the person is not there. The object is a substitute that is sought especially when the child is hungry, tired, or distressed, just as the parent is sought. They stand for the absent parent. Transitional objects are effectively used by children to shut out environmental stimuli and to calm themselves when upset. Supporting this view, Brazelton regards the child's use of transitional objects as representing "a crutch for the transition from dependence on mother to independence" (Brazelton, 1969). The selection of a special object may occur as early as 7 to 8 months but usually occurs between 1 and 2 years of age (Stevenson, 1965). Two thirds of children in the United States have a transitional object; other cultural groups have a lower rate (Lozoff et al, 1985), perhaps because the cultural drive for and value of independence is less. This object may take many forms—a blanket, a doll, toy, or piece of the child's clothing. Although most children discard the transitional object as they approach 3 or 4 years of age when the separation process is more complete, some children retain these attachments into their school years without evidence of psychopathology (Sherman et al., 1981).

Some parents may perceive the ever-present cuddly object as a weakness rather than a strength. Embarrassment may develop as they may view it as a negative reflection on their parenting or the child's ability to cope. Parents and the child may also receive pressure from extended family or child-care providers. The child's clinician can help parents appreciate their child's resourcefulness and emerging independence, which are expressed through the developmental transitional object.

Firstborn children use transitional objects more frequently. Some studies suggest that developmentally precocious children more frequently use transitional objects. These objects have their own lifetime of usefulness in the adaptation from infancy to childhood.

SLEEP AS A SEPARATION

Sleep represents a separation experience from parents in contemporary American society. We value independence and autonomy, and we usually associate nighttime with personal space for self and spouse. The night wakening that often occurs at 8 months is a violation of that expectation. Parents may feel that this is a regression to an earlier time rather than a manifestation of a new developmental stage. The child comes to wakefulness regularly at this age as she has always done, but now she can imagine the missing parent and makes bids for attention. As autonomy becomes an important daytime theme, it is often balanced by increasing dependency at night with accompanying bids for comfort and interaction.

The transitional objects can help the child through this minor nightly stress. Simple verbal and tactile reassurances, a night light, or a transitional object are supportive measures a parent can provide (Zuckerman and Blitzer, 1981). The goal is to allay anxiety while supporting the child's own efforts to go back to sleep. Too vigorous an intervention just further awakens the child, making it all the more difficult to settle. There is no evidence that bringing a child into the parents' bed is either uncommon or leads to disturbance (Lozoff et al., 1984). If the sleeping issue continues to be seen as a problem, the clinician must consider whether the *parent* may have difficulty separating from the child at night and be unable to allow the infant to settle herself back to sleep. For single parents, working parents, or parents who harbor unfounded fears regarding the child, the separation of sleep may be just too stressful in the face of their own need to stay close. The night wakening is perceived as a bid for closeness and help rather than a manifestation of growth. These parents cannot let the child solve this issue on her own. The motivations and emotional needs of the parents must be addressed openly if night wakening is frequent and problematic. Temperamental issues in the child and particular cultural or family issues may also be the source of barriers to achieve uninterrupted sleep.

DATA GATHERING

OBSERVATION

At the beginning of the office visit when the infant is 6 to 9 months old, on entering the examination room, you may observe either a wary expression on the child's face or a sobering infant. Observe the child's *social distance*—the limits of proximity that the child allows you before showing signs of distress. This "extra data" is obtained without special effort, merely the systematic observation of the child as you begin your encounter. The parent's response to the child's distress will reveal the interactive style of the mother or father. Are the child's needs for comfort easily met (e.g., during the physical examination, when weighing the child, or at the time of an immunization)?

Some infants at this age will accept the examiner's presence and manipulations during the physical examination without fuss. If so, is this response typical of the child's temperament at home? Does the child appear depressed, or is this an infant who has not, as yet, developed an affective response to strangers? Be aware of the signs of infantile depression in children who have experienced prolonged or particularly stressful situations.

HISTORY TAKING

How does she respond when she sees new people? Has she begun to be a bit wary of people she sees infrequently? How do you feel when she behaves this way? If she cries vigorously at these encounters, how do you respond?

Does she have a "lovey"—a special toy or object? Ask if the parent notes any pattern to the child's associated behaviors when she wants the object (e.g., fatigue, hunger, stress). How do you feel about the use of the object?

At this office visit or earlier, the mother's activities outside the home should be discussed in terms of their impact on the child. Is the child left with a regular care provider? What is the leave-taking routine? Is the baby's response different now than before? What helps the baby with these transitions?

ANTICIPATORY GUIDANCE

- The cognitive basis for emerging stranger anxiety should be clearly explained. This puts it in a positive normative framework.
- Children should never be forced to show affection for a new person if they are distressed. This protest behavior must be seen as developmentally based and protective.
- Leave-taking rituals should be well established by this time. The routine helps children to cope with separations. This includes sleep.
- When moving from room to room, parents should keep voice contact with children and reappear regularly.
- Baby-sitters should be introduced while the child is in the parent's arms, should approach slowly, and should give the child a chance to know them.
- Parents should never sneak away or go out after the child is asleep, if possible. The child's protest should be expected and tolerated rather than violating the child's basic trust.
- Discuss separation issues as parents plan trips, vacations, and other separations. Discuss what can be done to support the child at times of necessary separations.
- Avoid changes in placement or custody between 6 and 18 months if at all possible.
- Avoid hospitalizations, if possible, during this time.
- If a child needs a medical procedure, encourage the parent to stay with the child. The child may cry *more,* but the stress of the situation will be less. Decreased crying is not necessarily the desired endpoint.
- Suggest the sharing of the infant's care with other adults if no other adults are regularly in the family. The child needs to be introduced to friendly strangers as opportunities for growth.
- After a separation, hold the child close until *she* signals she is ready to play or move away.
- Discuss the night wakenings often seen at this age. Discuss management through allowing the child opportunity to get back to sleep. Avoid overfatigue.
- Establish falling asleep rituals that can be replicated by the child when she awakens. Do not put a child fully to sleep by holding unless you are prepared to do that all night long.

- Suggest support in choosing a transitional object for the child or family who is having trouble with these separations.
- Beware of the chronically ill child who "likes everybody" in the hospital or the foster child who goes too easily to your arms. These children may have a serious derangement in attachment and may need extensive remedial work.

REFERENCES

Ainsworth MDS: *Infancy in Uganda: Infant Care and the Growth of Attachment.* Baltimore, Johns Hopkins Press, 1967.

Batter B, Davidson C: Wariness of strangers: Reality or artifact? *Child Psychol Psychiatry* 1979; 20:93–109.

Bower TGR: *A Primer of Infant Development.* San Francisco, WH Freeman & Co, 1977, p 61.

Bowlby J: *Attachment.* New York, Basic Books, 1969a, vol 1.

Bowlby J: *Separation: Anxiety and Anger.* New York, Basic Books, 1969b.

Brazelton TB: *Infants and Mothers.* New York, Dell, 1969.

Bremer JG: *Infancy.* New York, Basil Blackwell, 1988.

Bronson G: Infants' reactions to unfamiliar persons and novel objects. *Monogr Soc Res Child Dev* 1972; 37:148.

Goin-DeCarie T: *The Infant's Reaction to Strangers.* New York, International Universities Press, 1974.

Green M, Solnit AJ: Reactions to the threatened loss of a child: A vulnerable child syndrome. *Pediatrics* 1964; 34:58.

Lozoff B, Paludetto R, Lotz S: Transitional object use in the United States, Japan and Italy. Paper presented to the Ambulatory Pediatric Association, Carmel, Calif, 1985.

Lozoff B, Wolf A, Davis N: Cosleeping in urban families with young children in the United States. *Pediatrics* 1984; 74:171–182.

Maccoby EE: *Social Development: Psychological Growth and the Parent-Child Relationship.* New York, Harcourt Brace Jovanovich, 1980.

Mahler M, Pine F, Bergman A: *The Psychological Birth of the Human Infant: Symbiosis and Individuation.* New York, Basic Books, 1975.

Piaget J: *The Origins of Intelligence in Children* (1952), Cook M (trans). New York, WW Norton Co, 1963.

Ross HD, Goldman BD: Infants' sociability toward strangers. *Child Dev* 1977; 48:638–642.

Rutter M: Separation experiences: A new look at an old topic. *J Pediatr* 1979; 95:147–154.

Sherman M, Hertzig M, Austrian R, et al: Treasured objects in school aged children. *Pediatrics* 1981; 68:379–386.

Spitz RA: The smiling response. *Genet Psychol Monogr* 1946; 34:57–125.

Sroufe A, Waters E, Matts L: Contextual determinants of infants' affectional response, in Lewis M, Rosenblum L: *Origins of Fear.* New York, John Wiley & Sons, 1977.

Stevenson HW: Social reinforcement of children's behavior, in Lipsett LP, Spiker CC (eds): *Advances in Child Development and Behavior.* New York, Academic Press, 1965, vol 2.

Tennes KH, Lampl EE: Stranger and separation anxiety in infants. *J Nerv Ment Dis* 1964; 139:247–254.

Willemsen E: *Understanding Infancy.* San Francisco, WH Freeman & Co, 1979.

Winnecott DW: Transitional objects and transitional phenomena, in *Collected Papers: Through Pediatrics and Psychoanalysis.* London, Tavistock Publications, 1958.

Zuckerman B, Blitzer E: Sleep disorders, in Gabel S (ed): *Behavioral Problems in Childhood: A Primary Care Approach.* New York, Grune & Stratton, 1981.

ADDITIONAL READINGS

Brazelton TB; *On Becoming a Family: The Growth of Attachment.* New York, Delacourt Press, 1981.
Brazelton TB: *Working and Caring.* Reading, Mass, Addison-Wesley Publishing Co, 1985.
Clarke-Stewart A: *Daycare.* Cambridge, Mass, Harvard University Press, 1982.
Doyl AB: Infant development in day care. *Dev Psychol* 1975; 11:655.
Dunn J: Distress and comfort, in Bruner J, Cole M, Lloyd B (eds): *The Developing Child Series.* Cambridge, Mass, Harvard University Press, 1977.
Kagan J, Kearsley R, Zelazo R: *Infancy.* Cambridge, Mass, Harvard University Press, 1978.
Morgan GA, Ricciuti HN: Infants' responses to strangers during the first year, in Foss BM (ed): *Determinants of Infant Behavior.* New York, Barnes & Noble, 1969, vol 4.
Moskowitz D, Schwartz JC, Corsini DA: Initiating daycare at 3 years of age: Effects on attachment. *Child Dev* 1977; 48:1271–1276.
Scarr S: *Mother Care: Other Care.* New York, Basic Books, 1984.

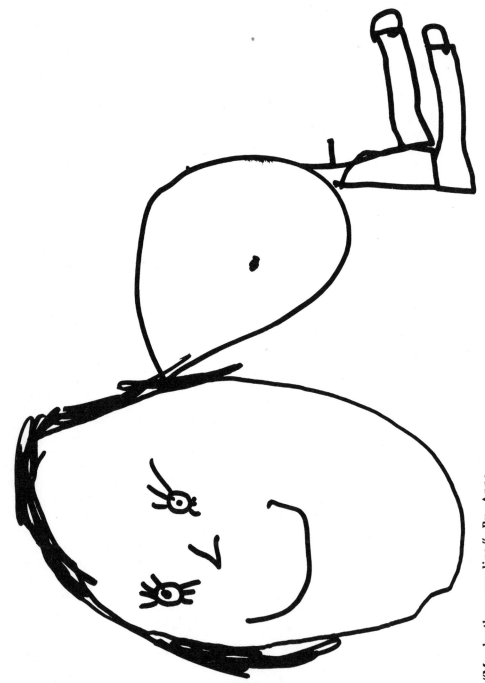

"My brother crawling." By Anne Atkinson, age 5½.

CHAPTER **14**

Nine to Ten Months: Active Exploration in a Safe Environment

PAMELA KAISER, M.N., C.P.N.P.
SUZANNE D. DIXON, M.D.

KEY WORDS

SAFETY
CHILDPROOFING
FEEDING
COGNITIVE DEVELOPMENT IN INFANCY
INFANT STIMULATION
INTERVENTION

Becky Jones, a 9-month-old obese child, was brought to the emergency room by her frantic mother. The child had a small scald burn to her left forearm and a large "goose egg" on her forehead but appeared alert as she whimpered in her mother's arms. Mrs. Jones said her daughter had pulled over the coffee pot, spilling coffee on herself. Mrs. Jones said she did not even know that she could go that far, because she really had not been crawling until recently. Becky sat quietly at her mother's feet, playing with some papers from the desk while her mother got out some tissues. Your office notes say Becky was in last week, was noted to be anemic, and was drinking 48 oz of formula each day. You counseled more solids and gave an iron preparation. She had always been a quiet baby who slept long hours and ate well. Mrs. Jones had said that the baby does not like solids but that she would try to offer them again.

The energy of the 9-month-old makes this an exciting time. The child learns about the world in a more active mode than ever before through increases in mobility and with improved use of her hands. The parents' work is to shape the environment in such a way as to enhance the child's sense of mastery and willingness to explore. The clinician will learn more about the child and family at this time by devoting a large part of the visit to a play session to watch these processes unfold on line and by taking a focused history.

LEARNING THROUGH DOING: COGNITIVE DEVELOPMENT IN THE FIRST TWO YEARS OF LIFE

With increased mobility and facility with reach and grasp, the child has new capacities to learn about the world. During this sensorimotor period described by Piaget (1952), the

193

TABLE 14-1.
Stages in Cognitive Development

Stage	Approximate Age (mo)	Basic Issue	Examples of Behavior
1	0–1	Expansion of reflexes	Learns how to breast or bottle-feed, coordinates body position
2	1–4	Expansion of reflexes; repeats actions that have pleasurable outcome	Sucks on hand to quiet self; quiets to mother's voice; gets excited with bath water sounds
3	4–10	Making things happen	Bats repeatedly at mobile; squeals to get attention; finds a hidden object
4	10–13	Old behaviors in new situations: the experimenter	Crumples paper; follows a disappearing ball; puts things inside other things
5	13–18	New behaviors in new situations	Looks for mechanism in wind up toy; Follows the hidden object through several displacements
6	18–24	New strategies without rehearsal	Looks for a dog on hearing a bark; walks through a cylinder on seeing it

child learns about her world through direct perception and action on the environment. Basic concepts about the material world and people are acquired through active experimentation in a predictable sequence of stages. All children throughout the world appear to go through these stages in their self-generated efforts to order their experience of the world around them. The rate of progress in each area may vary from child to child but not the sequence in acquisition of skills. The development of one or several processes may proceed at a faster rate in one child than in another, but the sequence and the endpoint remain the same. Each stage allows the child to perceive and act on the world around her in different ways. New capacities in understanding the permanency of objects, the concept of causes for observable events, and an appreciation of the play possibilities of three-dimensional space make the last half of the first year an exciting time in cognitive growth for the child and an enriching, insightful time for parents as they focus on these activities.

The child learns through an active process of ordering experiences. Passive infusion of information by parents or verbal instructions of any length are not useful. Parents support cognitive growth at this age by allowing the child to experiment with simple daily objects and toys in an environment that is stimulating and developmentally appropriate. Specific observations that the clinician can make with simple objects in the office or by a focused history are listed in Table 14-1.

STIMULATION VERSUS INTERVENTION

The nature of learning in early childhood has strong implications for the way in which we support development in children. For those with deficits or barriers, as well as those without, the approach is the same. A sensitive caregiver—parent, teacher, nurse, daycare provider, or therapist—will note a child's own developmental level. This may be subconscious or through review of explicit assessments. Then activities are set out *with* the child that capture newly emerging skills and concepts. Efforts are made to direct and sustain attention and to change the activity when interest drifts. Activities of *moderate* novelty will elicit most attention and learning throughout childhood. Interesting, but not overwhelming, situations elicit the most learning. When a task is mastered, the child is allowed to repeat the task ad lib (wallow in success) to get a sense of inner competency. Then the task may be changed slightly to reinfuse novelty, such as more objects or a new container placed further away; play is changed when no further interest is evident or the child withdraws behavior. Positive reinforcement is gained primarily by success with the task but is strengthened by praise and interactional excitement of the caregiver. Children put the most interest and energy into these newly emerging skills. Spontaneous play always gives a clue as to the developmental edge of the child's competency.

Children presented with tasks below their developmental level will show boredom by moving away, changing the task (e.g., throwing the blocks), or changing the agenda (e.g., poking the caregiver in the nose). School-aged children have more elaborate strategies to signal boredom. Tasks that are too overwhelming (e.g., a jack-in-the-box with a loud pop), too menacing (e.g., an object looming toward your face), or just plain too difficult will elicit avoidance behaviors as well.

Intervention for both the normal and special needs child means finding that zone of moderate challenge and setting up opportunities for the child to teach herself through active exploration. This calls for full participation by the child. Stimulation, on the other hand, implies that the adult does something *to* the child who passively soaks it all up. Learning does not occur in that passive way. Stimulation also implies that the child is an inactive lump until someone comes by and shakes her up. Au contraire, the child's senses and activities are always active, and there is an inner drive for mastery that propels the child forward, provided there is not undue physical or psychological stress. Finally, stimulation implies that more is better—more mobiles, more toys, more lights and sounds. Many studies now show that most "deprived" environments are full of stimuli but, unfortunately, are not consistent, are not interactive with the child, and are chaotic (like most intensive care nurseries). Overstimulation is far more pernicious in most homes than understimulation, except in the most extreme cases of neglect. Most restructuring of these environments involves simplification of the learning milieu.

Parents eager to support development must appreciate these distinctions to be effective. Play programs that promise fantastic developmental gains are likely to be stressful to parents and children alike, run counter to sound developmental principles, and may be unsuccessful in the long run. They direct attention away from the child's behavior and onto bright toys and boxes. Interaction orchestrated with sensitivity with the real world promotes successful development.

CHILD-PROOFING THE ENVIRONMENT AS A PARENTAL INDEX OF DEVELOPMENTAL SENSITIVITY

Parents should anticipate safety issues as a result of understanding the child's individual developmental capacities. The emerging motor skills at 9 months provide the opportunity to lay out this connection so that safety issues will *always* be thought of with developmental change. Parents also need to have a sensitivity to individual temperamental differences when considering the safety needs because these traits are also likely to be long standing, influenc-

TABLE 14–2.
Age-Appropriate Safety Guidelines

Age	Child's Activities	Dangers/Risks	Questions and Suggestions for Parents
0–6 mo	Swimming reflex	Drowning, water intoxication, stress	Counsel on early swimming lessons.
	Immobile	Fire, smoke dangers	Place smoke alarm near infant's sleeping quarters.
	Rolling over	Falls, rolling off table	Use appropriate bathing facilities, restraints, safe changing area, padded floor.
	Attempts to sit up	Flipping out of infant seat (3 mo)	Keep child restrained in infant seat; remove infant seat at 3 mo.
	Sucking/mouthing objects	Ingestion, aspiration, strangulation from pacifier string	
	Motor excitement	Slipping in bath	Lower temperature of hot water heater ($<120°F$?).
	Reaching for objects	Burns, cuts	
7–12 mo	Crawl, pull to stand, cruising	Burns; falls down stairs, into toilet bowl, falls in tub	Blocked stairs; eliminate walker.
	Increased curiosity	Ingestions (medicines, plants/chemicals, household cleaning agents)	Have poison control telephone numbers and ipecac available; lock cabinets.
	Pincer grasp	Aspiration of small objects, e.g., marbles and toy parts, pills, seeds, plants	
	Puts everything in mouth	Electric cord bites, ingestions, aspirations, lead poisoning	Offer safe toys.
	Goes after hidden objects	Aspiration, strangulation (cords)	
	Pulls objects down	Hot liquid burns, objects on tables	Put heavy or hot objects out of reach.
1–2 yr*	Walking, running	Traffic accidents	Does the child have access to the street?
	Loves to be chased (18–24 mo)	Runs away, into streets	
	Climbing (tables, desks, counters)	Ingestions, falls, burns	How are medications stored? Put chairs away from counters.
	Goes after hidden objects	Ingestions, electrocution	Are medications in purse? Are outlets covered?
	Increased independence and curiosity	Ingestions, burns, drownings	Is access to pool blocked?
2–3 yr*	Expanding world (backyard, garage, friend's house)	Ingestions	Is there access to garage, backyard?

TABLE 14–2.

—Continued

Age	Child's Activities	Dangers/Risks	Questions and Suggestions for Parents
	Imitative behavior	Climbs, follows older children, ingests pills	
	"Swim" classes	Drownings, drinking pool water with hyponatremia	Avoid. Be sure of full parent participation. Do not expect child to be drown-proof.
	Introduction to adult foods (nuts, popcorn, gum)	Aspiration	Avoid access to nuts, popcorn, and gum.
	Resists constraints (e.g., carseats)	Car accidents	Possess and *use* carseat.
	False maturity leading toward less parental supervision (2-yr-olds)	All accidents	
3–5 yr	Improved motor development:		
	Reaches high "safe" places	Ingestions, burns, falls	Supervise play.
	Tricycles/big wheels	Spoke injuries, traffic accidents	Provide safe places.
	Expanded world (school, neighborhood)	Car accidents, falls	Has traffic safety been taught?
	Continued drive to discover world	Burns (matches)	Discuss fire safety.
	Role playing, superhero imitations	Burns, ingestions, falls	
	Resists constraints (e.g., carseat)	Car accidents	Possess and *use* carseat.
6–14 yr	Independence, away from home	Bike, skateboard and car accidents; drownings	Wear helmets. Skateboard off streets, hills. Use inline skates with wrist and knee pads and helmets. Swim in groups, supervised. Take swimming and water safety classes.
	Unsupervised activities	Burns (fireworks and matches), alcohol and drug exploration or overdose	
15–17 yr		Car accidents	Take driver education.
		Drug/alcohol use	Discuss peer-proofing and other drug education programs. Apply reasonable curfews. All parties should be supervised.

*Highest accident rates of all groups

197

ing parental decision making. Building a safe environment, then, is both an important experience in establishing parenting skills and an outcome of a parent's understanding and sensitivity to an individual child.

Anticipation of children's activities ensures safety. Age-appropriate guidelines for child-proofing are given in Table 14–2. Booklets given to parents at specific stages should reinforce the developmentally based approach.

SPECIFIC SAFETY ISSUES

CAR RESTRAINTS

Children in the last quarter of the first year are likely to resist the carseat in an effort to resist being held down. Although a laudable trait, there must be no compromise at this (or any other) stage. *Any* deviation from the car safety routine confuses the child and sets this area up as one for negotiation. That message would be unfair to the child trying to understand the regularities in her environment.

WATER SAFETY

Children less than 3 years of age are the most vulnerable group for drowning. Victims of bathtub drownings are usually unsupervised, youngest children in low-income, large families experiencing high stress (Pearu and Nixon, 1977). Toddlers have drowned in toilets. The bathroom should be off limits except with constant adult supervision. Child abuse is a cause for some drownings. Swim classes *do not* make a young child water safe or drown-proof. They may teach infants and toddlers relaxation in the water, but the child and the parents may develop a false sense of reassurance. Unsupervised, the same child who accidentally falls in a pool may "swim" in the wrong direction! Water intoxication may result from infant "swimming" programs. Caution should be given to parents who are contemplating this participation.

BURNS

Ninety percent of burns occur in children less than 4 years old, usually by scalds of spilled food substances. At 9 months, the kitchen must be reevaluated from the floor looking up to see cords, containers, and dangerous appliances. An average (140°F) setting on a hot water heater causes full-thickness, deep burns with less than 5 seconds of exposure, whereas a lower setting of 120°F causes deep burns only after ten minutes exposure. Water set at this level allows even the youngest children to withdraw safely if exposed.

INGESTIONS

The most common ingestions are medications, cleaning substances, plants, cosmetics, personal care products, and hydrocarbons (Pearu and Nixon, 1977). Although the use of child-proof caps has reduced considerably some of the risk from medication (notably that of aspirin), a substantial number of ingestions still occur. Accidental ingestions occur in the toddler and young preschool child in association with their exploratory and imitative capacities. Pills of all types, purses, cleaning solutions, and plants should be moved up and out of the way. Child-proof latches on all cupboards should be installed before the child is 9 months old. Poison center numbers should be available near every telephone. Medications prescribed for parents and siblings should be stored carefully and all old medications thrown out. Visiting grandparents' luggage should be off limits for the same reasons.

ACCIDENTS

Accidents occur most often around dinnertime or during times of increased family stress (e.g., marital discord, a recent move, a financial setback) and are concentrated in families who live with constant stress. Under these circumstances parents are less vigilant and less attentive to a child's developmental capacities and age-appropriate activities. Research on children who experience repeated accidents (accident proneness) points to contributions from the child, as well as the environment. These children themselves usually are impulsive and very active. Their personal and family emotional lives are often labile, chaotic, and disorganized. These children and their families need help through an evaluation of physical, social, and psychological factors that contribute to accident-prone behavior, even when it occurs in infancy.

Nonaccidental trauma must be considered when the child's injury is inconsistent with the child's developmental competency or even temperamental issues or opportunities. The care provider must match the history and physical findings with observations of the child's age and developmental level. It is unreasonable to think that a 5-month-old could fall out of a crib or that a 1-year-old could turn on hot bath water. Referral to a child abuse team or the child welfare authorities would be indicated. The clinician is in a unique position to match the child's behavioral competencies with the described injury.

FEEDING: ITS DEVELOPMENTAL ROLE

Although in pediatric care our focus is often on the delivery of adequate nutrients to the child, the role of feeding in psychological development cannot be ignored. By the end of the first year, a major transition to self-feeding should be in process; this is an opportunity to see this daily event in a new light.

In early infancy, the symbiosis between infant and child is clearly seen in the act of breast-feeding. The reciprocal, contingent, and consistent interaction that this sets up is the foundation for psychological development. Built on a prepackaged set of reflexes, breast-feeding quickly becomes a learning opportunity for infant and mother. Breast-fed infants are held more and are given more tactile and vestibular input. As the child's social world widens at 3 months, the feeding interaction changes with more social time, more anticipation by the child of feeding routines, and more interest in the feeding of others.

Solid foods are best introduced when tongue-thrusting behavior is decreasing, when milk no longer satisfies the infant, and when she has enough head and trunk control to allow a prop or held sit position. Drinking from a cup is introduced when the child can sit steadily. Finger foods should be introduced when the child has developed a pincer grasp and good hand-eye coordination. The opportunity to explore the texture, smell, color, and taste of food means a mess. This learning opportunity must not be violated by overly neat expectations by parents. Children's bids for autonomy in this area should be respected and self-feeding encouraged as much as possible. A child's response to new foods often reflects temperamental characteristics that are seen in other areas as well—wary versus enthusiastic, positive versus negative, cautious versus exuberant. A focused history of the child's response often reveals these general traits.

The motorically active 1-year-old must be fed in short bursts of five to six small meals. The autonomy issues of the second year are played out around being in control of what you eat; a parent must make the child think it is his own idea. A positive interaction with family during meals is important for all children, no matter how messy.

The feeding interaction, so central to care and developmental change, has been shown to reflect the general patterns of interaction between a child and caregiver and is useful in providing insight into these basic interactional aspects of the parent-child relationship (Barnard, 1978; Spietz, 1978). In considering atypical feeding patterns (e.g., hourly feedings) dysfunctional feeding (failure to thrive or obesity), or developmental arrest ("he will not take solids"), one should consider whether this is a problem with the child, the parent, or both. A feeding history and a direct office observation are often the most efficient way of obtaining data around this issue. As in play interactions, the important data in these observations center around the parents' responsiveness to the infant's cues and needs, as well as that of the child's competencies. Table 14-3 lists this developmental approach to feeding.

DATA GATHERING

It is important at each clinical encounter to inquire about a child's *current* play activity because this usually reflects his cognitive level, provided the environment is not overly restrictive. His newest "trick" (i.e., new developmental skill) will reveal a child's developmental stage. Examples of specific questions that reflect cognitive growth in the young child are given in Table 14-4.

The child's immediate environment with regard to safety issues can be explored in a developmental context. Safety advice takes on a more interesting child-centered meaning when discussed in terms of newly acquired skills. For example,

As you know, Susie has more motor and social skills that allow her to explore your home with both inquisitiveness and mischievousness! Getting into cabinets and drawers, picking up small objects like pills, and using her mouth as a receptacle must seem like daily events. Safety has become an important issue in her life. Can you tell me what you've done to make your home safer?

Examples are included in Table 14-2.

Injuries sustained while riding unrestrained in cars are the major accidental health hazard in *all* age categories. Inquire about car-restraint usage at each well-child office visit. It is not enough to ask if the child has a car restraint. Is it being used each time the child rides in the car, both at home and on vacations? There is no valid excuse for a child to ride unrestrained in a car. Parents who cannot supply that structure and set absolute limits in this area will have even greater difficulty when there is some equivocation possible.

The way the feeding history is taken will in itself connect the child's developmental progress with changes in feeding. For example, "So he's sitting up now; it's time to begin to introduce a cup," or, "She's using her fingers very well now; it's time to let her feed herself some soft finger foods." If feeding difficulties are encountered, it is often helpful to elicit a detailed specific history from one specific day (e.g., yesterday).

One should pursue how a family is coping with their child's bid for autonomy during mealtime. How are they responding to the child's normal desire to participate in and control the feeding situation as evidenced by food jags, ritualism, and dawdling? Parents may dislike the messiness and unrealistically insist on good table manners. These predictable and developmentally normal behaviors can be interpreted to parents in terms of expected growth in the child's cognitive, social, and emotional life.

TABLE 14-3.
Behavioral and Developmental Abilities Related to Feeding

Newborn–2 mo	Primitive reflexes (rooting, sucking, swallowing) facilitate feeding and quickly become organized into a whole pattern of behavior; hunger cry initiates feeding interaction; minimal vocal, visual, or motor activity during feeding
2–4 mo	More alert and interactive during feeding; explosive cough to protect self from aspiration; beginning ability to wait for food; associates mother's smell, voice, and cradling with feeding; hand to mouth behavior quiets infant, increases interest in mouthing activities
4–6 mo	Readiness for solids; excellent head and trunk control; reaching for objects; raking grasp; increased hand to mouth facility; loss of extrusion reflex of the tongue; may purposefully spit out food as part of food exploration; adaptation to introduction of solids may be affected by infant's temperament
6–8 mo	Sits alone with a steady head during sitting feedings; chewing mechanism developed; holds bottle; vocal eagerness during meal preparation; much more motor acitivty during feeding
8–10 mo	Finger-food readiness; thumb-forefinger grasp (i.e., inferior pincer); grasps spoon but cannot use it effectively; feeds self crackers, etc; enjoys new textures, tastes; emerging independence
10–12 mo	Increasing determination to feed self; neat pincer grasp; drops food off highchair onto floor to see where it goes; holds cup but frequently spills it; more verbal and motor behavior during feeding
12–15 mo	Demands to feed self without help; decreased appetite and nutritional requirements; improved cup use (both hands); uses spoon, fills poorly, spills, turns at mouth; can use spoon as extension of the hand; messy play
15–18 mo	Eats rapidly, short feeding sessions; wants to be motorically active (too busy to eat); fairly good use of spoon and cup; enhanced ability to wait for food; plays with/throws food to elicit response from parent
18–24 mo	Feeds self, using combination of utensils and fingers; verbalizes "eat, all gone," asks for food; negativism emerges, says no when really wanting offered food; wants control of feeding situation
2–3 yr	Uses fork; ritualistic, repetitive at mealtimes; food jags, all one food at a time; dawdles; likes to help set/clear table; may begin to help self to refrigerator contents
3–4 yr	Spills little; uses utensils well; washes hands with minimal help; likes food preparation; reasonable table manners while eating out
4–5 yr	Serves self; choosy about food; resists some textures; begins to request foods seen on television ads (especially junk food); makes menu suggestions; likes to assist in washing dishes; helps in food preparation
5–6 yr	Uses knife; assists in preparing and packing own box lunch; can be responsible for setting/clearing table; aids younger siblings' requests for food or drink
6–8 yr	Does dishes independently and willingly; increases pressure to buy junk food; interested in, often critical of, and attempts to negotiate about daily menu; manages money for school meal ticket
8–10 yr	Enjoys planning and preparing simple family meals; wants supplemental spending money to buy snacks when away from home; more reticent to trying new foods; resists kitchen chores

TABLE 14-4.
Questions That Reflect Cognitive Growth

Age	Questions
1–4 mo	Does he sometimes seem to anticipate feeding, i.e., search for the nipple? Does he spend a lot of time looking around, checking out his environment? Does he swipe at the mobile to make it move?
6 mo	Does he explore objects, e.g., toys? Does he seem a bit bored by familiar objects?
7 mo	Does he prefer mom to other people? Is he wary of strangers?
9 mo	Does he drop food over the side of the highchair and then peek over to see if it is on the floor?
12 mo	Does he try to remove obstacles that are in front of his goal, e.g., a pillow placed in front of a toy? Does he try to imitate sounds or noises that you make?
15 mo	Does he experiment with his toys, exploring the properties of the object, e.g., a ball: drop it, squeeze it, throw it, kick it?
18 mo	Does he try to produce new sounds? Does he search for objects that he has actually seen hidden? Does he use objects for their appropriate function, e.g., drink from a cup rather than mouth the handle?
2 yr	Does he sometimes imitate someone or something he observed the day before, e.g., temper tantrums? Has he begun to "pretend" while playing? Does he have nightmares?

Anticipation of the feeding issues that will come up will help parents to cope and struggles to be avoided. This discussion is best linked to the start of finger feeding by the child. Parents of toddlers often are worried about their child being a "picky" eater. When the clinician asks, "Tell me about mealtimes," a tense, unhappy picture may be depicted. In addition to the preschooler's choosiness about food, there is often a related issue of parents' need for control. Explore how the parents have attempted to handle the situation (e.g., child made to sit at the table for extended periods). This information provides important clues to parent-child interactions at these moments in the day. It may act as a springboard into other areas of communication between parents and their young children. When getting a 24-hour dietary history, listen for a preponderance of snacks, juice, and junk food. The mother of an obese infant may be unconsciously holding onto the relationship she had in her child's earlier infancy with her completely dependent child. Maternal depression or isolation may be the basis for it, and those basic issues need exploration and help.

EXAMINATION

The agenda of the 9-month visit may be substantially altered to allow for observation of the child during free play. Motor competencies, visual motor skills, early gesture and verbal language, and the interaction with the primary caregiver can be observed.

In any child whose developmental level is unknown, start with a presentation of blocks with the child in a sitting position. This will quickly tell you about reach and grasp and will proceed to tower and bridge building, color, and number in the older child. If one hides the block with a paper towel, object permanence can be assessed. A 10-month-old should look for the block without hesitation, whether it is under the cloth or over the side of the table.

Most children will do their own developmental test if given the opportunity. For example, the capacity of the 9- to 10-month-old for anticipating events and the emerging awareness of spatial relationships (i.e., on, in, behind) can be demonstrated at this time. One technique is to move a stethoscope around the child and watch as he tracks it, then turns to await its return into view on the opposite side.

The 15- to 18-month-old demonstrates the trial-and-error searching for the cause of visible events by turning the light in the examination room on and off. He illustrates the fully developed concept of object permanence by repeatedly removing and then replacing the toys from the bottom drawer of the examination table. The 18- to 24-month-old displays the emergence of symbolic thought as he lines up several 1-in. cubes (e.g., Denver kit toys) and pushes them along, making choo-choo sounds to accompany his newly created train. These observations, along with a parental questionnaire, are adequate for most children and families without a risk condition.

The condition of an infant or toddler who does not demonstrate age-appropriate cognitive milestones deserves further evaluation. Unwarranted reassurance that the child will catch up may be misleading. A reasonable approach is to ask the family back for a specific evaluation using directed parent observations at home and a second developmental assessment. A screening test as opposed to a questionnaire may be utilized. The follow-up examination should be arranged at a time when the infant is most alert, such as in the morning after a feeding period. It should occur within a brief time frame after the initial examination with suspicious findings.

Delays that are evident at 9 months are unlikely to resolve unless they are the result of a significant illness that is resolving or intercurrent psychosocial deprivation. Even in such extreme cases there may be residual concerns after a period of developmental catch-up. A 2-month time frame is a reasonable one in which to reassess developmental status. Many infant intervention programs have special eligibility requirements that may include referral by 1 year. The clinician's wishful thinking should not limit program availability for an individual child and family (Parmelee, 1980). Referral to a developmental pediatrician, psychologist, or other professional experienced in the care of young children should be the next step.

If feeding or growth are issues, a specific oral-motor assessment, evaluation of reach and grasp, and other evidence of physical illness in the child should be assessed. The mother should be asked to feed the child to assess the nature of this issue. Direct observation of the parental behavior and interaction with the child may be helpful.

ANTICIPATORY GUIDANCE

- The clinician should provide a narrative of the child's developmental skills during the course of the examination.
- The child's need to freely and safely explore the environment should be highlighted.
- Safety advice should be specifically linked to developmental competencies: For example, block stairways and doors as the child crawls; cover table and shelf corners as the child cruises. This may be laid out in a handout and reinforced by the clinician.
- Suggest that parents will minimize behavioral conflicts by having lots of interesting things around that the baby can explore, such as a bottom kitchen drawer filled with plastic objects. Encourage the use of distraction at moments of frustration and the provision of acceptable substitutes. The clinician can role model these techniques if parents do not intervene appropriately during the visit, for example, if the child attempts to

investigate electrical outlets in the office (which should be covered with a plastic guard). Urge parents to be consistent and emphatic about the things the infant must absolutely not touch, such as fireplace and electric outlets and cords. Ensure the child's safety near the stairs with a safe barrier.

- Emphasize the need that all parents have to periodically review home safety. Suggest that they use subsequent health supervision visits as the day to reexamine the home safety needs of their child and update safety measures.
- Discuss the ongoing importance of car restraints at each health supervision visit.
- Ensure that your waiting and examination rooms are child-proofed. Besides providing a safe environment for idle children, it sets a good example for parents and underlines your related patient teaching.
- Visual aids should be made available to augment, not substitute for, verbal guidance in the office. Well-written safety checklists for specific age groups and other literature are available from the local poison control center and the American Academy of Pediatrics (e.g., TIPP, the Injury Prevention Program). A display board with examples of safety devices can be mounted in the waiting room. The American Automobile Association (AAA) and the state transportation department offer numerous materials, including superb, convincing films on car restraints and unsupervised children in traffic, both available without cost to service organizations and schools.
- Parents who provide a developmentally appropriate and nutritionally sound diet for their child deserve enthusiastic praise and encouragement from the clinician. One should acknowledge their response to the constant challenge to adjust to changing dietary habits and developmental changes of their child. New materials are available to provide concrete suggestions. One approach is to suggest that a child get 24 oz of milk per day, two protein servings (small), and three bread servings. A multivitamin daily obviates the need for conflicts around vegetables and other foods often resisted by kids.
- Parents must be given explicit instructions on feeding. Inability to follow those means that there is a difficulty in the child, the parent, or the interaction. Difficult children, children perceived as vulnerable, and tenuously attached or tightly entangled children often come in labeled as having a feeding problem. The clinician must be prepared to explore these issues and, perhaps in some cases, make a referral.
- The changing pattern of food intake at the first year should be anticipated. Frequent small feedings for the child on the go are adaptive.
- Encourage parents to provide small portions of soft finger foods and allow the child to set his own pace. Stress that the nutritional goal is not for the child to clean his plate but to satisfy hunger needs, whereas the developmental goal is to explore independently new textures, colors, and tastes through finger foods and the use of a cup.
- Parents worry about the "picky eater" that their toddler has become or the food jags he exhibits.
- Helping them gain insight into possible underlying control issues as the older child asserts his independence may be helpful. Control may be bidirectional because the parents may be unconsciously seeking to control the child's behavior by means of rigid nutritional expectations or behaviors at meal time. At times, this no-win feeding situation may necessitate an explicit back-off imperative from the clinician. Monitoring of health and growth should be the clinician's responsibility, and this should be the measure of adequate eating.

REFERENCES

Barnard K: *Nursing Child Assessment Feeding Scales.* Seattle, University of Washington, 1978.

Parmelee AH: Assessment of the infant at risk during the first year of life, in Sell E (ed): *Follow-up of High-Risk Infants: A Practical Approach.* Springfield, Ill, Charles C Thomas, Publisher, 1980.

Pearu J, Nixon J: Prevention of childhood drowning accidents. *Med J Aust* 1977; 1:616.

Piaget J: *Origins of Intelligence in Children,* Cook M (trans). New York, WW Norton & Co, 1952.

Spietz A: Why look at feeding? in Barnard K: *NCAST-Nursing Child Assessment Feeding Scales.* Seattle, University of Washington, 1978, pp 5–14.

ADDITIONAL READINGS

Berger L: Childhood injuries: Recognition and prevention. *Curr Probl Pediatr* 1981; 12:1–59.

Brown MS, Murphy A: Well child management: Childhood safety, in Brown MS, Murphy MA: *Ambulatory Pediatrics for Nurses.* New York, McGraw-Hill Book Co, 1975, pp 107–126.

O'Grady R: Feeding behavior in infants. *Am J Nurs* 1971; 71:736–739.

Rubin R: Food and feeding: A matrix of relationships. *Nurs Forum* 1967; 6:195–205.

Spietz A: Mother-infant adaptation over the first year, in Barnard K (ed): *Nursing Child Assessment Satellite Training Project (NCAST) Learning Resource Material.* Seattle, University of Washington, 1980, pp 75–81.

Telzrow R: Developmental considerations in infant feeding, in Howard RB, Herbold MH: *Nutrition in Clinical Care.* New York, McGraw-Hill Book Co, 1982.

"A girl-baby walking." By Anne
Atkinson, age 5.

CHAPTER 15

One Year: One Giant Step Forward

SUZANNE D. DIXON, M.D.
MICHAEL J. HENNESSY, M.D.

KEY WORDS

WALKING
GROSS MOTOR DEVELOPMENT
GAIT ANALYSIS
INDEPENDENCE
TEMPERAMENT AND STYLE IN GROSS MOTOR DEVELOPMENT

In response to the question, "Do you have any other concerns?" asked at the end of a health supervision visit, the mother of a 12-month-old exclaimed, "Her left foot looks odd!" Developmental history revealed normal motor, language, and social skills in a child who took a few unaided steps 1 week before the visit. Physical examination was normal. The left foot was moderately inverted when standing; it was thought to be secondary to a mild positional deformity. The mother was reassured.

At the 15-month visit, she reminded her pediatrician that "the left foot looks odd!" Examination revealed a normal foot and leg when examined passively but inversion of the foot when standing and walking. To the pediatrician's surprise, the left calf circumference was 0.5 cm smaller than the right side, and the left foot exerting muscles were weak. Strength, tone, sensation, and DTR's were otherwise normal and symmetrical. A magnetic resonance image of the spine demonstrated a congenital syringomyelia. Surgical exploration, drainage, and shunting prevented further neurological deterioration.

Parents often reveal to us important information that at first may not seem significant or pertinent. Active listening is a learned clinical skill. Some parents need permission to reveal their hidden agenda. Initiating an interview with the question, "What are some of your concerns?" and terminating the visit by asking, "Do you have any other concerns?" will help some parents to feel comfortable enough to allow important issues or problems to surface.

The one developmental milestone that most clinicians remember without hesitancy and parents focus on most prominently is the age of walking. Independent gait is greeted by parents as a source of pride and assurance of normality; any delay in its appearance may trigger worry and dire prognostication. Everyone, including the child, feels better when the baby walks, as if a big hurdle has been successfully overcome. The child's perspective on the world and how he sees himself changes dramatically when he can alter his location. The visit when the child is 1 year old offers the opportunity to look at ambulation and gross motor development in general. The goal is to see this area of development in the broader context of the whole child and in its importance to the family. The manner of emergence of this milestone provides great insight into a child and family from more than the motor vantage point.

THE EMERGENCE OF WALKING

In spite of our own expectations, most children are *not* walking on their first birthday. The mean age for walking is about 60 weeks, with a 2 SD range of 9 to 17 months (Bayley, 1969; Illingworth, 1970). Variation in gross-motor skill *appearance* (i.e., doing the activity), as well as *competency* (i.e., being able to do it without choosing to exercise that skill), is quite marked and is related to temperamental, familial, ethnic, and, to some degree, experiential factors (Chase et al., 1978). Parental expectations regarding this developmental process vary widely as well, reflecting broader cultural views of what a child is, what is the nature of development, and what is the role of parenting (Hopkins and Westra, 1989). Parental dating of this skill varies even by what is perceived as independant ambulation. Although regularity in the sequence of gross-motor development offers support for a prominent maturational component in this area of development, there is a clear role played by environmental factors acting with neuromotor growth. Familial patterns of late walking may be related to a slower course of nerve myelinization, to an inherited behavioral style, or to a deemphasis on gross-motor activities. Neuromotor precocity and these temperamental factors may be the basis for the observed early acceleration of motor development in several groups, including blacks, Mexicans, East Indians, and Middle Eastern children, when compared with that of white Americans (Willemsen, 1979). A basic motor competency appears to be present at birth in these groups that propels the infants forward at a faster rate and also leads to different patterns of handling (Dixon et al., 1982) that build on this early competency. *Severe* experiential deprivation is necessary before any systematic effect on motor development is noted. Dennis' study (1940) of Hopi Indian infants placed on cradleboards demonstrated no alteration in the maturity or timing of walking, with more recent studies confirming these findings (Harriman and Lukosius, 1982). These children, in spite of some early confinement, have ample opportunity for free movement and developed normally (Chisholm, 1983). Specific training of motor skills (e.g., climbing) appears to have no effect on the time of emergence of those skills (McGraw, 1945). The use of infant walkers in particular seems to have no effect on the appearance of independent walking (Crouchman, 1986; Ridenour, 1982), although safety may be impaired in all children riding these devices, and extensor postures may be solidified in children with lower extremity hypertonia.

Peripheral nerve myelinization and cerebellar growth increase rapidly from 6 to 12 months, and these changes appear to coincide with the movement changes that occur during that time. Physical growth factors such as height and leg length may influence patterns of motor development (Hennessy et al., 1984). A maturational readiness seems to be within a child, so motor skills emerge within a supportive but noninstructive environment. The environment alone can take little credit or blame for gross-motor achievements, but it acts with other factors synergistically. Or, as stated by Wolff (1981), "Neither intrinsic developmental timetables nor experience is a sufficient condition for motor skill acquisition. At every stage motor development depends not only on experience and quality of the stimuli, but also on brain mechanisms that *assimilate and organize information from the environment and from action in progress.''* Motor skills are not acquired automatically and, like cognitive skills, require the child herself to exercise active learning.

MOTOR MILESTONES

The incredible importance placed on walking is curious. The age of independent ambulation, except if it is delayed into the third year, means absolutely nothing at all. It is not a diagnostic marker. Accelerated motor development in general does not testify to superior mental skills; late motor development, except in the extreme, does not indicate mental deficiency. As stated by Bower (1977), "Motor skills seem by and large to be self-contained." The rate of change in gross-motor achievement is not generally correlated with achievement in other areas of development in most children. Delayed walking in children *with perinatal difficulties* is associated with an increased incidence of broader developmental delay; without this history, the age of walking has poor prognostic value (Chaplais and MacFarlane, 1984).

Some of the earliest perspectives on the regularities of early childhood development came from the observations of gross-motor milestones made by Gesell (1938), McGraw (1945), and others. This sequence came out of careful longitudinal and cross-sectional observations of normal children. The pediatric perspective on development has been strongly based on these schemes of milestones following from a neuromaturational model (see Chapter 2). Although we now know that not every aspect of gross-motor development can be accounted for by this model, the regularity and the readily observable nature of these achievements form a core of developmental assessment, as shown in Figures 15–1 and 15–2. Physical milestones in infancy are presented in Table 15–1. Wide individual variation is evident.

Through a chronicle of regular achievement of these skills, clinicians are assured of neurological adequacy. This basic matrix then allows us to add on other developmental expectations that are temporarily associated. Language, social, affective, and cognitive milestones can be linked in our minds and in the activities of our patients to this sequence of motor skills.

WALKING: A CHANGE IN PERSPECTIVES

From the child's perspective, new motor competencies dramatically change the child's view of himself and his world. His placement in space is under his own control. He now can choose (within limits) *what* he will explore, not just *how* he will investigate the objects within vision or reach. This provides an enormous sense of power (Brazelton, 1974). These skills allow him to perceive, learn, and experience in entirely new ways by movement through space. He can now choose to go away from or go toward his caregivers. That new option is both exciting and scary. Everything changes because of this change in perspective. Selma Fraiberg (1959) describes the overwhelming changes that a child experiences when he learns to walk.

In the last quarter of the first year, the baby is no longer an observer of a passing scene. He is in it. Travel changes one's perspective. A chair, for example, is an object of one dimension when viewed by a six month old baby propped up on a sofa. . . . It's when you start to get around under your own steam that you discover what a chair really is [pp 52–53].

FIG 15–1.
Progression of prone posture. **A,** newborn in flexed posture. **B,** infant at about 1 month, head up briefly; some extension at hips and knees. **C,** infant about 1 to 2 months old; head up to about 45 degrees; active legs. **D,** infant about 3 to 4 months; up easily on forearms; head steady, able to be turned with minimal bobbing. **E,** infant about 5 to 9 months; up on hands. May use arm to pull self forward. May push with thighs and knees. Creeping. **F,** infant 7 to 11 months, crawling; reciprocal movement of legs and legs with hands. **G,** crawling on feet. **H,** child 8 to 18 months of age; climbs stairs.

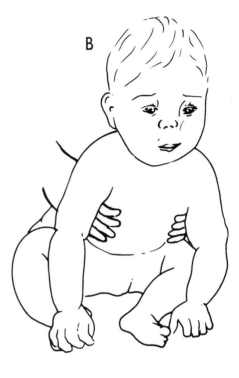

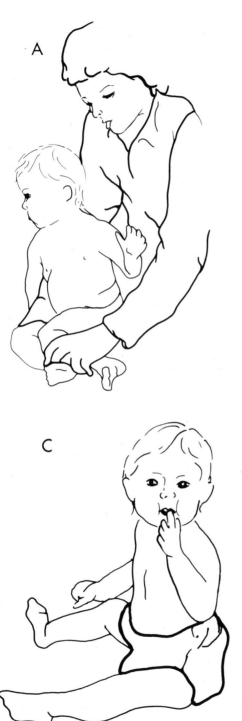

FIG 15–2.
Sitting progression. With each time period
steadiness and control of head increases;
back becomes straighter from upper portion
down; arms are held naturally further back,
with external rotation at the shoulder. **A,** age
1 to 2 months, sits with truncal support.
Head and shoulders steady. Lower back still
rounded. **B,** age 4 to 7 months, sits in a pivot
position with slight truncal support. All
energy directed at maintaining postures. **C,**
age 5 to 9 months, independent sitting. Back
straight. Able to pivot without losing
balance.

TABLE 15-1.
Physical Milestones in Infancy*

Behavior	Age Range (mo)	Average Age (mo)
Raises self by arms while lying face down	0.7–5	2.1
Sits with support	1–5	2.3
Sits alone momentarily	4–8	5.3
Sits alone 10–30 sec or more	5–8	6.0
Rolls from back to stomach	4–10	6.4
Sits alone quite steadily for long periods	5–9	6.6
Stands up holding onto furniture	6–12	8.6
Walks while adult holds hands	7–12	9.6
Sits down after standing	7–14	9.6
Stands alone	9–16	11.0
Walks alone	9–17	11.7
Walks sideways	10–20	14.1
Walks backward	11–20	14.6
Walks up stairs with help	12–23	16.1
Stands on left foot alone	15–30	22.7
Jumps off floor with both feet	17–30+	23.4
Stands on right foot alone	16–30+	23.5
Jumps from the last stair step to floor	19–30+	24.8
Walks up stairs alone with both feet on each step	18–30+	25.1
Walks a few steps on tiptoes	16–30+	25.7
Walks down stairs alone with both feet on each step	19–30+	25.8
Jumps from the second stair step to the floor	21–30+	28.1
Walks up stairs alternating forward foot	23–30+	30+

†5th to 95th percentile.
*From the Bayley Scales of Infant Development, Motor Scale Record. Psychological Corp, 1969. Used by permission.

The first time the baby stands unsupported and the first wobbly independent steps are milestones in personality development as well as in motor development. To stand unsupported, to take that first step is a brave and lonely thing to do [p 60].

All of development is fueled by the ability to change position in space and to move away from a completely dependent vantage point. Or as pointed out again by Fraiberg (1959):

The discovery of independent locomotion and the discovery of a new self usher in a new phase in personality development. The toddler is quite giddy with his new achievements. He behaves as if he had invented this new mode of locomotion and he is quite in love with himself for being so clever. From dawn to dusk he marches around in an ecstatic, drunken dance, which ends only when he collapses with fatigue [pp 61–62].

A motorically handicapped child suffers secondary disabilities because of limitations on visual, perceptual, and tactile experiences in his expanding world. Seen in this context, therapies, surgical procedures, and external supports and braces for these children should be considered or evaluated from the perspective of their impact on these areas of development. Just normalization of position or posture is not enough.

There is an internal consistency within a child that allows for some anticipation of gross-motor skills. For example, a late sitter is likely to be a late walker. The style with which a child approaches motor skill development is also consistent (Brazelton, 1974). Some children charge ahead to pull-to-stand, cruise, and walk with lots of energy and lots of falls. Others will take a more contemplative approach, studying the task well, winding up slowly and feeling assured at each step before trying the next. The clinician will learn more about a child by monitoring *how* she achieves gross-motor skills than by focusing exclusively on the timing of these behaviors.

MOTOR SKILLS: GENERAL PRINCIPLES

Walking must be seen in the context of other gross-motor accomplishments. These all share, in addition to their regular sequence, certain characteristics. First, these skills are built on neuromotor tone (Wyke, 1975). Behaviors, skills, and patterns are determined by this base. Hypotonic children, from whatever cause, will have delays in postural maturation and skill acquisition. Hypertonic children, with prominence of extensor postures, will have predictable "pseudoaccelerations" (e.g., rolling over, weight-bearing, and pull-to-stand) and delays (e.g., sitting).

Second, volitional behavior is preceded by reflex behavior. For example, the newborn reflex patterns of reciprocal kicking and automatic stepping clearly foreshadow the movements of walking seen near the end of the first year of life. These early patterns disappear at approximately 2 months of age to later reappear in the progressive emergence of independent gait. This sequence is usually thought to result from increasing suppression of the primitive reflexes by maturing cortical centers, leading to their reorganization into volitional patterns. Concomitant with increased strength and improved balance, the child learns to control the reflex pattern and use it to walk. Alternatively, it has been suggested that a more continuous movement pattern characterizes motor development, avoiding this adaptation of primitive reflex patterns (Thelen, 1984). Reflex hand grasp precedes volitional grasp. These reflex patterns foreshadow movements that come under conscious control. Conversely, a delay in the disappearance of early infant reflexes is associated with a comparable delay in the emergence of voluntary motor skills. The mechanism of association between reflex behavior and volitional behavior is unclear (Wolff, 1981), and the linkage does not imply causality. Whether reflexes "dissolve" or are subsumed in more complex volitional patterns is not known. However, the regular unfolding and then disappearance of first reflex behavior and then the emergence of skilled movement offer the clinician an opportunity to point out to parents the integrity and internally regulated nature of the child's maturation.

A third principle of gross-motor development is that maturation entails an increasing efficiency in the energy expenditure that is required to move through space. The child becomes an increasingly efficient movement machine (Burnett and Johnson, 1971; Sutherland et al., 1980). Fourth, the child increases in both speed and accuracy of movement with time. These last characteristics (gains in efficiency, accuracy, and speed) are demonstrated in the specific developmental course of gait.

THE ONTOGENY OF GAIT

Adult human ambulation is remarkably consistent in terms of angles of displacement of the joints involved; the relationships between cadence, stride length, and velocity; and the

TYPICAL NORMAL WALK CYCLE

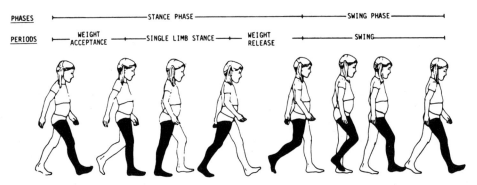

PHASES	STANCE PHASE				SWING PHASE		
PERIODS	WEIGHT ACCEPTANCE	SINGLE LIMB STANCE		WEIGHT RELEASE	SWING		

FIG 15–3.
Phases of the normal gait in childhood. (From Hennessy M, Dixon S, Simon S: *Child Dev* 1984; 55:844–853. Used by permission.)

timing of these events through the gait cycle (Perry, 1967). The gait cycle of events that occurs from heel strike to the next heel strike is illustrated in Figure 15–3. These biomechanical events have specific durations, timing of muscle groups, and shifts of weight that mature over time as shown in Table 15–2. The observation of gait throughout these phases allows for a more accurate characterization of gait in both normal and abnormal conditions.

All these parameters are aimed at maximal displacement in space with a minimum of energy expenditure. The body's center of gravity moves forward in nearly a straight line in a mature gait, the path of least energy expenditure. The extremity movements work together toward that end. Each of these parameters has its own developmental course demonstrated by high-speed film analysis coupled with floor force plate and analysis of electromyographic (EMG) data. These studies have allowed for a more complete and technically refined description of gait; they specify what the clinician can learn by careful additional observation (Hen-

TABLE 15–2.
Gross Motor Development—3–15 Yr*

Age (yr)	Gross Motor Development
3	Stands on one foot; walks upstairs alternating feet
4	Pedals tricycle; runs smoothly; throws ball overhand
5	Walks downstairs alternating feet; skips; marches with rhythm; catches bounced ball
6	Hops; jumps
7	Pedals bicycle
8	Has good body balance
9	Engages in vigorous bodily activities, especially team sports
10	Balances on one foot 15 sec; catches fly ball
12	Motor awkwardness secondary to uneven bone and muscle growth
15	Gradual correction of motor awkwardness

*Adapted from Sahler OJZ, McAnarney ER: *The Child From Three to Eighteen.* St Louis, CV Mosby Co, 1981.

nessy et al., 1984; Sutherland et al., 1980). These techniques are also useful in populations where gait is abnormal and surgical correction is contemplated.

The young child undergoes predictable changes in these biomechanical parameters (Burnett and Johnson, 1971; Ogg, 1963; Scrutton and Robson, 1968). The toddler's stance is broad based; his knees and hips are flexed even while standing; ankle movement is minimal, and there is a flat-footed foot placement. When the child is first walking, the arms are abducted and flexed at the elbow and move little throughout the gait cycle. Acceleration forces are much stronger than inhibitory deceleration forces, so forward momentum is difficult to check. With maturation the base narrows absolutely and relatively to leg length; knee extension is added; knee flexion decreases; and a heel strike appears consistently after 30 months. Hip displacement becomes less; the center of gravity movement stabilizes throughout the gait cycle, and truncal rotation decreases. The arms come down, the hands relax, and reciprocal arm movements are added (Sutherland et al., 1980). The maturity of the gait can be demonstrated through the observation of the arm posture of a child who is walking (Fig 15–4), with an adult pattern seen within several months of independent walking (Clark et al., 1988). Angles of displacement at all joints approach adult values with maturation. The feet go from toeing out to a straighter alignment. Step length and walking speed increase and cadence decreases, gradually approaching a fixed relationship. Stopping is reliable and can be combined with a pivot. By 5 years of age, gait has matured to nearly adult patterns (Figs 15–5 to 15–7), clinically and biomechanically. The EMG patterns show adult patterns of muscle firing (Berger et al., 1987).

The energy required by the toddler to walk is tremendous. Not only is he relentless in practicing this new skill, he is very inefficient. Early walking burns up incredible numbers of calories. Many children thin out after becoming bipedal; the fat stores of the second six months of life might seem to anticipate that demand.

The biomechanical precursors of gait are the reciprocal hip and leg movements of the kicking and crawling child, not standing or pull-to-stand (Thelen et al., 1981; Thelen, 1984). These very early spontaneous movements have the biomechanical characteristics and interrelationships of gait, the coordination and rhythm of gait. Not every child will crawl, and this is of no concern with regard to either motor or cognitive development. In fact, crawling may be the most overrated motor milestone in the first year. But all normal children will demonstrate ongoing reciprocal movement of the lower extremities that becomes smoother and more rhythmic and efficient from 9 to 12 months of age (Fig 15–8). Spontaneous "swimming" movements are seen with bathing at about 9 months. These spontaneous movements are important to monitor (e.g., when a child is supine on an examining table) during the first year rather than merely checking off specific skill acquisitions, a process that can be misleading.

FORCES FOR LEARNING MOTOR SKILLS

Most children will cruise by 12 months, walking while holding on to objects at shoulder height, as shown in Figure 15–9. Some children may resist any attempts at steps if their hands are held up because this eliminates the usefulness of arm position and truncal rotation that provide stability. Cruising *on one's own* provides the opportunity for real practice, the development of firm prototypes of movement that can be applied to varying demands, for example, walking on a carpet versus walking on grass, going up the stairs or down an incline versus

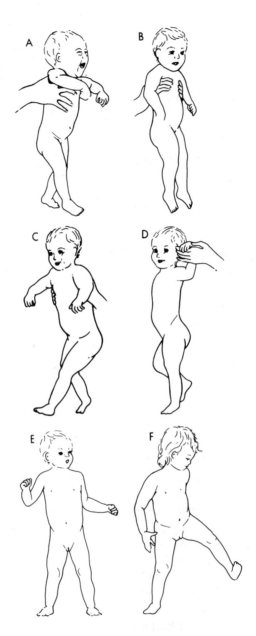

FIG 15–4.
Progression of gait development in toddlers and preschoolers. **A,** reflex walk of the newborn, usually disappears at 3 to 4 weeks of age. **B,** before 3 months, infant bears little weight on legs. **C,** after 7 months, infant will walk with much truncal support. Excessive hip flexion with a forwardly displaced center of gravity means child is not ready for walking. **D,** near 1 year of age child's center of gravity is over the hips and child can walk with help. **E,** during toddler years, positions of child's arm and feet testify to the level of maturity of gait. **F,** it is not until 3 to 5 years of age that child can balance steadily on one foot, with all the reciprocal truncal, hip, and arm adjustments that are required.

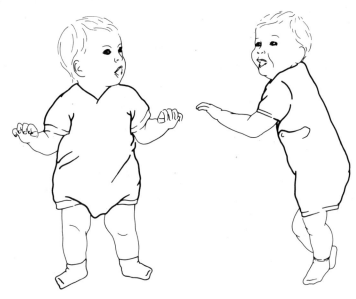

FIG 15–5.
Toddler's gait. Wide based, flexion at hip and knees, abducted feet, arms up and fixed.

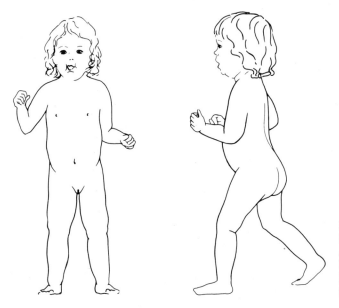

FIG 15–6.
Gait of the older toddler. Arms still used as part of balance. Feet out turned. Relative lordosis with trunk over hips.

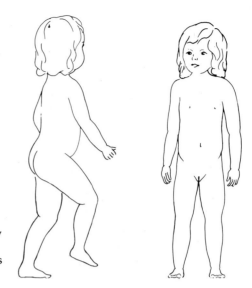

FIG 15–7.
Gait of the preschooler. Biomechanically
nearly at adult patterns. Heel strike
present. Neck, shoulder, hips, and knees
nearly vertical.

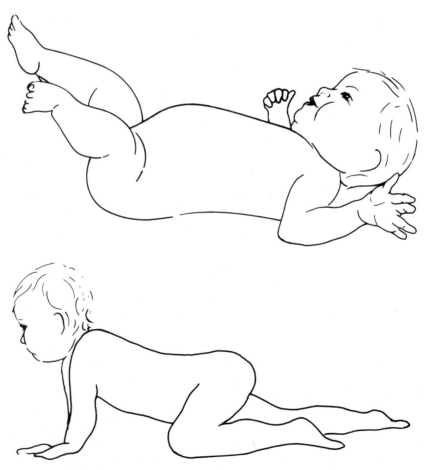

FIG 15–8.
Spontaneous reciprocal hip movements take a variety of forms. Practice opportunities are
provided in prone.

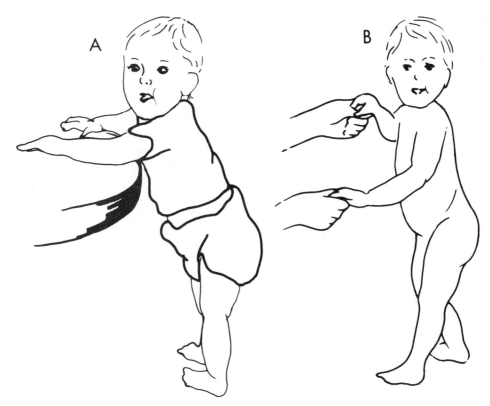

FIG 15–9.
Getting upright, cruising. **A,** cruising on one's own provides opportunities to practice and explore. Most children do this by 12 months. **B,** walking with help. Many families enjoy this activity. There is no evidence that this harms the child or accelerates walking. Some children resist holding on with both hands.

walking on a flat plane. The child is experimenting with new approaches to motor activity, rather than simply repeating fixed actions. Or, as discussed by Young (1977), real practice of motor skills is the application of a set of motor competencies in several different circumstances so that the skill is elaborated as it becomes established. It is not rote repetition of a single activity in a single circumstance many times over. For example, an adult could not claim competency in skiing if she had only gone down one hill, no matter how expertly that hill had been skied. Learning the skill (in the child's case walking, for the adult skiing) includes actively assimilated experiences in many circumstances and conditions. Passive practice or repetitive exercise of only motor skills in isolation has *no* effect on skill acquisition (Held and Hein, 1963) although range of motion may be maintained in a disabled child.

Self-initiated actions, active movement, and exploration of the possibilities of movement are the necessary components of motor development. Infant exercise programs for normal children do not support motor development except insofar as they energize the child and family through the enjoyment of movement. Therapy programs for disabled children that rely on passive movement only keep joints flexible and improve muscle tone, but they do not ensure or augment skill acquisition. Children locked in by tone abnormalities, primitive reflexes, or stereotyped movements may have difficulty in this expanded meaning of practice of motor activities. Therapies should be designed to liberate them from these constraints to allow for active exploration and self-initiated movement. There is no evidence that repeated practice of motor movements (i.e., patterning) has any effect on the development of the handicapped or learning impaired child (American Academy of Pediatrics, 1982). Pediatricians must actively put down proponents of such programs because they have the potential for incredible harm. The ability to explore the world freely has implications for cognitive, emotional, and social growth, and every child's opportunities should be maximized.

LATER MOTOR DEVELOPMENT

Although we often place the greatest emphasis on gross-motor development in the first 2 years of life, this sequence continues beyond walking (Sahler and McAnarney, 1981). These competencies are based on increasing ability to balance on one side and to lateralize more and on other varying motor activities. Children of 4 years of age should be able to ride a big wheel adeptly and those of 7 years should be able to ride a bike. Skateboarding and inline skating, activities we can neither condone nor stop, can be done by 7 to 8 years.

There are therapeutic implications and considerations based on these increasing skills. For example, a big wheeler *may* be able to walk with crutches; certainly a biker can learn this if needed.

EFFECTS ON OTHER AREAS

Cognitive competencies have an impact on how a child learns new motor skills. It is not until midlatency or even adolescence when a youngster can use preknowledge of outcome to improve motor performance; younger children must experience the outcome of their motor activities to alter them (Young, 1977). The ability to sequence concepts parallels the ability to sequence motor behaviors; only the older grade schooler or high school student can do this. This has implications for the coaching of sports. Children can refine movements only through practice and suggestions while engaged in the activity. Lengthy discussions of sport skills may not be useful for grade-school children. Sports activities, both individual and group, should be accompanied by individual and direct feedback to each child while they are engaged in the sport. Complex group plays can only be understood often when there is a "run-through," with each child experiencing the way all members should act together. Coaching from the sidelines is helpful only when closely associated with the child's own action.

The impact of perceptual input on gross-motor development is illustrated through the motor development of congenitally blind infants (Adelson and Fraiberg, 1974). These infants demonstrated all the postural readiness (e.g., excellent truncal tone) and static skill acquisitions (e.g., stepping in place with support) at the same time as sighted children. However, they were predictably delayed in any movement through space: crawling, walking, and climbing. These skills did not begin to emerge until the children were able to reach sound-dependent cues alone, a landmark met by all children between 8 and 12 months. That is, until the children were able to use perceptual input other than vision to map their environment, to be able to understand the consistency of three-dimensional space, they were unwilling to risk moving about. In addition, the fueling that walking receives by way of visual input did not sustain the efforts of these children through all the falls and uncertainties. It is a lot of work to walk, and the rewards must be there. Enhanced feelings of independence, greater perceptual input, and the attainment of goals (e.g., getting a toy) make the effort worthwhile.

The drive to mastery that energizes all of development is never more obvious than in the child just learning to walk. The revelation that one's placement in space can be changed while visually monitoring and even holding onto an object is so overwhelming for a child that all else pales by comparison. Routine things such as feeding, diaper changes, and sleeping are terrible interferences with this new activity. A child's new interest in motor activities may even invade his sleep time with wakefulness and restlessness. Difficulties, as well as regressions, in other areas of functioning should be anticipated at the time he is learning to walk. The expression of joy in accomplishment and a tangible excitement should be apparent in every child even if accompanied by looks of panic and wariness.

PARENTS' ROLE

The sparkle of joy testifies to the walking child's own sense of internal reward for a growing sense of competency. The sparkle is generalizable to other areas in which a child achieves mastery. An internal reward system is fueled as the child learns walking for walking's sake.

FIG 15–10.
Parenting support. Gentle, well placed, but not compelling.

An external reward system cannot have the energy or longevity of the internal one. The parents' role in this instance is to encourage, assure safety in exploration, prevent overtiredness, and enjoy (Fig 15–10). It is not to exercise, instruct, or overwhelm the child with excessive praise.

Walking changes a child's perspective of himself and of those around him. His sense of independence and his ability to separate himself from his parents is enhanced by this accomplishment. As he separates, he individuates (Mahler et al., 1975). He can play by roaming the environment with clear planning and direction. He is no longer as dependent on caregivers to supply toys and orchestrate his day. He can get into more trouble, and he can have more fun. The ability to ambulate independently heralds a whole new era. The infant becomes a toddler.

DATA GATHERING

WHAT TO OBSERVE

At every encounter during the first 2 years, the child should be allowed free movement so that the clinician can observe the child's motor competencies. Place the child both supine and prone on the examining table to observe increasing head control, truncal stability, arm support, movement at the hip, and the smoothness and rhythmicity of the movement.

Observe the amount of support the child requires to do other things such as reach for a stethoscope. Note a decreasing need for support with sitting and increasing weight bearing on the lower extremities.

Observation of the child walking with help and then alone should begin when the child is 9 months of age and continue until school age or beyond, if there is a question. The walking base, the foot position, truncal rotation, and movement at the knee should be observed. The hand and arm position should change over time. The child's stopping and pivoting should improve. The rising to stand, stooping, and recovering all will become smoother with time. The style, interest, and excitement of the child with motor activities should be noted at every encounter. At 3 years of age, there should be good knee and ankle motion, and a heel strike should be present. Children can broad jump at 3 years, balance briefly on one leg or the other at 4 years, and hop at 5 years.

A simple two-step climbing device kept in the examining room against the examining table can provide observations of increasing motor competencies. This apparatus will allow demonstration of lower extremity movement, proximal muscle strength, and coordination in climbing. A line on the floor provides guidance for the child's directed walking. An area of some reasonable length (e.g., a hallway) must be provided for free-walking assessment.

A parent's handling of the child can give clues to both the child's competencies and the child's motor abilities. A parent who carefully supports the infant's head at all times when the child is 3 months old may either rightfully anticipate that this infant's head control is poorer than that of the usual 3-month-old, or the parent may be evidencing a lack of appreciation for the child's growing motor competencies. Children around the world will be ready for upright packaging with or without attachment (e.g., backpacks, wrapping on the hip or back, cradleboarding) by 3 to 4 months. If they are being carried like a neonate, there is something wrong. Parents who cannot allow a 4-year-old to climb up on an examining table may anticipate that the child will be unsuccessful or awkward. Excessive "coaching" of a child during the motor assessment may also be a clue that there is a worry about function in this area.

WHAT TO ASK

Parents will usually find reporting of gross-motor skills the easiest of all areas of development. Because motor milestones reflect dramatic changes in skill acquisition, they are readily apparent to most observers. In addition to asking what the child can do, ask *how* the child approaches the task (e.g., with caution at one extreme, or with abandon and impulsively at the other). The manner or style in which these skills are performed may reflect the emerging personality, family expectations, or difficulty with motor coordination. The parents' response about the child's accomplishments may provide data about any underlying anxiety or specific worries. By beginning questions at a lower level of functioning than anticipated, the clinician can both find the floor of the child's performance and convey the importance of individual expectations in motor development.

By linking questions about other areas of development with those about motor skills, the clinician highlights the interrelationships between areas of development. As the clinician's questions link motor, social, and language skills, the parents' perspective about the significance of changing motor competencies surfaces; in other words, what *else* can he now do and how does he see himself in relationship to others and to new activities? This approach to history taking provides a broad data base and extends guidance to parents in a subtle, automatic, and effective way.

The child's temperament is revealed in *how* he goes about moving in space. A single detailed description of one event (e.g., moving toward a desired toy, learning to climb stairs or ride a bike) provides more information than an exhaustive checklist of motor skills.

Children practice newly emerging skills in motor development, as well as in other areas of development. The relatively invariant order of motor-skill acquisition allows the clinician taking a history for a generally normally developing child to simply ask what kind of new movements or activities he is doing. The internally regulated and self-fueling nature of this area of development is highlighted in this approach.

A child whose motor development is not synchronous with other areas of development needs a more detailed history. Disorders of movement vs. disorders of tone and posture can be specified through history, coupled with a careful examination. Perinatal difficulties must alert the clinician to the need for a very careful evaluation of gross motor competencies, particularly if walking is delayed beyond 18 months (Chaplais and MacFarlane, 1984; anon., 1990).

EXAMINATION

In addition to observation of posture and movement throughout the encounter, when talking to the parent or examining the child, the clinician should assess passive motor tone of all extremities throughout the first 3 years. Both slow and rapid motions should be applied to the limbs to elicit any lowered threshold to a stretch reflex. This will vary with state and will be predictably altered in prematurely born children. Deep tendon reflexes should also be monitored. Asymmetries of tone or reflexes, provided the child's head is in midline, need very careful follow-up. Persistence of these signs may require further neurological evaluation. Early evidence of spastic cerebral palsy is evident by noting tight heel cords with limited flexion of the foot. Scissoring of the lower extremities when the child is held upright reflects adductor spasm. An obvious limp requires complete neurological and orthopedic assessment by an experienced specialist.

Head and truncal tone should be assessed through the pull-to-sit, prone, and in the position of the child being held over the hand. In addition, the child's head and body control when being held upright, at the shoulder, or under the arms in front of the examiner should be assessed during the first year.

Placing the baby both prone and supine offers the chance to assess increasing shoulder girdle tone and strength, as well as control of the lower body. Alternating hip movements appear at 5 months of age but significantly increase in some form after 9 months.

Weight-bearing on the feet is observed in children from the age of 5 months to walking. Persistent standing on the tiptoes is abnormal after 9 months. Walking with help should be attempted after 9 months but may not be present until after the first birthday.

Climbing up stairs is seen from 8 to 18 months. After the age of 2 years, children will attempt to do this with feet only, two feet on the step. Only after $2\frac{1}{2}$ to 3 years of age do children alternate feet on steps.

Gait should be observed during the second through the sixth years and beyond if indicated. As the toddler begins to walk independently, his gait is typically wide based, accompanied by waddling hips and intermittent toe walking. With each observation, the base should narrow, the arms come down, and reciprocal movement should be added. The waddling at the hip should decrease; knees should move a bit more; ankle movement should increase, and a heel strike should be present at the age of 3 years. By the age of 5 years, a sticker placed below the umbilicus should move very little except forward as the child walks. Forward movement, either walking or crawling, should be, by and large, smooth and rhythmic.

Children can stoop about 6 months after independent walking. They bounce to music at 15 to 18 months of age. Getting up to sit or stand should be by a smooth roll to the side by 15 months.

Children who are consistently 3 to 6 months behind on motor-skill acquisition need a second look. Muscle tone, deep tendon reflexes, and the persistence of primitive reflexes and postures need careful evaluation. Cerebral palsy, hypotonias, muscular, and metabolic diseases must be considered. Through a careful history and assessment over a period of time, the primary care provider may determine whether the delays are global or are confined to the motor area. Further evaluation and intervention can become more focused with this in mind.

ANTICIPATORY GUIDANCE

The clinician can support the parents' feelings of assurance and pride in their child's motor accomplishments. She can also highlight the individual temperamental characteristics of the child that affect all areas of development. Anxiety about individual patterns of development should be diffused and the child's integrity confirmed.

Parents support development in this area by providing opportunities for free exploration of the environment within safe limits. Excessive "practice" (adult perspective) and even overwhelming praise squelch the child's own innate drive for mastery and competency. Enthusiasm and joy in movement, in exploration, and in opportunities for seeing the rewards of that activity are what parents can provide. Toys and interesting safe activities in every room of the house provide that atmosphere. A safe play area and encouragement of daily gross-motor activities for girls and boys in nonrestrictive, nonfussy clothes support that activity. Walkers should be avoided for all children but especially those with increased tone in the lower extremities.

On the floor exercises, wrestling sessions, and ball playing for both sexes are also good activities if they are done in a relaxed, social manner. Baby gymnastics, swimming classes, and therapy programs are fine if they are done with those principles in mind; the activities themselves do not magically enhance development.

Swimming lessons in particular may be dangerous for young infants (AAP, 1980; Bennett, et al., 1983; California Medical Association, 1984), and it is unrealistic for children to reliably sequence and coordinate the motor activities of swimming before the age of 4 years. Primitive reflexes are the basis for most behaviors in the water at younger ages.

Beginner walkers are very energy inefficient. They require about 1,200 kcal/day to sustain their new activities. This has to be delivered in six small meals because they usually cannot sit still long enough for larger meals. Clinicians can anticipate these changes in feeding for parents. Children less than age 4 years should never be allowed to eat and walk at the same time because of the danger of aspiration.

In spite of its name, the infant walker may not enhance a child's ability to walk (Crouchman, 1986). Head injuries are common in young children in walkers. Children with lower extremity extensor hypertonicity do "very well" in walkers. However, that posture only exaggerates their own abnormal preponderance of extensor tone. These children need to be on the floor, moving freely, and practicing reciprocal hip and knee movement. Every child can push walkers out doors, down stairs, and out into streets. They contain children poorly and thwart prewalking progression. Individual therapy programs may include walkers for specific children to stabilize the trunk. Other than in that context, it is better to actively discourage their use, particularly in populations of former premature infants, who may have either transient or fixed dystonias.

Programs based on the concept that all learning is facilitated through an integration of motor acitivites have no basis in science and have had no demonstration of effectiveness. These programs prescribe a rigid series of motor activities to be done by the parent so that "patterns," either accelerated or remedial, can be established in the child. These activities consume up to 8 hours per day of "therapy" by the parent. Failures are attributed to noncompliance. These programs, under several names throughout the country (AAP, 1982; Holm, 1984), victimize parents of handicapped children who are looking for anything to improve their child's outcome. An appeal is also made to parents who want to provide extra help for their normal children in academic skill acquisition. There is no evidence that patterning is important for development at all. There is certainly no evidence that learning to crawl has anything to do with learning to read. Secondary gain from increased parental attention, social interaction, and fun may have some benefit for some children in some circumstances, but the formal activities of those programs are incidental. Clinicians should be informed of what programs are operative in their communities and examine them carefully. Parents should be offered that professional input.

One final point is often raised by parents: The type of shoes a child wears is not critical to gait. The develoment of the foot and its participation in emerging gait are best supported by either no shoes or soft shoes that allow the foot to bend and move. Parents appreciate learning that shoes are to be used to protect the feet from injury. They should not be rigidly supporting the ankle or hampering movement. Expensive shoes are not necessarily the best shoes. Soft running shoes, properly fit and regularly replaced for a good fit on a growing foot, are probably as good as any. Good shoes for the toddler have much the same function as good parents in the support of motor development, that is, to provide protection from injury; to allow the child to move about freely; to avoid any untoward rigidity or expectation; to mold to the individual child; and to share daily new adventures and new discoveries.

REFERENCES

Adelson E, Fraiberg S: Gross motor development of infants blind from birth. *Child Dev* 1974; 45:114–126.

American Academy of Pediatrics, Committee on Pediatric Aspects of Physical Fitness, Recreation and Sports: Swimming instructions for infants. *Pediatrics* 1980; 65:847.

American Academy of Pediatrics: The Doman-Delcato treatment of neurologically handicapped children. *Pediatrics* 1982; 70:810–812.

Anonymous: Children who walk late [editorial]. *Lancet* 1990; 336:540–541.

Bayley N: *Bayley Scales of Infant Development.* New York, Psychological Corp, 1969.

Bennett HJ, Wagner T, Fields A.: Acute hyponatremia and seizures in an infant after a swimming lesson. *Pediatrics* 1983; 72:125–127.

Berger W, Quinlern J, Dietz V: Afferent and efferent control of stance and gait developmental changes in children. *Electroencephalogr Clin Neurophysiol* 1987; 66:244–252.

Bower TGR: *A Primer of Infant Development.* San Francisco, WH Freeman & Co, 1977.

Brazelton TB: *Toddlers and Parents: A Declaration of Independence.* New York, Delacorte Press, 1974.

Burnett CN, Johnson, EW: Development of gait in children: Parts I and II. *Dev Med Child Neurol* 1971; 13:196–215.

California Medical Association: Risks of toddler swimming programs. *Health Tips* June 1984; 454.

Chaplais JZ, MacFarlane IA: A review of four hundred and four late walkers. *Arch Dis Child* 1984; 59:512–516.

Chase RA, Fisher JJ, Rubin R, et al: *Infant Development Guide.* Skillman, NJ: Johnson & Johnson Baby Products Co, 1978.

Chisholm JS: *Navajo Infancy.* New York, Aldine Publishing Co, 1983.

Clark JE, Whitall J, Phillips SJ: Human interlimb coordination: The first six months of independent walking. *Dev Psychobiol* 1988; 21:445–456.

Crouchman M: The effect of baby walkers on early locomotor development. *Dev Med Child Neurol* 1986; 28:757–761.

Dennis W: Does culture appreciably affect patterns of infant behavior? *J Soc Psychol* 1940; 12:305–317.

Dixon S, Tronick E, Keefer C, et al: Perinatal circumstances and newborn outcome among the Gusii of Kenya: Assessment of risk. *Infant Behav Dev* 1982; 5:11–32.

Fraiberg SH: *The Magic Years.* New York, Charles Scribner's Sons, 1959.

Gesell A, Thompson H: *The Psychology of Early Growth.* New York, Macmillan Publishing Co, 1938.

Harriman AE, Lukosuis PA: On why Wayne Dennis found Hopi Indians retarded in age of onset of walking. *Percept Mot Skills* 1982; 55:79–86.

Held R, Hein A: A movement-produced stimulation in the development of visually guided behavior. *Compr Physiol Psychol* 1963; 56:872–876.

Hennessy M, Dixon S, Simon S: The development of gait: A study in African children ages one to five. *Child Dev* 1984; 55:844–853.

Holm V: A western version of the Doman-Delacato treatment of patterning for developmental disabilities. *West J Med* 1984; 139:553–556.

Hopkins B, Westra T: Maternal expectations of their infants' development: Some cultural differences. *Dev Med Child Neurol* 1989; 31:384–390.

Illingworth RS: *The Development of Infant and Young Child: Normal and Abnormal,* ed 4. Baltimore, Williams & Wilkins Co, 1970.

Mahler MS, Pine F, Bergman A: *The Psychological Birth of the Human Infant: Symbiosis and Individuation.* New York, Basic Books, 1975.

McGraw M: *The Neuromuscular Maturation of the Human Infant.* New York, Hafner Press, 1945.

Ogg HL: Measuring and evaluating the gait patterns of children. *J APTA* 1963; 43:717–720.

Perry J: The mechanics of walking. *Phys Ther* 1967; 47:778–801.

Ridenour MV: Infant walkers: Developmental tool or inherent danger? *Percept Mot Skills* 1982; 55:1201–1202.

Sahler OJN, McAnarney ER: *The Child from Three to Eighteen.* St Louis, CV Mosby, 1981.

Scrutton DR, Robson P: The gait of 50 normal children. *Physiotherapy* 1968; 54:363–368.

Smart MS, Smart RC: *Development and Relationships: Infants.* New York, Macmillan Publishing Co, 1978, vol 1.

Sutherland DH, Olshen RA, Cooper L, et al: The development of mature gait. *J Bone Joint Surg (Am)* 1980; 62:336–353.

Thelen E: Learning to walk: Ecological demands and phylogenetic constraints. *Adv Infancy Res* 1984; 3:213–250.

Thelen E, Bradshaw G, Ward JA: Spontaneous kicking in month old infants: Manifestation of a human central locomotor program. *Behav Neural Biol* 1981; 32:45–53.

Willemsen E: *Understanding Infancy.* San Francisco, WH Freeman & Co, 1979.

Wolff P: Theoretical issues in the development of motor skills, in Lewis M, Taft L (eds): *Developmental Disabilities: Theory, Assessment and Intervention.* New York, Spectrum Publications, 1981.

Wyke B: The neurological basis of movement: A developmental overview, in Holt K (ed): *Movement and Child Development.* London, Heinemann Medical Books, 1975.

Young G: Manual specialization in infancy, in Segalowitz SJ, Gruber FA (eds): *Language Development and Neurological Theory.* New York, Academic Press, 1977.

"A baby in the park." By K.P., girl, age 10.

CHAPTER 16

Eighteen Months: Asserting Oneself, A Push-Pull Process

MARTIN T. STEIN, M.D

KEY WORDS

AUTONOMY VS ATTACHMENT
RAPPROCHEMENT
PREDICTABLE REGRESSIONS
DISCIPLINE
SELF-DETERMINATION
TRANSITIONAL OBJECT
BEHAVIOR MODIFICATION

The mother of an 18-month-old girl asks if she should be concerned about her daughter's preference for a bottle—during the day and at bedtime. A standard response might be, "A child this age no longer needs her bottle. It's bad for her teeth and may encourage ear infections. My advise is to take it away and let her drink from a cup. She's a big girl now— she needs to grow up!"

An alternative approach would encourage a response based on a developmental history. Recognizing that maintaining a preference for the bottle represents holding onto an earlier, more dependent stage of development, an exploration of other milestones that reflect her autonomy might be useful. Focused questions to the mother as well as office observations revealed that this toddler fed herself independently with a spoon and drank from a cup, soothed herself to sleep each night with minimal fussing and responded to her parents' verbal constraints at times of conflict. She enjoyed the care of a regular babysitter and did not cry when her parents occasionally left her at night. In the office, she was observed to play by herself with toys. Periodically, she would check in with her mother and then return to the toy box. She seemed happy and able to move back and forth between the security of her mother and the autonomous, self-initiating play.

The child's development demonstrates a strong attachment to her mother while simultaneously becoming more independent in social and motor skills. While the use of a bottle may be viewed as a residual symbol of infancy, perhaps this remarkably healthy girl needs a temporary "crutch" in the form of a bottle in order to negotiate the more demanding achievements of the second year.

The discrepancy between what a parent tells you about behavior and development and what you observe in the office setting is perhaps most striking at the visit when the child is 18 months old. Although a parent may describe a child who now feeds herself, has the capability to express her needs, can follow simple directions, and is a "delightful child," the clinician frequently observes someone quite different. In the office, the same child may be suspicious of your kind and gentle approach, cling firmly to her parent, scream at any touch, and resist initial social interchange with a toy or an examining tool. How can this behavior be understood in a way that provides some insight into each child's development for the clinician and for the parents?

The behavior of an 18-month-old does contain many contradictions. She seeks to be more independent in all areas but needs additional nurturance to refuel that push toward autonomy. She needs parents for additional security but at the same time seems to be always assertive in pulling away. The resistance and the negativism of this age try the patience of parents. Simultaneously, these forces supply the energy needed to act independently.

The toddler appears to have an innate resource of energy to master new skills in her even more complex world. Unfortunately, attention span, cooperation with playmates, motor dexterity, and, perhaps the most significant, tolerance for frustrating events are limited. Although drive for mastery of the environment appears to be built in (some parents describe it as "driven . . . striving . . . searching"), the child's psychological tasks inevitably apply limits and precipitate conflicts as the child reaches out for more independence. Frustration is a fact of life for a child struggling to do more things, explore more places, and push at the limits of her behavior and the restraints of the real world around her.

The 18-month-old has developed a strong emotional tie with her parents; events in the outside world are measured against that link. At this age, the child frequently checks back with a parent as if to say, "Is it safe? Can I continue to play . . . to move forward?" She uses her parents as a secure base from which to explore (Ainsworth, 1979). This behavior can be seen in day-care centers and playgrounds when the toddler is brave and independent and then suddenly searches and runs to a secure area when the social environment changes or becomes threatening. For some toddlers, even the benevolent approach of a physician or nurse threatens a fragile internal stability; in the office, the child runs quickly to the parent, seeking a sanctum and security. The same child might have appeared more secure with the clinician during the first half of the second year, but by 18 months a "rapprochement" (Mahler et al., 1975) with the parent and outer world produces what, on the surface, appears to be more infantile behaviors (clinging to a parent, crying at a stranger, or refusing the approach of a playmate). It is as if the maturation of the central nervous system has produced greater awareness of the external world (e.g., other children, other adults, toys, furniture), and this awareness now comes into conflict with a previously secure, parentally modulated environment. Cognitive skills have matured enough so that a child can imagine a threat (Kagan, 1984). Communication is appreciated as important in handling of the world, but an 18-month-old cannot effectively communicate with strangers. She is lost without her parents' translation and interpretation.

Helping parents through this period is made easier when the clinician's observations and expectations of behaviors are based on these developmental phenomena. The patterns of interaction that are established at this time have great longevity. Parents must see the struggles for mastery and independence as both inevitable and a positive sign of the child's emotional and social growth. This will sustain them through the "first adolescence."

Three aspects of behavior and development often surface at this age either in the questions parents bring to the office visit or in what a clinician observes in the office setting: (1) discipline and temper tantrums; (2) toilet training; and (3) changes in feeding patterns. All of these can be seen within the context of this drive for independence.

DISCIPLINE

The newly discovered capacity to walk, run, and climb opens up new pathways of exploration for the toddler. Not only can she get to things, she now can manipulate objects into new forms that follow from her imagination. Fine-motor and visual-perceptual skills allow her to shape, invent, and explore objects; these manipulations give definition and form to her world. Simultaneously, receptive language function is developing rapidly; she now *understands* many words, follows simple directions, and can even point to some parts of her body when the name is sounded by a parent.

These new skills emerge rapidly and must be incorporated into a psychological framework that previously was dependent on caretakers passively manipulating the child's environment. The sudden awareness that through language, motor, and perceptual skills the child can shape and pattern her world brings about inner conflict for most children. These conflicts can be seen when a tower of neatly stacked blocks fall; when a playmate, benign and benevolent at one moment, commits the awful sin of touching a child's toys momentarily; or when a parent removes a child from one enjoyable activity to another (e.g., from playing with toys to the dreaded highchair). The toddler now is aware that she can make a choice about a toy, a playmate, or a meal. Infringement on those choices produces inner disharmony that may lead to anger and aggression. The young toddler does not possess the psychic structure to delay gratification, to suppress or displace angry feelings, or to manage these difficult situations through verbal communication. She cannot wait, see things from another's point of view, anticipate compound effects of her actions, or cope effectively.

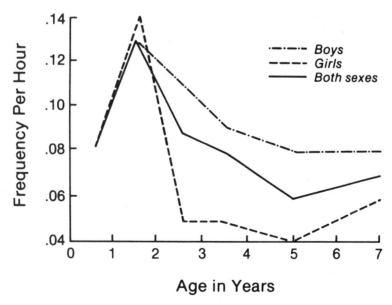

FIG 16–1.
Frequency of anger outbursts, with peak between 18 months and 2 years. (Adapted from Goodenough FL: *Anger in Young Children.* St Paul, University of Minnesota Press, 1931, and cited in Helms DB, Turner JS: *Exploring Child Behavior: Basic Principles.* Philadelphia, WB Saunders Co, 1978.)

As an alternative, she pouts, cries, becomes morose, or has a temper tantrum. Behavior outbursts by the 18-month-old can be viewed as developmentally predictable (Fig 16–1). The frequency and intensity with which an individual child manifests these behaviors is dependent on many factors, including (1) the degree of attachment to parents, (2) the toddler's individual personality and her way of adapting to new and stressful situations, and (3) the parents' style of responding to various behaviors in the child.

Emotional attachment to parents is a major goal of the first year of life; whereas in the second year, children need to be encouraged to broaden the focus of that attachment and become more independent. (In fact, some observers of human development have suggested that the guiding psychological goal throughout life after the first birthday is to disattach from one's parents!) Parents can be encouraged to allow self-play, mistakes, mishaps, and consequent frustrations in their child. If a parent is too protective and limits the development of independent skills by providing an overly protective environment, infantile attachment behaviors become more secure and lock the child into an earlier phase of development. New situations—without mommy or daddy or when frustration is inevitable—become intolerable. When a toddler is allowed, even encouraged, to experience *modulated* amounts of frustration during the course of play, she learns to manage angry feelings, feelings that may be directed toward parents, play objects, or a playmate. These kinds of experiences assist the child in the gradual journey of becoming more independent from parents.

The toddler's personality is reflected in the style in which she responds to conflict, with self, others, and the environment. Toddlers vary significantly in the energy released when a frustrating experience arises. A youngster with a high level of adaptability to change and a positive approach to new stimuli is likely to move quickly from a conflictual situation to one that is harmonious. At the opposite end of the spectrum is a child with intense expressions of mood and negative withdrawal responses to new situations. This child may be easily frustrated at seemingly minor conflict. The intensity and duration of crying, screaming, and level of consolability will, in part, relate to these innate aspects of temperament. Although most children are somewhere between these temperamental extremes, a clinical appreciation for them can be helpful in assessing a particular child and the parents' responses to that child (Carey, 1982).

Finally, parental styles of responding to a toddler's tantrums effect the resolution of the episode, as well as the nature of future tantrums. Children are sponges of adult attitudes and actions at this age. They learn how to handle their own anger, aggression, and frustration as they observe parents and other caretakers. Often those parents who seem able in managing toddler tantrums are less threatened by their child's aggressive moments and emerging independence. They do not get drawn into the struggle themselves. They recognize, often unconsciously, the strengths of this autonomous act and can freely assist the child in handling her feelings. Other parents may feel challenged or threatened by the child's bids for independence and respond only with anger. Styles of parenting the child at this age often reflect a parent's own sense of self-effectiveness and her own experiences from childhood. The toddler can call forth feelings and responses that many parents did not even know were within them.

Discipline at this age means teaching, guiding behavior, and showing the child how to cooperate. It is not simply the parents' response to a tantrum. When viewed constructively, discipline can be seen as a process of teaching the toddler to place limits or boundaries on her own behavior within family and cultural limits; to learn to "use words" to express anger; to feel comfortable with feelings of anger; and to learn to cope with the inevitable frustrations of normal life. It may be useful to compare tantrums to a blown fuse. The tantrum serves a purpose in itself; it releases tension as it provides an exit for bound-up energy that momentarily finds no other outlet. Occasional toddler tantrums viewed in this manner can be accepted, understood, and allowed to occur by the understanding parent. In the healthy toddler, occasional tantrums usually cannot be stopped and should even be seen as helpful.

Psychologically viewed, "discipline solidifies the boundaries as well as the core of the ego" (Brazelton et al., 1984). It offers the child a way to manage conflictual feelings and unacceptable behaviors. Because the fragile ego is developing a sense of self at this time, conflicts directed at parents, peers, siblings, and toys are necessary. These conflicts collectively define the child's emerging ego; simultaneously, the child needs an adult to define acceptable limits of behavior. Pushing and testing those limits may be the only way to be sure of their firmness. The push-pull process of a toddler's development is now seen in terms of both the child's behaviors and the parental responses to those behaviors.

TOILET TRAINING

Five milestones are required before a toddler is ready to master bowel and bladder control: (1) maturation of the central and peripheral nervous systems to the degree where voluntary control of the anal and urethral sphincters is possible, (2) an ability to sit on a potty seat quietly for a moderate period of time with the conscious intent to have a bowel movement or to urinate, (3) the desire to gain satisfaction from the successful completion of defecation and urination—to recognize the pleasure in the supervising parent and within oneself through growth in competency as a form of positive reinforcement, (4) an ability to understand the sequence of requirements of the task; and (5) the drive to imitate is greater than the drive to oppose parents. These milestones of development reflect mastery of motor, social, and language skills that usually come together after the second birthday; for some, it may be a few months earlier; for others, developmental readiness may not be apparent until 3 or more years of age (Table 16–1). From the child's viewpoint, there is no advantage to either too early or too rapid training. It may be detrimental if it lays out expectations she cannot handle. When viewed from the standpoint of the child's needs, toilet training demands a level of complex, multistepped, voluntary control that could not be obtained previously. Motor, social, and receptive language skills come together to make this a big event in a child's life. It is an opportunity for growth and increased feelings of self-esteem.

As a form of anticipatory guidance, it is helpful to discuss toilet training at the visit when the child is 18 months old for three reasons: (1) to prevent parents from rushing into training before the child is ready, (2) to bring out the developmental significance of training as a way to assist parents in understanding and responding to the broader developmental events at this age, and (3) so that parents can begin to set the stage for this process later on.

Clues that a child is physically and emotionally ready for potty training may be observed at some time between 18 months and $2\frac{1}{2}$ years of age in most children. The child will demonstrate that she has made the connection between the feeling (muscular contractions) of urination or defecation and what is produced. This connection will be communicated to the parent as the child points or looks at her urine or bowel movement. The child will have

TABLE 16–1.
Guide to Toilet Training Readiness: A Developmental Approach

Child's Behavior/Competencies	Parental Response
Complex, multistep behavior; completing household tasks; completing tasks in correct sequence	Child watching parent or siblings at toilet while parent narrates the process
Undresses self	Allow child to undress self; loose, easily removed clothes are preferred; praise the child while mentioning that she will soon use a potty seat
Shows interest in a potty seat	Keep potty seat in a regular place in the bathroom; let the child know she can sit on it and what it is used for; some children can learn about the seat initially by sitting on it with diaper on
Demonstrates ability to understand requirements of various tasks	
Points to, looks at, or announces BM* in diaper	Put diaper/BM in seat; dispose of it later; acknowledge the production
Increasing periods of daytime dryness	Training pants during the day
Ability to sit quietly on potty seat for a moderate period	Praise the child that she now knows about the seat and discuss its use; encourage sitting on the seat
Shows satisfaction in having BM	Praise moderately by showing pleasure in completion of task
Asks to use potty seat or uses it in self-directed manner	Encourage use of potty seat after a meal (gastro-colic reflex) or (for some children) at a time when she usually has a BM
Desire to please by imitating parents	Praise the child by pointing out that "my big girl is now ready to use her potty seat"
Partial voluntary control of anal and urethral sphincters, demonstrated by having a BM or urinating at a planned time on the potty seat	Show pleasure in task completion while expecting setbacks, both at times of stress and spontaneously
Interest in successful use of potty seat	Try training pants; encourage child to remove training pants by self

*BM = bowel movement.

increased periods of daytime dryness (i.e., increased bladder capacity and sphincter control), will tell you that she has had a bowel movement or urinated, and can sit quietly for a period. She will show interest in the toilet, will show imitative behavior in other areas (e.g., dressing, household tasks), will be interested in compulsively putting things away, and will not be violently negative. At this time, parents can be encouraged to introduce a potty seat, explaining its function to the child and making it available to her. Parents must take children into the bathroom with them and discuss the process; older siblings may complement the parents in this instructive role. Having the child on a potty chair (initially with the diaper attached) is a first step in getting acquainted with the chair. The parents should be positive toward the behavior and the product (feces). The child will see the bowel movement as a part of self; parents should not regard it as "yucky." Parents can be encouraged to show their pleasure at a successful movement, but overenthusiasm is not warranted, because this exaggerates the importance of this, adding stress to the child and inviting negative behavior. Conversely, parents whose 2-year-old does not seem interested in a potty chair should be encouraged to wait a few months. It is often helpful to point out to parents that just as some normal children do not walk until after 15 months, some toddlers require more time to attain consistent voluntary sphincter control and to be willing to exercise it! It is not a measure of intelligence on the child's part or of adequacy of child rearing on the parents' part.

The initiation and continuation of toilet training is dependent on the child's personal health and environmental events. External events such as intercurrent illness, birth of a new sibling, a family vacation, or absence of a parent for a prolonged period can be expected to delay or cause a setback in the mastery of toilet training. When some of these events are predictable, potty training may be delayed by the parents. Regressions without any explanations also should be expected. The child's self-respect should be preserved in these circumstances. Parents should be informed that other less predictable changes in the family function may delay mastery of this new skill. Boys generally train $2\frac{1}{2}$ months later than girls. Firstborn children are 1.7 months delayed compared with children born later. In most families, the whole process may take months.

FEEDING AND SELF-DETERMINATION

As fine-motor skills and visual-motor coordination advance, the 18-month-old finds herself enjoying the use of a cup and spoon. Self-feeding represents a significant form of mastery, as well as psychological separation from dependency on parents. It is helpful to point out to parents that although messy and seemingly disorganized, allowing a child the freedom to feed herself assists her development and mastery at several levels: (1) fine-motor skills, (2) hand-to-eye coordination, (3) independent actions yielding an enjoyable response, and (4) learning to choose from and enjoy different food textures and colors.

As with any new skill, learning may progess at different rates for children of various temperaments, and setbacks (or regressions) may occur after intercurrent events in the family. As with most new experiences that require mastery, feeding, in particular, is vulnerable to individual differences and fluctuations. Particular attractions or dislikes for certain foods are common at this time. Prolonged periods of refusing one food group are common (i.e., food jags). As long as the child's physical growth has not been compromised, parents need reassurance that the fluctuations in diet are normal and self-limited. Demonstrating the child's rate of growth on a standard growth curve is often reassuring to the parent who perceives the toddler as "starving herself." More important, from the developmental point of view, an explanation about the importance of self-directed feeding in terms of emotional independence is helpful. The more the clinician can do to assist the parent of a toddler in understanding these new skills as a reflection of mastery and "separation" from infantile dependency on the parent, the better equipped the parent will be for "letting go" through continued guidance and surveillance without squelching further growth. A parent has never won a feeding battle with a child. Ingenuity and patience are required to set up feeding to be a source of good nutrition, physical and psychological (Brazelton et al., 1984).

The "push-pull" process that characterizes this stage of development can be viewed as one of daily increments of psychological growth achieved by mastery of more complicated skills. These skills require adequate maturation of the toddler's nervous system and the parents' ability to simultaneously stimulate and pull back, that is, to encourage self-feeding, potty seat recognition, and creative play while letting the child master these objects and events independently. To be sure, it is a delicate balance that requires parental skill that will vary in different families. The child's clinician can point out the developmental necessity of this balance. It can be demonstrated during the physical examination with toys or examining instruments or when observing the child's play during the interview with the parent.

DATA GATHERING

OBSERVATIONS

Watching the 18-month-old child, both at independent play and while she is interacting with her parent, provides insight into the developmental goals of this age. As the history is recorded, helpful observations include:

1. Does the child play independently? Does she make use of toys in the examining room?
2. Fine-motor dexterity and visual-motor skills can be observed through play. Does the child play spontaneously with toys in the office? Does she make a tower out of four cubes? Does she scribble spontaneously? Does she remove her clothes by herself?
3. Does the child have a transitional object? Was it brought to the office? If so, how is it used by the child?
4. Does the parent allow the child to move around the examining room independently, to experiment with the available toys?
5. How does the parent modulate the child's play, verbally and nonverbally?
6. When you walk into the room, what is the child doing? Does she change activity in your presence?
7. What is the intensity and duration with which the child clings to the parent? How does the parent respond?
8. What is the content and style of the parent's verbal interactions with the child?
9. Assess the child's response to your examination.

HISTORY

To discover the point on the developmental pathway from dependency to autonomy for a particular toddler, the clinician may ask a parent to describe a typical morning at home with the child. Motor, language, and social milestones are documented. Feeding styles, behaviors, disciplinary responses, and play content are often discussed spontaneously by looking in detail at one time interval. If not, focused questions can be directed, with the goal of assessing psychological independence:

1. Does she play alone? What kind of toys interest her? Is she allowed to explore safe cabinets in the home? Is there a place for her in every room?
2. Does she experience temper tantrums? What appears to set her off? When do these occur? How intense are they? What are your usual responses? How do they make you feel?
3. Do you and your spouse agree on expectations for and management of the child's behavior?
4. Does she have a favorite thing she carries around or takes to bed? How do you feel about it? Do you always make it available to her?
5. When she is doing something that is off limits, how do you respond to her? What do you say? What do you do?
6. Many parents of toddlers find it hard to say "no" so many times each day. How do you manage to change behaviors without always saying "no"?

7. Have you thought about toilet training? If so, what ideas do you have about when and how to accomplish it?

EXAMINATION

Approach the child cautiously. If when you enter the examining room, the toddler is on the floor or at a table playing with toys, you might bend down to the child's level. Sitting on the floor and engaging the child with a ball or other toy may yield a temporary alliance permitting effective interaction with the child. A simple, brief comment about the toy she is playing with or a color (or pattern) on her clothes may be helpful.

Frequently at this age the toddler may react with alarm at your entrance into the examining room. She usually seeks out the mother and either clings to her or sits quietly on her lap. Reassure the parent that this is normal and expected behavior at this age. In fact, it represents an emotionally close attachment between the child and parent.

The physical examination is usually performed optimally with the child in the parent's lap. Relatively high-yield physical abnormalities can be assessed accurately while the child is held by the parent. In the same manner, assessment of language, motor, and social skill can be successful when the child is sitting on the parent's lap. The extent of the stranger-awareness response will determine how much developmental information can be observed; other data can be obtained from the parent's history.

Because the move toward independence is in progress at this stage, coupled with the unfamiliar examining room, many assessments of development at the age of 18 months appear more developmentally delayed than they are. Explaining this to parents is helpful. They should not feel embarrassment when their toddler screams and clings to mother at the clinician's approach.

ANTICIPATORY GUIDANCE

The pediatric perspective for parent education at this examination should focus on (1) the anticipation of either behavioral or developmental problems based on the clinician's data base during the interview and physical examination and (2) assisting parents with the next developmental stage by pointing to new milestones and anticipated behaviors.

The child's temperament, behavioral responses to new situations, progress in self-directed feeding, and independent play will guide the discussion of anticipatory guidance. Not every visit at 18 months will require the discussion offered in these guidelines. For some parents, reassurance that development is on track will suffice. Insight into broader meanings of new skills is appreciated by all parents.

Behavioral and developmental education for parents of an 18-month-old may include the following topics:

THE CONCEPT OF RAPPROCHEMENT (MAHLER ET AL., 1975)

Without using the term rapprochement, which may be confusing or misleading to some parents, an explanation of the child's anticipated behavior is helpful. It refers to the frequently observed and normal change from independent play and exploratory activity to a period of clinging to the parent in the presence of other children and adults. It is usually seen between 18 and 24 months and may last for a week to several months. It is age appropriate, transient, and, for some children, a developmental necessity before achieving greater independence in play, language, and motor skills.

SELF-FEEDING AS AN EXPRESSION OF CONTROL AND INDEPENDENCE

Talk about feeding time in terms of the *child's* needs, not only the need for nutrients but also for self-directed mastery over an important part of her environment. Point out that appetites are often erratic at this age, but toddlers do not starve themselves. Let parents know that the appetite control mechanism in the hypothalamus is well developed and that given the availability of nutritious foods, the 18-month-old will choose adequate nutrients over time. Discourage force feeding or battles over food intake. Redirect the discussion to help the parents to view feeding in developmental terms, as an expression of learning to be satisfied through a self-directed task. Let parents know that messy feeding behaviors are both expected and appropriate at this age. Praise them for allowing the toddler to exercise new visual-motor skills that provide the hand-eye coordination to use a cup and spoon successfully. Socially accepted eating patterns are nurtured over time by a positive approach to these social situations.

THE TRANSITIONAL OBJECT (WINNICOTT, 1958)

About two thirds of toddlers will have an inanimate object that is used for comforting, especially when they are falling asleep and at times of stress. Some parents need the reassurance that these old threadbare blankets, dolls, or toys are a reasonable way to find the security required at certain moments in each day. Their use may persist until the third or fourth birthday and occasionally later. Developmental assessments at 10 years old, comparing children who used a transitional object (TO) with those who did not possess an obvious TO, showed no significant differences in behavioral or educational outcomes. Some youngsters seem to need it. Parents may appreciate the theoretical insight about the meaning of the TO as described by Winnicott et al. (1958).

TOILET TRAINING READINESS

This examination (usually the last health supervision visit prior to the second birthday) is an ideal time to anticipate the parents' expectations, knowledge, and plans for the initiation of toilet training. Readiness skills have been discussed earlier. Ask the parents, "What are your ideas or plans for toilet training?" Providing developmentally appropriate information at this time in terms of motor, social, and receptive language skills goes a long way in preventing either a too rigid or too lenient program for the child. Table 16–1 provides guidelines for the early stages of the process. It is helpful to teach parents that learning to use a potty seat is an important milestone in the toddler's ability to take control of the environment while gaining a sense of mastery and feeling good about herself. The focus should be on the *child's* control and not the parents.

ANTICIPATING DISCIPLINARY PROBLEMS

To assist parents in understanding the expected development of negative behavior in the form of emotional outbursts is a significant task for the child's clinician at this time (AAP, 1983). It should be explained and interpreted in terms of the toddler's striving for psychological independence, whereas his ability to manage independently his anger and frustrations is limited by both language and attachment to parents. It is the child's bid to have a say in what is going on, to have his perspective appreciated. Some parents find it difficult to accept or understand the push-pull nature of toddler behavior, even when provided with an explanation of the behavior as a requirement for psychological independence. These parents may have experienced a rigid or strict form of child rearing from their own parents, some may have been physically abused as children, and others may have a rigid personality structure with a limited capacity to tolerate conflict. They may also be struggling with issues of autonomy themselves. Whatever their background, these parents need special guidance in behavior management.

Parents must see how easy it is to be drawn into conflict and that this is always a no-win situation. They must see how the child's needs for control are undercut by a power struggle on the one hand and lack of control on the other. Secure limits that are consistently and kindly presented are the needs of the child. It may be helpful to provide parents with guidelines to assist them in clarifying their perception of the child's problem and a strategy for intervention. Critical questions for effective interactions by parents include (Vaughan and Litt, 1990):

1. "What am I trying to teach?"
2. "Why is this important to me?"
3. "How am I trying to teach it?"
4. "What is my child learning?"

Anticipating problems, the clinician may use this and subsequent visits to explore various change strategies.

COMMUNICATION SKILLS

Teaching parents that the toddler often has a receptive vocabulary at least ten times her expressive vocabulary may encourage some parents to talk to their children more effectively. The use of simple, clear phrases and sentences that express parental emotions and directions can be encouraged. Clear directives that are brief, are unequivocal, and do not imply a choice when there is none are best (e.g., "It's time to go to bed" versus "Would you like to go to bed?").

ANTICIPATING AND SHORT-CIRCUITING EXCESSIVE FRUSTRATION

Many children at this age experience a tantrum as their immediate environment overheats (e.g., a supermarket, a large family gathering, dinner preparations causing a busy end of the day). The excessive sensory stimulation may be visual, auditory, tactile, or, as is often the case, a combination of sensory inputs. The time of the day may be a contributing factor (e.g., in the morning when parents are busy preparing for work or school, end of the day when parents and older siblings return home, or bedtime). Many parents are not aware of the temporal and situational patterns that tantrums follow. It may be helpful to suggest change indirectly by asking, "do you think that changing some of these situations may help your child by decreasing moments of frustration?" Specific suggestions might include shopping at a different time (when the child is more rested or, if possible, without the child), providing an alternative activity when dinner preparations are under way (e.g., watching Sesame Street or some other child-oriented television program or videotape, or arranging for an older sibling to play with the toddler).

CONSISTENCY IN DISCIPLINE

Children at this age require consistency in all aspects of their life. Too many caretakers, too many different activities, and too many different people giving different cues confuse expectations and responses of the toddler. It is not surprising that parents often have inconsistent approaches to child rearing in general and to toddler discipline in particular, because they are products of different families and often conflicting parenting styles. In addition, the inconsistencies in behavior responses may be between a grandparent and parents or between the parents and day-care personnel. When inconsistency in discipline becomes apparent, the clinician should point out the advantages, indeed, necessity, of providing consistency. A conference with both parents is often required to explore and solve this problem. Basic philosophies, as well as very specific issues, must be discussed in a frank, open manner within a family. This process ideally starts in the first year; it becomes a clear necessity in the second.

BEHAVIOR MODIFICATION

The reinforcement of positive behaviors while not recognizing or discouraging negative behaviors is important. Some parents encourage negative behavior unconsciously by either overreacting to minor outbursts of anger or by frequent demeaning statements when behavior is contrary. Point out that this kind of attention only raises the child's interest in pursuing negative behaviors. Conversely, frequent praise for positive behaviors teaches the child that parental attention and appreciation is the reward for doing things well, such as drinking from a cup independently, using a potty seat, asking for a toy or milk, or making something with toys (Showalter, 1977).

DEALING WITH TANTRUMS

When parents recognize that most tantrums in children at this age are a result of acute frustration, the simple, but very effective, method of distracting the child from the situation that appears to be associated with the frustration usually is effective. In fact, distraction as a way of life may be the method of survival for some families at this stage of development! Suggest that the child can be physically removed from the conflictual or unsafe environment and placed in a less conflictual or safer place. An alternative toy, a book, or an interactive game with a parent or other person usually serves to ameliorate the screaming child if given with a hug or loving touch. Bodily contact is important.

Other tantrums will require a verbal dialogue between parent and child. Removing the toddler from the conflictual environment and sitting with her in a quiet place is the first step. Holding her closely while talking is settling and reassuring for some children. Asking a question that reflects the child's feelings at the moment gives the child an opportunity to reflect on the emotional content of her behavior, a feeling or thought that may not be available to her unless it is articulated by a person she trusts (Table 16–2). Examples of this form of communication are:

1. "Gee, you sure are upset right now!"
2. "Sometimes we get real angry and upset inside us when things aren't going well."
3. "Isn't it awful when you can't do something you really want to do?"
4. "You seem really mad at me now."

Although the intensity of the tantrum, the child's temperament, and the parent's ability to confront emotional material will predict the effect of this method, it is a very powerful tool—not only as a method of response to negative behavior but also, more significantly, as a potential foundation for parent-child communication about feelings (Gordon, 1975).

TABLE 16–2.
Expressing Emotions Through Ideas*

Greenspan's model for child development emphasized the interaction between emerging emotional capacities and thought processes at different ages. He has pointed out that the 18 month old exhibits **specific behaviors to express emotions through ideas:**

Dependency and security—Caring for and holding a doll or stuffed toy

Pleasure—Showing smiles and excitement to accompany play; indicating fondness for certain food or a special toy

Curiosity—Hide-and-seek or exploring drawers or closets; search play with dolls or stuffed toys

Assertiveness—Making needs known verbally; putting doll or stuffed toy in charge of activities of other toys

Protest and anger—Using words such as "mad" to express anger; getting mad at an uncooperative toy

Setting self-limits—Punishing a doll or stuffed toy for being naughty; responding to parental "no"

In this model, "a tantrum is seen as the result of a frustration—an inability to master a task, to communicate a desire, to understand why things are as they are." Following a calming-down period, the parent can then reengage him in the world of ideas and teach a valuable lesson: closeness between parent and child can occur even after a disruptive emotional experience. By teaching a child to label feelings, to learn to make use of pretend play and by using words to discipline, the child's emotional and cognitive skills are blended to encourage growth.

Greenspan offers the following example of managing a toddler temper tantrum:

"Jimmy enjoys taking care of his stuffed dog in pretend play but has temper tantrums when frustrated. Today, his mother cannot find his green car just when he wants it. He manages to say, 'Car. Green,' and then when it doesn't instantly appear, he turns red in the face and starts kicking, stomping, and throwing things all over the place in a full-fledged tantrum. At moments of rage like this, your teaching about ideas obviously needs to wait until you have calmed the child down. So Jimmy's mother yells a little, threatens a little, and physically stops Jimmy from kicking until he quiets down. The two then sulk in mutual annoyance for a few minutes with Jimmy going off by himself and starting to play. At this point, his mother sits next to him, becomes a partner in his play, and then gives him a hug to show that everything is all right. While she is giving him a hug, she also says, 'Are you still angry?' This gives the child a chance to learn the word for the emotions he felt as well as the idea that emotions can be labeled. Gradually, his mother explains about patience and how to look for things he cannot find right away. Later on, when he wants his green car again, his mother might be able to convince him to be patient and look further. She can show him, even in hide-and-seek fashion, how to look. 'Is Mr. Green Car in the closet? No, he's not here. Under the chair?' etc. This use of ideas will probably not work each time, but he may be willing to wait and look rather than throw a tantrum at least some of the time. Your ability to tolerate intense emotion and to reconnect with your child will encourage his use of ideas to express feelings."

*Adapted from Greenspan SI: *Psychopathology and Adaptation in Infancy and Early Childhood: Principles of Clinical Diagnosis and Preventive Intervention.* New York, International Universities Press, 1981; and Greenspan S, Greenspan NT: *First Feelings: Milestones in the Emotional Development of Your Baby and Child.* New York, Penguin Books, 1985.

TIME-OUT PERIOD FOR EXCESSIVE TANTRUMS

When a child with a severe tantrum does not respond to verbal communication or being picked up, it may be helpful to give the toddler a time-out period in her room. An explanation is required ("you will stay in your room until you stop crying; mommy (or daddy) is in the kitchen, and you can come to me after you stop crying"). For some children this technique redirects out-of-control behavior, allows the anger to run its course, and provides a time for reinvestment with the parent as the tantrum terminates (Drabman and Jarvie, 1977).

For some parents, reading one or two books on behavior during this period may be helpful (see Chapter 32). Other parents may benefit from play groups, a parent group, or day care.

The child's clinician can be helpful as a guide to parents who are going through the experience of a toddler with tantrums. However, it is important to refrain from simply providing parents with a "recipe" for behavior change. Behavior modification techniques are helpful as

TABLE 16-3.
Discipline in Early Childhood Management: Concepts for Clinicians*

Achieving a helping relationship
Parent should perceive the child's clinician as someone available to discuss behavioral outbursts and other negative behaviors.
Identifying problem areas
Through a screening checklist or focused questions, developmentally predictable behavioral problems should be queried.
Explore genetic, historical and social predisposing factors
Include questions on maternal depression, prenatal events, perinatal stress, the health of siblings, the vulnerable child syndrome, substance abuse and the parents' own childhood memories.
Viewing parenthood as a developmental process
Recognize that parenting skills are established through maturation, knowledge, experience and guidance. Development of effective parenting skills takes time.
Encourage parents to take an active role in deciding how to manage the child's behavior.
Explore methods previously used by the parents and provide support for their ways or suggest modifications that might be more effective.
Respect different parenting styles.
Cultural, social class and past experience provide parents with variable responses to child behaviors. Variations in child rearing among families can be instructive for the clinician. A "best" way to manage a behavioral problem does not exist.
Providing appropriate models
Increase parental awareness that children imitate and identify with their parents' behavior. While role modeling healthy adult behavior, the clinician can be a useful guide to the parent.
Consistency
Rules are essential for discipline. For toddlers, the number of rules should be limited and parents should enforce only the important rules. This should help with consistency.
Talking about discipline
Parents (and other child care providers) need to discuss with each other expectations for the child's behavior and agree on management approaches. Discuss acceptable conduct as well as unacceptable behaviors.
Rewarding appropriate behavior
Praise, encouragement and rewards increase a child's happiness, security and self esteem.
Punishment to discourage some behaviors
Consistency
Design to motivate socially approved behaviors and to be specific for a particular offense.
Explanation must accompany punishment.
Carry out as soon as possible following inappropriate behavior.
Administer in context of a warm parent-child relationship.
*Modified from Smith EE, VanTassel E: Problems of discipline in early childhood. *Ped Clin North Am* 1982; 29(1):167–176.

part of an overall management plan that includes an understanding of the many variables contributing to the child's problems. Listening carefully to parents and children, observing parent-child interactional styles in the office, and communicating with them through active listening skills will often provide a sufficient foundation for the parent to understand both the nature and response to various negative behaviors. Prescriptions for behavior change can give the clinician a false sense of security. Teaching parents about their toddler rather than how to change their toddler's behavior has a bigger payoff in the long run. Having said this, there are some specific guidelines that often help parents in distress (Tables 16–3 and 16–4).

TABLE 16–4.
Discipline in Early Childhood Management: Concepts for Parents*

- Provide exemplary models.
- Frequently discuss with each other behavioral expectations and agree on uniform approaches to management.
- Limit number of rules and consistently enforce them.
- Discuss rules and appropriate behavior with your child at a calm time.
- Expect your child to need several trials to learn appropriate behaviors.
- Compliment your child frequently concerning correct behavior.
- Establish and maintain schedules and routines.
- Give your child choices when appropriate.
- Anticipate and avoid unnecessary conflict situations.
- Use punishment sparingly but consistently.
- Individualize punishment for particular offenses and provide simple explanations as to why you are punishing.
- Be mindful of individual and marital needs apart from your child.

*Modified from Smith EE, VanTassel E: Problems of discipline in early childhood. *Ped Clin North Am* 1982; 29(1):175.

ANTICIPATING PARENTAL DISTRESS

The rapid changes in the development of a toddler may be overwhelming for some parents, especially for the single adolescent mother, the socially isolated family, families experiencing economic poverty, and the family undergoing a significant life event (e.g., divorce, illness, or an unplanned move).

Young children are barometers of the family's emotional life. Although regressions in recently acquired milestones are common for all children at this stage, they are predictable among children in families experiencing increased stress. Developmental regressions in toddlers include refusal to use the potty seat, throwing food when in the highchair, screaming with seemingly mild frustrations, and increased periods of night awakening. Although these behaviors are transient setbacks in development, they are particularly frustrating to the parent in distress. The child's demands may be just too much for the parent to handle. He or she may not be able to see beyond the behavior. Some parents internalize the child's behavior and seem to see it as a failure in parenting ("She was so good at eating by herself and using the potty seat a few weeks ago. What have I done to cause these new behaviors?"). Along with guilt, these parents experience anger and fatigue as the toddler's infantile responses become more difficult to manage in the presence of acute or chronic family distress. An astute clinician will either anticipate or recognize the accompanying anxiety or depression in the parent (or its effect on the child), explore the severity or chronicity of the problems, and, when appropriate, offer assistance in the form of a referral to a parent group or a counseling resource.

In concluding the office visit, the clinician will find a summary statement about the child's current stage of development beneficial when it is then followed by what the parents might anticipate. At 18 months, the emphasis should be on:

1. Language skills will develop with the emerging use of two- and three-word phrases and mimicking as a way to communicate and reflect on experiences.

2. The importance of play should be stressed with self-initiated play in a safe environment that provides the arena to utilize new motor skills, followed by parallel play with other toddlers.

3. Behavioral changes that allow for increasing levels of tolerance for frustrating events such as limit setting during play time, bedtime behaviors, feeding behaviors, and toilet training, should be anticipated.

REFERENCES

Ainsworth MDS: Infant-mother attachment. *Am Psychol* 1979; 34:932.

American Academy of Pediatrics, Committee on Psychosocial Aspects of Child and Family Health: The pediatrician's role in discipline. *Pediatrics* 1983; 72:373–374.

Brazelton TB: *Toddlers and Parents.* New York, Dell, 1974.

Brazelton TB, Gatson RL, Howard RB: Developmental feeding issues, in Howard RB, Winter HS (eds): *Nutrition and Feeding of Infants and Toddlers.* Boston, Little, Brown & Co, 1984.

Carey WB: Clinical use of temperament data in pediatrics, in Porter R, Collins GM (eds): *Temperament in Infants and Young Children.* Ciba Foundation Symposium no 89. London, Pitman Books, 1982.

Drabman RS, Jarvie B: Counseling parents of children with behavior problems: The use of extinction and time-out techniques. *Pediatrics* 1977; 59:78–85.

Gordon T: *P.E.T.: Parent Effectiveness Training.* New York, Plume Books, 1975.

Kagan J: *The Nature of the Child.* New York, Basic Books, 1984, pp 43–48.

Mahler M, Pine F, Bergman A: *The Psychological Birth of the Human Infant.* New York, Basic Books, 1975.

Schowalter JE: The modification of behavior modification. *Pediatrics* 1977; 59:130–131.

Sherman M, Hertzig M, Austrian R, et al: Treasured objects in school aged children. *Pediatrics* 1981; 68:379–386.

Vaughan VC, Litt IF: *Child and Adolescent Development: Clinical Implications.* Philadelphia, WB Saunders Co, 1990, p 204.

Winnicott DW: Transitional objects and transitional phenomena, in *Collected Papers.* London, Tavistock Publishing, 1958, pp 229–242.

"A baby learning to talk." By Ryan Hennessy, age 7.

CHAPTER **17**

Two Years: Learning the Rules—Language and Cognition

SUZANNE D. DIXON, M.D.

With contributions from HEIDI FELDMAN, M.D., Ph.D., and ELIZABETH BATES, Ph.D.

KEY WORDS

LANGUAGE DEVELOPMENT
PRESCHOOL THINKING
LANGUAGE DELAYS/PROBLEMS
HEARING
SPEECH DIFFICULTIES

Jared, age 2, comes in for an ear check after an otitis episode. His tympanic membranes now appear nearly normal. Upon questioning, his mother says that he has about 10 to 20 single words and hasn't put together any words except "gimme me." The fourth child of this family, born 8 years after his next older sibling, Jared had a mildly difficult birth, but recovered well. He has had four episodes of otitis since birth. His mom says that he doesn't talk more because all of his sibs do everything for him— "There's no need for him to say anything, or even point, for that matter." She feels he's "younger" than the other kids were at his age but she says she's to blame—she really enjoys her "baby." Jared doesn't say anything in the office.

The second birthday falls in a period of time during which the child begins to interact with the world around her through an understanding of rules or patterns that are now becoming explicit. The child orders her response to the world with some problem-solving abilities that depend on new mental competencies. At around 2 years of age, the child develops the ability to use true creative language and the expanded cognitive skills that go with it. These abilities, language, and growth in cognitive structures allow for an entire new kind of activity. She can pretend, recall, and share unique observations of the world around her. A new plateau is reached—the era of the talkative, questioning, active 2-year-old. The clinical assessment of these children can be either a struggle or a delightful opportunity to explore these two inter-related areas of functioning. The level of satisfaction for the clinician and the family will be substantially greater if the latter course is chosen.

247

COGNITIVE ABILITIES

Some background information can add perspective on the behavior of this demanding 2-year-old. Sometime around her second birthday, a child begins to reason qualitatively differently about the world around her (Piaget and Inhelder, 1969). She can explore things and events mentally but her organization (Kagan, 1981) and understanding of these events is often faulty from an adult perspective. Her ordering of her world is dependent on her own rules. The system on which she operates is "egocentric," that is, from her own perspective. She can see the world from only her own rather than another's viewpoint or from her own rule system. Her beliefs and actions are logical from that point of view. This essential difference in cognitive abilities is a source of much delight and some misunderstanding. Two-year-olds remain resistant to information that is at odds with their own scheme; new events add to the richness of experience but are ordered according to the principles of "preoperational" or "intuitive" thought (Piaget and Inhelder, 1969). This development of an idiosyncratic rule system marks the beginning of logical thought and problem solving. The 2-year-old is very interested in placing physical objects in order—"put away," "tidy up," and place things inside. This behavior mirrors the internal drive to order or explain events in the environment at a new level of mental organization.

The young preschooler sees all natural events as occurring with her at center. Most inanimate objects are seen as having thoughts and feelings like herself (animism). Particularly things that move have life and are alive. Inanimate objects and actions seem to be geared around the child's own needs and desires. For example, the moon is seen to follow her at night; grass was made for her to walk in; the ocean is there for her to swim in. Spanking a table on which you bumped your head is logical if this is borne in mind. Seemingly unrelated events are causally related if they are perceived together by the child. This "transductive reasoning" leads to linkages of particular phenomena that often throw adults off guard. This process should, in fact, be interpreted as evidence of the child's genuine drive to put order in her own life experience. For example, a child may believe she had to take medicine because her physician put an otoscope in her ear. Another may be sure that she is ill because she did not put her trucks away as if these events were temporally related. Seeing dad in a tie (or for another child, in work jeans) may trigger anxiety about separation, for the tie (or jeans) is the usual sign of her father leaving for work in the morning. Adults should explore a child's understanding of events around her, offer explanations that might fuel a reorganization in the child's thinking, but not be surprised if the child's logic persists. The appreciation of a child's "mistakes" calls attention to the active mental processing that is now the regular way that the child orders the events around her (Piaget and Inhelder, 1969).

The 2- to 4-year-old cannot describe a scene as it might appear to another person positioned differently around it; she cannot place herself in another position. History taking or conversation with such a child has difficulties stemming from the fact that the child assumes that you already know everything about her and her life. She becomes impatient with your endless questions about things she is sure you already know, because of course *she* does. Similarly, the child cannot understand how another child feels as a result of her actions. Training in model social behavior must bear this in mind. "Just think how Jason feels now that you hit him; you wouldn't like it, would you?" is the kind of statement that can have no meaning for the young preschooler except through the tone of voice in which it is delivered.

The child cannot possibly imagine how Jason feels; she can only understand the anger she felt as she hit Jason. Other data suggest that with strong emotional displays, children of 2 to 3 years of age can have empathy for another, as in comforting someone who is crying.

LANGUAGE DEVELOPMENT COURSE

The specific patterns of language development have been summarized by many workers (e.g., Brown, 1973; Cazden, 1981; Dale, 1976; de Villiers and de Villiers, 1979; Elliot, 1981; Garvey, 1984). The following represents a synthesis of these works.

Language development begins before birth as the infant perceives the sounds of the womb, quiets to their steady rhythm, and begins to synchronize his movements to his mother's voice and body sounds. There is increasing evidence that the fetus responds to environmental sounds long before birth and begins to develop some memory of these. The responsivity and the interactional synchrony between infant movement and maternal sound and rhythm are well developed and specific in the newborn and become more and more differentiated within the first days and weeks of life (Condon and Sander, 1974). Discrimination of even very similar sounds (e.g., pa, ba) is present in the first weeks of life. Expressive language follows the growth in receptive (Peterson, 1980). Cooing, the production of vowel sounds without the formation of syllable units, begins in the first months of life. Loudness of cooing begins to vary at about 1 month of age (de Villiers and de Villiers, 1979; Eimas, 1974). Pitch variation emerges at 3 to 4 months of age. These sounds are present even in children who are completely deaf. Babbling, the production of sounds containing both vowels and consonants, often is heard by 6 months of age and is heard among all language groups around the world (Ferguson, 1964; Nakazema, 1962). Babbling requires a marked increase in fine-motor control of all the oral pharyngeal musculature. It appears to exercise these speech organs and to allow the child to discover that he can talk. The quantity and quality of babble is less in children who have absent or reduced hearing or who are rarely interacted with in a verbal setting. Imitation of adult speech, called jargon, with the phonetic and intonational parameters of the child's specific language occurs regularly by the ninth month; in some children, often earlier. Pointing at objects begins between 9 and 12 months and is a highly reliable predictor of language competence. By the age of 1 year, a child usually has 4 to 10 "words," short utterances that are produced in a specific context or to identify a specific person, event, or object. The minimum competency would be one word other than "mama" and "dada" and following one-step commands and gestures.

The infant's communicative intent, gestures, and speech all are evidence of the child's emerging language abilities (Peterson, 1980). This becomes linked to identification of things by pointing, sharing his growing perception of the world around him. These utterances also serve to identify special needs. Pointing at objects in the first year is a key linguistic marker. Symbolic gestures at 13 months are also highly correlated with later language ability (e.g., recognizing a telephone by lifting it toward the ear, categorizing a shoe by touching it to the foot, or labeling a toy car by moving it back and forth on the floor). Children with a rich gesture communication system at this time are likely to develop normal linguistic skills even if they are late bloomers in language production. Children without such gestures are likely to have persistent language difficulties (Thal and Bates, 1989).

The toddler both overextends (e.g., using the word "doggy" for all interesting animals) and overly restricts (e.g., using the word "doggy" only for the family dog) the meaning of these early utterances in his struggle to order and understand the world around him. The acquisition of new words during the period from about 12 to 18 months tends to be quite slow. These words tend to be simple, salient, and overgeneralized naming that allow for the child's needs to be met and the primitive sharing of simple observations. The average vocabulary of an 18-month-old is between 50 and 100 words, but this is extremely variable and may even fluctuate periodically within a given child. Words will appear and disappear in seemingly random fashion. The child may depend more on others' gestures in the context of her family's simplified, overemphasized speech to increase her own receptive language capacities (Bellugi, 1970). Families do expand and clarify these utterances through a process that may help to fuel further language development.

The apparent lag period in language development is often followed by an explosion in either words or phrases. The second half of the second year and the beginning of the third are characterized by rapid increases in vocabulary and the use of verbs, concomitant with the cognitive development that occurs at the same time. However, the most significant event is the creation of original linkages of words that express a complete and original thought (e.g., "da da come," "dight hot," "now night dark"). These combinations imply a subject, verb, and perhaps an object or modifying word, although they are telegraphic or without connecting words over three fourths of the time (Brown, 1973). They are in contrast to the simple naming of objects or expression of simple demands (e.g., doggy, water) that are characteristic of the prelanguage heard earlier.

The child of 2 years shows that she understands the rules of language through her differential ordering of words to alter their meanings, such as "go car" versus "car go" (Garvey, 1984). In addition, her confusion is obvious when requests are stated in her own telegraphic style (Brown, 1973). She anticipates that her language will be interpreted by those around her, and correct grammatical form will be spoken to her. New constructions ("I like it") for the child of this age are sometimes learned in their entirety and applied in several contexts (Bellugi, 1970). However, some 2-year-olds do not seem to learn by trial and error but seem to absorb the whole system of rules in this simple form nearly all at once. When this new level of language development is used, the construction of sentences is qualitatively different than the word utterances of the young toddler. Language becomes both the outcome and the tool of early cognitive thought, problem solving, and the sharing of experiences of past events in relating to others through the media of words. The 2- to 3-year-old child may use more than 200 words, nearly half the number that adults use in everyday conversation. She may delight in just trying out this new skill, both in public and in private. "Crib speech" is an active experimental forum where words, word order, intonation, and intensity are varied and practiced (Garvey, 1984). She delights in drawing adults into conversations and relies on them for expansion, clarification, and refueling of her efforts. The creation of original utterances is part of an expanded interactional world of people and events.

The years between 2½ and 5 years of age are characterized by a gradual expansion in sentence complexity marked by a much more consistent application of rules. Tenses are added in orderly sequence (Brown, 1973); systems of negation and the form of questions also have their own specific developmental course. The 2-year-old can communicate with his family easily; the 4-year-old should be intelligible to almost anyone who speaks his language.

After five years of age, all of the basic components of language are in place, although these forms become more accessible and usable with time. Poetry, puns, and jokes are enjoyed by early grade school. The study of grammar is appreciated with relish, and foreign languages have particular interest for the child at this time. Vocabulary increases should be a life-long process, and sentence complexity increases into adult life. The developmental progression is shown in Table 17–1.

GENERAL PRINCIPLES

Some general principles distinguish language development from other areas of psychological and physical growth. First, language development, especially expressive language development, is more variable in timing than other areas of development. Individual, temperament, family, and even cultural differences influence the pace of language development. Within expressive language, some general patterns hold. Children generally start to produce word combinations when their vocabulary reaches about 50 words, accompanied by an increase in rate of vocabulary expansion; verbs and adjectives appear at about this time as well. This burst in the size and shape of vocabulary occurs on the average between 17 and 20 months. There is a second burst in the size and complexity of sentences from 20 to 30 months.

Many of our tools of language assessment weigh heavily on expressive language, but there is reason to believe that receptive ability is a better predictor of long-term language outcome (Bates et al., 1988). In addition, performance in language is an "acute-phase reactant"; whenever a child is physically or psychologically stressed, it is one of the first abilities to regress or appear abnormal temporarily.

The clinician may have a difficult time eliciting performance in the office setting because the assessment itself involving a verbal interaction with a strange adult in the unfamiliar setting is a stress for a child. In many cultures and subgroups in our own country, children are not accustomed to interacting verbally with adults so that the sociocultural variable may prohibit them further from participating in the office-based language assessment (Super and Harkness, 1978). Careful, explicit, and focused history taking with a parent has been shown to be accurate in these circumstances if the period under discussion and recall is short and recent. Recall of *past* linguistic performance is notoriously faulted. The clinician may also structure his interaction with the child to allow for speech assessment early in the visit, with other interactions to follow later. Playful commentary about a toy kept in the room, the child's clothing, or the parent's dress or behavior may begin a dialogue between the child and the clinician. Language assessment is facilitated by the establishment of this early and seemingly casual evaluation. Focused questions to the parent will then allow for further data collection. Most important, the astute clinician will have watched the orderly progression of all aspects of language function from birth on and will not be thrown off base by temporary delays and an office-based assessment of expressive language alone. In addition, these predictable errors in child language will catch the clinician's attention and thereby will give clues to the orderly progression of language development through these expected stages. Specific tools of language development can easily be added to a previsit questionnaire given in the waiting room or sent out ahead of time.

All children overgeneralize the rules of language so that their mistakes are often just log-

TABLE 17–1.
Clinical Evaluation of Language Skills

Age	Receptive Skills	Expressive Skills	Specific Indication for Referral
0–1 mo	Recognizes sound with startle; turns to sound and looks for source; quiets motor activity to sound; "prefers" human speech with high inflection	Differentiated crying; body language of positive and negative response	No response to pleasing sound when alert; neonatal sepsis; meningitis; neonatal asphyxia; prematurity; congenital infection; familial deafness; renal abnormalities; aminoglycoside therapy
2–4 mo	Prolonged attention to sounds; responds to familiar voice; watches the speaking mouth; enjoys rattle; attempts to repeat pleasing sound with objects; shifts gaze back and forth between sounds	"Ee, ih, uh" (hind mouth vowels); cooing, blows bubbles; enjoys using tongue and lips; reciprocal cooing; play dialogues; loudness varies	No response to pleasing sounds; does not attend to voices
5–7 mo	Seeks out speaker; localizes sounds; understands own name, familiar words; associates word to activity (e.g., bath, car)	Initiates sounds; pitch varies; babbles with labial consonants ("ba, ma, ga"); uses sounds to get attention, express feeling; sounds directed at object	Decrease or absence of vocalizations
8–12 mo	Begins word comprehension; responds to simple commands: "point to your nose," "say bye-bye"; knows names of family members; responds to a few words, i.e., words associated with specific objects	First words, 5–6: "mama, dada"; inflected vocal play; repeats sounds and words made by others; "oo, ee" (foremouth vowels); intentional gestures	No babbling with consonant sounds; no response to music
13–20 mo	Single step element commands; identifies familiar objects	Points to objects with vocalization; vocabulary of 10–50 words, pivot and open class words, rate and content varies; jargon with proper stress and intonation, monologues and dual monologues; word combinations begin	No comprehension of words; does not understand simple requests
18–24 mo	Recognizes many nouns; understands simple questions	Telegraphic speech; vocabulary of 50–75 words; 2-word sentences, phrases; stuttering very common	Vowel sounds but no consonants No words
24–36 mo	Understands prepositions; can follow story with pictures	Identifies body parts; vocabulary of 200 words; dependent upon phrases, 3-word sentences; uses words for expressive needs; pronouns; early grammar	No words; does not follow simple directions No sentences

TABLE 17-1.
Clinical Evaluation of Language Skills

Age	Receptive Skills	Expressive Skills	Specific Indication for Referral
30–36 mo	Understands some syntax (difference between car hit train and train hit car); understands opposites; understands action in pictures	Sentences 4–5 words, 3 elements; tells stories; uses questions: what, where; uses negation; uses progressive and past tense, all regular form; uses plurals, regular form	Speech largely unintelligible to stranger; dropout of initial consonants; no sentences
3–4 yr	Understands 3-element commands	Talks about what she is doing; uses "I," grammar by her own rules; vocabulary 40–1,500 words; speech intelligible to strangers; "why" questions; commands; uses past and present tense; passive speech, in spontaneous speech; nursery rhymes; colors, 1–4 numbers, tells sex, full name; articulation: "m,n,p,h,w"; 4-word sentences	Speech not comprehended by strangers; still dependent on gestures; consistently holds hands over ears; speech without modulation
4–5 yr	Understands 4-element commands; links past and present events; decreasing ability for second language acquisition	2,700-word vocabulary; defines simple words; auxiliary verbs: "has, had"; conversationally mature; "How and why" questions in response to others; articulation: "b,k,g,f"; 5-word sentences; "normalizes" irregular verbs and nouns; increases in accessibility of forms	Stuttering; consistently avoids loud places
5–6 yr	Understands 5-element commands; can follow a story without pictures; enjoys jokes and riddles; can comprehend 2 meanings of word	Correct use of all parts of speech; vocabulary 5,000 words; articulation: "y,ng,d"; 6-word sentences; corrects his own errors in speech; can use logic in recounting story plots	Word endings dropped; faulty sentence structure; abnormal rate, rhythm, or inflection
6–7 yr	Asks for motivation and explanation of events; understands time intervals (months, seasons); right and left differences	Articulation: "l,r,t,sh,ch,dr,cl,bl,gl,cr"; has formal (adult) speech patterns	Poor voice quality, articulation
7–8 yr	Can use language alone to tell a story sequentially; reasons using language	Articulation: "v,th,j,s,z,tr,st,sl,sw,sp"	
8–9 yr		Articulation: "th,sc,sh"	

ical extensions of newly learned language rules. For example, in the third year, all plurals are formed by the addition of "s" (e.g., "mices"), and the past tenses by "ed" (e.g., "goed"). In the fourth and fifth years, these forms may reappear as the child reaches a new level of rule acquisition and rigidity and form in language. The clinician must be sensitive to the fact that some "mistakes" are perfectly normal, a sign of progress in the acquisition of linguistic rules.

WHY DO CHILDREN SPEAK?

This question raises considerable controversy among psychologists and is not satisfactorily answered by any one school of thought. *Innate theorists* contend that children speak because a predetermined neurosensory capacity (e.g., language acquisition device) kicks in at some point in development (Chomsky, 1964). These theorists make note of the regularity in language development across all cultural and language groups and the production of sounds in even young deaf infants. However, this school cannot account for the experientially determined disturbances of language in a neglected and emotionally disturbed child or for the interactional variables from child to child that strongly influence language development.

The *social learning theorists* (e.g., Bandura, 1971, see Chapter 2) and behaviorists maintain that children speak because they imitate the speech around them and are rewarded in their efforts. Language emerges from the need to name objects, make demands, and comply with the verbal environment around them, based on the models provided for the child. Certainly, children in isolation do not learn language, and children learn the language and dialect to which they are exposed. However, these theorists do not account for the unsolicited and private babble and practice done by the infant and young child (Bullowa, 1979; Lewis, 1951), even up through the school years that serves no communicative intent. In addition, as mentioned earlier, there are predictable developmental "mistakes" in grammar and syntax made by children at certain periods that have no parallel in adult speech. These detours cannot be accounted for by imitation. Indeed, they are temporarily unavailable to specific adult correction. In fact, adults rarely correct or negatively reinforce these language errors in their children (Snow, 1972). Adults respond to the content, the factual correctness, rather than the form of the child's speech (Garvey, 1984). In general, practicing speech with a child does not improve the quantity or quality of his language, so direct imitation does not explain the bulk of language development. Or, as stated by Cazden (1981) "as 'foots' and 'goed' and 'holded' show, children use language they hear as examples of language to learn from, not samples of language to learn." Although a model for speech is necessary, children translate adult speech into their own grammar or rule system.

The *interactionalist school* says that children speak as an outgrowth of their interactions with parents and significant others. These important people in a child's life respond to, elaborate on, and clarify early utterances and these interactions fuel the child's growth in language. Children exposed to only mechanical speech (e.g., television) do not speak. Language is an outgrowth of adequate emotional development and serves the emergence of new cognitive skills.

The amount and variety of babbling and imitative speech production at 9 to 18 months to some extent is a reflection of the amount of the mother's (or significant caretaker's) speech that the child has experienced. However, during that late infancy–early toddler period, subsequent growth in language competency is dependent on the amount and variety of *respon-*

sive speech around her (Ringler, 1981; Snow, 1972). In other words, the development of language is built on early interactions with caregivers and is augmented later by the presence of a rich interactional verbal environment. The presence of both the early dialogues with the child, building and expanding on her own utterances, and the later enriched verbal reinforcements around the child are directly related to early language acquisition.

As clinicians, we can make use of all elements from these different ways of conceptualizing language development. Children speak because they have a basic neurosensory and cognitive readiness, because there is speech around them to provide models, and because this speech is fun, both alone and, more important, with significant others. Deficits in any one of these areas will be reflected in abnormal or delayed language development.

LANGUAGE AND COGNITION

Language development is intricately entangled with cognitive development. Much discussion and research have been devoted to the question of whether language is necessary for cognition (i.e., whether or not we need words and semantic structure to think) or whether language is merely an outcome or reflection of growth in mental capacity (Brown, 1973; Elliot, 1981). This chicken-and-egg question aside, the clinician will find that language assessment becomes increasingly enmeshed in other areas of functioning as a child grows, because the usual evaluation of language, using standard instruments, is really one of cognitive growth and vice versa. Most often language and cognitive development *are* linked in an individual child but not necessarily so. Language development, particularly in a population of handicapped children, is highly predictive of overall functioning, and language remains the best predictor of cognition. School systems are heavily biased to verbal skills, so it is not surprising that school performance and linguistic abilities are linked. Early language disorders are highly predictive of learning difficulties in school. Most studies show that greater than 40% of children with early language difficulties will have learning difficulties in school (Aram and Hall, 1989).

Emotional and cognitive deficits may be secondary to primary language disorders, particularly in a society that places so much emphasis on verbal competency and formal schooling performance in its children (Stevenson and Richman, 1978). Conversely, emotional disorders may present as language delays (Rubin, 1982). In any case, the language delayed child must be carefully and comprehensively assessed to look for these associated difficulties.

VARIATIONS IN LANGUAGE DEVELOPMENT

As we have seen, there is significant variation in the normal population of children in both receptive and expressive language (Thal and Bates, 1989), with the former preceding the latter in most children. In addition, there are style differences, with some children adopting "frozen" phrases in their entirety (e.g., "I wuv you") and others hesitantly building sentences from a large stock of available words (e.g., "Daddy bottle Julia"). Those late talkers who do catch up are more likely to have a rich gesture communication system and to have normal comprehension.

Minority groups in this country are often at a disadvantage in language and its close relative, cognitive assessment, as measured in the school setting for several reasons: vocabulary differences, unfamiliarity with verbal interchange with adults in a test situation, and systematic differences in grammatical structures that lead to misunderstandings and assumptions. Analysis of dialect differences show that black English includes a highly complex well-structured system of grammar of its own based on the complex language of West Africa (Dillard, 1972). A minority child in a majority setting may be inhibited from using the advanced language structures that he has available to him. Compounding the problem is the tendency for even well-intentioned teachers to interact verbally with students who are verbal, take verbal initiatives, and respond with longer utterances (Cazden, 1981).

Socioeconomic class differences in language development may additionally reflect other differences in verbal environment (Elliot, 1981). Middle-class children experience a richer verbal environment, have instructions given in a complex verbal form, and are required from an early age to use verbal interchanges. Firstborn children generally have accelerated expressive language development; children born later may appear delayed in contrast, although there are no long-term differences in birth order vis a vis language. Birth order effects are minimal and transient at most. Girls usually develop verbal abilities ahead of boys throughout childhood after the first birthday.

Bilingual children often appear to have temporary delays in expressive language ability. Bilingualism is a broad term that can involve many kinds of multiple language exposure, no one of which has been well studied (Elliot, 1981). However, preliminary observations indicate that bilingual children will mix the syntax and vocabulary of both languages until 2 years of age, mixing the two languages in a single utterance but using only one word for a given object consistently over time. Later on they will begin to separate these two languages and use them appropriately in context. There is no evidence that early exposure to more than one language compromises language development; there is some suggestive evidence that this experience facilitates language acquisition later on. However, language confusion and difficulties beyond the second year in the child who is exposed to more than one language may be only a symptom of broader cultural and interfamilial conflicts rather than an isolated, primary language disturbance. This larger issue should be identified early by a primary care provider (Grosjean, 1982). In summary, there is no scientific foundation for explanatory statements regarding language delay such as, "he'll grow out of it," "he doesn't talk because his brothers get him everything he wants," "he doesn't talk because the maid speaks to him in Spanish," or "he's just lazy," in response to a child with language delays. These findings must be evaluated carefully, anticipating a continuance of cognitive and social issues into adolescence.

ASSESSMENT OF LANGUAGE

GENERAL PRINCIPLES

There are some general principles that should raise concern no matter when they occur. These have been outlined by Lillywhite et al. (1970) and are shown in Table 17–2. First, a marked decrease in verbalization at any time should always elicit further inquiry. This may be a sign of stress, but it may also indicate compromises in hearing.

Second, consistently loud or explosive speech, whenever it occurs, should be further evaluated. All children reflect their enthusiasm periodically in loud talk but not consistently so unless they have a hearing loss or anticipate that their listeners will ignore them.

Third, if a child is embarrassed or disturbed by his own speech at any time, this deserves

TABLE 17-2.
Speech and Language Problems*

The child is not talking at all by the age of 2 yr.
Speech is largely unintelligible after the age of 3 yr. No sentences by 2½.
There are many omissions of initial consonants after age 3 yr.
Sounds are more than 1 yr late in appearing, according to developmental sequence.
There are many substitutions of easy sounds in child's speech.
The child uses primarily vowel sounds in his speech.
Word endings are consistently dropped after age 5 yr.
Sentence structure is noticeably faulty at 5 yr.
The child is embarrassed and disturbed by his speech at any age.
The child is noticeably nonfluent after age 5 yr.
The child is distorting, omitting, or substituting any sound after age 7 yr.
The voice is a monotone, extremely loud, largely inaudible, or of poor quality.
The pitch is not appropriate to the child's age and sex.
There is noticeable hypernasality or lack of nasal resonance.
There are unusual confusions, reversals, or telescoping in connected speech.
There is abnormal rhythm, rate, and inflection after age 5 yr.

*Adapted from Lillywhite H, Young NB, Olmsted RW: *Pediatrician's Handbook of Communication Disorders.* Philadelphia, Lea & Febiger, 1970; Coplan J, et al: *Pediatrics* 1982; 70:677–683; 14:203–208; Thal D, Bates E: *Pediatr Ann* 1989; 18:299–305.

referral. In addition, hoarseness or consistently abnormal pitch should raise questions of local lesions, such as laryngeal edema polyps (secondary to screaming), or generalized neurologic syndromes or even endocrine disorders such as hypothyroidism or premature puberty. Awkward or absent inflection or rhythm that is consistent requires referral.

Historical factors—a family history of hearing difficulties and/or speech–language delays, perinatal complications, including asphyxia, prematurity, drug exposure, long-term treatment with aminoglycosides, and prolonged exposure to isolette noise—all should raise levels of concern and particular monitoring. One third of children with a significant hearing loss have it on a genetic basis, and up to two thirds have associated handicaps. About one half of children with language delays have delays in other areas (Kolvin and Fundudis, 1982). Behavioral problems are more frequent in older children with language delays (Levine et al., 1980). In this manner, language disorders must be placed in the context of a comprehensive history and a general physical and developmental examination in a primary care setting.

Atypical language progression as well as delay and play and/or social interactional difficulties should raise the possibility of pervasive developmental disorder or autism. Subtle forms of this disability are relatively common and yet require very specialized forms of intervention and education.

OFFICE ASSESSMENT

Assessment of speech and language in the office requires a quiet, nonthreatening atmosphere, small familiar toys to name and manipulate (e.g., model animals), a simple book of single element pictures, and cards or books in which an action is portrayed. Children will also be drawn into a conversation about a toy that changes or moves (e.g., a windup toy) more readily than static interactions. Language and speech evaluation before the physical examination often gives better clues to the language function than an assessment after a disturbing physical examination. Children beyond the age of 3 years should be asked to describe a recent experience. Observation of the child's verbal interaction with her parents and in response to requests clearly presented in sequence of one, two, and three steps are critical. The Early Language Milestone Scale (Coplan et al., 1982) has been developed for office use. Its division into visual, auditory receptive, and auditory expressive sections is helpful in separating these functions. Other parent questionnaires or assessment tools include the MacArthur CDI (1991) and the Receptive and Expressive Evaluation of Language (REEL).

Some specific questions for the parents of young children can add further focus, if needed, for a particular child (Capute and Accardo, 1978). These are presented in Table 17–3.

Receptive language disorders can be more elusive than expressive disorders in that they are not identified as the chief complaint and usually appear later in life, masked as global developmental delay or school difficulties (Levine et al., 1980).There may be an early history of poor command following; there may be a family history of "hearing" or "learning" problems. The child with a receptive language disorder may have had difficulty in attending in school but not in other situations (e.g., building models, watching television). The verbal demands of the school environment will trigger his inability to process language input in that setting. He may be slow to understand verbal commands that lack visual or gestural clues in the examination room; verbal commands given very rapidly may cause confusion and consternation in the child, and he may become anxious, wish to withdraw, or change the subject. Requests may need to be repeated time and time again. The child may become confused over words that sound alike or spell things in a manner that approximates the visual form of the word rather than its phonetic sound (Levine et al., 1980). The clinician can evaluate these functions in the office setting. Evaluation by an education or clinical psychologist or a speech pathologist is the next step.

Speech difficulties must be differentiated quickly from language difficulties because these often have very different etiologies, concomitant difficulties, remediation approaches, and

TABLE 17–3.
Sample Questions for Parental Reporting of Sequential Items*

When did your infant smile at you when you talked to him or stroked his face?
When did your infant produce long vowel sounds such as "eeee," "aaa"?
When did your baby first give you the "raspberry"?
When did your child first babble? (i.e., "ba ba," "ma ma")?
When did your child say "dada" or "mama" but inappropriately?
When did your child begin to use "dada" and "mama" appropriately?
When did your child say his first word other than "dada" and "mama"?
When did your child first point at objects?
When did your child begin to follow simple commands (e.g., "Give me _____" or "Bring me _____")
  accompanied by a gesture?
When was your child able to follow simple commands without an accompanying gesture?
When did your child begin to speak jargon—to run unintelligible words together in an attempt to make a sentence?
How many body parts can your child point to when named? Which ones?
When did your child start to put two words together?
When did your child use three pronouns?

*Adapted from Capute AJ, Accardo P: *Clin Pediatr* 1978; 17:847–853.

TABLE 17–4.
Various Disorders of Speech*

Deficits of resonance: These disorders are characterized by abnormal oronasal sound balance. Deficits most commonly appear as hypernasality (e.g., in cleft palate) or hyponasality (e.g., in adenoid hypertrophy).

Voice disorders: These problems are manifested as deviation in the quality, pitch, or volume of sound production. Such impairments have either psychological or physiological bases.

Fluency disorders: These disorders reflect disruption in the natural flow of connected speech. The most common type of fluency disorder is stuttering.

Articulation disorders: Such disorders include a large group of problems often encountered by the physician. They are characterized by imprecise production of speech sounds. Most articulation "problems" are common at certain ages and are, in fact, normal. However, their persistence often requires intervention.

*From Levine M, Brooks R, Shonkoff JP: *A Pediatric Approach to Learning Disorders.* New York, John Wiley & Sons, 1980. Used by permission.

---

more favorable prognoses. Speech can be defined as the ability to communicate through the production of spoken sound, the output of the cognitive structures associated with language.

The delineation of difficulty as confined to expressive language only begins this process. The classes of expressive speech difficulty are given in Table 17–4. The Denver Articulation Test (Drumwright, 1971) is helpful in delineating specific problems of articulation. Speech therapy should be considered for any preschooler and particularly for any child after the age of 4 years if there is abnormal development or substantial delay in these areas.

Central expressive and receptive developmental language delay problems may have all of the problems of specific speech disorders, but other clues may also be present. The child may have difficulty in putting thoughts together, telling a story, or relating an experience. His verbal exchange will be sparse, filled with substitute words and circumlocutions and hesitancy. Vocabulary will be small and immature. He will have difficulty naming familiar objects or pictures. Written work in school will be difficult (Levine et al., 1980). This child needs a full psychological evaluation in addition to a speech analysis. The clinician can direct his referrals by a clear delineation of expressive versus receptive language disorders and with further delineation of an isolated speech disorder as opposed to language problems. These must, of course, be distinguished from global mental retardation and pervasive developmental disorder or the autism spectrum.

ANTICIPATORY GUIDANCE

Parents can support language development by talking *with* their children, engaging them in dialogues, asking questions, and encouraging them to narrate experiences. The linkage of tactile and verbal games and the reading of body language cues in the first year begins this process. The playful use of language in the second year through rhymes and jingles fuels interest in words. Expanding the child's expressions and speaking clearly and simply with correct words and grammar are also important. When one is talking about a present object or event, beginning the description with "look" or another orienting word allows the child to focus attention. Important words should be repeated. Narration of parental activities and caretaking events provides a rich verbal environment. However, telling children things and correcting grammar are also important. Encouraging the use of words rather than actions to express feelings and wishes is to be encouraged. The reading of stories and other quiet listening activities in the third year are helpful. All of these should be consciously modeled by the clinician in the interaction with the child.

Reading together supports language development with its own developmental course. Parents who may find it awkward to know what to say to their young children may be supported in their efforts at verbal exchange through the specific use of books together. Beginning in the first year, parents may point to objects and identify them. This progresses to the child pointing and naming things in the early second year of life. Picture explanation with brief descriptions of the immediate action grows into short story telling by 2 to 3 years of age. Children who are 3 and 4 years old will expand the action beyond the picture and can follow stories and anticipate events through the medium of books. Stories without pictures are regularly enjoyed by children older than 7 years. Jokes and riddles for the 5- and 6-year-olds are often based on words with double meanings or the vagaries of language. Enjoyment of these by parents and their kids reinforces this new plateau of language development. Poetry and other interesting use of language can be introduced at this time, if not earlier. The physician should have a stock of simple jokes and puns in mind to highlight this new skill in a clinical setting.

Screening audiometry is a valuable tool in an office setting. Both high false positive and false negative rates are expected in the nonstandard setting of an office. However, repeated assessments add further confidence in this evaluation tool of the child's hearing. Tympanography can also assess the presence and the resolution of middle ear disease. A referral for formal audiometry is indicated at any age when screening procedures are consistently abnormal. Brainstem evoked audiometry and visual evoked response testing is appropriate for the infant and should be routine for those who fall into high-risk groups (see Chapter 8). Many toddlers and preschoolers can be conditioned to respond reliably in the visual reinforced audiometry with an audiologist skilled in this tool and with this age child. Parents and physicians should accept with caution the results of school screening audiometry done by commercial firms who make money through follow-up of their own positive screening findings. Screening done impartially within the school system should be supported by the pediatric clinician (Palfrey et al., 1980).

Stuttering in the young child, with multiple hesitations, repeats, and irregular cadences, is a symptom of a mind going faster than the tongue and should not raise concern, in general. Stuttering after 4 years of age, or even at 3 years, if the hesitancy involves only certain initial consonants, should be the occasion of a referral. Parents should never call attention to stuttering because there is no evidence that this is under volitional control or that it can ever be helped by scolding. Those with true stuttering should be under the care of a speech therapist.

SUMMARY

The language of the third year of life is a landmark of change for the child and the family. The child can now share his observations of events around him, recall past events to himself and others, and communicate his original thoughts and feelings to those around him. For most children, this is a liberating and exciting event. For parents, this often marks the undeniable end of infancy. Their child becomes more of an individual and an active participant in family life. Much of the work of exposing children to objects and events, talking to them without obvious response, and learning about their child through body language and non-verbal response now pays off as the child speaks. The joy, amazement, and amusement of toddler speech is tainted by the loss of the totally receptive infant. This step requires developmental work for the whole family. Language acquisition marks another step in individuation for the child and a separation for the family. It may also represent the single most significant developmental process in that it may be unmatched in its complexity and in the fact that it makes the child particularly human.

REFERENCES

Aram DM, Hall NE: Longitudinal follow-up of children with preschool communication disorders: Treatment implications. *School Psychol Rev* 1989; 18:487–501.

Bandura A (ed): *Psychological Modeling.* Chicago, Atherton, Aldine, 1971.

Bates E, Bretherton I, Snyder L: *From First Words to Grammar: Individual Differences and Dissociable Mechanisms.* New York, Cambridge University Press, 1988.

Bellugi U: Learning the Language. *Psychol Today* 1970; 4:32–35.

Brown R: *A First Language: The Early Stages.* Cambridge, Mass, Harvard University Press, 1973.

Capute A, Accardo P: Linguistic and auditory milestones during the first two years of life. *Clin Pediatr* 1978; 17:847–853.

Cazden CB: *Language in Early Childhood Education.* Washington, DC, National Association for the Education of Young Children, 1981.

Chomsky N: Formal discussion, in Bellugi U, Brown R (eds): The acquisition of language. *Monogr Soc Res Child Dev* 1964; 29(92):35–39.

Condon W, Sander L: Neonate movement is synchronized with adult speech: Interactional participation and language acquisition. *Science* 1974; 183:99–101.

Coplan J: Evaluation of the child with delayed speech or language. *Pediatr Ann* 1985; 14:203–208.

Coplan J, Gleason JR, Ryan, R, et al: Validation of an early language milestone scale in a high-risk population. *Pediatrics* 1982; 70:677–683.

Dale PS: *Language Development: Structure and Function.* Hinsdale, Ill, Dryden Press, 1976.

de Villiers PA, de Villiers JG: *Early Language.* Cambridge, Mass, Harvard University Press, 1979.

Dillard JL: *Black English: Its History and Use in the United States.* New York, Random House, 1972.

Drumwright AF: *Denver Articulation Screening Exam.* Denver, University of Colorado Medical Center, 1971.

Eimas PD: Linguistic processing of speech by young infants, in Schiefelbusch RL, Lloyd LL (eds): *Language Perspectives: Acquisition, Retardation, and Intervention.* Baltimore, University Park Press, 1974.

Elliot J: *Child Language.* New York, Cambridge University Press, 1981.

Ferguson C: Baby talk in six languages. *Anthropology* 1964; 66:114–130.

Garvey C: *Children's Talk.* Cambridge, Mass, Harvard University Press, 1984.

Grosjean F: *Life With Two Languages.* Cambridge, Mass, Harvard University Press, 1982.

Kagan J: *The Second Year of Life: The Emergence of Self-Awareness.* Cambridge, Mass, Harvard University Press, 1981.

Kolvin I, Fundudis T: Speech and language disorders of childhood, in Apley J, Ounsted C (eds): *One Child.* London, William Heinemann Medical Books-Spastics International Medical Publications, 1982.

Levine M, Brooks R, Shonkoff JP: *A Pediatric Approach to Learning Disorders.* New York, John Wiley & Sons, 1980.

Lewis MM: *Infant Speech.* New York, Humanities Press, 1951.

Lillywhite HS, Young NB, Olmsted RW: *Pediatrician's Handbook of Communication Disorders.* Philadelphia, Lea & Febiger, 1970.

Nakazema S: A comparative study of the speech developments of Japanese and American English in childhood. *Stud Phonol* 1962; 2:27–39.

Palfrey J, Hanson M, Pleszczynska C, et al: Selective hearing screening for young children. *Clin Pediatr* 1980; 19:473–477.

Peterson R: *The Communication Game.* Johnson & Johnson Round Table Series. Skillman, NJ, Johnson & Johnson Baby Products Co, 1980.

Piaget J, Inhelder B: *The Psychology of the Child.* New York, Basic Books, 1969.

Ringler NM: The development of language and how adults talk to children. *Infant Ment Health* 1981; 2:71–83.

Rubin SS: Expressive language deficits in preschool children and faulty development of the self. *Orthopsychiatry* 1982; 52:58–64.

Snow CE: Mothers' speech to children learning language. *Child Dev* 1972; 43:549–565.

Stevenson I, Richman N: Behavior, language and development in three year old children. *J Acad Child Schizophr* 1978; 8:299-313.

Super C, Harkners S: Why African children are so hard to test, in Adler LL (ed): *Cross Cultural Research at Issue.* New York, Ethos, 1978.

Thal D, Bates E: Language and communication in early childhood. *Pediatr Ann* 1989; 18:299–305.

ADDITIONAL READINGS

Allen DA, Rapin I, Wiznitzer M: Communication disorders of preschool children: The physician's responsibility. *J Dev Behav Pediatr* 1988; 9:164–170.

Bullowa M: *Before Speech.* New York, Cambridge University Press, 1979.

Cantwell D, Baker L: Clinical significance of childhood communication disorders: Perspectives from a longitudinal study. *J Clin Neurol* 1987; 2:257–264.

Fischel J, Whitehurst G, Caulfield M, et al: Language growth in children with expressive language delay. *Pediatrics* 1989; 83:218–227.

Howlin P: Language, in *Developmental Psychiatry.* Baltimore, University Park Press, 1981.

Piaget J: *The Origins of Intelligence in Children.* New York, International Universities Press, 1952.

"A scary dream." By Ryan Hennessy,
age 6½.

CHAPTER **18**

TWO AND ONE-HALF TO THREE YEARS: THE EMERGENCE OF MAGIC

SUZANNE D. DIXON, M.D.

KEY WORDS

TELEVISION
FANTASY
DREAMS AND NIGHTMARES
FEARS IN CHILDHOOD
IMAGINARY FRIENDS
LYING

Mr. Jackson brings in his 3-year-old because the boy does not tell the truth about drawing on the wall and spilling milk. He says he has an imaginary friend who is always sitting in his chair at home. He also seems to be afraid to take a walk after dinner with his dad, a thing he used to enjoy. He has nightmares at least twice per week, which he had never had before. His dad wonders if he is turning into "a wimp" and needs more discipline.

Although the charm and fascination of childhood imagination are apparent to all caretakers of children, we rarely reflect on the developmental significance and function of fantasy. Fantasy and language are conceptually and functionally related as manifestations of symbolic formations—a child's ability to let something stand for something else without any direct or objective linkage between the object and the symbolic meaning. The early development of fantasy and language becomes obvious and functional at about the same time in any given child. The primitive beginnings of both capacities are seen earlier and continue to develop far beyond childhood. The third year of life, however, sees both fantasy and language in their most exciting growth phase. The visit when the child is 1 to 3 years old offers the clinician and the family the chance to assess the emergence and the significance of this important basic component of development.

COGNITIVE BASIS FOR SYMBOLIC FUNCTION

The capacity to assign a novel function, meaning, or identity to an object or person grows out of the child's ability to go beyond one's immediate sensory or motoric experience of the object. It implies a mental action, linking two things—the object and its fantasized or imag-

265

ined meaning. This new level of cognitive functioning was called the *preoperational* period by Piaget (1952) (Ginsberg and Opper, 1969). This new mental capacity, like any new skill, emerges with apparent rapidity and is exercised frequently, or, as stated by Fraiberg (1959), "A child's contact with the real world can be *strengthened* by periodic excursions into fantasy in a world where the deepest wishes can achieve imaginary gratification." The child uses mental actions to link events, actions, sounds, and meanings, although his reasoning may still be based on his own mental processes rather than objective reality. Nevertheless, the ability to use imagination and fantasy opens an entire new world for a child. Previously this world was limited to the direct experience around him. The perceptions of everything from a child's experience in a pediatric office to the causes of day and night change with the ability to fantasize. The child of this age can review, rework, and repetitively process the events of daily life through actions, language, and "mental movies."

In addition, the ability to fantasize enables the child to mentally experiment with new sensations, an enhancement or elaboration of cognitive structures. The child can try out new roles for himself, new functions for toys, and new sequences of events. These *novel* creations of fantasy will be seen more clearly in the 4-year-old. The base seen in the third year begins that process. Fantasy, then, can serve, as well as define, cognitive growth throughout the preschool years.

THE TOOL OF AFFECTIVE GROWTH

Fantasy also serves affective growth in that it allows children to try out new roles for themselves in imagined forms: roles of the opposite sex, their parent, a monster, or an animal (Winnicott, 1971). Negative feelings can be expressed in safe ways, especially when those feelings are directed toward loved ones. It provides the ability to work through interactive difficulties with siblings and playmates, parents and caregivers. The child has strength and power in his fantasy life that he cannot achieve in real life. Costumes, puppet play, and doll play are forums and props for this developmental work. Expressive language abilities lag behind the child's cognitive capacities, so these nonverbal forms of fantasy are particularly important for the child to both work through and communicate his feelings, frustrations, anxieties, and wishes in safe ways (Murphy, 1962).

Imaginary friends are very useful to young people. They are created by many children, but particularly girls, firstborn, and only children. These magical creatures serve many functions, such as the missed presence of the parent, an idealized parent, a playmate, the willing slave of a toddler struggling with power and autonomy issues, or the victim in a power struggle. These friends can be the scapegoats for misdeeds, a comforter after discipline, or even a jolly companion for a long afternoon or a dark night. These useful magic people are id, ego, and even superego as the occasion calls for them. However, too careful scrutiny of them by adults makes them disappear, because they are the precious property of the developing child. They should be prized as being the product of a creative, adaptive, and developing person.

An active imagination is a healthy sign at this age even if it appears as "untruths." Children do not intentionally lie, in other words, in a preconceived way plan to deceive another. However, their reports of events most often reflect how they perceived things, how they "creatively" processed those impressions, how they wished things were, or how they thought things should be to please. These perceptions are real even if the events are not. These stories are not formed out of moral lassitude (Kohlberg, 1974). They should be seen as "creative coping" with a situation that may be stressful for the child. Parents should reflect on the underlying issue rather than struggle with the content of the "story."

IMAGINATION AND TELEVISION

The active nature of a child's imagination makes him particularly vulnerable to the effects of television, movies, and, to a lesser extent, stories. Although many studies have shown that television has many harmful effects on children (Lesser, 1974; Zuckerman and Zuckerman, 1985), it remains a major influence on them. Children may become more tolerant of violent behavior (Surgeon General's Committee, 1972), become more aggressive themselves, and participate in group decisions to inflict violence on others after viewing standard television shows containing aggressive behaviors (Liebert et al., 1973). Just as troublesome, other studies have shown that children become more passive toward their environments after extensive television viewing. Children cannot distinguish television advertising from other programming and, as such, are particularly vulnerable to commercial aspects of television (Lewis and Lewis, 1974). Television images fall on indiscriminately fertile ground when placed before the child with the capacity to fantasize, retain these images, and allow them to grow. In addition, television may draw time and developmental energy from other developmental work (Brazelton, 1974). Even very young children are influenced by television and have memory for these displays (Meltzoff, 1988).

The capacity to fantasize is highly developed in the preschool years and is readily fueled by television. At this time, this input is not tempered by the concrete thinking of the school-aged child, who can evaluate, reason, discuss, and dismiss what he sees and hears. Without monitoring, clarification, and reflection, television input in the preschool years is like gasoline on a campfire. With the appropriate adult input, however, television can have a major impact on a child's social and cognitive development (Kaye, 1974). Parental monitoring, participation, selection, and interaction will determine these effects. Limits should be placed on the amount of television time, as well as its contents.

FANTASY AND PLAY

The emergence of fantasy allows a child to play with other children in new ways (Chance, 1979; Garvey, 1977). The assumption of imaginary roles, however brief and ever changing, allows for longer and more elaborate play periods, as well as solitary and cooperative play with other children. One child can be caught up in another's imaginative structure and have fun and learn from it (Bruner, 1975). Even solitary play has an extended quality when fantasy enriches it. Solitary language (i.e., "crib speech"), often heard at this age, appears to have many functions, including (but not limited to) the practice of language (DeForest and Echols, 1983).

Parents cannot provide an exciting enough play experience in isolation at this point in development. Children in the third year need other children—relatives, neighbors, a play group, or a preschool group. Learning to get along with other children and to develop mutual play interactions are the goals rather than any structured learning. Play becomes more cooperative through the use of many symbolic skills—language, role playing, shared fantasy, and imaginative games. Parents should approach play at this age as an outreach experience for the child, not a substitute for their primary social experiences in the family. Introduction of a preschool experience should be gradual and responsive to the child's needs and in line with the family's needs and values.

FEARS IN CHILDHOOD

The child's fears now assume a more complex nature. The child can imagine fearful things that *might* happen, that *may* happen, or that *did* happen in the past. Current and future events can be feared not just for their immediate effects but for what is perceived as anticipated or ongoing danger. The ability to fantasize can enlarge and modify these real or perceived dangers. The child's increased sense of time can now be filled with worries of dangers, real and imagined.

The fears of children have their own expected developmental course (Jersild and Holmes, 1935; Lewis and Rosenblum, 1975; Rutter, 1981); these are presented in Table 18–1. Although subject to both individual and circumstantial flavoring, these objects of fear are remarkably consistent in their appearance throughout early childhood. *Fears may have many developmental functions and are healthy sources of emotional and cognitive growth* (Fraiberg, 1959). Note that some developmental fears appear regressed. For example, a fearless 5-year-old may be afraid of a monster in the closet when she becomes 6 years old. No child can be protected from working through these fears. The types of fears seem to be linked to cognitive

TABLE 18–1.
Fears in Childhood*

0–7 mo	Change in stimulus level, loss of support; loud, sudden noises
8–18 mo	Separation, strangers, loud events, sudden movements toward, touching, physical restraints, large crowds, water, being bathed
2 yr	Loud sounds, dark colors, large objects, large moving things, hats, mittens, changes in location of physical things, going down the drain or toilet, wind and rain, animals
2½ yr	Movement, familiar objects moved, moving objects, unexpected events linked (e.g., Grandma in mom's hat)
3 yr	Visual fears, masks, old people, people with scars, deformities, the dark, parents going out at night, animals, burglars
4 yr	Auditory fears, the dark, wild animals, mother's departure, imaginary creatures, recalled past events, aggressive actions, threats
5 yr	Decrease in fears; injury, falls, dogs
6 yr	Fearful age; supernatural events, hidden people, being left or lost, small bodily injuries (e.g., splinters, small cuts), being left alone, death of loved ones, the elements, fire, thunder
7 yr	Spaces (cellars), shadows, ideas suggested by television, movies, being late for school, missing answers in school
8–9 yr	School failure, personal failure, ridicule by peers, disease, unanticipated events
10–11 yr	Wild animals, high places, criminals, older kids, loss of possessions, parental anger, remote possibilities of catastrophe (e.g., earthquake), school failure, pollution
12–17 yr	Physical changes in one's own body, isolation, sexual fears, loss of face, world events

*Adapted from Jersild AT, Holmes FB: *Child Dev Monogr* 1935; 20:358; Ilg FL, Ames L, Baker SM: *Child Behavior*, rev. New York, Harper & Row Publishers, 1981.

development (i.e., bright children have precocious fears; delayed children have fears consistent with their mental age [Mussen et al., 1980]). Children's fears, especially in early childhood, seem to cross cultural barriers (Gray, 1971; Konner, 1972), although the intensity of the child's response and the *specific* circumstances that intensify fears vary from child to child and across groups (Mussen et al., 1980). Children signal their fears in nonverbal ways that vary from child to child. These may be manifested by sleep refusals, increased visual vigilance, increased or decreased talk or activity, seemingly nonspecific irritability, or increased cleanliness.

As children are exposed to increasingly complex issues and adult developmental issues (Elkind, 1981), we might anticipate that the situations and concerns that evoke fears may also grow in diversity and complexity. Children may be exposed to issues far sooner than they have been previously. To support mental health for children, clinicians and parents need a guide for dealing with a child's fears that is built on an understanding of a child's developmental capacity. This generic approach to a child's fears allows a clinician and parent to see things from the child's perspective. This vision is necessary for age-appropriate action, no matter what the issue or the family's values or circumstances.

Sibylle Escalona (1962), a noted developmental psychologist, developed guidelines for parents based on cognitive and social developmental levels to use in discussing nuclear threat with their children. Although this issue is of widespread and increasing concern for children (Beardsley and Mack, 1962), Escalona's guide can be applied to a parent-child (or clinician-child) discussion on many fears, from monsters in the closet to worldwide hunger. Her overall perspective is laid out in the following comments and formulations.

The levels of a child's fears follow an expectable developmental course. (These ideas concerning levels of a child's fears are presented in the following sections; from Level II onward they are adapted from Escalona's work.)

LEVEL I: TODDLERS

Toddlers fear large, loud, overwhelming things. Objects that are very strange and do not act in expected ways, noises, and falling or danger of falling are toddlers' greatest sources of fearfulness. It is healthy to fear barking dogs, noisy streets, and large crowds of strangers. Adult strangers who approach quickly in a strange situation without a significant caretaker present arouse the most fear (Rutter, 1981). Parents should appreciate the appropriateness of these tendencies and not attempt to break them down with admonitions to pet every dog or kiss every stranger. Respect and protect these adaptive fears. Children lose innate fears of other children between 12 and 20 months, although many children adapt sooner if exposed to other children frequently (Mussen et al., 1980). If the adult stranger waits until the child makes an approach before moving in, the child's fear will be dissipated. The clinician can model this in the examination.

The toddler's greatest fear is separation from familiar caretakers (see Chapter 13). When separations are necessary, the child should be told who will be there for him, when the caretaker will return, and what will happen during the separation. Although he may not be able to use all of this information, the calm assurances serve to contain some of the fears. Prolonged separations, particularly in strange settings, are to be avoided because the child has no cognitive skills to sustain himself. During illness, these fears and lack of coping strategies increase.

LEVEL II: PRESCHOOLERS

Preschoolers have many fears that are born of their own inner fantasies and take on many shapes, animate and inanimate. These fears invade both waking and sleep time. The preschooler is frightened by anything that is noisy, violent, uncontrolled, or suggestive of destruction. He is struggling to control very similar feelings in himself; external things that echo these inner feelings and go beyond his ability to control may lead to fearfulness. The preschooler fears feeling defenseless in confronting his own inner turmoil, as well as the external events that parallel these internal monsters.

Nightmares are testimony to the ability to use fantasy to work through the expectable fears of life. They begin to emerge at about the same time as language, role playing, and other manifestations of imagination. They peak in incidence from 4 to 6 years of age. As a manifestation of growth and as tools of emotional growth, nightmares should be greeted warmly unless they are excessive or particularly repetitive. In those cases, the clinician should look for the reason why the child is bogged down rather than achieving mastery over the anxiety or fear.

Although most parents would naturally wish to protect all children from fearful things, fears come out of the normative developmental processes (Fraiberg, 1959) and cannot and should not be kept from a child. In a study of children ages 4 to 6 years, Bauer (1976) demonstrated that about three fourths of these children had frightening dreams and were afraid of monsters and ghosts, and almost half were afraid of animals. The fear of animals peaked at 3 years of age, fear of the dark peaked at 4 to 5 years, and fear of imaginary creatures was variable throughout this period (Rutter, 1981). Jersild and Holmes (1935) likewise found that the majority of children in the preschool years fear imaginary creatures, the dark, being alone, and bodily injury. It does not take much adult imagination to see that much of even the most benign medical encounter has one or more elements that call up fears in the preschool child. Minimizing the fear in this situation means evaluating the elements of that experience from the child's level.

Preschool children love stories that may seem quite violent and aggressive to adults. Bettelheim (1976) emphasizes that these reflect the child's inner feelings and serve as an important support of emotional maturation through the medium of fantasy. He advises that these stories should *not* be modified by parents to eliminate the fearful things nor interrupted by adult logic. Children will take and use from each story what they need to serve their own mental growth. In contrast, television does not allow that selective filtration of material, so that adult censorship is well advised.

The facing and meeting of manageable fears can be sources of growth, learning, and an increased sense of mastery that are both healthy and unavoidable. How, then, do parents ensure that these fears have positive effects rather than negative ones? The parents' primary course of support builds upon the child's own built-in safety device. This is the child's belief that his parents are all powerful and can protect him from his fears, or in Escalona's (1962) words:

> Reassurance of our love and protection does most to keep a preschooler feeling safe. No matter what a preschooler's fear is about on the surface, his real fear is that he may be hurt or lose the protective closeness of his parents.

Arguments built on pointing out the illogic of a preschooler's fears are very rarely effective. Their fears rise as easily from imagined dangers as from real ones. In addition, these discussions may lead to a feeling that the parent does not understand the fear and, therefore, is not available for protection. Factual information should be presented briefly and to the point. A detailed explanation of why a monster could not *possibly* be in the closet is futile. The message to be conveyed is that parents understand the perceived problem and will take care of the child.

Overstimulation by violent, incomprehensible, or overwhelming images on television, in movies, or in the news clearly creates anxiety in most children. These images may or may not lead directly to violent or aggressive behaviors. Fears that come from these situations are rarely sources of growth. Each parent is responsible for modulating the child's exposure to these images dependent on each child's response, based on the child's developmental level (Wolman, 1978).

Many fears may be based on simple misunderstandings, for example, going for an ear checkup means an injection or having to take off one's clothes. Parents and clinicians should explore fears briefly to see if this is the case. These misunderstandings, not the fear, should be simply attacked by a clear explanation and a layout of what to expect insofar as that can be done honestly.

LEVEL III: SCHOOL-AGED CHILDREN, 6 TO 12 YEARS

The thought processes of a child 6 to 12 years of age are dominated by an understanding of a system of rules, logical explanations, and regularities in things and events that can be anticipated (see Chapter 22, and Piaget, 1952). These cognitive capacities give a child additional strategies to deal with fears, but they do not free him of his worries. By second grade, the monsters are gone, but nightmares are still there, sometimes both at night and in the day. Most of their fears are of relatively remote possibilities now rather than an exaggeration or elaboration of an immediate event. This makes the source of fearfulness a bit more elusive, requiring very patient listening from a developmental perspective.

School-aged children usually fear that they themselves will not measure up to their peers in school, in sports, in the neighborhood (see Chapters 22 and 23). They may even fear the real aggression of others, or, more commonly after the age of 10 years, they may have fear of rejection or other social anxieties. They have (hopefully) also learned a sense of inner competence that allows them to rely on themselves. This competence is built upon feelings of ability to meet what lies ahead, based on abilities acquired in the past. Schoolchildren counter their anticipated fears by trying to find out everything there is to know about a given threatening situation. The more he knows, the more he can anticipate and call forth his own strategies to meet the challenges. Medical procedures or a move to a new classroom become less fearful if the child knows enough to rehearse his own response, to develop action plans, and to talk himself through the experience mentally. Remote possibilities must be considered and resolved because these may be very real. The careful explanations that may only increase anxiety for the preschooler will be well utilized by the grade-school child.

Schoolchildren cope with stress and fear by looking to those whom they admire; as Escalona (1962) states:

School age children learn that confidence comes with knowing how to do a thing and having tools to do it with. They are impressed by parents, teachers, older children and . . . heroes and all those who seem to them to embody the strength they themselves still lack.

The identification with heroes (see Chapter 19) and older persons is an adaptive and effective tool in dealing with fears.

Parents can support this adaptive strength by sharing in some measure their own worries and concerns with their older children. They can openly share problem-solving processes and their own views on fearful concerns that have no solution. Subjects that *are not* discussed become fearful for the school-aged child, because he must assume that all of the remote possibilities are true and that no one around him can deal with these issues. Children may harbor a sense of hidden worry about subjects that parents refuse to discuss. Parents should listen carefully to what children say—to guide the topics of discussion, the real concerns about issues, and to clear up misunderstandings. Parents who do not know where to begin on any subject (e.g., child abuse, sex education) should start with open-ended questions to the child to set the specific topics and to stay at an appropriate level. Children will ask for the information they are ready to hear if parents give the message that they are ready to listen and that no question is forbidden or no topic so fearful that it cannot be discussed.

School-aged children need to "rehearse" fearful situations with parents, teachers, and clinicians. By emphasizing events and actions, adults can prepare children to meet fearful situations with confidence. Role playing and dialogues with relaxed adults about such issues as threatened sexual molestation or an approach to a medical procedure dissolve fears and give children real resources to deal with these and other situations they might encounter in reality or in their minds.

Each child will have a distinct coping style in dealing with fears—denial, increases in aggressiveness, withdrawal, regression, etc. And all children use these defenses from time to time. Parents and clinicians should respect these style differences, while still being vigilant for any persistent or maladaptive pattern. Fears should be respected, not shamed or ridiculed. Never force a child to face a fear; he will conquer it on his own if given the chance and assurance. Do not be impatient with the child, and do not think the fear is your fault or the child's. If a child overtly approaches a fear, he may need to be given some controls. For example, a fire-fearing child may then wish to start fires. Lighting candles under supervision is a safe way to work that out.

Excessively fearful children should have their interpersonal environment examined to see if there is a lack of support for resolution of their fears or if the environment is too overwhelming for their ability to cope. Clinicians can model for parents ways of discovering their child's *basic* fears through a sensitive clinical interview. Then appropriate responses can be modeled commensurate with the child's developmental level. This is advocacy in its purest, most direct form.

A child's fears should never be dismissed as trivial. They offer clear testimony to a child's affective, cognitive, and social level. Fears are the other side of fantasy, and both are to be respected as sources of and testimony to mental growth. The fear is real even if the object of the fear is not.

DATA GATHERING

WHAT TO OBSERVE

The clinician should observe the following:

1. The child's use of toys in the office; suggest the use of puppets, small doll figures, blocks, small cars, blackboard

2. Ability to fill in empty times (e.g., time in the waiting room or during mother's interview) with imaginary events

3. Interest in books

4. General response to the office environment and any manifestations of fear, wariness

5. Mechanisms to cope with fear, such as withdrawal, seeking caretaker support, increase in activity, or verbal activity

WHAT TO ASK

The clinician should ask the following questions during the examination:

1. How does the child use fantasy at home? Ask what his favorite toys are and how he uses them. Does he have imaginary friends or enemies; an interest in costumes, role playing, assignments? What types of books does he like; does he make the transition from realistic books with familiar objects to "impossible" stories and pictures?

2. Does the child discuss imaginary events, sequences, creatures? What role do they serve?

3. How much television does he watch? What programs? Are parents present?

4. Does he sing television jingles, talk about advertised products?

5. Is the child assigning new functions to familiar objects (e.g., toothbrush becomes a spaceship)?

6. Is the child having dreams or nightmares?

7. What things make him fearful?

8. What is the parent's response to nightmares, fearful situations?

9. Who does the child play with? In what activities do he and his friends involve themselves?

ASSESSMENT

The following factors should be assessed during the examination:

1. Does the child move into puppet or doll play?

2. Can he accept and use your own fantasy suggestion (e.g., tongue blade becomes a car)?

3. Can the child tell you about his friends?

4. Will he accept a nonsense word for a familiar object?

5. What does the child do with some nondescript objects (e.g., several tongue blades, paper clips, paper cup)?

6. Can he do clay play with imagination?

ANTICIPATORY GUIDANCE

1. Limit television to 2 hours per day *maximum* of child-oriented programs *of value*. Parent (or other adult) viewing participation with children should be for at least half of that time. Reflection on the show content should occur during and following the show, in other words, make it a social and active event. Caution that few "children's programs" are really made with the developmental needs of the child as paramount. Suggest reading in this area for some families (e.g., Brazelton, 1977; Kaye, 1974; Lesser, 1974).

2. Encourage the use of toys that require at least two thirds of their use to be child determined (e.g., blocks, balls, toy buildings, dolls, puppets, crayons and paper, and simple vehicles).

3. Reflect to parents the usefulness of stories, imaginary friends, role playing, and "untruths." Discipline or reality explanations are not appropriate for the typical "lies" of preschool life. These mental structures will disappear after they have spent their usefulness. Point out that imagination can help a child learn, cope, and experience.

4. Reflect on the emergence of dreams and nightmares as markers of this new phase of cognitive and affective development. Welcome them as indicators of healthy mental development. Parents should respond to the child's reaction to the nightmare rather than content of it. Brief reassurance of the parent's protection should be central to this response. Never dismiss or attempt to explain away this or other frightening experiences.

5. Stories should be read with minimal interruption, and the discussion to follow should be directed by the child's interest and questions. For some children a time lag between presentation and digestion is needed as they savor imaginative stories. Parents should preview books and perhaps develop good library habits or exchanges with friends beginning in the third year of life.

6. Old clothes and simple costumes are good props for this phase of development.

7. Never ignore a child's fears. They tell of the child's inner life and developmental level. Listen patiently.

8. Do not overdo or elaborate your own concern about a situation that frightens the child. Assurance of your protection and support is most important.

9. Never force the child to meet the object of his fears. Do not ridicule or threaten him for being afraid.

10. If a child appears excessively fearful or nightmares are very frequent, look at the child's daily experience for evidence of overstimulation and exposure to emotions or situations that are overwhelming.

REFERENCES

Bauer DH: An exploratory study of developmental changes in children's fears. *J Child Psychol Psychiatry* 1976; 17:69–74.

Beardslee E, Mack J: The impact on children and adolescents of nuclear developments, in *Psychological Aspects of Nuclear Development*. Task Force Report no 20 of the American Psychiatric Association, Washington, DC, 1982, pp 64–93.

Bettelheim B: *Uses of Enchantment*. New York, Random House, 1976.

Brazelton TB: *Toddlers and Parents*. New York, Delacorte, 1974.

Brazelton TB: How to tame the TV monster, in *Doctor and Child*. New York, Delacorte, 1977.

Bruner J: Children at play, in Lewin R (ed): *Child Alive*. Garden City, NY, Anchor Press, 1975.

Chance: *Learning Through Play*. New York, Johnson & Johnson Co, 1979.

DeForest M, Echols C: The role of crib speech in the acquisition of language. Paper presented at the Conference on Child Language, Boston University, Boston, October 1983.

Elkind D: *The Hurried Child: Growing Up Too Fast. Too Soon*. Redding, Mass, Addison-Wesley Publishing Co, 1981.

Escalona S: *Children and the Threat of Nuclear War.* New York, Child Study Association of America, 1962.

Fraiberg S: *The Magic Years.* New York, Scribner, 1959.

Garvey C: *Play.* Cambridge, Mass, Harvard University Press, 1977.

Ginsberg H, Opper S: *Piaget's Theory of Intellectual Development.* Englewood Cliffs, NJ: Prentice-Hall, 1969.

Gray JA: *The Psychology of Fear and Culture.* New York, McGraw-Hill Book Co, 1971.

Jersild AT, Holmes FB: Children's fears. *Child Dev Monogr* 1935; no 20, p 358.

Kaye E (ed): *The Family Guide to Children's Television.* New York, Pantheon Books, 1974.

Kohlberg L: Development of moral character and moral ideology, in Hoffman ML, Hoffman LW (eds): *Review of Child Development Research.* New York, Russell Sage Foundation, 1974, vol 1.

Konner M: Aspects of the developmental ethology of foraging people, in Blurton-Jones N (ed): *Ethological Studies of Child Behavior.* New York, University of Cambridge Press, 1972.

Lesser G: *Children and Television.* New York, Random House, 1974.

Lewis C, Lewis M: The impact of television commercials on health related beliefs and behaviors of children. *Pediatrics* 1974; 53:431–435.

Lewis M, Rosenblum M (eds): *The Origins of Fear.* New York, John Wiley & Sons, 1975.

Liebert R, Neale JM, Davidson ES: *The Early Window: Effects of Television on Children and Youth.* New York, Pergamon Press, 1973.

Meltzoff AN: Elimination of television models by infants. *Child Devel* 1988; 59:1221–1229.

Murphy B: *The Widening World of Childhood.* New York, Basic Books, 1962.

Mussen, PH, Conger JJ, Kagan J: *Essentials of Child Development and Personality.* New York, Harper & Row Publishers, 1980.

Piaget J: *The Origins of Intelligence,* Cook M (trans). New York, International University Press, 1952.

Rutter M (ed): *Scientific Foundation of Developmental Psychiatry.* Baltimore, University Park Press, 1981.

Surgeon General's Scientific Advisory Committee on Television and Growing Up: *The Impact of Televised Violence.* Washington, DC, US Government Printing Office, 1972.

Winnicott D: *Playing and Reality.* New York, Basic Books, 1971.

Wolman BB: *Children's Fears.* New York, Grosset & Dunlap, 1978.

Zuckerman DM, Zuckerman BS: Television's impact on children. *Pediatrics* 1985; 75:233.

"A picture of me." By T.W., boy, age
4¾.

CHAPTER **19**

Four Years: A Clearer Sense of Self

NICHOLAS PUTNAM, M.D.
SUZANNE D. DIXON, M.D.

KEY WORDS

INDIVIDUAL IDENTITY
GENDER IDENTITY
AGGRESSION
INITIATIVE
MORAL DEVELOPMENT
SEXUAL DEVELOPMENT
SEXUAL EXPLORATION

Daniel, age 4, is brought in by his mother at 4:30 p.m. after she received an urgent call from his child care center. He had bitten another child ("drawn blood") and the school wanted a complete assessment including an AIDS test and evaluation to be sure he'd never do that again. Mrs. Harris, after a full day's work as a supermarket clerk, is frazzled and tearful as she pulls Daniel into the examining room. She feels that the school wants to throw him out—a center where he has been since 18 months of age. She also complains that she has noticed him having some accidents in his pants lately, a new behavior. Daniel appears unusually quiet. He is wearing baggy pants, a Ninja Turtle sweatshirt, a baseball cap, and a string of purple beads. His fingernails are polished red. He sits quietly coloring a picture while you interview the mother.

The 4-year mark often begins "real childhood" when a child becomes his own person with independent actions and with interactions based mostly on words. Four-year-olds are remarkably engaging patients because of their explorations of new "persona," their ability to converse, and usual willingness to cooperate. This developmental stage is marked by rapid growth in language and motor skills, which in turn enables the child to take important steps in social and emotional development. The magical inner workings of the 3-year-old now share space with those of a little more rational person who is intensely curious about the specifics around him. In the preschool child, development is marked by the emergence of sex specific behaviors and gender-role identification associated with parental models. Also apparent are the emergence of a conscience, the capacity for collaborative play, and finally the beginnings of mastery over sexual, emotional, and aggressive impulses. The preschool child begins to develop a clear sense of who he is and how he should behave: new, clearer, self-perceptions with long-lasting consequences. Throughout this period, the child is increasingly ready to join his peers in social settings that are marked by less adult supervision and demand more self-control such as preschool classrooms and playgrounds and day camps and classes. The degree to which the child, with the help of his family, has successfully accomplished this growth forms the focus of the developmental evaluation of 4-year-old children.

LANGUAGE AND MOTOR DEVELOPMENT

Language skills blossom during this period. The child's vocabulary increases from several hundred to several thousand words—"too many to count." Speech begins to contain all the elements of adult speech with regard to syntax and grammar. Although speech is still imperfectly articulated, the child is, for the most part, intelligible to strangers virtually all the time. She can give her first and last name, age, sex, and names of siblings, although usually little useful information about where she lives. She will understand what it means to be tired and cold or hungry. Most interactions are based upon language. By the age of 4 years, most children understand a number of prepositions and can identify colors and common animals. A few will recognize letters, and many more can recite the alphabet. This capacity naturally leads the child to increased exploration and interactions with her environment. The functions of objects and the ongoing action in pictures can be identified. "Reading" a story by pictures shows elements of continuity and of cause and effect. Elements such as motivation and consequence of actions are beginning to be appreciated.

Improved motor skills also allow for a greater variety of play and social experiences. The child will actively seek out opportunities for climbing, swinging, modeling of clay or sand, drawing or painting, and often physical contact with other children. Riding a three-wheeler and jungle gym play are compelling activities for most children. The 4-year-old walks down stairs with alternating feet, catches a large ball most of the time, skips, and can do a broad jump. Gross- and fine-motor skills, however, are still not well coordinated so that the preschooler still appears "childlike" in her motor activities. Thus, competence in activities that demand greater accuracy or careful timing and sequencing, such as baseball, ballet, soccer, or football are still several years off. Cooperative group games, excursions to the park, and craft activities involving more than one step can be learned and enjoyed. Four-year-olds can assume more responsibility for dressing themselves, so the sequencing and fine motor skills are relatively coordinated.

COGNITIVE DEVELOPMENT

The child's thinking during this period continues to be "magical" (Fig 19–1). A preschooler may even feel as though her thinking can influence the outside world. Piaget (Flavell, 1963) described the thinking of children in this preconceptual stage as egocentric, animistic, and artificialistic (Table 19–1). The child has much difficulty in seeing any point of view other than her own and may feel that events in nature occur for her benefit (egocentrism). The child may assign human feelings and motives to inanimate objects and animals (animism). The child also may indicate she believes that everything, including natural objects and events, are caused by other human beings (artificialism).

In fact, cause and effect relationships are quite poorly understood by the preschooler. The child may confuse temporal relationships with causal relationships. For example, she may

FIG 19–1.
The magical quality of a preschool-aged child is illustrated in this picture in which inanimate objects are assigned human feelings and motives (animism).

TABLE 19–1.
The Nature of Early Childhood Thought*

Sample Questions	Typical Answers
	Egocentrism
Why does the sun shine?	To keep me warm.
Why is there snow?	For me to play in.
Why is grass green?	Because that's my favorite color.
What are TV sets for?	To watch my favorite shows and cartoons.
	Animism
Why do trees have leaves?	To keep them warm.
Why do stars twinkle?	Because they're happy and cheerful.
Why does the sun move in the sky?	To follow children and hear what they say.
Where do boats go at night?	They sleep like we do.
	Artificialism
What causes rain?	Someone emptying a watering can.
Why is the sky blue?	It has been painted.
What is the wind?	A man blowing.
What causes thunder?	A man grumbling.

*From Helms DB, Turner JS: *Exploring Child Behavior: Basic Principles.* Philadelphia, WB Saunders Co, 1978. Used by permission.

feel the birth of a sibling is causally related to the death of a pet if the two events happen to be temporally related. This thinking persists even while language now appears more rational.

The level of cognitive development in children about 4 years old has a profound effect upon the child's conception of illness and medical care. It is not uncommon for the preschooler to see illness as resulting from bad behavior on her part. Treatment is then viewed as a form of punishment. Inanimate objects such as X-ray machines may be endowed with animate characteristics and motivations by the child. Parents may unwittingly support such notions in children by warning a child that she may become ill or require a doctor's visit and/ or an injection if she does not obey. It is not surprising that a large percentage of sick children associate their illness or routine medical care with some recent disobedience or expression of anger on their parents' and clinicians' part. The facade of being "a regular kid" belies the thought processes that are still full of idiosyncratic reasoning and associations.

SOCIAL AND EMOTIONAL DEVELOPMENT

Much of the developmental work of this period has to do with the acquisition of self-control over sexual, emotional, and aggressive impulses through identification with important adults and older children in the child's life. Freud (1965) emphasized the strong attachment that children, beginning at 3 and 5 years old, show for the parent of the opposite sex. Physical closeness, fantasies, and play activities are often directed toward positive interchanges between boys and mothers on the one hand, and girls and fathers on the other. This closeness to the parent of the opposite sex is often associated with a certain amount of anxiety that motivates the child (at about 6 years of age) to redirect her attachment to the parent of the same sex. The successful negotiation of the "Oedipal phase," according to Freud, sets the pattern for later intimate relationships as well as providing the child with his or her own sexual identification. This also helps to instill the beliefs, morals, and behavioral manner of the parents, including the parental roles based upon gender. Four-year-olds want to please parents and assume the expected role definitions.

Emotional growth in childhood can be conceptualized in terms of the child's relationships to significant adults in his life. Termed "object relationships," this developmental line begins with the *symbiotic* closeness of the infant and mother in the first 6 months, and moves into the period of *separation-individuation* from about 6 months to 2 years when transitional objects serve to maintain psychological harmony in the absence of parents. This continues into the complex relationships characteristic of the preschool period (Mahler, 1975). As children traverse this pathway over the first 6 years of their lives, they experience different levels and types of psychological attachment to significant adults (usually, but not always, parents). This early experience significantly affects the quality and style of the child's future important relationships.

Erik Erikson (1963) extended Freud's theory to include the child's social experiences during this period as well. He emphasized the conflict between the feelings of initiative and guilt, which occurs in preschoolers. A 3- to 4-year-old should have a sufficient sense of autonomy from his earlier development to take initiative in his relationships with both peers and adults without experiencing excessive guilt or anxiety. Observations of preschool children at play provide good examples of the initiative children show at this age. One may see boys building the highest of towers, the longest of trains, and at times, intruding into the play and work activities of other children and adults. During this period girls will be seen to build enclosures, capture other children, and entice others into conversations and activities with them. Learning to take these kinds of social initiatives (without ever feeling excessively guilty or impinging excessively on the rights and feelings of others) is a sign of healthy emotional development during the preschool period. The child has confidence in her role and place in a group so initiating activities and actively participating does not cost much in anxiety.

During the period between 3 and 5 years of age, sex role differentiation becomes increasingly complex and assumes a functional rather than a nominal definition. Children begin to group clothes, behaviors, activities and friends into sex-specific groups. Little girls practice behaviors that they believe are characteristic of women; little boys do things they learn typify men. Children of both sexes become increasingly eager to behave in ways that firmly establish their position with reference to gender (Jacklin and Maccoby, 1983).

The roles of both sexes may be explored periodically during this time; this is entirely normal. Children will try to be other people, trying on identities is part of finding out more about themselves. This identity testing includes gender roles as well as others. Even in the presence of permissive adults who avoid sex-role stereotyping in play activities or toys, children today still show differences in interests in play activities related to their gender identity. These seem to be developmentally-based tasks, with social and cultural dimensions. Cultural and familial definitions of sex-appropriate behaviors or personality characteristics influence how children perceive these roles so that by the age of 5 years most children show preferences in their activities related to their sex and play preferentially with same sex groups.

MORAL DEVELOPMENT

Through a gradual assumption of an identity of parents, the foundation for moral development is laid down. The 4-year-old shows increasing reasoning ability and can apply this to some moral issues, but he is still "flawed" in judgment because of his idiosyncratic thought processes. The gains here are worth highlighting. The 4-year-old can understand promises but can't always keep them himself (Leach, 1986). He can recognize the difference between truth and fantasy but doesn't always tell the truth. "Inaccurate talk" is a better term than "lies." He can recognize the rights of others ("It's Johnny's turn now.") but not always respect those rights. Property rights often are a little vague. On the other hand, the 4-year-old demonstrates a good sense of justice and can show unselfish sympathy and concern for others. Moral judgments must be confined to the immediate instance as abstraction is a ways away. On the other hand, the 4-year-old wants to please, wants approval, and may even become a bit self righteous.

SEXUAL EXPLORATION

Preschool children show a great deal of interest in the "private area" (roughly that part of the body covered by a bathing suit) on themselves and others. Games involving undressing or exploration of another child's body are common by age 4. "Toilet talk" becomes particularly interesting as the structure and function of these private areas are verbally explored. Sex play sometimes played as "mother and father" or "doctor" is common in preschool children. Children of this age often attempt to engage in physical contacts with other family members, such as fondling their mother's breasts; both "exhibitionistic" and "voyeuristic" activities are common and normal. These behaviors should be seen in the positive sense that they testify to the child's work on the resolution of these important relationships. They do not predict continuance of these behaviors.

Such behavior in children can lead to conflict between parent and child and also create strained relationships between parents with differing views on management. It is helpful for the pediatric clinician to be able to reassure parents that sexual play among preschool children is a natural consequence of growth in the child's cognitive, emotional, and social development. One can tell parents that children of this age are intensely interested in learning about themselves and their bodies, and that this interest extends to other children and adults as well. In fact, this is the age at which children are most likely to notice differences between individuals, including differences in weight, race, and eye color, as well as sex organs. Again, observing and noting these differences helps the child obtain a clearer sense of herself as a unique individual with specific traits and characteristics.

At what point parents need to set limits on sexual exploration by preschool children is a matter for each family to decide, consistent with their own values and tolerance for such behavior. Parents may be told, however, that overreacting to sexual play in childhood may only temporarily suppress such behavior, actually heighten sexual curiosity, and create unnecessary anxiety in the child. On the other hand, parents who are overly permissive may expose their child to situations that are beyond his ability to handle. This, in turn, may be anxiety-provoking for the child. In general, parents should be helped to communicate to their children that an interest in the genital organs is healthy and natural; at the same time they can teach children that nudity and sex play are generally not acceptable in public, between children and adults, or when forced upon anyone. The degree of nudity allowed in a family should be discussed between parents to allow for consistency. Parents also should tell children of this age that no other person (including friends and family) has permission to touch them on their "private area." Such conversations between parent and child should take place on numerous occasions prior to adolescence if the child is to incorporate such values as his own level of understanding matures. "Sex education" begins in infancy with establishing comfort with physical touching and emotional closeness. It becomes explicit in this preschool period when children begin to connect sex organs with reproduction and sensual pleasure, and it includes the development of the ability to set limits and not be forced to closeness on any level. Children should be given the freedom to ask questions about this area. Parents should provide accurate answers for the questions asked, following the child's lead.

AGGRESSIVE BEHAVIOR

Overly aggressive behavior may become a problem during preschool years as emotions, a sense of self, and identification with powerful figures are developmental themes. A child engages in aggressive behavior when she shows a disregard for the feelings, property, rights, or physical safety of other individuals. Aggressive behavior can often be distinguished from assertive behavior in which the child attempts to satisfy her needs in a direct, energetic, perhaps even willful manner, while still respecting the basic rights of other children. The 4-year-old must learn to assert herself without being aggressive. Like sexual exploration, aggressive behavior is a natural consequence of a child's cognitive, physical, and emotional growth. She must struggle to keep aggression under *her own control* while becoming appropriately assertive.

Some theorists find that aggression is a biological instinct and believe that the better child-rearing practices channel this aggressive instinct into socially acceptable behaviors (Lorenz, 1963). Other theorists view the development of aggressive behavior as a response to frustration in the early life of a child, to positive reinforcement for aggressive behavior that occurs in some families, and to modeling by children after powerful adults who exhibit aggressive behavior (Martin and Beezley, 1977). The former theory of aggression as instinct is supported by the ubiquity of aggressive behavior in preschool children. Films taken of children in preschool settings indicate that boys engage in aggressive acts toward their peers many times each hour. Other evidence shows that girls too will engage in frequent aggressive behaviors, provided they feel relatively assured of going undetected; girls may also be particularly verbally assaultive. On the other hand, theories that view aggression as a learned response are supported by studies that show that many aggressive preschoolers come from homes in which the parent-child relationship is of a hostile, rejecting type or where violence is often present. Such children may also have aggressive models in the home and may, in fact, merely be imitating their parents' disciplinary behaviors or interpersonal style. Aggression may be the only consistent response they experience within their interpersonal space.

To understand a particular child's aggressive behavior, the clinician can take an appropriate history from the parent. The more serious the aggressive behavior is, the more frequently it occurs, the more widespread the settings (home, school, and community) are, the more likely it is that the child has a significant problem with aggression. Isolated instances of aggressive behavior, *regardless of the degree of actual physical or property damage incurred,* can be a part of a normative growth process. The child who appears chronically angry or anxious is more worrisome than a child whose aggressive act comes out of a positive, open approach to life in general. The angry child may not feel good about himself or his place in family or society. These issues need further exploration, suggestions for support for a more positive self-image, or, occasionally, a referral to a mental health professional. Behaviors that are really disguised aggression (include fecal soiling if a change in regular bowel habits and smearing), self-destructive behavior, and destructive behavior directed at objects. These behaviors must usually be interpreted as angry, aggressive acts. The "accident prone" child may likewise be aggressive toward self. He may be anxious, and carelessness and/or impulsive actions may ensue.

OBSERVATIONS

While the clinician takes a history, he can often observe whether the child is successful in modulating her behavior. During this period of waiting, the child may experience anxiety, frustration, or boredom. A well-socialized child will show evidence of self-control as she seeks to deal with these uncomfortable feelings. She may approach the parent for comfort or information and in so doing may either show a capacity for delay of gratification or she may intrude to the extent of disrupting the interview between clinician and parent. The clinician will also observe the parent's response to the child's intrusion into the adult conversation—a model for how mildly antisocial behavior is handled within a family. The pediatrician may also observe whether the child separates easily from the parent when toys are available and during the physical examination. Does the child assist in her own undressing, and does the parent allow it? The child's clothes may reveal a sex identification or a specific window into the child's sense of self. Does the child respond to verbal commands such as, "Hop up on this table," or does she require physical assistance? Are the parent's limit-setting activities balanced by expressions of affection for the child? Is the child's speech easily understood? Most children are reluctant to get undressed at this age. By 4 years old, they should be appropriately sensitive about uncovering their "private area." This should be avoided as long as possible, doing as much of the exam as possible with the clothes on.

Emotionally healthy preschool children are fascinated by the simple toys that can easily be provided in a physician's waiting room. Puzzles, shape boxes, puppets, and toy vehicles are almost uniformly appreciated by children of this age. An observer can note whether or not the child's play with these toys is functional, i.e., the toy hammer is used for pounding and the toy car to simulate driving. Children with serious developmental delays may use toys in a nonfunctional manner, for example, pounding on a book with a toy truck. The older preschool child, particularly if companions are available, may engage in "thematic play" in which the toys are used by the child to tell a story, express a fantasy, or develop a game about the same subject.

Additional data may be obtained in a conversational manner during the physical examination of the child. The clinician should direct some questions to the child, others to the parent, and listen attentively to the responses of both (Table 19–2). Children of this age are often quite candid in expressing their opinions and observations of the world and can provide valuable, uncensored information. The clinician may organize his thinking around the following areas without committing himself to a particular sequence of questions.

ANTICIPATORY GUIDANCE

- Assess the appropriateness of the child's preschool setting. Does she need more or less structure? What are her relationships with the other children? Does she have friends and engage in thematic play?

TABLE 19–2.

Questions to Be Asked During Examination

Questions for Children	Objective
	Physical Health
How are you feeling today?	Communicate to the child that you value the information he/she can provide about his/her own health
I am glad to see you today; do you know why mommy/daddy brought you to see me today?	Understand the child's beliefs about the reasons for medical examination and/or treatment; provide an opportunity to clarify common misconceptions, e.g., medical care is a form of punishment
(If the child is ill or in pain) What would you like mommy/daddy or me to do to help you feel better?	Obtain information regarding the child's beliefs relating to the illness or symptom and to medical treatment, as well as allow the child to feel like a participant in the medical care process at an early age
	Cognitive Development
How old are you? Do you have any pets? What color is your dog? What color is mommy's purse? How many brothers and sisters do you have? What are their names? What is your mommy's name? What is your daddy's name?	The child's general fund of information, vocabulary, speech, and even his/her degree of sociability will become apparent in his/her answers to simple questions such as these; pediatricians will develop their own age norms for evaluating children's responses by repeatedly asking the same questions to a large number of preschool children
What makes the sun come up in the morning? What makes the clouds move in the sky?	To assess the child's belief regarding causality and, perhaps, illustrate for the parents important differences in the way younger children reason
Ask the child to copy a circle, a cross, and a square	Assess the child's competence in increasingly difficult fine-motor tasks
Ask the child to draw a man	About 50% of 4-year-olds are able to draw a man with three parts; by age 5 most children can draw a man with eight parts
What do you do when you are cold . . . tired . . . hungry?	Most 4-year-olds can give appropriate answers to two of three of these questions used in the Denver Developmental Screening Test (DDST) to assess language development; a number of similar examples are provided in the DDST, which is a useful tool for the clinician to use in this age group
	Social and Emotional Development
Who is a good friend of yours? What's her (his) name?	Assess the child's progress in forming relationships outside the home; does the child name adults rather than peers as friends? He should have named at least one friend of preschool age
What do you like to do?	While enhancing rapport with the child, it provides the clinician with an opportunity to determine the nature of the child's solitary play with respect to complexity, activity vs. passivity, gender appropriateness, etc.
What do you like to do when you are with your friends?	Assesses the child's capacity for true collaborative play with peers. Does the child use his imagination to differentiate roles in group play, e.g., "we play hospital and I'm the doctor and my friend is the patient."
What is it like to have a baby brother/sister? What is it like to have a big brother/sister? When do you have fun with your (sibling)? When does your brother/sister make you mad?	Assess the degree of sibling rivalry present, child's capacity to express positive and negative affect, and child's perception of his place in the family

TABLE 19–2.
Questions to Be Asked During Examination

Questions for Children	Objective
Is there a dog living at your house? Is it a boy or girl dog? How can you tell?	Assess the child's awareness of sexual differences; if the clinical situation suggests any confusion in the child's own gender identity, clinician may follow up with questions such as, "How can you tell if you are a boy/girl? What do you like about being a boy/girl? Is there anything you don't like about being a boy/girl?"
What do you do when you want something and mommy/daddy says you can't have it?	Assess the child's perception of his own responses to parental limit setting: does the child admit to throwing tantrums that he later regrets (a good sign)? Does the child relate a number of different levels of responding to frustration, e.g., "sometimes I cry, but sometimes I just go to my room and play."
How do you like your preschool/daycare center, etc.? (by name if possible)	Assess the child's reaction to and success in separation from family members

Questions for Parents	Objective
What kinds of play activities does your child enjoy?	Parental reports can provide much information about the child's actual motor skills (e.g., can he ride a three-wheeler) and social skills
What does the child's preschool teacher (babysitter, grandparent, etc.) say about him/her?	Obtain additional information about the child's personality and behavior while separated from parents, and at the same time assess parents' openness to feedback about their child from outside the home; some parents find difficulty in accepting any negative feedback about their child, while other parents seem surprised at favorable reports from outsiders about a child with whom they are experiencing difficulty
What do you like most about your child? What would you say is his/her most troublesome quality?	Determine the parents' capacity to identify and articulate the child's positive and negative qualities; inability to report some highly positive quality is unusual for parents and should be a sign for further evaluation by the clinician
How often does he/she misbehave? What kinds of things does he/she do? What do you usually do when this happens?	An assessment of discipline practices at this age is absolutely essential; the clinician should be alert to the presence of inappropriately high or low behavioral expectations during this period; disciplinary techniques may be inconsistently applied, too harsh, or otherwise ineffective
Can you take him/her out to dinner at a friend's house or a restaurant?	Assesses the parents' comfort with their efforts to help the child meet social expectations outside the home; regardless of the parents' standard of behavior, parents should have a degree of confidence in their child's behavior by age 4 or 5
How does he/she act when he/she is angry? What does he/she usually do when another child grabs something away from him/her?	Allows the parents to discuss concerns regarding the child's aggressive behavior or lack of aggressive behavior
How does he/she show you that he/she knows that he/she is a boy/girl?	Allows the parent to discuss the child's gender identity formation and their own degree of comfort with it

TABLE 19–2.
Questions to Be Asked During Examination

Questions for Children	Objective
What are his/her play activities?	
Has your child expressed an interest in his/her body by asking questions, or examining himself/herself or other people?	Allows the parent to discuss evidence of sexual curiosity in the child, while defining this as a normative process
Does your child behave differently around his/or her father/mother than he does around you? In what way are his/her relationships different with each of his/her parents?	Provides opportunity for the parents to discuss the Oedipal phenomenon at its various stages, while allowing the clinician to assess and comment on the age appropriateness of this behavior

- Discuss the normalcy of sexual exploration at this level. Discuss with the family appropriate limit setting, management, the importance of consistency within the family.
- Discuss toys and play vis a vis broad range of interests but with expectations of sex-specific activities.
- Explain the importance of reviewing television and movies that children watch, limiting exposure to violent and or sexual themes and sex stereotyping (see Bibliography section on videos).
- Explain the importance of peer play and help a family orchestrate playmates if this does not occur naturally. A child this age should bring kids home or the parents should find out why they have not.
- Explain the basis for outbursts against the same sex parents and "over" attachment to the opposite sex parent. Physical closeness should continue, with parents alert to the need to limit overly sexualized behaviors.
- Read fairy tales and other stories through without comment. Discuss the story at the end, with any social/moral themes.
- Discuss sex education for the preschooler. This usually includes providing names for all genital parts, showing baby's form and explaining breasts are used for feeding. Follow the child's questions and do not overload with too much information at the same time.
- Children need to be counseled about their own private parts—they are for no one to touch except parents and health providers. Children should be empowered to resist all touches that feel bad. Parents should give them permission to discuss these. All reports of "bad touches" should be taken seriously.
- Caution parents about the differences between "inaccurate talk" and "lies" and the difficulty with respecting the property rights of others at this age. Aggressive behavior should be discouraged but *not* answered with aggression as that gives a mixed message and has been shown *not* to be successful.
- Differences between people (due to individual, ethnic, or handicapped characteristics) should be discussed openly, neutrally and positively. Children's curiosity about these issues should be respected.
- Children enjoy going through baby books and seeing old pictures of themselves as they struggle with a sense of self. Going over a baby book or displaying baby pictures are good ideas.

REFERENCES

Erikson E: *Childhood and Society,* ed 2. New York, WW Norton, 1963.

Flavell, J: *The Developmental Psychology of Jean Piaget.* Princeton, NJ, D VanNostrand Co, 1963.

Fraiberg S: *The Magic Years.* New York, Charles Scribner's Sons, 1959.

Freud S: *New Introductory Lectures on Psychoanalysis.* New York, WW Norton, 1965.

Gesell A, Amatruda C: *Developmental Diagnosis.* New York, Harper & Row Publishers, 1964.

Helms D, Turner J: *Exploring Child Behavior: Basic Principles.* Philadelphia, WB Saunders Co, 1978.

Jacklin C, Maccoby E: Issues of gender differentiation, in Levine MD, et al (eds): *Developmental-Behavioral Pediatrics.* Philadelphia, WB Saunders Co, 1983.

Leach P: *Your Baby and Child.* New York, Alfred A Knopf, 1986.

Lorenz K: *On Aggression.* New York, Harcourt Brace and World Inc, 1963.

Maccoby ET, Jacklin CN: *The Psychology of Sex Differences.* Stanford, Calif, Stanford University Press, 1974.

Mahler M: *The Psychological Birth of the Human Infant: Symbiosis and Individuation.* New York, Basic Books, 1975.

Martin H, Beezley P: Behavioral observations of abused children. *Dev Med Child Neurol.* 1977; 19:373.

Millar S: *The Psychology of Play,* New York, Penguin, 1968.

Perrin E, Gerrity P: There's a demon in your belly: Children's understanding of illness. *Pediatrics* 1981; 67:841–849.

Piaget J: *The Child's Conception of Physical Causality.* New York, Basic Books, 1930.

Piaget J: *The Child's Conception of the World.* Totowa, NJ, Littlefield, Adams & Co, 1965.

Rutter M: Child development, in Rutter M (ed): *Helping Troubled Children.* New York, Plenum Press, 1975.

"A girl and boy get on the bus. Their parents are watching." By Colin Hennessy, age 5½.

CHAPTER **20**

Five Years: Entering School

PHILIP R. NADER, M.D.

KEY WORDS

ENTERING SCHOOL
READINESS
KINDERGARTEN ENTRY
DEVELOPMENTAL VARIATION
MATCHING CHILD AND SCHOOL

FOCUS OF DEVELOPMENTAL WORK

It has been suggested that even though "play" is the "work" of the preschooler, "school is the work of the child." Contemplating the schooling of a child, therefore, holds realistic promises and realistic perils for both the child and the family. The transition to school represents the "proof" of child-rearing up to this time. How that transition is negotiated and when and what is experienced and learned in the early school years by the child and family often has long-lasting effects on several areas of psychological well-being. These include future achievement or lack of achievement, personal sense of worth, ability to contribute to others, and satisfaction with life. The developmental tasks facing the child at school entry include separation, increasing individualization, the putting together of cognitive skills required to learn to read, the ability to form relationships with other children and adults, the ability to participate in group activities and follow rules and directions, and the gradual formation of a sense of self or identity, both inside and outside the family environment. Rutter (1979) points out the profound and enduring influence of the school environment on the child. Getting off to a good start is of critical importance.

THEORETICAL FRAMEWORK

A variety of theoretical models of development have relevance for the pediatrician approaching the task of evaluation of school readiness. Conceptual models of Freud (1965), Erikson (1959), Piaget and Inhelder (1968), and Gesell and Ilg (1946; see Chapter 2) illustrate many of the critical tasks and substrata on which interaction of the individual with the environment is to unfold. Recent formulations of cognitive social learning theory (Bandura, 1977) are also of value in understanding the reciprocal interactions that shape an individual's sense of competence (see Chapter 2).

This comprehensive theory of learning is useful to those involved with the education and socialization of young children. Bandura (1977) points out the important influences of modeled and observed behavior to learning. The formulation also stresses the importance that mastery of a given task gives to the child's developing sense of competence as an individual. Bandura's theory takes into account the mutual influences of the individual, the physical and psychosocial environment, and the task or behavior to be learned. All of these factors are important to learning.

The skilled and experienced pediatrician approaches the evaluation of the child's school readiness with a healthy caution. This caution is appropriate because individual variation in "normal" behavior and cognitive function at this age is great. *Readiness at a given age does not necessarily imply either accelerated or retarded development.* The purpose of a readiness evaluation should be placed not in the context of prediction of disease or dysfunction but in the context of attempting to optimize the chances of a successful early school experience. The limitation of existing tools for assessment, coupled with the potential power of a "medical" pronouncement, also support the need for proceeding with caution in the evaluation of school readiness.

The time before school entry is an opportunity for the pediatrician to systematically review a 5-year data base that should be available to critically assess the potential fit or lack of fit between child, family, and school factors. It is unlikely that moderate to severe developmental problems, handicaps, or illnesses will have gone undetected up to this time. Naturally the pediatrician will already have been involved in the care plans and management of schooling or special education interventions for such children. Public Law 94-142 mandates an equal educational opportunity for the handicapped from ages 3 to 21 years; there is a probability that this mandate will be extended to an earlier age.

It is the more subtle developmental and behavioral variations that present problems for detection of potential inimical influences on schooling. Two children may be very similar in their temperamental characteristics, social behavior, ability to attend, ability to screen out distractions, visual motor abilities, and language development. Yet, how they do in school may be quite different, depending on parental views and expectations and the style and expectations that the school environment places on the children. It is very important, therefore, to first determine the attitudes, values, and expectations of the parents. It is also wise to ascertain those that seem to be prevalent in the community as expressed in the educational philosophy of the school (Rutter, 1979). For example, parents may describe an "active, inquisitive, independent, and creative" 5-year-old who is later described by a teacher as "restless, stubborn, resistant, and rebellious." Parental desires and expectations for performance should be determined, and comparison of these hopes with their own school experiences can sometimes be helpful in forming more realistic expectations of the child. Problems result when "underexpectations" and "overexpectations" are placed on the child's anticipated school performance (Wright and Nader, 1983).

Despite the wide variation in normal, several critical areas within the child deserve special attention at this time. These developmental requisites provide some touchstones in the evaluation process. They include the presence or absence of potential biological insults to the nervous system, the presence or absence of indicators of language dysfunction, the presence or absence of indicators of problems in attention and impulsivity, and the presence or absence of a successful socialization or separation experience from the parent or parents.

BIOLOGICAL FACTORS—We know the potential impact of gestational maturity at birth and maternal nutrition and illness factors in the prenatal period. We are becoming increasingly aware of more subtle effects on learning abilities and specific areas of cognitive function such as memory and attention. These arise from a number of perinatal and early life experiences. Minor surgical procedures, hospitalizations, self-limited illnesses, and other medical or biological events were previously thought to have little bearing on issues of education and future learning. Now it appears that such events may have a significant influence on *specific* cognitive abilities, emotional factors, or motor competencies. The impact of allergies and recurrent ear infections on subtle hearing deficits with subsequent impact on cognitive function is receiving greater recognition. Even straightforward issues of physical stature may impact the early school experience. For example, there are data suggesting that short children who also enter school at a relatively young chronological age may show poor self-esteem and become underachievers by adolescence, no matter what their level of cognitive function.

LANGUAGE—The presence of a delay in language development has been shown to be the best single predictor of later learning problems. We should also be alert to how the child's language develops; were there problems in fluencies, comprehension, and the naming of objects? Expected language milestones are shown in Table 20–1 and discussed in greater detail in Chapter 17. These language developmental milestones may also reflect other cognitive functional areas that are important to the tasks of new learning that will be expected

TABLE 20–1.
Selected Language Guideposts*

Skill	Age 2 yr	Age 3 yr	Age 4 yr	Age 5 yr
Comprehension	Follows simple commands; identifies body parts; points to common objects	Understands spatial relationships (in, on, under); knows functions of common objects	Follows 2-part commands; understands same/different	Recalls parts of a story; understands number concepts (3, 4, 5, 6); follows 3-part commands
Expression	Labels common objects; uses 2- or 3-word sentences; uses minimal jargon	Uses 3- to 4-word sentences; uses regular plurals; uses pronouns (I, me, you); can count 3 objects; can tell age, sex, and full name	Speaks 4- to 5-word sentences; can tell story; uses past tense; names 1 color; can count 4 objects	Speaks sentences of 5 words; uses future tense; names 4 colors; can count 10 or more objects
Speech	Intelligible to strangers 25% of the time	Intelligible to strangers 75% of the time	Normal dysfluency (stuttering)	Dysfluencies resolved

*From Levine MD, Carey WB, Crocker AC, et al: *Developmental and Behavioral Pediatrics.* Philadelphia, WB Saunders Co, 1983. Used by permission.

in school. Most developmental tests overemphasize verbal skills in estimating intellectual competency. However, when performance in school is considered, these verbal skills and the cognitive function that underlie them may be of central importance. Bilingual or non–English-speaking families present special difficulties in assessment of children's language development. The pediatrician should be wary of ascribing learning and language problems entirely to bilinguality. It is often noted that true language delay is present in both English and the natal language. By school age, confusion in the use of the two languages should be gone and the child should have no one area of language dysfunction because of bilinguality.

ATTENTION PROBLEMS—The presence at or before the age of 3 to 4 years of a high degree of activity, lack of ability to sustain attention, and impulsive behavior with little ability to delay gratification is a cluster of behaviors that has been associated with a high risk of school learning problems. The progressive improvement in a child's ability to focus and to select what is important to a task from what is not is often a key factor in how well the child can master early learning skills in the standard school environment. The child who can sustain attention only when information is given in one mode or another or when all distractions are eliminated will have difficulty when faced with the complexities of the usual classroom (Levine, 1983).

SOCIALIZATION AND SEPARATION—It is increasingly rare for a child not to have some outside-the-home or away-from-parents experience before school entry. The pediatrician will wish to obtain direct (from preschool teacher) and indirect (from parent) information on how the child functioned in separating and on how the child got along with new adults and other children in a preschool environment, if one was attended. Nursery school teachers' written observations when blindly rated on such characteristics as peer relationships, teacher-pupil relationships, independence, participation in group activities, leadership characteristics, task orientation, attention span and persistence, self-confidence, and immaturity were found to be relatively good predictors of school achievement and behavior in later elementary school (grades 2–6), as reported by Chamberlin and Nader (1971). Both parental and child factors come forth as the child faces school entry. Not only is the child required to successfully negotiate a partial separation from the parents, but the parents themselves must be able to separate from the child. The best predictor of a successful separation and entry into school is a previous successful experience. Parental views on their child's vulnerability and the pattern of child-rearing up to this time will impact on this process. As in other areas of medicine, a good focused history will help the clinician to identify problems to work on and strengths to reinforce.

DATA GATHERING

The assessment before school entry should include a complete update and review of the child's medical and the family's medical and social history. Previous day-care or preschool experience should be reviewed. Data should also be obtained on preschool resources, expectations, requirements, and educational programs and philosophy. The examination and formal assessment procedures should include a general physical examination if one has not been recently completed. It should include a neurological screening and recent evidence of visual and auditory acuity. Finally, some paper and pencil tasks or assessment tools can be administered.

TABLE 20–2.
Observations to Be Included in Examination

Observation	Assessment
Is the child quiet, reserved? Outgoing? Verbal? Inquisitive? At ease or frightened? Does he initiate questions or comments?	Child's social interaction during interview and examination. How does the child handle interactions with adults, parents, and non-family members?
Is the child active, passive, slow to warm?	Child's temperament and behavior in examination situation
Can child be completely understood? Is language appropriate for age? Are sentences clear, compound, and complex? Is articulation clear? Does the child modulate speech well?	Child's language and verbal skills (can use items from Denver Developmental Screening Test)
Does child show excessive dependence or independence? Observe separation effect(s) if occasion arises. What does the mother allow the child to do?	Mother-child interactions
Can child follow 1- to 3-step instructions, assist with examination by holding still, looking at a specific point, cooperating on the neurological examination? Is child easily distracted by environmental stimuli?	Ability to attend and cooperate
Does child show evidence of ability to solve hypothetical problem, does child ask questions, does child draw interesting pictures?	Curiosity, creativity, problem-solving ability

WHAT TO OBSERVE

The clinician should observe the child carefully during the examination to make certain assessments regarding development. Factors to be evaluated are outlined in Table 20–2.

WHAT TO ASK

Questions that should be asked during the examination are presented in Table 20–3.

EXAMINATION AND ASSESSMENT

After a careful history has been obtained and the physician has a good data base plus observation and some talking with the child, it is time to examine. The drawings, paper and pencil tasks, and games of developmental assessment can often be done first unless there is some pressing reason to perform selected portions of the physical examination immediately.

Pediatricians need not become psychologists but may wish to build into their repertoire a battery of tasks they believe they can administer in a reproducible, standardized way. The Denver Developmental, Draw-a-Person, geometric figures, the Beery-Buchtanika test of visual motor integration, the Pediatric Examination of Educational Readiness (PEER), and others can be utilized. Part or all of these tests can be done by office personnel and the data reviewed by the physician.

A collection of age-appropriate behaviors is shown in Table 20–4. Familiarity with these

TABLE 20–3.
Questions to Be Asked During Examination

Question	Objective
Tell me about _____. What words would you use to describe _____?	Determine parents' views of child, what characteristics they mention first; it is better to have parents describe behavior rather than make judgments about it ("he gets along well with other children")
What happens when _____ is with friends or playmates? To the child: Do you have any friends? What do you do with your friends? How are you the same/different from your friends?	
Who in the family is _____ like; you, his/her father, or who? Why? How do you expect _____ to do in school? Why?	Follow-up of this line of questioning can open up areas of parental concern, expectations, and their own experiences with the education system
Tell me what you know about the school where ____ will be starting.	Should bring out real or imagined view of today's school; whether or not there has been a visit to the school or discussion of the school with neighbors may indicate degree of parental investment or interest
Describe how he uses crayons, pencils, scissors.	One child may laboriously use scissors to cut out a doll, while another will be engaged in a task, use the scissors, lay them down, and proceed with the next task
What does he like to do? Dislike?	This may help in determining leisure time use, amount of television viewing, interest in reading or being read to
If _____ does that, what do you do?	Helping parent to focus on behavior will give information on discipline methods, parental ability to cope, guide, direct, and support child

behaviors, drawn from the most popular tests for young children, will assist the pediatrician in the assessment process.

Observation of how the child approaches the various tasks, including those to facilitate the physical examination, can be revealing: Can the child follow auditory directions spoken with no visual clues? Can these be one-, two-, or three-step directions? How attentive to the task is the child? How facile is the child with pencil tasks? Is it easy or slow and pressured?

Performance of the so-called amplified neurological examination to detect "soft" neurological signs has been given attention. The testing of various higher central nervous system (CNS) functions in sensory, coordination, and motor, as well as spatial, areas is supposed to detect areas of developmental dysfunctioning as opposed to the more static permanent CNS dysfunctions (Hartlage and Lucas, 1973). If the clinician decides to proceed with such an examination, several caveats need to be kept in mind:

1. Always precede the soft neurological examination with enough of a standard neurological examination to ensure the absence of mild neurological deficits (e.g., mild cerebral palsy).

TABLE 20–4.
Appropriate Abilities at Various Ages*

Years	Abilities
3	Picks longer of 2 lines
	Can point to chin and teeth on request
	Cuts with scissors
	Makes 3-cube pyramid in about 15 sec
	Copies a circle
	Jumps with 2 feet together
4	Goes upstairs and downstairs one foot per step
	Copies cross (+)
	Washes hands
	Can tell "how many" when shown 2 circles
	Completes "A hat goes on your head, shoes on your. . . ."
	Can button
5	Dress self (except tying shoe laces)
	Copies square
	Can count 6 objects
	Can answer: "Why do we have houses, books, clocks, eyes, ears?"
	Can tell: "What is a chair made of? A dress?"
	Knows (or can be taught): Address, phone number, where mother/father work
	Finger counting (how it is done—pointing to or not) and finger identification
	Digit span—should be able to repeat 4 digits forward
6	Tells how a crayon and pencil are same and different
	Can tell differences between common objects: dog/bird; milk/water
	Can complete "A lemon is sour, sugar is . . ."
	Can tell what a forest is made of

*From Hoekelman R, Blatman S, Brunell PA: *Principles of Pediatrics.* New York, McGraw-Hill Book Co, 1978. Used by permission.

2. Remember to rigorously standardize the instructions and procedures of the specific tests.

3. Be aware of the age range when failure on a specific item or task may be suspect for indication of neurological dysfunction. Most occur in children at least 8 to 9 years of age who are well beyond the age of school entry.

4. Many clumsy and uncoordinated people are very successful in life and do well in school, both socially and academically.

No child should be entering school without the benefit of a formal vision and hearing acuity test. Many schools have such screening programs in place for school entrants. Updating routine immunizations and other health screening tests are now universal requirements in the United States (all 50 states) to enter and remain in school.

STANDARDIZED EVALUATIONS FOR SCHOOL READINESS

Because there is increasing pressure on schools to ensure academic success of their students, some have instituted testing to determine so-called readiness for formal schooling.

Such tests are often unstandardized and untested with regard to reliability and predictive validity. The decision to enter school is always based on legal age of entitlement. No child should be deprived of this right, although the learning environment should be adapted to individual needs. There is a distinction to be made between tests of academic readiness, which evaluate the child's ability to perform basic learning skills, and developmental screening tests, which attempt to evaluate a child's level of gross-motor, fine-motor, language, and personal-social development in comparison with the performance of age-mates. What one has learned at home does not ensure ability to profit from a specific educational environment. Conversely, lack of academic skills does not predict school failure.

Most pediatricians are familiar with the items from the *Denver Developmental Screening Test* and with the tasks of copying geometric figures; the ability to copy a circle (3 years), a cross (4 years), a square (5 years), a triangle (6 years), and a diamond (7 years). It should be remembered that the forms should be presented to the child to copy and that the clinician should not routinely demonstrate drawing the form. A summary of expected neuromotor accomplishments is presented in Table 20–5. Special attention to these tasks should be called forward for former premies or those with a difficult perinatal course (see Chapter 8).

The Beery-Buchtanika test of visual-motor integration (VMI), in a structured way, yields information on visual-motor and perceptual skills similar to that obtained by administering the Bender-Gestalt. A psychologist is not required for administration or interpretation. It can be ordered from Follett Publishing Co., 1010 W. Washington Blvd.; Chicago, IL 60607.

The PEER is a combined neurodevelopmental, behavioral, and health assessment designed primarily for children 4 to 6 years of age. It requires a substantial amount of time, plus familiarization with test administration before it can be utilized. Thus, it could not be considered as a front-line, quick screening instrument. However, it may be a useful tool for the clinician to use with a child when there are questions about the child's abilities in one or

TABLE 20–5.
Neuromotor Accomplishments*

Age (yr)	Gross-Motor Skills	Fine-Motor Skills
2	Runs well	Builds tower of 6 cubes
	Kicks ball	Imitates vertical crayon stroke
	Goes upstairs and downstairs (one step at a time)	Turns book pages singly
3	Goes upstairs (alternating feet)	Copies circle
	Jumps from bottom step	Copies cross
	Pedals tricycle	
	Stands on one foot momentarily	
4	Hops on one foot	Copies square
	Goes downstairs (alternating feet)	Draws person with 2 to 4 parts
	Stands on one foot (5 sec)	Uses scissors
	Throws ball overhand	
5	Stands on one foot (10 sec)	Copies triangle
	May be able to skip	Draws person with body
		Prints some letters

*From Levine MD, Carey WB, Crocker AC, et al: *Developmental and Behavioral Pediatrics.* Philadelphia, WB Saunders Co, 1983. Used by permission.

more areas. It can be ordered from Educator's Publishing Service, Inc., 75 Moulton St., Cambridge, MA 02238-9101.

ANTICIPATORY GUIDANCE

The greatest danger in assessment of school readiness is a tendency to overinterpret findings. The pediatrician should avoid dogmatic pronouncements of prognosis. Strive to describe the child in the most accurate way possible. The child's particular strengths should be brought into focus so that the parents and the school may build on these. Areas of concern should be clearly identified. For most of these it will not be possible to predict the possible outcomes. Concentrated efforts at support can evolve, and occasionally remediation will be indicated. Examples of such summaries follow:

Johnny, age $5\frac{1}{2}$ years, is an only child. He has no serious health or medical problems; he displays the behavior, skills, and knowledge of most 5- to 6-year-old children. His ability to handle paper and pencil tasks is more like that of a 4-year-old. The parents, college graduates, describe him as fun loving, able to concentrate on things, and having several good friends. He had a good preschool experience, and preferred large-motor activities, sand box, cars and trucks, to drawing and puzzles. My knowledge of the Park Elementary School kindergarten program is that attempts are made to take children at the speed they can work, and formal prereading skills are introduced after the first month of school.

Jennifer, age 5 years, is the third of five children and the only girl. She has had a past history of recurrent ear infections, but her hearing at this time has been tested as normal. She is slightly overweight for height. She tends to be shy, apprehensive in new situations, and quiet in large groups. However, her neurological examination and developmental assessments show her to perform at or above age level. She learns most readily to visually presented materials. Her parents describe her as "serious." She has two close friends. Jefferson School's small class size should be ideally suited to bring out the skills of this lovely girl and to encourage gross-motor activities.

The pediatrician in these situations can be optimistic and encourage the parents to be regularly involved in visits at open houses and to listen to the child's descriptions of the school experience. Ongoing monitoring of each child's progress and fit with the school is indicated.

Parents may ask the pediatrician for advice on what type of school, public, private, parochial, or specialized to select from if they have a choice. The pediatrician will inquire from the parents a little more information before venturing a suggestion. Are the parents concerned about ethnic or minority mixing? Are they under any misconceptions regarding the quality of education that can be obtained? What are the traditions and social expectations of the family? What was the parents' experience with the schooling they received? What is the profile of the children in a given school? Will this child fit in, be able to make friends, and succeed?

In general, quality education is available in most schools and is often highly dependent on the teacher. Therefore, a visit to a prospective school is advised. This is advisable even if no choice is anticipated, because all children do better if parents are visible and involved from the start. A classroom environment that is able to adapt to the needs of a wide variety of levels of development would be the most ideal. Public schools, for the most part, have more access to a greater range of specialized services for children with special needs than private or parochial schools.

Parents may frequently ask if the pediatrician thinks the child should be kept out of school, at home for another year. Such a decision should almost never be made because of the delay in socialization and learning and school readiness activities that are often exactly what is needed. Such questions can serve as a springboard into exploring reasons for the parents' concerns. If it turns out on evaluation that serious, previously undetected, developmental problems are present, appropriate diagnostic and remediation efforts should be instituted. These efforts often involve school-based resources and special programs. When in doubt, the pediatrician should encourage school attendance, even with a modified program, in contrast to continued day care or remaining at home. Close contact with the kindergarten teacher is mandatory, especially if the patient entering school is a boy, very close to barely making the 5-year-old age cutoff, and is small (at or below the 25th percentile for height).

When the child experiences difficulty or adjustment and learning do not occur, further evaluation and referral are indicated for psychological testing aimed at formal evaluation of cognitive and other factors that may be impeding progress. Waiting 1 year for the child to "mature" may only serve to delay necessary remediation. In the event that the educational expectations are found to be excessive and the child is within range of normal abilities for age, adjustment of the environment is required rather than labeling the child as deviant. Repeating kindergarten as a remedial step without formal evaluation and program restructuring is not indicated and is invariably nonproductive.

The pediatrician's door will always be open to a discussion of how the child is doing in school. Any response less than a superlative from a parent deserves a little further exploration. Simply carrying out the preschool assessment sets the stage for ongoing monitoring of family and school behavior and achievement. In this way the pediatrician can be alert to early signs of "lack of fit" between what the child brings to the situation and what the parents and school expect. Also, in this way the pediatrician can share in the joy and excitement of a young school-aged child's successful social and intellectual growth.

REFERENCES

Bandura A: *Cognitive Social Learning Theory.* Englewood Cliffs, NJ, Prentice Hall, 1977.
Chamberlin RW, Nader PR: Relationship between nursery school behavior patterns and late school functioning. *Am J Orthopsychiatry* 1971; 41:597–601.
Erikson EH: *Identity and the Life Cycle,* New York, International Universities Press, 1959.
Freud S: *New Introductory Lessons in Psychoanalysis.* New York, WW Norton & Co, 1965.
Gesell A, Ilg F: *The Child From Five to Ten.* Harper Brothers, 1946.
Hartlage LC, Lucas DG: *Mental Development Evaluation of the Pediatric Patient.* Springfield, Ill, Charles C Thomas, Publisher, 1973.
Levine MD: Middle childhood, in Levine MD, Carey WB, Crocker AC, et al (eds): *Developmental and Behavioral Pediatrics.* Philadelphia, WB Saunders Co, 1983, pp 108–132.
Piaget J, Inhelder B: *The Psychology of the Child.* New York, Basic Books, 1968.
Rutter M: *Fifteen Thousand Hours.* Cambridge, Mass, Harvard University Press, 1979.
Wright G, Nader P: Schools as milieux, in Levine MD, Carey WB, Crocker AC, et al (eds): *Developmental and Behavioral Pediatrics.* Philadelphia, WB Saunders Co, 1983, pp 276–283.

ADDITIONAL READINGS

Buros OK: *The Mental Measurements Yearbook,* ed 6. Highland Park, NJ, Gryphon Press, 1985.

Elkind D: Miseducation: Preschoolers at Risk. New York, Alfred A Knopf, 1988.

ERIC Series. Prepared by ERIC Clearinghouse on Higher Education, George Washington University. Washington, DC, American Association for Higher Education, 1982.

Flavell JH, Ross L (eds): *Social Cognitive Development.* New York, Cambridge University Press, 1981.

Hoekelman R, Blatman S, Brunell PA, et al: *Principles of Pediatrics.* New York, McGraw-Hill Book Co, 1978.

"Reading in School." By Ryan Hennessy, age 6.

CHAPTER 21

Six Years: Learning to Use Symbols

NICHOLAS PUTNAM, M.D.
MARTIN T. STEIN, M.D.

KEY WORDS

CONCRETE THINKING
DECODING TASKS
ATTENTION DEFICIT
SCHOOL REFUSAL
SEPARATION ANXIETY
TRUANCY

Bryan, age 6 years, was referred at his school's request to see if "something couldn't be done" about his activity level. His first grade teacher thought him much more active than the other boys in her class, frequently speaking out of turn, moving about the classroom during less structured class periods, and invading his peers' workspace and private conversations. He was an only child whose parents both worked. He was adored by all four grandparents, who lived nearby and provided much of his daily care. His parents had encouraged his outgoing personality and excellent verbal skills and were quite tolerant of his high energy level during their times alone with him. His pediatrician found him to be physically healthy, with no neurological abnormalities and with a history of excellent language and motor development. He was rather presumptuous in his stance toward the pediatrician, asking the doctor what kind of car he owned and how much the examination would cost. His mother had difficulty concealing her amusement at this inquiry by Bryan. Psychometric evaluation by the school psychologist documented Bryan's academic achievement at above grade level in all academic areas.

The pediatrician convinced Bryan's parents to work closely with his teacher in making clear to Bryan their support of classroom behavioral expectations. His parents began to follow through with the teacher's rewards and consequences for unacceptable behavior at school. Improvement in impulse control was not dramatic, but by second grade his teacher commented that Bryan was a "challenging but gratifying student to have in class."

The 6-year-old child stands on a threshold of exciting new cognitive and social experiences. With regular school attendance actually required for the first time, this age marks the beginning of a lifetime of obligations and adherence to schedules and routines imposed outside of the familiar family environment. This time of transition may present a crisis to the child or her family while at the same time providing an opportunity for rapid cognitive, social, and emotional growth.

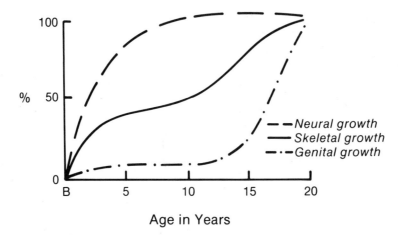

FIG 21–1.
Organ growth curves, drawn to a common scale by computing values at successive ages in terms of growth. (Adapted from Harris JA, et al: *The Measurement of Man.* Minneapolis, University of Minnesota Press, 1930.)

The accelerated physical growth of the preschooler begins to slow as children enter the years of middle childhood. By age 5 years the brain has attained approximately 90% of its adult weight, and over the next 2 years the final myelinization of the central nervous system will be completed (Fig 21–1). The nearly mature central nervous system coincides with qualitative advances in cognitive capacities. Simultaneously, the child may participate in activities requiring the integration of fine- and gross-motor skills, such as dance, sports, and, in the classroom, handwriting and arts and crafts projects.

COGNITIVE DEVELOPMENT

The 6-year-old begins to show less evidence of the cognitive stage described by Piaget (1952) as "preoperational" thinking—thinking marked by so-called magical qualities. The sensitive observer will find most first graders questioning many of their previous assumptions about the world. The typical 6-year-old does not take fantasy for granted and may question magical events. Nevertheless, she may have difficulty in performing mental operations that involve simultaneous changes in more than one variable. Instead, she may continue to focus on one aspect of a situation, a phenomenon known as *centration.* For example, the child may believe that a tall narrow bottle of soda contains more soda than a short wide bottle with an equal volume merely because the former is taller. Likewise a child may be able to make her way from home to school with great accuracy but may be unable to mentally reverse the directions so as to appropriately plan the trip home. She may be able to participate in a multifaceted game but will have difficulty learning it from verbal directions alone or explaining the rules with clarity. She may resent a sibling whose birthday "comes before hers" without consolation from the sense that soon thereafter the situation will be reversed.

Piaget (1952) was able to demonstrate preoperational thinking and the transition to concrete operations with simple techniques using readily available materials. For example, one can form a ball of clay for a child and ask him to form a similar ball with "as much clay" as the first ball. When the child agrees that both balls have exactly the same amount of clay, one can flatten one of the pieces, roll it into a narrow cylinder, or break it into two or more chunks. If the child is asked which of the original two balls now has the most clay, his answer and reasoning may reveal his capacity to *conserve mass* cognitively despite the physical manipulations that were carried out before his eyes. The child of about 6 years or less may demonstrate an absence of conservation of mass by his answer and reasoning, perhaps stating that the original ball of clay now contains more clay, because it is now longer than the other ball, or less clay, because it is now flatter. The child who *retains* the concept of mass despite these changes in appearance has achieved, in part, a new level of reasoning, "concrete operations" (Fig 21–2).

There is a great deal of variablity in the age at which children demonstrate these changes in cognition, often beginning around age 6 years and gradually evolving over the next 4 to 5

FIG 21–2.
This child is proudly able to appreciate that equal volumes of water are maintained when the shape of the container is changed: a demonstration of conservation of mass in a child who has entered the stage of concrete operations.

years (Elkind, 1974). By age $5\frac{1}{2}$ years, most children demonstrate that they understand the concept of the conservation of length. Many younger children will maintain that a long string and a shorter wooden stick are the same length if they are arranged so that the ends of the string coincide with the ends of the stick. Conservation of mass and weight are accomplished mentally by most children 1 year or more later, and conservation of volume is achieved much later when children reach the last 2 years of grade school.

Six-year-olds continue to demonstrate many of the preconceptual qualities of thinking typical of preschoolers (see Chapter 17). First graders may still believe the sun and moon were made artificially and move because man or God makes them move. They may feel sorry for a car that is heavily loaded with passengers as if the car had feelings. In fact, even adults may think in egocentric, magical ways depending on many factors, including the context of the cognitive task. The ways in which children think and attain knowledge as they develop into middle childhood are apparently less rigidly tied to specific Piagetian cognitive stages as was once thought (Hobson, 1985).

As children move through the early years of grade school, they do manifest more of the qualities of thinking that Piaget described as "concrete operational thought." This stage is marked by the ability to consider multiple variables concerning objects or situations simul-taneously, perform mental operations relating to concrete objects (e.g., adding or subtracting objects, creating maps), understand serial relationships (e.g., ordering pictures, number con-cepts), and appreciate classification systems. Classification tasks, common in modern school-work, require the identification of a common factor in groups and subgroups.

Although the thinking process of the 6-year-old child is qualitatively different from the thinking of older school-aged children, the typical 6-year-old should manifest those qualities that make possible productive classroom participation and learning. Most 6-year-olds are either in or about to enter the first grade, where academic rather than mainly behavioral, social, and emotional demands are being made on children. Academic failure in the first grade results when children cannot demonstrate in school that they have the capacity to perform the primary *decoding tasks* of reading, solving simple addition and subtraction problems, and writing simple sentences with properly spelled words (Levine and Oberklaid, 1980). Although these skills are generally taught to all children at about the same age, normal children vary substantially in the age at which they achieve the capacity to read, spell, and work with num-bers. A modest delay in the development of these abilities, though not otherwise significant, can create serious psychological and behavioral difficulties for a child whose self-image is tarnished by the experience of academic failure at an early age.

Academic difficulties in the first grade may diminish the child's self-esteem, color her future attitude toward school, and result in considerable anxiety in parents. It is important that the pediatrician begin to help the parents understand the source of their child's academic difficulty and collaborate with the child, her parents, and the school in designing a program to address the child's specific needs.

A useful model to evaluate academic success in the first grade curriculum requires that children have both the *cognitive power* and *cognitive style* to deal effectively with the class-room environment (Kinsbourne and Caplan, 1979). The child with insufficient cognitive power may be generally dull, with mild or borderline mental retardation that does not become apparent until the child is faced with the academic demands of first grade; or there may be selective cognitive deficits (i.e., learning disabilities) in a child who otherwise shows normal intelligence. The child with general backwardness may have a history of delayed attainment of early milestones in language development. Another child with a selective learning disabiltiy may seem bright with a good fund of general knowledge and normal developmental milestones but develops difficulty with specific academic tasks during the first grade in a way that is quite unexpected by parents and teachers who usually perceive the child as normal in intelligence and demonstrating good work habits.

The diagnosis of a learning disability must be based on more data than the physician can obtain during the interview with the family and examination of the child (Cantwell, 1975). It is essential to obtain the results of psychological and educational testing or to ask that such tests be performed if necessary. Difficulties with cognitive style may not always be apparent in the pediatrician's office, an environment that differs from a classroom environment in many important ways. Data on the child's attention span, social, and behavioral adjustment can be obtained by contacting teachers directly with the parent's permission. Teachers are often eager to have an opportunity to discuss the children whom they find most challenging. A number of standardized teacher report forms are also available if the pediatrician wishes to obtain a more formal profile of the child's behavior in school (Levine et al., 1980).

The collection of test and observational data from the school may reveal a child who has the cognitive power to succeed academically but may have difficulties with temperament, emotions, or behavior that result in academic failure. To succeed in the classroom, the first grader must be capable of focused and sustained attention for periods of 25 minutes to 1 hour. Good students in standard settings are not easily distracted, are selective in what they attend to, and must be able to shift the focus of attention rapidly. Parents and teachers are not surprised when a child who lacks these qualities earns low marks in the first grade, often after experiencing a difficult time in kindergarten. Such a child may be seen as so unhappy, so distractible, or so preoccupied that his academic failure can be predicted early in the school year. Often children have both specific deficits in cognitive power and behavior or emotional problems that interfere with learning. Children with difficulties in learning required skills may try to avoid obvious failure by withdrawing, increasing social interactions with teachers or other students, or engaging in disruptive behavior.

ATTENTION DEFICIT AND LEARNING

Perhaps the most common disorder of cognitive style in the differential diagnosis of academic failure is the attention-deficit hyperactivity disorder (ADHD). Teachers identify far more children as overactive than do parents or clinicians, and there continue to be striking differences in reported prevalence even among English-speaking countries. A child with a primary attention disorder is presumed to suffer from intrinsic inefficiencies in maintaining selective attention (Table 21–1). A history of temperamental difficulties, perinatal stress events, sleep disorder, and inattention in multiple settings and situations may be obtained. Minor neurological abnormalities or signs of neuromaturational delay may be apparent on physical examination (Stein, 1975). However, the diagnosis is made largely on the basis of history, including teacher questionnaires and psychometric testing, rather than physical examination (Table 21–2). A positive history for ADHD provides evidence for problems with hyperactivity, inattention, and impulsivity beginning before age 7 years and lasting at least 6 months.

TABLE 21–1.
A General Classification of Chronic Inattention in School-Aged Children*

Subtypes†	Descriptions	Frequently Observed Associations
Primary attention disorder	Intrinsic inefficiencies of selective attention	Early onset of temperamental dysfunction Perinatal stress events Signs of neuromaturational delay Inattention in multiple settings and situations
Secondary attention disorders	Inattention secondary to deficits in information processing	Sleep disorders Visual perceptual disabilities Developmental language disabilities Deficits of sequential organization and short-term memory Signs of neuromaturational delay
	Inattention secondary to psychosocial and emotional disturbances	Family problems Emotional disturbance in other family members Primary depression and anxiety
Tertiary inattention	Apparent inattention resulting from inappropriate expectations, perceptions, or educational circumstances extrinsic to the child	Tendency toward inattention only in specific settings or situations Discrepant perceptions of child by adults
Mixed forms	2 or more subtypes	Relevant to subtypes

*From Levine M: *Pediatrics* 1976; 58:146. Used by permission
†Common denominators of the subtypes: (1) Purposeless selection of stimuli, (2) weak resistance to distraction, (3) impersistence, (4) inefficiencies of motor activity, (5) insatiability, (6) impulsivity, (7) academic failure, (8) social failure, (9) performance inconsistency, and (10) diminished self-esteem. Some or all of these manifestations are seen in each subtype of attention disorder.

The diagnosis of an attention-deficit disorder should be made with careful deliberation. It is important that parents understand that this diagnosis is largely descriptive of the child's behavior and does not reveal the etiology of the problem, dictate treatment, or predict the individual child's prognosis. Children with early-onset, severe ADHD do carry a significant risk for serious maladjustment in adolescence and beyond (Mannuzza et al., 1991). Other children with less pervasive attentional problems may eventually do quite well. Feedback to the parents should emphasize specific problem behaviors that have been identified and focus on possible strategies that might mitigate these problems and enhance adjustment to school. The use of stimulant medication may improve the behavior of children who have this disorder, perhaps making them more ready to learn. Medication will not improve academic achievement directly. Improved progress will be achieved through clear behavioral management (perhaps including medication) and a focused educational intervention using all avenues of learning available to the child. Stimulant medication will not by itself turn Ds into As and will not correct a specific learning disability. An unjustified shift to a medical versus an educational diagnosis may lead to unduly high expectations from the medication and the lack of a directed specific educational program.

The evaluation and management of children with chronic inattention involves continuing

TABLE 21-2.
Attention-Deficit Hyperactivity Disorder*†

A disturbance of at least 6 mo during which at least 8 of the following are present:
1. Often fidgets with hands or feet or squirms in seat (in adolescents, may be limited to subjective feelings of restlessness)
2. Has difficulty remaining seated when required to do so
3. Is easily distracted by extraneous stimuli
4. Has difficulty awaiting turn in games or group situations
5. Often blurts out answers to questions before they have been completed
6. Has difficulty following through on instructions from others (not due to oppositional behavior or failure of comprehension), e.g., fails to finish chores
7. Has difficulty sustaining attention in tasks or play activities
8. Often shifts from one uncompleted activity to another
9. Has difficulty playing quietly
10. Often talks excessively
11. Often interrupts or intrudes on others, e.g., butts into other children's games
12. Often does not seem to listen to what is being said to him or her
13. Often loses things necessary for tasks or activities at school or at home (e.g., toys, pencils, books, assignments)
14. Often engages in physically dangerous activities without considering possible consequences (not for the purpose of thrill-seeking) e.g., runs into street without looking

*From American Psychiatric Association: *Diagnostic and Statistical Manual of Mental Disorders*, ed 3, revised. Washington, DC, American Psychiatric Association, 1987.
†NOTE: Consider a criterion met only if the behavior is considerably more frequent than that of most people of the same mental age. The items are listed in descending order of discriminating power based on data from a national field trial of the DSM-III-R criteria for disruptive behavior disorders.

contact with the school, as well as referral to educational and mental health specialists, when indicated. This is equally true when stimulant medications are prescribed. The pediatrician must therefore develop an alliance with the child, parents, and teacher such that a long-term collaboration is possible. An environment that supports the child's efforts to maintain focus on tasks and be successful can be created only by this collaborative effort.

The case of Bryan provides an example of how a child's temperament and experiences in the family can result in disruptive behavior in school. Attention-deficit hyperactivity disorder is only one of a number of disruptive behavior disorders occurring in childhood. In Bryan's case, it would not be appropriate to label his difficulties in school as a disorder, because they resulted from normal variations in the personalities of child, parents (and grandparents), and teacher.

Specific learning disabilities most often become apparent during the first grade, although other specific subtypes of academic difficulty may emerge initially in fourth or fifth grade (see Chapters 22 and 23), and still others become apparent for the first time in junior high school (see Chapter 25). It is essential that physicians routinely inquire about the progress of 6-year-olds in the first grade. Any concerns raised should not be dismissed as "adjustment" problems or entirely maturational in origin (e.g., "he will grow out of it"). This will provide a data base that may reveal the sequence in which academic problems develop and provide for appropriate remediation before the establishment of a cycle of failures. If evaluated soon enough, children with a primary learning disability will show academic difficulties in the absence of attentional, behavioral, or emotional problems. However, such children may subsequently develop low self-esteem and disturbances in emotions and conduct as a result of academic frustration. These secondary effects of academic failure will make accurate diagnosis much more difficult later. Because the best medicine is preventive medicine, it is important that learning disabilities be recognized early so that specific remedial measures may be undertaken to lessen the occurrence of secondary problems with emotions and conduct.

SCHOOL REFUSAL

All clinicians who work with children sooner or later will evaluate a child who refuses to attend school (Nader et al., 1975; Eisenberg, 1958). Unexcused absences from school follow a bimodal pattern of incidence, with peaks in the early primary grades, particularly first grade, and a second peak again in junior high school. The physician should carefully and systematically determine the reason the child is not attending school before developing an approach to the problem. Some children are kept home from school by parents, although most unexcused absences from school are attributable to school refusal by the child.

Most first graders who refuse to attend school, do not roam the community (truancy) but spend the school day at home. These children may have a variety of physical complaints including stomachaches, headaches, dizziness, and fatigue, which often subside as the day progresses (Fig 21–3). Although a few of these children may be suffering from an actual phobia (Schmidt, 1971) of school itself or some particular aspect of the school experience such as travel on the bus, most first graders who refuse to attend school appear to be suffering from separation anxiety. When examined in the pediatrician's office, these children usually appear healthy and have a normal physical examination, although some initially appear pale, sad, and emotionally depressed.

These children are experiencing stress in response to leaving their parents and familiar surroundings for a full day of school. It may be diagnosed by the pediatrician and often responds to simple behavioral measures combined with supportive counseling of the parents. Such children may be unusually sensitive to the anxiety that is normal in all children who begin their grade school experience. In addition, some mothers may transmit their anxiety about separating to the child and thereby exacerbate the problem. Such families need to be reminded that school attendance in the first grade is compulsory and that the separation from family at this time is a healthy and predictable stage of maturation.

The child's clinician must be sympathetic to the physical complaints and initiate a reasonable medical evaluation. Excessive medical attention to the physical complaints, which may occur when a large number of laboratory tests or specialty referrals are ordered, should be avoided when nonorganic disease is suspected. The clinician must make it clear to the family that the child is to attend school on a daily basis unless the symptoms are of such severity as to require a visit to the physician's office. The parents may be reassured that the child will usually settle down in school if he comes to understand that his parents expect and will demand school attendance. Often the school can collaborate with the parent in keeping the child in school. Children with separation anxiety disorder become rapidly asymptomatic as their school attendance becomes more regular. When school refusal does not respond to these measures or when pediatric evaluation of the child or family suggests a serious emotional disorder, a specific mental health referral may be indicated.

School refusal in early adolescence often leads to a more extensive differential diagnostic

SICK

"I cannot go to school today,"
Said little Peggy Ann McKay.
"I have the measles and the mumps,
A gash, a rash and purple bumps.
My mouth is wet, my throat is dry,
I'm going blind in my right eye.
My tonsils are as big as rocks,
I've counted sixteen chicken pox
And there's one more—that's seventeen,
And don't you think my face looks green?
My leg is cut, my eyes are blue—
It might be instamatic flu.
I cough and sneeze and gasp and choke,
I'm sure that my left leg is broke—
My hip hurts when I move my chin,
My belly button's caving in,
My back is wrenched, my ankle's sprained,
My 'pendix pains each time it rains.
My nose is cold, my toes are numb,
I have a sliver in my thumb.
My neck is stiff, my spine is weak,
I hardly whisper when I speak.
My tongue is filling up my mouth,
I think my hair is falling out.
My elbow's bent, my spine ain't straight,
My temperature is one-o-eight.
My brain is shrunk, I cannot hear,
There is a hole inside my ear.
I have a hangnail, and my heart is—what?
What's that? What's that you say?
You say today is . . . Saturday?
G'bye, I'm going out to play!"

FIG 21–3.
(From Silverstein S: *Where the Sidewalk Ends.* New York, Harper & Row Publishers, 1974.
Used by permission.)

evaluation. If the junior high school student spends school time in community areas such as malls and engages in varying degrees of antisocial behavior, one must suspect a conduct disturbance. Those adolescents who remain at home may have physical complaints similar to the 6-year-olds and may be suffering from an anxiety disorder. Some of these youngsters are home because they are fearful and have been threatened or mistreated by peers. A further, small number are experiencing the onset of a serious, but usually treatable, psychiatric disturbance such as depression or schizophrenia. School refusal in adolescence that is not clearly truancy should be carefully examined and every effort made to prevent a tragic early withdrawal from school.

DATA GATHERING

Six-year-old children may not be as candid in providing information to the physician as they once were. Just as the clinician may observe increasing modesty during physical examination at this age, he may also find the child withholding or distorting his answers to questions about personal, school, and family life. Obtaining information with the child and parent present is the most productive technique for 6-year-olds. As with the preschool child, it is important to communicate to the child that you value information provided by the child about his health and his feelings. Asking the child first to describe his or her physical complaints and beliefs about the reasons for the medical examination may provide an opportunity to deal directly with the 6-year-old's lingering misconceptions about the reasons for the medical encounter. In the course of evaluating the child's physical health, the clinician may gather data about the child's development in the following areas:

COGNITIVE DEVELOPMENT

Questions for Children	Objective

Where do you go to school?
  What grade are you in?
  What are you learning in school?
  Are there some things you do at school that you really like?
  Are there things about school that you don't like?
	The 6-year-old should be able to provide physicians with acceptable answers to nearly all of these questions. Such answers may suggest that the child is having difficulty in particular areas. When the child is reluctant to talk about school or provides very little information, the physician should then invite the parent to enter the discussion.

What town do you live in?
  On what street?
  Do you know your address?
  Do you know your telephone number?
	To assess the child's attention to basic information important to his well-being as he spends increasing amounts of time away from his family; to assess visual or auditory memory skills.

Ask the child to copy a cross (4-year-old), a square (5-year-old), a triangle (6-year-old), and a diamond (7-year-old).	To observe the child's handedness, his ability to grasp and control a writing instrument, and his competence in increasingly difficult fine-motor and visual-perceptual tasks.
Ask the child to draw a person while you are interviewing the parent.	An estimated mental age may be obtained by using Goodenough's scoring criteria (see Appendix). In addition, information may be obtained about the child's attentiveness, tendency to cooperate, compulsivity, and even

What makes the sun come up in the morning?
  What makes the clouds move in the sky?
  How can you tell if something is alive?

emotional health if the drawing is atypical (see Chapter 31).

To assess the child's beliefs regarding causality and to help parents understand that the child remains in a transitional period relative to his cognitive abilities. Most 6-year-olds, regardless of intelligence, will respond to these questions with magical thinking characterized by animism and egocentricity. For example, "The sun comes up in the morning so that I can play," or "It's alive because I see it and talk to it."

How do you get to your house from school?

Children at this age continue to be highly egocentric in their ability to give directions and will often leave out important details. This may be interpreted to parents as a normal developmental stage and will also help parents understand why it is difficult for children to reverse directions or see the world from another person's perspective.

Do you ever have dreams?
  Do the dreams ever really happen?
  Where do the dreams take place?
  What really happens to the people on televison who fly or get hurt?

To assess the child's capacity for distinguishing between reality and fantasy, which should be well developed at this age.

Questions for Parents

Does (name) have a problem concentrating or paying attention? Do you think that (name) is more active, less attentive than other children his age?

Do you frequently find yourself repeating directions or instructions?

How is school going?
  Have you had a conference with teacher?
  How does (name) fit in with the classroom?
  What are the teacher's expectations for (name)?

Objective

To assess the parent's perception of the child's ablity to attend to a classroom learning environment.

To assess auditory processing maturation.

To assess the parent's understanding and involvement with the school; to model the expected close interaction between parent and school personnel.

SOCIAL AND EMOTIONAL DEVELOPMENT

Questions for Children

Do you know the name of the team that plays baseball or football for your city?
  What is your favorite movie?
  What is your favorite television show?
  Where did you go on your vacation?
Who are your good friends?

Objective

To assess both the child's general fund of information and the child's interest in and retention of information about events that occur outside the home.

By this time a child should have formed several close relationships outside the home. The child should name one and preferably more friends close to his age. A child who does not name anybody or names an adult, a family member, or a much younger child requires further eval-

What games do you like to play?

uation. The parent may be asked to comment on the child's response.

To assess the child's preferences for solitary versus peer activities. Is he comfortable with the give and take of peer group activities? Does he understand the necessity for and the nature of rules? Is he involved in organized community-wide activities, such as team sports or a religious-based peer group?

Who lives at your house?
  What do you think about your brother/sister/ the new baby?

To assess the child's capacity to express both positive and negative affects relating to family members and the degree of sibling rivalry that may be present.

Questions for Parents	**Objective**
How long is (name) in school?	To assess the overdemands on the child's and family's circumstances, arrangements.
What does (name) do after school?	
What jobs does (name) do around the house?	To assess family responsibilities that the child shares.
How much television does (name) watch each day? What programs?	

REFERENCES

Cantwell D: *The Hyperactive Child: Diagnosis, Management and Current Research.* New York, Spectrum Publications, 1975.

Eisenberg L: School phobia: A study in the communication of anxiety. *Am J Psychiatry* 1958; 114:712.

Elkind D: *Children and Adolescents: Interpretive Essays on Jean Piaget.* New York, Oxford University Press, 1974.

Hersov L: School refusal. *Br Med J* 1972; 3:102.

Hobson RP: Piaget: On the ways of knowing in childhood, in Rutter M, Hersov L (eds): *Child and Adolescent Psychiatry: Modern Approaches.* Boston, Blackwell Scientific Publications, 1985.

Kinsbourne M, Caplan P: *Children's Learning and Attention Problems.* Boston, Little, Brown & Co, 1979.

Levine MD, Brooks R, Shonkoff J: *A Pediatric Approach to Learning Disorders.* New York, John Wiley & Sons, 1980.

Levine MD, Oberklaid F: Hyperactivity: Symptom complex or complex symptom? *Am J Dis Child* 1980; 134:409.

Mannuzza S, Klein R, Bonagura N, et al: Hyperactive boys almost grown up. *Arch Gen Psychiatry* 1991; 48:77–83.

Nader P, Bullock D, Caldwell B: School phobia. *Pediatr Clin North Am* 1975; 22:605–617.

Piaget J: *The Origins of Intelligence in Children.* New York, International Press, 1952.

Schmidt B: School phobia: The great imitator. A pediatrician's viewpoint. *Pediatrics* 1971; 48:433.

Stein M: Minimal brain dysfunction: A cautious note. *Clin Pediatr* 1975; 125:840.

family

scool

T-ball

Waltcube

By Neil Hennessy, age 7.

CHAPTER **22**

Seven to Ten Years: Growth and Competency

NICHOLAS PUTNAM, M.D.

KEY WORDS

LATENCY AGE
CONSCIENCE
MORALITY
DEVELOPMENTAL OUTPUT FAILURE
ENCODING DIFFICULTIES
NERDS

Michael, age 9 years, and his mother come for a visit requesting a "motor evaluation" and "some therapy" to help Michael with coordination. His mother says that he has been teased by the other kids on the basketball team in spite of his large size. Last week he got so upset and confused after tripping on the court that he passed the ball to an opponent. On questioning, Michael's mom says he has few friends and spends most of his time doing mathematical computer games. His teacher describes him as bright and eager, often asking and answering questions. He does not do well with group projects. You observe that he is wearing a neat striped, collared knit shirt, corduroy pants, and brown tie leather shoes. He is reading a magazine and then wanders over to the window during your interview.

Middle childhood is a time set aside, in all cultures, for children to learn those skills that are necessary for survival and productive living. Children of primitive societies become competent in obtaining food, shelter, and clothing. In our complex society children develop competence in reading, writing, and mathematics. They acquire the basic knowledge necessary to master the demands of adult life, both within the home and in the community. The cognitive, social, and emotional growth seen during this period follows the near completion of central nervous system growth by the age of 7 years and precedes the rapid growth of the reproductive organs in early adolescence. A developmental assessment during this period should focus on the child's capacity to function effectively in a number of settings, including the family, the school, the playground, and the community. Increasing competency in each of these areas marks appropriate development.

The years of middle childhood were once thought to be a period of "latency" during which sexual and aggressive drives were unlikely to interfere with the learning of new cognitive and social skills (Freud, 1965). Theories of development emphasized that the child was relieved of the pressure of these feelings and was better able to focus his attention on academic and extracurricular activities as a result. Common experience with grade-school children, as well as scientific evidence, indicates that this is not the case (Rutter, 1977). Sexual and aggressive feelings continue throughout the grade-school years and gradually increase from year to year. The functional capabilities of the prepubertal gonad and gonadotropin-secreting cells of the hypothalamus are established and appear to be a miniaturization of those found in the adult (Grumbach et al., 1974). Research has shown a gradually increasing interest throughout middle childhood in sexual matters (Martinson, 1981). Children who live in highly permissive cultures do attempt adult sexual activity during the middle childhood years. In cultures with tighter norms of behavior, children learn the culturally appropriate levels of control and safe ways to express impulses.

Both younger children and adolescents are more likely to express sexual and aggressive impulses than school-aged children. The so-called latency-aged child is more subtle and indirect in expressing impulses of several types. The healthy child, during this middle part of childhood in Western cultures, expresses normal sexual and aggressive impulses through the sophisticated use of fantasy and intense participation in organized activities with peers. This emotional energy is coupled with increasing cognitive, social, and physical capacities in the achievement of new levels of mastery.

THE ROLE OF FANTASY

Sarnoff (1976) has emphasized that the psychological work of latency involves the active use of fantasy and identification with real and imagined characters who do what the child can only wish to do. This allows the emotionally healthy school child to express feelings without losing self-control. The boy who identifies with a professional athletic team may find expression for aggressive feelings by loudly denouncing a rival team (e.g., "I hate the Raiders!"). Though the child may have only recently outgrown a variety of fears, he may boast of his prowess versus the unknown by wearing a Ghostbusters T-shirt or communicate to others and to himself his capacity for aggression by wearing military clothing and engaging in mock but fierce battles with real or imaginary opponents. A school-aged girl may identify strongly with the sensuality of a popular actress or singer or with the controlled aggression of a woman tennis champion or ballerina.

The physical, aesthetic, and aggressive actions of these heroes provide an outlet for normal, age-appropriate sexual feelings and drives. Their presence in a child's life can be demonstrated in the clinician's office by asking specific questions ("Who would you most like to be?"), by observing and commenting on the child's clothing and favorite possessions, and by reviewing a child's artwork.

It is essential that the child at this age be able to spend some of her energy in such fantasy and yet also express herself through active participation in the real world. Emotional problems may occur when a child becomes lost in fantasy and fails to gain a sense of competence in dealing with the actual world. Behavior problems may occur if a child fails to learn to use fantasy as a means of expressing feelings and instead acts out many of her impulses in real situations.

DEVELOPMENT OF CONSCIENCE AND MORALITY

During this time the child continues to consolidate her identification with important adults in her life. In this process the same-sexed parent is an important role model. Other adults inside and outside of the child's family also serve as examples for the child, augmenting the primary organizing force of the immediate family. Freud (1965) pointed out the continuing growth during these years of that part of the child's mental life that represents internalized parental values—the superego, or internalized conscience. Emotional and cognitive growth interact and result in the early development of a more personal conscience with less emphasis placed by the child on adult authority or conventional rules. This growth in conscience crosses cultural and religious boundaries. The specific belief systems and norms of behavior are developed within the context of the family and, increasingly, that of society as a whole.

Moral development begins long before this age when the 2-year-old realizes that some behaviors are "good" and some are "bad." Preschoolers accept rules from parents and other adults without completely understanding the reasons behind them. They come to understand that actions have consequences and to anticipate consequences of their behavior. Moral behavior may be dependent on those consequences—approval, punishment, isolation—that follow certain behaviors. The magnitude of the crime is determined by the magnitude of its consequences rather than the knowledge or intent of the perpetrator. In middle childhood, children come to understand that rules are the product of mutual consent and respect and that rules may be changed under certain circumstances.

Piaget (1952, 1968) demonstrated how children of grade-school age increasingly take context and motivation into account in making moral judgments. In clinical practices it is sometimes worthwhile to tell a child a simple story and ask her to make a moral judgment to ascertain whether the child remains in the stage of *moral realism*, where certain behaviors are wrong regardless of the situation and the rules are always sacred.

Kohlberg (1981) has demonstrated that grade-school children vary in their apparent level of moral development. Many behave well mainly to earn some tangible reward or avoid punishment, others are beginning to conform to win more general approval from peers and adults, and still others respect the social order that a rule system generates. Others are oriented to "doing their duty" to a higher authority, such as "God and my country," although this is more common among adolescents.

Children conceptualize their conscience in different ways as they move through middle childhood (Stilwell et al., 1991). Before age 6 years, they see their conscience as an *external* force, an outside authority either praising or admonishing. By age 7 years, many children designate a particular body part as a storage site for rules about right and wrong, describing a *brain* or *heart* conscience. By age 12 years, the thinking (brain) and feeling (heart) aspects of conscience become integrated into a *personified* conscience, an abstract entity within the child that can generate feelings such as guilt. Early adolescents may be quite *confused* about their consciences before *integrating* diverse moral options into a more mature conscience by early adulthood.

COGNITIVE DEVELOPMENT

The dramatic changes in cognitive powers that occur during the early grade-school years were discussed in Chapter 21. Piaget (1952) described the way in which children can perform increasingly complex "concrete operations" mentally, such that mental operations can take the place of actual physical manipulation of objects. For example, the typical 7-year-old appreciates that the amount of liquid remains the same regardless of the shape of the container into which it is poured. An 8-year-old with the capacity for concrete operations will appreciate that a lump of clay still contains the same "amount" (or mass) and weighs the same, regardless of the shape into which it is molded.

The school-aged child is able to consider two or more aspects of a situation simultaneously. In making comparisons, he takes into account more than one variable. He appreciates that a tall, narrow lump of clay can be made short and wide without any net gain or loss of clay. Such reasoning extends to the child's capacity for making a variety of judgments. He may appreciate for the first time another child who is clumsy but bright, a teacher who is strict but fair, or medicine that is difficult to swallow but brings down a fever. For the first time the child has the mental capacity to appreciate that a surgical procedure will cause discomfort yet produce a desired result. Clinicians should take advantage of this increased capacity for understanding and yet not forget that under stress children (and adults) may revert to patterns of thinking about health and illness that were typical of the preschool years.

INDUSTRY VERSUS INFERIORITY

Erikson (1963) observed that the school-aged child wins recognition by producing things himself or by becoming an eager part of a productive situation. He believed that the important psychological milestone of this period was the development of a sense of industry. A child may produce book reports, spelling tests, batting averages, stamp collections, healthy pets, or turnips in a garden. Even the successful completion of chores may reinforce his sense of competence. The school system, athletic teams, and hobby groups usually emphasize practice, motivation, and accomplishment through the application of learned rules. A child who experiences repeated failure in several areas may develop a sense of inferiority or inadequacy that can persist into later life. It is for this reason that the identification and remediation of or compensation for a child's specific liabilities are so important during this period of development.

ACADEMIC ACHIEVEMENT

In our society much of the work of the child takes place in the classroom. By age 7 years, most children have become proficient in *decoding* basic symbols. Levine et al. (1981) have pointed out that academic demands change qualitatively midway through grade school. A child without any learning disability may develop a "working disability" manifested by low productivity and difficulty *encoding* information.

During the encoding process, the child may be asked to access previously gained knowledge, organize it, and express it verbally or in writing. Writing an essay and solving a numerical word problem are examples of encoding tasks. Levine et al. (1981) have termed this disability "developmental output failure," and it may be seen in children for the first time as late as junior high school. Such children form an extremely heterogenous group with respect to the underlying disorders responsible for their generally poor productivity. Expressive language deficits, attentional deficits, fine-motor problems, and even emotional problems may interact to produce the same clinical picture. These children may be seen as "lazy," and although a few students put little energy into their work on the basis of individual temperamental style, many students are handicapped by real disabilities that can be addressed. For example, some children with fine-motor difficulties benefit from being given the opportunity to present their work orally, use a typewriter, or present less work of better quality. The clinician serves such children by helping families, teachers, and the children themselves to see the problem in terms of underlying neurodevelopmental disabilities rather than to look at it simply as "work refusal." Through effective advocacy, the clinician can identify these children for further evaluation and educational remediation.

As demand for output increases, so does the complexity of the academic tasks that face the child in grades 2 through 4. Mussen et al. (1969) have pointed to five additional aspects of the learning process that are a result of a higher level of central nervous system maturation: *perception,* the detection, organization, and interpretation of information from both the outside world and the internal environment; *memory,* the storage and later retrieval of information; *reasoning,* the use of information to make inferences and draw conclusions; *reflections,* the evaluation of the quality of ideas and solutions; and *insight,* the recognition of new relationships between two or more bits of information. Successful learning requires an ability to attend in the classroom coupled with these cognitive and perceptual attributes.

The clinician can examine the child's capacity for such thinking by asking a series of questions that assess increasingly sophisticated educational skills, including memory ("Where did you go on your vacation?"), reasoning ("Why did your family decide to go there?"), reflection and analysis ("What did you like best and least about the trip? Why?"), and even insight and creativity ("Where would you like to go if you could go anywhere? Why?"). The nature of the child's answers may reveal his capacity to make use of and communicate the knowledge he has, a task that is increasingly important as the child progresses through school.

PROGRESS IN SOCIAL DEVELOPMENT

The social development of the school child occurs as interest is transferred from the home into the outside community. By second grade, many children are more concerned about their friends' opinions than the opinions of either parents or teachers, and this trend accelerates into adolescence. Children also begin to learn by experience how to initiate, maintain, and, when appropriate, terminate friendships. This is the beginning of a lifelong learning process, marked by periods of relative social success and failure. If a child's emotional development is proceeding in a healthy direction, he will be able to name several favorite companions in whom he begins to confide and will spend much time, even overnight, in the company of friends.

During these early grade-school years, some children suffer continuing social failure. More often boys, these youngsters exhibit difficulties in social relationships despite a strong desire for companionship. They have trouble reading social cues, presenting themselves in a favorable light, and adopting contemporary jargon and dress. They may have difficulty taking part in imaginative play or appreciating the arts. They are sometimes clumsy and usually have difficulty fitting into team activities. They are genuinely bewildered by their lack of acceptance. They do not know intuitively when to stop answering teachers' questions in class, how to choose a responsive friend, and when or how to express feelings. Bright and logical but unable to act "cool," these children are most often labeled as "nerds" by peers. If this problem goes unnoticed by parents and adequate social skills training and engineered social success experiences are not provided, these children will become symptomatic, with depression and conduct disturbance increasing as social pressures peak in early adolescence. Diagnostically, these youngsters suffer from a mild but pervasive developmental disorder (Putnam et al., 1990).

Although children of this age do spend more time out of the home, it is also true that they may become better companions to their parents as they begin to appreciate a wider variety of learning and play activities that adults also enjoy. Children should be truly integrated into the family's home and leisure life. Participation in the planning, work, enjoyment, and evaluation of family projects enhances growth.

Participation in organized athletic and artistic activities becomes an important part of the life of most school-aged children (American Academy of Pediatrics, 1983). By 6 years, children become aware of their abilities in various areas and in comparison with other children. At this age they may participate in team sports competitively while relying on adults to structure the activity; at times they may have difficulty in maintaining interest throughout the game. They may even be unclear about the outcome of a game in which they were involved. Nevertheless, by 10 years, many children have participated in sports and other performance activities that include intense training, commitment, physical risk, and physical contact. The child involved in such activities learns basic skills, rules, and the meaning of teamwork and discipline. He or she also has fun and develops friendships, and this may be reason enough to participate.

DATA GATHERING

A clinician familiar with the developmental trends previously discussed will find working with school-aged children most enjoyable. He or she will also be in a position to assess the development of competence in his or her patients. Data may be obtained in a conversational manner with the child and parents during routine physical examination or perhaps during a minor illness episode. In a clinical practice, data about the development of school-aged children can be limiting when questions are directed primarily to the parents. By 7 years, most children have the expressive language capacity to respond to detailed questions concerning their health, their feelings, and their relationships with others. The clinican will be rewarded, and perhaps astonished, at the richness of information obtained from a series of questions directed to the child. The clinician may find it helpful to organize his thinking around the areas presented in Table 22–1 without committing himself to a particular sequence of questions.

The clinician who asks questions such as those suggested in Table 22–1 during the examination of a school-aged child will be rewarded with a broad understanding of the child's development. He will soon recognize responses that are immature or otherwise unusual and be able to decide which children require further evaluation. He will communicate to the child

TABLE 22-1.
Questions to Be Used in Data Gathering

Question	Objective
Physical Growth	
How are you feeling today?	Communicate to the child that you value the information he/she can provide about his/her own health.
For all children with acute or chronic illness: How do you think you got sick? What do you think will help you get better?	Provide an opportunity to enhance the child's understanding of the way his body functions while correcting misconceptions. At the same time, the clinician warns about the child's "explanatory model" for disease.
How do you usually feel—pretty well or sometimes not so well?	Invite the child to discuss directly somatic complaints, e.g., headaches and stomachaches that commonly occur in this age group. Obtain information about the child's own view of his health.
Do you have any questions about your body or how it is working?	Lay groundwork for a candid physician/patient relationship during adolescence.
For children with chronic illness: Some children with _____ (e.g., CF,* diabetes, asthma) forget to take their medicine at times or don't like using them when friends are around. Does this ever happen to you?	Assess compliance to a chronic medical regimen and the degree to which the child accepts the need for continuing treatment.
For children with chronic illness: Has your _____ (e.g., CF, diabetes, asthma) ever kept you from doing something with your friends or at school that you wanted to do, like spend the night away from home or eat dinner at a friend's house?	Become aware of unnecessary infantilization of children with chronic medical problems.
Cognitive Development	
What day is it today? What month? What year? What is the next holiday? Who is the President of the United States? What is the name of the team that plays baseball for your city?	The child's general fund of information, vocabulary, and ability to express himself may become apparent in his answers to simple questions about the world in which he lives. (Pediatricians will develop their own age norms for evaluating children's responses by repeatedly asking the same questions to a large number of school-aged children.)
What is your address and telephone number?	Failure to answer this question correctly by the end of the first grade would raise a significant question about the child's cognitive growth.
How do you get from your house to your school?	Assess the child's capacity to hold a mental image of routes and direction and communicate these without assuming the listener shares his knowledge.
What makes the clouds move?	Assess the child's beliefs regarding causality and, to a limited extent, his knowledge of the natural world.
How can you tell if something is alive? Is a chair alive? Are clouds alive? Is a tree alive?	Assess the child's ability to distinguish between animate and inanimate objects as well as the degree of sophistication present in the child's concept of both life and death.
Point to my right ear with your left hand.	Assess whether, by age 10 yr, the child is able to mentally "put himself in another's place" by responding correctly to this task.

TABLE 22–1.
Questions to Be Used in Data Gathering

Question	Objective
Social and Emotional Development	
Who are your best friends? What do you and your best friend like to do together?	Assess the degree of commitment to and success in forming positive relationships outside the home.
If you were able to take a special trip or visit an amusement park, who would you choose to bring along?	Assess the degree to which the child desires to include persons outside the family in positive experiences.
After asking the previous question: Who else would you take with you? What about your brother/sister?	Assess the degree of rivalry among siblings or perhaps with one's parents.
Who would you take with you if you were shipwrecked on a desert island? (Who else?)	Assess the degree to which the child feels dependent on members of the immediate family.
What do you do to help out around the house?	Sanction the expectation that the child can be involved in constructive activities that help the family.
Do you ever get in trouble at home or in school?	Invite the parent to comment on disturbances in the child's conduct or to commend the child for good conduct. Also allow the child and parent to comment on disciplinary techniques (e.g., "What usually happens when you get in trouble?").
If you had 3 wishes, what would they be? If the child answers, "Money," ask, "What would you do with the money?" If you could change your life in some way, how would you change it?	Allow the child to express his concerns and his hopes about himself and his family.
What do you think of _____, e.g., the new freeway they're building across town? Why do some people want the freeway built and why are there some people who are against it?	Assess the child's awareness of current developments in his community, as well as his ability to discuss both sides of a conflict.
How do you help your mom and dad around the house?	Assess the child's sense of responsibility toward the family, as well as the expectations and "maturity demands" of the parents.
Suppose a boy broke 10 dishes while trying to wash them and his brother broke only 1 by sailing it out the window. Who deserves to be punished, and who did the worse thing?	Assess the child's moral reasoning, i.e., does he take context and motivation into account in making moral judgments?

*CF = cystic fibrosis.

that he is interested in the child as a whole person. The child may feel, for the first time, that he can speak for himself to the physician. Such an interview with the child in the parents' presence may enhance the parents' understanding of their own child.

ANTICIPATORY GUIDANCE

The clinician can anticipate with the family the school-aged child's increasing need for a sense of competency. She can encourage parents to give the child responsibilities in the form of chores along with an allowance to manage, if possible. She can advise the parents to be sensitive to the sense of inferiority that can develop in children of this age so that appropriate measures may be taken to support the child's self-esteem. If it appears that the child's difficulties are related to academic failure, the pediatrician is often in the best position to initiate and coordinate an evaluation of the problem.

The clinician should develop some understanding of each family's attitude toward their child's participation in organized activities outside the home. Do the parents encourage the child to develop individual interests and abilities? Do they recognize the value of regular physical activity? Do they recognize their child's reasonable physical and mental limits? Do they emphasize excellence and winning, or do they understand the value of participation? Parents may overschedule their child's free time, a situation Elkind (1981) termed the "hurried child syndrome." Conversely, they may do little to help the child develop skills and healthy habits in the use of leisure time.

Parents can expect that children by 8 years of age will begin to understand for the first time the inevitability of certain losses such as death of a parent. The clinician can reassure parents whose children begin at this age to express fears relating to the loss of a parent, provided these fears do not interfere with the child's daily functioning. Children who become depressed over such concerns or who become so fearful that they avoid their usual activities outside the home require a more careful psychological evaluation.

Clinicians may also anticipate with parents the conflicts that arise in children as they are increasingly exposed to the world outside the family. Children today are aware of violence on a global scale through the media and will almost certainly need help from their parents to deal with the news of events that produce anxiety even in adults and adolescents. Many of today's chidren are exposed to sexual material that may be perverse or even bizarre through television and the movies. Parental guidance in such matters is supported by society in a number of ways, from the existence of community groups such as the Parent-Teacher Association to the movie rating system that has been refined to include a "PG-13" rating. As a children's advocate who is aware of the potential toxicity of exposure to excessive amounts of television (as well as other forms of passive entertainment), the pediatrician has a responsibility to raise the issue of television viewing with parents (Rothenberg, 1975). Parents need to understand the confusion and anxiety such material can engender in the child 7 to 10 years old. Parents can be encouraged to limit the child's exposure and provide an atmosphere in which the child feels free to share her concerns and clear up misconceptions.

REFERENCES

American Academy of Pediatrics: Counseling parents, in *Sports Medicine: Health Care for Young Athletes.* Evanston, Ill, American Academy of Pediatrics, 1983.

Elkind D: *The Hurried Child: Growing Up Too Fast, Too Soon.* Reading, Mass, Addison-Wesley Publishing Co, 1981.

Erikson EH: *Childhood and Society,* ed 2. New York, WW Norton, 1963.

Freud S: *Introductory Lectures in Psychoanalysis.* New York, WW Norton, 1965.

Grumbach M, Grave G, Mayer F: *Control of the Onset of Puberty.* New York, John Wiley & Sons, 1974.

Kohlberg L: Essays on moral development, in *The Philosophy of Moral Development.* New York, Harper & Row Publishers, 1981, vol 1.

Levine MD, Oberklaid F, Meltzer L: Developmental output failure: A study of low productivity in school age children. *Pediatrics* 1981; 67:18–25.

Martinson FM: Preadolescent sexuality, in Constantine LL, Martinson FM (eds): *Children and Sex: New Findings/New Perspectives.* Boston, Little, Brown & Co, 1981.

Mussen P, Conger J, Kagan J: *Child Development and Personality.* New York, Harper & Row Publishers, 1969.

Piaget J: *The Origins of Intelligence in Children.* New York, International University Press, 1952.

Piaget J, Inhelder B: *The Psychology of the Child.* New York, Basic Books, 1968.

Putnam N: Revenge or tragedy: Do nerds suffer from a mild pervasive developmental disorder? in Feinstein S (ed): *Adolescent Psychiatry: Developmental and Clinical Studies.* Chicago, University of Chicago Press, 1990, vol 17.

Rothenberg M: Effect of television violence on children and youth. *JAMA* 1975; 234:1043–1046.

Rutter M: Normal psychosexual development. *J Child Psychol Psychiatry* 1977; 12:259–283.

Sarnoff C: *Latency.* New York, Aronson, 1976.

Stilwell BM, Galvin M, Kopta S: Conceptualization of conscience in normal children and adolescents, ages 5 to 17. *J Am Acad Child Adolesc Psychiatry* 1991; 30(1):16–21.

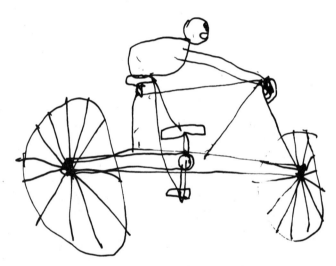

"Boy rides his bike." By Ryan Hennessy, age 7½.

CHAPTER 23

Seven to Ten Years: The World of the Elementary School Child

ROBERT D. WELLS, PH.D.
MARTIN T. STEIN, M.D.

KEY WORDS

MASTERY
COPING STYLES
STRESS RESPONSE
SCHOOL PERFORMANCE
FRIENDS AND ACTIVITIES

Aaron, age 9 years, was brought to you after a 1-week history of headaches. He is a fourth grader in a school for gifted children and has been earning excellent grades. You know the family well, because he has two younger siblings (ages 3 and 6 years) and his mother often calls and visits the office with acute concerns. Aaron was born after 5 years of infertility. His father is an attorney who is even-tempered and serious. His mother is a part-time teacher in computer sciences and has always been intense. She is very concerned that Aaron's headaches are the result of a brain tumor, because he has also had a major change in his behavior. His paternal grandfather died of an astrocytoma when Aaron was 2 years old. Although he always was an intense but sociable child, he is now withdrawn, irritable, and demanding. He has been out of school for 1 week. His mother is unaware of any specific changes or stressful events but did note that there have been recent problems with friends in the neighborhood. You decide to speak with Aaron alone to assess his developmental and behavioral functioning to help determine its potential significance in creating or maintaining his symptoms.

On physical examination, Aaron is a depressed-appearing child with dramatic complaints of headache that are not well localized. A complete examination, including neurological assessment and visual acuity, is normal. The child is afebrile and appears well.

When Aaron is interviewed alone, he initially denies with irritation specific concerns. He easily discusses his baseball card collection. When asked about his strengths, Aaron is unable to tell you what he does well.

He says his headache keeps him from doing his schoolwork and admits to hating school despite his great success. He admits to feeling lonely at times and wishes he had more friends. This is his first year out of the neighborhood school. To attend the gifted program, he must travel to the other side of town and thus far has not met any of his fellow students out of school.

The assessment suggests that Aaron's headaches may stem from stress overload after the loss of a friendship. His social skills appear somewhat limited by his intense preoccupations. His coping style has always been to withdraw and distract by occupying himself with more pleasant stimuli. His parents' responses have often tended to heighten concern and to further reinforce his symptomatic behaviors. His social skills in developing and maintaining friendships appear lacking.

After ruling out serious physical illness, his parents were reassured. They were encouraged to decrease the secondary gains (i.e., increased attention, new baseball cards, no chores, no homework) and to return him to school. He was allowed to use acetaminophen for pain analgesia but was also forced to be out of his room and out of his house for approximately 1 hour per day. His father was encouraged to involve Aaron in league baseball and to practice regularly with his son to build up his stamina and sense of resilience. The family was also encouraged to have Aaron arrange to bring friends over to the house. Within 1 week Aaron's headaches were gone and his social and academic functioning returned to normal. He continues to be a child of somewhat increased risk as a result of a family history of emotional problems and his own difficult temperament and problematic social skills. On the other hand, his intelligence, his organized and concerned family, and his general competence may serve as important moderators in helping him maintain a positive adjustment.

The middle school-aged years are, for most children, a time of robust physical health filled with surges of competencies and vulnerabilities in behavioral and developmental areas. This places the primary care physician in a challenging position as visits become less frequent during a time when many behavior and learning problems may become evident. Self-awareness, control over new feelings and desires, interpersonal engagement, and other psychological processes deepen and evolve.

A significant number of school-aged children face additional obstacles in their way toward developing these competencies. Ten percent to 20% of children must cope with a chronic illness (Gortmaker and Sappenfield, 1984) and thus require additional care during a period of heightened independence and self-responsibility. Learning problems, traumatic events, and social and family dysfunctions all pose significant risks for the development of a wide range of behavioral, academic, and psychosomatic disorders.

DEVELOPMENTAL TASKS

Mastery, though always a focus of child development, takes on special meaning during the school-aged years. Erikson (1963) labeled this stage as one contrasting industry and inferiority, thus linking achievement with self-concept. The ability to compete productively in academic, extracurricular, social, and family realms in large part determines the child's sense of self-efficacy. Highly self-efficacious individuals believe in their relative ability to master and control the situation such that goals and rewards are realized. In the face of failure and disappointment, children with moderate to high self-efficacy will reapply themselves in an industrious fashion and develop a range of skills for overcoming obstacles. In contrast, low self-efficacy may be both the result and the cause of personal failure in developing social and academic skills.

Although earlier explorations into separation have been experienced, the school-aged years are filled with a need to separate from parents for more prolonged periods. The ability to master these outings (e.g., sleepovers, camp) and to utilize independent coping skills when away from home appear critical for healthy development. While the separation process progresses, the child must still manage to function in the home in a manner that allows for recognition of his new responsibilities. Chores and homework become frequent testing grounds for conflict resolution skills. With the child's increased cognitive and verbal sophistication, arguments between parent and child can take on the appearance of a court room with each side arguing with righteousness over the obvious logic and illogic of the case.

Achievement at school becomes more demanding and complex at this time. Tests, grades, and special classes exert a significant effect on school-aged children. Repeating a grade level is one of the most stressful events for an elementary school child, outranking the death of a close friend and just below having a visible congenital deformity (Heisel et al., 1973). The expectations placed on students by their parents, teachers, and, ultimately, themselves has a significant impact on learning rate, academic ranking, and the child's sense of self-worth (Rosenthal and Jacobson, 1968; Samuels, 1977). Children with exaggerated optimistic or pessimistic expectations will demonstrate significant problems in work motivation and frustration tolerance (Elkind, 1989). Distinct learning disabilities and learning styles may become most obvious during this time as the cognitive operations required in class become increasingly complex, sequential, and reading based. For mastery to occur, it is important for the child to recognize her capacity to meet the expectations of teachers and parents by assuming responsibility and developing the skills to complete assigned tasks.

School-aged children immerse themselves into sports, clubs, crafts, organizations, music, baseball cards, current fads, and a variety of other activities. These pursuits reflect a drive to master specific motor, social, and artistic skills that are fashioned out of individual experiences and cultural expectations. Some children spend hours drawing, whereas others shoot basketball, write poetry, or build remote control cars. Doing the "in thing" becomes extremely important at this age, and most school-aged children pursue sex-stereotyped activities with same-gender friendship groupings. Every child should have at least one such area of activity to which she, not her parents only, is committed.

Perhaps most central to the school-aged years is the quest for social involvement and social acceptance. Most children seek to find a place for themselves among a cohesive group of friends. Their success in maintaining a positive sense of self during the vicissitudes of making and breaking of friendships is in part dependent on the resilience of their coping and social skills (Asher et al., 1982). Children with positive peer relations tend to give and receive positive attention to others, conform to classroom rules, and perform well academically. They are also able to initiate social contact in a positive manner, and they tend to develop pleasant social interchanges with others (Ollendick et al., 1989).

Social skills may encompass a good sense of humor, an ability to make others feel wanted, a willingness to share, a positive mood, creativity, leadership, and negotiation skills. These abilities are developed typically through observation of others (e.g., peers, parents, siblings, teachers, and even television), and for most children, friendships develop naturally as social involvement is pursued. On the other hand, scapegoating, teasing, bullying, and self-isolation become social dynamics that can seriously hinder the child with poor social skills. Social skills can be specifically taught to a child if these negative difficulties are caught early.

The child's temperament appears to be an important contributor in the school-aged child's ability to develop competency at play and in making and losing friendships (Murphy and Moriarty, 1976). Children with difficult, high-strung temperaments generally show greater mood intensity and lability and have a greater tendency to develop behavioral and psychosomatic symptoms. Children with poor frustration tolerance, those with difficulties sharing, and those who stand out as different based on cultural, psychosocial, or physical conditions are at high risk for an array of behavioral, somatic, and developmental conditions. One study found that being labeled by a teacher as a school-aged child who "failed to get along" was the most predictive of adolescent and adult criminality than any other single factor (Janes and Hesselbrock, 1978).

RISK AND PROTECTIVE FACTORS

Adjustment disorders constitute the majority of emotional problems among school-aged children seen by primary care clinicians (Goldberg et al., 1979). This condition describes changes in behavior, mood, or academic performance after a stressful life event. One million children each year experience the breakup of their families because of divorce (National Center for Health Statistics, 1986). Domestic violence is also rampant, and there are estimates that almost one-half million children are directly affected by child abuse (Garmezy, 1988). Natural disasters, violence, and serious accidents or illness in a family member can also have significant emotional effects on the developmental work of school-aged children (Frederick, 1985; Pynoos and Eth, 1985; Terr, 1985).

The impact of any loss is experienced by school-aged children with growing awareness of its permanence and a feeling of being responsible for events around them. Psychologically significant losses during this age takes many forms. From the strikout at the plate to the loss of a best friend, the need to develop skills for experiencing, expressing, and tolerating these uncomfortable emotions provides the school-aged child with the opportunity to learn new adaptive coping strategies and skills.

When stress exceeds coping resources, maladaptation results. Some children will respond to stress overload by becoming depressed, anxious, or preoccupied with body functions, whereas others may become provocative, angry, and demanding. The array of psychological dysfunctions have been conceptualized as fitting into two broad groupings of disorders: *internalizing* and *externalizing* (Achenbach and Edelbrock, 1983). Internalizing disorders include psychosomatic complaints, depression, withdrawal, and anxiety. Disruptive behaviors, negativism, hyperactivity, and conduct disorders reflect externalizing disorders. Some children exhibit both concurrently with agitated complaints of sadness and anxiety intermixed with temper outbursts, noncompliance, and negativism. A difficult temperament in a boy is associated with externalizing disorders, whereas internalizing disorders are more common among girls with a slow to warm up temperament.

Recurrent symptoms of headache, abdominal, and limb pain are frequent during the school-aged years (Oster, 1972) and in some cases may lead to difficulties in functioning in several areas (Table 23–1). Although the majority of these recurrent pains are idiopathic with negative physical examination findings (Appley, 1975), growing evidence suggests that the parents of these children have higher rates of depression and somatic preoccupation (Hughes and Zimin, 1978; Routh and Ernst, 1984), suggesting a familial pattern of underlying stress. Habit problems are also very prevalent in school-aged children. Affected children and their parents become increasingly concerned about nocturnal enuresis, encopresis, thumb sucking, nail biting, hair pulling, and other childhood habits as social ostracism becomes more fervent (Schaefer, 1979).

Poor school performance may be the result of stress overload, sensory-perceptual limi-

TABLE 23–1.

Behavioral-Somatic Symptoms Common During School-Aged Years*

	Psychosomatic Conversion Reaction	Maturational Behavior
Headache	+++	
Recurrent abdominal pain	+++	
Limb pain	++	
Chest pain	+	
Enuresis	+	+++
Encopresis	+	
Thumb sucking	+	+
Hair pulling	+	
Nail biting	+	
Ritual behaviors		+++
Sleep disturbance	+	+

*__Psychosomatic conversion reactions__ = symptoms that typically result from situational stress or depression in either the child or parent; **maturational behavior** = residual behaviors seen in some normal children from an earlier stage in development but that are not associated with stress or depression; +++ = common symptom (10%–15% of school-aged children); + = less common symptom (less than 5% of children).

tations, learning disabilities, behavioral disorders, retardation, or a host of other potentially contributing factors (Dworkin, 1985). Three percent of elementary-aged children have a hearing impairment, almost 25% have visual defects, and 1% have a major speech articulation disorder. In addition, 10% to 20% have a definable learning disability in reading, arithmetic, attention, visual-spatial skills, or other areas of neuropsychological functioning. Children with disabilities that limit their capacity for learning are at twice the risk for developing school avoidance, disruptive behavior problems, depression, and psychosomatic reactions. Concern about poor academic performance may bring a child to the clinician; at other times it is the child's emotional or psychosomatic response to the disability that raises parental concern. Behavioral symptoms and somatic functioning that manifest during school days but either lessen or resolve during holidays and weekends may be an important clue to discovering related developmental disorders.

Children with chronic medical diseases carry an additional burden for behavioral and developmental adjustment disorders. Children with central nervous system dysfunction are at three to four times the risk for behavioral, emotional, and learning problems when compared with the general population of children (Rutter et al., 1970). Differences in adjustment capacities do not correlate with the type of illness; they are most affected by family functioning (Breslau, 1990). In particular, the quality of the parent-child relationship, emotional disorder in the parents, and marital discord are the strongest predictors of child maladjustment for both chronically ill and healthy children (Lewis and Khaw, 1982). In addition, the extent of functional limitation imposed by the illness and its treatment contribute toward increasing the risk for maladaptation (Stein et al., 1987).

School-aged children with greater intelligence, those with easier temperaments, and those coming from more organized families are at reduced risk for significant behavioral and developmental problems (Garmezy, 1988). Flexible coping skills, an internal sense that one can have a positive effect on events and people, and good physical health are also important moderators of stress (Block and Block, 1979; Werner and Smith, 1979).

Family functioning appears to be both the strongest risk and the strongest protective factor. Genetic predisposition to depression, alcoholism, obesity, learning disabilities, conduct problems, and psychosomatic preoccupations will become apparent often only through a focused family history interview. Of equal importance is the extent to which a family is successful in helping their child develop the necessary skills for social and academic success. Studies of resilience emphasize the parental modeling of coping skills and the need to maintain predictable rules and expectations at home. Social support from friends, family, and others exerts significant effects in moderating the range of acute and chronic stress. Although peer friendships are important in helping children become socialized, studies of resilient children suggest that having one healthy, interested, caring, and predictable adult can do a great deal for children facing numerous barriers to their development (Anthony and Cohler, 1987).

The target for assessment, strengthening, and intervening remains the child's environment, which includes the family unit as always, but for the school-aged child it also includes the school and outside activities.

ASSESSMENT

Developmental and behavioral assessment of the school-aged child should broadly assess the child's functioning at home, in school, with friends, and in the community. The child and parents can be interviewed together, but some time with the child alone will be important to establish your sense of her as an independent and competent individual. While one is engaged in developing rapport and expanding one's data base, observations of the child and family will be helpful. In particular, note the child's and parent's general mood and level of interaction. Is the child's behavior appropriate for age, pseudomature, or delayed? How well does the parent allow the child to speak for herself? Are there indications of underlying anger, distrust, or worry? How age appropriate are the child's basic skills of speech, concentration, attention, and compliance? How close do the parents seem with each other, and how close are they with this child? How do the parents respond when their child seems anxious, angry, or embarrassed? How much do they control his or her behavior during the visit? How easy or difficult is it to relate to this child and family?

Questions regarding the child's functioning should focus on strengths and successes, as well as concerns and weaknesses. Such terms as "problems" and "failures" should be avoided. Helping the family keep a balance while discussing their child is extremely important to avoid belittling the child in a disrespectful and potentially harmful fashion. To spend some time with the child, explain that this is part of your standard practice with children who are on their way to being teenagers. Showing an interest in getting to know her and wanting to give her a chance to discuss things in a more private way are also important goals to convey. Clarifying that you will treat her like any competent patient by keeping her communications confidential is also helpful.

Interviewing the school-aged child can be a challenge, but there are certain skills and attitudes that will help. If one is to recognize her concerns about competency, the first rule is to focus on her abilities and strengths. This will allow her to present herself in a controlled fashion, which will help in the development of trust. Early questions about stressful events or feelings should be avoided until the child settles down and appears more comfortable. Consequently, questions about the three arenas (family, school, and social functioning) can be ordered such that the least stressful area is discussed first and the most worrisome is left for last. Predictions about this can be made from the information gained from parents, your own observations, and the presenting problem.

DATA GATHERING

FAMILY FUNCTIONING

- How is everybody at home getting along?
- What are you allowed to do now that you couldn't when you were younger?
- Tell me about what the family enjoys doing together.
- What chores do you have at home? How easy is it to do them? What happens if you forget?
- If you have a problem at school or with a friend, who do you talk to about it?
- How much fighting goes on between you and your brother or sister?
- What are the most important rules at home?
- What type of punishment do your parents use?
- How important is it to your parents that you succeed in school, sports, or chores?
- What new freedoms do you expect to get over the next few years?
- What parts of your parents do you wish to be like when you have children?
- Tell me about a usual Sunday. What happens? Who does what with whom?
- What do your parents worry about with you?
- What do you worry about at home?

SCHOOL FUNCTIONING

- What do you like about school the most?
- What do you dislike about school?
- What subjects are easy? Which ones are hard?
- What kind of grades are you getting this year? How about last year? Are you happy with them?
- What is your teacher like this year?
- Do you ever worry that it is extra hard for you to do something he or she asks?
- Have you ever gotten into trouble for the way you behave at school? What happened?
- How much school have you missed recently?
- Do you ever visit the nurse's office or feel sick in school?
- How do you get along with the other children at school? Do you have friends? Do you have enemies or people who pick on you?
- If you were the principal or teacher, what rules would you change?
- What jobs or careers do you think you would enjoy?
- Do you like to read? Do you read for fun?

SOCIAL FUNCTIONING

- What kinds of things do you like to do after school and on weekends?
- What are you good at? What types of things do you enjoy and do well?
- Who is your best friend? How long have you known him/her? How often do you get together? What do you like about him/her?
- Can you talk about worries and problems with your friends?
- Have you ever lost a friend? What happened? How did you cope?
- Do you and your friends ever fight or have problems sharing? How do you settle it?
- Do your friends have special problems at their home? Do they worry about their parents?
- Have you slept over at their home? Have they stayed with you?
- What types of things do you wish you could do or learn?
- Have your friends gotten interested in boys/girls? What kind of grades do they get? Are they experimenting with cigarettes, alcohol, or drugs? What are they good at?
- Do you belong to any teams, groups, or clubs?
- How well do you behave when you are out in the neighborhood? Do you get in any fights?
- Has anyone ever hurt you or made you do something you didn't want to do?
- If you could have anything or change anything, what three things might you wish for?
- What is the hardest thing you have ever had to deal with?
- If you could be any age, what age would you pick?
- Is this year going better, worse, or about the same as last year? How come?

ANTICIPATORY GUIDANCE

The child's clinician can offer specific guidance to the child and family directed toward the development of responsible, competent behaviors. Counseling about accident prevention recognizes the school-aged child's cognitive ability to connect an event with an outcome while focusing on the innate interest in controlling one's environment. Thus, the need for seat belts, responsible bike riding, skating, and roller blading should be mentioned because these continue to be the leading causes of death in children. When family risk factors for obesity are determined, a balanced diet (low in saturated fats, refined carbohydrates, and salt) and regular exercise for all family members should be encouraged. Responsibility can be enhanced by having clear expectations of the child for initiating and completing chores and homework. Gradual increases in independent activities can be used as encouragement for child behaviors that demonstrate trustworthiness and competence. Extracurricular activities should be supported, but care should be taken to avoid the "hurried child syndrome" (Elkind, 1989) where the pressures to excel far outweigh the pleasures to explore and experience. Parents may be encouraged to maintain reasonable, predictable, and observable boundaries and rules so that the child can accurately predict the parents' positive and negative responses to her behavior. Children need to learn a variety of skills, including delay of gratification and frustration tolerance, which can be developed only when negative events are experienced and tolerated. Parents can be helped to consult with their child on their concerns, but they are wise to avoid premature suggestions or advice in favor of supporting their child's problem-solving efforts. The clinician can identify areas of stress for the child and invite family-initiated solutions. Changes in the school and social environments that will support positive growth should be encouraged. Parents must get involved to understand the impact of that milieu on their own child and to effect positive change. Finally, for those children who experience a major life stress such as a divorce, death, or school failure, the clinician should be an advocate for the child by keeping the child's developmental needs in focus and coping strategies intact. At least one domain should be seen by the child as positive and successful as the struggles continue in others. At the close of each visit, the child and parent should be complimented on their particular strengths. Families will come to anticipate these office visits as an opportunity to share their child's achievements, as well as a place to explore current behavioral and developmental concerns.

REFERENCES

Achenbach TM, Edelbrock C: *Manual for the Child Behavior Checklist and Revised Behavior Profile.* Burlington, Vt, University of Vermont, 1983.

Anthony E, Cohler B: *The Invulnerable Child.* New York, Guilford Press, 1987.

Appley J: *The Child With Abdominal Pains.* Boston, Blackwell Scientific Publications, 1975.

Asher S, Renshaw P, Hymel S: Peer relations and the development of social skills, in Moore S, Cooper C (eds): *The Young Child: Reviews of Research.* Washington, DC, National Association for the Education of Young Children, 1982, vol 3.

Block J, Block J: The role of ego-control and ego-resiliency in the organization of behavior, in Collin WA (ed): *Minnesota Symposium on Child Psychology.* Hillsdale, NJ, Erlbaum, 1979, vol 13.

Breslau N: Does brain dysfunction increase children's vulnerability to environmental stress? *Arch Gen Psychiatry* 1990; 47:15–20.

Dworkin P: *Learning and Behavior Problems of School Children:* Philadelphia, WB Saunders Co, 1985.

Elkind D: *The Hurried Child: Growing Up Too Fast, Too Soon.* Reading, Mass, Addison-Wesley Publishing Co, 1988.

Erikson EH: *Childhood and Society,* ed 2. New York, WW Norton, 1963.

Frederick C: Children traumatized in small groups, in Eth S, Pynoos R (eds): *Post-Traumatic Stress Disorders in Children.* Washington, DC, American Psychiatric Press, 1985.

Garmezy N: Stressors of childhood, in Garmezy N, Rutter M (eds): *Stress, Coping and Development in Children.* New York, McGraw-Hill Book Co, 1988.

Goldberg ID, Huxley DA, McInerny TK, et al: The role of the pediatrician in the delivery of mental health services to children. *Pediatrics* 1979; 63:898–909.

Gortmaker SL, Sappenfield W: Chronic childhood disorders: Prevalence and impact, in Haggerty R (ed): *Pediatr Clin North Am* 1984; 31:1.

Heisel JS, Ream S, Raitz R, et al: The significance of life events as contributing factors in the diseases of children. *J Pediatr* 1973; 83:119–123.

Hughes M, Zimin R: Children with psychogenic abdominal pain and their families: Management during hospitalization. *Clin Pediatr* 1978; 17:569–573.

Janes CL, Hesselbrock VM: Problem children's adult adjustment predicted from teacher ratings. *Am J Orthopsychiatry* 1978; 48:300–390.

Kashani JH, Simonds JF: The incidence of depression in children. *Am J Psychiatry* 1979; 136:1203–1205.

Lewis BL, Khaw K: Family functioning as a mediating variable affecting psychosocial adjustment of children with cystic fibrosis. *J Pediatr* 1982; 101:636–640.

Murphy L, Moriarty A: *Vulnerability, Coping and Growth.* New Haven, Conn, Yale University Press, 1976.

National Center for Health Statistics: Annual summary of births, marriages, divorces and deaths for 1986. *Monthly Vital Stat Rep* 35(12), Hyattsville, Md, Public Health Service.

Ollendick T, Oswald D, Francis G: Validity of teacher nominations in identifying aggressive, withdrawn and popular children. *J Clin Child Psychol* 1989; 18:221–229.

Oster J: Recurrent abdominal pain, headache, and limb pains in children and adolescents. *Pediatrics* 1972; 50:429–436.

Pynoos R, Eth S: Children traumatized by witnessing acts of personal violence: Homicide, rape or suicide behavior, in Eth S, Pynoos R (eds): *Post-Traumatic Stress Disorders in Children.* Washington, DC, American Psychiatric Press, 1985.

Rosenthal R, Jacobson L: *Pygmalion in the Classroom.* New York, Holt, Rinehart & Winston, 1968.

Routh D, Ernst, A: Somatization disorder in relatives of children and adolescents with functional abdominal pain. *J Pediatr Psychol* 1984; 9:427–436.

Rutter M, Tizard J, Whitmore K: *Education, Health and Behavior.* London, Longman Group, 1970.

Samuels S: *Enhancing Self-Concept in Early Childhood. Theory and Practice.* New York, Human Sciences Press, 1977.

Schaefer C: *Childhood Encopresis and Enuresis: Causes and Therapy.* New York, Van Nostrand Reinhold, Co, 1979.

Stein R, Gortmaker S, Perrin E, et al: Severity of illness: Concepts and measurement. *Lancet* 1987; 2:1506–1509.

Terr L: Children traumatized in small groups, in Eth S, Pynoos R (eds): *Post-Traumatic Stress Disorders in Children.* Washington, DC, American Psychiatric Press, 1985.

Werner E, Smith R: An epidemiologic perspective on some antecedents and consequences of childhood mental health problems and learning disabilities. *J Am Acad Child Psychiatry* 1979; 18:292–306.

"My family." By E.Y., girl, age 14.

CHAPTER 24

Overview of Adolescence

MARIANNE E. FELICE, M.D.

Adolescence is the developmental phase between childhood and adulthood marked by rapid changes in physical, psychosocial, moral, and cognitive growth (Felice, 1992). Adolescence generally spans a 10-year period but is not one long decade of similar development; rather it consists of three substages: early, mid-, and late adolescence. Early adolescence generally includes 11- to 13-year-olds, mid-adolescence usually refers to 14- to 16-year-olds, and late adolescence, as a rule, denotes teenagers 17 years or older and may even extend to youths in their twenties. These age ranges are variable and arbitrary. For example, some 15-year-olds are clearly still in early adolescence, others are clearly in late adolescence, but most are in mid-adolescence.

Besides chronological age, many factors contribute to the adolescent's placement in early, mid-, or late adolescent development, including gender, cultural background, socioeconomic class, and health status. For example, girls usually mature earlier than boys, particularly in the younger age ranges (Tanner, 1962), and in some subcultures, adolescents are expected to grow up faster than in others. Chronic disease may delay adolescent development as the teenager with chronic illness copes with his dependency on medication, ongoing support by parents and physicians, and struggles with body image and the limitations imposed by his illness (Buhlmann and Fitzpatrick, 1987; Long et al., 1984). Finally, the timing of puberty may affect the age at which a youngster progresses through the developmental phases: "late bloomers" in pubertal development may also be late bloomers in psychosocial development. The concept of distinct adolescent substages is also important because the needs of younger adolescents are different from the needs of older adolescents, and the evaluation of younger and older youth may need to focus on different issues (Lohner, 1987). This developmental change across time will allow for a changing and targeted approach to primary care.

PSYCHOSOCIAL GROWTH TASKS

The psychosocial growth tasks of adolescence are summarized in Table 24–1. The key issues are separation and independence, sexual identity, cognitive expansion, moral maturation, and preparation for an adult role in society. In other words, during adolescence the individual must ask himself: Who am I? Where am I going? How am I getting there?

TABLE 24–1.
Developmental Growth Tasks of Adolescence*

Gradual development as an independent individual
Mental evolvement of a satisfying, realistic body image
Harnessing appropriate control and expression of sexual drives
Expansion of relationships outside the home
Implementation of a realistic plan to achieve social and economic stability
Transition from concrete to abstract conceptualization
Integration of a value system applicable to life events

*From Felice M: Adolescence, in Levine MD, Carey WB, Crocker AC (eds): *Developmental-Behavioral Pediatrics.* Philadelphia, WB Saunders Co, 1983. Used by permission.

Mastery of all these growth tasks is necessary for healthy adulthood and personal maturity. However, like all psychological growth, progress does not occur in a straight line. There are peaks, valleys, and plateaus, and progress in one area may influence progress in another area. Teenagers probably struggle to varying degrees through all of the tasks concomitantly, but it does appear that each of the three phases of adolescence concentrates on different aspects of the tasks at different times. Table 24–2 is a summary of the psychosocial tasks by developmental phase. The following three chapters will focus on the growth tasks emphasized in each substage of adolescence.

TABLE 24–2.
Growth Tasks by Developmental Phase*

Task	Early: 10–13 yr	Mid: 14–16 yr	Late: 17 yr +
Independence	Emotional break from parents; prefers friends to family	Ambivalence about separation	Integration of independence issues
Body image	Adjustment to pubescent changes	"Trying on" different images to find real self	Integration of a satisfying body image with personality
Sexual drives	Sexual curiousity; occasional masturbation	Sexual experimentation; opposite sex viewed as sex object	Beginning of intimacy/caring
Relationships	Unisex peer group; adult crushes	Begin heterosexual peer group; multiple adult-role models	Individual relationships more important than peer group
Career plans	Vague and unrealistic plans —————————————————————→		Specific goals/specific steps to implement them
Conceptualization	Concrete thinking ————————————————→	Fascinated by new capacity for thinking	Ability to abstract
Value system	Drop in superego; testing of moral system of parents	Self-centered ——————→	Idealism; rigid concepts of right and wrong; other-oriented, asceticism

*Adapted from Felice ME: Adolescence, in Levine MD, Carey WB, Crocker AC (eds): *Developmental-Behavioral Pediatrics*, ed 2. Philadelphia, WB Saunders Co, 1992.

SPECIFIC ADOLESCENT ISSUES

Besides being knowledgeable about the psychosocial growth tasks, physicians should be aware of other issues regarding adolescents. For example, clinicians must become accustomed to interviewing adolescents and parents separately (Felice and Friedman, 1982; Felice and Vargish, 1984). This not only enables the clinician to obtain sensitive information from the adolescent in private but also emphasizes the emerging independence of the youngster and helps to establish rapport. Also some pediatric practices and clinics find it useful to use health-survey questionnaires to obtain additional information in an efficient manner from the young people they serve. These questionnaires are not always appropriate, particularly if the teenager is brought to the clinician against his will (in which case he may feel hostile toward the assignment to complete the questionnaire) or if the youngster has an inadequate reading ability, does not speak English, or is frightened by the visit (Felice, 1992). Other adolescents may find a health-survey questionnaire reassuring because the questionnaire implies that he is not the only adolescent with a given concern or worry. If questionnaires are used, they must never take the place of patient contact and should be used only as an adjunct to the individual physician-patient interview. Clinicians who care for teenagers will also find it helpful to have the waiting room stocked with reading materials appropriate for youth. In this way, those areas that the teenager may be reluctant to ask about or the physician may neglect to inquire about will still be addressed.

Adolescence is a developmental period that may baffle parents, frustrate health care providers, and cause confusion for adolescents themselves. The industrious school-aged child who was hard working, compliant, and quiet, is suddenly seen as rebellious. The wide-eyed shy child who was previously in adoration of his parents, teachers, and pediatricians is now viewed as insolent and outspoken. Furthermore, adolescents often evoke uncomfortable feelings in the adults around them, usually memories of the adult's own uncomfortable adolescence. Rather than be frustrated in caring for teenagers, physicians may find that interaction with them is uplifting and a constant reminder of the idealism of youth. Most youth go through this time without delinquency, school failure, parenthood, or drug addiction. Clinicians must not be afraid that these extremes will affect the majority of patients. There is a persistent myth that adolescence is tumultuous in all cases, leading to caregiver dread and avoidance (Weiner, 1990). The outspoken young person is really in the midst of an age of wonderment and is someone who is searching to find himself while learning to make his contribution to society. One would miss a great deal by not encouraging the maintenance of a cohort of adolescents in a practice, particularly those followed from early childhood, as these youngsters make the journey to adulthood.

REFERENCES

Buhlmann U, Fitzpatrick SB: Caring for an adolescent with a chronic illness. *Primary Care* 1987; 14:57–68.

Felice ME: Adolescence, in Levine MD, Carey WB, Crocker AC (eds): *Developmental-Behavioral Pediatrics,* ed 2. Philadelphia, WB Saunders Co, 1992.

Felice ME, Friedman SB: Behavioral considerations in the health care of adolescents. *Pediatr Clin North Am* 1982; 29:399–412.

Felice ME, Vargish W: Interviewing and evaluation of the adolescent, in Kelley VE (ed): *Practice of Pediatrics.* New York, Harper & Row Publishers, 1984.

Lohner T: Adolescent psychosocial growth and development. *Primary Care* 1987; 14:13–23.

Long TJL, Fitzpatrick SB, Reese JM, et al: Basic issues in adolescent medicine. *Curr Probl Pediatr* 1984; 14:1–50.

Tanner JM: *Growth at Adolescence.* Boston, Blackwell Scientific Publications, 1962.

Weiner IB: Distinguishing healthy from disturbed adolescent development. *J Dev Behav Pediatr* 1990; 11:151–154.

My brother's friends.
by Colin Hennessy, age 11

CHAPTER **25**

Eleven to Thirteen Years: Early Adolescence—The Age of Rapid Changes

MARIANNE E. FELICE, M.D.

KEY WORDS

PUBERTY
TANNER STAGES
JUNIOR HIGH/MIDDLE SCHOOL
PEER GROUP IDENTITY

Mrs. Martin sat self-consciously at one side of the waiting room. She had asked the receptionist if her (Mrs. Martin's) clothes looked okay to her because Jeremy had asked her on the way over why she always dressed so funny. Mrs. Martin wrote on the questionnaire sheet that she was concerned about Jeremy's posture and "early development." In the interview she said he had become "slumped," and she had found pictures of nude girls behind his bed. Jeremy, emerging from the opposite side of the waiting room, was wearing a black shirt emblazoned with a skull. He said his only concern was whether you did ear piercing in this office. He had grown 6 in. since his last visit.

This case represents common themes that the pubertal stage of development evoke in parent-child interactions. Associated with accelerated physical growth and the progression of secondary sexual characteristics, Jeremy is now identifying more with peers than his family. Symbols of that identification process take on a new importance. The more dramatic those symbols, often the greater the tensions between parent and child. His provocative shirt, desire for an earring, hidden pictures of nude girls, and criticism of his mother's appearance are clear and appropriate reflections of Jeremy's early adolescent development.

The pediatric clinician can be helpful by respecting Jeremy's separation process from his family. A positive comment on his chosen apparel may go far in cementing a therapeutic relationship. A few moments with Jeremy alone can be used to discuss pubertal change—physical and emotional—while exploring his own concerns. The desire for an earring should be discussed with regard to medical concerns about the procedure; his mother and Jeremy should be encouraged to explore the decision further. The clinician can help his mother by providing a developmental perspective; the earring is a concrete way for Jeremy to express his individuality and peer group identification. If the parents decide that this issue is not negotiable, a compromise might be struck by accepting one of Jeremy's wishes (e.g., a new haircut or piece of clothing).

At each moment during the visit, active listening skills and advice should be directed toward specific, predictable developmental tasks and milestones. This approach ensures nonjudgmental counseling and suggestions that can be tailored to a specific child and family.

Early adolescence, sometimes called preadolescence, is characterized by the onset of puberty with resulting body consciousness and the gradual emergence of independence from the family. It is an important transition time that calls for developmental work on the part of both parents and their growing youngsters. The tasks here are to understand and anticipate these changes and to support the young person in the gradual assumption of more autonomy.

PHYSICAL DEVELOPMENT

To understand the behavior of early adolescents, one must be familiar with the normal pattern of puberty and appreciate the dramatic physical changes that are a part of it (Tanner, 1962). Pubescence begins in most girls in the United States with the development of breast buds, sometime between the ages of 9 and 11 years; in most boys in the United States it begins with scrotal enlargement and lengthening of the penis, which occurs sometime between the ages of 10 and 12 years (Marshall and Tanner, 1970). The other signs of puberty then occur over the next 2 to 6 years after a well-described pattern that is summarized in Table 25–1 and Figure 25–1 (Marshall and Tanner, 1970). Until puberty, the only body changes most youngsters experience are quantitiative: steady increases in height and weight each year. These increases can be anticipated by youngsters. With puberty, physical changes are much more dramatic, much more rapid, and are qualitatively different from what had previously been

TABLE 25–1.
Maturational Staging Criteria for Secondary Sexual Characteristics*

Breast Stage	Female	
B1	No visible breast mound	
B2	Breast buds: a small amount of subareolar breast tissue	
B3	Amount of breast tissue increases	
B4	Nipple is distinct from areola; areola forms a mound above breast tissue	
B5	Areola recedes to the contour of breast	
Genitalia	Male	
G1	Infantile genitalia	
G2	Scrotal skin reddens and thins; testes increase in size; minimal or no enlargement of phallus	
G3	Continued enlargement of testes; phallus lengthens	
G4	Continued enlargement of testes; increased length and circumference of phallus and glans penis	
G5	Adult-sized testes (>20 cc) and adult-sized phallus; deeply pigmented scrotum	
Pubic Hair	Female	Male
PH1	No pubic hair	No pubic hair
PH2	Long, downy hair on labia majora	Long, downy hair at base of phallus
PH3	Coarse, curly hair in small amount on labia majora and mons pubis	Coarse, curly hair in small amount at base of phallus
PH4	Increased amount but not on median aspect of thighs	Increased amount, but not on median aspect of thighs
PH5	Triangular-shaped escutcheon; hair extends to median aspect of thighs	Triangular-shaped escutcheon; hair extends to median aspect of thighs

From Long TJ, Fitzpatrick SB, Reese JM, et al: *Curr Probl Pediatr* 1984; 14:1–50. Used by permission.

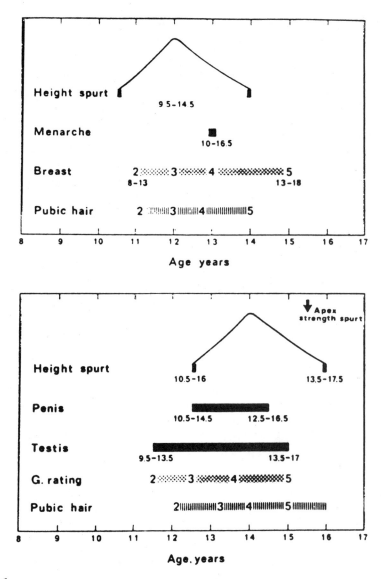

FIG 25–1.
Top, pattern of pubertal development of girls. **Bottom,** pattern of pubertal development of boys. (From Marshall WA, Tanner JM: *Arch Dis Child* 1970; 45:13–22. Used by permission.)

seen (Fujii and Felice, 1987). Height increases suddenly; hair becomes coarse and appears to grow where it never grew before; there are major changes in the distribution of body fat and musculature; skin becomes oily; apocrine glands begin to secrete; genitals enlarge; and breasts develop (Barnes, 1975; Daniel, 1985; Reiter and Grumbach, 1982). Furthermore, these physical changes may be asynchronous; that is, the body organs and subsystems may appear to grow at different rates, so that arms, legs, nose, or chin may seem to enlarge individually with no apparent respect for overall body harmony (Stone and Church, 1975). The youngster may not know what to anticipate next and may become very anxious about the seemingly out of control maturation he is experiencing. Mild acne may become a problem and may be fantasized as much worse than it really is; braces often become neccessary. Young adolescents may be unaware, or acutely aware, of the need for frequent bathing and the use of deodorants. This is a time for agonizing self-consciousness and painful sensitivity to one's bodily changes. For the health care provider, this means that the physical examination must be done with sensitivity and awareness of the young adolescent's shyness and perhaps exaggerated embarrassment (Felice, 1992, Felice and Friedman, 1982; Long et al., 1984). For example, the clinician should give clear directions concerning disrobing and gowning in preparation for a physical examination. If the physician expects underwear to be removed, he should say so. And, of course, the physical examination should be undertaken behind closed drapes or in an enclosed cubicle or room to protect the adolescent's privacy.

The young adolescent is well aware that not only is he changing but also his friends are changing. Not all youngsters grow at the same time or at the same rate. Hence, a seventh grade class picture may show 12-year-olds in all sizes and shapes. Youngsters are acutely aware of how *their* physical changes compare with their friends and harbor some anxiety about the comparison. Some youngsters feel that they are growing too fast or too slowly, too soon or too late (Gross and Duke, 1983). These apprehensions are most often revealed by nonverbal or obtuse patterns of communication. Hence, the girl whose breasts are developing more quickly than those of her peers may adopt a hunched posture in her development. The boy whose genitals are not quite as big as those of his friends may suddenly find excuses not to take gym or go to the locker room. It is not unusual for an adolescent to spend hours before a mirror or in the bathroom becoming acquainted with his own body and noting the changes that appear to take place on a daily basis. Even the youngster whose maturation keeps pace with his peers may feel out of step. This is the age of gangliness and gawkiness and feeling gauche. Although these youngsters may feel awkward, they often develop superb motor skills in some particular area or sport. Sometimes the changes that are observed are worrisome to the young teen, and they may harbor their own "explanatory model" for these events. For example, the pubertal boy who has gynecomastia may be alarmed that he is developing breasts like a girl or that he has breast cancer; the girl who has been inadequately prepared for menstruation may believe that her first period is a result of internal injury or a symptom of serious illness. *All young adolescents are concerned about their bodily changes,* whether they easily reveal this or not. It is important for the clinician to reach some of these concerns and subjective diagnoses. Correct and personal information provides the fuel for the young person to accept these changes and build a positive self-image. Specific affirmation of normal examination findings rather than a noncommittal "hmmm" or "it's normal" is very helpful at this stage. The narration of even normal findings during the physical examination demystifies the clinical encounter as it provides informative and valuable information.

SOCIAL AND SEXUAL DEVELOPMENT

As the young adolescent ponders the various changes taking place in his body, he begins to have an acute interest in sexual matters (Freud, 1975) but is not usually sexually active, nor does the young adolescent usually have a dating partner. As an 8-year-old, a youngster may scorn romantic movies as "mush" and be embarrassed or even disgusted to see a couple kissing or embracing. As a 12-year-old, the same youngster may be fascinated by such matters and may even be caught spying on older adolescent couples to learn from them. This is the age when parents may find "girlie" magazines hidden under an adolescent's bed. Parents usually are caught off guard by this "early" interest in sexual matters. They may interpret this interest as indicating that the child is sexually active. That anxiety may lead them to act more restrictively or punitively than they have in the past, feeling their own loss of control.

This is also the age when adolescents may begin to masturbate or have nocturnal emissions ("wet dreams"). There are many myths concerning masturbation (e.g., masturbation causes blindness, acne, or hairy hands), and young adolescents need reassurance that those myths are indeed wrong. Occasionally a male adolescent may be frightened by the occurrence of wet dreams because the event happens beyond his control or because he believes the emission is the result of an infectious disease. Similarly, about 6 months before menarche, the female adolescent may begin to have a vaginal leukorrhea, which typically appears as a clear, mucoid discharge in her underpants. Both she and her parents may be alarmed at this occurrence, erroneously believing that she has a sexually transmitted disease.

Anxiety concerning sexuality may prevent parents from supporting the other developmental task of early adolescence, the emergence of independence from the family. During latency, youngsters generally identify strongly with their own families and role model after their own parents. With adolescence, youngsters have an appropriate psychological need to separate from their parents and establish their own identities as individuals (Erikson, 1968). It is important to be known as Bobby Jones, rather than "Mr. Jones's son." In most young adolescents, this is generally accomplished quietly without open rebellion through the media of clothes, hair, music, and the increased importance of close friends. However, in some families, this process may still pose difficulties. For example, parents of close-knit families are often bewildered and hurt that 12-year-old Johnny prefers to be with his friends than to join in family activities. Parents become entrapped in futile and potentially harmful arguments about clothes, cosmetics, and other superficial matters. They cannot risk letting go at all for fear of loss of all influence and control. This struggle recalls that of an earlier era, the second year of life. Then the bids for independence heralded the transition from infancy to childhood; now these bids are renewed as the child begins the journey from childhood to adulthood. Most parents need that perspective clearly laid out.

As the adolescent separates from his parents, he turns to his peer group. This provides a safe psychological shelter for growth outside the family. The peer group also provides a sounding board against which the young teen can test his ideas, and it serves as a barometer against which he can compare his own physical and psychological growth. In other words, the peer group provides an important supportive structure to the adolescent's psychosocial development. Most adolescents have "a number of friends, with whom they spend considerable time and share a variety of interests and activities" (Weiner, 1990). The adolescent must move away from his family, and a prerequisite for this step is the support of a peer group. The adolescent often needs to define the differences between what his friends say or do and what the family's position is on any issue. However oddly they might view them, most adolescents do not hate their parents or view their home as an unpleasant place.

In early adolescence, the peer group generally consists of members of the same gender.

The girl's peer group usually consists of two or three friends with whom she shares every intimate detail of her day (Faust, 1960). Boys usually belong to a larger group that is often informally considered a boyhood "gang." This same gang in childhood often had a secret meeting place, a secret code or password, or other rituals that were hidden from outsiders, particularly adults (Mannarino, 1979). As young adolescents, the secret codes may no longer exist, but some rituals or habits may persist, for example, meeting at the same place each day at certain times.

Members of the peer group often dress exactly alike, even to the last detail. Girls spend hours on the telephone checking one another's planned outfits for any given occasion. Boys often wear similar jackets emblazoned with a team name or T-shirts with the same inscription or insignia. Haircuts are alike. To verify these statements, an individual need only to visit a shopping mall for the afternoon and observe a group of youngsters walking by. The tendency to dress alike continues through all of adolescence but is most exaggerated in early adolescence. It signals the important work of separation and peer-group identification, and in that sense it is an indicator of developmental progress. Social isolation or alienation is not normal.

Early adolescents are usually in junior high school (seventh, eighth, and ninth grades). For most seventh graders, this is a completely new social experience. Junior high is a completely different milieu from elementary school, and the youngster must adapt to the home room structure, to changing classes and to a variable homework load and testing schedules (Simmons et al., 1979). This may be the first time that a young person is exposed to children outside his own neighborhood. He may meet others of different races, religions, and socio-economic status. These new experiences may make him uncomfortable. Most young people make this transition with minimal anxiety, tempered by the comfort of knowing that one's grade-school companions are in the same predicament. Those youngsters who must attend a new school with all new classmates may be more anxious and frightened. For example, this anxiety may manifest as psychosomatic complaints, school avoidance, or school difficulties. Hence, all adolescents with school dysfunction must have a social, as well as physical, neurological, and academic, evaluation (Cannon and Compton, 1980). Junior high "transition" should last weeks, not months. Continuing school difficulty must be taken seriously and evaluated broadly.

COGNITIVE DEVELOPMENT

Because of the assumption of pseudoadult mannerisms or the emulation of older models, it is easy for both parents and clinicians to overestimate the cognitive abilities of young adolescents (Elkind, 1967, 1978). When evaluating a child in early adolescence, one must realize that 11-year-olds usually think concretely; that is, they do not yet have the cognitive ability to think abstractly, to develop contingency plans, to conceptualize. They may still be in Piaget's concrete operational stage of cognitive development and may still have difficulty in organizing large bodies of data or inferential tasks (Piaget, 1969; see Chapter 2). This means that they may not relate present actions with future consequences. This has important implications for health care counseling and the management of illness and treatment regimens. In addition, physicians who care for young adolescents frequently proclaim that they are difficult to interview because they answer questions with only monosyllabic answers. This probably means that the physician is not being specific enough for a concrete-thinking youngster. For example, instead of saying, "Tell me about yourself," the clinician may be more successful in saying, "Tell me what you do on the soccer team." Because of limitations in conceptualization, young adolescents may be unable to sustain lengthy verbal interviews (Felice and Vargish, 1984). Other youngsters may view a physician's questions as a test and interpret the medical interview as an examination at school, with right or wrong answers. In those instances, the physician may glean more information by interacting with the young teen by playing checkers or drawing pictures. Some children 11 to 12 years old may "talk" more freely in such a play environment. In addition, the young adolescent may be more able to describe specific behaviors, beliefs, and attitudes in her peer group than in herself. The clinician will do well to respect these distancing maneuvers, and may even use those approaches in his own data gathering.

DATA GATHERING

Components to be included in the examination of the child in early adolescence are presented in Table 25–2.

SPECIAL REFERRALS

1. Adolescent girls who have not begun breast development by the age of 14 years should be carefully evaluated for pubertal delay.

2. Boys who have not begun pubertal development by the age of 16 years should be evaluated for pubertal delay.

3. Boys or girls who do not follow the *pattern* of pubertal development may need endocrine evaluation (e.g., menstruation before breast development).

4. Adolescents in this age group should be seen annually to mark progression along physical and psychosocial maturation growth curves.

5. Families that are in prolonged conflict during this time may need another session to identify areas of disagreement and to put the patterns of mutual respect in negotiation. Family counseling may be indicated in some cases. Some turbulence is expected in all families, but a decline in functioning or prolonged conflict is not to be expected.

6. Children who are adjusting poorly to middle or junior high school after 6 weeks may need special psychological or educational assessments, tutoring in special areas, or counseling to assist in social interactions. Declining school performance should never be attributed to benign causes.

7. Youngsters who do not have a peer group of friends need careful psychological or psychiatric evaluation. This signals significant social isolation and this is a serious matter.

ANTICIPATORY GUIDANCE

FOR THE ADOLESCENT

FURTHER PHYSICAL DEVELOPMENT

Young teenagers need much reassurance concerning their bodies. Explain the pattern of physical and sexual maturation to each youngster. For example, if a girl has not begun to

TABLE 25-2.
Components of Examination (Early Adolescence)

What to Observe	Objective
Interactions between adolescent/parent	To assess whether they communicate well or if the mother/father answers all the questions for the adolescent or allows the youngster to answer for himself; these interactions may reveal the status of the separation process
The adolescent's willingness to be interviewed and/or examined alone without parental presence	To determine the adolescent's willingness to begin to act independently from his parents

What to Ask	Objective
Inquire about the young adolescent's school and school activities (e.g., "Tell me what happens to you on an average day at school. What is your favorite class? Why is that class so special? Who is your favorite teacher? What's so special about that teacher? Is yours a friendly or a not so friendly school? If you were having difficulty in school to whom would you go to talk? How far away from your home is your school?")	To determine if the youngster is in the right grade for his age and to begin the interview on generally neutral grounds To assess the youngster's attitude toward school
Inquire about the adolescent's function with a peer group (e.g., "Do you have a best friend? What is his name and age? What kind of things do you do together? What's so special about Tommy? How long have your known him? Do you ever spend time at each other's homes? Do you ever stay overnight in the other's home? Do you and Tommy belong to a group of friends? How long have you known these friends? What do you do together? Is there another group you wished you belonged to, but do not?")	To determine whether the youngster belongs to a peer group and if this group is perceived as supportive
Inquire about the adolescent's function in his family (e.g., "Are you the oldest or youngest? What's it like being the oldest, youngest, or only child in your family? Do you have your own room? What kind of duties do you have around the house? Who are you closest to in your family—your mother or father, brother or sister? What do you do if you become angry? What happens in your family if someone is angry with you? How are you punished?")	To determine whether the patient is beginning to develop independence from the family; to assess this child's role in the family; to assess patterns of interaction within the family from the youngster's perspective
Inquire about the adolescent's feelings about himself and his body (e.g., "In your class, are you the tallest, shortest, or in between? What is it like being the tallest or shortest in your class? As most young people grow up, their bodies change . . . is there anything about your body's changes that has you worried? Is there anything about yourself that you wish were different?")	To determine the youngster's concerns about his body; to determine the youngster's information base about the physical changes that are taking place or will soon occur

Continued.

TABLE 25-2.—*Continued*

Physical Assessment	Objective
Height, weight	To have a baseline to mark the adolescent's percentile on a growth chart
Blood pressure	As a baseline to rule out hypertension if it develops later
Tanner maturational staging (see Table 25–1 and Fig 25–1)	To determine baseline and progress for physical maturation
Check carefully for scoliosis	Scoliosis is most apparent during the adolescent growth spurt and should be carefully assessed as early as possible in this phase of development
Note the presence of gynecomastia in boys	Gynecomastia is common in pubertal boys and is generally a source of concern
Careful palpation of thyroid gland	Adolescent goiter is common and may be pronounced in this age group

Psychosocial Assessments	Objective
The adolescent's comfort during the physical examination	To assess the adolescent's feelings concerning his body
Affect regarding this visit (anger, fear, anxiety, sulking)	May help explain responses/actions in this patient
The report of the importance of peer group; the style of hair or dress	To assess the important identification with a peer group

menstruate but has begun breast development, the clinician can outline for her the expected pattern of growth, including approximate time of menarche. The physician may say, "Mary, I notice that you have begun to develop as a young woman. Have you been wondering what happens next?"or "Jack, when I did your physical examination, I noticed that you are starting to have pubic hair. Have you wondered what would happen next?"

MENSTRUATION

All girls should receive an explanation of menstruation whether they have started menses or not. It is usually helpful to ask the teenager what she already knows about menstrual periods and then build on her knowledge. It is important that young women be exposed to a *positive* attitude toward menstrual periods rather than a negative attitude. Pamphlets do not substitute for personal counseling by the health provider within the context of an interaction.

MASTURBATION AND NOCTURNAL EMISSIONS

Adolescent boys may need reassurance concerning masturbation and nocturnal emissions, but it may be inappropriate and embarrassing to *directly* ask a young teen about these issues. It is usually more helpful to say, "Many boys your age start to notice more sexual urges now than they did when they were younger. Sometimes these urges occur at night, resulting in a sticky, white discharge in their pajamas. I don't know if this has happened to you yet, but I want you to know that this is normal."

PUBERTAL DEVELOPMENT OF THE OPPOSITE SEX

Both boys and girls may be ignorant of the development of the opposite sex. Others may be too embarrassed to ask questions concerning this area. It is usually helpful to say, "What have you learned at school about the changes that boys (or girls) experience at your age? Is this something you'd like to learn more about?" A brief explanation is usually sufficient accompanied by pamphlets to take with them.

FOR PARENTS

PUBERTAL DEVELOPMENT

Parents should be informed when a youngster has begun the process of puberty, a fact that may not be obvious to the parent. A simple explanation concerning the expected progression of pubertal development is usually appreciated by most parents, with specific emphasis on those matters that will be most noticeable to parents rather than to someone outside the family. For example, let parents know that when doing the laundry, they may notice leukorrhea in a girl's underpants for 4 to 6 months before the onset of menarche. This knowledge will enable the mother to be prepared for a girl's menarche to occur, so that sanitary pads or tampons will be available. Sexual interest is appropriate and does not necessarily indicate sexual activity. Assumptions of inappropriate behavior may become a self-fulfilling prophecy.

NEED FOR PRIVACY

Parents need to be informed that with the onset of puberty, young adolescents must have privacy to be by themselves. This is best accomplished by allowing the teen to have his own room; if this is not possible, he should have his own section of a room where he can go and be by himself and not be bothered by older or younger siblings or by parents.

SENSITIVITY TO TEASING

Parents should be advised that it is not appropriate to tease youngsters about their pubertal development. Most teenagers are exquisitely self-conscious about their development and may be acutely embarrassed by this teasing. This advice is best given by asking a parent about his or her own early adolescent days. In that context, most parents will recall their own self-consciousness and be more likely to be more sensitive to their own child's needs. Siblings' comments may need to be restrained.

QUEST FOR INDEPENDENCE

Parents must be reassured that the teenager's quest for independence is normal and should not be interpreted as parental rejection by the adolescent. Give parents examples of this situation, such as (1) young teenagers may not want to join the family on all family outings, and (2) young teens may not want the parents around the school or at social functions in a chaperone capacity. If possible, another authority figure may do better; (3) young teens may begin to confide in an adult outside the family rather than in mothers or fathers as in previous years; and (4) parents should avoid arguments about trivial things. It is best to concentrate on basic hygiene, physical safety, and school attendance.

REFERENCES

Barnes HV: Physical growth and development during puberty. *Med Clin North Am* 1975; 59:1305–1317.

Cannon IP, Compton CL: School dysfunction in the adolescent. *Pediatr Clin North Am* 1980; 27:79–96.

Daniel WA Jr: Growth of adolescence. *Semin Adolesc Med* 1:1985;15–24.

Elkind D: Cognitive structure and adolescent experience. *Adolescence* 1967; 2:427–434.

Elkind D: Understanding the young adolescent. *Adolescence* 1978; 13:127–134.

Erikson EH: *Identity, Youth and Crisis.* New York, WW Norton & Co, 1968.

Faust M: Developmental maturity as a determinant of prestige in adolescent girls. *Child Dev* 1960; 31:173–184.

Felice ME: Adolescence, in Levine MD, Carey WB, Crocker AC (eds): *Developmental-Behavioral Pediatrics.* Philadelphia, WB Saunders Co, 1992.

Felice ME, Friedman SB: Behavioral considerations in the health care of adolescents. *Pediatr Clin North Am* 1982; 29:399–412.

Felice ME, Vargish W: Interviewing and evaluation of adolescents, in Kelley VE (ed): *Practice of Pediatrics.* New York, Harper & Row Publishers, 1984.

Freud S: The transformation of puberty, in Esman AH (ed): *Psychology of Adolescence.* New York, International Universities Press, 1975, pp 86–99.

Fujii CM, Felice ME. Physical growth and development: current concepts. *Primary Care* 1987; 14:1–12.

Gross RT, Duke PM: Effects of early versus late physical maturation on adolescent behavior, in Levine MD, Carey WB, Crocker AC (eds): *Developmental-Behavioral Pediatrics.* Philadelphia, WB Saunders Co, 1983.

Long TJ, Fitzpatrick, SB, Reese JM, et al: Basic issues in adolescent medicine. *Curr Probl Pediatr* 1984; 14:1–50

Mannarino AP: The interactional process in pre-adolescent friendships. *Psychiatry* 1979; 41:308–312.

Marshall WA, Tanner JM: Variations in the pattern of pubertal changes in boys. *Arch Dis Child* 1970; 45:13–22.

Piaget J: The intellectual development of the adolescent, in Caplan G, Levovici S (eds): *Adolescence: Psychosocial Perspective.* New York, Basic Books, 1969, pp 22–26.

Reiter EO, Grumbach MM: Neuroendocrine control mechanisms and the onset of puberty. *Annu Rev Physiol* 1982; 44:595–613.

Simmons RG, Blyth DA, Van Cleave EF, et al: Entry into early adolescence: The impact of school structure, puberty and early dating on self-esteem. *Am Sociol Rev* 1979; 44:948–967.

Stone LJ, Church J: Pubescence, puberty, and physical development, in Esman AH (ed): *Psychology of Adolescence.* New York, International Universities Press, 1975, pp 75–85.

Tanner JM: *Growth at Adolescence,* ed, 2. Boston, Blackwell Scientific Publications, 1962.

Weiner IB: Distinguishing healthy from disturbed adolescent development. *J Dev Behav Pediatr* 1990; 11:151–154.

"My friend." By Steven Fitz, age 15.

CHAPTER 26

Fourteen to Sixteen Years: Mid-adolescence — The Dating Game

MARIANNE E. FELICE, M.D.

KEY WORDS

SEXUAL IDENTITY
DATING
PROMISCUITY
PEER INTERACTION
DELINQUENCY

The major developmental task of mid-adolescence, approximately the ages of 14 to 16 years, is the achievement of sexual identity (Felice, 1992). This means becoming comfortable with one's sexuality, as well as learning to express sexual feelings in an appropriate manner and to receive sexual advances from another in a comfortable way. It means the assumption of culturally defined sexual roles, including behaviors and activities.

THE REFINEMENT OF THE SELF-IMAGE

For the adolescent to become comfortable with his sexuality, he must be comfortable with his body. Most mid-adolescents have already experienced puberty, but they may not yet be comfortable with the results (Lohner, 1987). Hence, both mid-adolescent girls and boys spend much time, money, and energy trying to improve their faces and figures. Girls usually experiment with makeup, and both sexes experiment with clothing styles in an effort to "try on" different images and find the real self. It would not be surprising to observe a 15-year-old adolescent girl in pigtails at one medical visit and see her wearing a sophisticated hairstyle 2 weeks later at another visit. This experimentation is evidence of developmental work.

The emphasis on bodily development is one part of the pervasive self-centeredness of many mid-adolescent teenagers (Lohner, 1987). Because *they* are spending so much time thinking and looking at themselves, they presume that others are thinking and looking at them as well. This preoccupation with self may seem to border on paranoia, hysteria, or frank narcissism, but it is completely normal. One example of this self-centered behavior is easily observed by watching a group of same-sex adolescents in a public place being approached by a group of adolescents of the opposite sex. Each teenager acts and feels like all attention is on him or her, that everybody is looking directly and completely at him or her. No wonder then that so much effort is spent on the development of an image! This self-centeredness and heightened self-awareness may account for the hair grooming, clothes straightening, and makeup activities that continually take place in any gathering of mid-adolescents.

SOCIAL DEVELOPMENT

The supportive approval and the combined efforts of the peer group fuel self-confidence under the imagined scrutiny of the opposite sex. Even when not dating, adolescents benefit from interactions with members of the opposite sex as they learn to expand the peer group from a unisexual group to a heterosexual one, from a local neighborhood clique to selected groups with individuals of similar interests or talents. Frequently these interactions are initiated through school-based activities such as team sports, clubs, academic societies, or elected positions. In these organizations, the mid-adolescent has the opportunity to socialize even when not actually dating. For some teens, this is a safer, more comfortable environment than a formal dating situation. Not only are relationships with members of the opposite sex expanded, but all relationships outside the family are expanded. Mid-adolescents, typically high school sophomores and juniors, usually make some new friends of the same sex, frequently develop a strong attachment to one or two adults, and begin to care about and for younger children. These are important interactions and expose mid-adolescents in depth to life-styles and philosophies different from their own families. During mid-adolescence, teens may begin to try on these different lifestyles in dress, manner of speech, and political viewpoints to the chagrin of parents. But these excursions are normal developmental explorations, and by young adulthood, adolescents usually have political and philosophical opinions similar to those of their parents. In fact, for most adolescents, constant conflict and recurrent turmoil are the exception rather than the rule (Offer et al., 1989), and most adolescents love and respect their parents in spite of disagreements about everyday issues (Weiner, 1990).

SEXUAL DEVELOPMENT

It is sometimes stated that sexual and aggressive drives may be stronger during adolescence than at any other time of life. Learning to express and control these drives is a major and formidable task of the teenage years, and the need to master these drives is most acutely felt during the mid-adolescent years, a time when the individual may seem least equipped to control them. Responding to strong biological sexual drives, most mid-adolescents begin to date members of the opposite sex (Coles and Stokes, 1985). However, one characteristic of mid-adolescent sexuality is that the opposite sex is often viewed as a sex object, and both boys and girls may see the relationship as an opportunity for social gain (Lohner, 1987). The degree of attractiveness of one's sexual partner provides an important measure of one's own self-worth.

Most mid-adolescents engage in some aspect of sexual experimentation, the extent of which varies from one socioeconomic group to another and one subcultural group to another. In the 1970s, the mean age of coitarche among unmarried females was reported to be 15.5 years for blacks and 16.4 years for whites (Zelnick and Kantner, 1980) but these ages may be lower for all racial groups in the 1990s because young adolescents (15 years or younger) are engaging in premarital sexual intercourse in increasing numbers, and there is no evidence that this trend is decreasing (Hofferth et al., 1987). In spite of these alarming figures, one cannot presume that all mid-adolescents are sexually active, but one can assume that all mid-adolescents are interested in sexual issues.

Some adolescents are homosexual (Remafedi, 1987), but survey questionnaires of large numbers of adolescents of all ages indicate that few mid-adolescents claim to be homosexual (Coles and Stokes, 1985) at this time. These data are in contrast to interviews with adult homosexual men and lesbian women who acknowledge that even in their youth they knew that they were different from their same-sex adolescent peers in their sexual preferences (Marmon, 1976). This apparent discrepancy may exist because many mid-adolescents may not realize or are not able to admit that they are homosexual. This realization may not be faced until late adolescence (Stewart, 1987). In the process of establishing sexual identity, many adolescents normally wonder if they are homosexual. It is common for adolescent girls to develop crushes on girlfriends or women teachers, and it is certainly not unusual for adolescent boys to experience an erection in the company of other males. Such experiences happen frequently and do not indicate that an adolescent is necessarily lesbian or homosexual. With time, the teenager's sexual preference will become clear.

With the knowledge that mid-adolescents are heavily invested in sexual identity, the clinician must be capable and willing to discuss sexual issues with the adolescent patient (Felice and Vargish, 1984). This means that the clinician must be comfortable with his own sexuality and comfortable with and knowledgeable of the subject of sex. Clinicians must be aware of their own limitations and biases in this area and must try not to impose their biases on the adolescent patient.

It is essential to take a sexual history from every adolescent. Although one may ask adolescents directly if they are sexually active, such an approach may be viewed warily. Incorporating questions about sexuality into the review of systems (e.g., menstruation, the genitourinary system) is usually more helpful (Stewart, 1987). Adolescents should be asked questions about sexuality only in private and not in the presence of parents. All adolescents should be assured of confidentiality concerning sexual matters, and the clinician should be aware of the laws governing informed consent and treatment of minors without parental consent in the local community. Many states now permit clinicians to provide health care to teenagers for contraception, the diagnosis and treatment of sexually transmitted disease, the diagnosis of pregnancy, the treatment of abortion, and, in some states, the treatment for drug use and abuse without parental knowledge or consent. Because these laws vary from one community to another, it is important that the physician know what the regulations regarding the treatment of minors are in a particular locale.

COGNITIVE AND MORAL DEVELOPMENT

Another characteristic of mid-adolescents is progress in cognitive growth. Most mid-adolescents have developed the capacity for abstraction and are usually capable of introspection. In other words, they can think about thinking and can now reflect on their own thought processes in an "objective" manner. This stage of cognitive development is known as *formal operational thinking* and is a giant step in mental development (Piaget, 1969). The mid-adolescent may become fascinated with his newfound intellectual tool, and this aspect of growth may be another factor contributing to the self-centeredness of mid-adolescence, because they can now think about themselves thinking (Elkind, 1967). A marvelous sense of self-cleverness may contribute to a positive self-image or a slight disdain for the archaic thought processes of adults.

With the development of conceptualization, adolescents have new capacities for moral decision making (Kohlberg and Gilligan, 1972). In younger years, children are in a stage of moral growth in which good behavior results in reward and misbehavior results in punishment. Hence, good or bad is determined solely by physical consequences. A second level of morality is marked by the need to meet the expectations or follow the rules of one's family, peer group, or nation. In fact, maintaining the rules of the group becomes a value in itself. The third stage of moral development consists of a major thrust toward autonomous moral principles that have validity apart from the authority of the group and is based on the individual's own beliefs and conclusions concerning what is right or wrong. This is called *adult morality*. This last stage of morality usually begins in mid-adolescence. The mid-adolescent may be capable of making moral judgments based on the principles of a moral code, but, unfortunately, the self-centered behavior of mid-adolescents also results in a narcissistic value system, "what is right is what makes me feel good," "what is right is what I want." This self-centered attitude partially explains the sexual exploitation described previously. Indeed, many activities during the mid-adolescent years may be impulsive, with little thought about consequences. Hence, cognitive capacities may be superseded by other psychosocial processes.

COUNSELING PARENTS

During the child's mid-adolescent years, the physician may begin to see the adolescent patient regularly without the parent's presence, but this does not mean that the role of the parent is unimportant. Indeed, the mid-adolescent years are considered the "heart" of adolescence and may be the most difficult time period for parents to face (Leiman and Strasburger, 1985). Children in the mid-adolescent years are characteristically ambivalent about their relationship with their parents as they struggle with self-identity. Having already progressed through *early* adolescence, they have declared their need for independence in one way or another. But being wiser than their younger selves, they realize that complete independence from parents may be frightening. So, typically, the mid-adolescent "flirts" with a close relationship with his parents, sometimes asking for help and at other times rejecting all offers of assistance for fear that the parents' assistance will engulf him and suffocate his independence. This ambivalence is normal. Parents must realize that to be of most benefit to a teenager, they must remain a constant and consistent figure, willing to be a sounding board for the youngster's ideas without overtaking and dominating the mid-teen. Mid-adolescents must learn to think through problems to evolve solutions, and parents are a valuable resource to assist in that task.

DATA GATHERING

Components to be included in examination of a child in the mid-adolescent period are outlined in Table 26–1.

TABLE 26–1.
Components of Examination (Mid-Adolescence)

What to Observe	Objective
The relationship between the teen and his parent if the parent accompanies the teen to the physician.	To determine the nature of the relationship and interactions between the mid-adolescent and the parent
Who made the appointment?	Knowing this may explain some of the adolescent's behavior/attitude during the interview and examination
Dress and clothing style of the patient.	Observing clothing styles of the adolescent may give insight into how he sees himself at the present time

What to Ask	Objective
Ask how the adolescent is doing in school (e.g., in what activities is he engaged? Does the patient belong to any clubs or is he/she involved in sports? What is the most fun about being in school? Who is the favorite teacher and why? What are the social activities that take place at school? Are there any areas at school that give the patient difficulties?)	To determine the adolescent's perception and function in the school setting as well as involvement with a social group
Ask about the adolescent's function in the family, e.g., "Are you involved in many activities with your family? Do you accompany the family on many outings? What are your responsibilities around the house? Most adolescents have curfews, do you? Do you feel that your parents are fair in their treatment of you concerning dating and outside events? Most adolescents and their parents disagree on certain issues . . . what issues do you and your parents disagree on? What do you do if you disagree with your father or mother on a certain issue? Who are you closest to in your family?"	To determine relationships in the family
Ask questions about the peer group and dating, e.g., "Do you have a best friend? How long have you been friends? What kind of activities do you do together? Do most of your friends have a steady boyfriend or girlfriend? How are your friends different from you? Do you have a steady boyfriend or many boyfriends? Some teenagers your age have begun to be sexually active—what are most of your friends doing about sexual activity? Have you ever felt forced to have sex when you didn't want to? Many adolescents today find that at school they are exposed to drug usage—is this true at your school? What are most of your friends doing about drugs? Have you ever felt that you were forced to take drugs when you didn't want to?"	To determine the adolescent's function in his peer group and his comfort with dating/sexual issues
Ask about the adolescent's feelings about himself. ("Most young people your age have experienced a lot of changes in their bodies. Are you satisfied with the way your body has turned out? Is there anything about yourself you wish you could change?")	To determine the adolescent's comfort with himself

Continued.

TABLE 26-1.—*Continued*

Physical Assessment	Objective
Height and weight	To follow the progress on a growth curve
Blood pressure	Essential hypertension often begins in adolescence
Sexual maturation by Tanner staging (most mid-adolescents are Tanner III–V)	To mark progress on the maturational curve

Psychological Assessment	Objective
Comfort during the physical examination	To determine the adolescent's comfort with his adultlike body
Maturity of answers to questions (e.g., monosyllabic responses to questions vs. complete sentences, or even paragraphs; formal thinking; moral dilemma)	To determine cognitive development

SPECIAL REFERRALS

THE PROMISCUOUS TEENAGER

Although many teenagers are sexually active, sexual activity is usually confined to one partner at a time and is an expression of affection. Adolescents who have multiple partners at the same time are outside normal behavior. Promiscuity may be a sign of difficulties in the adolescent's life and may be the means by which an adolescent tells the adults around her that she is having difficulties. For example, an adolescent girl with very poor self-esteem and self-image may seek many sexual partners to affirm that she is attractive, or a young woman who is not getting along well at home may deliberately flaunt her newfound sexual prowess in an effort to antagonize her parents. In other words, sexual intercourse may be used for nonsexual reasons such as hostility, rebellion, self-destruction, or a search for comfort and love (Cohen and Friedman, 1975). And although this may be true of any teenager involved in a sexual relationship, these are almost always factors in promiscuous teens.

THE ADOLESCENT WHO IS A LONER

Adolescents should be involved in a peer group and engage in multiple social activities. Those who do not belong to a peer group (e.g., choir at school, chess club, organized sports, dating regularly) are defined as loners and are worrisome. Adolescents who are loners may be very depressed and at risk for suicide (Hodgman, 1990); they may be involved in truancy and drugs (AAP, 1988); or they may be in early stages of psychosis because adult forms of schizophrenia may begin to manifest themselves in mid- to late adolescence (Weiner, 1990).

DECLINE IN SCHOOL PERFORMANCE

Adolescents whose grades deteriorate from usual should not be viewed lightly. Reasons for declining grades, such as a learning disability (Black, 1987), drug use or abuse (AAP, 1988), or clinical psychosis (Weiner, 1990), should be investigated. Poor grades in high school may be the first clue to emotional disturbance, because such youth often begin to think in strange ways during the mid-adolescent years (Weiner, 1990). These maladaptive thought processes may interfere with cognitive function to such an extent that a young person is unable to sustain his usual grades.

SERIOUS DELINQUENT BEHAVIOR

Adolescents who are in trouble with the law need careful evaluation (Weiner, 1990). Although many adolescents are arrested each year, most offenses are minor and are not repeated. Minor offenses (e.g., stealing hubcaps) by young adolescents may not signify a major psychosocial problem and might reflect the young adolescent's struggle with independence and peer group approval. Even at a young age, this behavior should not be ignored. But young people who commit major crimes against people or property may be having severe difficulties, including sociopathic tendencies.

ANTICIPATORY GUIDANCE FOR THE ADOLESCENT

ISSUES RELATING TO SEXUAL ACTIVITY

SEXUAL INTERCOURSE

It is not unusual for adolescents to have questions about the sexual act, although they may be embarrassed about making the inquiry or about what terminology to use. Young people who are unskilled in love-making may not know whether their experiences are normal. They may simply need information about anatomy or physiology, or they may actually require counseling concerning sexual dysfunction. To discuss sexual intercourse with adolescents, the clinician must be comfortable with the topic itself and with her own sexuality.

SEXUALLY TRANSMITTED DISEASE

The incidence of sexually transmitted disease in adolescents has grown to epidemic levels (Cates, 1990). Gonorrhea, chlamydia, syphilis, genital herpes, genital warts, and acquired immunodeficiency syndrome are the sexually transmitted diseases of greatest current importance. Adolescents should be informed about the different types of sexually transmitted diseases and instructed to recognize signs in themselves or their sexual partner. Many clinicians find it helpful to have pamphlets in the waiting and examining rooms for adolescents to take home and read. These do not substitute for the clinician's direct invitation for questions in this area or an open attitude on these issues. Condom use is to be encouraged to prevent disease spread, particularly HIV.

BIRTH CONTROL

The words "birth control" have different connotations for different adolescents. To some it simply means the birth control pill. When an adolescent girl requests birth control pills, it may signify that she has already been sexually active for many months (Zelnik et al., 1979). Any inquiry should be met with a positive response. The adolescent should be commended for taking responsibility for her actions. It is usually helpful to have a contraceptive kit available to use in discussions with both teenage girls and boys. The kit should include various forms of contraception: condom, foam, intrauterine device (IUD), diaphragm, and birth control pills. The physician or nurse should calmly discuss the pros and cons of each form of contraception. Sometimes teenagers know immediately what they want to use, but others are more timid and need to talk it over with a boyfriend or girlfriend. It is inappropriate to push a teenager into accepting one form of contraception or another or to demand that a teenager use contraception. After a contraception discussion, it is often helpful to arrrange for a follow-up visit in 7 to 10 days so that the adolescent may express his or her wishes concerning contraception. It is often enlightening to invite the teenager to bring his girlfriend or her boyfriend to the health care provider for the follow-up appointment. The discussion of birth control should be seen in the broader context of individual decision making, taking responsibility for one's actions, and planning for the future. These developmental skills have obvious applicability in many areas.

TEENAGE PREGNANCY

Many times, a mid-adolescent girl will be seen by the clinician for the first time when she is actually pregnant. The physician should be prepared to make the diagnosis of pregnancy and to discuss the adolescent's options with her. All options should be presented to the adolescent, who should be encouraged to make her own decision through information provided by the clinician. It is always the adolescent's decision as to what to do about pregnancy, not the physician's. She should be encouraged to discuss the pregnancy with her parents, and this can often be done in the physician's office. The clinician may play an important mediator role in this setting. The teenager should also be encouraged to discuss her pregnancy with the father of the baby to explore his wishes.

ISSUES RELATING TO GOOD HEALTH HABITS

ROUTINE PAPANICOLAOU SMEAR

When teenagers become sexually active, it is a good time to instill good health habits concerning their own bodies. Those girls who are sexually active should have a yearly Papanicolaou (Pap) smear (Emans and Goldstein, 1982). The purpose of the Pap should be explained in simple language, not to scare a teenager but to educate her about her body and to encourage her to take responsibility for it.

BREAST EXAMINATION

Most mid-adolescent girls have reached Tanner stage IV breast development and are ready to be taught to do a breast self-examination (Cromer, 1989). Although breast cancer is uncommon in teenage girls, this practice instills good health habits at an early age and supports the process of being comfortable with one's own body. Show the girl what her breast feels like by having her palpate her breast after you. To explain what an abnormal lump will feel like, have her place her tongue in her cheek and feel her face over that area; that firm rubbery lump is very much like an abnormal breast mass. Models are available from medical supply houses.

TESTICULAR EXAMINATION

Testicular cancer is very rare, but when it does occur, it often occurs in the adolescent male. Hence, boys should be taught the testicular self-examination (Klein et al., 1990) and instructed that if they find lumps or bumps on the testis or in the scrotal sac, they should have an immediate checkup by a physician. This discussion itself acknowledges and verifies a new attitude toward the genitalia.

DRUGS, CIGARETTES, AND ALCOHOL

Although children are exposed to drugs even in grade school, the pressure to use drugs is not usually as threatening as it is in mid-adolescence. When adolescents begin dating, they may also begin substance use and misuse. Many adolescents experiment with drugs and alcohol (AAP, 1988), but they may be reluctant to admit using these substances if an authority figure asks them directly. Sometimes it is productive to ask about peer group usage of substances rather than about the individual teen's use. In spite of the information available on the risks of heavy cigarette smoking, about 20% of high school students smoke cigarettes daily and the proportion of young women who smoke has steadily increased (Miller and Slap, 1989). It is usually not helpful to lecture to the adolescent about substance abuse and alcohol and cigarette use. Rather, it is helpful to provide factual information usually related to health (e.g., the adolescent girl who wishes birth control pills should be informed that smoking increases her risk for strokes and is a reason to stop). Although it is common for adolescents to experiment with alcohol and marijuana, it is not normal for adolescents to be habitually drunk or "stoned," and it is not normal for adolescents to use "hard drugs" such as cocaine, phencyclidine (PCP), or amphetamines. When adolescents do admit to using alcohol or drugs, it is appropriate to ask frequency and amount. The experienced clinician will usually double or quadruple the figure given. Some symptoms of drug abuse are a drop in school performance, truancy, and stealing money (often from parents) to purchase drugs. These youngsters need special help (AAP, 1988). Adolescents who abuse drugs should be referred for drug counseling by mental health workers experienced in drug counseling of youth. Frequently this requires residential treatment, and pediatricians should become familiar with drug rehabilitation agencies in their area of practice. Drug usage that alters a youngster's functioning cannot be dealt with in an ordinary pediatric office setting.

ACCIDENT PREVENTION

AUTOMOBILES

The mid-adolescent is usually a newly licensed or about to be licensed driver and, as such, is inexperienced in the skill of driving. The physician may inquire whether the teenager has a driver's license or plans to obtain one and whether the teenager has taken a driver's education course. It is doubtful whether a discussion on automobile safety between the teenage patient and the physician is useful in preventing automobile accidents, but most sensitive adolescents give at least transient thought to the physician's observation that more teenagers die from accidents than from any other cause.

HELMET USAGE

Many teenagers ride motorcycles and bicycles and yet do not use helmets. A physician may inquire whether the teenager uses a helmet and then explain that the most common result of not wearing a helmet when riding a bike or motorcycle is serious head injury, with paralysis and permanent handicaps. Again, it is not helpful to preach to the adolescent but merely to give facts with which he can make his own decisions.

ANTICIPATORY GUIDANCE FOR PARENTS

LIMIT SETTING VERSUS A POWER STRUGGLE

It is not unusual for mid-teens to "test" all authority figures, including parents, but this does not mean that they do not need or want rules or regulations. Indeed, most mid-adolescents appreciate reasonable parental limit setting as evidence of parental concern and as a safe bounded area in which to function. But there is a difference between limit setting and power struggle. Limit setting refers to rules and regulations concerning behavior; power struggle occurs when authority itself is at stake regardless of the issue being discussed. Limit setting is neccessary; power struggles should be avoided because someone (usually the teenager) always loses face and is inevitably resentful and bitter. One example of limit setting is the curfew. Teens and their parents should decide together on a reasonable curfew; also, in advance, the parent and teen should discuss the consequences to follow if the curfew is missed. In contrast, a power struggle may involve an argument over one person being "right" and the other person "wrong." Usually the subject matter is unimportant; being "right" is all that counts. Since limit setting consists of rules, these may need to be modified as the adolescent matures or the situation changes. Adolescents and parents should be encouraged to communicate as these changing needs arise.

CROSS-SEX PARENT ATTACHMENTS

As adolescents cope with sexual identity, it is common for adolescents to experience renewed attraction for the opposite-sex parent. This is the reemergence of the oedipal complex. In healthy families, this attraction may be used to bolster the adolescent's self-esteem and provide reassurance to the young person that he or she is developing into a very attractive normal adult. In most families, this phenomenon is expressed in normal parental-filial affection and pride. In other families, the cross-sex parent attachment is a threatening experience or a source of conflict or pain. In such instances, the conflict is almost always the result of a parental problem. Some parents become frightened by their child's attentions, particularly because it occurs at a time when the youngster is sexually blossoming. A parent may become aloof and distant from a youngster who, in turn, finds such action confusing. For example, a father may tell his daughter that she's "too big to be hugged anymore," even though he continues to hug the younger children. Another father may inappropriately respond to his daughter's attentions by taking sexual liberties in the form of incest. It is normal for parents to find their adolescent children attractive. In fact, the son or daughter usually resembles the parents at a younger age or looks like the spouse looked when the parents married. If the spouse was attractive enough for the parent to marry, it is not unusual that the teenage youngster is also seen as attractive. It is *not* normal to act on that attractiveness or to take advantage of the teen's stage of development for personal parental sexual gratification. All cases of suspected incest should be referred to the appropriate authorities for investigation.

VICARIOUS SATISFACTION IN AN ADOLESCENT'S ACTIVITIES

Sometimes the parents of adolescents unconsciously encourage adolescents to misbehave because the teenager is acting out the parent's own fantasies (Anthony, 1975). For example, a mother may warn a daughter to remain a virgin until marriage yet buy her revealing or provocative clothing. If so, this area should be explored and brought to the parent's attention.

THE EFFECT OF PARENTING AN ADOLESCENT

It is not easy to be a parent, and the mid-adolescent years may be the most difficult for some parents. Parents should be prepared for the fact that there are commonly experienced conflicts for parents raising adolescents. For example, for the first time, parents may face unresolved issues from the adolescent's childhood and unresolved issues from their own adolescence, and they may find their authority as parents repeatedly challenged. Parents should be reassured that the best approach to their teenagers (and to themselves) is to keep lines of communication open. In most families, parents find themselves growing in wisdom as they struggle with the issues that teenage children force parents to face.

REFERENCES

American Academy of Pediatrics: *Substance Abuse: A Guide for Health Professionals.* Elk Grove, Village, Ill, American Academy of Pediatrics, 1988.

Anthony EJ: The reactions of adults to adolescents and their behavior, in Esman AH (ed): *The Psychology of Adolescence: Essential Readings.* New York, International University Press, 1975, pp 467–493.

Black JL: Adolescents with learning problems. *Primary Care* 1987; 14:203–223.

Cates W: The epidemiology and control for sexually transmitted diseases in adolescent. *Adolesc Med State Art Rev* 1990; 1:409–427.

Cohen M, Friedman SB: Nonsexual motivation of adolescent sexual behavior. *Med Aspects Human Sexuality* 1975; 9:31.

Coles R, Stokes G: *Sex and the American Teenager.* New York, Harper & Row Publishers, 1985.

Cromer BA, Frankel ME, Keder LM: Compliance with breast self-examination instruction in healthy adolescents. *J Adolesc Health Care* 1989; 10:105–109.

Elkind D: Egocentrism in adolescence. *Child Dev* 1967; 38:1025–1034.

Emans SJH, Goldstein D: *Pediatric and Adolescent Gynecology,* ed 2. Boston, Little Brown & Co, 1982.

Felice ME: Adolescence, in Levine MD, Carey WB, Crocker AC (eds): *Developmental Behavioral Pediatrics.* Philadelphia, WB Saunders Co, (in press).

Felice ME, Vargish W: Interviewing and evaluation of the adolescent, in Kelley V (ed): *Practice of Pediatrics,* ed 2. New York, Harper & Row Publishers, 1992.

Hodgman CH: Adolescent depression and suicide. *Adolesc Med State Art Rev* 1990; 1:81–95.

Hofferth SL, Kahn JR, Baldwin W: Premarital sexual activity among US teenage women over the past three decades. *Fam Plann Perspect* 1987; 19:46–53.

Klein JF, Berry CC, Felice ME: The development of a testicular self-examination instructional booklet for adolescent. *J Adolesc Health Care* 1990; 11:235–239.

Kohlberg L, Gilligan C: The adolescent as a philosopher: The discovery of the self in a post-conventional world, in Kagan J, Coles R (eds): *12 to 16: Early Adolescence.* New York, WW Norton & Co, 1972, pp 144–179.

Leiman AH, Strasburger VC: Counseling parents of adolescents. *Pediatrics* 1985; 76(suppl):664–668.

Lohner T: Adolescent psychosocial growth and development. *Primary Care* 1987; 14:13–23.

Marmon J: Homosexuality and Sexual Orientation, in Sadock BJ, Kaplan HI, Freedman AM (eds): *The Sexual Experience.* Baltimore, Williams & Wilkins Co, 1976, pp 374–391.

Miller SK, Slap GB: Adolescent Smoking: A review of prevalence and prevention. *J Adolesc Health Care* 1989; 10:129–135.

Offer D, Ostrow E, Howard K: Adolescence: What is normal? *Am J Dis Child* 1989; 143:731.

Piaget J: The intellectual development of the adolescent, in Caplan G, Lebovici S (eds): *Adolescence: Psychological Perspectives.* New York, Basic Books, 1969, pp 222–239.

Remafedi G: Homosexual youth: A challenge to contemporary society. *JAMA* 1987; 258:222.

Stewart DC: Sexuality and the adolescent: Issues for the clinician. *Primary Care* 1987; 14:83–99.

Weiner IB: Distinguishing healthy from disturbed adolescent development. *J Dev Behav Pediatr* 1990; 11:151–154.

Zelnik M, Kantner JF: Sexual activity, contraceptive use and pregnancy among metropolitan area teenagers: 1971–1979. *Fam Plann Perspect* 1980; 12:230–237.

Zelnik M, Kim YJ, Kantner JF: Probabilities of intercourse and conception among US teenage women, 1971 and 1976. *Fam Plann Perspect* 1979; 11:177–183.

"Self portrait." By Eileen Fitz, age 18.

CHAPTER 27

Seventeen to Twenty-One Years: Late Adolescence

LYNN I. RICE, R.N., C.P.N.P.
MARIANNE E. FELICE, M.D.

KEY WORDS

OCCUPATIONAL IDENTITY
SCHOOL DROPOUT
JOBS
HOMOSEXUALITY
AIDS
ETHICS AND MORALS
EMANCIPATION PANIC

James, a 17-year-old senior in high school, comes in for a general physical examination. He hands in two physical forms for your completion, one for the local junior college and one for the Navy. He waits outside until called into a room. He says he has been having a lot of headaches lately and has a cold he cannot get rid of. He is having trouble concentrating, and his schoolwork has dropped off. He says he has changed to a more healthy diet and has been meditating with a small group of friends but still feels "nervous" all of the time. His nurse hands you a telephone message from James's mother to be sure you fill out the college application form.

The major task of late adolescence (age range approximately 17 to 21 years) is, in the words of Erikson, "the development of an occupational identity" (Erikson, 1968). Children and adolescents of all ages are frequently asked the question, "What do you want to be when you grow up?" The answer that is given is stated in the psychological shelter of knowing that the individual answering the question is still quite young. In other words, the 9-year-old who says he is going to be an astronaut when he grows up may answer that safely because no one expects a 9-year-old to actually be an astronaut. Whereas the 18-year-old who says he is going to be an astronaut when he grows up must take action and hence risks failure when he gives his response. So it is safer to answer the question in one's childhood than it is in late adolescence when it is no longer a theoretical question but, rather, a confrontation with reality. Hence, each teenager in late adolescence must decide how he or she is going to contribute to society as a responsible adult.

371

EDUCATION AND JOBS

This major developmental task is true for all adolescents, even those who are not in the formal educational system and have chosen to drop out of school. For the majority of adolescents, the beginning of late adolescence generally coincides with the final year of high school. This means that high school seniors are particularly enmeshed with this growth task and must face hard decisions: Should college be pursued? Should the work force be tackled immediately or prolonged to a future date? What kind of job can I do best? Should I get married now or later? Will I ever be able to get married? How soon do I want to become a mother or a father?

Many young people choose to continue their education beyond high school. This may only prolong economic dependence, because most college youth are, at least in part, financially dependent on their parents. Indeed, graduate school and postgraduate education may further delay one's independence and may be a source of conflict or concern for some youth (Felice, 1992). Some young people may choose to go on to college only as an effort to avoid decision making concerning their futures, with the hope that something may simply happen and they will not have to actively make choices.

Erikson (1968) notes that occupational identity may be a serious problem for some young people, and it may be appropriate for an individual to drop out of the usual track, find out what is comfortable for him, and only later pursue the career, job, or education that he finally selects. Indeed, this approach is healthier than the one that is pursued by other adolescents who find a final career choice so difficult that they actually avoid all decision making and simply go along with whatever decisions are made for them by parents or teachers. Eventually these young people do pay an emotional price and may end up resenting the adults who made those decisions for them. Clinical experience suggests that the adolescent who struggles with the decision-making process and eventually does what *he* wants to do rather than what *someone else* wants him to do is more likely to achieve personal career satisfaction (Felice, in press). In other words, it is important for each individual to have self-determination if a satisfying outcome concerning career choice is to be expected.

WORKING DURING ADOLESCENCE

It is during late adolescence that many teenagers seek jobs to earn their own spending money. In previous years, adults have nurtured this concept, believing that holding a job "builds character" in young people. Recent studies (Greenberger and Steinberg, 1986) suggest that this may not be true. Although employed adolescents have more purchasing power than nonemployed teens, they also tend to do less well in school, have higher rates of drug use and delinquency, and appear to be more cynical about work and employment. This may be partially explained by the types of jobs available to the young, as well as by the hours worked. Clinicians who care for adolescents may wish to present these issues to teenagers and their parents.

SCHOOL DROPOUTS

It is estimated that 20% to 30% of young people who begin high school do not graduate from high school and drop out of the formal education system (Weitzman et al., 1982). These high school dropouts include a wide variety of individuals: pregnant teenagers, delinquents, teens with learning disabilities, drug users, depressed youngsters, psychotic adolescents, and others. Some teens drop out of school because they are bored, because they are actually highly gifted in one or more areas, or because they wish to avoid decisions concerning the future during the last year of high school. Some youngsters drop out of high school because a formal education is not viewed as important or their adult role models do not emphasize the need for a high school diploma. The most common reason that teenage girls drop out of high school is pregnancy. Young women who become pregnant when they are less than 15 years of age are more likely to drop out of school than those who become pregnant at the end of high school and have only a few months left until graduation (Furstenberg, 1976a). Young pregnant women who drop out of high school have a high chance of becoming pregnant again before the end of adolescence and severely curtail their chances of finding a meaningful job in the work force (Furstenberg, 1976b). Perhaps some of these young women have made the choice of how they wish to contribute to society, and this choice includes early motherhood and may even be based on the role models around them. It is believed that other young women first drop out of school and *then* become pregnant (Felice et al., 1987). Regardless of which pattern a pregnant teen follows, it is important to encourage teenage mothers (and teenage fathers) to continue or return to their educations. Many communities have special schools for pregnant teens, and these programs may be a good resource for the adolescent and her family.

Many young people who do drop out of school for nonscholastic reasons later realize that schooling is an important component to their futures (Furstenberg et al., 1987). It may be that for these young people it was neccessary to drop out of school to find themselves and to struggle with the question of occupational identity. These youth should be directed to adult education classes, job training programs, and community-based occupational assistance programs. Those young people who opt to return to school of their own volition have a very good chance of succeeding in whatever goals they pursue with support of the adults around them.

SEXUAL DEVELOPMENT

Part of the task of developing an identity includes the task of finding a life partner with whom to share that identity. Unlike their mid-adolescent peers, late adolescents are generally capable of shedding the strong need for a peer group in favor of a close, intimate, caring relationship with another individual (Aten and McAnarney, 1981). All friendships are generally more intense; the superficiality of interactions seen in previous years is dissipated. These new bonds are particularly strong in individuals working toward a common goal or task, such as college roommates, sports team members, or military recruits. For many youth, finding a life partner or significant other becomes a major search. In previous generations, being in love automatically led to marriage. In today's society, many young people choose to live together or cohabitate for a period of time. This lifestyle may be a trial marriage to test compatibility, or it may be a tactic to delay the legal bonds of marriage for economic or psychological reasons. But the intimate relationship of late adolescence is clearly different from the dating relationship of mid-adolescence, which often has an exploitive component (Lohner, 1987). Intimacy, or caring for another, is a core component of the heterosexual relationship of the older adolescent. This may include sexual relations and often involves lengthy, intense conversations.

As noted in previous chapters, it is often during late adolescence that some young people face for the first time the realization that they are homosexual (Remafedi, 1987). As noted previously, not all adolescents who worry about being homosexual actually are homosexual, and it is not uncommon for younger adolescent boys to mutually masturbate or to have an erection in the presence of other males. It is not unusual for younger adolescent females to develop crushes on girls their own age or older women such as teachers. By late adolescence, these phenomena are less common and, if they do occur, are more likely to suggest that the teenager may indeed be homosexual. For some young people, facing the realization of being homosexual is a relatively easy task with easy acceptance. For others, it is quite painful. Such youngsters desperately need to be able to talk to trusted adults about their concerns. The physician may be such an individual, but many young people complain that physicians (even open and caring physicians) make it difficult for a youngster to "confess" that he or she is homosexual. Physicians must be wary of presuming that all teenagers are engaged in heterosexual relationships when questions about sexuality are asked (Stewart, 1987). Physicians must convey acceptance and understanding to give permission to teenagers to discuss their homosexuality.

FINDING AN ETHICAL CODE

In contrast to the narcissistic value system of mid-adolescence, late adolescence is marked by a rigid sense of morality and ethics (Kohlberg and Gilligan, 1972). Late adolescents are characterized by high moral standards, idealism, and even perhaps asceticism. This follows from advanced cognitive development (Piaget, 1972). It is also theorized that the self-serving behavior of the mid-adolescent is frightening and anxiety producing to the teenager, particularly as he anticipates living on his own without parentally imposed rules and regulations (Aten and McAnarney, 1981). If these impulses have no check, he may feel out of control. To guard against this outcome, the older adolescent may establish his own rules and standards that may be more rigid than the rules of the adults around him. Hence, the late adolescent appears to be "other" oriented and may embrace many causes with zeal. Teenagers in this age group often join movements such as religious groups or the Peace Corps in an effort to act on the idealism that they profess. Indeed, in many cultures and societies, it is expected that young people in the late-adolescent age group give service to society. In the Mormon Church, for example, young people are expected to give service to the mission of the ministry for a specified period of time during late adolescence. In some countries, all young people are drafted into military service. In the 1960s, President Kennedy appealed to youth to join the Peace Corps, a very successful request. During late adolescence, young men and women may enter the priesthood or the convent in Christian religions. It is also a time when adolescents are at high risk for being swept up by fringe religious movements. In other words, late adolescents join causes.

Although justice is championed by the late adolescent, there is intolerance for different or opposing points of view on nearly all topics. Older teens have a tendency to view all issues in severe terms as either right or wrong, with no in between, often with self-righteous indignation (Miller et al., 1978). Many adults, particularly parents, may find it difficult to carry on a conversation with such a young person. It has been noted that 19-year-olds have an opinion on everything, even those topics about which they know very little. The transition to adulthood usually occurs when an individual finds that there are suddenly more gray issues in life than black and white ones. At the same time, a tolerance for other points of view becomes apparent. This transition takes place at various ages, but in most individuals it occurs sometime in the mid- to late twenties.

THE ROLE OF PARENTS

The role of the parents during late adolescence should be one of support. Most parents will find that their teenagers have a better relationship with them in late adolescence than they did in the early teen years (Leiman and Strasburger, 1985). This is probably a result of many factors, one of which is that the late adolescent has already established his need for independence and no longer needs to struggle with emancipation from parents. The most common fault noted in parents of older adolescents is overprotection. Parents appropriately fear that a young person who is ready to embark on adulthood will make serious mistakes in career or spouse selections. It is painful for most parents to watch a son or daughter struggle with major decisions while resisting the impulse to make choices for their son or daughter. For example, one mother may *know* that her son would make an excellent lawyer, or physician, or teacher and try to impose that observation on the adolescent. The wise parent will refrain from imposing such an observation and allow the youngster to come to that conclusion on his own. Parents often find themselves criticizing members of the opposite sex with whom teenagers become intimately involved at this age. Parents may become concerned that a young person will marry inappropriately or commit himself to a spouse who would not be right for him. In many instances, the parent is correct, but it rarely does any good to impose that observation on the young person, who may interpret the observation as being unjust, prejudiced, or unfair, and push him or her further into the affection of the individual disliked by the parent.

In general, late adolescence is less of a struggle for parental-child relationships than earlier years. Parents should avoid solving all problems for a youngster when a problem is presented. For example, the teenager who makes the decision to move into his own apartment should be commended for making such a decision and gently asked how he expects to pay for it, what are his plans for maintaining the apartment, does he need any help in moving. Such an individual should be expected to find his own apartment and make plans for stocking it, cleaning it, and paying for it in an appropriate manner. The parent who seizes the opportunity to find an apartment for the teen and then moves the youngster into the apartment is taking over an important task of the late adolescent who must learn these skills for the future. By the end of adolescence, parents may find that they like and enjoy their offspring as an emerging young adult.

DATA GATHERING

Components to be included in the physical examination of the late adolescent are presented in Table 27–1.

TABLE 27–1.
Components of Examination (Late Adolescence)

What to Observe	Objective
Physical presentation of the adolescent: How old does the adolescent look? How does he dress?	Observing if the adolescent looks his stated age may give a clue as to how he feels about himself and is treated by others. Usually young people are treated by how they *look*, not how old they actually are.
Note who made the appointment for the adolescent.	By late adolescence, teenagers should be responsible for making and keeping their own medical/dental appointments and should be responsible for their own health care.
Observe who accompanies the adolescent to his appointment.	By late adolescence, most teens should come to physician's office alone or accompanied by a friend. If parents continue to accompany the late adolescent on medical appointments, it may (although not necessarily) suggest a problem with independence by the adolescent or his parent.

What to Ask	Objective
Ask whether or not the youngster is still in school. If so, ask about his activities at school and his plans following graduation. ("What kind of extracurricular activities are you involved in at school? Do you think you are ready for graduation and leaving school? What are your plans when graduation is over? Where do you expect to live next year? Do you have any worries about going to college? Have you wondered what it would be like to live away from home? Who has most influenced you in the decisions you've made for your future?")	To determine whether the older adolescent has realistic plans concerning his future; to assess undue stress and anxiety concerning his future.
If the youngster is not in school, ask about the teenager's activities and his future plans. ("At what point in your education did you decide to drop out of school? What influenced you to drop out of school? Have you been happier out of school than in school? How have you been supporting yourself? Have you wondered whether or not it is possible to go back to school? Have you explored any agencies or programs that are developed for persons who quit high school like yourself? Where are you living these days? Alone or with your family? Do you have any worries about getting a job and supporting yourself?")	To determine whether the adolescent has realistic plans concerning his future; to assess undue stress and anxiety concerning his future.
Ask about the teenager's relationship with others his own age. ("Are you still good friends with the friends you had a few years ago? What kinds of things do your friends talk about with you? Are most of your friends still in school like you? Or, have most of your friends dropped out of school like you? Do you have a best friend? When you want to discuss issues that are troubling you, to whom do you go?")	To determine whether the teenager has continuing close personal relationships with others his own age.

Continued.

TABLE 27-1.—*Continued*

What to Ask	Objective
Ask about the teenager's relationship with the opposite sex. ("Have you started to date yet? Do you have a steady girlfriend/boyfriend? How long have you and she/he been going together? What are the qualities about him/her that attracted you in the first place? Is he/she the type of person you hope to spend your life with? If you do not have a boyfriend/girlfriend, does this bother you, or worry you? Do you think you have a different attitude towards boys/girls than you did a few years ago? In what way?")	To explore whether the older adolescent is beginning to develop an intimate relationship with a member of the opposite sex.
Ask about the teen's sexual relationships. ("Many young people your age have begun to be sexually active. Is this true for you? Since you have decided not to be sexually active, will you share your thoughts about this? If you are sexually active, with how many partners have you been sexually active? Have all of your sexual relationships been with members of the opposite sex? Have you ever been approached concerning a sexual relationship with somebody of your own gender? Does this worry or bother you? Are you taking any precautions against pregnancy or sexually transmitted disease in your sexual activity?")	To inquire about the adolescent's sexual relationships; to give the adolescent permission to discuss his cares and concerns about sexuality with you.
Ask about family relationships. ("Who are you closest to in your family at the present time? Who are you most like? Are you closer to your family now than when you were younger? How do your mother and father feel about you leaving home next year for college? Have your parents put any pressure on you to leave home? Who has influenced you in your family the most regarding these decisions? If you move away from home next year, do you think you'll return for visits? Do you think your parents worry about you more than your friends' parents worry about them?")	To determine whether the older adolescent has made appropriate plans to be independent from his family; to determine his/her perceptions of the relationships between himself and family members.

Physical Assessment	Objective
Height and weight	To determine if the adolescent is at his final adult height. This is determined by plotting on the growth curve that has been kept since infancy and childhood. Late adolescent boys who have not begun a growth spurt should be referred for evaluation by an endocrinologist.
Blood pressure	To screen for essential hypertension. Essential hypertension often begins during the teenage years, particularly in black adolescents. It is important to pick up an elevated blood pressure as early as possible to influence final outcome.

Continued.

TABLE 27–1.—*Continued*

Physical Assessment	Objective
Tanner maturational staging	To determine whether or not the adolescent is at full sexual maturation. Most late adolescent girls are at Tanner stage IV for breasts and Tanner stage V for pubic hair. Most adolescent males are at Tanner stage IV/V for genital and pubic hair development. Late adolescents who have not reached full sexual maturation may need to be referred for endocrine evaluation. Girls who have not begun to menstruate by 16–17 years of age should be referred for evaluation.

Psychosocial Assessment	Objective
Comfort with independence	To determine whether or not the adolescent's responses to previous questions indicate that he is ready to become independent from his family.
Cognitive growth	To listen to the adolescent's responses to questions listed previously and assess if the adolescent is truly capable of planning for the future and has logically thought out his options.
Moral development	By asking the adolescent about current events and current moral issues, the clinician can assess the adolescent's sense of morality; e.g., the physician may ask the teenager's thoughts about abortion, cheating on scholastic examinations, or some world crisis, e.g., hunger in Africa or war in the Mid-East. Youngsters who have given thought to these issues usually have a highly developed sense of morality.

SITUATIONS REQUIRING SPECIAL REFERRALS

EMANCIPATION PANIC

Some older adolescents find it extremely difficult to leave home, live on their own, support themselves, or make decisions concerning a future career. Indeed, in some adolescents there is an entity known as "emancipation panic." These young people (often from middle socioeconomic classes) become very anxious as high school graduation approaches or the first day of college nears. This anxiety may actually incapacitate them so that they cannot maintain their usual activities. They may become a recluse or fearful, or may have multiple psychosomatic complaints. It is, of course, normal to become anxious about completing high school, starting a new job, or going to college, but these young people are actually panicked in their anxiety and should be referred for professional counseling to a psychologist or psychiatrist experienced in adolescent issues.

FEELINGS CONCERNING HOMOSEXUALITY

As mentioned earlier, late adolescence is often the age when some young people come face to face with their own homosexuality. For some youth, this is an easy acceptance, but for others it is painful. If a youngster is ashamed or frightened of his homosexual status, these are criteria for referral for professional counseling so that the teenager may better understand and accept his sexual preferences. A referral should be made to an understanding, compassionate clinician who is familiar with psychosexual issues. A youngster who is at ease with her homosexuality may not need to be referred for counseling but may benefit from the opportunity of being able to discuss her homosexuality with her own physician.

ANTICIPATORY GUIDANCE FOR OLDER ADOLESCENTS

GOOD HEALTH HABITS

KNOWLEDGE ABOUT ONE'S BODY

Older adolescents are generally less self-conscious about their bodies than younger adolescents and hence may be more receptive of education concerning self-examinations. Young women who have not yet required a pelvic examination may be ready to have a baseline pelvic examination and may be receptive to the use of a mirror during the examination to learn about female genitals. Young men may be more receptive than during younger years to receive instruction concerning testicular self-examination. The reasons for doing this examination should be explained (Klein et al., 1990). The reasons for the frequency of doing a testicular examination and having a pelvic examination should be explained to the young person.

In addition, the clinician should educate the older adolescent about his past medical or psychosocial history, emphasizing those points that will be important for future medical care. For example, the physician may review the adolescent's immunization status and tell him when it is necessary for a future tuberculosis screening or tetanus inoculation. The clinician should summarize the medications that have been prescribed for the adolescent in the past and remind him of the reasons for those prescriptions. The youngster's past medical, social, and psychological history should be reviewed. The drawings done over the years as part of the visits can provide the focus for this discussion.

LIFE STYLE ISSUES

AN EXERCISE PROGRAM—As most older adolescents are making plans for the future, it is important to emphasize the need for exercise, even during times of stress in college or on-the-job training. The dangers of overexercise should be explained and discouraged.

NUTRITION AND DIET—Unlike younger adolescents who have a strong need to identify with a peer group and do whatever the peer group does, the older adolescent may be more receptive to information regarding good nutrition. Teaching the older adolescent about the four basic food groups and emphasizing the need for healthy diets may be helpful, because older adolescents frequently will be responsible for preparing or choosing their own meals. As mentioned previously, preaching to adolescents is generally ineffective, but supplying the adolescent with factual information may be worthwhile.

ALCOHOL CONSUMPTION AND SMOKING—Older adolescents who live away from home may need to be reminded of the dangers of smoking and drinking alcohol. Those young people who have chosen not to begin smoking cigarettes should be commended and advised that being in a room with others who do smoke may be harmful to their lungs. Both adolescent boys and girls should be warned about the dangers of drinking too much alcohol, as well as the danger of drinking and driving. This information should not be given in a pedantic, lecturing manner but in the spirit of one adult advising another adult (Miller and Slap, 1989).

DRUGS—Illicit drug use is a common danger. The clinician should supply facts about the danger of this use and support peer counseling efforts. Adolescents with a problem should be referred to a specialized program. The dangers of anabolic steroids should be discussed with all, but particularly with those young people involved in competitive athletics and those concerned with fitness and physique.

ACQUIRED IMMUNODEFICIENCY SYNDROME—Although only 1% to 2% of all acquired immunodeficiency syndrome (AIDS) cases in the United States are in adolescents, the number of U.S. adolescents diagnosed with AIDS is rapidly increasing (Vermund et al., 1989). This figure does not include those youths who become infected in their teenage years and symptomatic in their twenties. The extent of human immunodeficiency virus (HIV) positivity in adolescents is not known, but limited seroprevalence data suggest that there are geographic pockets of high seropositivity rates in the young (Kipke and Hein, 1990). Certain subgroups of adolescents may be at particularly high risk for HIV infection, including gay males, runaways, teen prostitutes, intravenous (IV) drug users, and some sexually abused teens. Teenage girls whose older boyfriends engage in high-risk behaviors (e.g., IV drug use or bisexual behavior) may not realize that they, too, are at risk for HIV infection in themselves and their babies (Hein, 1989).

Alerting all adolescents of the dangers of AIDS is important, but it has been well demonstrated that adolescents are not likely to alter their risk-related activities based on knowledge alone (Jaffe et al., 1988). This is probably because of immature cognitive development and the inability to relate current behaviors to future consequences. Hence, late adolescence, when abstract thinking is developing, may be the earliest time that high-risk youths may be open to suggestions concerning AIDS vis-à-vis risk reduction and testing.

Screening adolescents for HIV infection is a complicated issue with major medical, ethical, legal, psychological, and social implications (Kipke and Hein, 1990). Guidelines for screening adults may be inappropriate for screening adolescents when one considers adolescents' concrete thinking, perceived invincibility, and egocentrism. Certainly HIV testing should occur only in a setting that includes developmentally appropriate and age-sensitive pretest and posttest counseling. In fact, posttest counseling may require several sessions to ensure that the adolescent understands the implications of test results whether the results are positive or negative. Unfounded fears in this area must also be explored.

CHOOSING AN ADULT HEALTH CARE PROVIDER

Young people who are moving out of town should be advised about how to obtain health care in a strange city. Explaining the various types of health care services is important, and if a referral can be made to a clinic, health care provider, or hospital in the city in question, it is usually reassuring to the adolescent to have this information. Furthermore, older adolescents should be transferred to adult health care providers when they become adults. Transferring care from a pediatric base to internal medicine or family medicine further emphasizes the adolescent's strides toward adulthood and his newfound independence. Family medicine physicians continuing to see the youngster should emphasize the shift in relationship through separate appointment slots and so forth. Adolescents should be made aware of the prominent health issues in their family and provided with a plan of screening given their own risk status. Sometimes pediatric-based health care providers have more difficulty with the transition than the adolescent himself. When the adolescent is transferred to the adult health care provider, he should be advised as to how often he needs appointments and the reasons he needs those appointments.

CAREER CHOICES

Many times, older adolescents welcome the opportunity to discuss career options with a clinician. This is generally done when the adolescent trusts the clinician and respects his life-style. Adolescents with chronic illnesses are particularly prone to asking for advice from their physicians and often find themselves expressing the desire to enter the health care field. Health care providers should be cautioned to realize that this may or may not be a realistic goal, and in some instances it may be the adolescent's need to "identify with the aggressor." The physician and the health care team may be of great benefit to the youngster with a chronic illness in helping him to make realistic plans concerning his career options and the choices available to him (Bellamy et al., 1985; Buhlman and Fitzpatrick, 1987). Teenagers should not be encouraged to pursue careers in which it is certain that they will fail, but neither should they be completely discouraged from tackling something that may be challenging. There is danger of deviation in both directions. A career counseling component associated with a rehabilitation center may provide needed services in some cases.

REFERENCES

Aten MJ, McAnarney ER: *A Behavioral Approach to the Care of Adolescents.* St Louis, CV Mosby Co, 1981.

Bellamy GT, Wilcox B, Rose H, et al: Education and career preparation for youth with disabilities. *J Adolesc Health Care* 1985; 6:125–135.

Buhlman U, Fitzpatrick SB: Caring for an adolescent with a chronic illness. *Primary Care* 1987; 14:57–68.

Erikson EH: *Identity, Youth and Crisis.* New York, WW Norton & Co, 1968.

Felice ME: Adolescence, in Levine MD, Carey WB, Crocker AC (eds): *Developmental and Behavioral Pediatrics,* ed 2. Philadelphia, WB Saunders Co, 1992.

Felice ME, Shragg GP, James M, et al: Psychosocial aspects of Mexican-American, white, and black teenage pregnancy. *J Adolesc Health Care* 1987; 8:330–335.

Furstenberg F: The social consequences of teenage parenthood. *Fam Plann Perspect* 1976a; 8:148–164.

Furstenberg F: *Unplanned Parenthood.* New York, Free Press, 1976b.

Furstenberg FF, Brooks-Gaunn J, Morgan SP: Adolescent mothers in later life. New York, Cambridge University Press, 1987.

Greenberger E, Steinberg L: *When Teenagers Work.* New York, Basic Books, 1986.

Hein K: AIDS in adolescence: The next wave of the HIV epidemic. *J Pediatr* 1989; 114:114–119.

Jaffe LR, Seehaus M, Wagner C, et al: Anal intercourse and knowledge of AIDS among minority group female adolescents. *J Pediatr* 1988; 112:1005–1007.

Kipke MD, Hein K: AIDS in adolescents. *Adolesc Med State Art Rev* 1990; 1:429–449.

Klein JF, Berry CC, Felice ME: The development of a testicular self-examination instructional booklet for adolescent. *J Adolesc Health Care* 1990; 11:235–239.

Kohlberg L, Gilligan C: The adolescent as a philosopher: The discovery of the self in a post-conventional world, in Kagan J, Coles R (eds): *12 to 16: Early Adolescence.* New York, WW Norton & Co, 1972, pp 144–179.

Leiman AH, Strasburger VC: Counseling parents of adolescents. *Pediatrics* 1985; 76(suppl):664–668.

Lohner T: Adolescent psychosocial growth and development. *Primary Care* 1987; 14:13–23.

Miller J, Piaget J, Kohlberg L, et al: Developmental implications for secondary education. *Adolescence* 1978; 18:236.

Miller SK, Slap GB: Adolescent smoking: A review of prevalence and prevention. *J Adolesc Health Care* 1989; 10:129–135.

Piaget J: Intellectual evolution from adolescence to adulthood. *Hum Dev* 1972; 15:1–12.

Remafedi G: Homosexual youth: A challenge to contemporary society. *JAMA* 1987; 258:222.

Stewart DC: Sexuality and the adolescent: Issues for the clinician. *Primary Care* 1987; 14:83–99.

Vermund SV, Hein K, Gayle H, et al: AIDS among adolescents in NYC: Case surveillance profiles compared with the rest of the U.S. *Am J Dis Child* 1989; 143:1220–1225.

Weitzman M, Klerman LV, Lamb G, et al: School absence: A problem for the pediatrician. *Pediatrics* 1982; 69:739–746.

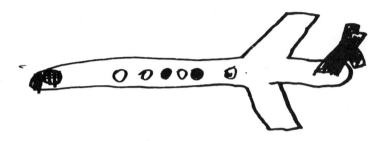

"My cousins coming to see their dad." By Ryan Hennessy, age 8.

CHAPTER **28**

Special Families

ROBERT D. WELLS, PH.D.

NICHOLAS PUTNAM, M.D.

MARTIN T. STEIN, M.D.

Shelly, an 11-year-old girl, was seen by her pediatrician for recurrent abdominal pain. She lived with her mother, a 52-year-old nurse administrator, and her father, a 63-year-old retired physician. Shelly had been complaining of abdominal pain on almost a daily basis for the past year. At first, her parents had dismissed it as "just nerves." When she was sent home from school, her parents became more concerned. Shelly was evaluated by her pediatrician, who did not determine an apparent cause for her pain after an initial history, review of symptoms, and complete physical examination. Results of screening laboratory tests, including a complete blood cell count, erythrocyte sedimentation rate, urinalysis, chemistry panel, and a stool examination for occult blood and ova and parasites, were normal. While performing the medical assessment, her pediatrician was impressed by Shelly's depressed and anxious demeanor.

When Shelly's mother was questioned alone, she quickly became tearful and disclosed that her husband was severely handicapped by multiple sclerosis and was abusing opiates to control his pain and depression. Marital conflict was extremely high, and she admitted to being involved in an extramarital affair, which Shelly knew about for 1 year. She also wondered how Shelly was coping with taking care of her dad after school.

Shelly was then interviewed alone. She indeed appeared quite depressed and worried. She described a recurrent fear that she would return home from school to find her father dead or severely injured. She hated having to take care of him and longed for her mother's return from work. She did not volunteer any information about her mother's affair but did admit to worrying about her mother's adjustment. She saw her as a "workaholic who was always stressed out" and quick to anger. It was clear that Shelly experienced a tremendous amount of stress and anxiety related to her special family circumstances.

Both Shelly and her mother were referred to a pediatric psychologist by her pediatrician. Her mother was eventually referred to an adult psychiatrist for psychopharmacologic treatment of a significant depression. Through counseling, she made a decision to place her disabled husband in a chronic care facility. She recognized that she and Shelly were unable to sustain him in their home without severe chronic stress. She also hoped that detoxification in a structured setting would assist in his long-term adjustment.

Shelly was responsive to individual counseling. In the context of a warm, supportive relationship, she enjoyed the mutual detective work of understanding and modifying her stress and pain. After the third visit and without direct interpretation, Shelly verbalized the belief that her anxious state and frequent stress were associated with her abdominal pain. As she was helped to see the special nature of the stressors in her family, her feelings of anger, worry, and sadness were now viewed as a natural outcome of stress overload. Her love for both parents was constantly reaffirmed in the counseling sessions, but

385

she was also helped to get in touch with her anger and frustration at their excessive demands on her. Her abdominal pain declined steadily and resolved completely shortly after the placement of her father. She continued to visit him in the nursing home where he was able to resolve his substance dependency.

The rapid changes in family constellation in the United States over the past 40 years have created great diversification in the makeup of families. The divorce rate has doubled since 1965, as have the number of mothers who are now working full time. If our definition of the typical family is restricted to those homes with two parents, the majority of children come from special families. The most recent census indicates that 25% of children are raised by single parents, and greater than 50% experience a divorce; demographers predict that 33% of all children will live with a stepparent in the home before they turn 18 years old. It may well be that over the next decade, the child with both parents present will be seen as special and unique.

There is no evidence that a particular family constellation is either "good" or "bad" for children. However, the way in which a family functions to support the growth and development of its children is important. Characteristics of families that are important for children, regardless of the specific constellation, include the following: (1) provision of life necessities, including food, housing, clothing, and medical care; (2) demonstrated warmth, unconditional love, and constructive limit setting for the child; (3) continuity and stability in caregiving for the child; (4) appropriate models of development of healthy sexuality; (5) cooperation among involved caretaking adults; (6) lack of violence toward, and respect for, all members in the family; (7) lack of excessive stress such as significant physical or mental illness of the caretaking adults, including depression, alcoholism, and drug abuse; (8) adequate support for caretaking adults from relatives, friends, neighbors, and community; (9) stimulation of cognitive development; (10) capacity for meaningful interpersonal relationships, good communication, problem-solving capacity, and motivation to achieve; and (11) fostering socialization by helping children function as cooperative members of society. These are basic aspects of family functioning that are necessary if children are to acquire a sense of security and self-esteem, learn to socialize, respond to rules, and limit and control their anger and aggression (personal communication: Committee on Psychosocial Aspects of the Child and Family, American Academy of Pediatrics, 1991).

All families provide varying levels of concrete resources, discipline, expectations, modeling, and emotional support to their children. After significant acute or chronic loss, most families appear to suffer some reduction in their capacity to meet the needs of their children. When the functional capacity of these special families is assessed, it is important to avoid value-laden expectations in favor of a more objective appraisal of relative strengths and weaknesses. Specifically, it is not how different from the norm the family is but how well they go about meeting the needs of the various family members while remaining effective members of the wider community.

The term "special families" is used in this chapter to delineate a variety of circumstances in family constellation that may affect child health, behavior, and development. Such a definition includes foster, adoptive, step-parent, and single-parent families, in addition to families facing severe strain because of poor parental health or adjustment. Although differing from each other in important ways, their commonality lies in the effects of loss on the child. In this manner, intact, nuclear families can be seen as "special" if they indeed subject the child to certain risks as a result of loss or threatened loss. Farm families who are facing bankruptcy, inner-city homeless families, and immigrant families who have had to flee their home-lands should be considered special because of the uniqueness of the loss that children and adults experience. For clinicians, recognition of these special circumstances focuses our behavioral and developmental assessment on each family and promotes individually tailored anticipatory guidance for greater effectiveness.

The assessment of children in special families must take into account the extent of loss expe-rienced, the amount of time that has elapsed, the child's age, the degree to which stressors are acute, chronic, or recurrent, and the adaptive capacity of the child and parenting figures. Although the values and beliefs of the clinician should be restrained from entering into the equation, the values of the family's community should be considered. Unique family constellations are more or less acceptable in certain contexts. Teenage pregnancy in some middle class neigh-borhoods is associated with greater ostracism than in a neighborhood where it is more com-mon and acceptable. Similarly, having homosexual, adoptive, or handicapped parents will be less of a strain on those children living in communities where it is not considered unusual.

Even when large numbers of families experience similar losses (e.g., after natural catas-trophes), the actual severity of the loss is highly subjective. Some parents find that the divorce process is a considerable strain, whereas others find it energizing and liberating. Death of a family member is typically stress producing, but a study of Amish families has documented their relative ease of adjustment (Bryner, 1986). Loss and stress are clearly subjectively deter-mined experiences (Lazarus, 1966). The implications for clinicians is that the family and child must be asked about their sense of the severity of loss or upheaval rather than relying on one's own impression.

The amount of time that has elapsed since the change or loss is also important in deter-mining the nature of an individual child and family's adjustment. Studies of bereavement and divorce indicate significant upheaval during the first year after the loss, with the majority of children returning to baseline functioning during the second year (Wallerstein and Kelly, 1980). Consequently, early disruptions in a child's behavior or academic functioning during the first year after divorce are not unusual and may not signify serious maladaptation, whereas such behavior after the second year is far more serious.

The age and developmental skills of the child also play an important role in determining the child's state of adjustment to special family circumstances. Infants require responsive and predictable caregiving behaviors, and the biological relatedness of the caregiver is relatively unimportant. Separations or changes in caregivers are particularly stressful between about 8 and 18 months when the developmental theme of attachment is prominent. Similarly, losses because of divorce or death during infancy and the preschool years are less obviously sensi-tizing than when they occur during the school-age and adolescent period (Wallerstein and Kelly, 1980). Divorce itself may not be so stressful for the preschool child, but the necessity to adjust to two homes may require significant adjustment and provoke behavioral stress. In general, children will be more vulnerable to special family circumstances from school age to middle adolescence.

The effects of multiple, chronic, and severe stressors on children appear most dramatic and disabling. Ongoing domestic violence, parental substance abuse, and dire poverty are particularly devastating and appear to have long-standing effects on child development and adjustment. Acute stressors such as natural catastrophes, divorce, sudden loss of income, and death of a parent can also pose a profound challenge to the child and family. Longitudinal studies suggest that a period of adaptation follows the initial shock. For children and parents alike, this may lead to decreases in academic and occupational functioning, moodiness, depression, anger, behavioral, and sleep disturbances.

After the initial trauma, the quality of a child's adaptation is determined primarily by the parent's ability to model effective coping strategies while maintaining family rules and expectations (Block and Block, 1980; Murphy and Moriarty, 1976; Sameroff et al., 1984; Wallerstein and Kelly, 1980; Werner and Smith, 1982). When the child's clinician focuses family energy toward the augmentation of parental recovery, she encourages the child's adaptation and recovery as well. Self-help groups, religious organizations, and more formalized mental health services may be helpful, especially when the parent and the child have few friends or available family.

Prediction of developmental outcome of a particular child reared in one class of special families is usually not possible. However, some generalizations about the ways in which families influence children can be made from the available literature. There is clear evidence that children can be successfully reared in special families despite some evidence that an intact family with both biological parents present and reasonably compatible provides children with the best opportunity for healthy growth and development. One study concluded that poor, single-parent families entail the highest risk of social maladaptation and psychological problems in their children (Kellam et al., 1977). The presence of second adults in these families did have important ameliorative functions. Families headed by mother and grandmother were nearly as effective in producing socially and emotionally healthy first graders as were mother-father families. The powerful ameliorative effects of social support has clearly been documented.

Developmental and behavioral problems in children may not be related directly to the loss of the nuclear family. Rather, it is family discord and harsh parental discipline, associated with isolation, financial stress, and parental mental states, that seems to lead to delinquent behavior in children (Patterson, 1988). Family discord may occur, of course, in either an intact family or a special family. Children exposed to continuing family discord either before or after a divorce are at much greater risk for developing conduct disturbances (Rutter, 1975).

All special families need reassurance and guidance from the community, and especially from the child's clinician, as to their capacity to successfully undertake the tasks of family life. Stepparents and adoptive parents may need considerable *external validation* of their roles as parents, and the child's clinician is often in a unique position to provide such support. In her role of advocate for the child's development, the clinician may assist parents through timely support and guidance in understanding the changes the family is experiencing in terms of the best interest of the child or children while supporting the needs and emotional responses of the parents.

These general principles of understanding and determining the specific needs of the individual family and child should assist the child's clinician. The following sections provide more specific information about different types of special families.

DIVORCING FAMILIES

The effects of the divorce process on the development of children has been studied extensively over the past 20 years (Heatherington et al., 1985; Kappelman and Black, 1980; Wallerstein and Kelly, 1980). Most children respond to the initiation of separation and divorce with significant feelings of depression, anxiety, and anger (Hoyt et al., 1990). Infants and preschool-aged children appear less affected than their older counterparts. Notable declines in academic performance may occur for both boys and girls during the first year. Boys tend to respond to this loss with increased emotional outbursts, noncompliance, and other external behavior problems. Withdrawal, sadness, and anxiety, characterized as internalizing behaviors, are more commonly observed in girls, and their difficulties may be overlooked for longer periods of time. Some data also suggest that some young women suffer from a "sleeper" effect, whereby an initial adjustment is realized, but when they enter young adulthood, a reawakening of anxieties regarding male-female relationships may occur (Wallerstein and Johnston, 1990).

Recent evidence refutes the general belief that by the second year the majority of children adjust to their altered family circumstances. In a longitudinal study, 37% of children were doing poorly (i.e., academic underachievement, behavior problems at school, home, or both) at 5 years after divorce. At the 10-year follow-up, 41% were still maladjusted, which suggests that the years following a divorce continue to be stressful for a large number of children (Wallerstein and Johnston, 1990).

During the 10-year period since divorce, these investigators reported that only one of seven children saw their parents happily remarried, 50% experienced a new divorce, 60% felt rejected by at least one parent, and 50% grew up in families in which the parents remained intensely angry at each other. The economic consequence of a divorce is also quite significant. Twenty-five percent of children who experienced a divorce were living with a parent with significantly reduced financial resources. The social, psychological, and economic adjustments after the divorce made by the parents as individuals and as partners in parenting determine the long-term effects on children.

A number of factors may predict the relative risk of maladaptation after divorce. If open family conflict decreases after divorce, better outcomes are predicted. In contrast, children who have been sheltered from parental conflicts and awaken to open conflict during and after the divorce are often the most grievously injured. Frequently the emotional availability of the parent or parents is often diminished during the separation and divorce process. If this continues unabated, children face tremendous obstacles in meeting their own, their siblings', and their parents' needs. Although age (younger) and sex of the child (female) are predictors of a better outcome in general, appropriate ongoing relationships with both parents is the most important factor in predicting resilience. An easy child temperament, social support, physical health, and intelligence also contribute to better outcomes.

The clinician's role in helping families who experience divorce should precede the actual separation. During regular pediatric health supervision visits, families should be made aware of the clinician's interest and need to know about significant family events that might affect the child. Periodic focused questions that serve to update the clinician about family function will both inform and cement the relationship between the parents and the clinician. If separation occurs, specific guidelines can be offered regarding how and what to tell the child. Attention can be focused on ways to support the child's coping skills and to maintain appropriate contact with both parents, friends, and concerned others. Parents frequently need help in controlling their own emotional state, and this should be directly addressed. Distinguishing their own needs and feelings from those of their child is also recognized as important.

Predicting the types of reactions they and their child may experience is usually helpful. Monitoring subsequent responses of both the child and parent is then critical for effective clinical assessments, and at times referral to a mental health professional may be appropriate.

STEPFAMILIES

As the divorce rate remains high and the rate of remarriage continues to increase, stepfamilies have become an important part of our culture. Although these reconstituted families usually function as effectively as nuclear family units, a number of salient differences should be appreciated by responsive clinicians (Herndon and Combs, 1982). Each member of the family has experienced significant losses. Children who are depressed and anxious after a parent separation now must cope with sharing their biological parent with a new adult. The biological parent who may also be functioning with diminished coping resources must contend with playing a "middle man" role, leaving neither side satisfied. The stepparent will quickly appreciate that the parent-child bonds preceded his or her involvement; issues of loyalty and alliance by the biological parent may lead to a sense of isolation and rejection by the stepparent. Most stepchildren continue to visit the other biological parent. Differences in rules between the households and jealousies between the biological noncustodial parent and the stepparent may lead to further disruption (Visher and Visher, 1985).

Despite these challenges, studies suggest that children from stepfamilies do not differ significantly from children in other family structures (Ganong and Coleman, 1984). They achieve effective family functioning with developmentally appropriate levels of adjustment and are equally prone to maladaptation in the face of family discord. Family functioning is optimal when there is positive marital adjustment, strong parent-child attachment, generalized family cohesiveness, and effective problem solving (Anderson and White, 1986). When stepfamilies were dysfunctional, they were characterized by strong parent-child coalitions (in comparison with parent-to-parent coalitions) and a lack of mutual decision-making skills. Adolescents appear particularly vulnerable to developing both internalizing and externalizing problems when their stepfamilies are characterized by chaotic rules, punitiveness, excessive dependency, and frequent major life events (Garbarino et al., 1984).

The sensitive and alert clinician may at times become confused about the nature of the alliance between natural parents, stepparents, and children. Attempts should be made to maintain contact with all adults who serve as psychological parents while complying with the legal rights and restrictions to information as stipulated in custody agreements. Keeping in mind the nature of loss experienced by children in reconstituted families, it is helpful to expect some early adjustment difficulties with eventual remission in the majority of cases. Specific attention should be paid to developing well-recognized rules of behavior in the home. Stepparents can be counseled to develop a role as an independent caregiver, in addition to supporting their spouse's actions. Parents, children, and the clinician need to maintain some patient hopefulness that over time rules and roles will become more comfortable and acceptable. The clinician should express clear support for the importance of the noncustodial parent's right to visit, obtain information about the children, and discuss concerns. Finally, stepparents should be encouraged to maintain nonparental, romantic, and supportive roles with each other so that the alliance between the adults remains balanced and strong. When adjustment problems predominate or become chronic, or when fixed maladaptive roles and alliances have developed, referral for family counseling is indicated and often helpful.

SERIOUS ILLNESS AND DEATH OF PARENTS

The psychosocial effects of growing up with a parent with a serious, life-threatening physical illness is perhaps one of the least studied stress events in childhood. In contrast, the effects of parental mental illness on children has been more extensively studied (Anthony, 1987; Garmezy, 1981). Children with a schizophrenic parent benefit significantly when they have a healthy relationship with a caring and predictable adult. This was also the conclusion among families with mothers who were diagnosed with breast cancer, diabetes, or fibrocystic breast disease (Lewis et al., 1989). Children in these families showed the most adaptive behavior when fathers maintained frequent interactions with their children. Not surprisingly, marital harmony was also correlated with improved child functioning.

For the clinician treating children with highly stressed, physically ill parents, special attention should be directed to guilt reactions in children. Psychosomatic conditions, school avoidance, separation anxiety, and depression are common responses to a sudden threat to a parent's health. Temperamentally easy children may show a tendency to develop "pseudo-maturity" where they appear to be the psychological parent for the family. Extra effort is needed to keep them out of the family's decision-making process for them to experience and benefit from a normal period of growth and development. Parents may need to be explicitly informed that they not seek counsel from children acting in this fashion, and they should be encouraged to develop more adaptive and supportive relationships with other adults and health care providers. Children should be encouraged to continue their normal scholastic and extracurricular activities. Family communication about the parent's illness and treatment should be encouraged, particularly when the focus is on the feelings and reactions that are naturally evoked.

The clinician may find it useful to maintain contact with the ill parent during the course of illness. There are often different questions on the mind of the well and ill parent regarding what, how, and when to tell children about predictable and frightening events. In the majority of circumstances, open and honest communication with children is the best advice. Concerns about the death of a parent must be addressed to minimize the child's tendency to fantasize catastrophic outcomes or miraculous cures. Most important, the clinician should take the time to empathize with the child regarding her worries about the parent. She should be encouraged to ask questions about her parent's condition and to call for an appointment if she becomes confused, overwhelmingly anxious, or depressed.

Because of the small number of well-controlled prospective studies, the effect of parental death on children is also poorly understood. Worden and Silverman (1990) have been following 70 families who had experienced the death of a parent and a matched sample of intact families. Three distinct types of bereaved responses have been delineated: (1) affective responses (e.g., crying, sleep disorders, and impaired concentration), (2) attempts to maintain connection to the deceased (e.g., dreaming of the parent, feeling being watched by the parent), and (3) coping through involvement with friends, family members, and classmates. The researchers noted that although the children were indeed grieving, they did not see serious psychological disharmony in the majority of children. Indeed, children examined 1 year after the death of a parent reported less crying, better concentration, and improved sleep in comparison with their reaction 8 months later. There was also an increase in concern about their own health and worries about the safety of the surviving parent. These children had more headaches, abdominal pain, and other somatic manifestations than did control children. Those children who lost a mother tended to face additional changes in living arrangements that led to further stress and maladaptation.

When families who are anticipating or experiencing the death of a parent are counseled, care should be given to help support the emotional health of the surviving parent. They should be encouraged to use friends and family members for support and to allow themselves time for emotional reactions. Care should be placed in helping them maintain important home rituals that the children have come to expect. Additional disruptions such as moving or a change in school should be avoided if possible. Open communication with the child by both the surviving parent and the clinician is important. Normalizing various psychological and psychosomatic reactions to death by speaking about other children who have survived this experience is also helpful. When interested, children should be supported in their efforts to participate fully in the funeral ceremony. Those children who demonstrate a particular desire to avoid the service should be supported in their decision. Some have counseled caution in allowing a child to attend open casket services.

Children should be encouraged to maintain thoughts and contact with the deceased parent. It is not uncommon for children to report seeing or hearing the parent, even while awake. When possible, children can be helped to maintain some effective contact with the deceased by having an object or photo that is reminiscent and evocative. As the mourning progresses, the child will tend to let go of these transitional phenomena. Referral for counseling should be made if the child continues to function poorly.

SINGLE-PARENT FAMILIES

Financial concerns are by far the most serious problem faced by single parents. Earning a living and caring for the needs of children can easily consume the full-time energy of more than one adult. Remarkably, many single parents find ways to spend as much or more time with their children than they would if they were involved in a marriage, although certain sacrifices must be made. Frequently single parents have to sacrifice some "adult time" that would ordinarily be spent meeting their own emotional needs to meet both their financial and family obligations. When appointments are broken or arrival to the office is late, when anxiety levels are heightened or when payment for medical service is delayed, the child's clinician should be sensitive to these added stresses among single parents.

Clinicians can be helpful to single parents by accepting them as healthy family units capable of providing for the needs of their children (Wessel, 1960) while being sensitive to the special pressures felt by single parents. Isolation from other adults is a particular problem for some single parents, and at times they need to share their experiences with another adult. The child's clinician may be the most respected and available adult who can utilize this position therapeutically by providing feedback, empathy, and validation in their role as parents.

Single parents can be encouraged to share some of their parenting obligations with other responsible adults. Depending on the situation, this might mean encouraging contact with grandparents or noncustodial parents or utilizing the support of various social agencies such as Big Brothers and Big Sisters organizations and single-parent clubs. The pediatric office can make available a directory of single-parent support groups in the community. Finally, a number of joys and strengths can result from single-parenting experiences (e.g., learning self-sufficiency as a parent), and those positive aspects of single parenting can be emphasized to members of single-parent households.

ADOPTIVE FAMILIES

Adoption provides a caring and responsive home and a family for children who might not otherwise have one while at the same time providing children for couples who wish to parent. Like other special families, both the children and adults bring their own unique strengths and liabilities together for the purpose of providing a warm environment for healing prior losses and developing new capacities. Although most adoptions are formulated when relatives become the adoptive parents, many unrelated families are adopting infants and older children with the help of adoption agencies and private attorneys. The clinician may be asked to help review birth and health information of their soon-to-be adopted child. The parents may have many questions regarding ways to best help make their infant or child's transition to a new family as smooth and enjoyable as possible.

Adoptions outside the family involve at least three participants, referred to as "the adoption triangle" (Sorosky et al., 1978). At one corner of the triangle is the biological parent or parents, often a single woman in her early twenties who has chosen adoption for her fetus or newborn. Frequently she is under considerable emotional stress, supported by neither the biological father of the baby nor her own parents. Although many adoptions are arranged during pregnancy, a significant number of babies are placed after birth as a result of neglect or abuse. To avoid a tendency to blame or stigmatize the biological parent, the clinician should bear in mind the difficult circumstances in which many parents live. In general, the decision to relinquish a child demonstrates the parent's capacity to recognize the predominance of the child's needs. The biological parent's adjustment is aided by having the opportunity to know her neonate and "say goodbye." Reassurance of the child's well-being from the clinician also aids adjustment.

At another corner of the triangle are the adoptive parents who have long dreamed of and contemplated the wonderful effects of having children. Although many families are well counseled by the time adoption becomes a reality, some couples may have unresolved feelings related to their decision to adopt, and most parents worry about their own reactions to the parenting role. Anger and grief over infertility may still be present. Over the years adoption has become far less stigmatizing, though some parents may still experience unsupportiveness in extended family members and friends. Adoptive parents also live with many unanswered questions about the child's biological genetic background and the possibility of intrauterine substance exposure or other unknown pregnancy complications.

The adopted child forms the final part of the triangle. This child may have experienced many prenatal stresses related to the biological mother's age, emotional state, and physical health and habits during pregnancy. Placement for varying periods of time at critical ages in one or more foster homes may have occurred. When placement is within the first 6 months of life, the infant is likely to avoid the experience of significant loss that is often apparent in older children. The quality of care they experienced before placement has significant effects

on the level of trust they exhibit. When there is a background of abuse, neglect, and unpre-
dictability, children will develop a very different set of expectations, and parents may find
the attachment process to be lengthened and more complex. The child's temperament is also
an important aspect to consider when determining risk factors and level of adjustment, with
easier temperaments leading to more rapid family integration. Ethnic differences, in appearance and cultural identification, may be additional challenges for the racially mixed adoptive
family.

When caring for adopted children, clinicians should realize that all three parties in the
adoption process have their own emotional needs and civil rights. Over time, open adoptions
are becoming the norm, whereby all three members of the triangle are encouraged to maintain
contact. In open adoption, the biological and adoptive parents agree beforehand on the level
of involvement that each will have with the child. This can range from sending a picture
during Christmas time to regular weekly visitations. In general, full awareness and select visitation with biological parents appears to be beneficial to all three parties involved. The biological parent is helped to assuage his or her concerns about the child's circumstances, and
the adoptive parents come to appreciate the character and heritage of their child. Just as with
divorce, the child is powerfully influenced by the ability of the biological and adoptive parents
to form an effective alliance and to function without insecurity and jealousy.

Helping parents feel comfortable in talking with a child about her adoption is a matter in
which physicians can be quite helpful. Families should be encouraged to include the child's
adoption as an important part of the family's story. Children's books can be used to help
portray the adoption process. Even when children grow up with early knowledge of their
adoption, it is in the school-aged years that many first come to awareness that adoption meant
loss and relinquishment by their biological parent. The child may demonstrate signs of
mourning and will be helped by sensitive questions by the parent after either subtle or overt
behaviors or questions. Physicians will occasionally come in contact with school-aged children and adolescent patients who were adopted but have not yet been told, and parents will
at this point seek consultation on when and how to break the news to their child. In most
instances, families should be encouraged to share this information at the earliest opportunity
to avoid a sense of rejection and mistrust. These exchanges should be done as a process over
time and need to be responsive to the types of questions asked by the child. The clinician can
be particularly useful in helping adoptive parents find ways to explain the reason for adoption
and difficulties experienced by the biological parent. Avoidance of the idea of having "been
chosen" by the adoptive parents is important, because this concept can introduce the thought
that one can be "unchosen." Clinicians should avoid such pejorative terms as "natural" or
"real" mother. The adoptive parents are real and natural; the term "birth mother" is
preferred.

FOSTER FAMILIES

In the United States, approximately one-half million children receive foster care services.
Foster care provides children with a home and a family life when the child's parents are
unable to do so, usually in her known community. At one time, foster care was used primarily
to serve the needs of temporarily displaced children. Currently, children in foster care are
likely to have been placed there because of severe psychological, social, or behavioral prob-

lems in the child, the parents, or both. Unlike adoption, the goal of foster care placement is to preserve and hopefully improve the child's relationship with her biological parents. Like adoption, this creates a triangle consisting of the child, the foster parents, and the biological parents. Like the stepchild, the foster child may feel as though she is a member of two (or more) homes and families concurrently and that this circumstance is beyond her control.

Foster parents volunteer to take children into their homes and are infrequently given any specific training in the complexities of foster parenthood. Foster parents must attempt to provide for the present needs and perhaps even rehabilitate the children entrusted to their care. They must also make room in the family for the new child. The birth children of foster parents may experience feelings akin to sibling rivalry on the arrival of a foster child into their home. Conversely, they may benefit by exposure to children less fortunate or infants who are the result of irresponsible behavior on the part of others. Foster parents must also maintain a collaborative relationship with the foster care agency and be open to investigation and periodic evaluation of their intimate family life. They must often fight for services and deal with mounds of paperwork. The foster family must establish a relationship with the birth parents of the child and such relationships are often quite challenging. Finally, foster parents must work through issues of attachment and separation with their foster children and within themselves related to the continuous process of bonding and then separating from foster children.

When foster children present the foster family with challenging problems, a variety of reactions can occur. Some foster parents distance themselves from these problems, citing the child's lack of biological relationship to the foster family, as well as the previously poor conditions in which the child lived. Other foster families assume that the child's maladaptive behaviors are a response to the foster family and feel frustrated or rejected. In working with these parents, the clinician should help them realize that children bring a significant past history into their foster family relationships. In fact, perhaps after a brief "honeymoon," the child may test to the limit the structure provided by the foster family. In some cases it may even appear that the child has set out to prove that he is unmanageable in any home and therefore should be returned to his biological parents. With a high rate of physical and mental illness, and often unmet care needs, these children meet these challenges with diminished resources.

In helping a foster child, the health care provider must understand the effects of separation from natural parents in children at various developmental levels. Most children react to the loss of their relationship with the biological parent in the same ways that children react to the loss of a parent through divorce or death. There is a period of grief, a sense of failure, angry feelings expressed toward the present caretaker, and perhaps behavioral acting out or depression and withdrawal. Many children will develop somatic complaints, and there may be a loss of previously achieved developmental milestones. Children who are placed in foster care between the ages of 6 and 18 months may show the classic patterns of reaction to separation from parents described by Bowlby (1980). These include reactions of protest, despair, and finally a period of "detachment" in which the child may appear to have adjusted to the new home but has become dangerously superficial in his relationships to important adults. These signs of infantile depression must be recognized and a permanent placement sought with urgency. The clinician should advocate for no further changes, if possible, and certainly not during this critical period in affective development.

A physician may have a relationship with a child that continues despite the child's various living arrangements with natural or foster parents. Whenever possible, one should develop a relationship with the child that allows the child to express feelings about foster placement and allows the physician to help these children and their foster parents deal with a variety of problems that arise. The physician may act as the child's advocate in his relationship with the foster parents and the foster care placement agency in helping to determine the individual child's needs and current state of development. The foster child's clinician should encourage continuity of medical records as the child moves from one foster home to the next or into an adopting family. Physicians should be supportive of the children in foster care by seeing them with priority, delineating their physical and mental health needs in detail and communicating these to the child welfare agency. The tendency to avoid these complex, often recordless cases should be resisted to advocate for the best interests of these at risk children (Sokoloff, 1979).

HOMELESS FAMILIES

Families are the fastest growing segment of the homeless population in America (Edelman and Mihaly, 1989). As such, more and more children are living in cars, vans, low-cost hotels, shelters, or simply on the street. They are exposed to severe poverty, violence, and profound deprivation. Approximately one half of these children suffer from severe depression, anxiety, and learning and behavior problems (Bassuk and Rubin, 1987). Their parents are typically aware of these problems but do not have resources for dealing with them.

When treating homeless children, the clinician should pay particular attention to their school attendance and functioning. Collaboration with teachers, public health nursing, social workers, and mental health personnel is useful. Concrete recommendations for the parents about community resources and customary guidance about growth and development are important. With the high rates of violence and substance abuse among the homeless, these children should be screened carefully for developmental delays, depression, posttraumatic stress disorder, and conduct problems.

As a result of the tremendous disorganization commonly found among homeless families, clinicians may become frustrated by their lack of follow-up during planned medical visits. It is useful to keep in mind Maslow's hierarchy (1970), whereby motivation for higher goals of achievement, self-esteem, and identity are based on achieving earlier goals of safety, comfort, and love. As with all special families, issues of safety, predictability, and organization can help overcome the effects of prior losses. It is likely that more children will be growing up in these disruptive environments, and clinicians will need to be particularly sensitive to the frustration experienced by parents who are unable to meet their child's needs because of extraordinary social circumstances.

CONCLUSION

The needs of children living in specific forms of special families (single-parent families, stepfamilies, adoptive families, and foster care families) have been described. Other types of special families, in which a child's development may be affected in unique ways, are increasing in contemporary America. These include children living with a grandmother as a primary parent, homosexual parents, and live-in situations. Openness, respect, and a desire to talk about the effect of these special family environments on the development of children should be the goal of the child's clinician. Helping parents to guide the development of children who live in special families is an appropriate goal—and challenge—in a developmentally focused clinical practice. The generic functions of a family unit must be kept clearly in mind when the circumstances in which a child lives, no matter how "special" she seems, are evaluated.

REFERENCES

Anderson JZ, White GD: An empirical investigation of interaction and relationship patterns in functional and dysfunctional nuclear families and stepfamilies. *Fam Process* 1986; 25:407–422.

Anthony EJ: Children at risk for psychosis growing up successfully, in Anthony EJ, Cohler B (eds): *The Invulnerable Child.* New York, Guilford Press, 1987.

Bassuk EL, Rubin L: Homeless children: A neglected population. *Am J Orthopsychiatry* 1987; 57:279–286.

Block JH, Block J: The role of ego-control and ego-resiliency in the organization of behavior, in Collins WA (ed): *Development of Cognition, Affect and Social Relations. The Minnesota Symposia on Child Psychology.* Hillsdale, NJ, Lawrence Erlbaum Associates, 1980, vol 3.

Bowlby J: Loss: sadness and depression, in *Attachment and Loss.* New York, Basic Books, 1980, vol 3.

Bryner KB: The Amish way of death: A study of family support systems, in Moos RH (ed): *Coping With Life Crises: An Integrated Approach.* New York, Plenum Press, 1986.

Edelman MW, Mihaly L: Homeless families and the housing crisis in the United States. *Child Youth Services Rev* 1989; 11:91–108.

Ganong LH, Coleman M: The effects of remarriage on children: A review of the empirical literature. *J Appl Fam Child Studies* 1984; 33:389–406.

Garbarino J, Seves J, Schellenbach C: Families at risk for destructive parent-child relations in adolescence. *Child Dev* 1984; 55:174–183.

Garmezy N: Children under stress: Perspectives on antecedents and correlates of vulnerability and resistance to psychopathology, in Rabin AI, Aronoff J, Barclay AM, et al (eds): *Further Explorations in Personality.* New York, John Wiley & Sons, 1981.

Heatherington EM, Cox M, Cox R: Long-term effects of divorce and remarriage on the adjustment of children. *J Am Acad Child Psychiatry* 1985; 24:518–530.

Herndon A, Combs LG: Stepfamilies as patients. *J Fam Pract* 1982; 15:917–922.

Hoyt LA, Cowen EL, Pedro-Carroll JL, et al: Anxiety and depression in young children of divorce. *J Clin Child Psychol* 1990; 19:26–32.

Kappelman MM, Black J: Children of divorce: The pediatrician's responsibility. *Pediatr Ann* 1980; 9:48–64.

Kellam S, Ensminger M, Turner R: Family structure and the mental health of children. *Arch Gen Psychiatry* 1977; 34:1012–1022.

Lazarus RS: *Psychological Stress and the Coping Process.* New York, McGraw-Hill Book Co, 1966.

Lewis FM, Woods NF, Hough EE, et al: The family's functioning with chronic illness in the mother: The spouse's perspective. *Soc Sci Med* 1989; 29:1261–1269.

Maslow AH: *Motivation and Personality,* ed 2. New York, Harper & Row Publishers, 1970.

Murphy LB, Moriarty AE: *Vulnerability, Coping and Growth.* New Haven, Conn, Yale University Press, 1976.

Patterson GR: Stress: A change agent for family process, in Garmezy N, Rutter M (eds):

Stress, Coping and Development in Children. Baltimore, Johns Hopkins University Press, 1988.

Rutter M: Families, in Rutter M (ed): *Helping Troubled Children.* New York, Brunner-Mazel, 1975.

Sameroff AJ, Barocas R, Seifer R: The early development of children born to mentally ill women, in Watt NF, Anthony EJ, Wynne LC, et al (eds): *Children at Risk for Schizophrenia: A Longitudinal Perspective.* New York, Cambridge University Press, 1984.

Sokoloff B: Adoption and foster care: The pediatrician's role. *Prediatr Rev* 1979; 1:57.

Sorosky AD, Baran A, Pannor R: *The Adoption Triangle.* New York, Doubleday Publishing, 1978.

Visher EB, Visher JS: Stepfamilies are different. *J Fam Ther* 1985; 7:9–18.

Wallerstein JS, Johnston JR: Children of divorce: Recent findings regarding long term effects and recent studies of joint and sole custody. *Pediatr Rev* 1990; 11:197–204.

Wallerstein J, Kelly J: *Surviving the Breakup: How Children and Parents Cope with Divorce.* New York, Basic Books, 1980.

Werner EE, Smith RS: *Vulnerable but Invincible: A Longitudinal Study of Resilient Children and Youth.* New York, McGraw-Hill Book Co, 1982.

Wessel MA: The pediatrician and adoption. *N Engl J Med* 1960; 262:446.

Worden JW, Silverman PR: Childhood bereavement: One year later. Paper presented at the 98th Annual Meeting of the American Psychological Association, Boston, 1990.

"A sick boy." By Colin Hennessy, age 5 (sick)

CHAPTER **29**

Children's Encounters With Illness: Hospitalization and Procedures

MARTIN T. STEIN, M.D.

KEY WORDS

SEPARATION EXPERIENCE
OBJECT CONSTANCY
STRANGER WARINESS
PROTEST/DESPAIR/DENIAL
EXPLANATORY MODELS OF ILLNESS
DEVELOPMENTAL REGRESSION/PROGRESSION

The hospitalization of a child represents the removal of that child from a characteristically safe and nurturing environment within the home to a place populated by strangers, to a crib or bed that is unfamiliar, to a place with walls and floors that are different from home colors, and sounds that are new and, at times, cacophonous. The child may experience people in uniforms for the first time. Procedures, examinations, and treatments may be perceived as frighteningly invasive or affrontive to the child. Any hospitalization, no matter how well managed, is a stress for the child. That stress can be a source of growth in experience and competence (Parmelee, 1985) or can create additional illness complications and delay healing in its broadest sense.

Attention to behavioral patterns of hospitalized children has received increasing emphasis in the past 50 years from a research, clinical, and child advocacy vantage (Vernon et al., 1965). In association with the emergence of hospitals and wards designed specifically for the needs of children, more attention has been given to the emotional needs and developmental capacities of children in hospitals. The American Association for the Care of Children in Hospitals has provided leadership to effect these changes. Hospitals in general are better able to respond to the unique needs of children now more than ever before. However, the clinician cannot rely on the institution alone to be supportive of his or her patient during the stress of hospitalization.

IMPACT OF HOSPITALIZATION

The impact of hospitalization for children is significant when viewed from the perspective of a sudden environmental change. There are predictable alterations that a hospital environment brings to a child's relationships with family members, peers, and school activities. Perhaps most significantly, going to the hospital means a loss of independence that is appropriate to the child's developmental level. Because the quest for independent activity and psychological autonomy begins at birth and is the energizing force fueling developmental work, most children are affected by the loss of independence when hospitalized. In addition, they may be stripped of their usual patterns of coping with the stresses of life. This leaves them in a vulnerable, psychologically naked position. We expect their behavior to be altered.

Children develop attachments to important people throughout childhood. A child relies on these to carry him through developmental hurdles and times of stress. Hospitalization has a variable meaning to children dependent on the quality of those attachments and the developmental level of the child. In this context, the experience of separation (from mother, father, or another significant caretaker) is the major psychological event that occurs when a child is hospitalized (Rutter, 1979). She is deprived of the trust and security of the loving person or persons being present at all times of need. The psychological, and resulting physiological, effects of separation are dependent on the child's ability to maintain the image of primary caretaker or caretakers in her mind. This milestone in development is known as *object constancy* (see Chapters 2 and 13). It is one cognitive skill that is necessary but not sufficient for the child to weather the stress of separation. With this skill the child may be able to call forth that image of her primary caretaker without experiencing an overwhelming feeling of abandonment. The attachment figure's presence is maintained throughout the separation if it is relatively short and if the bond has been a strong one.

These concepts can be illustrated by expressing the development of object relationships and separation reactions in terms of the primary developmental theme at each age group from infancy to adolescence (see Table 3–1). At less than 6 months of age, most infants seem to tolerate hospital experiences with minimal long-term behavioral or physiological reactions to separation experiences. Although recent studies have demonstrated that very young infants do distinguish parents and strangers in social interactions, the young infant in the hospital is usually cared for by a stranger (e.g., nurse, physician, technician) without significant changes in behavior. However, the clinician will appreciate behavioral differences in the child when cared for by the parent rather than by a nurse. These differences are data to support or refute the attachment between the parent and child. Although the close bond with the mother is described as "symbiotic" (Mahler, 1975), the infant less than 6 months old has not reached the stage of perceiving himself or herself as an independent being to the point where separation appears threatening. Occasionally even a young infant may show behavioral reactions (fussiness, inconsolability, sleep disturbances) or physiological reactions (vomiting, constipation, poor weight gain, poor feeding) in response to a hospital experience. Young infants will begin to establish new relationships with sensitive, consistent caretakers and will build on these very quickly. Similarly, they re-establish patterns of interactions with parents very quickly after the separation, if brief, has ended. Alterations in sleep patterns and feeding may be a consequence of the impact of these on the child's schedule and state regulation.

Behavioral changes in the toddler, who is undergoing a "separation-individuation" phase (Mahler, 1975), are both more dramatic and require a longer recovery phase. As she develops independence through motor and language functions, there is the accompanying awareness of the psychological impact of separation. The toddler's concern is, "Will mommy come back?" The bravado of the toddler making bids for independence covers a need to fall back on a secure attachment periodically. The phenomenon of stranger wariness (see Chapter 13) is reflected in the toddler by the ability to appreciate cognitively and emotionally a strange environment without the parent's presence and to perceive it as threatening. She also lacks a sense of time so that she cannot appreciate a promise of a prompt return by the parent. Her anxiety remains chronically high. Temper tantrums, listlessness, refusal to eat, and sleep disturbances are characteristic responses of the toddler to a hospital setting or to any separation experience. It reflects the normal development of a strong attachment to the primary caregiver and is testimony to appropriate psychological growth. It is not a problem but a reflection of normal psychological development. Regressive behavior in this situation should be seen as adaptive and appropriate, because it allows for conservation of energy and a bid for help during this "crisis" situation. It usually subsides after hospitalization as long as the separation experience has not been too intense or prolonged.

Normal toddlers who experience abrupt or prolonged separation from parents undergo a progression of behavioral patterns. Originally described by Bowlby (Robertson, 1970), these phases allow the clinician to monitor the child's response to stress. The first stage is one of *protest reaction* (tantrums, refusal to eat, aggressive behavior). It is followed by *despair* (a quiet, withdrawn, sad appearance). This may be followed by a *denial* phase when the previously depressed, despairing toddler now appears outgoing and responsive but flat in affective relations, as if the separation experience did not occur. The child represses her feelings, especially for her mother and father, and simultaneously shows more interest in her emotionally neutral environment, her nurse, physician, and other patients and parents. This third stage attests to a severe stress for the child who is now resistant to engaging in deep relationships or unwilling to risk wide excursions in either negative or positive emotions. It is a conservative psychological mechanism and is evidence of the severity of the insult. Red flags should appear when a child becomes the favorite of every nurse on the floor, offers no objection to examinations, or makes extraordinary efforts to elicit interactions with every passerby.

Language may play an important role in the toddler's reaction to hospitalization. Before age 18 months, the child's expressive language is limited, and she may not understand hospital personnel. She is a stranger in a land that does not understand her. After about 1 year, the toddler becomes acutely aware of this dissonance. After 18 months, the acceleration of expressive and receptive language provides the toddler with the equipment to interact with others in a more advanced form and, therefore, to understand, or at least anticipate, some of the strange manipulations she is experiencing.

In contrast to the toddler, the preschool child's response to hospitalization may call forth newly developed skills of imagination, verbal questioning, and magical thinking to understand and deal with the acute stresses of a strange environment (Robertson, 1970). The 4- to 5-year-old can tolerate the absence of parents for a longer period of time, because she now understands that out of sight is not out of mind. Her memory is better developed and does not require props such as blankets and "loveys" to sustain that image. At the same time, cognitive thinking at this age may produce distortions (Perrin and Gerrity, 1981) about causality, with associated fears, fantasies, and body distortions. Children at this age may feel personally responsible for their illness or that they did something wrong that caused their parents to bring them to the hospital (Bibale and Walsh, 1980). Causal relationships may depend on the child's perception of the temporal or spatial placement of events. This linkage occurs automatically as the child generates her own hypotheses regarding events around her. These "explanatory models" (Klineman et al., 1978) may be very resistant to change, no matter how many "facts" the parents or clinician may provide. Because the preschool child has the emotional and developmental equipment to tolerate separation experiences and to exercise these newly developed capacities, she may learn new coping skills and emotionally grow from hospitalization. This will depend on the strength of her primary attachments, her past history of separation, and the environment. The provision of a supportive environment, appropriate preparation, and outlets for expression of feeling will assist the preschool child in adapting to the hospital experience.

The hospitalized school-aged child is often able to develop peer-group friendships and attachments to nurses, physicians, and other personnel that may buffer the feelings arising from a new environment. Increasing verbal skills and the capacity to understand causality allow the school-aged child to gain more control over the situation. In addition, the child may be able to exercise more options in his treatment and participate in his own care. This is the age of superego (i.e., conscience) development (see Chapter 22), which provides the school-aged child with an internal control over her behavior and an emerging sense of right and wrong. However, because these new cognitive and psychological skills are developing, the hospital experience may become stressful and the school-aged child may experience a loss of internal controls, with subsequent behavioral manifestations of either depression or anxiety or behavioral regression. The concept of "locus of control"—a feeling of either internal or external control of events or an illness—at times may be useful in understanding and navigating a child through a stressful hospital experience (Lefcourt, 1976). The loss of school relationships and fear of getting behind scholastically and socially may add to this distress.

As the child reaches adolescence, the toddler theme of independence versus dependence takes on a more advanced stage of negotiation in the form of a quest for personal identity. A hospital experience, as well as the disease process, confronts the adolescent's identity directly. The loss of an idealized self as a result of the disease, coupled with an abrupt separation from the peer group and the idealized self, may bring about psychological conflict in the hospitalized teenager. The disease process, coupled with invasive hospital procedures, may distort the adolescent's concept of her body image and disrupt future plans. Although the adolescent possesses the cognitive ability to understand causality with regard to illness and the need for hospitalization and procedures, the psychological turmoil may be dominant. The fantasies for the future may be encroached on by visions of deformities and disabilities.

DEVELOPMENTAL REGRESSION

Children of all age groups can be expected to demonstrate a loss of some developmental milestones during and after a hospital experience (Table 29–1). The intensity and duration of developmental regression are controlled by several determinants that have both preventive and therapeutic implications for the clinician:

1. The child's developmental level with regard to social and language skills.
2. Object constancy—has the child been able to separate from parent(s) prior to hospitalization without significant behavioral problems?
3. Personality and temperament—what kind of child was she before hospitalization?

TABLE 29-1.
Consequences of Hospitalization*

Regression
  Immature behavior
    Thumb sucking, enuresis, encopresis, baby talk, clinging, crying
  Feeding dysfunction
  Increased dependency
  Decreased attention span
  School refusal
Sleep disturbance
Anxiety
  Refusal to leave home (separation anxiety)
  Fear of physicians/nurses
Aggressive behavior
  Increased temper tantrums
  Hitting and biting
  Self-mutilation
Progression
  Increased self-esteem
  Accelerated development

*Adapted from Thornton SM, Frankenburg WK (eds): *Child Health Care Communication.* Pediatric Round Table Series no 8. Skillman, NJ, Johnson & Johnson Baby Products Co, 1984.

Can you describe your child's personality? (The quality of the reaction to a separation experience will vary not only with developmental level but also with the unique temperament of each child.)

4. Previous styles of coping with new situations.

5. Characteristics of the illness—duration, acuteness, severity, invasive procedures, immobilization, isolation.

6. Family's response to illness—the behavioral reactions of close relatives may influence the child's behavior. Is denial, rejection, or overpermissiveness apparent (Azarnoff, 1984)?

7. Fears and fantasies—ask the child, "What do you think is wrong with you?" or "Why are you in the hospital?" Observation of play or review of the child's drawings may uncover the fears or fantasies that are based on her own explanatory model of the illness.

In an attempt to lessen the adverse reactions of children to the hospital experience, pediatric professionals should not lose sight of the fact that *developmental regression symbolizes both a stress and a protective maneuver* to defend against the loss of parent or parents and settle into the hospital experience. In this sense, behavioral alterations while in the hospital may be adaptive and represent a healthy response to the separation experience. For example, mild to moderate protest followed by despair in the toddler may be an appropriate adaptation to a strange new world inhabited by a new crib, an intravenous line, and numerous nurses and physicians. Preparing parents for these reponses to hospitalization may help them to understand their adaptive significance (Visintainer and Wolfer, 1975).

TABLE 29–2.
Communicating With Hospitalized Children*

Ages 0–3 yr
 Allow child prior, nonstressful exposure to new perceptual experiences: lights, masks, uniforms, smells, restraints
 Allow child to establish sense of control by handling equipment, performing procedures on dolls
 Provide parent information and allow expression of concerns
 Assure child about return of parents
Ages 4–7 yr
 Provide child with models of coping responses
 Allow child to rehearse coping responses to painful/stressful procedure
 Help child distinguish attainable goals: blood tests cannot be avoided but can be shortened by child's action
 Explore concepts of illness, hospitalization, and procedures
  Misconceptions include
   Illness and procedures are punishment
   Do not believe what can't be seen, e.g., spots only caused externally
   Lumping organ systems: the heart pumps when you breathe
   Blood is a fixed quantity that can be permanently depleted
   All diseases are contagious
   Procedures that hurt are not therapeutic
 Explore concerns about separation, mutilation, physical pain, guilt
Ages 8–12 yr
 Explore concerns about impact on peer relations, especially sense of inferiority
 Explore illness concepts
  Misconceptions include
   Inability to consider simultaneously numerous causes or factors in disease
   Failure to recognize changes in mood, motivation, state, and role accompanying illness
   Failure to understand interdependency among organ systems
   No awareness of preventive action
Ages 13–18 yr
 Explore concerns about body image, independence, sexual identity; interference with ability to establish identity
  especially likely
 Tendency to deny or minimize severity of illness
 May desire more information about etiology and prognosis than physician provides

*Adapted from Thornton SM, Frankenburg WK (eds): *Child Health Care Communications.* Pediatric Round Table Series no 8. Skillman, NJ, Johnson & Johnson Baby Products Co, 1984.

MEASURES TO HELP CHILDREN WITH HOSPITALIZATION

Pediatricians and other providers of health care for children may be advocates for their patients when hospitalization is considered by attending to the following issues (Table 29–2):

1. *Avoid hospitalization when possible.* When diagnostic or therapeutic procedures can be accomplished without hospital admission, it should be encouraged. Outpatient procedures usually allow for more parent participation, which may lessen the stress on the child. Outpatient surgical units for children provide the child a hospital experience without an overnight stay. For example, recently, cardiac catheterization has been accomplished in these units.

2. *Provide parents and the child with an age-appropriate explanation for the hospitalization.* Ask the verbal child, "Why do you think you must come to the hospital?"

3. *For elective procedures (e.g., hernia repair, cardiac catheterization, myringotomy), provide*

the child with a description of the hospital setting and the procedures that will be encountered before anesthesia. Children's books (see Chapter 32), coloring books, and doctor-nurse toys may assist the child in preparing for the new experience. Suggest to parents that acting out a hospital scene at home may help to acquaint the child with the new environment. Some hospitals arrange for tours through the children's facility to acquaint parents and children with the setting, uniforms, and routines before hospitalization. Although these forms of preparation may produce some increase in anxiety during hospitalization, they have been shown to lessen fears, fantasies, and behavioral symptoms during the following year.

4. *Encourage flexible visiting hours that allow for visits from working parents.*

5. *Encourage a rooming-in policy for parents.* The parent's presence in the hospital may assist the child in her adaptation to the new setting by helping her to master separation anxiety, to master self-control of bodily functions, and to overcome ambivalent feelings toward parents. Rooming in may give parents the opportunity to assist in the care of the child and may lessen parental feelings of losing control over the child. Parent participation in hospital care is so beneficial to the well-being of children that it outweighs the occasional problems that parents may bring to the nursing or medical staff. When one nurse from each shift cares for the child during the entire hospitalization, the child and the parents may benefit by developing feelings of attachment and trust.

It is the practice in some hospitals for children to involve parents during the induction of anesthesia. This is carried out in a special room adjacent to the operating room. Although it is difficult to document a beneficial behavioral effect from these child-oriented interventions, they deserve consideration in planning hospital policies along with further careful study.

6. *Hospitalize children in a pediatric setting that is appropriately designed for children.* Colors and pictures on the walls should be child oriented. Toys in a play room that provide flexibility of movement should be available; play is the "work" of childhood, and in this role it provides children with an opportunity for symbolic expression of concerns and fantasies. The mere act of playing can be therapeutic. Encourage the parents to bring a few familiar toys and books as a way to dampen the effects of the separation.

7. *Be truthful about procedures.* Children are not helped by statements such as, "It won't hurt." An age-appropriate description of the hospitalization should be given. When painful procedures are planned, an explanation just before the procedure that "It will hurt for a moment" prepares the child more than 2 years of age in an honest manner. Provide realistic options for the child and age-appropriate opportunities for her to participate in her own care. Set clear, simple limits on behavior and outline for the parents what you think are the necessary limits (e.g., length of stay, mobility, diet).

8. *When possible, allow the child to participate in medical care.* Child-centered health care allows children to feel that they have some control over their bodies, even at a time of illness. For example, ask the older child, "Which arm would you like the blood test from?" An anesthesiologist may offer a child a choice between a clear oxygen mask or an opaque mask during the preinduction period.

9. *Sensory information and coping strategies.* A description of each part of a planned procedure and the purpose behind it may focus on particular sensations that the child will experience. When a venipuncture is planned, a description about the sensation of a tourniquet, the smell of the alcohol, and the feeling of a needle inserting through the skin will desensitize many children to the accompanying fears and pain. As an adjunct to sensory information,

coping strategies—relaxation techniques, self-talk, distracting imagery—can be combined to block out unpleasant sensations (Peterson and Shigetomi, 1981; Siegel and Peterson, 1980). In some pediatric centers, pain management has reached sophisticated levels in the form of hypnosis (Olness and Gardner, 1989) and other distraction/relaxation techniques (Zeltzer et al., 1989 and 1991).

The desired outcomes for the hospitalized child are that the child heals as quickly and completely as possible, that he is supported in an appropriate manner through recognition of his developmental needs, and that he is given the opportunity to grow from the experience.

The clinician's role is to understand and support the child's developmental work while caring for the child's physical illness. The clinician must monitor the environment to assure that it is providing the appropriate support. The parents must be provided with expectations for their child's physical and psychological recovery. They should emerge from the experience of their child's hospitalization as better parents—better observers of their child's physical and mental health—better participants in the healing process—and with an enhanced sense of competency as guardians of their child's health. The child's physician must support these processes through knowledge and sensitivity.

REFERENCES

Azarnoff P: Parents and siblings of pediatric patients. *Curr Probl Pediatr* 1984; 14:1–40.

Bibale R, Walsh M: Development of children's concept of illness. *Pediatrics* 1980; 66:912.

Douglas JWB: Early hospital admissions and later disturbances of behavior and learning. *Dev Med Child Neurol* 1975; 17:456.

Klineman A, Eisenberg L, Good B: Culture, illness and care. *Ann Intern Med* 1978; 88:251–258.

Lefcourt HM: *Locus of Control: Current Trends in Theory and Research.* Hillsdale, NJ, Lawrence Erlbaum Associates, 1976.

Mahler M: *The Psychological Birth of the Human Infant: Symbiosis and Individuation.* New York, Basic Books, 1975.

Olness K, Gardner GG: *Hypnosis and Hypnotherapy With Children,* ed 2. Philadelphia, Grune & Stratton, 1989.

Parmelee AH: Childhood illness as a source of psychological growth. Presidential address, Society for Research in Child Development, 1985.

Perrin EC, Gerrity PS: There's a demon in your belly: Children's understanding of concepts regarding illness. *Pediatrics* 1981; 67:841.

Peterson L, Shigetomi C: The use of coping techniques to minimize anxiety in hospitalized children. *Behav Ther* 1981; 12:1–14.

Robertson J: *Young Children in Hospital,* ed 2. London, Tavistock Publications, 1970.

Rutter M: Separation experiences: A new look at an old topic. *J Pediatr* 1979; 95:147–154.

Siegel LJ, Peterson L: Stress reduction in young dental patients through coping skills and sensory information. *J Consult Clin Psychol* 1980; 48:785–787.

Vernon DTA, Foley JM, Sipowicz RR, et al: *The Psychological Responses of Children to Hospitalization and Illness: A Review of the Literature.* Springfield, Ill, Charles C Thomas, Publisher, 1965.

Visintainer MA, Wolfer JA: Psychological preparation for surgical pediatric patients: The effects on children's and parents' stress responses and adjustment. *Pediatrics* 1975; 56:187–202.

Zeltzer LK, Dolgin MJ, LeBaron S, et al: A randomized, controlled study of behavioral intervention for chemotherapy distress in children with cancer. *Pediatrics* 1991; 88:34–42.

Zeltzer LK, Jay SM, Fisher DM: The management of pain associated with pediatric procedures. *Pediatr Clin North Am* 1989; 36:1–24.

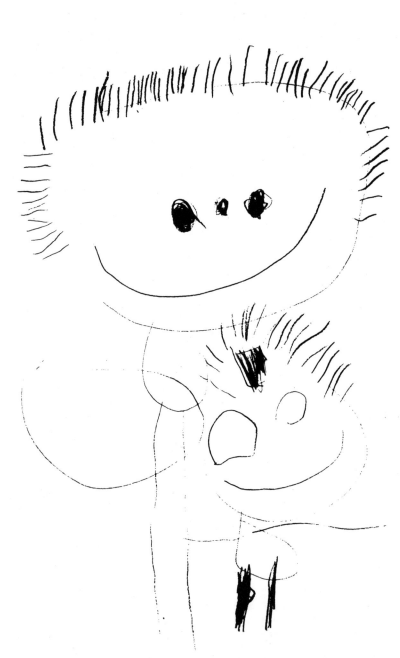

"A grownup and a kid." By Colin Hennessy, age 4½.

CHAPTER **30**

Child Advocacy: A Pediatric Perspective

MARTIN T. STEIN, M.D.

SUZANNE D. DIXON, M.D.

JOHN E. SCHANBERGER, M.D.

The term "child advocacy" is a functional definition for all the work of the practicing pediatric clinician, encompassing the needs of the individual child, the family, and the community as a whole. These concentric circles of care and influence are both the forum and medium of change for the child. These circles are the territory where the pediatric clinician belongs (Fig 30–1).

The advocacy role for children, as it applies to the practice of medicine, encompasses the social, psychological, and biological needs of children. These needs and their solutions are the contents of those concentric circles of influence. The characteristics of the pediatric role in child advocacy require that:

1. The child's *needs* in the broadest sense are given top priority.

2. The child's problems are observed, diagnosed, and remediated from the perspective of the child's *developmental and functional level* of performance as these change and emerge over time.

3. The *prevention* of childhood morbidity and mortality is the primary goal of any child advocacy program. This implies an anticipation of issues before they become in need of treatment.

4. The care of one problem implies consideration of the *consequences* of that problem in all spheres of the child's life.

5. *Environmental factors,* physical, psychological, social, and economic, have direct impact on the developmental processes that then become magnified with time and growth.

For example, diagnosing acute otitis media at an early age and providing appropriate therapeutic intervention, intubating the airway of a distressed newborn in the delivery room, providing oxygen at a moment critical to the child's life, assisting a parent of a "colicky" infant by explaining that behavior in the context of the child's own individuality and development tasks are forms of child advocacy for the individual child within a general pediatric practice that are very common. The focus for this advocacy is on the future for the clinician who already sees the child as growing toward new developmental stages, going over new physiologic hurdles and carving an individual place within the family. The pleasure of pri-

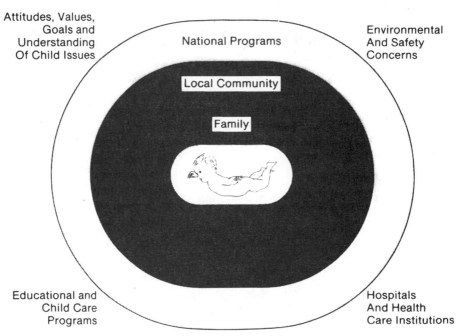

FIG 30-1.
Spheres of advocacy for children.

mary care involves seeing the history being made and anticipating a future—a going for-ward—for that child. To stay grounded in today's issues alone is inherently limiting in a primary care setting. The entire context of this book originated from the idea that the child's clinician is the most effective advocate for the provision of optimal physical and emotional growth of children. It is an advocacy that implies a relationship over time and a foresight that is built on a knowledge of pediatric medicine and child development.

PEDIATRICS: A DIFFERENT RESPONSIBILITY FOR THE INDIVIDUAL

The conceptual framework for child advocacy within the practice of pediatrics has no parallel in adult medicine. Although the clinician for an adult patient assumes that the patient will take appropriate responsibility for his or her health care needs, the child's clinician cannot rest on this assumption. Parents or other caretakers may lack knowledge, experience, skills, emotional stability, or the financial foundation to care adequately for the health of their child. Pediatricians are in a position to provide guidance and information that may assist parents in developing an appropriate physical and emotional environment for the child. Usually parents and the child's clinician can work collectively to ensure what is best for the child. At other, less frequent times, a recommendation from the clinician may conflict with parental beliefs or values. This type of conflict may occur in various clinical areas, such as treatment regimens, participation in contact or overly competitive sports at an early age, or approaches to discipline. Whenever possible, a common ground for discussion should be discovered and explored, starting with a clear elicitation of the parent's perspective. There are times, however, when the duality between the pediatrician as an educator or guide for the parents and the role of child advocate becomes striking. At these times, the child advocacy role and intervention must surface as primary to the task of pediatrics. The child's welfare assumes a central focus.

ADVOCACY DIRECTED AT THE FAMILY

The clinician's second area of care and influence is the next concentric circle—that of the family. The clinician can substantially change the way a family functions through issues related to the care of the individual child. Most (if not all) parents care about the welfare of their children, even when there are other physical and emotional drains on family resources. Parental concern can be mobilized around a child by the clinician working on building a sense of competency in the parents themselves (Belsky, 1984). Programs that assure success for parents with child rearing can energize the family unit to continue that attentiveness. Parental self-esteem in general, and in regard to caretaking in particular, is a necessary component to adequate parenting. Power struggles, confusing directives, or assignments of responsibilities beyond the level of ability of the parents will make the situation worse, and the clinician will thus do harm by creating such situations. Alternatively, situations that ensure success and growth in competency will do great benefit for the family as a unit. Counsel around any particular area must be given in such a way as to enhance parental competency and provide a format for future problem solving. This proactive direction to encourage a sense of parental control on the health of children is supported by recent studies that show that mothers who believe in their own control over their infants' health were more likely to utilize preventive health services on behalf of their infants and affect infant health status (Tinsley and Holtgrave, 1989). The clinician must see the small day-to-day issues as an opportunity for an investment in the family unit as a medium of care for the child. The advocacy for the child in these instances is through an enhancement of the caretaking unit. It extends beyond the immediate issues. Parental well-being and family stability are part of pediatric territory.

The effectiveness of child advocacy through the medium of family is demonstrated in studies of intervention for high-risk infants. Programs that are primarily home based with parental involvement and with recognition of the parents' and siblings' own needs do appear to optimize the development of the high-risk infant (Greenspan, 1985; Sigman and Parmelee, 1979; Beckwith et al., 1976). Individual therapies, toys, or activities do not appear (Leach, 1989) in and of themselves to be important toward a specific developmental outcome; these activities may serve as a media for specific changes in the basic way that parents interact with their children, anticipating the child's needs and wants within a developmental framework (Casey and Whitt, 1980).

The pediatric clinician can support that basic process through a sensitive inquiry about the parent's own concerns, ideas, and activities with a positive response to appropriate actions and questions. During the physical examination, modeling effective interactions with the child and reflecting on the individual child's style and needs is also helpful. Occasionally specific directives may be useful. However, to get any mileage out of these specific directions, the clinician must place them in a broader context of a child's developmental level, and the parent must demonstrate a clear readiness to hear what is offered. Asking a parent for observations, encouraging efforts at problem solving, and reviewing successes and failures around specific issues over a short time frame appears to be a more efficient and effective model in reinforcing the family unit around the child's care.

The clinician's own identification of issues through a sensitive clinical interview may be both an immediate and long-term form of advocacy. Recent recognition that maternal depression is common (10%), may not be recognized by pediatricians, and has adverse effects on child development, suggesting a role for the child's clinician (Zuckerman and Beardslee, 1987). Questions and sensitive observations about parental emotional health, as well as child behaviors, ensure recognition that the clinician is an advocate for the entire family. Physicians can become "enablers" of dysfunctional family situations by ignoring these problems or their consequences rather than directly identifying them and making a referral for help. In these circumstances (e.g., parental alcohol or drug abuse, depression), the general positive, supportive attitude must give way to appropriate intervention and often referral.

Inquiring about a child's worries not only identify an area of concern but also models an approach to the child with other fears. The clinician can identifies the *child's* perspective on a given event that is feared (e.g., a move to a new town) when other family members may not see it either because of their own concerns or because they lack a developmental perspective. In another example, family vacation plans that call for separation of the parent and child at a critical point in the child's life when she might be particularly vulnerable to even a brief separation might be discussed. The clinician does not decide the issue; she only infuses the developmental issue at hand into the family's decision process. If the child can engage in conversation, the clinician may elicit the child's own perspective on a concern, particularly if the family has been unable to bring this out. The clinician is a success as an advocate if both parents and children see the office as a "safe harbor" to bring their concerns, not for solutions but for some direction in their own problem solving.

CHILD-CENTERED INTERVIEWING

The sensitive and developmentally oriented pediatrician practices an important form of child advocacy with each clinical encounter that he or she may not be aware of. Our approach to children—the way we look at them, talk to them, play games with them, and handle them—has a twofold purpose; not only are we seeking a cooperative patient to obtain an adequate physical examination, but we are also providing for the parents a role model for adult interaction with their child. For some parents, there may be little to learn from these interactional encounters; for others, the way we approach their child may provide insight into their own child-rearing practices, as well as a fresh look at how their own child reacts to a different interactional setting. A parent may see her child as separate from her for the first time as the independent relationship the child develops with the clinician unfolds during an office visit.

The focus of all clinical interactions with children should be child centered. To successfully engage a young child requires an ability to tap into that child's world—to ask questions and make comments about things that are of interest or of importance to the child. "The Superman on your shirt sure looks strong." "That hat you're wearing tells me you like baseball." "What a fine drawing you just made . . . tell me about it." Instructive comments can focus on an illness: "I heard from the nurse that you have a sore throat . . . show me where it's sore; what made your throat sore? . . . a germ: how did it get into your throat? . . . What did you do for it at home?" These statements and questions help some parents to see ways in which they can communicate more effectively with their children. Some parents respond with surprise that their child is so communicative, animated, and interactive. As a general rule, office visits that are verbally and visually focused on the child's developmental age will yield potentially beneficial ways for parents to interact with their children (Gordon, 1975).

Child-centered interviewing in a pediatric office practice can have immediate therapeutic value and provide a model for parent-child communication. An encounter with a school-aged child or adolescent who is experiencing anxiety surrounding fear about a nuclear threat, kidnapping, or sexual abuse is a contemporary example of pediatric child advocacy in an office setting. Of course, this anxiety only rarely surfaces as a primary complaint; it is usually disguised in the form of recurrent abdominal pain, headaches, school refusal, or either withdrawn or aggressive behavior. A comprehensive pediatric history and physical examination will suggest a physical cause occasionally. Pediatricians who are sensitive to their patients' family and social milieu will allow the child to express fears and anxieties as the interview unfolds. Observations of facial expressions, play, and family drawings (see Chapter 31) can provide the material necessary to understand the child's concerns. The clinician can help parents discover the way a fear such as the nuclear threat or sexual abuse is expressed by children at various developmental ages; their expression is dependent on the child's level of cognitive and social development. The manner in which the clinician asks a child about these fears can be a model for further exploration by parents in the home.

Discipline is a special area of child advocacy. Many parents need guidelines with regard to the extent and appropriateness of discipline at various ages. The spectrum between over-permissiveness and strict physical and emotional limits on behavior can be seen in different families in most pediatric practices. Although the child's clinician should respect some degree of individual differences between families as to approaches to discipline, she can bring sound developmental principles into the discussion with parents. Simultaneous with these discussions, there may develop opportunities to demonstrate effective limit setting in the office with the active toddler who is into everything or the uncooperative preschooler. Modeling disciplinary experiences may benefit the parent and the child.

ADVOCACY DIRECTED AT THE ENVIRONMENT

The next stage of child advocacy takes place both in office practice and within a local or national community. Pediatricians have traditionally participated in these broader forums for the health care of children. These situations offer opportunities for advocacy within the community, the environment in which the family and the child function (Table 30–1). Preventive office practice with regard to child safety is an excellent example (Table 30–2). Office-based child advocacy is practiced when a clinician is assured that a newborn rides safely home in an infant carseat in the family's automobile after delivery and at subsequent times. Participation in local programs to support the use of child carseats and legislation that requires their

TABLE 30-1.
Child Advocacy: A Pediatric Perspective

Levels of Participation		
Office-Based	Local Community	State and National
Anticipatory guidance	Schools	American Academy of Pediatrics (and
Screening procedures	Day care	other national child advocacy
Role modeling of communication	Media	groups):
skills for parents	Human sexuality	Child health care legislation
Developmental assessment in terms	Education	Education and day-care funding
of psychosocial functioning	Drug abuse	Environmental safety
Child care outside the home	Sports participation	Nuclear threat
Environmental safety	Child abuse and neglect	Occupational health hazards
Child abuse and neglect	Nutrition programs	Pediatric medical research
Sexual abuse	Immunization programs	Television programming
Sports participation	Nuclear threat	Parent Action
Television usage	Television programming	Childrens Defense Fund
Immunizations	Water safety regulations	Child Welfare League of America
	Hospital environment	Private foundations
	Cardiovascular risk reduction	
	Juvenile justice system	

use exemplifies advocacy on the community level. Guiding parents with regard to toys (Greensher and Mofenson, 1985) and furniture that may be safe for children and providing information and early management of childhood poisonings, as well as supporting a poison information center, are areas of expanding pediatric concern. These are examples of child advocacy that a prevention-oriented pediatrician practices every day (Alpert and Guyer, 1985).

As a further extension of the advocacy role, the pediatric clinician can have a significant impact on the hospital environment for children. By working with hospital administration, nursing, and auxiliary staffs, a child- and family-centered environment can be established within a hospital. This should reflect a knowledge of behavioral and developmental phenomena experienced by children in hospitals. The presence of fathers in the delivery room, rooming in during the perinatal period, and a sibling visitation program at that time represent changes in many hospital environments, made by the continuous support of pediatricians who can bring a developmental and child-centered perspective to ensure the continuation of these programs. For older hospitalized children, the presence of a playroom supervised by a child-care specialist and a liberal family visiting policy make hospitals better places for the kids—an opportunity for growth, as well as physiological healing (see Chapter 28).

ADVOCACY DIRECTED AT COMPETITIVE SPORTS

A recent area of child advocacy that has aroused the interest of many pediatricians is that of competitive sports (Table 30-3). Whether individual or team sports, approval for participation in these activities requires an understanding of physical, social, and psychological needs of children at various developmental ages. Preparticipation physical examinations

TABLE 30–2.

Child Safety for Injury Prevention—Anticipatory Guidance to Parents: A Developmental Model*

Office Visit	Developmental Concerns	Information to Parents
Prenatal–2 mo	Rolling off a flat surface; need for full-time protection	Use a car safety seat on the first and every ride Use an undamaged crib with slats less than $2\frac{3}{8}$ in. apart; a snug-fitting mattress, when rail is raised a minimum of 26 in. from the top of the rail to the mattress set at its lowest level; secure and child-proof sidelocking mechanisms; no sharp edges or lead paint Pay constant attention to an infant on a diapering table, couch, bed, or in a bathtub; if interrupted, put infant in the crib, under arm, or on the floor Use smoke and fire detectors, fire extinguishers, and rope ladders in appropriate places; have family fire drills Set water heaters no higher than 130°F
2–4 mo	Grasping objects and putting them into the mouth Increasing activity, therefore, exposed to more hazards	Use a car safety seat correctly and continuously In the crib, eliminate strangulation hazards, e.g., pacifiers or toys with cords, low-hanging cradle gyms, straps, small objects, or window shade cords nearby Never leave an infant unattended where rolling off an elevated surface is possible Select toys that are too large to swallow, too tough to break, and that have no small parts, sharp points, or edges
4–6 mo	Reaching for and pulling objects Feeding self crackers and other items Activity increasing more	Lower the crib mattress before the infant can sit unassisted and to the lowest point before infant can stand Provide high, locked cabinets for poisonous items, never store them in other containers or near food Keep scissors, knives, razor blades, tools, and sharp objects out of reach Use a safe playpen Correctly use a car safety seat
6–9 mo	Crawling, sitting up, pulling self up to stand while holding on Coordinating eye and hand movements more to reach for objects	Install effective safety devices on windows, doors, and screens, at stairways, driveways, storage, and other hazardous areas; use gates at the top and bottom of stairs Keep hot liquids and foods, electric cords, irons, toasters, and coffee pots out of reach; place safety plugs in unused electric wall sockets Prepare foods to a suitable size and texture for the infant to chew and swallow

Continued.

TABLE 30-2.—*Continued*

Office Visit	Developmental Concerns	Information to Parents
9–12 mo	Investigating many places, objects, and substances	Continue use of a car safety seat
	Possibly climbing stairs and beginning to walk	Post the number of the physician's office, rescue squad, and poison control center near the telephone
		Have on hand a dispensed or purchased 1 oz bottle of ipecac syrup to treat poisoning, and follow the advice of the poison control center or physician
		Place the poison control center number also on the bottle of ipecac syrup; many centers have stickers with their number imprinted
		Continue to keep sharp objects out of infant reach
		Supervise infant on stairs
1–2 yr	Walking and climbing	Remove the child from the crib when she is nipple high to the rails (child approximately 35 in. tall)
	Inquisitively opening doors and drawers, taking things apart	
	Enjoys playing in water	Supervise all water activities constantly and competently, including bath or play near ditches, puddles, cesspools, wells; also private and public pools, which should be surrounded by a 4½ ft fence, at least
		Supervise all other inside and outside play and activity by the child alone and with other children
Toddler to 6 yr	Learning to ride a tricycle, then a bicycle	Use auto restraint
	Playing more with other children in areas other than the home	Choose a tricycle or bicycle to suit the child's present size and skill; supervise the child's riding it in safe, traffic-free areas
		Install and/or use playground equipment that is placed at least 6 ft away from walls, fences, other play equipment; anchor it firmly in a soft ground surface
		Supervise learning to cross driveways and streets

*Adapted from Feldman KW: *Pediatrics Rev* 1980; 2:75–82.

should not be limited to the child's physiological well-being (e.g., blood pressure determination, cardiovascular integrity, and musculoskeletal readiness) but should include an assessment of the emotional and social readiness of each child (Table 30–4). Some parents place excessive emphasis on winning or on physical workouts that are inappropriately too long, too frequent, or too vigorous for a particular child. Clinical sensitivity to these issues will sometimes require a frank discussion with an overzealous parent; clarifying to the parent that you are taking the role of the child's advocate may help you and the parent in these discussions.

TABLE 30–3.
Sports Participation: A Potential Influence on Development*

Characteristics of development
  Self-esteem
  Social competency—team sports may encourage an internal locus of control (seeing self as able to make change)
  Emotional adjustment
  Achievement motivation
  Aggression
Environmental factors
  Coaches
  Parents
  Teachers
  Media
  Professional sports personalities (heroes)

*Modified from Livingood AB, Goldwater C, Kurz RB: Psychological aspects of sports participation in young children, in Camp BW (ed): *Advances in Behavioral Pediatrics.* Greenwich, Conn, Jai Press, 1981, vol 2, pp 141–169.

Available research in this area points to the importance of adult models who promote fair play, participation, and improving skills over winning, while maintaining sensitivity to the potential frustrations of intensive competition (AAP, 1983; Smith, 1986).

ADVOCACY FOR CHILDREN WITH SPECIAL NEEDS

The educational system is an important part of the natural habitat of children and, therefore, it belongs to the territory of pediatric advocacy. Clinicians have opportunities to interface with that educational system at the individual and the community level. The child's phy-

TABLE 30–4.
Readiness Factors Influencing Sports Participation*

Motor readiness
  Basic prerequisites: running, throwing, hand-eye coordination
  Minor prerequisites: height, weight, skeletal age
  Specific skills for different sports: e.g., soccer vs. swimming vs. gymnastics vs. baseball
  General physical well-being
Psychological readiness
  Achievement motivation: desire to perform successfully—stages of development for team sport participation
    Capacity to evaluate own competence
    Capacity to compare own performance with others
    Integration of self and comparison evaluations
  Cognitive development (Piaget)—stages of understanding game rules
    Egocentric—play using personal rules
    Cooperative play
    Perception of rules as human productions that can be changed when participants agree
  Moral development (Kohlberg)—stages of moral reasoning:
    Self-gratification and avoiding punishment
    Desire to win approval
    Internal sense of ethics (i.e., internalization of a sense of fair play and sportsmanship)

*Modified from Livingood AB, Goldwater C, Kurz RB: Psychological aspects of sports participation in young children, in Camp BW (ed): *Advances in Behavioral Pediatrics.* Greenwich, Conn, Jai Press, 1981, vol 2, pp 141–169.

sician may identify problems, hurdles, strengths, special needs, and proposed changes for an individual child within a school setting. The clinician can ask the schools for observations, assessments, planning conferences, and participation in therapies. These activities can be accomplished only through a practical knowledge of the local educational community. Such an alliance can be an efficient and effective therapeutic modality for care of an individual child. That same knowledge can be applied to effect systematic changes in school systems at the local level for youngsters with special needs, those who are medically at risk, physically and perceptually handicapped, learning disabled, asthmatic, or diabetic, and those children in need of intervention programming from birth to 3 years of age. Advocacy for these groups within the educational community is a unique opportunity for the pediatric clinician. Additional areas of child advocacy within the educational system might include regular participation in curriculum development around sex education, chemical abuse, or cardiovascular risk reduction. The clinician may also become involved with local television and radio programming that influences issues of child health.

For some pediatricians, active participation in the juvenile justice system is an important part of their local activities. Educational and judicial systems are ready for collaborative programs with pediatrics around special needs children and families (Solnit et al., 1979). Although semantic, as well as organizational, differences exist between these areas, all of these disciplines see themselves as advocates for children. A true collaboration between them can only strengthen child advocacy programs on a communitywide basis and lead to professional enrichment.

An emphasis on developmental principles, coupled with selected use of pediatric research, adds substance to the pediatric child advocate role in the community. For example, while assisting parents of normal children and educators to accept the mainstreaming of a moderately developmentally disabled child into a regular classroom, the pediatrician might use available research to point out the social and psychological benefits to the normal children (Rosenbaum et al., 1986).

ADVOCACY AT NATIONAL LEVEL

At the national level, the pediatric community advocates for children through national organizations such as the American Academy of Pediatrics (AAP) and the Children's Lobby. Through membership in these organizations, the child's clinician, either directly or indirectly, is an advocate for the child's health at a broad level. Examples of these efforts have included support for legislation that requires (1) child-proofing of potentially dangerous medicines (Haddon, 1980), (2) legislation that mandates the use of child-restraint seats in automobiles, and (3) legislation that limits the maximum temperature on hot water heaters to prevent scald burns (Feldman et al., 1978; Feldman, 1980). The "Baby Doe" controversy is an example of pediatric advocacy at the national level as reflected in the major role of the AAP in the provision of guidelines during the controversial national debate. This ensures a balanced view toward the protection of children and families against inappropriate or unjustified medical or surgical interventions. The AAP has been a leader in developing and lobbying for legislation that ensures access to health care for all children, adequate early childhood care and education, and parental leave. Letters, telephone calls, and personal contacts from physicians have powerful influence on legislators.

OFFICE-BASED ADVOCACY

The extent to which a child's clinician participates in these activities is, of course, an individual matter. Participation at the local community, state, or national level usually attracts those clinicians with the interest, time, and capability to offer their advocacy service at the "macro" level. For the majority of child health providers, however, child advocacy remains largely in the domain of the office practice. Although objective documentation of efficacy is a research challenge (Casey and Whitt, 1980), clinicians are aware of the tremendous influence that advice and information from themselves and their office staff can have on parents and children. Always conscious of this phenomenon, the office-based child health clinician is in a unique position to organize health supervision visits to include both prevention-oriented information and clinical assessments, where appropriate, for various age groups of children. Pediatric practice by its nature is an exercise in child advocacy.

CONCLUSION

This book has included information at each office visit in many areas of child health advocacy. As pediatricians come to see themselves in terms of advocates for children, the effectiveness of this role, both in the office and at the community level, will be strengthened. In fact, historical landmarks of modern pediatrics provides an appreciation for the compassion and commitment to child advocacy that was expressed by the pioneers of pediatrics. When George Armstrong initiated the first clinic for the care of London children who lived in poverty, he certainly saw his child advocacy role (Charney, 1974). When Abraham Jacoby, one of America's first practicing pediatricians, provided the professional direction to decontaminate New York City's milk supply, he was a child advocate (Garrison, 1919). In fact, the beginning of the child advocacy movement in America (both within and outside the profession of pediatrics) might be said to have begun in the first decade of this century in association with the progressive movement. Pediatricians and other child health care advocates were active participants in the development of strict child labor laws, improved urban sanitation, and the formation of well-child health stations in America's largest cities (Leopold, 1967).

Certainly, the pediatrician's role as an advocate for children has changed since the turn of the century. Whether choosing to be an advocate for children at the macro or community level, or directing attention to individual issues as an office setting, the pediatric clinician has a unique advocacy role for the health and welfare of children.

> Five little monkeys, jumping on the bed
> One fell off and bumped his head.
> They called for the doctor, and the doctor said:
> "No more monkeys jumping on the bed!"
>
> Old nursery rhyme, Anonymous

REFERENCES

Alpert JJ, Guyer B (eds): Injuries and injury prevention. *Pediatr Clin North Am* 1985.
American Academy of Pediatrics: *Counseling Families in Sports Medicine: Health Care for Young Athletes.* Evanston, Ill, American Academy of Pediatrics, 1983, pp 6–16.

Beckwith L, Cohen SE, Kopp CB, et al: Caregiver-infant interaction and early cognitive development in preterm infants. *Child Dev* 1976; 47:579–581.

Belsky J: The determinants of parenting: A process model. *Child Dev* 1984; 55:83–96.

Casey PH, Whitt JK: Effect of the pediatrician on the mother-infant relationship. *Pediatrics* 1980; 65:815–820.

Charney E: George Armstrong: An early activist. *Am J Dis Child* 1974; 128:824–826.

Feldman, KW: Prevention of childhood accidents: Recent progress. *Pediatr Rev* 1980; 2:75–82.

Feldman KW, Schaller RT, Feldman J, et al: Tap water burns in children. *Pediatrics* 1978; 62:1–7.

Garrison FH: Dr. Abraham Jacobi (1830–1919). *Science* 1919; 50:1283.

Gordon T: *P.E.T.: Parent Effectiveness Training.* New York, Plume Books, 1975.

Greensher J, Mofenson HC: Injuries at play. *Pediatr Clin North Am* 1985; 32:127–139.

Greenspan S: Intervention programs in perspective, in *Zero to Three.* Washington, DC, National Institute of Clinical Infant Studies, April 1985.

Haddon JRW: Advances in the epidemiology of injuries as a basis for public policy. *Public Health Rep* 1980; 95:411–421.

Leach P: *Your Baby and Child,* ed 2. New York, Alfred A Knopf, 1989.

Leopold JS: *Abraham Jacobi,* in Veeder BS (ed): *Pediatric Profiles.* St Louis, CV Mosby Co, 1967, pp 13–19.

Rosenbaum PL, Armstrong RW, King SM: Improving attitudes toward the disabled: A randomized control trial of direct contact versus kids-on-the-block. *J Dev Behav Pediatr* 1986; 7:302–307.

Sigman M, Parmelee AH: Longitudinal evaluation of the high-risk infant, in Field T, Sostek A, Goldberg S, et al: *Infants Born at Risk.* New York, Spectrum, 1979.

Smith NJ: Is that child ready for competitive sports? *Contemp Pediatr* 1986; 3:260–270.

Solnit A, Freud A, Goldstein J: *Beyond the Best Interests of Children.* New York, Free Press, 1979.

Tinsley BJ, Holtgrave DP: Maternal health locus of control beliefs, utilization of childhood preventive health services, and infant health. *J Behav Dev Pediatr* 1989; 10:236–241.

Zuckerman B, Beardslee W: Maternal depression: Concern for pediatricians. *Pediatrics* 1987; 79:110–117.

"My family." By girl, age 13.

CHAPTER 31

The Use of Drawings by Children in the Pediatric Office

JOHN B. WELSH, M.D.

The regular use of drawing can make a number of contributions to a child's visit to his physician. It creates a nonthreatening, relaxing ambience in the office setting and allows the physician to make meaningful observations of the child at the same time. Fine-motor skills, how the pencil is held and manipulated, visual perception, visual-motor integration, and the process of copying geometric shapes and forms can be assessed beginning at 18 months and continuing through adolescence. Sequential drawings should be part of the medical record, to mark the child's progress, to monitor both ordinary and extraordinary adaptive stress, and to serve as a developmental screen.

A definite sequence, beginning with basic linear scribbles progressing to more complex diagrams and on to the designing of suns and mandalas, is seen early in the drawings of toddlers and young preschoolers. The human figure emerges by the time the child is $3\frac{1}{2}$ to 4 years of age. This sequence has been carefully documented through analyses of hundreds of thousands of nursery school scribbles (Kellogg, 1969). These seem to be universal and cross-cultural in their progression toward meaningful, symbolic representation of the human figure (Gardner, 1980).

Well-established norms have been documented for the sequence of copying forms: circles (3 years), squares (4 years), triangles (5 years), and diamonds (6 years). The Draw-A-Person (DAP) Test correlates with mental age and has been used for children more than 3 years of age. It has proved to be reliable for nearly 60 years as a general screening test for well children (Goodenough, 1926; Harris, 1963).

The evolution from subjective to objective realism marks cognitive maturation as the figures drawn progress from depicting the world as it seems to the child to the objective reality of the world as it really exists (Luquet, 1917). These changes correlate with the child's mental structures from "intuitive" or "egocentric" (see Chapter 2) to those of a logical thinker. The child at both stages reveals his perceptions of the world, as well as his ability to replicate these.

The development of a third dimension, depth perception and visual occlusion (not seeing the parts of a figure through another object, so-called x-ray visibility), are marks of intellectual maturity that gradually develop between the ages of 7 and 8 years through 10 and 12 years. Developmental psychologists learn much from the observation of the changes with the age of the child as seen in this progression toward photographic reality. Although the emergence of these elements is quite standard, their *utilization* by any given child remains the unique product of that individual. Temperamental, contemporary, cultural, and even sociopolitical influences shape how these emerging skills are used.

Drawing used as a projective technique in which the child reveals his inner feelings about himself and his world greatly strengthens their utility. This necessitates a wide range of symbolic interpretations to the readings and its effectiveness varies with the skill and experience of the viewer. There is a literature that supports this approach to children's drawings (DiLeo, 1970). Of particular importance are family drawings, especially kinetic family drawings (Burns and Kaufman, 1972). The child is directed to draw a picture with "everyone in your family, all doing something." Considerable sophistication and objective verification of the family drawings have established this technique in child development. Where individual members are placed in the picture, relative size and position on the paper, distortion of mem-

FIG 31–1.
A KFD by a 6-year-old boy who had a particularly close relationship with his mother. The mother is seen attached to a magnified left hand of the child, whereas the father (described as emotionally distant) is placed below the powerful hand and drawn as a smaller figure. An older brother is seen at the right side of the picture.

bers or parts of members, and omitted members can offer insight into family dynamics that may not be otherwise available. Studies employing grid analyses and computer evaluation have added considerable sophistication to these observations (O'Brien and Patton, 1974). Clinically, the child lays out his internal perception of his family through these drawings.

Psychological insights may be especially helpful to the drawings in the subjective reality states, that is, children less than 7 to 8 years of age. The threatening parent of the opposite sex, exaggeration of size, siblings missing, the magnified, nurturing mother, or the threatening, menacing father occur with such regularity as children go through important social and emotional stages that these are seen readily in drawings (Fig 31–1). Occasionally parents can gain insight into these special stages of development from their child's drawings in ways that may not be apparent from the child's behavior. The drawing tells more about deep-seated emotional issues than the child can tell in words or the parent can see in behavior (Fig 31–2).

Parents are often interested in interpretation of these drawings. Caution must be used to not overextend their meanings. At times, however, they can shed illumination on situations

FIG 31–2.
This drawing was done by a 9-year-old boy who had been admitted to the hospital on three occasions for severe abdominal pain and vomiting without a detectable organic cause. His parents had separated. In this KFD, the child demonstrates aggression toward his mother and separates his idolized father ("Bill") and a symbolized monster-sister ("Abby"). The child appeared depressed in the office, and his mother was concerned that "he wants to sleep all the time."

that would be otherwise obscure. The drawing, like a urinalysis or electrocardiogram, is only one piece of data at one point in time and must not be overinterpreted.

Of specific importance to pediatric practice are certain drawing configurations of children with psychosomatic complaints, such as recurrent abdominal pain and headache syndromes. The regularity with which these children produce characteristic pictures can be of considerable diagnostic aid in these clinical situations. Rigid, stiff body images; fixed, uniform smiles; perfect symmetry; short stubby fingers; and "cookie-cutter" figures often correlate with perfectionist, achieving children with significant need for approval and limited ability to ventilate feelings (Fig 31–3). These symbols represent a predisposition to the internalization of stress

FIG 31–3.
Drawing by an 11-year-old girl who is a high-achieving perfectionist. Her mother described her as one who "holds in her feelings." This KFD depicts a uniformity ("cookie-cutter") appearance that reflects internalized stress often manifested in recurrent functional somatic complaints.

and pressures, which results in recurrent somatic complaints. Reviewing these pictures with the child or family often serves to open up the discussion of the background and the dynamics of the complaint.

Assessing school readiness and appraisal of neurodevelopmental status is an important part of pediatric practice. A child's drawing adds a dimension to this evaluation (Fig 31–4). Studies of drawings of preschool children have identified particular characteristics that correlate with subsequent school dysfunction. Examples at this age include poor integration of torso, absence of eyes, ear, and so forth. Age-appropriate visual-motor integration and distortion of body image or other atypical features may point to psychosocial or emotional problems rather than visual-motor integration difficulty. Figure copying may be aberrant at this age in high-risk populations who may otherwise appear developmentally normal. Difficulties seen at this time call for early and *specific* assessment by school psychologists before school entry (Vohr and Garcia-Coll, 1985).

Making the child's drawing a regular part of the medical record gives it an individual identification, which extends over a period of time. Children naturally like to draw; their creations are given recognition and encouragement in an office setting. Drawing and symbolic representation lead naturally to writing and reading and may be useful precursors to the latter. Children are interested in their previous drawings; adolescents, in particular, are impressed with what they have done in the past, and this thread of continuity helps in their seeking a personal identity. Many studies have been made of the drawings of seriously ill children in hospital settings and clinics, and interpretation of these is said to be not only therapeutic for the children but, in some instances, may give useful clues to the developmental stage of the illness. Ill children or those undergoing procedures show cognitive regression, disintegration, and signs of stress. Recovery, in a psychological sense, is seen in subsequent drawings. Jungian analysts emphasize the importance of colors used in the drawings and subtle changes occurring in the course of succeeding pictures as evidence of internal state changes within the child that may precede clinical changes in the course of the illness. The drawings used in this book serve to emphasize the communicative power of these creations in identifying developmental issues, hurdles, and progress.

In summary, children's drawings regularly lessen the stress of the visit to the physician's office and may provide useful information about the developmental status, as well as the family relationships, of the child. Children can be asked routinely to "Draw a picture of your family" at all well-child visits beginning at 4 or 5 years of age.

THE DRAW-A-PERSON TEST

The purpose of the DAP Test is to give the clinician an approximation of the mental age of a particular child. The test assesses three areas of visual-motor development: (1) visualization of the human figure, (2) organization and interpretation (i.e., abstract conceptualization of form, etc.), and (3) reproduction through motor skills of the visualized image as it is seen and interpreted.

The child is given a large blank piece of paper and a pencil and is instructed to draw the picture of a person. He is told to take his time and to draw as complete a picture as possible. The child is left alone to make the drawing, because it is not unusual for a concerned parent to offer help or criticism. The fact that people are hovering over the child can also produce a

FIG 31–4.
A, drawing by a girl, 3 years and 10 months old, with advanced school readiness skills in language, social, and motor areas. This drawing would receive a mental age of 5 years 6 months. **B,** drawing by a 6-year-old boy who was small for gestational age and whose perinatal period was associated with distress and tremulousness in the nursery. Discipline problems characterize his early development. His drawing is atypical at school entry; it demonstrates a constricted sense of self with limited body parts, especially a paucity of facial features. Mental age assigned to drawing is 4 years 9 months. **C,** drawing by a 6-year-old boy with attention-deficit disorder associated with aggressive behavior and hyperactivity. At 4 years old, he had a viral encephalitis with a residual abnormal electroencephalogram. Mental age assigned to drawing is 6 years. **D,** drawing by a boy, 6 years 4 months old, which he described as "an engineer that signals to the train." He demonstrates advanced school readiness skills in areas of fine-motor, spatial, and conceptual skills. Mental age assigned to drawing is 7 years 6 months. (A 20-year follow-up visit revealed that he had completed a degree in architecture and was currently studying to become a stage designer.)

degree of anxiety that might cause the child to make a less complete drawing. The test is most suitable for children between 3 and 10 years of age.

SCORING

The child receives 1 point for each of the items that is present in his drawing. For each 4 points, 1 year is added to the basal age, which is 3. Thus, if the child scores 9 points, his mental age is $3 + \frac{9}{4} = 5\frac{1}{4}$ years. The criteria are shown in Table 31–1.

In addition to measuring mental age, the test can serve as a diagnostic aid as previously mentioned. Very poor drawings, rather than representing low intelligence, may indicate neurological or emotional difficulties, and the child should be examined carefully for physical or neuromuscular defects and emotional symptoms. One can go beyond the cognitive elements of the drawings to highlight certain projective psychological elements as described by Burns and Kaufman (1972) and as shown in Table 31–2.

KINETIC FAMILY DRAWINGS: SYMBOLIC INTERPRETATIONS

The older preschooler and grade-school child can be asked to do a family drawing as previously described. Colors can be used. There is a danger to overinterpretation and misin-

TABLE 31–1.
Scoring Criteria for Draw-a-Person Test

1. Head present
2. Neck present
3. Neck, two dimensions
4. Eyes present
5. Eye detail: brow or lashes
6. Eye detail: pupil
7. Nose present
8. Nose, two dimensions (not round ball)
9. Mouth present
10. Lips, two dimensions
11. Both nose and lips in two dimensions
12. Both chin and forehead shown
13. Bridge of nose (straight to eyes; narrower than base)
14. Hair I (any scribble)
15. Hair II (more detail)
16. Ears present
17. Fingers present
18. Correct number of fingers
19. Opposition of thumb shown (must include fingers)
20. Hands present
21. Arms present
22. Arms at side, or engaged in activity
23. Feet: any indication
24. Attachment of arms and legs I (to trunk anywhere)
25. Attachment of arms and legs II (to trunk anywhere)
26. Trunk present
27. Trunk in proportion, two dimensions (length greater than breadth)
28. Clothing I (anything)
29. Clothing II (two articles of clothing)

TABLE 31–2.
Draw-a-Person: Clinical/Projective Interpretation

Arms—Controllers of the physical environment; *arm extensions* as aids in controlling the environment may include cleaning implements (mops, brooms, vacuum cleaners), paint brushes (paddles?), and weapons; *long and powerful arms* reach out to control the environment; *lack of arms* represents feelings of helplessness; *folded arms* are usually produced by suspicious and hostile persons.

Belt, heavily emphasized—Suggests conflict between expression and control of sex or impulses.

Bilateral symmetry—If overemphasized, suggests an obsessive system of emotional control.

Broad shoulders—Need for physical power.

Buttons—Usually reflect dependency.

Cartoons, clown figures—Self-deprecating, defensive attitudes.

Cross-hatching—"Controlled shading," attempts to control *anxiety* through obsessive methods.

Disproportionately small body parts—Feelings of inadequacy in specific areas, denial, or repression.

Elevated figures—Numerous techniques will be used to elevate various figures; occasionally a dominant sibling will be elevated or it may represent children striving for dominance.

Erasures—Ambivalence, conflict, or denial.

Exaggeration of body parts—Enlargement or exaggeration of parts suggests preoccupation with the function of those parts.

Eyes—Are facial features that refer primarily to social communication; large eyes scan the world for information, whereas small eyes exclude it and may be paranoid in their wariness or crossed out in guilt.

Facial expressions—Faces depicting various emotions were believed by Machover to be one of the more reliable signs of inner feelings.

Feet, long—Need for security.

Feet, tiny—Dependence, constriction, instability.

Figures on the back of the page—Many children will have difficulty with certain figures and may finally ask whether they can put the person on the back.

Hanging, leaning or falling figures—Figures seen in precarious positions are usually associated with tension.

Long necks—Usually reflect dependency in children; because the neck connects the impulse-laden body with the controlling mind, the neck is a frequent area of conflict expression.

Mouth—Emphasis may be associated with feeding difficulties or speech disturbances; in children, overemphasis is frequently associated with dependency.

Omission of body parts—Suggests denial of function; conflict.

Omission of figures—Conflict; the figure cannot be drawn on either the front or the back of the paper; often seen with a new baby.

Precision, orderliness, neatness—Often reflects a need for a structured environment; overconcern with structure may be viewed as an attempt to control a threatening environment.

Pressure—The pressure used in drawing suggests outward or inward direction of impulse, i.e., the depressed person presses lightly, whereas the aggressive, acting-out individual uses excessive pressure.

Rotated figures—Feelings of being different, demanding attention.

Shading or scribbling—Shading in a drawing suggests preoccupation, fixation, or anxiety.

Size—Size suggests diminished or exaggerated view of the self; persons who feel inadequate usually draw a tiny person.

Teeth, prominent—Anger

---

terpretation of symbols that can be prevented by considering the totality of the individual who made the drawing. Viewing the drawings with a comprehensive pediatric medical and developmental perspective should prevent these mistakes (Burns and Kaufman, 1972). Some possible interpretations have been found to recur in kinetic family drawings. Repeated drawings, each with the context clearly laid out, are good for informal and clinical use in a pediatric setting. They provide suggestions and support for diagnostic formulations. They are not diag-

TABLE 31–3.
Interpretation of Elements in Kinetic Family Drawings

As—Associated with an emphasis on high academic achievement.

Beds—Relatively rare; associated with sexual or depressive themes.

Bikes—A common activity of normal children; when overemphasized, may reflect the child's (usually a boy) significant strivings; more common in adolescents when the power of the bike and motorbike become particularly important.

Brooms—A recurrent symbol; particularly in the hands of mothers who put much emphasis on household cleanliness.

Butterflies—Associated with the search for elusive love and beauty.

Cats—Often symbolic of conflict in identification with mother; a dominant symbol in many KFDs,* particularly girls; the "furry cuddliness" combined with teeth and claws—*ambivalence, conflict.*

Clowns—A preoccupation often seen in a child with significant feelings of inferiority.

Cribs—A new baby in the family often produces jealousy in older siblings; because of their "magical thinking," they may insist on staying home from school out of a fear that something will happen to the baby.

Dirt—A theme of digging or shoveling dirt is associated with negative connotations about dirty thoughts or dirty clothes.

Drums—Displaced anger.

Electricity—An extreme need for warmth and love.

Fire—An intense need for warmth and love; the fact that love may turn into hate—a destructive force (most fire setters are passive-aggressive personality types).

Flowers—Love of beauty, the growth process; in girls, flowers below the waist reflect feminine identification.

Garbage—"Taking out the garbage" for many children is equivalent to taking out the unwanted and "dirty" parts of the family existence; frequently found in KFDs when there is a new baby in the house, or a new foster child; without young infants, garbage may reflect significant guilt about feelings of ambivalence and rivalry toward a younger sibling.

Heat—Need for love and warmth.

Horses—A safe comfortable sexual symbolic identification found universally in Western culture among adolescent girls.

Ironing board—With an "X" by adolescent boys may reflect conflict and ambivalence toward mother; the *iron* may reflect the intensity of the feelings.

Jump rope—The encapsulation of a rival or protection for the self.

Kites/balloons—Attempts to escape from restrictive family environments; escape and freedom.

Ladders—Tension, precarious balance.

Lamps—The need for warmth and love.

Lawnmower—A cutting symbol that is usually associated with a castrating figure; usually drawn by boys.

Leaves—Dependency; a symbol of that which clings to the source of nurturance.

Light bulbs—Need for warmth and love; also *flashlights.*

Logs—Hypermasculinity or masculine strivings.

Paint brush—Often an extension of the hand and associated with a punishing figure.

Rain—Associated with depressive tendencies.

Refrigerators—Associated with deprivation and depressive reactions to deprivation; the refrigerator is a source of nurturance but is still a cold object.

Skin diving—Usually drawn by boys; associated with withdrawal and depressive tendencies.

Snakes—An infrequent but well-known phallic symbol.

Stars—Associated with deprivation—physical or emotional; stars are usually cold and distant.

Stop sign—"Keep out"; attempts at impulse control.

Sun—In young children, the sun is stereotyped and has little meaning; a darkened sun drawn by older children may reflect depression; the sun's face may reflect pertinent emotions; if figures are facing the sun—the need for warmth and love; if facing away from the sun—rejection.

*KFDS = Kinetic family drawings.

nostic in themselves. Some may have *no* symbolic meanings (Koppety, 1968). Interpretive elements are laid out in Table 31–3.

SUMMARY

Children's drawings are a delightful, cost-effective way of highlighting a child's developmental progress, emotional and social concerns, and needs for further evaluation. This low-cost diagnostic aid adds vitality, veracity, reflection, and insight into every pediatric encounter. Facility with this tool should be in every black bag.

REFERENCES

Burns RC, Kaufman SH: *Actions, Styles and Symbols in Kinetic Family Drawings: An Interpretive Manual.* New York, Brunner-Mazel, 1972.

DiLeo JH: *Young Children and Their Drawings.* New York, Brunner-Mazel, 1970.

Gardner H: *Artful Scribbles: The Significance of Children's Drawings.* New York, Basic Books, 1980.

Goodenough FL: *Measurement of Intelligence by Drawings.* New York, World Books, 1926.

Goodnow J: *Children Drawing.* Cambridge, Mass, Harvard University Press, 1977.

Harris DB: *Children's Drawings as Measures of Intellectual Maturity.* New York, Harcourt Brace & World, 1963.

Kellog R: *Analyzing Children's Art.* Palo Alto, Calif, National Press, 1969.

Koppety EM: *Psychological Evaluation of Children's Human Figure Drawings.* New York, Grune & Stratton, 1968.

Luquet GF: *Les Dessins d'un Enfants: Etude Psychologique.* Paris, Alcain, 1917.

O'Brien RP, Patton WW: Development of an objective scoring method for kinetic family drawings. *J Pers Assess* 1974; 58:156–164.

Vohr B, Garcia-Coll CT: Neurodevelopmental and school performance of very low birth weight infants: A seven year longitudinal study. *Pediatrics* 1985; 345–350.

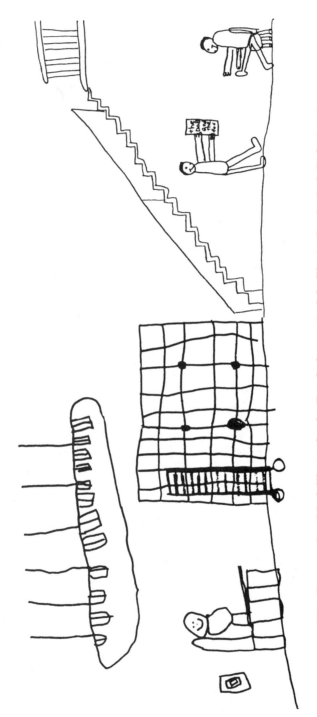

"Reading together." Left illustration by Ben Stein, age 5; right illustration by Josh Stein, age 8.

CHAPTER **32**

Books for Parents, Videos for Kids: An Annotated Bibliography

PAM KAISER, M.N., C.P.N.P.

MARY CAFFERY, R.N., M.S.N.

HEDI J. BREHM

SUZANNE D. DIXON, M.D.

MARTIN T. STEIN, M.D.

MARIANNE E. FELICE, M.D.

Pediatric professionals recommend books for parents to read for various reasons. Books often serve as an adjunct to the teaching done in the office. Some parents need and/or request additional information on topics discussed briefly in the office visit. Books can provide a reinforcing or differing view, as needed. Parents with children with special needs, e.g., twins, prematurity, may be especially appreciative of such resources.

Several factors should be considered before recommending a book. These include: the parents' particular need, the child's developmental level, the parents' ability to use written material, what is affordable and available, and parental motivation. Written information cannot replace the valuable personal, direct interaction between a parent and the clinician around particular issues. Clinicians should be clear about the goals to be achieved in recommending books. There is the pernicious belief that parenting can only be done by professionals and that more information automatically ensures better parenting. The clinician can unconsciously support those beliefs and add to anxiety by wholesale or routine reading suggestions.

Maximal availability of the books will offer the opportunity for ready utilization. Strategies include keeping copies of selected books in the waiting room and/or examining room, having books available to purchase at cost in the office, compiling a lending libary, and requesting a nearby bookstore to stock selected favorites.

A few cautions are in order. First, it is essential for the clinician to read the books. One must be familiar with the author's philosophy and recommendations to determine if the book would be compatible with the clinician's own philosophy and information imparted to parents in the office.

Second, the following list has been selected from the vast and ever-growing literature available for parents. Criteria for selection include:

1. Clarity—succinct, easy to comprehend vs. wordy and rambling;
2. Organization—well-defined topics, headings, and subheadings;

3. Author's attitude—condescending and guilt-inducing vs. reassuring, and supportive;
4. Author's qualifications.

The clinician should periodically peruse the child-development section at the local bookstore in order to be familiar with the most current books.

BIBLIOGRAPHY FOR PARENTS

CHILD DEVELOPMENT

1. Ames LB, Ilg F: **Your One Year Old: The Fun Loving Fussy** (1982); **Your Two Year Old: Terrible or Tender** (1976); **Your Three Year Old: Friend or Enemy** (1976); **Your Four Year Old: Wild and Wonderful** (1976); **Your Five Year Old: Sunny and Serene** (1979); **Your Six Year Old: Loving and Defiant** (1980). New York, Dell Books. *Codirectors of the Gesell Institute of Child Development, these authors display their knowledge, experience and sense of humor in their uncanny skill of depicting accurate portraits of children's behavior. Very practical advice combined with a reassuring style make these books invaluable reading for a frustrated parent.*

2a. Brazelton TB: **Infants and Mothers.** New York, Dell, 1969. *In describing the behavior of three normal babies, Dr. Brazelton makes it extremely clear how different infants can be. His descriptions of the interactions between average, quiet, and active babies and their families during the first year of life make worthwhile reading for new parents and also for parents who make frequent comparisons between their infant and other babies.*

2b. Brazelton TB: **Toddlers and Parents.** New York, Dell, 1974. *With empathy and humor, Dr. Brazelton presents a realistic family profile in the turbulent life of a child from the ages of 1 to 2½ years. He explores the toddler's developmental work of self-assertion, as well as the issues of toilet training, sibling rivalry, working parents, and single parents.*

2c. Brazelton TB: **On Becoming a Family.** New York, Dell, 1983. *The case-vignette style is extended to the exploration of attachment, social development, parenting issues, and care in the immediate newborn period; a section on prematurity is included.*

2d. Brazelton TB: **Working and Caring.** Reading, Mass, Addison-Wesley Publishing Co, 1985. *Sensitive work on all aspects of family development when mother works. Essential reading for all families in all parts of society struggling with making things work.*

2e. Brazelton TB: **To Listen to a Child.** Reading, Mass, Addison-Wesley Publishing Co, 1984. *Discussion of several behavioral/developmental problems in a sensible, positive manner. Helpful with older children's issues as well as those of younger children.*

3a. Caplan F (ed): **The First Twelve Months of Life.** New York, Grosset & Dunlap, 1973. *Recognizing that parenting is a difficult job, Caplan has brought together much of the most recent research on infants in an effort to help parents understand why babies behave as they do. In addition to interesting descriptions of a baby's month by month development, the book contains numerous photographs and growth charts. Sensitive to individual differences among infants, Caplan is also sympathetic to the feelings of new* *parents. This excellent book has a wealth of information, which is both fun to discover and helpful to know.*

3b. Caplan F, Caplan T: **The Second Twelve Months of Life.** New York, Grosset & Dunlap, 1977. *This companion volume to The First Twelve Months of Life is also written in an easy-to-read format accompanied by photographs and growth charts. A highly recommended resource for parents.*

4. Chase R, Rubin R (eds): **The First Wondrous Year.** Johnson & Johnson, Child Development Publications, New York, Collier Books, 1979. *An innovative resource on social, emotional, and physical development from birth to the age of 1 year. An excellent and extensive section on play and learning with numerous, simple play-stimulation suggestions. A major strength of the book is the 1,200 well-selected photographs that are particularly useful teaching tools for the parent not having an extensive inclination toward reading, and/or needing concrete ideas on how to interact with the baby.*

5. Comer JP, Poussaint AF: *Black Child Care.* New York, Simon & Schuster, 1975. *A general guide to parenting directed toward black families but not nearly as ethnic-specific as it could be.*

6. Fraiberg S: **The Magic Years.** New York, Charles Scribner's Sons, 1959. *Child psychoanalyst Fraiberg discusses early psychological development (birth to 6 years) as if the reader were experiencing the child's inner world. More theoretical than most books, it discusses typical developmental problems and their management. Very sensible observations. A big favorite for pediatricians in the making and established.*

7. Hagstrom J, Morrill J: **Games Babies Play.** New York, A & W Publishers (Pocket Books), 1979. *A series of suggested play activities with infants to capture developmental competencies. Helpful for parents who would like or need very specific suggestions in getting going with their young infant. Avoid prescribing this book too rigidly.*

8. Rubin R, Fisher J, Deering S (eds): **Your Toddler.** Johnson & Johnson, Child Development Publications, New York, Collier, 1980. *This resource provides down-to-earth explanations of the many developmental issues that occur from 1 to 3 years of age. As in The First Wondrous Year, the book's major strength is the section on play and related practical suggestions accompanied by well-chosen pictures.*

9. Rubin R, Fisher J: **Your Preschooler.** Johnson & Johnson, Child Development Publications, New York, Collier, 1982. *The same format as the previous two on development during the ages of 3 and 4 years. Includes a discussion of preschools, television, and peer relationships.*

10. White BL: **The First Three Years of Life**. New York, Prentice Hall, 1989 ($10.95). *Solid theoretical material and practical advice. Weekly accounts of all aspects of development. Language, titles, and background material are really geared for the well-educated parents who want the background developmental issues.*

PARENTING

1. Ames LB: **He Hit Me First: When Brothers and Sisters Fight.** New York, Debner Books, 1972. *This child developmentalist explains the dynamics of sibling rivalry in a reassuring and readable way. Loaded with practical suggestions.*

2. Barber V, Skaggs M: **The Mother Person.** New York, Schocken Books, 1975. *The book gives a candid description of the challenging experience of motherhood. The authors*

explore such issues as expectations of self, family, and society and the struggle with emotions like anger, depression, guilt, and ambivalence. Well-written in a forthright manner by these mothers, the book is geared to educated women and is also illuminating for pediatric professionals who are not parents themselves.

3. Brazelton TB: **Families: Crisis and Caring.** New York, Ballantine Books, 1989 ($12.95). *Insightful and useful description of families in transition including divorce, stepparenting, parenting rivalry, infertility, loss of a parent, adoption and illness. The case histories and dialogues describe family members' reactions to a crisis and the strategies used by the family to regain balance.*

4. Ferber R: **Solve Your Child's Sleep Problems.** New York, Simon & Schuster, 1985. *Excellent explanations of the developmental basis of sleep disturbances in a family context. Very specific, sensible suggestions for problem solving from sleep rhythm disturbances to enuresis. Highly recommended; for educated parents only.*

5. Gordon T: **P.E.T.: Parent Effectiveness Training.** New York, Plume Books, 1975. *One of the best books in presenting the basic essential communication skills needed in families: how to listen, how to communicate your feelings, how to solve conflicts. Recipe format. Gives parents a concrete place to manage issues and sets up an approach to problem solving.*

6. Greenspan S, Greenspan NT: **First Feelings.** New York, Viking, 1985 ($3.95). *This book chronicles the stages of emotional and cognitive development from birth through age 4. Six stages in the emotional life of the young child are seen as critical to healthy development: the awakening of the infant, the discovery of communication, the deepening of relationships, the developing sense of self and the ability to create new ideas and complex feelings. Descriptions of children and families are strategically used to clarify each stage. Practical advice to assist parents as they encounter the range of children's emotions, fears and struggles. College educated audience.*

7. Greenspan S, Greenspan NT: **The Essential Partnership.** New York, Penguin, 1989 ($8.95). *This book builds on the information presented in* First Feelings, *offering guidelines on everyday childrearing issues from infancy through age 4. The authors discuss relationship building, self-esteem, independence, anger, aggression, tantrums, and peer relationships. Case histories, including single and dual career families, clarify concepts and offer practical advice. Offers an excellent discussion on the use of play time or "floor time" as an opportunity to observe and learn about children.*

8. Hopson DP, Hopson D: **Different and Wonderful. Raising Black Children in a Race Conscious Society.** New York, Prentice Hall, 1990 ($19.95). *Black children in America are born into a society with strong racist undercurrents that can damage self-esteem and reduce control over their environment. Black parents are faced with the challenge of raising children with a positive sense of self worth in a society that judges blacks as less intelligent, attractive, and trustworthy.. This book guides black parents through each phase of child development in the context of race issues and self esteem. Explores tough issues affecting black middle class families. Provides parents with practical tools for recognizing their own racial attitudes, instilling ethnic pride and discussing race related issues. Offers a resource guide to direct parents toward children's books and toys that celebrate African-American culture.*

CHILD HEALTH AND PHYSICAL CARE

1. Eisenberg A, Murkoff HE, Hathaway SE: **What to Expect the First Year.** New York, Workman, 1989 ($12.95). *Comprehensive guide to newborn and infant care. Offers up-to-date practical information. Format is easy to read as chapters identify issues at monthly stages. Useful sections on nutrition, language development and safety-proofing.*

2. Hillman S: **The Baby Checkup Book.** New York, Bantam Books, 1982. *Gives parents expectations for health supervision visits, outlining the issues, concerns, and procedures. This book shouldn't be necessary if the clinician has good communication skills and a developmental focus. Provides a check on the clinician.*

3. Johnson SA: **First Aid for Kids.** New York, Quick Fox, 1981. *A brightly colored, clearly organized presentation of the proper handling of both minor and major emergencies. Supports parents' and teachers' sense of competence in dealing with everything from insect bites to burns, cuts, and common diseases.*

4. Kelly P: **First Year Baby Care.** Meadowbrook Press ($6.95). *Brief handling of issues from the most basic forward. Checklists, charts, and instructions will be helpful with a lot of backup by the health care provider.*

5. Leach P: **Your Baby and Child,** ed 2. New York, Alfred A Knopf, 1989 ($17.95). *A developmental psychologist, Penelope Leach has written an outstanding encyclopedia for parents of children from birth to 5 years. Her developmental approach to everyday care and common behavioral issues is accessible to most parents and families. Subtitles within the chapter, and a superb index with definitions, facilitate reading this comprehensive book. Many excellent drawings and pictures contribute to its practical, easy to use, and acceptable style.*

6. Leach P: **Your Growing Child.** New York, Alfred A Knopf, 1989. *An encyclopedia of child care issues, from health to nutrition to development. Solid, clear, although brief sections. Alphabetical format a bit difficult to use. However, it does cover issues through adolescence, with a strong section on the teenage issues.*

7. Pantell R, Fries JF, Vickery DM: **Taking Care of Your Child: A Parent's Guide to Medical Care,** ed 3. Reading, Mass, Addison-Wesley Publishing Co, 1990. *Pediatrician Pantell and his colleagues outline many aspects of health promotion, approaches to common symptoms, and home management for parents. Through a series of algorithms designed for parents faced with specific symptoms, the format is especially lucid and practical.*

8. Pomeranz VE (MD): **The Mothers' and Fathers' Medical Encyclopedia.** Signet ($4.95). *The new "Merck Manual" for pediatric issues, this book contains everything from illnesses to accidents, drugs and diseases. The section on medical emergencies is particularly good.*

9. Schmitt BD: **Your Child's Health: A Pediatric Guide for Parents.** New York, Bantam, 1987 ($12.95). *Clearly written, practical guidebook on children's common illnesses, behavior problems, and health promotion from infancy through adolescence. Offers parents appropriate and safe home remedies and guidelines for seeking emergency and nonemergency medical care. The behavior modification protocols for common developmental problems are readily accessible and practical to most parents.*

10. Shelov S (ed): **Caring for Your Baby and Young Child: Birth to Age 5.** New York, Bantam Books (for American Academy of Pediatrics), 1991. *Written especially for new parents, this well written guide for parenting in the first 5 years of life was developed by the American Academy of Pediatrics. Details about physical and psychological growth, development and common problems of early childhood are described in appropriate detail to be of help to all parents. The index and organization of the book provide quick access to questions and concerns.*

11. Spock B, Rothenberg MB: **Dr. Spock's Baby and Child Care.** New York, Pocket Books, 1985 (softcover, $5.95); EP Dutton (hardcover, $19.95). *This classic, revised for the nineties, contains an impressive quantity of useful information. New parents will appreciate the question-and-answer format used for Dr. Spock's suggestions regarding the recognition and appropriate management of both common and uncommon physical and emotional problems. The index provides quick responses to concerns of new parents. A must for all clinicians as well as parents!*

12. US Department of Health and Human Services: **Infant Care.** DHHS Publication No HRS-M-CH-89-2, 1989, 109 pp. *A short and easy-to-read manual, it contains helpful information for new parents. Basic information that new parents need include care of the baby, special problems that may develop (such as illness or accidents), developmental characteristics of infants, ways to enhance their growth through play, and a discussion of temperamental differences among babies. Available in Spanish. A single copy is free from the National Maternal and Child Health Clearinghouse, 38th and R Streets NW, Washington, DC 20057. Additional copies can be purchased for $1.50 each.*

13. US Department of Health and Human Services: **Your Child From 1 to 6.** Superintendent of Documents, US Government Printing Office, DHHS Publication No OCD 91-30026, 1991. *This 92-page booklet begins where* Infant Care *leaves off. It contains material relating to the emotional and intellectual development of the child, as well as medical information. It makes helpful suggestions for handling special situations, such as going to the hospital, moving, handicaps, illnesses, and accidents. Available in Spanish. A single copy is available free from the National Maternal and Child Health Clearinghouse, 38th and R Streets NW, Washington, DC 20057. Additional copies are $1.00 each.*

14. Wessel M: **Parents® Book for Raising a Healthy Child.** New York, Ballantine Books ($3.95). *This collection of articles published in* Parents Magazine. *Solid advice, easy reading, good suggestions for problem solving. Alphabetical sections of diseases, procedures, medications, etc.*

DAYCARE

1. Katzev AR, Bragdon NH: **Child Care Solutions.** New York, Avon Books, 1990 ($7.95). *Comprehensive guide for the selection of day care from infancy to after-school care. Identifies strategies for parents to use as they search for, evaluate, and choose among various child care environments. Includes practical advice for parents as they manage day-to-day child care issues and strive to work effectively with providers.*

2. Scarr S: **Mother Care/Other Care.** New York, Basic Books, 1984. *The most up-to-date discussion of all the issues, as science can delineate them. Thorough, scholarly, the*

best summary work so far available. For educated parents. Be prepared to discuss this book with families.

3. US Department of Health and Human Serrvices, Office of Human Development Services, Daycare Division: **A Parent's Guide to Daycare.** Superintendent of Documents, US Government Printing Office, 1980. DHHS Publication No (OHDS) 80-30254. *A practical, readable, and inexpensive booklet for parents. Part I discusses the components of quality day care and pragmatic considerations to be made before seeking day care. Part II details the step-by-step process of finding day care arrangements. The checklists are particularly valuable. In addition to noting the age-related needs of children and individual parent preferences, special situations such as nighttime care, single parenting, and children with special needs are considered. Part III covers a multitude of common day-care problems and suggestions for management. Part IV offers resources of organizations and agencies that may be useful when selecting day care for children with handicapping conditions as well. In addition to the manual's reasonable length (75 pages), sections are designed to enhance finding the particular information needed by having headlines in the left column and boldface headings in the text. Highly recommended.*

4. Woolever E (ed): **Your Child: Selecting Day Care.** Des Moines, Iowa: Better Homes and Gardens Books, 1990 ($2.95). *Brief, but thorough review of issues that parents face as they evaluate and select child care. Includes checklists for evaluating the child care providers, identifying the quality among programs and their safety. Provides excellent information on parent/child care provider relationships.*

FAMILIES WITH SPECIAL NEEDS

PREMATURITY

1. Harrison H: **The Premature Baby Book.** New York, St. Martin's Press, 1983. *Parents will appreciate this book as the* most complete *compilation of information about preemies. Written by the mother of a preemie with extensive consultation from neonatology experts, this is a superb resource. Numerous vignettes of families' responses and adaptation make this a "must" for neonatal staff as well.*

2. Metcalf S: **Getting to Know Your Premature Baby.** March of Dimes, 334 E Broadway, Room 131, Louisville, KY, 1978. *This 20-page booklet is written in a simple, readable way to assist parents who have had a premature infant. Nurse author Metcalf describes the preemie's appearance, sensory skills, and stimulation needs. This very inexpensive (50 cents) pamphlet is easily understood by a person with a seventh-grade reading level.*

3. Nance S: **Premature Babies: A Handbook for Parents.** New York, Arbor House, 1982. *A full text, written by and for parents, but very useful to professionals as well; covers parenting, medical, behavioral, and family services. Vignettes, letters, and pictures add vitality to presentation. A list of resources is in the back.*

4. Shosenberg N: **The Premature Infant: A Handbook for Parents.** Toronto, The Hospital for Sick Children, 1980. *An excellent 60-page booklet with numerous photographs, which follow a preemie's course from admission to the special-care nursery to discharge home. Content includes explanations of the preemie's physical appearance and physical problems (e.g., respiratory distress syndrome, jaundice), as well as practical advice regard-*

ing home care. The compassionately written section on parents' feelings reflects the nurse author's experience with this patient population. This affordable ($3.00) booklet would make a perfect supplement to teaching given by the nursery staff. Best understood by persons at a high-school reading level.

TWINS

1. Theroux R, Tingley J: **The Case of Twin Children: A Common Sense Guide for Parents.** The Center for Study of Multiple Gestation, 333 E Superior St, Suite 463-5, Chicago, IL, 1978. *Two nurses draw on their research as well as their own experience as mothers of twins in providing common-sense suggestions for parents of twins. The chapters are separated by age (birth–teens) covering basic care, logistical advice, and developmental issues. A most useful resource for parents of a multiple birth. A complete list of twin-care booklets and pamphlets is available from National Organization of Mothers of Twins Clubs, Inc, 5402 Amberwood Lane, Rockville, MD 20853. Information sheets on twins are available in Spanish.*

HANDICAPPED

1. Cunningham C, Sloper P: **Helping Your Exceptional Baby: A Practical and Honest Approach to Raising a Mentally Handicapped Child.** New York, Pantheon Books, 1978. *Cunningham and Sloper, researchers of early development of mentally handicapped children, present an extensive, supportive, and down-to-earth program of exercises, games, and other forms of stimulation that parents can employ to help their child master the skills of the first 2 years—from basic processes of turning and reaching to more complex actions such as crawling. A realistic guide, particularly for teaching babies with Down syndrome under 3 years of age.*
2. Freeman RD, Carvin CF, Boese RJ: **Can't Your Child Hear? A Guide for Those Who Care for the Deaf.** Austin, Texas, ProEd, 1981. *Complete, clear guide for a child with any degree of hearing impairment from birth onward. Good resource for professionals, too.*
3. Schleichkorn J: **Coping With Cerebral Palsy.** Austin, Texas, ProEd, 1983. *This paperback book provides concise guidelines toward an understanding of the issues facing children with CP, definitions of medical terms, psychosocial issues, and educational concerns. It has a particularly valuable section which describes issues that affect the older child and adult and a further list of readings. Appropriate for beginning a discussion with a family after an initial post-diagnosis adjustment period.*
4. Stewart MA, Wendkos-Olds S: **Raising a Hyperactive Child.** New York, Harper & Row, 1973. *This book teaches parents to think and act positively with these challenging children. Medically a little dated but this doesn't appear to jeopardize the value of the advice.*
5. Thompson CE: **Raising a Handicapped Child.** New York, William Morrow and Co, 1986. *Written by a pediatrician and mother, this book addresses issues facing a family with a major handicapping condition. There is a significant portion dedicated to the feelings of parents and helpful approaches to coping. Strategies for working with medical and*

educational systems are discussed. This book is for parents of a child with an established disability, particularly for those in a "dawn time" of grief, frustration or hopelessness.

GIFTED CHILDREN

1. Ehrlich VZ: **Gifted Children: A School for Parents and Teachers.** Englewood Cliffs, NJ, Prentice-Hall, 1982. *General overview for parents with children who have special educational needs that are not being met by standard or enriched programs. The focus is on schooling issues.*
2. Laycock F: **Gifted Children,** Glenview, Ill, Scott Foresman & Co, 1979. *Theoretical and historical perspectives on this population. Sociologic and political issues sprinkled in with practical suggestions.*

DIVORCE AND STEPFAMILIES

1. Bernstein AC: **Yours, Mine and Ours.** New York, Norton, 1990 ($10.95). *This book explores how families change when remarried parents have a child together. Based on the author's experiences as a stepmother/family therapist and on interviews with "mixed" families, this book explores the psychology and social influences of stepfamilies. Bernstein details the interdependent roles of each member in a stepfamily and analyzes the issues of resentment, competition and anger.*
2. Evans MD: **This Is Me and My Single Parent** (1989); **This Is Me and My Two Families** (1988). New York, Magenation Press. *Fill in the blanks workbooks for parent(s) and children to do together in order to open up discussion on the stress points in these "special families."*
3. Grollman EA: **Explaining Divorce to Children.** Boston, Beacon Press, 1969. *Discusses divorce as it affects all members of the family from several vantage points. Although somewhat negative, the issues are identified for parents. Tends to be slightly dry, but complete.*
4. Kalter N: **Growing Up With Divorce.** New York, Free Press, 1990 ($22.95). *Informative discussion of the impact of divorce on children at specific ages with practical suggestions for parents. Focus is on the need to observe the individual child, respect the stage of development and communicate clearly. Case histories provide insight into children's perceptions of the immediate and long-term issues in divorce and the ways families have learned to cope with their children's anger, fears, and maladaptive behaviors.*
5. Maddox B: **The Half-Parent.** New York, Evans, 1975. *A common-sense, short, and easy-to-read book dealing with the problems of stepparents, covering legal, financial, emotional, and sexual issues, as well as exploring myths and roles. Maddox, a stepmother herself, writes with insight about her own experiences as well as those of the 100 other stepparents she interviewed.*
6. Register C: **Are Those Kids Yours? American Families With Children Adopted From Other Countries.** New York, The Free Press, 1991 ($22.95). *Comprehensive look at the issues for families contemplating interracial adoption or for those with a multi-ethnic family. Explores real issues facing such families as they mature together.*
7. Roosevelt R, Lofas J: **Living in Step.** New York, Stein & Day, 1976. *Particularly popular with stepparents. Easy-to-read account of the experiences of the authors and a number of persons they interviewed about stepfamily problems.*

8. Wallerstein J, Blakeslee S: **Second Chances: Men, Women, and Children a Decade After Divorce.** New York, Ticknor and Fields, 1989 ($9.95). *The authors interviewed 60 families with 131 children at the time of their divorce and again at 5- and 10-year intervals. The long-term psychological effect and economic impact of divorce is analyzed. Descriptions of the effect of divorce on children's thoughts and feelings, social relationships, work, family life, and economic stability are candid and comprehensive. The psychological stages of divorce are defined for children and adults. Case vignettes add a valuable personal dimension to the research findings.*

CHILDHOOD SERIOUS ILLNESS AND DEATH

1. Family Living Series: **Children Die Too** and **Why Mine?** Omaha, Centering Corp, 1981. *Two simply and sensitively written, brief (20 pages) booklets, which can be used at any stage of parental grief. An added dimension of support and insight through quotes from parents. Recommend purchase in bulk by health care professionals as an adjunct in their support offered to parents. Free catalogue available from: Centering Corp, PO Box 3367, Omaha, NB 68103.*
2. Howe J: **The Hospital Book.** Association for the Care of Children's Health, 1981 ($13.95).
3. Thomas JR: **Saying Goodbye to Grandma.** Association for the Care of Children's Health, 1988 ($13.95).

CHILD SAFETY RESOURCES

The following organizations and agencies provide pamphlets and leaflets dealing with child safety resources:

1. Action for Child Product Safety, 358 Woburn St, Lexington MA 02173.
2. Committee on Accident and Poison Prevention, American Academy of Pediatrics (AAP), 141 Northwest Point Blvd, Elk Grove Village, IL 60009.
3. Kaye E: **The ACT Guide to Children's Television.** Boston, Beacon Press, 1979. *A complete examination of the effect of television on children, with suggestions on how parents may begin to set their own limits and guides. Developed by Action for Children's Television, an advocacy group that continues to be legislatively active, to provide ongoing monitoring of television and to provide educational materials. A good mailing list to be on.*
4. US Consumer Product Safety Commission (Washington, DC 20207): **Because You Care for Kids** (numerous hazards); **Safety Sampler** (baby equipment and toys); **Super Sitter** (advice to babysitters).

HEALTH CARE

1. Azarnoff P: **Health, Illness and Disability: A Guide to Books for Children and Young Adults.** New York, RR Bowker Co, 1983. *A thorough reference book for health professionals; the bibliographic guide annotates over 1,000 fiction and nonfiction books about children's health and disabled bodies. The author includes such pertinent information as suggested reader level, cost and length of book, and designation of fiction vs. nonfiction. The subject index includes almost 300 areas. Utilization of the book is maximized by the inclusion of a title index, subject guide, and directory of publishers. Children and*

parents alike would undoubtedly be grateful to their health-care provider for a list of books related to that child's particular experience with disability and medical treatment.

2. **Child Care Series.** Omaha, Nebraska, Centering Corporation, 1981. *Fifteen simply written, short coloring booklets, each one creatively covering the basic details of such medical procedures as spinal tap, insertion of intravenous lines, various types of x-ray films, and surgery. Inexpensive (60 cents, each) teaching aids for older toddlers to children who are 12 years old, with appropriate participation of parents and health team members. Free catalogue available from: Centering Corporation, PO Box 3367, Omaha, NE 68103.*

3. Pediatrics Projects Inc, Dept B, PO Box 1880, Santa Monica CA 90406. *A nonprofit corporation distributing publications and medical toys to people who work for children and families in health care. Bibliographies of children's books are provided for a nominal fee. Separate lists of numerous topics are available that may be otherwise difficult to find. Examples are obesity, child abuse, emergencies, blood, alcohol abuse, attitudes toward disability. At least 35 citations on each list.*

NUTRITION

1. Baker S, Henry R: **Boston Children's Hospital Parents' Guide to Nutrition.** Reading, Mass, Addison-Wesley, 1989 ($9.95). *Comprehensive, sensible, and usable information on nutritional issues from infancy to adolescence. The authors review the latest research, demystify fad diets, and provide nutritional recommendations. The format is easy to read and recipes are included.*

2. Satter E: **Child of Mine.** Palo Alto, Calif, Bull, 1987 ($10.95). *This nutritional guidebook offers information on the developmental and social aspects of feeding from infancy through adolescence. Behaviors that encourage the formation of healthy eating patterns are reviewed and technical nutrition information is translated into practical and basic concepts.*

BOOKS FOR CHILDREN

DEVELOPMENTAL AND SITUATIONAL CONFLICTS

1. Arnstein H: **Billy and Our New Baby.** New York, Human Sciences Press, 1973. *One of several books in a series of psychologically relevant themes approved by a panel of child-development experts. Designed to help children cope with various conflicts, e.g., sibling rivalry, death, divorce. Often available at public libraries.*

2. Berenstain S, Berenstain J: First Time Books; **The Berenstain Bears Go to the Doctor; The Berenstain Bears Go to Visit the Dentist; The Berenstain Bears Moving Day; The Berenstain Bears and the Sitter.** New York, Random House, 1981. *Inexpensive ($1.25) picture books that highlight some stressful experiences. Written for older toddlers and preschoolers in pleasant and reassuring manner. Available in bookstores and children's stores.*

3. Berger T: **I Have Feelings.** New York, Human Sciences Press, 1977. *Nice reflective book for kindergarten through sixth grade. An example of several books that help children to reflect on themselves through another child's eyes.*

4. Fassler J: **Helping Children Cope: Mastering Stress Through Books and Stories.** New York, The Free Press (Division of Macmillan Publishing Co, Inc), 1978. *A strongly recommended resource for health-care providers and parents alike. Child psy-*

chologist Fassler reviews and recommends contemporary children's literature, including such topics as death, illness, hospitalization, divorce, adoption, moving, birth of a sibling, natural disasters, separation experiences, and visits to the doctor and dentist. She suggests questions to initiate discussion between children and parents in helping children reduce their fears and anxieties. A bibliography of professional literature for each topic is included.

5. Pediatric Projects Inc, PO Box 1880, Santa Monica, CA. *A nonprofit organization distributing publications and medical toys to people in health care. Materials include short booklets on topics such as having a cast, going to the hospital, allergies, and disabilities. Adult-level books for parents and professionals are also annotated and made available. Clinicians would do well to be on the mailing list.*

6. Tomlinson W: Books for and about children. **Pediatric Currents** 1981; 29: January. *A handy booklist reference for health-care professionals developed by an academic pediatrician with extensive private-practice experience. The many categories of books include: nature, sciences, birth, sexual maturation, death and aging, hospitalization, illness, handicaps, child development, and behavior (books for adults and books for children). He offers a very brief description and opinion of numerous books. Age-indexes provided. Copies available through your Ross representative.*

SPORTS AND CHILD DEVELOPMENT

1. Schreiber LR: **The Parent's Guide to Kids' Sports.** Boston, Little, Brown & Co, 1990. *This book provides essential information on the physical, psychological, and social issues in children's sports. Parental involvement, coaching, competition, and girls' participation in sports are emphasized. Exercise, nutrition, and injury prevention are also reviewed. It is a useful guide to the equipment needs, costs, and injuries in common sports. A bibliography and resource list is included.*

BOOKS FOR TEENAGERS

1. Edelstein B: **The Women Doctor's Diet for Teenage Girls.** Englewood Cliffs, NJ, Prentice-Hall Inc, 1980. *This is a good book for bright parents and their teenage girls from the middle to upper-middle class. The author offers sound guidelines for losing weight tailored to the needs of young women. It is sensitive to issues of body image, junk food, crash diets, and family pressures. Although the book is written for teens, parents (AND DOCTORS!) may find it helpful.*

2. Lindsay JW: **Pregnant Too Soon: Adoption Is an Option.** Buena Park, Calif, Morning Glory Press, 1980. *This soft-cover book utilizes case histories of pregnant teenagers to illustrate the problems of young women who become mothers in their teen years. The author emphasizes the option of adoption to pregnant teens, and this book serves as a good resource for pregnant teenagers who want to learn or read more about the process of adoption.*

3. Mayle P: **What's Happening to Me?** Secaucus, NJ, Lyle Stuart Inc, 1975. *This delightful, slim, inexpensive illustrated soft-cover book is described as a guide to puberty and is produced by the same authors who wrote "Where Did I Come From?" With amusing drawings and a brief compassionate narrative, the authors present various aspects of pubertal development from breasts to erections. This book is probably best suited for those in early adolescence.*

4. McCoy K, Wibbelsman C: **The Teenage Body Book.** New York, Simon & Schuster, 1978. *This book is based upon questions commonly asked by teenagers concerning their bodies and bodily changes. The authors are a former editor of Teen Magazine and a physician who specializes in adolescent medicine. The authors cover a wide range of topics, including normal physical development and birth control. Case vignettes and examples of letters from teens are used to illustrate various problems. Detailed line drawings are plentiful and excellent. This book is more appropriate for those in mid to late adolescence and may be too sophisticated for younger adolescents.*

SEX EDUCATION

1. An eight-page annotated bibliography of books on sex education (and sibling preparation/rivalry), with age-level recommendations developed by and available from nurse-mother Philothea T Sweet, RN; Obstetrics Clinic, Outpatient Department; University of Minnesota Hospitals; Minneapolis, Minn. *A free, annotated resource list of sex-education books is available from the local Planned Parenthood Association. List has separate sections for parents, teens, and children. Free reprints of some articles also available.*

2. Gordon S, Gordon J: **Raising a Child Conservatively in a Sexually Permissive World.** New York, Fireside, 1989 ($8.95). *This book offers useful guidelines for parents who would like to talk with their children about sexual, social, and moral issues. The author believes that parents have the responsibility to be their children's primary sex educators and that informed children will grow into responsible adults. The format is well organized and the writing is thoughtful and readable. Sample questions that children ask are included in order to anticipate a child's curiosity at different developmental stages. This book also provides a comprehensive bibliography with recommendations for parents who want to know more.*

3. Lewis HR, Lewis ME: **The Parent's Guide to Teenage Sex and Pregnancy.** New York, St Martin's Press, 1980. *The authors are professional medical writers who also happen to be a married couple with teenage children. The authors are sensitive to the concerns of parents but are also honest and factual concerning adolescent sexuality. Information is presented in a forthright manner but also includes suggestions for helping the parent cope with his or her adolescent's sexuality. Individual chapters are devoted to such topics as sex talks, helping children to resist premature intercourse, veneral disease, what to do if one's daughter is pregnant, and many other issues. Although well-written and intended for the lay public, this book may seem like a heavy textbook to some parents but fills a need for scholarly information for other parents.*

4. Maderas L: **What's Happening to My Body? A Book for Girls;** and **What's Happening to My Body? A Book for Boys;** ed 2. New York; New Market Press, 1983, 1988, respectively. *Excellent and comprehensive books to be read with preadolescents. New edition has information on AIDS and sexually transmitted diseases.*

5. Weisman BA, Weisman MH: **What We Told Our Kids About Sex.** San Diego, Harvest/Harcourt, Brace, Jovanovitch, 1987 ($4.95). *This concise book offers parents guidelines for sensitive and factual discussion of human sexuality. Recognizing the emotional nature of sexual issues and human values, the authors recommend that parents begin discussing sex and family values prior to the teenage years. Chapters are designed to be read as background for a discussion or by a preteen.*

HOME VIDEOS: PROMOTING DEVELOPMENTAL GROWTH: A PARENT GUIDE*

With the introduction of video recorders into the homes of most American families, the opportunity to expose children to a variety of people and thematic material has become possible. Used wisely and selectively, this contemporary form of home entertainment can enrich and expand the experience of children with people, cultures, and situations that are outside their own lives.

Parents can be encouraged to control television habits of their children rather than allowing the TV to control the family. Prerecorded video tapes provide a vehicle not only for planning but allow a choice in subject, language, and context not as readily manageable in commercial television.

The videos selected in this guide for parents are intended to simultaneously entertain and educate. The guide has been organized in order to give parents some choice of subjects with regard to stages of development (e.g., autonomy), values (e.g., honesty, patience, sportsmanship), emotions (e.g., envy, jealousy, anger, aggression), life events (e.g., adoption, divorce, illness), and cultural issues (e.g., child abuse, crime, and poverty). This list of videos for children is not comprehensive. It is selected with the intent to inform the school-age child and adolescent while providing a vehicle for dialogue between children and their parents. Viewed together in the home, these videos are an opportunity for developmental growth. A bowl of popcorn may help the process!

1. **Pinocchio** (1940 Disney/RKO G: 7–12-yr-old. *A Disney cartoon classic of the timeless story of a wooden puppet and his creator who wants nothing more than for the puppet to become a real life boy. Pinocchio falls into bad company, only to become a real boy when he mends his ways.*
2. **The Parent Trap** (1961) Disney/BV NR: 9+-yr-old. *Fast-paced slapstick Disney comedy about twins separated at birth by the divorce of their parents. They are reunited at summer camp, discover their relationship, and proceed to plot a scheme to reunite their parents.*
3. **Captains Courageous** (1937) MGM NR: 7+-yr-old. *A very spoiled child falls overboard from a luxury liner and is rescued by a salty fisherman who teaches him the value of a good attitude and a compassionate soul. This film also teaches the valuable lesson of taking responsibility and dealing with the death of a loved one.*
4. **Johnny Tremain** (1957) BV NR: 8+-yr-old. *A Revolutionary War film about an uncommitted young man who changes his views about the cause of freedom and becomes caught up in the conflict of these tumultuous times.*
5. **The Black Stallion** (1979) United Artists PG: 10+-yr-old. *A great story about a boy who develops a deep relationship with a wild Arabian stallion that saves his life in a shipwreck. Suspense, joy, and fantasy ensue as the boy and his older friend train the stallion to be a champion race horse. The film explores the value of bravery and coping with the changes associated with life's unexpected turns.*

---

*Authored by Hedi J. Brehm. Credits: Guy Hanford, Winnie Hanford, and Pan Cisneros of Kensington Video, San Diego; Randy Pittman of The Video Librarian; E.P. Carsman, Ph.D., of The Children's Video Review Newsletter; and William C. Brehm.

6. **Hoosiers** (1986) Vestron PG: 10+-yr-old. *A small town Indiana basketball coach gets a second chance in life and one of his star players learns to cope with his father's alcoholism as their underdog, but inspiring, team struggles to reach the state tournament finals.*

7. **Cinderella** (1950) Disney/RKO NR: 7–13-yr-old. *An excellent Disney animation about a poor young woman who is mistreated by her sisters and relatives, but through her fairy godmother meets a prince who falls in love with her. A good movie to begin discussion about child abuse.*

8. **The Sound of Music** (1972) Fox G: 9+-yr-old. *The value of freedom can be learned by children of all ages in this musical film about the seven singing children of Captain Von Trapp, a widower, who, along with their governess, must escape the Nazis by trekking through the Austrian Alps.*

9. **Ordinary People** (1980) Paramount R: 14+-yr-old. *A powerful story about a family as they attempt to cope with the accidental death of a son and brother. The "R" rating is limited to the language in one scene between the surviving son and his psychiatrist.*

10. **Old Yeller** (1957) Disney/BV NR: 13+-yr-old. *A Disney film set in Texas in 1869 about a boy and his dog and how he must cope with the dog's death.*

11. **The Diary of Anne Frank** (1959) CBS/Fox NR: 13+-yr-old. *A dramatic true story about a young Jewish girl who was hidden in the attic of a Dutch family for 2 years in order to escape the Nazis. This film can open up a dialogue about prejudice, kindness, and patience.*

12. **African Queen** (1949) United Artists NR: 11+-yr-old. *A romantic World War I adventure about an alcoholic river boat skipper and a missionary's daughter who, through determination, avoid capture by the enemy. In the process, the two of them develop a mutual respect and love for one another.*

13. **The Pride of the Yankees** (1942) RKO NR: 8+-yr-old. *A sentimental, entertaining film about baseball hero Lou Gehrig's determination and courage that marked his life in sports and coping with serious disease.*

14. **Mother Theresa** (1986) Today Home Entertainment NR: 9+-yr-old. *A documentary which explores the accomplishments of this patient and hard-working Nobel Prize-winning woman. The value of patience, love, and dedication to healing societal ills is exemplified by this woman who is often referred to as a saint.*

15. **The Journey of Natty Gann** (1985) Disney/BV PG: 8+-yr-old. *A Depression era drama about a determined tomboy who becomes friends with a wolf as she travels from Chicago to Seattle in search of her father.*

16. **Pollyanna** (1960) Buena Vista NR: 8+-yr-old. *Set in a small town in 1912, this is the story of an orphan girl who is adopted by her wealthy aunt and wins the affection of the townspeople with her ever-optimistic ways.*

17. **The Adventures of Robin Hood** (1938) CBS/Fox NR: 6+-yr-old. *An adaptation of the classic Sherwood Forest tale of Robin Hood and his fellow band of merry men, how they cooperate and compromise in their adventures against the Sheriff of Nottingham.*

18. **Oklahoma** (1955) Magna Theatres G: 8+-yr-old. *The Rogers and Hammerstein musical about the love affair between a cowboy and country girl and Jud Fry who has difficulty controlling his anger and hate.*

19. **The Red Balloon** (1956) Nelson NR: 5+-yr-old. *A classic short children's film without words about a young French boy who unties a stray balloon from a lamppost. The*

balloon follows him wherever he goes. The film develops sympathy for victims of violence and crime and creates a case against bullying and selfishness.

20. **Angels With Dirty Faces** (1938) Warner Brothers NR: 9+-yr-old. *The tale of two boyhood chums who take different paths in life—one toward criminal behavior and the other toward the priesthood and helping others.*

21. **Stand and Deliver** (1988) Warner Brothers PG: 9+-yr-old. *A true story of an inner-city high school teacher, assigned to teach remedial math, who accomplishes the amazing feat of challenging and encouraging his students to take and pass the college entrance exam for calculus.*

22. **The King and I** (1956) Fox NR: 9+-yr-old. *A musical love story about a widowed British school teacher hired by the powerful King of Siam to teach his children. The king is old fashioned and stubborn, but he believes that education is important for his people.*

23. **The Miracle on 34th Street** (1947) Fox NR: 7+-yr-old. *An enduring Christmas film about a department store Santa Claus who claims to be the real Saint Nick. Despite his detractors, he continues to promote kindness and goodness.*

24. **Goodbye Mr. Chips** (1939) MGM NR: 9+-yr-old. *Set in England in the 1800s, this film depicts the story of a shy British school teacher who guides several generations of students from boyhood to manhood.*

25. **Bang the Drum Slowly** (1973) Paramount PG: 8+-yr-old. *The sentimental and heartwarming story of a baseball player with leukemia who struggles to play one more season before he dies. His effect on his teammates and opponents is explored.*

26. **A Tree Grows in Brooklyn** (1945) Playhouse Video NR: 10+-yr-old. *The story of a troubled Irish family, an alcoholic father, and his daughter who live in a Brooklyn tenement in the early 1900s. This film conveys a genuine empathy for children who live with an alcoholic parent.*

27. **Secret Life of Walter Mitty** (1947) Embassy NR: 8+-yr-old. *A story about a shy man who feels inadequate and cowardly but fantasizes a world where he leads an exciting life.*

28. **Swiss Family Robinson** (1960) Disney G: 7+-yr-old. *A family learns to accept change in their living environment after the ship they are travelling on is shipwrecked en route to New Guinea. They build a paradise of their own in their new world.*

29. **Breaking Away** (1979) CBS/Fox Home Video PG: 10+-yr-old. *A comedy about four working class boys in middle America who challenge the more well-to-do college fraternity members to a bicycle race during a summer before entering the reality of adult life. An informative exploration of mid to late adolescence.*

30. **Damn Yankees** (1958) Warner Brothers NR: 12+-yr-old. *A film version of the hit Broadway musical about a baseball fan who uses the devil to change his life from that of an ordinary person to a star player. Sportsmanship and succeeding at any cost are illustrated.*

31. **The Great Santini** (1979) Warner Brothers PG: 12+-yr-old. *The story of a gung-ho, frustrated Marine Corps fighter pilot who treats his family and his 18-year-old son, in particular, like boot camp recruits. This film will open up discussions in the family about child and spousal abuse in its more subtle forms.*

32. **My Life as a Dog** (1985) Paramount Home Video PG: 13+-yr-old. *A film about a young Swedish boy's glimpse at some of adult life concerns: sex, loss, and the need for*

companionship. Contains some nudity and sexual references. Suitable for children over 13 and to be watched with parents.

33. **To Kill a Mockingbird** (1962) MCA Home Video NR: 10+-yr-old. *A film portraying childhood adventures in a racially divided town in Alabama in the 1930s. Gregory Peck plays the lawyer who represents a black man accused of raping a white woman. A poignant look at prejudice through a child's eyes.*

34. **Sounder** (1972) Fox G: 9+-yr-old. *A southern black family struggles to survive as sharecroppers in the Depression. This family film portrays poverty, racism, persecution, but most of all, hope.*

35. **Yours, Mine and Ours** (1968) Desilu/United Artists NR: 7+-yr-old. *Henry Fonda and Lucille Ball star in this satirical comedy about a widow and widower who fall in love and merge their two large families. Portrayed in a comical and heartwarming style, the story is about adoption, sibling rivalry, stepparenting, and the importance of families sticking together.*

36. **Cheaper by the Dozen** (1950) Fox G: 7+-yr-old. *A story about an efficiency expert father and a psychologist mother who have 12 children. This comedy, set in the 1920s, explores the closeness of family life and the need for family cooperation.*

37. **Little Women** (1962) MGM NR: 7+-yr-old. *Based on the classic 1868 novel by Louisa May Alcott about a family of four sisters who live during the Civil War era. There are laughs and tears in this movie that focuses on the importance of family and family cooperation.*

38. **The Miracle Worker** (1961) MGM NR: 9+-yr-old. *The inspiring story of Helen Keller and her teacher's amazing struggle to overcome Helen's multitude of handicaps. It is as much a story of the family's ability to cope with Helen's handicaps and her teacher's dedicated unconventional methods as it is Helen's incredible accomplishments.*

39. **The Elephant Man** (1980) Paramount PG: 12+-yr-old. *The true story about a man horribly disfigured by a rare disease who becomes a respected member of society. The film teaches a sensitivity to the human condition and coping with a severe physical disability.*

40. **My Left Foot** (1990) Miramax R: 12+-yr-old. *The autobiography of Christy Brown, the writer and painter born with a severe case of cerebral palsy. The film deals realistically with Christy's struggle and triumphs with his disability and the profound effects it had on people he lived and worked with.*

41. **Heidi** (1937) Fox NR: 7+-yr-old. *Shirley Temple stars in this 1937 film about an orphan girl who is sent to live with her angry and distant grandfather. Heidi breaks through her grandfather's cold personality, but is then sent to her aunt to work in her service. While her grandfather tries to find her, Heidi perseveres and brightens up the lives of those around her.*

42. **National Velvet** (1944) MGM NR: 6+-yr-old. *The story about a young girl (Elizabeth Taylor) who trains a horse with the help of a friend (Mickey Rooney) with the goal of winning the Grand National Horse Race. They persevere in overcoming many obstacles which are relevant to both young and adult audiences.*

43. **The Yearling** (1946) NR: 8+-yr-old. *The story of a rural, impoverished family trying to make a living on their small farm following the Civil War. The main character is a young boy who raises a fawn, but is forced to kill the pet to protect the family's meager*

livelihood. The story conveys the struggle of poverty and overcoming adversity through family love and affection for animals.

44. **Bambi** (1942) Disney/RKO NR: 6+-yr-old. *An animated Disney classic about a fawn that grows up to be a magnificent stag—and the leader of the herd. The fawn could be any child who must overcome the adversity and trials associated with growing up.*

45. **The Music Man** (1961) Warner Brothers NR: 8+-yr-old. *A film version of the Broadway musical about a con-man from the big city who organizes a boy's band in order to sell their parents musical instruments. A light and airy look at the value of honesty and truthfulness.*

46. **Beauty and the Beast** (1947) Lopert Films NR: 8+-yr-old. *Based on the classic fairy tale, this film deals with a young girl who learns to look beyond the ugly exterior of a beast and finds the good heart within. Film version.*

47. **Cocoon** (1988) CBS/Fox PG: 13+-yr-old. *Extraterrestrials visit earth and become friends with a group of elderly people living in a Florida retirement community, granting them the fountain of youth. This film gives children insight into the feelings and issues of growing old in our society.*

48. **My Side of the Mountain** (1969) Paramount G: 8+-yr-old. *An entertaining and educational film about a young boy who leaves his family for a year in order to live in the wilderness like his hero, Henry David Thoreau. In the process he learns about survival, himself, and his relationship with his family.*

49. **Born Free** (1966) Columbia NR: 8+-yr-old. *A true story about a couple who adopt lion cubs after their mother was killed. One of the cubs is raised to adulthood, but the couple must face the fact that the lion cannot remain a pet and must return to the wild.*

50. **Chariots of Fire** (1981) Fox PG: 12+-yr-old. *A true story about two 1924 Olympic long distance runners, one of whom runs because of his commitment to God, the other who runs to compensate for religious prejudices. This film effectively deals with commitment to winning and the prejudices of antisemitism.*

51. **Incredible Journey** (1963) Disney NR: 7+-yr-old. *This Disney film is the story of three family pets (two dogs and a cat) that are left with a friend when their family moves miles away. The pets undertake a long journey to find their family. This film will help children feel more compassion for animals and their own pets.*

52. **Jungle Book** (1942) United Artists NR: 6–13-yr-old. *An adaptation of Rudyard Kipling's novel about a young boy who befriends animals in the jungle and in the process learns their ways.*

53. **On the Waterfront** (1954) Columbia NR: 13+-yr-old. *Powerful drama about a New York City boxer who exposes the corrupt longshoremen who control the waterfront union. It is appropriate for older children as it confronts directly the issues of honesty and telling the truth.*

54. **Somebody Up There Likes Me** (1956) MGM/United Artists NR: 11+-yr-old. *This autobiographical film about boxing champ Rocky Graziano's life, from reform school to champion, grapples with conflicts surrounding aggression and anger.*

55. **Spirit of St. Louis** (1957) Warner Brothers NR: 8+-yr-old. *The story about Charles Lindbergh's pursuit to become the first person to cross the Atlantic alone in an airplane. It effectively captures the thoughts and feelings of a true American hero as he pursues and accomplishes his dream.*

56. **Ben Hur** (1959) MGM/United Artists NR: 9+-yr-old. *An historical spectacle of a*

persecuted Jew in Roman times who becomes a courageous chariot racer and overcomes many adversities.

57. **David Copperfield** (1935) MGM NR: 9+-yr-old. *A movie adaptation of Charles Dickens' novel about a young boy growing up in 19th century England. This film makes a case against child abuse and how this problem can be overcome in later life.*

58. **Conrack** (1974) Fox PG: 12+-yr-old. *A southern, white man is hired to teach young, black children, most of whom are illiterate, in a small town on an island off the coast of South Carolina. This true story is an inspirational and heartwarming account of how this teacher faces the challenges of educating and how he deals with the prejudices of the time.*

59. **Twelve Angry Men** (1957) United Artists NR: 11+-yr-old. *This is the story about a cross section of jurors who must decide the guilt or innocence of an unspecified minority teenager who is accused of murdering his father. A gripping example of the inner workings of a jury and how one person's prejudices could influence an important decision.*

60. **Jacob I Have Loved** Wonderworks NR: 9+-yr-old. *This film is about twin sisters, one of whom is very jealous of the other's musical talents. This story depicts how futile it is to experience jealous feelings and how important it is to develop one's own place and talents.*

61. **The Gods Must Be Crazy** (1984) Playhouse Video PG: 8+-yr-old. *A box office smash that described life of a bushman in the Kalahari Desert of Africa who finds a Coke bottle that had fallen from an airplane flying overhead. With great difficulty, the bushman tries to dispose of the bottle because of the disharmony it causes among his tribesmen. This sensitively directed film will provide children with an understanding about living in harmony with nature and the impact of modern life on more fundamental patterns of family and community organization.*

62. **The Good Earth** (1937) MGM/United Artists NR: 11+-yr-old. *The story, set in China, is about a poor family struggling to survive, only to be overcome by the husband's greed.*

63. **The Treasure of Sierra Madre** (1948) Warner Bros. NR: 8+-yr-old. *After three Americans discover gold in Mexico, jealousy, envy and greed untangle their friendship. A wonderful (and entertaining) film that shows older children how newly acquired wealth can adversely affect character development.*

64. **It's a Mad, Mad, Mad World** (1963) CBS/Fox NR: 12+-yr-old. *A comedy film that treats the subject of greed by utilizing virtually every Hollywood comedian of its day. A madcap search to recover hidden loot from a robbery is the storyline.*

65. **The Lost Weekend** (1945) Paramount NR: 12+-yr-old. *A New York writer's pain and terror due to his addiction to alcohol.*

66. **The Man With the Golden Arm** (1955) Fox NR: 12+-yr-old. *A film classic about a man's withdrawal from heroin addiction, it should be viewed by the adolescent prepared for a raw, honest depiction of drug addiction. The film includes powerful scenes depicting physical withdrawal from drug addiction. The music by Elmer Bernstein is unforgettable.*

67. **West Side Story** (1961) United Artists NR: 10+-yr-old. *This late 1950s Romeo and Juliet musical set in teenage, gangland New York City shows the futility of prejudice. Urban gang warfare combine with a love story and incredible dancing and singing to make this Leonard Bernstein musical simultaneously instructive and enjoyable.*

68. **Johnny Belinda** (1948) Warner Brothers NR: 11+-yr-old. *A touching story about a young deaf-mute woman who is raped, gives birth to a child, and overcomes adversity with courage and love. The rape scene is not explicit. The film shows how people can overcome severe impairments and hardships.*

69. **Fiddler on the Roof** (1971) United Artists G: 9+-yr-old. *A wonderful musical that depicts the story of Jewish immigration to America in order to escape the persecution of a homeland in turmoil. The characters are forced to adapt to many changes, accept new ways of looking at their culture, and explore changing transitions.*

70. **The Heart Is a Lonely Hunter** (1968) Warner Bros. G: 12+-yr-old. *A story about a good-hearted man who is a deaf-mute, this film illustrates sensitivity to those with special differences.*

71. **The Secret of Nimh** (1982) MGM G: 6+-yr-old. *This is an animated story about the importance of family cooperation. The plot revolves around a mother mouse trying to protect and move her family before they are harmed.*

72. **The Secret Garden** (1981) MGM G: 10+-yr-old. *This film shows the healing qualities that a good friendship can bring about. The story is about an orphan who, through transformation of a garden, brings very needed healing qualities to the household.*

73. **How Green Was My Valley** (1941) Fox NR: 10+-yr-old. *Inspirational film about a community and family in South Wales.*

74. **Anne of Green Gables** (1985) Disney G: 8+-yr-old. *A story of an orphan girl who became an inspiration to all those who got to know her. The value of education is strongly emphasized.*

75. **Gandhi** (1982) RCA/Columbia PG: 11+-yr-old. *The epic biography is about the life of Gandhi, the spiritual leader who led India to freedom from British colonial rule.*

76. **Shane** (1953) Paramount NR: 8+-yr-old. *This is a classic western film about a young boy who idolizes a gunslinger who comes to the aid of a homesteading family.*

77. **Little Lord Fauntleroy** (1936) United Artists NR: 8+-yr-old. *A young boy has to adapt to new surroundings and dramatically changes his values.*

78. **Les Miserables** Key Video NR. *A foreign film which asks the viewer the question, when is it appropriate to steal?*

79. **It's a Wonderful Life** (1946) Liberty Films NR: 12+-yr-old. *This film teaches the value of self, family, and community. It is the story about a man who contemplates suicide, but is able to overcome these feelings with the help of his family and friends. Not a movie for a young child.*

FILM RATING KEY

G   = General audience.
PG = Parental guidance.
R   = Parent supervision recommended.
NR = Not rated.

Topics	Title Code
Developmental stage	
Adolescent autonomy	29, 31, 32
Peer group pressure	1, 77
Elderly	47

Topics	Title Code
Values	
Compromise and cooperation	17, 75, 76
Courage and bravery	4, 5, 8
Determination	12, 13, 15, 55, 75
Developing a social conscience	75
Education	21, 22, 58, 74
Equality—case against racism & prejudice	33, 34, 50, 59, 67
Family interactions	28, 35, 36, 37, 48
Freedom	4, 8, 75
Friendship, kindness, helpfulness	23, 33, 72
Generosity and sharing	35, 36
Kindness to animals	49, 51
Living in harmony with nature	28, 52, 61, 62
Patience	11, 14, 38, 75
Responsibility and perseverance	3, 41, 42, 75
Sportsmanship	29, 30
Emotions	
Aggression and anger	18, 38, 54
Coping with physical or emotional disability	25, 38, 39, 40, 68, 70
Envy, jealousy, and greed	19, 62, 64
Vanity	46
Shyness and low self-esteem	24, 27, 60, 74
Spoiling	3
Sibling rivalry	7, 35, 60
Life events	
Adoption	16, 35, 72, 74
Adversity	44, 56, 79
Death	3, 9, 10, 25
Divorce, stepparents, and single parents	2, 35
Stealing	78
Suicide	79
Cultural-societal issues	
Alcohol and drug abuse	6, 26, 65, 66
Child abuse	7, 57
Violence and crime	19, 20

REFERENCES

1. *Consumer Guide Rating the Movies,* Lincolnwood, Ill, Beekman House, Ltd, 1989.
2. *Family Classics Films Ideally Suited for Family Viewing.* Evanston, Ill, Cline Books, Inc, 1988.
3. 100 Great Videos for Kids. *US News and World Report* 1990; Jan 22; 66–70.

Appendix

WELL-CHILD CARE RECORD

Patient Identification

Request Date

Source

DEVELOPMENTAL TASKS
S = Social
Fm = Fine Motor
L = Language
M = Gross Motor

( ) = Age at which 90% of children can do task.
White bars = age during which 75–90% of children accomplish task per Denver Developmental (DDST).
Check age in which task accomplished

ANTICIPATORY GUIDANCE
Sa = Safety
Sx = Symptomatic Rx
Fd = Feeding
Fl = Feeding
Se = Sex Education
Check if discussed

PROCEDURES
Mark if done

Column headings (mos/wks): 0 | 4w | 8w | 4m | 6m | 8m | 10m | 12m

Age	Developmental Tasks	(mos/wks)	Anticipatory Guidance	Procedures
Birth to <4 wks	S — Regards face	(1/0)	Sa — Car restraints / Bathing / Bedding	Hgt
	Fm — Equal movements	(birth)		Wgt
	Fm — Follow to midline	(1/2)	Fd — Breast Feeding / Propping, burping / Volume expectations	HC
	L — Responds to bell	(1/2)		
	M — Moro	( )	Sx — Nasal hygiene / Skin care	Vitamins
	M — Neck/elbow flexor tone	( )		
	M — Stomach—lifts head		Fl — Parents and siblings	Fluoride
≥4 to <8 wks	S — Smiles responsively	(2/0)	Sa — Falls (rolls over) / Car restraints / Bathing / Fire retardant clothing / Small objects out of reach	Hgt
	Fm — Follows past midline	(3/0)		Wgt
	L — Vocalizes, not crying	(1/3)		HC
	M — Stomach up 45°	(3/0)	Fd — Formula or breast / Future solids	DPT-1
			Sx — Thermometer use	OPV-1
			Fl — Sleep	HIB-1
≥2 to <4 mo	S — Smiles spontaneously	(5/0)	Sa — Crawling: objects out of reach / stairway "gate" / Risks of walkers, jumpers	Hgt
	Fm — Follows to 180°	(4/0)		Wgt
	Fm — Hands together	(3/3)		HC
	L — Laughs	(3/1)	Fd — Review solids / Spoon / Formula or breast	DPT-2
	L — Squeals	(4/2)		OPV-2
	M — Head steady, sitting	(4/0)	Sx — Diarrhea	HIB-2
	M — Prone, holds chest up	(4/1)	Fl — Behavior expectations	

Age		Milestones		Anticipatory guidance		Screening/Immunization
≥4 to <6 mo	S	Smiles at mirror (*)	Sa	Review crawling: objects, electric outlets, floor heaters; Food aspiration (beans)		Hgt
	Fm	Grasps rattle (4/2), Reaches for object (5/0)	Fd	Milk, Food selection, Feeding techniques		Wgt
	L	Coos (*)				HC
	M	Rolls over (4/2), Pulls-to-sit, no head lag (6/1)	Sx	URI, Review		DPT-3
			Fl	Stimulation–consistency		OPV-3
						HIB-3 (optional)
						Sickle screen if appropriate
≥6 to <8 mo	S	Feeds self crackers (8/0)	Sa	Review poisons		Hgt
	Fm	Rakes raisin, attains (7/3), Passes cube, hand to hand (7/2)	Fd	Review solids intro.		Wgt
	L	Turns to voice (8/1)	Sx	Ear infection		HC
	M	Bears some weight on legs (7/2), Sits without support (7/3)	Fl	Separation anxiety		Ipecac
			Se	Discuss discovery of genitalia, Parent knowledge/attitude		
≥8 to <10 mo	S	Works for toy out of reach (9/0), Plays peekaboo (9/0), Resists toy pull (10/0)	Fd	Finger feeding, Weaning, Feeding techniques		Hgt
	Fm	Thumb-finger grasp (10/2)	Sx	Dental hygiene		Wgt
	L	Mama, dada, nonspecific (10/0)	Fl	Experimentation, separation, Exploration		HC
	M	Pulls self to stand (10/0), Stands holding on (10/0), Gets to sitting (11/0)				TBE skin test
						Hct
≥10 to <12 mo	S	Plays pat a cake (13/0)	Sa	Streets, Climbing (poisons, falls, windows)		Hgt
	Fm	Bangs two cubes in hand (12/1)	Fd	Decreased appetite, Eating habits		Wgt
	L	Mama, dada specific (13/1)	Sx	Vomiting		HC
	M	Walks, holding on furniture (12/2)	Fl	Independence testing, Consistent limits		

FIG A–1.
Well-child care record (continues on following two pages).

() = Age at which 90% of children can do task.
White bars = age during which 75–90% of children accomplish task per Denver Developmental (DDST).
Check age in which task accomplished

DEVELOPMENTAL TASKS
S = Social
Fm = Fine motor
L = Language
M = Gross Motor

ANTICIPATORY GUIDANCE
Sa = Safety
Sx = Symptomatic Ṛ
Fd = Feeding
Fl = Feeling
Se = Sex Education
Check if Discussed

PROCEDURES
Mark if Done

Age	Developmental Tasks	(yrs/mos)	Check columns: 12m 18m 2y 2½y 3y 4y 5y 6y	Anticipatory Guidance	Procedures
≥12 to <18 mo	**S** Plays ball	(1/4)		**Sa** Car restraint	Hgt
	Drinks from cup	(1/5)		Window screens	Wgt
	Fm Neat pincer grasp	(1/2)		Running into danger	HC
	Tower two cubes	(1/8)		Scalds	DPT-4²
	Scribbles spontaneously	(2/1)		**Fd** Complete weaning	OPV-3(4)²
	L 3 words (other than mama)	(1/8)		Appetite slump	MMR #3
	M Stands momentarily	(1/1)		**Sx** Mouth-to-mouth resuscitation	(≥15 mo)
	Walks well	(1/2)		**Fl** Imitation of adults	
	Stoops & recovers	(1/2)		Tantrums	
	Crawls up steps	(*)		Strong preferences	
				Se Anatomical terms	
≥18 mo to <2 yrs	**S** Removes garment	(1/10)		**Sa** Water safety	Hgt
	Uses spoon, spills little	(1/11)		Matches	Wgt
	Helps with simple tasks	(1/11)		Sharp or electric objects	HC
	Fm Dumps raisin from bottle demonstrated	(2/0)		**Fd** Proper snacks	Hct
	Tower 4 cubes	(2/3)		**Sx** Toilet training	DPT-4
	L Points to 1 named body part	(1/11)		**Fl** "No"	OPV-3(4)
	Combines 2 words	(2/3)		Bedtime rituals	
	M Walks up steps	(1/11)		Night terrors	
	Kicks ball	(2/0)		**Se** Masturbation	
≥2 to <2½ yrs	**S** Independence	(*)		**Sa** Sibling torment	Hgt
	Bowel-bladder control	(*)		Car restraint	Wgt
	Fm Dumps raisins out of bottle spontaneously	(3/0)		Play, supervision	HC
	L Names one picture	(2/6)		**Fd** Good eating habits	Chol⁴
	Follows direction, (2 of 3)	(2/8)		**Sx** Constipation	
	M Throws ball overhand	(2/7)		**Fl** Discipline: Explanation & consistency	
				Need for play with peers	
≥2½ to <3 yrs	**S** Puts on clothing	(3/0)		**Sa** Teach child play safety: throwing sharp objects following ball into street	Hgt
	Washes/dries hands	(3/2)		**Fd** Small portions of food	Wgt
	Fm Imitates vertical line to within 30°	(3/0)		**Sx** URI—viral infections	Hct
	Copies "0"	(3/3)		**Fl** Decision making within limits	UA⁵
	Tower 8 cubes	(3/5)		Explaining "rules"	Vision
	L Uses plurals	(3/2)		Curiosity	Hearing
	M Jumps in place	(3/0)		**Se** Masturbation	
	Pedals tricycle	(3/0)			

≥3 to <4 yrs

	Developmental items	Ratio	Anticipatory guidance	Exam/Labs
S	Plays interactive games (tag)	(3/6)	**Sa** Supervised use of scissors, pencils; Street crossing; Water safety	Hgt
	Dresses up with help	(3/6)		Wgt
	Buttons up	(4/3)	**Fd** Table manners	BP
Fm	Picks longer line (3 of 3)	(4/4)		TB test[6]
	Copies "+"	(4/4)	**Sx** Nightmares	U[5]
L	Gives first & last name	(3/9)		
	Comprehends cold, tired, hungry (2 of 3)	(4/2)	**Fl** Imaginative play and fears; Sharing	
	Comprehends prepositions (3 or 4)	(4/6)		
	50% of speech intelligible	(*)	**Se** Birth, sex difference questions	
M	Balances on one foot 1 second	(3/3)		
	5 seconds, (2 of 3)	(4/3)		

≥4 to <5 yrs

	Developmental items	Ratio	Anticipatory guidance	Exam/Labs
S	Separates easily from mother	(4/9)	**Sa** Teaching "outdoors alone" safety; Travel to school; Neighborhood play; Bike safety	Hgt
	Dresses alone	(5/0)		Wgt
Fm	Draw a man—3 parts	(5/4)		BP
	Imitate ☐ demonstrated	(5/8)	**Fd** Teaching food selection	PPD
L	Recognizes colors (3 of 4)	(4/11)		Hgt
	Opposites: [] hot [] woman [] big	(5/0)	**Sx** Check regarding: school phobia; tummy aches	U[5]
M	Heel to toe walk (2 of 3)	(4/10)		DPT-5
	Hops on 1 foot		**Fl** Teaching respect for feelings and property of others; Home responsibility	OPV-4(5)
				MMR
			Se Curiosity, exploration	Vision
				Hearing[7]

≥5 to <6 yrs

	Developmental items	Ratio	Anticipatory guidance	Exam/Labs
Fm	Copies square	(6/0)	**Sa** Review 5 year items	School form
	Draw a man, 6 parts	(6/0)		Hgt
L	Defines (6 of 9): [] ball [] beach [] desk [] house [] banana [] window [] ceiling [] fence [] sidewalk	(6/3) 75% at 6/0	Teach: Parents' names; Home address; Home telephone number	Wgt
	Composition (3 of 3): [] spoon [] shoe [] door	(6/3)		BP
M	Balance on 1 foot 10 sec (2 of 3)	(5/10)		TB test
	Catches bounced ball (2 of 3)	(5/6)		U[5]
	Backward heel to toe (2 of 3)	(6/3)		Hct
				Vision
				Hearing
				Immunization Update

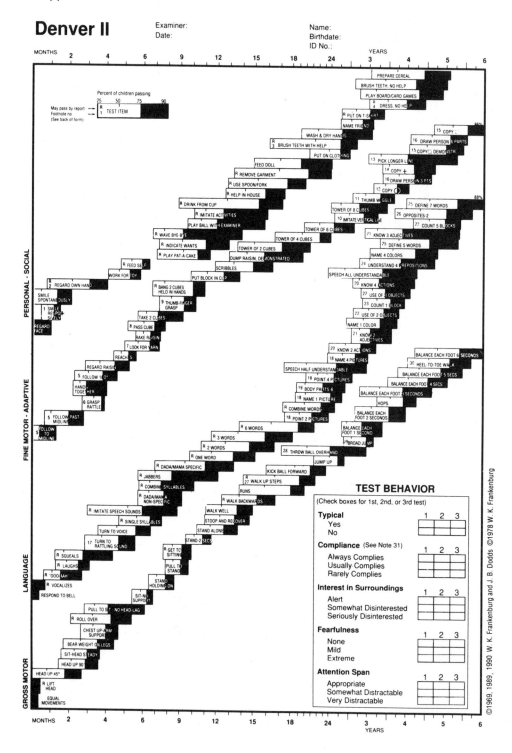

Denver II

Examiner:
Date:

Name:
Birthdate:
ID No.:

FIG A-2.
Denver Developmental Screening Test (appears left and continues on following two pages).

The Denver Developmental Screening test, first published in 1967, has been widely used by health providers in detecting potential developmental areas of concern in young children. It is a valuable tool for screening asymptomatic children for possible problems or in confirming intuitive suspicions with an objective measure. The Denver II is not an IQ test, nor a definitive predictor of future adaptive or intellectual ability. It should never be used as a substitute for a diagnostic evaluation or physical examination, nor as a predictor of later development.

The principle value of this test is to provide an organized, clinical impression of a child's development overall and to alert the user to potential developmental difficulties. It should be used primarily to determine how a child compares to other children.

The Denver II should be administered in the standard manner after training and familiarization with this edition of the test. (Courtesy of W. K. Frankenburg and J. B. Dobbs, 1990.)

DIRECTIONS FOR ADMINISTRATION

1. Try to get child to smile by smiling, talking or waving. Do not touch him/her.
2. Child must stare at hand several seconds.
3. Parent may help guide toothbrush and put toothpaste on brush.
4. Child does not have to be able to tie shoes or button/zip in the back.
5. Move yarn slowly in an arc from one side to the other, about 8" above child's face.
6. Pass if child grasps rattle when it is touched to the backs or tips of fingers.
7. Pass if child tries to see where yarn went. Yarn should be dropped quickly from sight from tester's hand without arm movement.
8. Child must transfer cube from hand to hand without help of body, mouth, or table.
9. Pass if child picks up raisin with any part of thumb and finger.
10. Line can vary only 30 degrees or less from tester's line. |/
11. Make a fist with thumb pointing upward and wiggle only the thumb. Pass if child imitates and does not move any fingers other than the thumb.

12. Pass any enclosed form. Fail continuous round motions.
13. Which line is longer? (Not bigger.) Turn paper upside down and repeat. (pass 3 of 3 or 5 of 6)
14. Pass any lines crossing near midpoint.
15. Have child copy first. If failed, demonstrate.

When giving items 12, 14, and 15, do not name the forms. Do not demonstrate 12 and 14.

16. When scoring, each pair (2 arms, 2 legs, etc.) counts as one part.
17. Place one cube in cup and shake gently near child's ear, but out of sight. Repeat for other ear.
18. Point to picture and have child name it. (No credit is given for sounds only.)
   If less than 4 pictures are named correctly, have child point to picture as each is named by tester.

19. Using doll, tell child: Show me the nose, eyes, ears, mouth, hands, feet, tummy, hair. Pass 6 of 8.
20. Using pictures, ask child: Which one flies?... says meow?... talks?... barks?... gallops? Pass 2 of 5, 4 of 5.
21. Ask child: What do you do when you are cold?... tired?... hungry?   Pass 2 of 3, 3 of 3.
22. Ask child: What do you do with a cup? What is a chair used for? What is a pencil used for?
    Action words must be included in answers.
23. Pass if child correctly places <u>and</u> says how many blocks are on paper. (1, 5).
24. Tell child: Put block **on** table; **under** table; **in front of** me, **behind** me. Pass 4 of 4.
    (Do not help child by pointing, moving head or eyes.)
25. Ask child: What is a ball?... lake?... desk?... house?... banana?... curtain?... fence?... ceiling? Pass if defined in terms
    of use, shape, what it is made of, or general category (such as banana is fruit, not just yellow). Pass 5 of 8, 7 of 8.
26. Ask child: If a horse is big, a mouse is __? If fire is hot, ice is __? If the sun shines during the day, the moon shines
    during the __? Pass 2 of 3.
27. Child may use wall or rail only, not person. May not crawl.
28. Child must throw ball overhand 3 feet to within arm's reach of tester.
29. Child must perform standing broad jump over width of test sheet (8 1/2 inches).
30. Tell child to walk forward, ⬭⬭⬭⬭➜ heel within 1 inch of toe. Tester may demonstrate.
    Child must walk 4 consecutive steps.
31. In the second year, half of normal children are non-compliant.

OBSERVATIONS:

Mark under the heading that best fits your child:

	Never	Sometimes	Often
Complains of aches and pains	_____	_____	_____
Spends more time alone	_____	_____	_____
Tires easily, little energy	_____	_____	_____
Fidgety, unable to sit still	_____	_____	_____
Has trouble with a teacher	_____	_____	_____
Less interested in school	_____	_____	_____
Acts as if driven by a motor	_____	_____	_____
Daydreams too much	_____	_____	_____
Distracted easily	_____	_____	_____
Is afraid of new situations	_____	_____	_____
Feels sad, unhappy	_____	_____	_____
Is irritable, angry	_____	_____	_____
Feels hopeless	_____	_____	_____
Has trouble concentrating	_____	_____	_____
Less interest in friends	_____	_____	_____
Fights with other children	_____	_____	_____
Absent from school	_____	_____	_____
School grades dropping	_____	_____	_____
Is down on him or herself	_____	_____	_____
Visits doctor with doctor finding nothing wrong	_____	_____	_____
Has trouble with sleeping	_____	_____	_____
Worries a lot	_____	_____	_____
Wants to be with you more than before	_____	_____	_____
Feels he or she is bad	_____	_____	_____
Takes unnecessary risks	_____	_____	_____
Gets hurt frequently	_____	_____	_____
Seems to be having less fun	_____	_____	_____
Acts younger than children his or her age	_____	_____	_____
Does not listen to rules	_____	_____	_____
Does not show feelings	_____	_____	_____
Does not understand other people's feelings	_____	_____	_____
Teases others	_____	_____	_____
Blames others for his or her troubles	_____	_____	_____
Takes things that do not belong to him/her	_____	_____	_____
Refuses to share	_____	_____	_____

FIG A–3.
Pediatric symptom checklist. (From Jellinek M, Murphy JM: Screening for psychosocial disorders in pediatric practice. *Am J Dis Child* 1988; 142:1153–1157. Used by permission.)

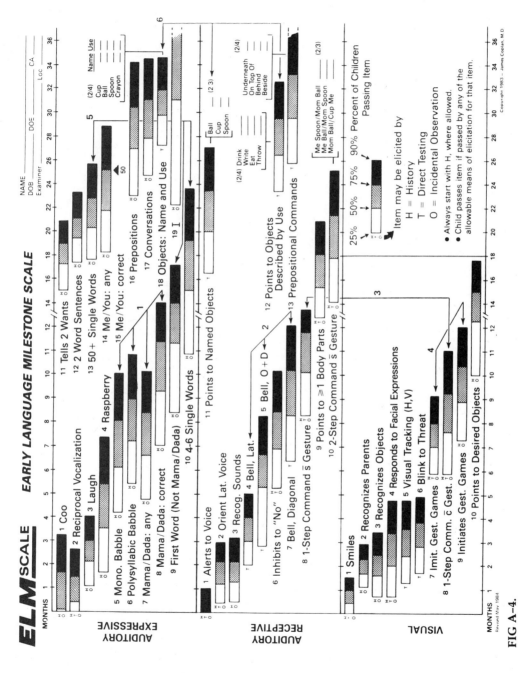

FIG A–4.
Early language milestone scale (continues on following two pages). (Courtesy Modern Education Corporation, Tulsa, Oklahoma.)

I. General Instructions
a) Draw vertical line down entire page at child's chronologic age (CA).
b) Work <u>backward</u> from CA, until 3 consecutive items in each Division (AE, AR, V) are passed (= Basal Level).
c) If child achieves Basal without failing any items already attained by more than 90% of children, then Stop. ELM screen is passed.
d) If 1 or more items which have already been attained by more than 90% of children are failed, then work <u>forward</u> from CA until 3 consecutive items in that Division are failed. (Exception: Child is permitted to fail <u>one</u> of the following without penalty: V3-V6). The 50% value of the highest item passed in each Division is the Ceiling Level.
If Ceiling Level ≥CA → ELM screen is passed.
If Ceiling Level<CA → ELM screen is failed.

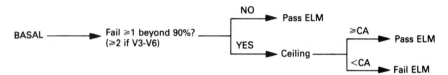

II. <u>Auditory Expressive (AE)</u>
AE1: Prolonged musical vowel sounds in a sing-song fashion (ooo, aaa, etc.), <u>not</u> just grunts or squeaks.
AE2 H: "Does baby watch speaker's face and appear to listen intently, then vocalize when the speaker is quiet? Can you 'have a conversation' with your baby?"
AE4 H: Blow bubbles or "bronx cheer"?
AE5 H: Isolated sounds such as ba, da, ga, goo, etc.
AE6 H: Repetitive string of sounds: "bababab a:, or "lalalalala", etc.
AE7 H: Says "mama" or "dada", but uses them at other times besides just labelling parents.
AE8 H: Child <u>spontaneously</u>, <u>consistently</u> and <u>correctly</u> uses mama or dada, <u>just</u> to label the <u>appropriate</u> parent.
AE9, AE10 H: Child <u>spontaneously</u>, <u>consistently</u> and <u>correctly</u> uses words. Do not count "mama", "dada", or the names of other family members or pets. <u>Do</u> list the particular words.
AE11 H. Uses single words to tell you what he/she wants. "Milk!", "Cookie!", "More!", etc. Pass = 2 or more wants. List specific words.
AE12 H: <u>Spontaneous</u>, <u>novel</u> 2 word combinations ("Want cookie", "No bed", "See daddy", etc.) <u>Not</u> rotely learned phrases which have been specifically taught to the child, or combinations which are really single thoughts (e.g. "hot dog").
AE14 H: Child uses "me", or "you", but may reverse them ("you want cookie" instead of "me want cookie", etc.)
AE15 H: Pronoun reversal gone.
AE17 H: "Can child put 2 or 3 sentences together to hold brief conversations?"
AE18 T: Put out cup, ball, crayon, & spoon. Pick up cup & say "What is this? What do we do with it (What is it for)?" Child must <u>name</u> the object, and give its use. Pass = "drink with", etc., <u>not</u> "milk" or "juice". Ball: Pass = "throw", "play with", etc. Spoon: Pass = "Eat" or "Eat with", etc., <u>not</u> "Food", "Lunch". Crayon: Pass = "Write (with)", "Color (with)", etc. Pass item if child gives <u>name and use</u> for 2 objects.
AE19 H: Does child ever refer to himself as "I"? (<u>Not</u> "me", "my", or "mine").

III. <u>Auditory Receptive (AR)</u>
AR1 H,T: Any behavioral change in response to noise (eye blink, startle, change in movements or respiration, etc.)
AR2 H,T: What does baby do when mother starts talking while out of baby's line of sight? Pass if any shift of head or eyes to voice.
AR3 H: Does baby seem to respond in a specific way to certain sounds (becomes excited at hearing parents' voices, etc.)?
AR4 T: Sit facing baby, with baby in mother's lap. Extend both arms so that your hands are behind baby's field of vision, and at the level of baby's waist. Ring a 2" diameter bell, first with 1 hand, then the other. Repeat x2 or 3 if necessary. Pass if baby turns head to the side at least once.
AR5 T: See note for AR4. Pass if baby turns head first to the side, then down, to localize bell, at least once. (Automatically passes AR4.)
AR6 H: Does baby understand the command "No" (even though he may not always obey)? T: Test by commanding "(<u>Baby's Name</u>) No!" while baby is playing with any test object. Pass if baby temporarily inhibits his actions.
AR7 T: See note for AR 4. Pass if baby turns directly down on diagonal to localize bell, at least once. (Automatically passes AR5 and AR4.)

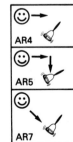

AR8 H: Will your baby follow any verbal commands, <u>without</u> you indicating by gestures what it is you want him to do ("Stop", "Come here", "Give me", etc.)? T: Wait until baby is playing with any test object, then say "(Baby's name), give it to me". Pass if baby extends object to you, even if baby seems to change his mind and take the object back. May repeat command x 1 or 2. If failed, repeat the command, but this time hold out your hand for the object. If baby responds, then pass item V8 (1 step command with gesture).

AR9 H: Does your child point to at least 1 body part on command? T: Have mother command baby "Show me your . . ." or "Where's your . . .", without pointing to the desired part herself.

AR10 H: "Can child do 2 things in a row, if asked? For example 'First go get your shoes, then sit down'?" T: Set out ball, cup, and spoon, and say "(Child's name), give me the spoon, then give the ball to mommy". Use slow, steady voice but do <u>not</u> break command into 2 separate sentences. If no response, <u>then</u> give each half of command separately to see if child understands separate components. If child succeeds on at least half of command, then give each of the following: "(Child's name), give me the ball and give mommy the spoon". May repeat once, but do not break into 2 commands. Then "Give mommy the ball, then give the cup to me". Pass if at least two 2-step commands executed correctly. (Note: Child is credited even if the order of execution of a command is reversed.)

AR11 H: Place a cup, ball, and spoon on the table. Command child "Show me/where is/give me the . . . cup/ball/spoon". (If command is "Give me", be sure to replace each object before asking about the next object.) Pass = 2 items correctly identified.

AR12 T: Put cup, ball, spoon, and crayon on table, and give command "Show me/where is/give me . . . the one we drink with/eat with/draw (color, write) with/throw (play with)". If the command "Give me" is used, be sure to replace each object before asking about the next object. Pass = 2 or more objects correctly identified.

AR13: Put out cup (upside down), and a 1" red cube. Command the child "Put the block underneath the cup". Repeat x1 or 2 if necessary. If no attempt, or if incorrect response, then demonstrate correct response, saying "See, now the block is <u>underneath</u> the cup". Remove the block and hand it to the child. Then give command "Put the block <u>on top of</u> the cup". If child makes no response, then repeat command x1, but do <u>not</u> demonstrate. Then command "Put the block <u>behind</u> the cup", then "Put the block <u>beside</u> the cup." Pass = 2 or more commands correctly executed (<u>prior</u> to demonstration by examiner, if 'underneath' is scored).

IV. <u>Visual</u>

V1 H: "Does your baby smile for you? Not just a gas bubble or a burp, but a real smile?" T: Have mother attempt to elicit smile by any means.

V2 H: "Does your baby seem to recognize you, reacting differently to you than to the sight of other people? For example, does your baby smile more quickly for you than for other people?"

V3 H: "Does your baby seem to recognize any common objects by sight? For example (if bottle or spoon fed), what happens when bottle or spoon is brought into view, but <u>before</u> it touches baby's lips?" Pass if baby gets visibly excited, or opens mouth in anticipation of feeding.

V4 H: "Does your baby respond to your facial expressions?" T: Engage baby's gaze, and attempt to elicit a smile by smiling and talking to baby. The scowl at baby. Pass if any change in baby's facial expression.

V5 T: Horizontal (H): Engage child's gaze with yours at a distance of 18". Move slowly back and forth. Pass if child turns head 60° to left and right from midline. Vertical (V): Move slowly up and down. Pass if child elevates eyes 30° from horizontal. Must pass both H & V to pass item.

V6 T: Flick your fingers rapidly towards child's face, ending with fingertips 1-2" from face. Do not touch face or eyelashes. Pass if child blinks.

V7 H: Does child play pat-a-cake, peek-a-boo, etc., in response to parents?

V8 T: See note for AR8 (always try AR8 first; if AR8 is passed, then automatically give credit for V8).

V9 H: Does child spontaneously initiate gesture games?

V10 H: "Does your child ever point with index finger to something he/she wants? For example, if child is sitting at the dinner table and wants something that is out of reach, how does child let you know what he/she wants?" Pass <u>only</u> index finger pointing, <u>not</u> reaching with whole hand.

INDEX